W9-DAS-055

The

NEW
AMERICAN
NATION

1775–1820

A Twelve-Volume
Collection of Articles
on the Development
of the Early American
Republic

Edited by

PETER S. ONUF
UNIVERSITY OF VIRGINIA

A GARLAND SERIES

THE NEW AMERICAN NATION
1775–1820

Volume
11

★

AMERICAN
SOCIETY
1776–1815

Edited with an
Introduction by

PETER S. ONUF

GARLAND PUBLISHING, INC.
NEW YORK & LONDON
1991

Library of Congress Cataloging-in-Publication Data

American society, 1776–1815 / edited with an introduction by Peter S.
Onuf.
    p.   cm. — (New American nation, 1776–1815 ; v. 11)
    Includes bibliographical references.
    ISBN 0-8153-0446-3 (alk. paper) : $49.99
    1. United States—History—Colonial period, ca. 1600–1775. 2. United
States—History—1783–1815. 3. United States—History—Revolution, 1775–
1783—Social aspects. 4. United States—Social conditions—To 1865. I.
Onuf, Peter S. II. Series.
    E164.N45   1991 vol. 11
    [E195]
    973s—dc20
    [973]
    [973]   91-13745
            CIP

Printed on acid-free, 250-year-life paper.
Manufactured in the United States of America

THE NEW AMERICAN NATION, 1775–1820

EDITOR'S INTRODUCTION

This series includes a representative selection of the most interesting and influential journal articles on revolutionary and early national America. My goal is to introduce readers to the wide range of topics that now engage scholarly attention. The essays in these volumes show that the revolutionary era was an extraordinarily complex "moment" when the broad outlines of national history first emerged. Yet if the "common cause" brought Americans together, it also drove them apart: the Revolution, historians agree, was as much a civil war as a war of national liberation. And, given the distinctive colonial histories of the original members of the American Union, it is not surprising that the war had profoundly different effects in different parts of the country. This series has been designed to reveal the multiplicity of these experiences in a period of radical political and social change.

Most of the essays collected here were first published within the last twenty years. This series therefore does *not* recapitulate the development of the historiography of the Revolution. Many of the questions asked by earlier generations of scholars now seem misconceived and simplistic. Constitutional historians wanted to know if the Patriots had legitimate grounds to revolt: was the Revolution "legal"? Economic historians sought to assess the costs of the navigation system for American farmers and merchants and to identify the interest groups that promoted resistance. Comparative historians wondered how "revolutionary" the Revolution really was. By and large, the best recent work has ignored these classic questions. Contemporary scholarship instead draws its inspiration from other sources, most notable of which is the far-ranging reconception and reconstruction of prerevolutionary America by a brilliant generation of colonial historians.

Bernard Bailyn's *Ideological Origins of the American Revolution* (1967) was a landmark in the new historical writing on colonial politics. As his title suggests, Bailyn was less interested in constitutional and legal arguments as such than in the "ideology" or political language that shaped colonists' perception of and responses to British imperial policy. Bailyn's great contribution was to focus attention on colonial political culture; disciples and critics alike followed his lead as they explored the impact—and limits—of "republicanism" in specific colonial settings. Meanwhile, the social historians who had played a leading role in the transformation of colonial historiography were extending their work into the late colonial period and were increasingly interested in the questions of value, meaning, and behavior that were raised by the new political history. The resulting convergence points to some of the unifying themes in recent work on the revolutionary period presented in this series.

A thorough grounding in the new scholarship on colonial British America is the best introduction to the history and historiography of the Revolution. These volumes therefore can be seen as a complement and extension of Peter Charles Hoffer's eighteen-volume set, *Early American History*, published by Garland in 1987. Hoffer's collection includes numerous important essays essential for understanding developments in independent America. Indeed, only a generation ago—when the Revolution generally was defined in terms of its colonial origins—it would have been hard to justify a separate series on the "new American nation." But exciting recent work—for instance, on wartime mobilization and social change, or on the Americanization of republican ideology during the great era of state making and constitution writing—has opened up new vistas. Historians now generally agree that the revolutionary period saw far-reaching and profound changes, that is, a "great transformation," toward a more recognizably modern America. If the connections between this transformation and the actual unfolding of events often remain elusive, the historiographical quest for the larger meaning of the war and its aftermath has yielded impressive results.

To an important extent, the revitalization of scholarship on revolutionary and early national America is a tribute to the efforts and expertise of scholars working in other professional disciplines. Students of early American literature have made key contributions to the history of rhetoric, ideology, and culture; political scientists and legal scholars have brought new clarity and sophistication to the study of political and constitutional thought and practice in the founding period. Kermit L. Hall's superb Garland series, *United States Constitutional and Legal History* (20 volumes, 1985), is another fine resource for students and scholars interested in the founding. The sampling of recent work in various disciplines offered in these volumes gives a sense of the interpretative possibilities of a crucial period in American history that is now getting the kind of attention it has long deserved.

Peter S. Onuf

INTRODUCTION

Historians locate the origins of modern American society in a series of epochal transformations taking place in the century after 1750. Profound changes in family life, the organization of labor, and social relations generally accompanied the triumph of the marketplace as the central institution in American life. There is intense historiographical debate about when and on what terms different groups across the country embraced the market and a correlative "liberal" system of values. But all scholars agree that social and economic conditions were changing with unprecedented rapidity. Traditional, corporatist values were subverted by the fluidity of class and status relations and the turnover of local populations through in- and out-migration.

The American Revolution accelerated the process of social transformation. Even while they destroyed property and disrupted the economy, the contending armies fostered the commercialization of the countryside by offering new markets to enterprising agriculturalists. The opening of frontier areas to settlement spurred the migration process, just as exposure to new regions prompted many soldiers to leave their old homes. Whatever their intentions, mobile Americans could not move beyond the imperatives or opportunities of expanding markets. Access to land itself was determined by a market in private and public lands that favored market-oriented commercial farmers.

Yet it does not follow that even market-oriented agriculturalists were simply profit maximizers. In *The Elusive Republic* (1980), Drew R. McCoy argues that Jeffersonian political economists sought to promote commercial agriculture in order to sustain the roughly equal conditions they considered essential to the survival of republican government. Similarly, as Alan Taylor and other historians of the early national frontier suggest, farmers cherished the republican "independence" that freeholds supposedly guaranteed, even while they sought to promote their families' welfare by production for distant markets. Students of early American artisanal culture have illuminated an equivalent complex of traditional values and bourgeois aspirations.

It would be mistaken to assume that frontier farmers or urban artisans necessarily felt deeply conflicted about the economic and social changes in which so many of them eagerly participated. But opportunities were by no means equally distributed: if some craftsmen flourished as merchant-manufacturers, many others were reduced to the status of hired labor; patterns of property holding on the frontiers quickly replicated those of long-settled regions, minimizing the chances of marginal producers and a surplus farm population. The characteristic answer to diminishing opportunity in cities and countryside alike was to move, but upward mobility in the burgeoning cities or newly opened frontiers increasingly depended on having some property to begin with. This was nowhere more true than on the slaveholding frontier of the old Southwest—one of the most prosperous areas in the country.

The dynamism and prosperity of the American economy was as unsettling and disorienting as the dislocation and displacement suffered by marginalized groups. Postwar changes made a mockery of the social aspirations of Anglicizing elites who had hoped to remake provincial American societies along British metropolitan lines. The fracturing of the old, never fully achieved synthesis of wealth, social status, and political power made the very idea of "gentility" itself problematic. Elite social authority was most conspicuously and successfully challenged in religious life as popular Christianity was invigorated by disestablishment, evangelical revivalism, and the proliferation of "democratic" Christian sects described by Nathan O. Hatch. The real "Revolution of 1800" may not have been the election of a wealthy Virginia planter to the presidency but the beginnings of a second Great Awakening, which had such a profound impact on the un- and under-churched South and West in the early nineteenth century.

The revolutionary democratization of social relations among white male Americans threw into sharp relief the boundaries of the new social order as well as the fundamental inequality in gender relations on which it was founded. Feminist historiography has illuminated the construction of new conceptions of "republican motherhood" and family life that justified emerging distinctions between private and public spheres—and the suppression of female agency and personality—in liberal bourgeois culture.

By contrast, Americans wasted little ideological energy in justifying the continuing enslavement and exploitation of African-Americans. Though Revolutionary idealism may have prompted gradual emancipation schemes in the northern states and private manumissions in the South, whites successfully resisted the claims of freedmen and women to civil rights and equal opportunity. Nor could Native Americans hope to gain a place—if they had wanted one—in the new democratic order. Anthony F. C. Wallace's *Death and Rebirth of the Seneca* (1970) provides eloquent testimony to the costs of white expansionism to the native population. However philanthropic their impulses, white Americans could not imagine a new world that long included primitive "savages," relics of an earlier stage of historical development in the onward and westward progress of civilization.

The essays collected in this and the next volume explore complementary themes. As many of the essays demonstrate, the distinction between "society" and "culture" is often arbitrary and misleading. My purpose in this volume is to illuminate some of the social changes, and their institutional and behavorial concommitants, that shaped the transformation of cultural values, attitudes, and expressions recounted in the concluding volume of the series.

Peter S. Onuf

Additional Reading

Ira Berlin and Ronald Hoffman, eds. *Slavery and Freedom in the Age of the American Revolution.* Charlottesville: University Press of Virginia, 1983.

Nathan O. Hatch. *The Democratization of American Christianity.* New Haven: Yale University Press, 1989.

Ronald Hoffman and Peter J. Albert, eds. *Women in the Age of the American Revolution.* Charlottesville: University Press of Virginia, 1989.

Rhys Isaac. *The Transformation of Virginia, 1740–1790.* Chapel Hill: University of North Carolina Press, 1982.

Linda K. Kerber. *Women of the Republic: Intellect and Ideology in Revolutionary America.* Chapel Hill: University of North Carolina Press, 1980.

Drew R. McCoy. *The Elusive Republic: Political Economy in Jeffersonian America.* Chapel Hill: University of North Carolina Press, 1980.

Donald G. Mathews. *Religion in the Old South.* Chicago: University of Chicago Press, 1977.

Howard B. Rock. *Artisans of the New Republic: The Tradesmen of New York City in the Age of Jefferson.* New York: New York University Press, 1979.

Bernard Sheehan. *Seeds of Extinction: Jeffersonian Philanthropy and the American Indian.* Chapel Hill: University of North Carolina Press, 1973.

Alan Taylor. *Liberty Men and Great Proprietors: The Revolutionary Settlement on the Maine Frontier, 1780–1820.* Chapel Hill: University of North Carolina Press, 1990.

Anthony F. C. Wallace. *The Death and Rebirth of the Seneca.* New York: Alfred A. Knopf, 1970.

Robert H. Wiebe. *The Opening of American Society: From the Adoption of the Constitution to the Eve of Disunion.* New York: Alfred A. Knopf, 1984.

Sean Wilentz. *Chants Democratic: New York City and the Rise of the American Working Class, 1788–1850.* New York: Oxford University Press, 1984.

CONTENTS

Volume 11—American Society, 1776–1815

Mary B. Norton, "Eighteenth-Century American Women in Peace and War: The Case of the Loyalists," *William and Mary Quarterly*, 1976, 33(3):386–409.

Barbara E. Lacey, "Women in the Era of the American Revolution: The Case of Norwich, Connecticut," *New England Quarterly*, 1980, 53(4):527–543.

Laurel Thatcher Ulrich, "'The Living Mother of a Living Child': Midwifery and Mortality in Post-Revolutionary New England," *William and Mary Quarterly*, 1989, 46(1)(Third Series):27–48.

Sylvia R. Frey, "Between Slavery and Freedom: Virginia Blacks in the American Revolution," *Journal of Southern History*, 1983, 49(3):375–398.

Jeffrey J. Crow, "Slave Rebelliousness and Social Conflict in North Carolina, 1775 to 1802," *William and Mary Quarterly*, 1980, 37(1)(Third Series):79–102.

Charles B. Dew, "David Ross and the Oxford Iron Works: A Study of Industrial Slavery in the Early Nineteenth-Century South," *William and Mary Quarterly*, 1974, 31(2)(Third Series):189–224.

Richard S. Dunn, "A Tale of Two Plantations: Slave Life at Mesopotamia in Jamaica and Mount Airy in Virginia, 1799 to 1828," *William and Mary Quarterly*, 1977, 34 (Third Series):32–65.

Richard D. Brown, "'Not Only Extreme Poverty, but the Worst Kind of Orphanage': Lemuel Haynes and the Boundaries of Racial Tolerance on the Yankee Frontier, 1770–1820," *New England Quarterly*, 1988, 61(4):502–518.

Shane White, "'We Dwell in Safety and Pursue Our Honest Callings': Free Blacks in New York City, 1783–1810," *Journal of American History*, 1988, 75(2):445–470.

Daniel H. Usner, Jr., "American Indians on the Cotton Frontier: Changing Economic Relations with Citizens and Slaves in the Mississippi Territory," Journal of American History, 1985, 72(2):297–317.

ACKNOWLEDGMENTS

Volume 11—American Society, 1776–1815

Richard D. Brown, "The Emergence of Urban Society in Rural Massachusetts, 1760–1820," *Journal of American History*, 1974–75, 61(1):29–51. Reprinted with the permission of the *Journal of American History*. Courtesy of Yale University Sterling Memorial Library.

J. S. Wood, "Elaboration of a Settlement System: the New England Village in the Federal Period," *Journal of Historical Geography*, 1984, 10(4):331–356. Reprinted with the permission of Academic Press, Inc. Courtesy of Yale University Sterling Memorial Library.

Allan Kulikoff, "The Progress of Inequality in Revolutionary Boston," *William and Mary Quarterly*, 1971, 28(3) (Third Series):375–412. Originally appeared in the *William and Mary Quarterly*. Courtesy of Yale University Sterling Memorial Library.

Thomas L. Purvis, "The European Origins of New Jersey's Eighteenth-Century Population," *New Jersey History*, 1982, 100(1-2):15–31. Reprinted with the permission of the New Jersey Historical Society. Courtesy of Yale University Sterling Memorial Library.

Dennis P. Ryan, "Landholding, Opportunity, and Mobility in Revolutionary New Jersey," *William and Mary Quarterly*, 1979, 36(4) (Third Series):571–592. Originally appeared in the *William and Mary Quarterly*. Courtesy of Yale University Sterling Memorial Library.

Sharon V. Salinger, "Artisans, Journeymen, and the Transformation of Labor in Late Eighteenth-Century Philadelphia," *William and Mary Quarterly*, 1983, 40(1)(Third Series):62–84. Originally appeared in the *William and Mary Quarterly*. Courtesy of Yale University Sterling Memorial Library.

Paul E. Johnson, "The Modernization of Mayo Greenleaf Patch: Land, Family, and Marginality in New England, 1766–1818," *New England Quarterly*, 1982, 55(4):488–516. Reprinted with the permission of the *New England Quarterly*. Courtesy of Yale University Sterling Memorial Library.

John D. Cushing, "Notes on Disestablishment in Massachusetts, 1780–1833," *William and Mary Quarterly*, 1969, 26(2) (Third Series):169–190. Originally appeared in the *William and Mary Quarterly*. Courtesy of Yale University Sterling Memorial Library.

Stephen Foster, "A Connecticut Separate Church: Strict Congregationalism in Cornwall, 1780–1809," *New England Quarterly*, 1966, 39(3):309–333. Reprinted with the permission of the *New England Quarterly*. Courtesy of Yale University Sterling Memorial Library.

Thomas E. Buckley, S.J., "Evangelicals Triumphant: The Baptists' Assault on the Virginia Glebes, 1786–1801," *William and Mary Quarterly*, 1988, 45(1) (Third Series):33–69. Originally appeared in the *William and*

Mary Quarterly. Courtesy of Yale University Sterling Memorial Library.

James David Essig, "A Very Wintry Season: Virginia Baptists and Slavery, 1785–1797," *Virginia Magazine of History and Biography*, 1980, 88(2):170–185. Reprinted with the permission of the Virginia Historical Society. Courtesy of Yale University Sterling Memorial Library.

Mary B. Norton, "Eighteenth-Century American Women in Peace and War: The Case of the Loyalists," *William and Mary Quarterly*, 1976, 33(3):386–409. Originally appeared in the *William and Mary Quarterly*. Courtesy of Yale University Sterling Memorial Library.

Barbara E. Lacey, "Women in the Era of the American Revolution: The Case of Norwich, Connecticut," *New England Quarterly*, 1980, 53(4):527–543. Reprinted with the permission of the *New England Quarterly*. Courtesy of Yale University Sterling Memorial Library.

Laurel Thatcher Ulrich, "'The Living Mother of a Living Child': Midwifery and Mortality in Post-Revolutionary New England," *William and Mary Quarterly*, 1989, 46(1) (Third Series):27–48. Originally appeared in the *William and Mary Quarterly*. Courtesy of Yale University Sterling Memorial Library.

Sylvia R. Frey, "Between Slavery and Freedom: Virginia Blacks in the American Revolution," *Journal of Southern History*, 1983, 49(3):375–398. Reprinted with the permission of the Southern Historical Association. Courtesy of Yale University Sterling Memorial Library.

Jeffrey J. Crow, "Slave Rebelliousness and Social Conflict in North Carolina, 1775 to 1802," *William and Mary Quarterly*, 1980, 37(1)(Third Series):79–102. Originally appeared in the *William and Mary Quarterly*. Courtesy of Yale University Sterling Memorial Library.

Charles B. Dew, "David Ross and the Oxford Iron Works: A Study of Industrial Slavery in the Early Nineteenth-Century South," *William and Mary Quarterly*, 1974, 31(2) (Third Series):189–224. Originally appeared in the *William and Mary Quarterly*. Courtesy of Yale University Sterling Memorial Library.

Richard S. Dunn, "A Tale of Two Plantations: Slave Life at Mesopotamia in Jamaica and Mount Airy in Virginia, 1799 to 1828," *William and Mary Quarterly*, 1977, 34 (Third Series):32–65. Originally appeared in the *William and Mary Quarterly*. Courtesy of Yale University Sterling Memorial Library.

Richard D. Brown, "'Not Only Extreme Poverty, but the Worst Kind of Orphanage': Lemuel Haynes and the Boundaries of Racial Tolerance on the Yankee Frontier, 1770–1820," *New England Quarterly*, 1988, 61(4):502–518. Reprinted with the permission of the *New England Quarterly*. Courtesy of Yale University Sterling Memorial Library.

Shane White, "'We Dwell in Safety and Pursue Our Honest Callings': Free Blacks in New York City, 1783–1810," *Journal of American History*, 1988 75(2):445–470. Reprinted with the permission of the *Journal of American History*. Courtesy of Yale University Sterling Memorial Library.

Daniel H. Usner, Jr., "American Indians on the Cotton Frontier: Changing Economic Relations with Citizens and Slaves in the Mississippi Territory," *Journal of American History*, 1985, 72(2):297–317. Reprinted with the permission of the *Journal of American History*. Courtesy of Yale University Sterling Memorial Library.

The Emergence of Urban Society in Rural Massachusetts, 1760-1820

RICHARD D. BROWN

CITIES, as Americans commonly think of them, are associated with massive concentrations of people, cement pavements, skyscrapers. Within recent decades great metropolitan centers have absorbed the majority of the population. Cities have become the focus of American social and economic life. Notwithstanding its vast territory and superabundant agriculture, the United States has become preeminently an urban nation.

Urban historians have directed primary attention to cities during the industrial era, when the physical character of today's city developed. The preindustrial origins of American urban development and the transition from rural to urban society have so far received little attention. When one seeks out urban studies in the preindustrial era, the works of Carl Bridenbaugh, which chronicle the emergence of five seaboard cities, and Richard Wade, who describes the rise of five inland cities, stand almost alone.[1] Moreover their methodology, essentially that of the urban biographer, has dominated the literature since Bridenbaugh's first major work appeared in 1938. Only in the last several years have alternative lines of analysis been explored, and the most important of these has come not from a historian but from a geographer, James T. Lemon.[2] Working on eastern Pennsyl-

Richard D. Brown is associate professor of history in the University of Connecticut.

[1] Carl Bridenbaugh, *Cities in the Wilderness: The First Century of Urban Life in America, 1625-1742* (New York, 1938); Carl Bridenbaugh, *Cities in Revolt: Urban Life in America, 1743-1776* (New York, 1955); Richard C. Wade, *The Urban Frontier: The Rise of Western Cities, 1790-1830* (Cambridge, Mass., 1959). See also David T. Gilchrist, ed., *The Growth of the Seaport Cities, 1790-1825: Proceedings of a Conference Sponsored by the Eleutherian Mills-Hagley Foundation March 17-19, 1966* (Charlottesville, 1967).

[2] James T. Lemon, "Urbanization and the Development of Eighteenth-Century Southeastern Pennsylvania and Adjacent Delaware," *William and Mary Quarterly*, XXIV (Oct. 1967), 501-42; James T. Lemon, *The Best Poor Man's Country: A Geographical Study of Early Southeastern Pennsylvania* (Baltimore, 1972). Significant approaches have also appeared in Charles Tilly, *The Vendée* (Cambridge, Mass., 1964), and Edward M. Cook, Jr., "Local Leadership and the Typology of New England Towns, 1700-

29

vania and Delaware in the eighteenth century, Lemon has created a systematic technique for charting the process of urbanization according to several key statistical indicators (especially occupational specialization and population growth) as well as community functions.

What is lacking, however, is a sustained attempt to assess the cultural dimension of urbanization or the character of social relationships in rural, semi-urban, or urban communities. Without examining the development of urban society the study of urbanization is so badly crippled as to preclude understanding why nineteenth-century Americans embraced urban development so enthusiastically for so long, in spite of the problems they knew it generated. One of the great American culture heroes of the century, Thomas Jefferson, expressed grave misgivings about cities, associating them with "degeneracy," yet millions of his agrarian worshipers flocked to urban centers or worked to transform their own rural hamlets into cities.[3] Urbanization was one of the great popular movements of the nineteenth century: to understand it requires exploration of the character and values of urban society.

No definition of urban society is universally accepted, nor is there unanimity on the particular set of values that is characteristically urban.[4] One cannot escape time and place. Society in a medieval city differs from that of Renaissance cities, just as both differ from industrial cities. National and ethnic character also shape the culture of particular cities. Nevertheless the term "urban" possesses meaning because common denominators are visible in diverse cities.

Urban society is a crossroads phenomenon, bound directly to exchange and communication, commercial as well as social and intellectual. Heterogeneity characterizes the social and economic life of the city. Historically this syndrome has been accompanied by cosmopolitan attitudes and acceptance of social and intellectual diversity. In urban society, individuals possess opportunities for voluntarily choosing their livelihoods and their personal associations and allegiances—choices that have usually been inaccessible to

1785," *Political Science Quarterly*, LXXXVI (Dec. 1971), 586-608. See also G. B. Warden, "L'urbanisation américaine avant 1800," *Annales*, XXV (1970), 862-79.

[3] Thomas Jefferson, *Notes on the State of Virginia* (New York, 1964), 158. From Thomas Jefferson's viewpoint urban society was alien to the American environment; he hoped permanently.

[4] Eric E. Lampard, "American Historians and the Study of Urbanization," *American Historical Review*, LXVII (Oct. 1961), 49-61; Oscar Handlin and John Burchard, eds., *The Historian and the City* (Cambridge, Mass., 1963); Charles N. Glaab, "The Historian and the American City: A Bibliographic Survey," Alexander B. Callow, Jr., ed., *American Urban History: An Interpretive Reader with Commentaries* (New York, 1969), 654-74.

villagers and country people. These characteristics of urban society—communication, heterogeneity, cosmopolitanism, and choice—are all relative and defy absolute definition or measurement.

Most studies of the emergence of urban society in the United States concentrate on the period between the Civil War and the Progressive era, when agriculture yielded to industry as the leading sector of the economy and when, according to the census bureau, the majority of the population came to reside in urban places. Yet urban society in America was much older, generations before railroads and electronic communications, before canals and turnpikes, and even perhaps before brick construction became routine. The Mathers' Boston and Benjamin Franklin's Philadelphia both possessed urban social life long before immense populations and industrial development became prominent features of cities. In these two ports commerce and cosmopolitanism flourished; printers disseminated information from all over the world. Both were centers of communication and administration and tolerated various religious denominations. Londoners found Boston and Philadelphia provincial, but in the American context they were centers of urban society.

In colonial America urban society was a highly restricted phenomenon, limited to port towns that were also administrative centers. Before independence less than a dozen towns had newspapers, and only a few possessed the range of organizations necessary to sustain urban social life. With rare exceptions, the churches and the government were the only organizations. Some localities experienced religious heterogeneity, but that was not typical; sectarian rivalries marked the limits of pluralism in the countryside. Local government was so highly personalized as to lose its institutional distinctiveness, operating instead as an instrument of the social structure. County government was the quasi-oligarchic enterprise of a handful of individuals. In the areas where town meetings were established their concerns were so intensely ingrown and local as to make urbanity alien. Everywhere communication beyond the immediate neighborhood was infrequent. To the degree that urban society penetrated the countryside it was an élite phenomenon, limited to a thin layer of social leaders—professional men and the outstanding merchants and politicians who were concerned with urban styles as part of their social status and who were in touch with the capital as an occupational necessity.[5]

[5] Bridenbaugh, *Cities in the Wilderness*; Bridenbaugh, *Cities in Revolt*; Lemon, "Urbanization and the Development of Eighteenth-Century Southeastern Pennsylvania and Adjacent Delaware"; Richard L. Bushman, *From Puritan to Yankee: Character and the Social Order in Connecticut, 1690-1765* (Cambridge, Mass., 1967); Jere R. Daniell,

By the middle of the nineteenth century these conditions had virtually disappeared. Population increased ninefold from 1776 to 1850. The number of urban communities multiplied even more dramatically: in 1776 there were fewer than a dozen cities of 5,000 or more inhabitants; by 1850 there were 147, twelve times as many.[6] Cities appeared everywhere, north, south, east, and west, coastal and inland. All were not equal sharers of urban society, yet they did all possess the variety of institutions characteristic of urban life—newspapers, post offices, churches, political groups, libraries, professional organizations, and other voluntary associations. Of equal significance, urban society had developed a broad social and geographic base in the countryside.

Economic development was necessary to sustain this diffusion of urban social patterns and to bring about the growth of regional and national commercial systems. But these phenomena alone did not lead necessarily to the cosmopolitan outlook or the variety of organizations characteristic of urban society. Existing scholarship does not explain whether economic development preceded or followed the diffusion of urban society, or whether the two processes occurred simultaneously. Current research will not now sustain a persuasive answer for the United States as a whole. But since Massachusetts experienced a transformation characteristic of the nation, one might propose that the dynamics involved in the expansion of urban society in Massachusetts were part of broader regional and national phenomena.

In the middle of the eighteenth century Massachusetts society was probably more distinctive than a century later. The peculiarities of its civil and ecclesiastical history cast a longer shadow in the colonial period than after the Revolution, which provided a more common American history. Nevertheless, even in the 1750s the structure of social life resembled that of other New England colonies. Its ethnic and religious homogeneity, the ways of local government and community life, and its agricultural, fishing, and forest economy made Massachusetts characteristic of New England. In Massachusetts, urban society was almost exclusively a Boston phenome-

Experiment in Republicanism: New Hampshire Politics and the American Revolution, 1741-1794 (Cambridge, Mass., 1970); Alfred F. Young, *The Democratic Republicans of New York: The Origins, 1763-1797* (Chapel Hill, 1967), 3-32.

[6] Stella H. Sutherland, *Population Distribution in Colonial America* (New York, 1936), xii; U.S. Department of Commerce, Bureau of the Census, *Historical Statistics of the United States: Colonial Times to 1957: A Statistical Abstract Supplement* (Washington, 1960), 14; George Rogers Taylor, "American Urban Growth Preceding the Railway Age," *Journal of Economic History*, XXVII (Sept. 1967), 309-39.

non. The predominant culture was that of rural communities.[1] As of 1760 the inhabitants of these rural communities were normally members of three overlapping organizations—family, congregation, and town. Membership in these corporations was largely a matter of birth, although individual choice did have some role. The family was the least voluntary of these connections. It is impossible to choose one's parents, but personal choice did operate in significant ways within the family. By 1760 individuals frequently chose marriage partners independently. Sometimes, they selected careers for themselves outside of family relationships. In pursuing their livelihoods people commonly faced the question of whether to remain in their hometown or move elsewhere, a decision that might remove them from the family orbit.

Given these possibilities, the common willingness to remain within the geographic reach of family relationships was voluntary.[2] But the hold of the family on individuals was also prescriptive, enforced by custom, social ideals, and practical functions. Families exercised an important, often decisive role in determining both the marriage partners and careers of their offspring. Magistrates sustained the cohesiveness of family relations by legislative acts and judicial decisions, while clergymen rendered moral support with homilies from the pulpit and by the hearth. In economic terms the family was often crucial, since it usually provided access to the necessary skills and capital required to earn a living. Because the moral, material, and legal sanctions reinforcing family membership were so pervasive and powerful, the role of the individual in the family organization was largely involuntary.

In religion the situation differed. Originally Puritan congregations had been classic voluntary associations. Membership was a voluntary act for the person seeking to join the church and for the members who controlled admission. By the latter half of the seventeenth century, however, Puritan congregations were approaching the status of territorial churches. Church membership remained voluntary and exclusive in a strict sense, even with the halfway covenant, but participation in the congregation was compulsory for everyone residing within the parish. Attendance and tithing laws were

[1] Kenneth A. Lockridge, *A New England Town: The First Hundred Years* (New York, 1970); Michael Zuckerman, *Peaceable Kingdoms: New England Towns in the Eighteenth Century* (New York, 1970).

[2] Philip J. Greven, Jr., *Four Generations: Population, Land, and Family in Colonial Andover, Massachusetts* (Ithaca, 1970); Lockridge, *New England Town*; J. M. Bumsted and J. T. Lemon, "New Approaches in Early American Studies: The Local Community in New England," *Social History*, 2 (Nov. 1968), 98-112.

systematically enforced. By 1700 it was public policy that everyone in Massachusetts was gathered in congregations.

Attendance and tithing laws formally expressed the involuntary character of parish membership. But they also signified that other behavior existed. As the decades passed attendance laws often fell into abeyance. By the middle of the eighteenth century in many communities church-going had become a voluntary act, particularly where settlement had dispersed families away from the meetinghouse. Doubtless those who did attend frowned on those who did not, but nonattendance occurred. Still membership was not entirely voluntary since the weight of habit, tradition, and the declared values of society continued to support participation in congregational life.

The appearance of Baptist dissenters and the Great Awakening, with its "old lights" and "new lights," increased the voluntary character of church membership. The choice had once been either joining in the parish or staying home. But by the 1750s many towns offered the choice of supporting an "old light," a "new light," a Baptist, or in a few places, an Anglican church. Church membership, more than family membership, furnished a range for individual choice in rural communities.

Public policy, however, still promoted church membership. Throughout the eighteenth century the Massachusetts electorate and their representatives affirmed public support for religion. Before the Revolution everyone, regardless of preference, was required to pay for the local established church. Postwar reforms permitted tithe support for other denominations, maintaining the idea that everyone must nourish the churches. Choice could be exercised within religion, but irreligion was unacceptable. With the vast body of opinion still warmly attached to the orthodox, established church, affiliation remained prescriptive for many people.

Membership and participation in the town was even less voluntary than church membership during the middle decades of the eighteenth century. Earlier, when towns were formed, they were voluntary associations like churches. But once towns passed into their second generation, the voluntary associations of the fathers became involuntary for the sons. One did not necessarily have to remain in the town of birth, but access to land together with family ties limited the scope of voluntary action. By the middle of the eighteenth century the potential economic advantages of migration to the frontier or to Boston were commonly overcome by the magnetism of the native town.[9]

At one level, admittedly, town membership was purely a matter of in-

[9] Greven, *Four Generations*; Kenneth Lockridge, "Land, Population and the Evolution of New England Society, 1630-1790," *Past and Present*, 39 (April 1968), 62-80.

dividual choice. No laws compelled individuals to remain where they were, and geographic mobility was a reality throughout the eighteenth century. By changing towns a person could leave family and congregation behind forever. If he moved to Boston, the center of urban society, he could avoid participation in these kinds of social corporations altogether. A Boston resident could be entirely unchurched, and he could convert town obligations into fines so as to avoid the web of civic responsibilities. If he left behind the family, the escape from these three basic associations might be complete. Hypothetically, to remain integrated into family, church, and town was a voluntary, individual act of will.

For most people this possibility was far removed from social reality. In contrast to the nineteenth century, eighteenth-century Boston was not thronged with country emigrants; the psychological, social, and economic functions of family, church, and town were indispensable for most inhabitants.[10] Alienation from these institutions was unknown, except for the ritual declamations of clergymen alienated from this sinful world. For most people the rural community was psychologically self-sufficient; they were content to be strangers to urban society.

In these communities, Michael Zuckerman has argued, individual relationships were subordinated to a "coercive" consensus owing to the overriding attachment to unity and harmony.[11] Common patterns of town and ecclesiastical politics, however, require significant modifications of Zuckerman's view. "Coercive" implies more active and purposeful denial of individual expression than was typical in Massachusetts towns, at least from the time of the Great Awakening onward. The multiplication and division of towns, districts, and parishes during the eighteenth century demonstrates that conflict was not always subordinated to ideals of unity and harmony. Imperatives of ecclesiastical and political self-determination were just as firmly embedded in the common value structure and often took precedence.

Still, as Zuckerman points out, the heterogeneity and cosmopolitanism of urban Boston were exceptional. Division and diversity were barely tolerated; before the Revolution they were never morally accepted. For this reason it became common to subdivide communities by forming new towns, districts, parishes, and precincts. Instead of developing variegated, heterogeneous

---

[10] G. B. Warden illustrates the absence of substantial migration to Boston from the countryside during the eighteenth century. In contrast, nineteenth-century Boston experienced much immigration from native as well as foreign areas. G. B. Warden, *Boston, 1689-1776* (Boston, 1970). See also Jesse R. Chickering, *A Statistical View of the Population of Massachusetts From 1765 to 1840* (Boston, 1846); Oscar Handlin, *Boston's Immigrants: A Study in Acculturation* (Cambridge, Mass., 1959); Peter R. Knights, *The Plain People of Boston, 1830-1860: A Study in City Growth* (New York, 1971).

[11] Zuckerman, *Peaceable Kingdoms.*

communities, people clung to the older unitary ideal where family, church, and town were interwoven into a single community, bound together by mutual interests and shared beliefs.

Participation in family, church, and town was so routinely expected that it was seldom a matter of conscious choice. The populace dwelt so comfortably within these institutions that participation was not coercive, merely involuntary. Nor was there any sense that it should be otherwise. Except in matters of faith and morality, society attached no premium to individual choice or the voluntary expression of will. Variety and heterogeneity were not seen as assets. If anything, the social ideology of the period displayed a contrary set of values, even in Boston.

The Revolution disrupted these time-honored patterns of community life and expectations. Their legitimacy eroded. New aspirations for community life, together with new experiences, came to supplant older attitudes and patterns of behavior. The organizational variety, heterogeneity, cosmopolitanism, and range of individual choice in personal associations that had once been peculiar to urban Boston now became a generalized feature of Massachusetts society.

One direct consequence of the Revolution was the new electoral system. Previously elections had been limited to the selection of familiar local notables to part-time duties. The new system, providing for statewide election of governor and lieutenant governor and district elections of state senators and (after 1788) United States congressmen, introduced anonymity and abstract issues as primary features of elections. Prior to 1780 the Massachusetts voter needed to know which of his townsmen he preferred to assess his property, act as selectmen, or represent his town's interest at the General Court. He chose local men for local needs. Now, suddenly, he began to choose strangers to serve largely unknown or indefinite interests of the state and the district. Voters' attention was necessarily directed toward supralocal concerns. The new system required a new cosmopolitanism.

This electoral cosmopolitanism would have had limited impact if local leaders had been able to unite in support of a single candidate and if townspeople had deferred to that choice. But as early as 1785 it became apparent that statewide electoral competition frequently divided voters within communities. In the gubernatorial election of 1785, when the popular John Hancock declined to run, most towns divided their vote fairly evenly among two or three candidates; less than one third returned majorities as high as 90 percent for one candidate.[12] Regardless of location or individual char-

---

[12] Compiled from Return of Votes, Governor and Lieutenant Governor, 1780-1820 (Massachusetts Archives, State House, Boston). Thirty-one percent of the 203 towns re-

acter, the overwhelming majority of communities divided over the question of which stranger should sit as governor. After Hancock died in 1793, electoral division became an annual institution, even before the onset of Federalist and Republican competition. Neither division nor competition was new to Massachusetts town politics, but now they were frequent, regular, and systematic. According to the new political ideology such division was legitimate.

By 1810, political sectarianism had become a durable feature of many localities. Federalists and Republicans created formal organizations at the town level. Loyalty to the local party chapter sometimes supplanted devotion to a town meeting that was often a battleground rather than a forum for consensus.[13] Throughout the state, political division and competition became commonplace. Elections were so vital to the state and national systems that the cosmopolitan politics of their operation inevitably became bound up with local personalities and grievances. By generating broad-based, vertically integrated electoral institutions, the Revolution provided a powerful stimulus to the diffusion of urban society.

The Revolution and the new electoral system extended urban social attitudes by enlarging the pool of community leaders.[14] Revolutionary civil and military activity multiplied committees and offices causing many people of very ordinary social qualifications to be drawn into active public roles. Their duties inevitably involved supra-local relationships, whether they were charged with raising and supplying troops, attending political con-

porting gave 90 percent or more of their vote to a single candidate in 1785. Later such displays of unanimity became comparatively rare; in 1820, for example, only 7 percent of the 256 reporting towns showed 90 percent or better for a candidate.

[13] James M. Banner, Jr., *To the Hartford Convention: The Federalists and the Origins of Party Politics in Massachusetts, 1789-1815* (New York, 1970); David Hackett Fischer, *The Revolution of American Conservatism: The Federalist Party in the Era of Jeffersonian Democracy* (New York, 1965), 59, 62, 65; Paul Goodman, *The Democratic-Republicans of Massachusetts: Politics in a Young Republic* (Cambridge, Mass., 1964); William T. Whitney, Jr., "The Crowninshields of Salem, 1800-1808: A Study in the Politics of Commercial Growth," *Essex Institute Historical Collections*, XCIV (Jan. 1958), 1-36, and *ibid.* (April 1958), 79-118; Charles Warren, *Jacobin and Junto, or Early American Politics as Viewed in the Diary of Dr. Nathaniel Ames, 1758-1822* (Cambridge, Mass., 1931); James Morton Smith, "The Federalist 'Saints' Versus 'The Devil of Sedition': The Liberty Pole Cases of Dedham, Massachusetts, 1798-1799," *New England Quarterly*, XXVIII (June 1955), 198-215; James H. Robbins, "The Impact of the First American Party System on Salem Politics," *Essex Institute Historical Collections*, CVII (July 1971), 254-67.

[14] John R. Howe, "Society and Politics in Revolutionary Massachusetts: Membership Patterns in the General Court, 1751-1800," paper presented at the annual meeting of the American Historical Association, Boston, Dec. 28, 1970; Jackson Turner Main, *The Social Structure of Revolutionary America* (Princeton, 1965); Jackson Turner Main, "Government by the People: The American Revolution and the Democratization of the Legislatures," *William and Mary Quarterly*, XXIII (July 1966), 391-407.

ventions, or serving as members of committees of correspondence, safety, and inspection.

Justifying these activities led to civic expectations approaching the values of urban society. Republican ideology emphasized information and communication as necessary for an enlightened citizenry; and it made adherence to abstract universals of freedom and justice crucial to American identity. As a result the old ethos of localism was fundamentally challenged. The new citizenship self-consciously demanded cosmopolitanism from everyone. The practical political effects of the Revolution furnished experience in acting out the new ideal.[15]

Widespread adherence to these civic aspirations was visible in the proliferation of formal voluntary associations during the generation or so following the Revolution. Once limited to urban Boston, and not very prominent there, they now multiplied rapidly all over Massachusetts (see Table I). Their development signified fundamental changes in community life.

In Boston charity societies, fire clubs, Freemasonry, and a handful of other organizations had been established by the mid-eighteenth century.[16] These, together with a host of informal clubs testified to the heterogeneity, perhaps even pluralism, that flourished in urban Boston. Elsewhere such variety was unknown.[17]

Between 1760 and 1820, however, over 1,900 voluntary associations were created. By the 1820s at least seventy were founded each year. They came in many varieties. Some, such as the associations of lawyers, doctors, and mechanics, were occupational and directed toward practical goals. At the other extreme were societies promoting good morals. In between lay a broad variety, including educational and cultural organizations, charities, civic groups, and profit-seeking corporations.

Their declared purposes were diverse. Some acted to supplement government services, such as providing for the poor and the sick, working to prevent and extinguish fires, educating children. A few acted as pressure groups for enforcement of statutes forbidding swearing and sabbath-breaking or

[15] Richard D. Brown, *Revolutionary Politics in Massachusetts: The Boston Committee of Correspondence and the Towns, 1772-1774* (Cambridge, Mass., 1970), 210-47; Gordon S. Wood, *The Creation of the American Republic, 1776-1787* (Chapel Hill, 1969), 91-255, 593-615.

[16] Early Boston societies included Scots Charitable Society (by 1684), Massachusetts Charitable Society (1672), Episcopal Charitable Society (1724), Charitable Irish Society (1737), St. John's Masonic Lodge (1733), Boston Marine Society (1742), Society for Industry (1754), and seven fire clubs (1717-1760).

[17] Salem, the second largest port in Massachusetts, with a population of about 4,250, had only two such organizations in 1760, a fire club and a library.

prohibiting wooden construction in Boston. There were even vigilante associations formed to stop horse thieves.[18]

The objectives of most were not seen as belonging to government, however essential they were regarded for individuals in a civilized society. Literary and debating clubs, libraries, and musical societies were formed to benefit participants and provide access to cosmopolitan culture. Societies organized to promote knowledge, whether marine, scientific, or historical, aimed at raising the general level of culture. Associations created for missionary purposes and religious education justified themselves in Christian or sectarian terms. They turned their adherents' outlook away from purely local church affairs toward the cosmopolitan concerns of their denomination, Christianity, or mankind in general. Whether secular or religious, voluntary associations encouraged cosmopolitanism and introduced a new heterogeneity into local communities.

In the past such urban society as existed in the countryside had been limited to a very thin layer of élite individuals. Now the proliferation of voluntary associations comprehended every social group. After 1790 women began to organize, both separately and with men, starting with charity clubs called "female fragment societies" and social libraries. By the 1820s, when the lyceum movement developed, participation by both sexes became routine. With the simultaneous creation of "mutual improvement associations," coeducational participation by youths between the ages of twelve and eighteen also became common.[19]

Though voluntary associations comprehended all social groups, including sailors and blacks, they were seldom egalitarian. Social libraries, for example, charged fees. Their rates, ranging from one to five dollars per year, indicate exclusiveness. A five-dollar library served the wealthy in port towns; even the one-dollar charge of a country library limited membership.[20] When

---

[18] Two examples that might be called pressure groups are the Pittsfield Auxiliary Society for Promoting Good Morals, started in 1814, and the Boston Charitable Fire Society, founded in 1794. Among the vigilante groups are the Horse-Thief Detecting Society of Milford, Mendon, and Bellingham and the Milton Horse-Thief Society.

[19] Kenneth C. R. White, "The American Lyceum" (doctoral dissertation, Harvard University, 1918); Carl Bode, *The American Lyceum: Town Meeting of the Mind* (Carbondale, Ill., 1968). Originally, lyceums were limited to men, but by 1830 both sexes attended. See [Josiah Holbrook], *American Lyceum, or Society for the Improvement of Schools, and Diffusion of Useful Knowledge* (Boston, 1829). Joseph F. Kett reports that "by 1820 the various denominations were competing for converts in the same towns and villages. Religious alternatives were at the parental door." Joseph F. Kett, "Adolescence and Youth in Nineteenth-Century America," *Journal of Interdisciplinary History*, II (Autumn 1971), 289.

[20] Examples of the varieties of exclusiveness are indicated by the following entrance requirements: Warwick Library Association was open to all women who paid twenty-five

TABLE I
VOLUNTARY ASSOCIATIONS FOUNDED IN MASSACHUSETTS BEFORE 1830[a]

| | Pre-1760 | | 1760s | | 1770s | | 1780s | | 1790s | | 1800s | | 1810s | | 1820s | |
	Boston	Mass.	Boston	Mass.	Boston	Mass.	Boston	Mass.	Boston	Mass.	Boston	Mass.	Boston	Mass.	Boston	Mass. and Maine
Charitable																
Missionary[b]	0	0	0	0	0	0	0	2	0	3	1	9	5	59	6	34
Needy	3	4	0	0	0	0	0	2	2	4	1	8	8	48	4	23
Reform[c]	0	0	0	0	0	0	0	0	0	2	0	0	3	43	3	91
Total Charitable	3	4	0	0	0	0	0	4	2	9	2	17	16	150	13	148
Civic																
Fire clubs	6	8	6	8	3	7	10	16	12	19	5	24	3	12	1	16
Law enforcement	0	0	0	0	0	0	0	0	0	2	0	0	0	4	0	3
Military	0	0	0	0	0	2	0	4	1	7	0	7	1	11	0	10
Political[d]	0	1	1	2	1	1	0	0	0	1	2	14	1	68	0	2
Total Civic	6	10	7	10	4	10	10	20	13	29	7	45	5	95	1	31
Education																
Academies[e]	0	0	0	1	0	1	0	4	1	25	0	37	0	12	1	34
Learned[f]	0	0	0	0	0	0	0	1	0	2	1	2	0	4	0	6
Debate, lit., music	0	1	0	1	0	3	0	3	1	3	0	13	4	1	1	28
Library	0	0	0	5	0	7	0	6	0	42	2	28	0	14	1	29
Lyceum	0	0	0	0	0	0	0	0	0	0	0	0	0	0	1	35
Religious	0	1	0	0	0	0	0	1	0	1	0	3	5	52	0	12
Total Education	0	2	0	7	0	11	0	15	3	73	3	83	9	83	4	144
Occupational																
Agriculture	0	0	0	0	0	0	0	0	0	2	0	3	0	16	0	9
Learned professions[g]	0	3	0	0	0	0	0	3	1	30	0	4	0	1	1	2
Marine	1	1	0	1	0	1	0	0	0	3	0	0	0	0	0	0
Mechanic	0	0	0	0	0	0	0	0	2	3	3	5	0	4	0	2
Merchant	1	1	1	1	0	0	0	0	1	1	1	1	1	3	1	1
Total Occupational	2	5	1	2	0	1	0	3	4	39	4	13	1	24	2	14

															Total
Profit-seeking															
Banks	0	0	0	0	0	0	1	1	1	6	1	17	4	33	6	40
Insurance	0	0	0	1	0	1	1		4	5	5	26	4	8	13	32
Manufacture	0	0	0	1	0	0	0	2	0	3	0	21	3	113	19	130
Utilities[h]	0	0	0	0	0	0	0		1	16	0	14	0	5	0	16
Total Profit-seeking	0	0	0	1	0	2	2	5	6	30	6	78	11	159	38	218
Worship and Ritual																
Christian	18	247	0	35	0	26	0	63	3	116	2	117	5	118	14	249
Freemason	3	3	4	5	3	13	1	4	3	46	3	54	1	32	1	50
Total Worship and Ritual	21	250	4	40	3	39	1	67	6	162	5	171	6	150	15	299
TOTALS	32	272	12	60	7	63	13	114	31	342	27	407	48	661	73	852
Supra-Local																
Intertown	0		1	0	0	0	2		12		15		18			26
County	1		0	0	0	0	2		4		16		41			29
Region	2		0	0	0	0	1		28		3		22			12
District of Maine	0		0	0	0	0			6		2		6			4
State	2		0	0	0	0	7		10		7		12			8
Nation	0		0	0	0	0	2		0		0		8			2
Total Supra-Local	5		0	0	0	0	14		54		43		107			81

a Secondary sources include: Redmond J. Barnett, "From Philanthropy to Reform: Poverty, Drunkenness and the Social Order in Massachusetts, 1780-1825" (doctoral dissertation, Harvard University, 1973); Fischer, *Revolution of American Conservatism*, 118; Jesse H. Shera, *Foundations of the Public Library: The Origins of the Public Library Movement in New England 1629-1855* (Chicago, 1949), 255-60; and White, "The American Lyceum," 373-82. Searches were also made of extant Massachusetts and Maine town histories, Massachusetts Registers, the Early American Imprint series, statutes, newspapers, and the central records and publications of associations. Further searches elsewhere yielded diminishing returns. This tabulation is certainly incomplete. Specialized studies exist for only some of the categories included in the list, and some town historians omitted voluntary associations from their writings. For inclusion in this tabulation the author required that the approximate date of founding be located. Some fifty associations whose origin or function could not be ascertained have been deliberately omitted. Because the sources vary in reliability and because the entire "census" is flawed by the circumstances cited above, readers are cautioned against making detailed statistical comparisons on the basis of this tabulation.

b "Missionary" includes domestic and foreign as well as class-oriented local missions.

c "Reform" includes morals, peace, and temperance.

d "Political" includes extralegal clubs and party groups.

e "Academies" includes colleges and private corporate secondary schools.

f "Learned" includes organizations such as the American Academy of Arts and Sciences, American Antiquarian Society, and Massachusetts Historical Society.

g "Learned professions" includes clergy, lawyers, and physicians.

h "Utilities" includes transport, wharves, aqueducts, and booms.

lyceums were founded during the 1820s, they aimed at inclusive membership and kept their annual charge to only fifty cents.[21] Literary societies were
more exclusive, since membership was by invitation, and they often formed
around friendship or kin groups composed of young grammar school and
college graduates.[22] Even fire clubs could be exclusive. John Adams remarked
in 1774 that "It is of some Importance in Boston to belong to a Fire Clubb
and to choose and get admitted to a good one."[23] Their tendency to remain
small and club-like is illustrated by the frequent formation of new fire clubs
by men excluded from the old ones.[24]

Masonry was exclusive as a matter of principle. Poverty was one barrier
to masonic lodges, in part owing to prudential considerations, since the
masons served as a mutual insurance society. But members were not all
wealthy, and factors such as adherence to "liberal principles" and religious
tolerance also counted. Generally, extreme or abrasive personalities were
unwelcome in an organization that stressed harmony, love, and order.
Lodges resembled contemporary social clubs and the secret fraternities that
were appearing at Harvard College, grouping people of similar attitudes
and social rank. Significantly, a separate lodge was organized by and for
blacks in 1787.[25] The increased social stratification and heterogeneity characteristic of urban culture were prominent consequences of the new voluntary associations.

By 1820 a new pattern of community organization had penetrated Massachusetts towns. Localism and insularity were being challenged, if not
actually destroyed. People remained bound to the old organizations of

cents annually (1815); Reading Library charged one-dollar membership plus twenty-five
cents annual dues; Deerfield Second Social Library admitted new members by unanimous
vote of old members and charged four to six dollars annually; Portland Library Association charged two dollars per year in 1784 and fifteen dollars by 1801.

[21] For example the Kennebunk Lyceum (1829) admitted any adult for fifty cents per
year, twenty-five cents for minors.

[22] The diary of Nathaniel Ames reveals the exclusiveness of Dedham literary circles.
Warren, *Jacobin and Junto*. The Literary and Moral Society of Kennebunk (1818) normally met in private but held one public meeting each year at which members performed
their own literary creations. The most grandiose of such societies was the Somerset
Halcyonic and Logical Society for the Promotion of Literature in the County of Somerset
(1809).

[23] John Adams to William Tudor, Jr., July 24, 1774, William Tudor Papers (Massachusetts Historical Society, Boston).

[24] Josiah Quincy, *A Municipal History of the Town and City of Boston, During Two
Centuries: From September 17, 1630, to September 17, 1830* (Boston, 1852), 153-59.

[25] Prince Hall first organized a lodge in 1775 under the auspices of an English military lodge. After the war, Boston masons refused to charter the lodge, so Hall appealed
to London and a charter was issued in 1784. Three years later the African Lodge installed its officers. Wm. H. Grimshaw, *Official History of Freemasonry Among the Colored People in North America* (New York, 1903), 67-83; *Proceedings in Masonry: St.
John's Grand Lodge, 1773-1792, Massachusetts Grand Lodge, 1769-1792* (Boston, 1895).

family, church, and town, but now they possessed additional ties, links that brought them outside their family, neighborhood, and congregation and into contact with strangers. Sometimes the contact was direct, if they traveled to a meeting or convention or if outsiders came to them as part of a political campaign, lyceum, temperance or missionary association. More often, the contact was psychological, coming from membership in a countywide or statewide organization and the publications such activities produced.

The expansion and decentralization of printing and postal service are indicative of the penetration of supra-local communications into the countryside. Although every one did not read newspapers or write letters, access to communications became almost universally available. The decentralization of printing began with the wartime dispersion of Boston printers. Isaiah Thomas, who moved his press from Boston to Worcester, explained that "After the establishment of our independence, by the peace of 1783, presses multiplied very fast, not only in seaports, but in all the principal inland towns and villages."[26] In 1760 Massachusetts had nine print shops (none in Maine), virtually all located in Boston. By 1820 there were 120 scattered throughout the state.[27]

Newspapers boomed. In 1760 Massachusetts possessed five newspapers, all located in Boston, whereas by 1820 there were fifty-three dailies and weeklies being published in twenty-three different towns (including the District of Maine).[28] Neither a newspaper nor a press was sufficient to make an urban milieu of a country town, but taken in conjunction with the new civic attitudes and behavior, the decentralization of printing was a significant element in the spread of urban society. Likewise the new periodicals of the early nineteenth century, with subscribers scattered throughout the state, were vehicles of urban society. The dramatic rise in the per capita consumption of printed materials indicates the shift toward cosmopolitan communications.[29] Word-of-mouth and face-to-face patterns con-

[26] Isaiah Thomas, *The History of Printing In America: With a Biography of Printers, with the Author's Corrections and Additions and A Catalogue of American Publications Previous to the Revolution of 1776: A Chronological Dictionary of All Books, Pamphlets, and Periodical Publications Printed in the United States of America from the Genesis of Printing in 1639 Down to and Including the Year 1820* (Albany, 1874), I, 18, 25.

[27] Compiled from Charles Evans and others, *American Bibliography* (14 vols., Worcester, Mass., 1903-1959), and Ralph R. Shaw and Richard H. Shoemaker, *American Bibliography: A Preliminary Checklist for 1801-1819* (22 vols., New York, 1958-1966).

[28] Compiled from Clarence S. Brigham, *History and Bibliography of American Newspapers, 1690-1820* (2 vols., Worcester, Mass., 1947). In 1765 the colonies had twenty-six newspapers; in 1800 the United States had 267.

[29] There is no way to determine precisely the per capita consumption of printed matter, in part owing to imports from other states and Britain. The ratio of newspapers to pop-

tinued within communities—the newspapers were virtually free of local reporting—but now supra-local communication became common, and printing was its normal mode.

Further evidence of the rise of supra-local communication may be found in the development of the postal system. Before the Revolution there was only one post office in the entire province. By 1820 Massachusetts (including Maine) had 443 post offices blanketing the state.[30] Now virtually every community possessed direct, official connection to the national communication system. Expanded postal communications together with the extraordinary growth of printing and voluntary associations demonstrate that key elements in the urban social syndrome—a cosmopolitan perspective and communications system as well as heterogeneous community organizations —now prevailed generally in Massachusetts.

Physically most Massachusetts towns were not much different in 1820 from what they had been in 1760. A countryside composed of woodland, orchards, and cleared fields remained, the houses still built of clapboard and shingles following popular adaptations of classical designs. The chief public buildings remained the churches; taverns continued as the neighborhood gathering places. Manufacturing was still small-scale, and railroads were a generation away. Physically Massachusetts was far from urban. Even its metropolis, Boston, with a population of 43,000 people, remained a township not a city.[31] Nonetheless, in advance of industrialization and urbanization as large-scale material phenomena, agricultural Massachusetts had developed a broad attachment to urban society.

Why should this transformation have occurred? Technology did not change so swiftly or dramatically as to alter existing capabilities. There were no "breakthroughs" in land or water transportation and no major alterations in printing techniques. Agricultural technology was similarly sta-

ulation climbed from two per 100,000 people in 1760 to five per 100,000 people in 1820, and the per capita number of separate titles published increased from thirty-two per 100,000 to seventy-five per 100,000 in the same period. Compiled from Evans and others, *American Bibliography*.

[30] One post office is listed at Boston in 1767. John Mein and John Fleming, *Massachusetts Register . . . For the Year 1767* (Boston, n.d.), 34. As late as 1774 the situation had not changed. *Mills and Hicks's British and American Register* [1774] (Boston, n.d.), 60. The Revolution produced significant changes, and by 1779 Falmouth (Portland, Me.), Newbury, Ipswich, Salem, Worcester, and Springfield all had post offices in addition to Boston. *Fleet's Register for the State of Massachusetts Bay in New England for . . . 1779* (Boston, 1779). Figures for 1820 were compiled from *Massachusetts Register . . . 1820* (Boston, n.d.), 136-41. As in the case of newspapers, the spread of post offices was a national phenomenon: there were seventy-five in 1790 and 4,500 in 1820. *Historical Statistics of the United States: Colonial Times to 1957*, p. 497.

[31] See Timothy Dwight, *Travels in New England and New York*, Barbara Miller Solomon, ed. (4 vols., Cambridge, Mass., 1969).

ble. There is nothing to suggest any significant increase in leisure time.[32] Explanations must be sought elsewhere in society. It appears that the reasons for the extension of urban society lay in the interaction between the Revolution, the Second Great Awakening and its secular counterpart, the flowering of a romantic view of progress, and commercial development and population growth. Together these events brought much of urban society to country villages, making their old cultural isolation obsolete.

The Revolution altered the political structure, especially elections, so as to promote supra-local perspectives. It generated a new definition of the citizen's role, one very different from prewar British subjects. Political participation and citizen initiative were held up as ideals in the new Republic. National patriotism superseded local identifications. These changes were institutionalized by the political parties that formed around 1800. Canvassing from door-to-door, in newspapers, parades, festivals, and orations, Federalists and Jeffersonians both promulgated the Revolutionary ideal of active citizenship and concern for supra-local issues. The aggressive politicking of their local organizations stigmatized parochial passivity. So effective were their organizations, so pervasive was the new ideal, that in peak years of statewide electoral competition, turnouts approached 75 percent of eligible voters.[33] The Revolutionary ideal of active citizenship penetrated virtually every community and household throughout Massachusetts.

Simultaneously the Second Great Awakening with its quest for individual regeneration reinforced secular development.[34] With saving grace illustrated by acts of piety, the regenerate were stimulated to band together for the promotion of pious goals. Sabbath schools and missionary societies were

[32] Roads were improved and canals were built as the consequence of new aspirations, not new technology. See Ram G. Deshmukh, "Development of Highways in Massachusetts" (doctoral dissertation, Harvard University, 1927). In printing one great stimulus to mass production was stereotype, which gradually appeared after 1810. The early years of the nineteenth century saw some movement toward scientific farming, but Clarence H. Danhof characterizes the decades prior to 1820 as essentially stable. Clarence H. Danhof, *Change in Agriculture: The Northern United States, 1820-1870* (Cambridge, Mass., 1969). Improvements in the quality and cost of lighting also came later, so there is no reason to suppose that technology had made evening activities any easier than before.

[33] On the behavior of the parties see Banner, *To the Hartford Convention*; and Goodman, *Democratic-Republicans of Massachusetts*. Turnout figures are based on comparison of adult male population with votes recorded in Return of Votes, Governor and Lieutenant Governor, Massachusetts Archives. The peak years were 1812 (74 percent), 1808 (64 percent), and 1816 (64 percent).

[34] John L. Thomas, "Romantic Reform in America, 1815-1865," *American Quarterly*, XVII (Winter 1965), 656-81; Donald G. Mathews, "The Second Great Awakening as an Organizing Process, 1780-1830: An Hypothesis," *ibid.*, XXI (Spring 1969), 23-43.

17

direct manifestations of these impulses. Religious concerns were evident in
Handel and Haydn societies aimed at improving the quality of sacred music. Libraries and literary clubs dwelt on religious subjects and often
avowed goals of moral and spiritual self-improvement. Charities to relieve
one or another group were informed by Christian impulses. Even a secular
figure, John Quincy Adams, emphasized Christian virtues in addressing
a charitable fire society.[35]

The impulse to active citizenship that sprang from awakened piety was
complemented by enlightened and romantic elements in contemporary
thought. Rational solutions to long-standing hazards like commercial risks
and fire became popular in the form of insurance companies (see Table I).
Gathering and communicating information was viewed as rational altruism,
encouraging libraries, debating clubs, learned societies, and occupational
associations. Simultaneously expectations for the perfection of society and
the individual were reaching romantic heights. For Americans self-devel-
opment, an idea connected to awakened Christianity, had become a primary
cultural ideal. This made passivity appear positively sinful. Cultural isolation was recognized as a serious handicap to self-improvement.

This new outlook is visible in Boston's response to fires. Unlike epidemics and earthquakes, fires were not purely natural disasters. Human
imprudence bore heavy responsibility. But even as late as 1760 the liberal
Jonathan Mayhew was preaching from the text "Shall there be evil in a
city, and the Lord hath not done it?" He concluded that "when God's
judgments are abroad in the earth, it is then more especially incumbent
upon the inhabitants thereof to learn righteousness." Mayhew thus treated
calamity as punishment to be accepted with soul-searching humility. Fire
prevention or fire control was extraneous, since the fire was "particularly
calculated to wean your affections from this evil world; and excite you to
seek, with greater diligence, the true spiritual riches."[36] Since Mayhew was
as "modern" a clergyman as pre-Revolutionary Boston possessed, it is no
wonder that civic activism possessed a limited appeal, especially in the
countryside.

In 1802 when John Quincy Adams addressed the Massachusetts Char-

[35] John Quincy Adams, *An Address to the Members of the Massachusetts Charitable
Fire Society, at their Annual Meeting, May 28, 1802* (Boston, 1802). The Boston Handel-
Haydn Society was "instituted for the purpose of associating together the admirers of
the great masters whose names they had adopted, for practice and improvement in the
performance of Sacred Musick." *Massachusetts Register for the Year 1825* (Boston, n.d.),
164.
[36] Jonathan Mayhew, *God's Hand and Providence to be religiously acknowledged in
public Calamities, A Sermon Occasioned by The Great Fire in Boston, New-England,
Thursday, March 20, 1760* (Boston, 1760), 5, 36, 29.

itable Fire Society his mood was utterly different. Although his rhetoric was permeated with Christian principles, his message was dominated by the idea that calamitous fires were the consequence of erroneous policy and shortsighted parsimony, not divine judgment. Clapboard and shingles, not sinfulness, were the culprits. By 1800 fires were not punishments to be borne; they must be combated with human ingenuity marshaled in voluntary associations.[37] Active citizenship, whether inspired by rationalism, religion, or romanticism, had become the proper response to social problems.

Commercial development and population growth accompanied these changes in outlook and nourished urban heterogeneity and cosmopolitanism. The correlation between associational activity, population, and commercial growth was apparent in Boston by 1760; after independence it became even more pronounced. One indicator is the volume of postal traffic in Massachusetts. Postal traffic was primarily a function of commercial activity and population. By the 1820s fifteen of the sixteen towns where associational activity was most fully developed were among the top 20 percent in postal revenues. Towns at the median level of associational activity appeared at the median of postal traffic.[38] Certainly there were other variables affecting the number of voluntary associations in a town and its participation in urban society; but wherever population and commerce flourished, voluntary associations and the other components of urban culture were sure to appear.

Massachusetts communities began to develop the organizational heterogeneity associated with urban society only after they had reached certain demographic and occupational thresholds. The population range necessary to generate and sustain multiple organizations was from about 1,000 to 2,000 people, roughly 200 to 400 families. It was important that at least 20 percent of the men be engaged in non-agricultural callings, in commerce, processing and manufacturing, or services.[39] There was no great rise in leisure time during this period, but there was significant growth among

[37] Adams, *Address to the Members of the Massachusetts Charitable Fire Society*, 9, 6-14. In the 1820s Mayor Josiah Quincy led the movement to create a public fire department. Quincy, *Municipal History*, 187-89, 204-06, 230, 253-54.

[38] Data on postal traffic are based on revenues in Walter Lowrie and Walter S. Franklin, eds., *American State Papers, Documents, Legislative and Executive, of the Congress of the United States from the First Session of the First to the Second Session of the Twenty-Second Congress, Inclusive: Commencing March 4, 1789, and Ending March 2, 1833: Post Office Department* (Washington, 1834), 163-64. Data are for 1826-1827 and are doubtless different from several years earlier, but there is no reason to believe that the basic pattern would not apply as of 1820.

[39] Population and occupational data are from the *Census for 1820: Published by authority of an Act of Congress, under the direction of the Secretary of State* (Washington, 1821).

occupations that permitted leisure, communication, and concentration in villages. During the years 1760 to 1820 the vast majority of Massachusetts towns surpassed these thresholds.

The emergence of urban culture was related to other social and geographic factors. Where a single town dominated commerce and communications in a county or region, urban social characteristics developed in that central town, but their appearance was retarded in the surrounding area. In the counties of Essex and Worcester, however, where commerce was particularly decentralized and where the social élite was distributed among many towns, communications and organizational activity became exceptionally developed in middle-sized towns of 2,000 to 3,000 people. Everywhere county seats that were centers of trade, administration, and communication and that possessed a higher than average proportion of people in non-agricultural occupations experienced higher levels of social urbanization.[40] Massachusetts towns remained predominantly agricultural, but it was the merchants, lawyers, printers, millers, and artisans who together created the secular society of Massachusetts villages. They exercised a disproportionate role in bringing urban culture to the countryside. Their outlook, less insular and more cosmopolitan than the typical farmer, gave them central roles in the transformation of community life.[41]

Commercial development and population growth were crucial to the spread of urban culture. But they were not sufficient to account for what happened. Before the Revolution there had been dozens of towns with 300 or 400 families that were tied to commerce. But such towns had shown few signs of urban culture. After 1780, life changed. The consequences of the Revolution, electoral competition, expanded communications, and the ideologies of active self-improvement stimulated a social transformation. Heterogeneity and cosmopolitanism became the common experience, and the human resources of average agricultural communities became sufficient to provide a modicum of urban society.

The expansion of urban society in Massachusetts preceded large-scale commercial and industrial development. Before the appearance of great cities and factories, the inhabitants had embraced values and patterns of community life that would promote city growth. An ideology emphasizing the social virtues of cities began to be expressed, challenging the old ideal

---

[40] County seats with high levels of social urbanization included Worcester, Pittsfield, Northampton, and Springfield.

[41] The relative traditionalism of farmers was noted by Levi Lincoln, *New England Farmer* (Boston, 1823), I, 180, quoted in Earl W. Hayter, *The Troubled Farmer, 1850-1900: Rural Adjustment to Industrialism* (DeKalb, Ill., 1968), 4.

of the self-sufficient, isolated, rural yeoman. The legendary yeoman survived in American mythology, but a rival vision of America as the land of thriving cities and cultural excellence emerged. In a lecture on "the Moral and other Indirect Influences of Rail-Roads," a lyceum speaker stated that "Society alone is a rich source of education and improvement, in all that is most desirable,—all that ministers to the elevation and perfection of human nature,—knowledge, morals, manners, taste, and personal appearance. . . . [And] society [is] better in cities than in towns, in towns than in villages, and in villages than in country places."[42] The yeoman had not yet become a "hayseed," but he was warned that if he stayed exclusively on his farm, he became a boor. He was isolating himself from "all that ministers to the elevation and perfection of human nature," and becoming a stranger to "good company; by which is meant, social circles possessed of correct morals, sound and well-informed intellects, and cultivated manners."[43] The city, before it became engulfed by industrial smoke and masses of aliens, possessed a romantic appeal based on the cosmopolitanism and richness of its social life.

Under these circumstances, people in Massachusetts, whether yeomen or artisans, commercial or professional, were eager to share the advantages of urban society though they lived in the countryside. Cosmopolitanism and the didactic benefits of voluntary social intercourse competed successfully with the older community ideal of homogeneous unity. Printing and the post office furnished easy access to information from anywhere in the world, while voluntary organizations provided opportunities for social intercourse within a circle of one's own choosing. Participation in traditional corporate groups—family, church, and town—was less prescriptive now that there were supplementary alternatives. The range of individual choices was expanding.

One consequence was that the focus of individual duties and obligations shifted. Prescribed duties to the town and the local community were now rivaled by obligations to new associations. These obligations might complement those of the community, as in the creation of academies and sabbath schools. Alternatively, they might bear no relation to communal duties, as in the case of learned societies. They might even conflict with the community as a whole. Masonic lodges were potentially divisive subcommunities. Occupational groups looked to their own interests first and to those of the entire community later. Similarly, preoccupation with a fire society or

[42] Charles Caldwell, "Thoughts Regarding the Moral and other Indirect Influences of Rail-Roads," *New-England Magazine*, II (April 1832), 290.
[43] *Ibid.*, 290.

the moral reform of the poor detracted from a comprehensive attachment to community goals. In time, the legitimation of political competition and voluntary associations brought legitimacy to the special interest group. Henceforth such organized interest groups would exercise a major role in defining the public good.

These conditions withered the old corporate insularity of towns. Tied by commerce, politics, and communications to the world outside its boundaries, the preeminence of the town as the focus of secular concern declined. Weakening of purely local allegiances and development of supra-local interest groups made the old compulsion to achieve consensus anachronistic. Townspeople were now members of many communities—their own organizations as well as the state and the nation.

People now left their hometowns readily to pursue careers elsewhere. New supra-local attachments had been formed while old localistic loyalties weakened. Communications had helped to make the outside world less alien and allowed nominal maintenance of old ties through the mail. Before the Revolution many sons had been reluctant to leave home; now they seemed almost eager to enter the larger world, whether they went west to farm or headed for the rapidly growing and multiplying cities.[44] The development of multiple allegiances that was tied to the dissemination of urban culture permitted individuals to free themselves from local bonds. It served as one of the psychological preconditions for the great nineteenth-century migrations to the cities and to the West.[45]

All these phenomena are associated with Massachusetts in the six decades following 1760. Whether they were generally common is less certain. But it seems unlikely that the emergence of urban society throughout Massachusetts was unique. Perhaps it merely occurred earlier and to a more exaggerated degree there than elsewhere owing to Massachusetts' political and cultural heritage and its unusually well integrated commercial and communications networks. To move from the particular case of Massachusetts

[44] Joseph F. Kett, "Growing Up in Rural New England, 1800-1840," Tamara K. Hareven, ed., *Anonymous Americans: Explorations in Nineteenth-Century Social History* (Englewood Cliffs, N. J., 1971), 1-16. Daniel Scott Smith maintains that parental control was diminishing in Massachusetts at the end of the eighteenth century and that autonomous behavior was increasing. Daniel Scott Smith, "Parental Power and Marriage Patterns: An Analysis of Historical Trends in Hingham, Massachusetts," *Journal of Marriage and the Family*, 35 (Aug. 1973), 419-28. Percy W. Bidwell, "The Agricultural Revolution in New England," *American Historical Review*, XXVI (July 1921), 700-01. On the growth and multiplication of cities see Taylor, "American Urban Growth."

[45] A broader view of this type of phenomenon is presented in Karl W. Deutsch, "Social Mobilization and Political Development," *American Political Science Review*, LV (Sept. 1961), 493-514.

to the United States in general may seem foolhardy, especially before the case is firmly established for Massachusetts. But since the key phenomena appeared throughout the northern United States—the Revolution, electoral competition, expanded communications, ideologies of active self-improvement, voluntary associations and interest groups, commercial development and population growth, and finally the extensive migrations and the growth of cities—one is tempted to conclude that the extension of urban society to rural America in the preindustrial era was one of the central events of the first half of the nineteenth century.

Journal of Historical Geography, 10, 4 (1984) 331–356

Elaboration of a settlement system:
the New England village in the federal period

J. S. Wood

Contemporary New England villages arose as nineteenth-century central places. The emergence of these commercial places reflected not the creation of something new out of whole cloth but an elaboration of an existing settlement system, a legacy of the colonial period and a manifestation of long-standing cultural habit. Town centers, more or less equally spaced and comprised of little more than a meetinghouse and a tavern, served as foci for town activities, as *auxiliary central places*. Most of the considerable localized economic exchange that characterized the colonial period occurred at *dispersed places*. The emergence of true central places about colonial town centers in the federal period marked a shift in scale or a general and widespread development of extra-local exchange, division of labor, and provision of centrality—the ability of a place to provide goods and services beyond the needs of its residents. Central places became accretions of full-time nonfarmers, of storekeepers, artisans, and professional people. Moreover, these places were interlinked to form a system of central places and, although a sorting process took place, the system was both a material manifestation of contemporary economic experience and an elaboration of the colonial settlement system.

The village one encounters today in the landscape of New England was formed in the federal period, in the last decades of the eighteenth century and the first decades of the nineteenth century. The villages were new places of commerce, not the simple agricultural-community centers thought to have dotted the colonial landscape. The new village was a central place, what geographers commonly call active market places that dominate and are central to a market area. Yet, the New England village was not immaculately conceived. The rise of these commercial villages reflected not the creation of something new out of whole cloth, but an elaboration of an existing settlement system, a legacy of the colonial period and a manifestation of long-standing cultural habit.

Elaboration here means the detailed working out or development (or decline) of the system of the New England villages in their historical and geographical context. Human geographic patterns reflect cultural habits of interaction and organization. Such geographic patterns, however, tend to persist long after the cultural habits that produced them have faded away. Because they persist, geographical patterns condition subsequent human activity. In New England, the town has always been the culturally significant unit of settlement. The colonial town center provided dispersed farmers with comfortable access to a centrally located meetinghouse by means of an elaborate town road network. When a meetinghouse proved too eccentric in its location for a portion of the congregation, division took place so that every family had its own town center nearby. Although local exchange was more than sufficient to support the

0305–7488/84/040331 + 26 $03.00/0 331

presence of central-place activities—by part-time practitioners—the rural economy simply did not support many central places, and commercial villages inland were few and far between.

The federal period, in contrast, witnessed a more commercial rural economy, or at least an economy able to support central places. Farmers left agriculture to take up full-time commerce, processing, and professions, and by relocating they gathered together to make central places out of what had been colonial town centers. A marked geographic separation of production and ultimate sale of goods had occurred, and town centers, already centrally and uniformly spaced and interconnected by town road networks, provided comfortable access for dispersed farmers to centrally located clusters of stores and shops. Even the directions in which goods flowed persisted. The flow of goods between commercial villages followed lines of credit and exchange developed by traders during the colonial period and, though turnpikes later captured flows of goods, such roads did not redirect flows. Hence, the New England village emerged within and came to comprise an increasingly elaborate regional system of central places, reflecting the level and intensity of activity that characterized the federal period but founded on a pre-commercial colonial settlement system. In short, the town center provided an appropriate site for a central place where New Englanders were predisposed to congregate. The settlement system persisted.

Theory of central places

Central place theory seeks to explain logically the localization of economic exchange at centrally located places and the resultant geographical distribution of such places.[1] The number and type of commercial functions performed in any market center are related to the size and relative location of the center and to the center's position in a hierarchy of market centers or central places. A central place, as distinct from any settlement, is a mediator of local commerce with the outside world. This "surplus importance" or "central importance" of the place, as it has been called, produces "centrality", or the ability of a place to provide goods and services in excess of the needs of its residents. A crossroads, even with a church and tavern or store, is not necessarily a central place without a degree of centrality. Centrality of a place, therefore, refers less to its location than to its function as a provider of central goods and services, including non-economic or cultural offerings that nevertheless seem to respond to laws of economic behavior.[2]

Theoretically, the service areas of central places will be arranged in such a way as to take on a hexagonal shape because this is the most efficient subdivision of space. New England towns, or settlement patterns anywhere, are rarely hexagonal, but the spacing of settlements is remarkably regular in reality. Because of this regularity, central place theory is often invoked to explain the evolution and arrangement of settlement patterns.[3]

Most historical geographers invoking central place theory have related the development of an expansive and hierarchical diffusion of a central-place system across the landscape, either in the Christallerian mode or, for instance, as Vance has predicated in his mercantile model.[4] What the New England experience of the federal period appears to illustrate, however, is something different. The development (and later decline) of the central-place system is not so much the emergence of new locations or places offering central goods as it is a shift in scale, the development of centrality at already established places, or the elaboration of the existing settlement system.

In a historical view, the relative importance of central places can change markedly over time. For instance, the appearance of functions and the proliferation of establishments should parallel population growth, though population growth alone is hardly an adequate measure of the centrality of a place.[5] Moreover, as McManis has previously noted, a central-place system was inherent in the New England town system, but exception should be taken to his inference that a particular site within each town was necessarily and consciously designated to be a future central place.[6] Nevertheless, as Christaller argued, "the rational scheme of the system is not itself changed; only the decisive factors are changed."[7] Put another way: "The rule is that the older system previously determined always determines the more recent system developed under other economic laws and conditions with other types of central goods and other ranges of these central goods."[8]

In this regard, the development of a central-place system should not necessarily be viewed as a diffusion of locations or places, but may also be viewed as a diffusion of the creation of centrality or the increased demand for central goods, giving rise to central places at existing settlement sites within a persistent settlement system. Change in centrality, because of a shift in the scale of a rural economy, can produce a shift in the scale of a central-place system and the proliferation or decline of central places.

Understanding of the notion of elaboration hinges on the distinction between a central place and what Christaller called *auxiliary central places* and *dispersed places*. The presence of institutions of exchange does not measure the central importance of a place. Only extra-local exchange is regarded as a basis for centrality and, notwithstanding clear evidence of exchange, few central places actually existed in colonial rural New England. Dispersed goods and services were provided at dispersed places, at the homes or farms of producers, the locations of which were hardly determined by any economic advantage with respect to other places.[9] In this regard, colonial New England towns, comprised of many dispersed places where localized exchange had taken place, have been misconstrued as central places.[10]

Many noneconomic activities, however, still required a measure of centrality. As a matter of cultural practice, the town center's meetinghouse provided a gathering place for social, political, and religious activities. The colonial New England tavern, too, had a role that went well beyond serving cider and rum to locals or providing meals and lodging to occasional passers-by. It was also a place where people gathered to exchange news and opinions or to engage in personal business. Meetinghouses were sited and resited to ensure a central location for the town's cultural activities. Many entrepreneurial New Englanders, fully conscious of the importance of a central location, thus located their tavern next door to the meetinghouse or urged that the meetinghouse be constructed nearby. The colonial town center was an auxiliary central place, dependent for its existence on the comings and goings of townspeople but hardly a place of much extra-local exchange.[11]

What follows is an abbreviated attempt to illustrate the notion of elaboration in a settlement system. In an analysis of the emergence of central places in early nineteenth-century New England, no K-systems are identified and no test of central place theory is intended. But it is clear from the New England experience

that well developed cultural habits of interaction and organization, not simply
the emergence of a commercial society, set the regular pattern of settlement
which the commercial society adopted. Culture underlies settlement patterns—
something of which Christaller was well aware.[12]

Settlement landscape of colonial New England

To understand the rise of New England villages in the federal period, one
must understand the colonial settlement landscape. Plans for nucleated
settlements and the term "village" are common enough in colonial records. As a
result of this evidence, along with the presumed cultural predisposition of
Englishmen toward nucleated settlement and the particular centripetal forces
operating in the New England wilderness, the settlement landscape, in the
seventeenth century at least, has long been thought to have resembled a large
pan of fried eggs—a community at each yolk and the community's resources
held in common in the whites.[13] The analogy is hardly correct, however.
Seventeenth-century settlement was not necessarily compact or nucleated.
Dispersed settlement has long been attributed to settlement in the eighteenth
century. But a closer look at the behavior of seventeenth-century Englishmen
has revealed that they too were less predisposed to nucleated settlement and
common-field agriculture and that, except in the upper Connecticut valley,
mutual defense was not the compelling centripetal force it has been thought to
be. Indeed, no single form of settlement or, as some have proposed, evolutionary
model of settlement form can account for colonial settlement, and regional
distinctions are apparent, reflecting the diversity of settlement practices brought
from England.[14] Commercial places, ranging in size from small landings to such
urban places as Boston, were important components of the settlement
landscape, though their number was relatively limited in the colonial period, and
they were concentrated along tidewater or within easy reach of tidewater.[15]
Agricultural settlements, what Christaller might have identified as dispersed
places or at best auxiliary central places, ranged in form from very compact,
such as at Hampton, New Hampshire, to the isolated farmsteads of squatters as
at Framingham, Massachusetts.[16] But most settlements—towns—regardless of
when settled, appear to have been composed of loosely gathered neighborhoods
of farmers. The modal form of settlement was dispersed.[17]

In the relative absence of compact villages from the early seventeenth century
on, the town itself formed the basis for settlement, and the meetinghouse was the
symbolic focus of the settlement, regardless of how compact or dispersed
settlement was in the town. The location of the meetinghouse might have been
planned from the start, or it might have been the result of considerable
controversy and negotiation. Meetinghouse sites located by legislative fiat or
before settlement took place were removed to a preferable site if they proved to
be "uncentrical".[18] Once the site for a meetinghouse had been set, however,
roads were laid out to it, which is to say that a maze of trails was established
within the town by common usage, so that all farmsteads might have access to
the meetinghouse. The location of the meetinghouse with respect to the
distribution of population within a town was therefore always more important
than geometric centrality.

Division of towns

Not everyone could be satisfied with the location of the meetinghouse. Many early settled towns, especially in Connecticut, were quite large and, as the population of a town increased and spread farther and farther from the meetinghouse, controversy over the location of the meetinghouse inevitably arose. The controversy was usually resolved by the establishment of a new community, whether as an ecclesiastical parish or immediately as a town.[19] The price of town growth in Massachusetts in the seventeenth century was internal strife and contentiousness, as residents of Watertown, Sudbury, Andover, and scores of other towns had all learned.[20] Only divine intervention could have kept "broyles" from developing within a town over the distance that one neighborhood or another might have to travel to the meetinghouse. Ultimately, separation from the parent town was the only means by which a new meetinghouse—as a symbol of a new local community and unanimity—could be obtained.[21] In Connecticut, parish status seems to have been more significant than in Massachusetts, and many neither petitioned for, nor were granted town status until after the 1760s.[22]

Town division was not an unforeseen event. Many early Massachusetts Bay grants stipulated that lands could extend six or ten miles or more from the meetinghouse to accommodate anticipated population increases and the development of new communities within a town. Windham, Connecticut, was laid out as three parishes initially.[23] But two conditions were usually necessary before a community was divided. A new community needed a population of sufficient density and geographic continuity. Moreover, there needed to be some hardship on the part of this population in getting to the meetinghouse, too great a distance or an intervening obstacle, such as a river. There also appear to have been critical thresholds for population size and distance. The experience of a large number of towns in Massachusetts suggests that division, usually to form a town, resulted when a new community had grown to about 30 or 40 families. Boxfield in eastern Massachusetts was denied separate incorporation from Rowley until 1685, when about 40 families had been settled. In 1673 the incorporation of Brookfield, beyond the frontier, required that the "Township" could not be divided until 40 or 50 families had been settled.[24] In Connecticut in the eighteenth century, on the other hand, successful petitions for parish status received by the General Assembly were usually granted when signed by 20 or 30 families. As important as a critical size was the distance that separated the petitioning families from the meetinghouse. Almost invariably the stated distance on Connecticut petitions, including hazardous river crossings, exceeded three miles and averaged about five or six miles.[25]

Town division continued throughout the eighteenth century as long as population spread out in large towns. Although population might continue to increase, however, the distance between meetinghouses soon stabilized in settled areas, and town division—or at least subdivision of towns into parishes—ran its course. Consequently, in granting petitions for separation, colonial assemblies seem to have taken it for granted, consciously or not, that a comfortable spacing between meetinghouses was about five to six miles and that this spacing provided a proper area for a New England town.[26] By the end of the colonial period this geographic *modus operandi* had created new congregations and the mosaic of towns across New England, and also created a network of town centers almost uniformly spaced from Boston to Lake Champlain.

When division generally ceased across inhabited New England in the last quarter of the eighteenth century, towns and the remaining parishes averaged about 35 square miles in area, and meetinghouses were thus spaced about six miles apart, the square root of the area.[27] The earliest settled towns and their parishes, especially about Massachusetts Bay and southeastern New Hampshire, were smaller than the average, having been considerably divided into areas of about 20 to 25 square miles and with meetinghouses spaced four and a half to five miles apart. Mainland towns of Rhode Island, Providence Plantation, where a meetinghouse could be built anywhere by anyone, were always larger; no permission was needed to form a parish or town in order to build a church. Towns and remaining parishes most closely matching the mean area were established in large number in the eighteenth century, especially through central New England. With the experience that town division had provided, the 30 to 40 square-mile size was confirmed when, in the 1730s and later, relatively standard-sized, approximately square towns with a reserved, central meetinghouse lot were laid out in the Massachusetts military grants and in the colony grants in Connecticut. The practice flourished in northern New England. Between 1760 and 1764 Governor Benning Wentworth of New Hampshire granted 129 standard-sized towns in great tiers west of the Connecticut River.[28] As these towns were settled, plans for the location of the town center and settling lots were usually ignored, but town boundaries and a sense of community from a common locale and a shared meetinghouse have remained largely unchanged.

The town center

The distinguishing feature of the colonial settlement landscape in the relative absence of compact settlement was the town center, symbolizing in tangible form the intangible web of human relationships that constituted the town. The meetinghouse was the material manifestation of the political and religious community. No particular sacredness was attached to the meetinghouse itself and not everyone was a church member, but relative proximity to the meetinghouse was a significant factor in rural life. The importance of roads was determined by their directness to the town center. Having a nearby meetinghouse was an overriding consideration in the expansion of settlement and, thus, the cause of town division.

The tavernkeeper–trader was the only townsman to do enough business to require a central location—aside the meetinghouse lot.[29] The tavern, often a farmhouse parlor, was the second most important public place in town, and few town centers were without one or more.[30] Besides being an important place for private business, socializing, and politics, it was not uncommon for public business to repair from the meetinghouse to the more comfortable quarters of the tavern. An influential citizen, or one who hoped to be influential, might have appropriated a lot for the meetinghouse and often the materials needed to construct it. The meetinghouse at Lexington, Massachusetts, was donated to the town by the local tavernkeeper. The Effingham, New Hampshire, meetinghouse was located on "Lord's Hill"—almost in front of Lord's tavern. And in Westmoreland, New Hampshire, an entrepreneur offered a barrel of rum to the teamsters moving the disassembled meetinghouse, if they would unload the meetinghouse next to his tavern. They did, and there it stood.[31]

In central-place terms, therefore, the town center was an auxiliary central place. The community or congregation provided the threshold, or minimum population, for the meetinghouse and other activities that might locate at the town center for local intercourse and exchange. The range, or the maximum distance over which exchange will occur, defined the effective boundary line between communities. Radial movement of traffic to the nearest central place (theoretically) causes centers with similar order activities—like New England town centers and later central-place villages—to be spaced at approximately equal distance from one another over a uniformly populated and productive area. Thus, in colonial New England, when the range of a meetinghouse was large and there was sufficient popultion to meet a threshold for a new community, division created a new town with its own town center. Across much of glacier-scrubbed, boulder-strewn, and later-settled New England, however, towns of standard size with town centers of standard spacing were laid down upon a map, and then upon the landscape, without regard to population density.

Economic and social context

The dispersed settlement that dominated in colonial New England was an appropriate manifestation of the rural economy. Yet, the rural economy was not fixed. Throughout much of the colonial period and especially in the eighteenth century, transformation from predominantly subsistence to increasingly, though never dominantly, advanced commercial agriculture occurred. It is conventional wisdom that the transformation gained momentum in the second half of the eighteenth century and culminated in a burst of commercial activity in the federal period.[32] Although it is not clear when this transformation began or how rapidly it took place, the corresponding rise of central places, the focus of concern here, clearly indicates change had occurred and a threshold of economic activity had been reached during the last half of the eighteenth century.

The colonial rural economy

Colonial New England yeomen made their living close to the land. Land ownership was an important ingredient of the rural economy, and inland almost everyone was a farmer first. Farmers lived comfortably by their standard and actually accumulated some wealth, but New England's hardscrabble seems hardly to have allowed much marketable surplus for one's endeavor: "Their farms yield food—much of cloathing—most of the articles of building—with a surplus sufficient to buy such foreign luxuries as are necessary to make life pass comfortably; there is very little elegance among them, but more of necessaries."[33] By producing as many different kinds of food and materials as his effort and time allowed, a farmer could maintain this standard of living with irregular participation in an exchange economy beyond the bounds of the town. Thus, extra-local trade would have been too sporadic and the rural economy alone not sufficient to support commerce at central places inland.[34]

The low agricultural productivity in New England appears to have resulted

not just because land was poor, nor from poor market opportunities or
inadequate transport, but mostly because of the cultural context. Colonial New
Englanders were enmeshed in a web of social relationships and cultural
expectations that may have inhibited the free play of market forces.[35] The land
was no different during the heyday of New England agriculture in the federal
period; colonial farmers were aware of market opportunities; and those near
coastal commercial villages could always find markets. But a deficiency in
pasturage and fodder, the inefficiency of technology based on hand sickles, and a
scarcity of labor combined to limit productivity and income. The inadequacy of
transportation, moreover, was a consequence and not a cause of agricultural
productivity. Given the marginal quality of most land, colonial New Englanders
were largely general farmers supporting most of their own agricultural needs and
marketing what surplus vegetable, grain, or animal products they could.[36]

This is not to argue that New England farmers were self-sufficient, and they
did not care to be. But as a result of relatively low agricultural productivity,
most did not participate greatly in regional markets. Long-distance trade, of
only a few score miles, was in luxuries and when opportunities presented
themselves but not generally in any great quantity of bulk goods. The economy
was fundamentally local, and trade was dominated by local society, not the
reverse. As a result, farmers developed special skills to supplement agricultural
surpluses, and most occupations were represented locally. In the aggregate, local
exchange was important to an extent hardly suggested by the meagerness and
pettiness of individual transactions. But local exchange could not very well
support full-time nonfarmers, if it did not require central places of any
magnitude or close geographical proximity. Production and exchange remained
largely dispersed within each town's geographic realm, and with the tangle of
credit relationships that developed within a community the community itself
became "a dispersed general store".[37]

Economic change

The transformation from an economy based on local exchange at dispersed
places to an economy focused on central places had clearly begun in New
England by the last quarter of the eighteenth century. There is good reason to
believe, as well, that change may have resulted in part from the economic
imperative of a local land crisis—overpopulation in short—which resulted in
new economic endeavors and increased social stratification in New England.[38]
Change was underscored by the considerable development in the early 1770s of
new port villages such as Norwich, Connecticut, or Wickford, Rhode Island.
The Revolutionary War, moreover, accelerated the change already underway in
the colonial rural economy and ushered in a quickening of the commercial
element in the rural economy throughout the region in the subsequent
generation.[39]

Because most rural New Englanders had not generally participated to any
great degree in extra-local trade, they suffered little harm when trade was cut off
by economic encumberances and retaliatory measures of nonconsumption and
nonimportation before the Revolution and by the war itself. On the contrary,
the war encouraged domestic industry and commercial agriculture and incited
rising expectations inland.[40] The immediate effect of peace in 1783, however,
was economic depression. Farmers were plagued by financial confusion, low

agricultural prices, and heavy taxation. As before the Revolution, many farmers found the market frustrating. The results showed. In 1790 real per capita income in the United States remained below the level it had achieved by 1770. But by 1790 the tempo of transactions appears to have increased and the regional economy to have become more productive and more complex. Per capita income was growing, accelerated by the increasing availability of currency and by commercial opportunities generated by European wars of the 1790s and early 1800s. Merchant capitalists, engaging in any trade that might prove profitable, came to dominate fast-growing places everywhere, and from 1781 to the Embargo Act in 1807 New England achieved considerable prosperity that led many New Englanders to seek new occupations off the farm and new means of increasing investments.[41] It was thus evident to an observer in the 1790s that: "Their imports have not been swelled in proportion to the increase of their population and wealth. The reason is clear, viz. the constant introduction of new branches of manufacture amongst themselves, and a great extension of the old branches."[42]

In agriculture as well as in household production no clear break occurred between the locally oriented rural economy of the colonial period and the increasingly outward oriented rural economy, but the balance had shifted. In relative terms, productivity remained low, communication and transportation poor, processing unsophisticated, and subsistence a persistent dimension of everyday life. Agriculture itself never became a flourishing enterprise for many New Englanders, but trade was far less localized than it had been in the colonial period. An increasing distance intervened between the locations of production and consumption as farmers became more dependent on outside markets, and thus central places, for the sale and purchase of goods. With regular exchange, favorable and stable prices, and cash, farmers slowly but consciously increased productivity.[43]

The change in agriculture was complemented by unprecedented organization and concentration of business enterprise. Corporations, franchised to carry out banking and insurance, internal improvements in transportation and communication, and pioneering in manufacturing, increased from 7 in 1780 to well over 300 in 1800. Another 1700 corporations were chartered in New England in the next 30 years, most reflecting the removal of manufacturing activities from independent household producers into the hands of entrepreneurs.[44] The widespread diffusion of banking was an especially important indicator of the percolation of enterprise and investment capital into the backcountry in the federal period. The 14 banks in New England in 1800 could only be found in the larger urban places. Within 20 years, however, there were over 100 banks widely spread across New England in over 60 central places, many of which had not existed before 1780.[45]

The turnpike epitomized the internal-improvement effort of the period and visibly manifested the invisible economic network that was spreading across New England. The first turnpike in New England was chartered in 1792, and charters reached their zenith with over 30 new charters a year when the economy peaked in the mid-1800s. A turnpike charter was a franchise to connect a number of towns with a passable road in exchange for collecting a toll. A corporation either took over responsibility for maintaining a string of local roads or laid out and maintained a new road between town centers. Successful turnpike corporations were those that properly judged the traffic they could absorb and generate, but turnpikes were never very lucrative investments in themselves. Investors counted more upon collateral returns than upon direct returns in the matter of tolls.[46]

Turnpikes were laid down on existing road networks as often as possible to strengthen existing traffic patterns. In long-settled areas of southern and eastern New England, traffic had always flowed to nearby commercial villages that acted as intervening collection and distribution points for Boston or New York. Especially in Connecticut, where no particular market center was dominant, turnpikes were used as means of improving existing roads, not of extending the road network. Most Connecticut turnpikes were thus short links between nearby towns. Litchfield, an important place in the colonial road network, was intersected by half a dozen turnpikes, and, "in due time, it became almost impossible to get into or out of our town without encountering a toll gate."[47] In northern New England trading patterns were not as well established as in longer settled areas. Long turnpikes were laid out like the spokes of a wheel to connect the new settlements to Portland, to Portsmouth, and to Boston, where trade had always gravitated and the source of much of the credit extended in New England.[48]

With more produce to be hauled than before, there was also a development in carriage. Until the federal period, the poor quality of what passed as roads meant that travel was generally by foot, horse, sled, or two-wheeled ox cart. Carriages were limited to the wealthy, and wagons were more common in the middle colonies. By the end of the eighteenth century, however, chaises and four-wheeled, horse-drawn wagons known as Pennsylvania rigs were frequent sights on New England town roads and turnpikes, and numerous town histories recorded with some emphasis the appearance of the first wagon or chaise in town. In 1789 there was a wagon in Meriden, Connecticut, and in the early 1800s in Brunswick, Maine, and, by 1790, a two-horse chaise in Framingham, Massachusetts. Wagons were considered unusual in Bedford and Billerica, Massachusetts, only until the turn of the century.[49]

Four-wheeled, horse-drawn stages were especially common means of carriage in the federal period. The first stage between Boston and New York began operation in 1772, and three six-day trips were scheduled a week in 1787. But with increasing demands for travel and improved roads, stage lines proliferated, and more and more towns were linked to one another. The first stage through Nashua, New Hampshire, in 1795 "was an occasion of great public interest." The covered vehicle pulled by two horses ran once a week from Amherst, New Hampshire, to Boston, with an overnight stop in Billerica, Massachusetts. A weekly stage between Boston and Charleston, New Hampshire, was operating by 1801, and there were three a week from Hanover, New Hampshire, to Boston in 1807.[50]

Merchants were not only moving increasing quantities of goods, but they were advertising their stocks or their particular demands for backcountry surpluses and doing so widely in the newspapers. After 1790 few merchants did without advertising, and few major towns were without their own "advertiser". Though New Englanders were highly literate, less than 20 newspapers were published in New England in 1780. By the close of the century, however, nearly 80 were being published and, although by 1820 there were still less than 100 newspapers, publication and readership were widespread even in the most recently settled areas of western and northern New England.[51] The postal service helped. The number of postal routes and offices expanded at an enormous rate after 1790 to meet the demand for increased communication.[52] New Englanders were now inextricably linked to the world outside the geographical limits of the town.[53]

The rise of the New England village

Questions remain as to how dramatic was the transformation in rural economy and how rapidly it occurred. Certainly over the period of several decades in the last half of the eighteenth century the rural economy became more complex and outreaching. At some point, moreover, a threshold was reached that let loose the rise of villages across New England in the federal period. Regular trade connections and increasing occupational specialization were now sufficient to support permanently gathered villagers. Many village entrepreneurs—like blacksmiths or local doctors and lawyers, for example—did not participate in the trade of agricultural and handicraft products that now extended beyond the bounds of the town. All, however, depended on and took advantage of the wealth that the new trade generated. Across New England, stores and shops and offices, courthouses and academies, and residences of nonfarmers—all material manifestations of the maturing of the rural economy—were gathered about hundreds of meetinghouse lots. Storekeepers, blacksmiths, lawyers, cordwainers, doctors, tanners, hatters, saddlemakers, harnessmakers, coopers, tinsmiths, and printers, all came to locate at these existing colonial town centers. At these central locations, now inextricably linked to the world beyond the colonial town, travellers by horseback, wagon, and stage, emigrants, and large numbers of independent teamsters driving along new turnpikes, all were stopping and transacting business.

The first store in Francestown, New Hampshire, was opened on the meetinghouse lot the year the Constitution was written. The following year a cabinetmaker opened a shop, and a doctor set up practice nearby. Within a generation a "lively and enterprising" commercial village had emerged (Fig. 1).[54] Several entrepreneurs planned a village in Pittsfield, Massachusetts, in the 1760s where their four settling lots came together. They built large frame houses but could attract neither the meetinghouse nor other activity. Twenty years later, however, an agglomeration of stores and taverns, a lawyer, a doctor, and a number of artisans and millers had gathered about the meetinghouse lot. By 1800 the town center was a substantial village (Fig. 2).[55] The village at Framingham, Massachusetts, started in much the same way. Between 1790 and 1805 the town center acquired a new tavern and a store, two blacksmiths, a hatter, a cordwainer, a tanner, a lawyer, a carpenter, a doctor, a saddlemaker, a mason, and an academy.[56]

Other places grew larger or remained smaller, but the same process of accretion was repeated in towns across New England. Regardless of regional differences in how long a town had been settled, what form colonial settlement had taken, or what the nature of the rural economy had been and now was, full-time storekeepers, artisans, and professionals, by locating at town centers, were creating commercial villages (Figs 3–4). By 1800 in Gorham, Maine, there were two stores, two coopers, two shoemakers, a blacksmith, and a joiner. In addition to having the first store in the county in 1790, the future shiretown of Middlebury, Vermont, was quickly accumulating a blacksmith, a cabinetmaker, a hatter, a physician, a saddle and harnessmaker, and even a college. Within 20 years it had become "one of the principal villages in Vermont". Burlington,

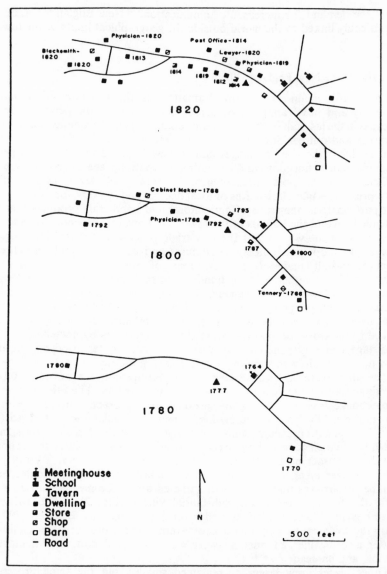

Figure 1. Francestown, New Hampshire, 1780–1820. Redrawn from W. R. Cochran and G. K. Wood, *History of Francestown, New Hampshire* (Nashua, N.H. 1895) 415

Vermont, also hardly 20 years old, had a "commercial village" of some esteem by the first decade of the nineteenth century. And in Walpole, New Hampshire, a business center was developing around the meetinghouse lot toward the end of the 1790s (Fig. 5).[57]

Stores, the connecting link for extra-local exchange and often outliers of mercantile firms, especially marked change. The first store in Hampton, Connecticut, was opened in the late 1780s and on the Hill in Thompson,

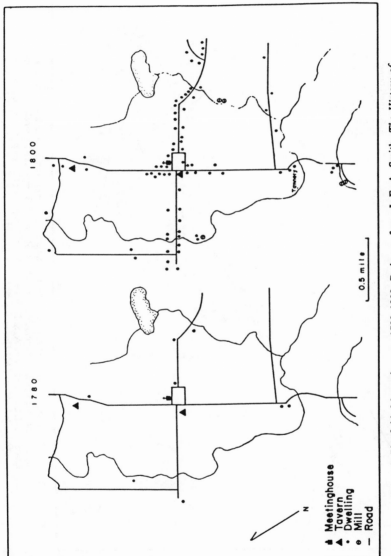

Figure 2. Pittsfield, Massachusetts, 1780–1800. Redrawn from J. E. A. Smith, *The History of Pittsfield, Massachusetts, 1800 to 1876* (Springfield Mass. 1876) 4

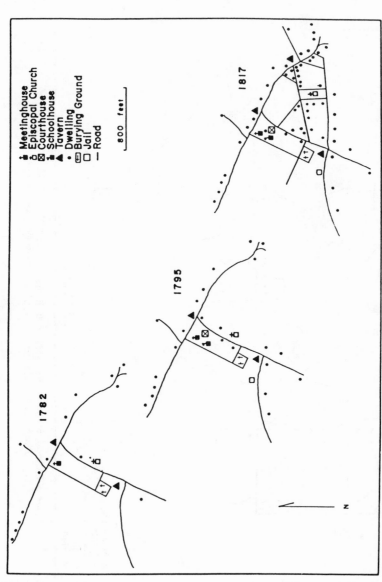

Figure 3. Dedham, Massachusetts, 1782–1817. Dedham was planted in the 1630s as an agricultural village, but that village had dispersed by the 1660s. Redrawn from a 1782 French Army map reproduced in H. C. Rice Jr. and A. S. K. Brown (eds), *The American Campaigns of Rochambeau's Army, 1780, 1781, 1782, 1783* (Princeton N.J. and Providence R.I. 1972) 2:158; and Dedham Village in 1817 *The Dedham Historical Register* 14 (1903) 39, 71

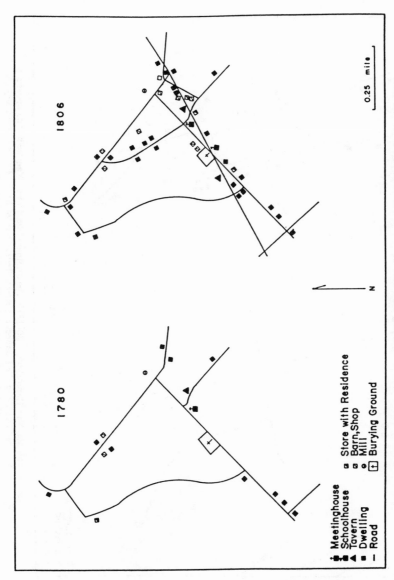

Figure 4. Meriden, Connecticut, 1780–1806. Meriden was a parish of Wallingford until 1806. Redrawn from C. B. Gillespie, *A Century of Meriden* (Meriden Conn. 1906) 342

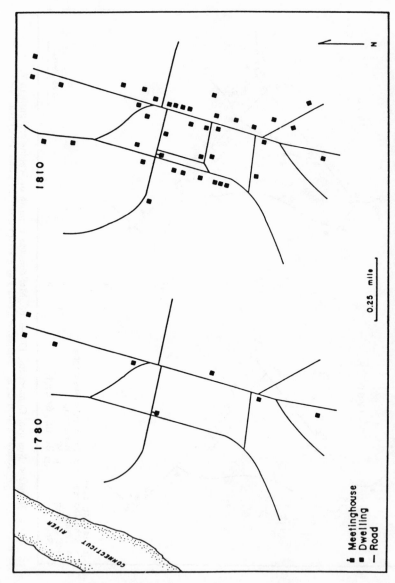

Figure 5. Walpole, New Hampshire, 1780–1810. The original settlement of Walpole was composed of farms stretched out along the Connecticut River. Redrawn from M. D. Frizzell, *A History of Walpole, New Hampshire* (Walpole N.H. 1963) insert

Connecticut, in 1794. Western Massachusetts towns competed in offering inducements to traders to settle in their communities in the 1780s. Ashfield, Massachusetts, had its first store about 1789, and one was built about 1795 near the meetinghouse in Bernardston, Massachusetts. A mercantile business began out of trading in miscellaneous articles at the tavern in Middlefield, Massachusetts; there was a separate store in 1804. First stores were opened in 1790 in Rindge, New Hampshire, and Springfield, Vermont; in Gilmanton, New Hampshire, in 1791; in Jaffrey, New Hampshire, in 1792; and before 1800 in Salem, New Hampshire. A village began to form in the 1790s around several traders and professionals in Buckfield, Maine; there was a store in Belfast, Maine, by 1796; and one in Turner, Maine, before 1800.[60]

Relative location

Because of some geographical variation in the division of towns during the colonial period, some geographical variation existed in the spacing of the new central places. Commercial villages were generally somewhat closer where town centers had been closer and farther apart where town centers had been farther apart. The distance between villages was sometimes short in long-settled areas, such as eastern Massachusetts; in areas where productive soils could support a denser population, as in the Connecticut River valley; in locations where mill villages had sprung up; and along major turnpikes. The distance was greater in late-settled areas of northern New England, in part because population remained more thinly scattered than in southern New England, but also because town centers were always more distant from one another.[61]

The underlying pattern of settlement set in the colonial period persisted in the upper reaches of the New England central-place hierarchy as well.[62] In the federal period most commercial villages of the colonial period grew into cities and were still the ultimate sources of credit and supplies and destinations for agricultural produce. The largest of these places, Boston, Providence, Portsmouth, and many Connecticut ports, all were still tied to the sea. By and large they retained their relative ranking locally, if not regionally, as development proceeded. Many inland commercial villages of the colonial period—Litchfield, Northampton, Worcester, and Concord—were still larger, more important places than their neighbors in the federal period. Other villages like Wickford, Rhode Island; Ipswich, Massachusetts; and Windham, Connecticut, failing to achieve the necessary threshold, remained small. In northern and western New England some town-center villages, such as Pittsfield, Massachusetts; Burlington and Windsor, Vermont; or Concord, New Hampshire, took on additional activities and grew large. Their growth represented a geographical extension and sorting of higher-order central places into later-settled northern New England.

Central-place sorting

No central-place system is static, and settlement patterns experience a constant sorting process. Notwithstanding the established settlement pattern of the colonial period, geography was ultimately cruel to many new central places. What often made—or broke—a village was its highways. Horace Bushnell

41

found that "it is possible to tell whether there is any motion in a society by
observing whether there is activity in its roads."[63] And to Josiah Temple, roads
were nothing less than the material foundation of moral virtue:

> The record of its highways is the history of the material growth, the public
> spirit, and the relative importance of a town. When its roads radiate from a
> common centre to the circumference, and that centre is the meeting-house,
> you will commonly find an intelligent, moral, and religious, as well as
> thriving community. The people have faith in God and faith in each other;
> are social and helpful; are mindful of individual prosperity, and the
> prosperity and position of the town. Where the roads mainly lead through
> or out of town, they give sufficient warning to strangers to continue their
> journey.[64]

Traffic, and thus the road network, determined in large measure where central
places would be located and which would ultimately flourish.[65] From the time a
town was first settled, a centripetal network of town roads had been laid out
from the meetinghouse or the meetinghouse had gravitated to an important
intersection in the road network. Because road networks focused on—or
radiated from—the town center and because through routes were strings of local
roads, an entrepreneur could expect townsmen and passers-by alike to be found
passing by the town center. The bustle of the federal period brought increased
traffic directed by the existing road network past the town center (Fig. 6).

Turnpikes, whether wholly new roads or not, generated additional trade and
focused it. In the 1790s a tavern, a blacksmith, and a couple of houses were all
that would be found at the town center at Thompson Hill, Connecticut. But the
traffic along the Providence and Springfield stage line that intersected a new
turnpike from eastern Connecticut to Boston on the Hill generated real estate
speculation in the early 1800s.[66] Other hilltop centers typically did not develop
or soon failed if access roads were too arduous or too steep. The courthouse of
Windham County, Vermont, on Newfane Hill, was removed in 1827 to nearby
Fayetteville because the latter was more accessible. The village that had emerged
on the Hill in the 1790s consisted of a courthouse, a jail, a meetinghouse, an
academy, three stores, two hotels (or taverns), a variety of shops, and some
twenty residences. But the hilltop location was too inaccessible, and by 1860 not
one building remained to mark the original site.[67]

New industrial places, such as Lowell, Lawrence, Manchester and many
smaller factory villages, began to bloom about mill sites as localization of
manufacturing took place in the federal period.[68] These places were laid down
on top of and largely independent of the long-standing settlement pattern, sited
as they were by water power. The system of factory places eventually was
merged with the system of central places. By the process of sorting
factory–place/central–place hybrids emerged more durable than many places
dependent only on trade or on manufacturing. The meetinghouse in Waitsfield,
Vermont, had become dilapidated by 1840, and the center of business had
entirely shifted away from the common to a nearby mill seat. Yet several
dwellings, two blacksmiths, a store, a potash works, and a physician had all been
located about the common in the first decade of the century. In Cummington,
Massachusetts, the shift of commerce from the hilltop center to Main Street
along a mill seat on the Westfield River began in the 1790s and was completed in

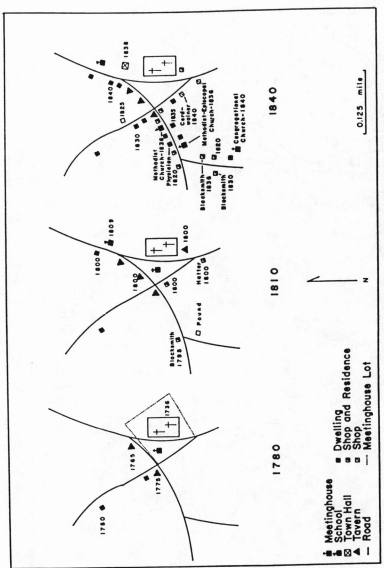

Figure 6. Salem, New Hampshire, 1780–1840. Increasing traffic warranted the number of taverns and general growth of Salem. Redrawn from E. Gilbert, *History of Salem, New Hampshire* (Concord N.H. 1907) 364

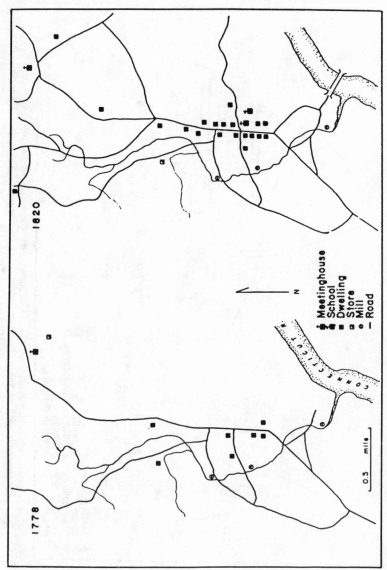

Figure 7. Norwich, Vermont, 1778–1820. The original town center in Norwich gravitated to a location closer to mill seats. Redrawn from P. A. White and D. D. Johnson, *Early Houses of Norwich, Vermont* (Norwich Vt. 1973) ii

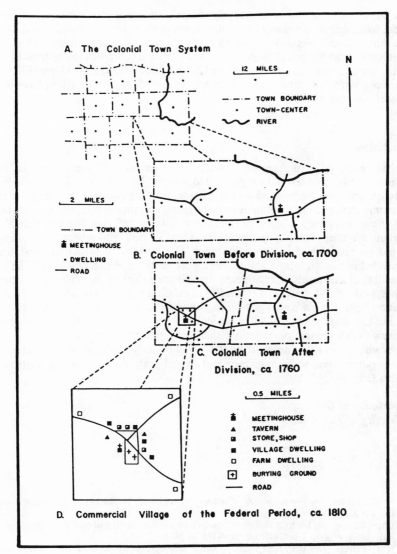

A. The Colonial Town System

12 MILES

- - - TOWN BOUNDARY
· TOWN-CENTER
~ RIVER

N

2 MILES

- - - TOWN BOUNDARY
🏛 MEETINGHOUSE
· DWELLING
— ROAD

B. Colonial Town Before Division, ca. 1700

C. Colonial Town After
Division, ca. 1760

0.5 MILES

🏛 MEETINGHOUSE
▲ TAVERN
▣ STORE, SHOP
■ VILLAGE DWELLING
□ FARM DWELLING
⊞ BURYING GROUND
— ROAD

D. Commercial Village of the Federal Period, ca. 1810

Figure 8. Elaboration of a settlement system

the 1840s. The store and tavern on the hill closed in 1841, two years after the church was removed, though growth at the new center peaked in that decade as well. Today Cummington Hill is marked by a solitary plaque.[69] The geographical character of the central-place system was distorted accordingly from the system of colonial town centers that had originally underlain it (Fig. 7).

In central-place terms, during the general increase in economic activity in the federal period, the thresholds of local commercial activities were exceeded, and central places sprouted across New England. The region was soon saturated with little central-place villages, and for many town centers in the later settled, less populated, upland areas, thresholds proved too high or ranges too low. There were simply too many towns and town centers for the limited population. A sorting process was soon underway: marginal sellers and marginal villages at each level of the hierarchy were eliminated from the central-place system. Many hilltop centers failed to develop or like Cummington Hill and Newfane Hill were abandoned in a "downhill slide" to better connected, more accessible places only a short distance away.

Conclusion

New England's nineteenth-century commercial villages were neither spontaneously conceived nor generated simply by the rise of central-place activities and then distributed across the economic landscape. The parameters of economic change in late colonial New England remain unclear, but the location and the morphology of new central-place villages reflected the colonial New Englander's long-standing geographical ideas of how and where communities should be established in the wilderness. The pattern of settlement was long embedded in the landscape before there were central places to speak of. The rise of central places resulted, it appears then, from a shift in the scale of economic activity—the development of centrality at existing places. Centrality and central location both gave advantage to villagers who kept shop by the meetinghouse lot, but the arrangement of town centers had long provided most New England farmers with a central place before there was ever need for central places. The rise of villages in the nineteenth century was both the material manifestation of contemporary economic experience and an elaboration of an existing settlement system (Fig. 8).[70]

Department of Geography
University of Nebraska at Omaha

Notes

[1] W. Christaller, *The central places of southern Germany* C. W. Baskin (trans.), (Englewood Cliffs N.J. 1967)

[2] Christaller, *op. cit.* 14–20, 140–1; and Bonnie Barton, The creation of centrality *Annals of the Association of American Geographers* **68** (1978) 34–5

[3] J. T. Lemon, *The best poor man's country: a geographical study of early southeastern Pennsylvania* (New York 1972); D. R. McManis, *Colonial New England: a historical geography* (New York 1975); E. Cook Jr., *Fathers of the towns: leadership and community structure in eighteenth-century New England* (Baltimore 1976); B. C. Daniels, *The Connecticut town: growth and development, 1635–1790* (Middletown Conn. 1979)

[4] Christaller, *op. cit.* 118–9; J. E. Vance Jr., *The merchants world: the geography of wholesaling* (Englewood Cliffs N. J. 1970)

[5] Barton, *op. cit.* 39; Christaller, *op. cit.* 107ff

[6] McManis, *op. cit.* 74

[7] Christaller, *op. cit.* 11

[8] *Ibid.* 122

[9] *Ibid.* 16–19, 139–40

[10] Barton, *op. cit.* 40–4; Daniels, *op. cit.* 160

[11] Christaller, *op. cit.* 17, 105, 152–5

[12] M. B. Newton Jr., Settlement patterns as artifacts of social structure, in M. Richardson (ed), *The human mirror: material and spatial images of man* (Baton Rouge La. 1974) 358
Also note P. Wheatley, *The pivot of the four quarters: a preliminary inquiry into the origins and character of the ancient Chinese city* (Chicago 1971) 225; P. L. Wagner, *Environments and peoples* (Englewood Cliffs N.J. 1972) 45–9; A. Rapoport, *The meaning of the built environment* (Beverly Hills Ca. 1982)

[13] Geographers who have maintained the view include E. Scofield, The origin of settlement patterns in rural New England *Geographical Review* 28 (1938) 652–63; G. T. Trewartha, Types of rural settlement in colonial America *Geographical Review* 36 (1946) 568–96; R. H. Brown, *Historical geography of the United States* (New York 1948) 51–6; F. G. Morris, Some aspects of the rural settlement of New England in colonial times, in L. D. Stamp and S. E. Wooldridge (eds), *London essays in geography* (London 1951) 219–27; McManis, *op. cit.* 53–63

[14] For elaboration on the colonial settlement landscape see J. S. Wood, The origin of the New England village (unpubl. Ph.D. thesis, Pennsylvania State University 1978); and *idem.*, Village and community in early colonial New England *Journal of Historical Geography* 8 (1982) 333–46

[15] McManis, *op. cit.* 72–84

[16] J. S. Wood, New England agricultural villages, circa 1780, in J. F. Rooney Jr., *et al.* (eds), *This remarkable continent: an atlas of United States and Canadian society and cultures* (College Station Tx. 1982) 40; J. Dow, *History of the town of Hampton, New Hampshire* (Salem Mass. 1893); J. H. Temple, *History of Framingham, Massachusetts, 1640–1880* (Framingham Mass. 1887) 2, 107–8

[17] Wood, Village and community, 334–9

[18] I. B. Sawtelle, *History of Town of Townshend, Massachusetts, 1676–1878* (Townshend Mass. 1878) 145

[19] A. B. MacLear, *Early New England towns: a comparative study of their development* (New York 1908) 31

[20] S. C. Powell, *Puritan village: the formation of a New England town* (Middletown Conn. 1963); P. J. Greven, *Four generations: population, land and family life in colonial Andover, Massachusetts* (Ithaca N.Y. 1970)

[21] H. R. McCutcheon, Town formation in eastern Massachusetts, 1630–1802: a case study in political area organization (unpubl. Ph.D. thesis, Clark University 1970); MacLear, *op. cit.* 31; O. E. Winslow, *Meetinghouse hill: 1630–1783* (New York 1952); R. L. Bushman, *From Puritan to Yankee: character and social order in Connecticut, 1690–1765* (Cambridge Mass. 1967) 60ff; M. Zuckerman, *Peaceable kingdoms: New England towns in the eighteenth century* (New York 1970); P. Boyer and S. Nissenbaum, *Salem possessed: the social origins of witchcraft* (Cambridge Mass. 1974) 39–45, described the process of division in Salem

[22] Daniels, *op. cit.* 34–43

[23] See J. Winthrop, *The history of New England from 1630–1649* (New York 1825–1826) 2:254; M. Egleston, *The land system of the New England colonies* (Baltimore 1886) 32–3; E. D. Larned, *History of Windham County, Connecticut* (Thompson Conn. 1880) 1:65; Bushman, *op. cit.* 81

[24] T. Gage, *The history of Rowley* (Boston 1840) 360–6; L. E. Roy, *Quabog Plantation alias Brookfield: a seventeenth-century New England town* (West Brookfield Mass. 1965) 56, referred to General Court records without citation

[25] Sample data for Connecticut before 1776 were collected from the Connecticut State Library, Archives, Ecclesiastical Affairs, and provided by Christopher Collier, University of Bridgeport. See also Daniels, *op. cit.* 14, 24, 34, 41, 183–5; W. Haller Jr., *The puritan frontier: town planting in New England colonial development, 1630–1660* (New York 1951) 18, suggested that a critical "zone of population" for splitting was about two hundred households. As household size generally ran about five or six, he may have meant about two hundred people, or some thirty-five head of household

[26] McCutcheon, *op. cit.* provided a wealth of detail on the division process. On Connecticut see Daniels, *op. cit.* 8–44, 183–5

[27] Calculations are based on state, county, and town records for towns and parishes in 1800. The radius for a meetinghouse was thus about three miles or an hour's journey on foot or by cart. C. A. Dioxiadis, Ancient Greek settlement: second annual report *Ekistics* 33 (1972) 80, argued that the basic underlying system of settlements everywhere was established on spacing of two hours' distance. J. E. Brush and H. E. Bracey, Rural service centers in southwestern

Wisconsin and southern England *Geographical Review* 45 (1955) 568, similarly suggested that places are generally four to six miles apart. The cultural tradition seems longstanding

[28] R. H. Akagi, *The town proprietors of the New England colonies* (Philadelphia 1924) 190ff; E. S. Stackpole, *History of New Hampshire* (New York 1916) 1:365

[29] Daniels, *op. cit.* 162, argued that town centers in eighteenth-century Connecticut were more generally inhabited and, thus, the central-place system more fully developed

[30] Barton, *op. cit.* 40, misconstrued the relatively insignificant extra-local role of the tavern in colonial times

[31] J. D. Cushing, Town commons of New England, 1640–1840 *Old Time New England* 51 (1961) 86–94; C. A. Staples, A sketch of the History of Lexington common *Proceedings of the Lexington Historical Society* 1 (1980) 17–37; E. A. Speare, *Colonial meetinghouses of New Hampshire* (Littleton N.H. 1938) 69, 147

[32] The changing character of the colonial rural economy, the causes of change, and the pace of change are elements in an ongoing argument. J. A. Henretta, Families and farms: *mentalité* in pre-industrial America *William and Mary Quarterly* Ser. 3, 35 (1978) 3–32, claims that commercialization began only after 1750. J. T. Lemon, Comment on J. A. Henretta's 'Families and farms: *mentalité* in pre-industrial America' (and Henretta's reply) *William and Mary Quarterly* Ser. 3, 37 (1980) 688–700, disagrees; for Lemon far more continuity existed with early English ways. See also J. T. Lemon, Early Americans and their social environment *Journal of Historical Geography* 6 (1980) 115–31; *idem.*, Spatial organization in early America: local, regional and household, Oxford Conference on Anglo-American Colonial History, Oxford University 1981 (mimeo); A. H. Jones, *Wealth of a nation to be: the American colonies on the eve of the revolution* (New York 1980) describes the relative wealth accumulated by New Englanders but does not provide a clear picture of market activity inland

[33] H. J. Carman (ed) *American husbandry* (New York 1939) 50; originally published in 1775, this anonymous tract has been quoted by Bushman, *op. cit.* 108

[34] See especially H. B. Hall, A description of rural life and labor in Massachusetts at four periods (unpubl. Ph.D. thesis, Harvard University 1917); M. G. Schumacher, The northern farmer and his markets during the late colonial period (unpubl. Ph.D. thesis, University of California 1948); C. S. Grant, *Democracy in the Connecticut frontier town of Kent* (New York 1961); G. A. Stiverson, Early American farming: a comment *Agricultural History* 50 (1976) 37–44; Jones, *op. cit.* 77–9, 111, 304; as well as R. C. Loehr, Self-sufficiency on the farm, 1759–1819 *Agricultural History* 26 (1952) 37–41; A. H. Clark, Suggestions for the geographical study of agricultural change in the United States, 1790–1840, and R. N. Parks, Comments on change in agriculture, 1790–1840, in D. P. Kelsey (ed), *Farming in the new nation: interpreting American agriculture, 1790–1840* (Washington 1972) 155–72, 173–80. See also F. B. Dexter (ed), *Extracts from the itineraries and other miscellanies of Ezra Stiles, D.D., LL.D., 1755–1794* (New Haven Conn. 1916) 409 (1790)

[35] D. B. Rutman, The social web: a prospectus for the study of the early American community, in W. L. O'Neill (ed), *Insight and parallels: problems and issues of American social history* (Minneapolis 1973); also see Henretta, Families and farms, 19; and Lemon, Early Americans, 128

[36] For a general overview of agriculture in colonial New England, see H. S. Russell, *A long deep furrow: three centuries of farming in New England* (Hanover N.H. 1976)

[37] Schumacher, *op. cit.* 88; Jones, *op. cit.* 152, 201–2. See also J. E. A. Smith, *The history of Pittsfield, Massachusetts, 1800 to 1876* (Springfield Mass. 1876) 46. Grant, *op. cit.* 69, noted that in the 1770s there was an average of twenty outstanding debts per adult male in Kent, Connecticut. W. Winterbotham, *An historical, geographical, commercial, and philosophical view of the American United States* (London 1795) 3:308–9. Temple, *op. cit.* 239, listed a large number of craftsmen in Framingham between 1710 and 1760, including at one time or another eight cordwainers, two weavers, two blacksmiths, two housewrights, a cabinetmaker, and a saddler

[38] D. S. Smith, The demographic history of colonial New England *Journal of Economic History* 322 (1972) 165, 171; K. Lockridge, Land, population and the evolution of New England society, 1630–1790 *Past and Present* 39 (1968) 62–8; Greven, *Four generations*; J. A. Henretta, The morphology of New England society in the colonial period *Journal of Interdisciplinary History* 2 (1971) 380; D. Rutman, People in process: the New Hampshire towns in the eighteenth century *Journal of Urban History* 1 (1975) 268–92. J. J. Waters, Family, inheritance, and migration in colonial New England: the evidence from Guilford, Connecticut *William and Mary Quarterly* Ser. 3, 39 (1982) 64–8; N. Osterud and J. Fulton, Family

limitation and age at marriage: fertility decline in Sturbridge, Massachusetts, 1730–1850 *Population Studies* 30 (1976) 492–3; R. A. Easterlin, Population change and farm settlement in the northern United States *Journal of Economic History* 36 (1976) 70; C. Forster and G. S. L. Tucker, *Economic opportunity and white American fertility ratios, 1800–1860* (New Haven Conn. 1972) address the demographic characteristics

[39] See M. Jensen, *The founding of a nation: a history of the American revolution, 1763–1776* (New York 1968); J. H. Andrews, Anglo-American trade in the early eighteenth century *Geographical Review* 45 (1955) 99–110; R. M. Hooker, *The colonial trade of Connecticut* (New Haven Conn. 1936); Schumacher, *op. cit.*; Bushman, *op. cit.* 135; R. A. Gross, *The minutemen and their world* (New York 1976) 87, 172–3

[40] L. N. Newcomer, *The embattled farmers: the Massachusetts countryside in the American revolution* (New York 1953) 109ff., 132; F. J. Saladino, The economic revolution in late eighteenth-century Connecticut (unpubl. Ph.D. thesis, University of Wisconsin 1964) 43; J. T. Schlebaker, Agricultural markets and marketing in the North: 1744–1777 *Agricultural History* 50 (1976) 35–6; Stiverson, *op. cit.*; T. Bender, *Community and social change in America* (New Brunswick N.J. 1978) 78–9; Zuckerman, *op. cit.*

[41] D. C. North, *The economic growth of the United States* (Englewood Cliffs N.J. 1961) 62; Jones, *op. cit.* 82–4. See also R. Doherty, *Society and power: five New England towns, 1800–1860* (Amherst Mass. 1977); E. A. Kendall, *Travels through the northern parts of the United States in the years 1807 and 1808* (New York 1809) 1:89; M. E. Martin, *Merchants and trade of the Connecticut River Valley, 1750–1820* (Northampton Mass. 1962) 13; B. W. Labaree, *Patriots and partisans: the merchants of Newburyport, 1764–1815* (Cambridge Mass. 1962); C. White, *Wickford and its old houses* (Wickford R.I. 1947)

[42] Winterbotham, *op. cit.* 3:304

[43] See for instance Christopher Clark, The household economy, market exchange and the rise of capitalism in the Connecticut Valley, 1800–1860 *Journal of Social History* 13 (1979) 169–89; Olson, *op. cit.* 9–10; Schumacher, *op. cit.* 144; McManis, *op. cit.* 101. See also W. Bidwell, The agricultural revolution in New England *American Historical Review* 26 (1921) 683–702; R. J. Purcell, *Connecticut in transition, 1775–1818* (Washington, D.C. 1918) 114, 158ff; and D. J. Cahill, Bozrah, Connecticut: the agricultural history of an 'insignificant township', 1796–1817 (unpubl. M.A. thesis, University of Connecticut 1970)

[44] See Massachusetts Secretary of State, *Report of the list of incorporations and their capitals, granted by the legislature of Massachusetts, from the adoption of the Constitution in 1780 to 1836*; E. M. Dodd, *American business corporations until 1860 with special references to Massachusetts* (Cambridge Mass. 1954) 196–7; O. Handlin and M. F. Handlin, *Commonwealth: a study of the role of government in the American economy: Massachusetts, 1774–1861* (Cambridge Mass. 1969); W. C. Kessler, Incorporation in New England: a statistical study, 1800–1875 *Journal of Economic History* 8 (1949) 45–7; Clark, *op. cit.*

[45] Old Sturbridge Village, Banks and banking in New England, 1784–1840 (Sturbridge Mass. 1962) (Typewritten) Appendices I–IV. See also map in Wood, Origin of the New England village, 211.

[46] See F. J. Wood, *The turnpikes of New England and evolution of the same through England, Virginia, and Maryland* (Boston 1919) especially 63; S. P. Mead, *Ye historie of ye town of Greenwich* (New York 1911) 186

[47] Parks, *op. cit.* 96; A. C. White, *The history of the Town of Litchfield, Connecticut, 1720–1920* (Litchfield Conn. 1920) 94–5

[48] Kendall, *op. cit.* 1:138–9; see also Smith, *op. cit.* 507; Wood, Origin of the New England village, 214

[49] *A statistical account of the towns and parishes in the State of Connecticut* (New Haven Conn. 1811) 22; Jones, *op. cit.* 331. See also Schumacher, *op. cit.* 67; Saladino, *op. cit.* 346–7; C. H. S. Davis, *History of Wallingford (and Meriden), Connecticut* (Meriden Conn. 1870) 149; G. A. Wheeler and H. W. Wheeler, *History of Brunswick, Topsham, and Harpswell, Maine* (Boston 1878) 216; Temple, *op. cit.* 342; L. K. Brown, *Wilderness town: the story of Bedford, Massachusetts* (Bedford Mass. 1968) 97

[50] Mead, *op. cit.* 185; Brown, *op. cit.* 97; C. J. Fox, *History of the old Township of Dunstable including Nashua, New Hampshire* (Nashua N.H. 1846) 193; M. D. Frizzell, *Second history of Charlestown, New Hampshire: Old Number Four* (Charlestown N.H. 1955) 257

[51] Winterbotham, *op. cit.* 2:14. See also Martin, *op. cit.* 15–17; C. S. Brigham, *History and bibliography of American newspapers, 1690–1820* (Worcester Mass. 1947); Clark, *op. cit.* 177; map in Wood, Origin of the New England village, 219

[52] W. E. Rich, *The history of the United States Post Office to the the year 1829* (Cambridge Mass. 1924) 182-3

[53] See R. Brown, The emergence of urban society in rural Massachusetts, 1760-1820 *Journal of American History* 61 (1974) 29-51; W. E. Nelson, *The Americanization of the common law: the impact of legal change on Massachusetts Society, 1760-1830* (Cambridge Mass. 1975); Bushman, *op. cit.* 288; Saladino, *op. cit.* 353-4; Massachusetts Secretary of State, *op. cit.*

[54] W. R. Cochrane and G. K. Wood, *History of Francestown, New Hampshire* (Nashua N.H. 1895(411—21

[55] J. E. A. Smith, *The history of Pittsfield, Massachusetts, 1734 to 1800* (Boston 1869)-142

[56] Temple, *op. cit.* 351-3

[57] H. D. McLellan, *History of Gorham, Maine* (Portland Me. 1903) 262; Kendall, *op. cit.* 3:241, 243; S. Swift, *History of the Town of Middlebury, Vermont* (Middlebury Vt. 1859) 235ff; D. Frizzell, *A history of Walpole, New Hampshire* (Walpole N.H. 1963) 569. Wood, Origin of the New England village, 221-71 further documents graphically the rise of villages

[58] Larned, *op. cit.* 2:240, 358. See Vance, *op. cit.*; K. Polanyi, *The great transformation: the political and economic origin of our time* (New York 1944) 56-60, for discussions of the "reach of trade" beyond the local community and its importance with respect to settlement patterns

[59] Newcomer, *op. cit.* 155, listed several newspaper advertisements for stores; see also Smith, *Pittsfield, 1800-1876* 46

[60] F. G. Howes, *The history of the Town of Ashfield, Franklin County, Massachusetts, 1742-1910* (Ashfield Mass. n.d.) 48; C. Kellogg, *History of the Town of Bernardston, 1736-1900* (Greenfield Mass. 1902) 70; E. C. Smith, *et al.*, *A history of the Town of Middlefield, Massachusetts* (Middlefield Mass. 1924) 94, 103; E. S. Stearns, *History of the Town of Rindge, New Hampshire, 1736-1874* (Boston 1875) 375; H. C. Hubbard and J. Dartt, *History of the Town of Springfield, Vermont, 1752-1895* (Boston 1895) 31; D. Lancaster, *The history of Gilmanton* (Gilmanton N.H. 1845) 136; A. Annett and A. E. E. Lehtinen, *The history of Jaffrey, New Hampshire* (Jaffrey N.H. 1937) 398; E. Gilbert, *History of Salem, New Hampshire* (Concord N.H. 1907) 362; A. Cole and C. F. Whitman, *A history of Buckfield, Maine, to 1900* (Buckfield Me. 1915) 94; J. Williamson, *History of the City of Belfast in the State of Maine, 1770-1875* (Portland Me. 1877) 209, 639; W. R. French, *A history of Turner, Maine* (Portland Me. 1886) 80

[61] Because existing patterns determine subsequent patterns, Vance *op. cit.* 2-3, is correct that Christaller's *Central places* is indeed a special regional case reflecting a system of medieval German villages. But Vance's model of an untouched world settled under European mercantilism (148) is also a special case. Both of Vance's arguments bolster Christaller's point (47-8) that the prevailing pattern of interaction determines the resultant pattern of central places. Christaller (191) also discussed reasons for differences in spacing between similar-order places.

[62] Theoretically a hierarchy is based on a geometric progression determining a prescribed number of central places to be found in each order. The geometric progression reflects the interaction pattern upon which the system is built. Christaller, *op. cit.* 60-80

[63] H. Bushnell, *The day of roads: a discourse delivered on the annual Thanksgiving, 1846* (Hartford Conn. 1846) 3

[64] Temple, *op. cit.* 156

[65] See Christaller, *op. cit.* 104, for elaboration

[66] Larned, *op. cit.* 2:358-9; Cochran and Wood, *op. cit.* 332; S. G. Wood, *The turnpikes and taverns of Blandford, 1733-1833* (Blandford Mass. 1908) 147

[67] *Centennial proceedings and other historical facts and incidents relating to Newfane, the county seat of Windham County, Vermont* (Brattleboro Vt. 1877) 25-8

[68] R. G. LeBlanc, *Location of manufacturing in New England in the nineteenth century* (Hanover N.H. 1969) 18

[69] M. B. Jones, *History of the Town of Waitsfield, Vermont, 1782-1908* (Boston 1909) 54, 117; H. N. Foster and W. W. Streeter, *Only one Cummington* (Cummington Mass. 1974) 346

[70] I am indebted to Martyn J. Bowden, Graduate School of Geography, Clark University, for challenging me to try to make sense out of the New England village as a central place

50

The Progress of Inequality in Revolutionary Boston

Allan Kulikoff*

O N February 2, 1785, the *Massachusetts Centinel* in Boston complained that "We daily see men speculating, with impunity, on
the most essential articles of life, and grinding the faces of the
poor and laborious as if there was no God," yet five months later to the
day, Sam Adams wrote to his cousin John, "You would be surprizd to
see the Equipage, the Furniture and expensive Living of too many, the
Pride and Vanity of Dress which pervades thro every Class, confounding
every Distinction between the Poor and the Rich."[1] As these quotations
suggest, opinion divided sharply in post-Revolutionary Boston on the
direction of major social change, and impressionistic evidence can be
found to sustain a broad range of interpretation. Relying on this material,
historians have perpetuated the contemporary diversity of opinion. Scholars of the Progressive era, like J. Franklin Jameson, tended to agree with
Adams that the Revolution had a leveling effect, while more recent
studies have found some change as whigs replaced tories and a new propertied class emerged, but less democratization than had been supposed.[2]

This essay attempts to discover the magnitude of change in Boston
from 1771 to 1790 by testing controllable, quantitative materials to answer the following questions: How did the town's occupational structure change? Did the distribution of wealth become more or less equal?
How closely related were wealth and status? Did political power become
more democratically shared? By how much did population increase?

* Mr. Kulikoff is a graduate student at Brandeis University. He would like to
thank Stuart Blumin, M. I. T.; John Demos, Marvin Meyers, and members of the
graduate seminar, Brandeis University; Kenneth Lockridge, University of Michigan;
and Paul Kleppner and Alfred Young, Northern Illinois University, for their advice
and criticism. David Fischer, Brandeis University, who directed the paper, made
numerous helpful criticisms.

[1] *Massachusetts Centinel* (Boston), Feb. 2, 1785; Samuel Adams to John Adams,
July 2, 1785, *The Writings of Samuel Adams*, ed. Harry Alonzo Cushing, IV (New
York, 1908), 315-316.

[2] J. Franklin Jameson, *The American Revolution Considered As a Social Movement* (Princeton, 1926); Richard D. Brown, "The Confiscation and Disposition of
Loyalists' Estates in Suffolk County, Massachusetts," *William and Mary Quarterly*,
3d Ser., XXI (1964), 534-550, surveys the relevant historiography.

What social and economic patterns of residence could be found? What changes occurred in the rate of geographic and economic mobility?

Before the Revolution, Boston had been an intensely unequal society. Wealthy men of high status dominated government and social life. The top 10 per cent of the taxpayers in 1771 owned nearly two-thirds of the wealth and held most of the important town offices. While demanding respect from the poor, many of the wealthy lived in the center of town, segregated from the impoverished. Poorer men possessed no significant political power, but held numerous minor town offices. And largely because many poor men and women were migrating from nearby towns, the poor in Boston were becoming more numerous.[3] These trends continued and accelerated during the war and the Confederation period. Not a less stratified, but an even more unequal society developed in Boston after the Revolution.

Late eighteenth-century Boston was a typical "consumer city" in Max Weber's phrase. It was a town of under 20,000 inhabitants in which "the purchasing power of its larger consumers rests on the retail for profit of foreign products on the local market . . . the foreign sale for profit of local products or goods obtained by native producers . . . or the purchase of foreign products and their sale . . . outside."[4]

The economy of Boston still rested squarely on foreign trade. Close to a quarter of her workers—merchants, mariners, captains, chandlers, and wharfingers—earned their livelihood from commerce. Another 15 per cent were indirectly concerned with trade. Retailers sold and distributed foreign goods; coopers made barrels bound for the sea; laborers supplied the manpower necessary to unload ships; and distillers used foreign sugar in their product.

Unlike Weber's "producer city," Boston was not an exporter of the goods she produced.[5] Most of those not engaged in commerce produced goods and services for the local market. No industrial group included large numbers of workers. About 7 per cent worked with cloth, 4 per

[3] James A. Henretta, "Economic Development and Social Structure in Colonial Boston," *Wm. and Mary Qtly.*, 3d Ser., XXII (1965), 75-92.
[4] Max Weber, *The City*, trans. and ed. Don Martindale and Gertrud Neuwirth (New York, 1958), 69.
[5] *Ibid.* Philadelphia closely resembled a "producer city." See James T. Lemon, "Urbanization and the Development of Eighteenth-Century Southeastern Pennsylvania and Adjacent Delaware," *Wm. and Mary Qtly.*, 3d Ser., XXIV (1967), 504-510.

52

TABLE I
BOSTON'S OCCUPATIONAL STRUCTURE, 1790*

Occupational Group	Number in Group	Number of Trades in Group	Percentage of Work Force
Government Officials	67	4	2.6
Professionals*	105	8	4.1
Merchants-Traders	224	3	8.7
Retailers	184	7	7.1
Sea Captains	114	1	4.4
Other Business*	66	6	2.6
Clerks and Scribes	66	2	2.6
Building Crafts	245	7	9.3
Cloth Trades	182	8	7.1
Leather Crafts	113	5	5.1
Food Trades	175	11	6.8
Marine Crafts	219	13	8.5
Metal Crafts	132	11	5.1
Woodworkers	106	7	4.1
Other Artisans	105	35	4.1
Transportation	80	6	3.2
Service	103	4	4.0
Mariners	117	4	4.5
Unskilled	188	4	7.4
Total Artisans	1,271	96	49.1
Total Other	1,314	49	50.9
Total Employed	2,585	145	100.0
Servants (white)	63		
Unemployed and Retired*	106		
Total	2,754		

Notes: * Boston Tax Taking and Rate Books, 1790, City Hall, Boston, Mass. Hereafter cited as Tax and Rate Books, 1790. These records were checked with the Boston city directories for 1789 and 1796, *Report of the Record Commissioners of the City of Boston* (Boston, 1876–1909), X, 171–296. Hereafter cited as *Record Commissioners' Report*. A total accounting of each trade is found in the Appendix.
  * Includes 20 untaxed clergymen counted in Thomas Pemberton, "A Topographical and Historical Description of Boston, 1794," Massachusetts Historical Society, *Collections*, 1st Ser., III (1794), 256–264.
  * Includes groups such as wharfingers, chandlers, brokers, and auctioneers.
  * Includes 23 gentlemen, 27 poor, 28 sick and poor, and 28 little or no business.

cent with leather, and 5 per cent with metals. Construction workers were
under a tenth of all those employed. The small proportion of innkeepers
(3 per cent) and men in the food trades (7 per cent) showed that Boston
was not a major food market; nor had a large bureaucracy developed,
since only 3 per cent of the labor force was employed in government—
and many of these worked only part-time.

Large enterprises were uncommon: the median number of workers
in ninety-six artisan crafts was only three, and the mean number thirteen.
The typical middling artisan employed his sons and several other workers. These young apprentices and journeymen lived with the families of
master craftsmen, not alone in rented rooms.[6]

There was an excess population in the working ages, composed mostly
of women and including many widows, who were outside the occupational structure. Between 1765 and 1800, the proportion of people in the
productive ages above fifteen years increased by 17 per cent, thereby providing workers for any factories that might open. There were 19 per
cent more women than men of working age in 1765, and 14 per cent more
in 1800. About a tenth of these women were widows, and three-quarters
of them supported dependents.[7]

[6] Tax and Rate Books, 1790, compared with *Heads of Families At the First
Census, 1790. Massachusetts* (Washington, 1906), 188-195; and "Names of the Inhabitants of the Town of Boston in 1790," *Record Commissioners' Report*, XXII,
443-511. Numerous dependent males over 16 years of age are found in the census,
but not in the tax lists. Almost all of them were in homes of artisans of middling
wealth. This suggests that many of them were transient journeymen and apprentices and not older sons hidden from the assessor. Tax and census records are the
source for any uncited comments.

[7] Lemuel Shattuck, *Report to the Committee of the City Council Appointed to
Obtain the Census of Boston for the Year 1845, . . .* (Boston, 1846), 4, 45. A sample
of every sixth column of the Washington edition of the census was checked for
widows; three-quarters had dependents. Joseph J. Spengler, "Demographic Factors
and Early Modern Economic Development," *Daedalus*, XCVII (1968), 440-443, defines productive ages as from 15 to 65 years. Data in Shattuck does not allow such
fine distinctions, but the percentage of people over 65 is probably too small to materially change the following statistics:

Age Ratios	Percentage over 15 yrs. old			Sex Ratios	Number of Men/100 Women		
	1765	1790	1800		1765	1790	1800
Total	44.30	...	61.93	All ages	95.48	82.07	90.27
Male	41.71	56.13	60.42	Over 15	81.42	...	86.14
Female	47.26	...	63.31				

Two small factories were operating in 1790, but they were not part of a general industrialization, and only one of them utilized this surplus laboring population. At a "duck cloth manufactory" employing four hundred workers in 1792, there were only seventeen male employees two years before. A few of the others were young girls; the rest were women. The factory had been established to promote American manufactures and at the same time to aid the poor. According to the *Massachusetts Centinel* in 1788, it and a small glass works "promise soon to be completed and to give employment to a great number of persons, especially females who now eat the bread of idleness, whereby they may gain an honest livelihood." By 1800, the duckcloth factory was out of business.[8]

About three-quarters of the one thousand workers in the other large enterprise, a cotton and wool card factory, were children. About a fifth of all the children in Boston from eight to sixteen years of age were probably employed there. The owners chose to hire them rather than women, since children could easily run the machinery and were paid less.[9]

At least until 1820, Boston's occupational structure remained close to the "consumer city" model. Less than one-tenth of 1 per cent of men listed in the 1820 directory were manufacturers, and the proportion of merchants, retailers, and building tradesmen remained almost the same. Domestic commerce was becoming more important as foreign trade declined. A reduction in the percentage of mariners, captains, and marine tradesmen from 17.4 per cent in 1790 to 10.6 per cent in 1820 illustrates the trend. Meanwhile, the town had become more important as a food market, with the proportion of men in the food trades climbing from 6.8 per cent to 10.7 per cent.[10]

Most of Boston's taxable wealth—real estate, stock in trade, and income from trade[11]—rested in fewer and fewer hands as time passed.

[8] *Mass. Centinel* (Boston), Sept. 6, 1788, quoted in William R. Bagnall, *The Textile Industries of the United States, . . .* (Cambridge, Mass., 1893), 112-116; Pemberton, "Description of Boston," Mass. Hist. Soc., *Collections,* 1st Ser., III (1794), 252-253, 279; Samuel Breck to Henry Knox, Sept. 12, 1790, Knox Papers, Mass. Hist. Soc., Boston.

[9] Nathaniel Cutting, "Extracts from a Journal of a Gentleman visiting Boston in 1792," Sept. 6, 1792, Mass. Hist. Soc., *Proceedings,* 1st Ser., XII (1871-1873), 61-62.

[10] See Table I; David Reed, Membership in the Massachusetts Peace Society, 1816-1820 (unpubl. seminar paper, Brandeis University, 1968), 60-63.

[11] *The Acts and Resolves, Public and Private, of the Province of Massachusetts Bay,* V (Boston, 1886), 1163, 1165.

Boston followed a pattern similar to both American towns and rural areas. Although in the seventeenth century wealth in American towns was typically less concentrated than in sixteenth-century English towns, where the poorer half of the population owned less than a tenth of the wealth and the richest tenth owned between half and seven-tenths, the English pattern soon reappeared in America and intensified.[12]

TABLE II

A. DISTRIBUTION OF TAXABLE WEALTH IN BOSTON, 1790[a]

Assessment in Pounds	Number in Category	Percentage of Taxpayers in Category	Wealth in Category in Pounds	Percentage of Wealth in Category
0	892	29.8	0	0.0
25	388	12.9	9,700	1.0
26–50	240	8.0	11,162	1.2
51–75	148	4.9	11,012	1.2
76–100	167	5.6	16,662	1.8
101–150	186	6.2	24,938	2.7
151–200	147	4.9	27,887	3.0
201–300	186	6.2	49,113	5.3
301–400	128	4.3	46,713	5.0
401–500	116	3.9	54,300	5.9
501–700	124	4.1	75,775	8.3
701–999	71	2.4	58,775	6.1
1000–1,999	122	4.1	159,875	17.2
2000–4,999	58	1.9	165,250	17.8
5000+	22	0.8	217,775	23.5
Totals	2,995	100.0	928,937	100.0

[12] W. G. Hoskins, *Provincial England* (London, 1963), 90-91; J. F. Pound, "The Social and Trade Structure of Norwich 1525-1575," *Past and Present*, No. 34 (July 1966), 50-53; Donald Warner Koch, "Income Distribution and Political Structure in Seventeenth-Century Salem, Massachusetts," *Essex Institute Historical Collections*, CV (1969), 54, 59; James T. Lemon and Gary B. Nash, "The Distribution of Wealth in Eighteenth Century America: A Century of Changes in Chester County, Pennsylvania, 1693-1802," *Journal of Social History*, II (1968-1969), 9-12; Stuart Blumin,

B. DISTRIBUTION OF WEALTH IN BOSTON, 1687 TO 1830[b]

Percentage of Taxpayers	Percentage of Wealth Held			
	1687	1771	1790	1830
Bottom 30	2.48	0.10	0.03	0.00
Low-Mid 30	11.29	9.43	4.80	7.92
Upper-Mid 30	39.63	27.01	30.47	26.94
Top 10	46.60	63.46	64.70	65.14
Total	100.00	100.00	100.00	100.00
Top 1%	9.51	25.98	27.14	26.15
Schutz Coefficient	.4896	.5541	.6276	.6370

Notes: [a] Tax and Rate Books, 1790. Group at 0 paid only poll tax; £25 was the first assessment. Untaxed widows found on the census are not included.
[b] See Table II A for 1790 figures; 1687 and 1771 figures are from Henretta, "Economic Development and Social Structure," *Wm. and Mary Qtly.*, 3d Ser., XXII (1965), 80, 82, with those paying only poll tax added; 1830 figures were estimated from imprecise, grouped data in Shattuck, *Report*, 95. The Schutz coefficient of inequality measures income concentration—0 equals total equality, 1 total inequality. Robert R. Schutz, "On the Measurement of Income Inequality," *American Economic Review*, XLI (1951), 107–122; Blumin, "Mobility and Change," in Thernstrom and Sennett, eds., *Nineteenth-Century Cities*, 204.

From 1687 to 1790, Boston's wealth became very concentrated. A glance at the Lorenz curves shows that the amount of change between 1687 and 1771 was similar to that between 1771 and 1790. Statistically, changes in the distribution of wealth measured by increases in the Schutz coefficient (see Table II B) were greater between 1771 and 1790 (.0735) than during the preceding 87 years (.0647). However, the proportion of wealth held by the richest tenth of the taxpayers had almost reached its peak by 1771 and 29 per cent were without taxable property both before and after the Revolution. The wealth of the lower middle group, where assessments

"Mobility and Change in Antebellum Philadelphia," in Stephan Thernstrom and Richard Sennett, eds., *Nineteenth-Century Cities: Essays in the New Urban History* (New Haven, 1969), 204-206; Robert E. Gallman, "Trends in the Size Distribution of Wealth in the Nineteenth Century," in Lee Soltow, ed., *Six Papers on the Size Distribution of Wealth and Income* (New York, 1969), 22-23; Merle Curti, *The Making of an American Community: A Case Study of Democracy in a Frontier County* (Stanford, Calif., 1959), 78.

Chart I
Distribution of Wealth in Boston, 1687-1790[a]

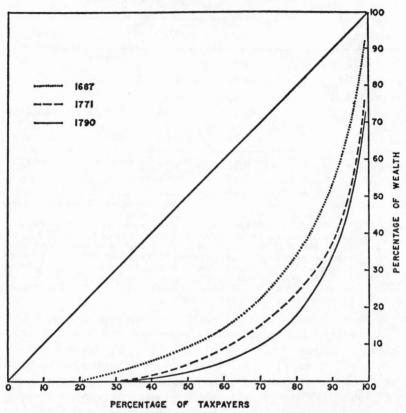

Note: [a]Drawn from Table II. The diagonal indicates an equal distribution; the area
between the dotted and dashed lines shows change between 1687 and 1771;
and the space between the dashed and solid lines shows change between 1771
and 1790.

ranged from £25 to £100, was cut in half. Three-quarters of this decline
was gained by the upper middle group, assessed between £100 and
£500.

The sale of forty-six loyalist estates in Suffolk County to ninety-six
men, two-thirds of whom already owned land in the county, had little effect on the overall distribution. The sale may have permitted a few poorer

men to enter the upper middle group, but the small gain in wealth between 1771 and 1790 made by the top tenth suggests that a wealthy group of patriots replaced an equally wealthy group of tories.[13]

Were the relatively poor becoming poorer? Brissot de Warville discovered full employment in Boston in 1788 and "saw none of those livid, ragged wretches that one sees in Europe, who, soliciting our compassion at the foot of the altar, seem to bear witness . . . against our inhumanity."[14] Brissot's European standard of comparison allowed him to underestimate the extent of poverty in Boston. At this time, a fifth to a third of those living in English and French towns were beggars, paupers, and others who could not make a living for themselves. Another third were the near poor of the English towns and the *sans-culottes* and *menu peuple* in French towns—persons who could become destitute in times of crisis.[15]

The poor and near poor were growing more numerous in Boston. The percentage of poor can be roughly estimated at 7 per cent of the population in 1771 and 10 per cent in 1790. The change is illustrated by the slow increase in the numbers of destitute, old, and sick men and women, and dependent children in the poorhouse at a time of relatively little population increase (see Table V): 146 in 1742, never over 180 before the Revolution, and 250 in August 1790, with 300 to 400 expected the following winter.[16] Because personal property was not taxed, it is difficult to determine the percentage of near poor, but an estimate can be made.[17] Composed of widows, blacks, seamen, laborers, and poorer arti-

[13] Brown, "Confiscation of Loyalists' Estates," *Wm. and Mary Qtly.*, 3d Ser., XXI (1964), 546-549.

[14] Jacques Pierre Brissot de Warville, *New Travels in the United States of America, 1788*, trans. Mara Soceanu Vamos and Durand Echeverria, ed. Durand Echeverria (Cambridge, Mass., 1964), 87, 98-100.

[15] In this paper, "poor" refers to the destitute, "near poor" to those living at or near the minimum level of subsistence. For Europe see Hoskins, *Provincial England*, 90-93; Hoskins, *Industry, Trade and People in Exeter, 1688-1800, . . .* (Manchester, Eng., 1935), 119; Pound, "Structure of Norwich," *Past and Present*, No. 34 (July 1966), 50-51; George Rudé, "La population ouvrière de Paris de 1789 à 1791," *Annales Historiques de la Révolution Française*, XXXIX (1967), 21-27; Jeffry Kaplow, "Sur la population flottante de Paris, à la fin de l'Ancien Régime," *ibid.*, 7-8; Pierre Deyon, *Amiens, Capitale Provinciale. Etude sur la Société Urbaine au 17ᵉ Siècle* (Paris, 1967), 349-357. I am indebted to Gerald Soliday, Brandeis University, for the French materials.

[16] See Table VI; *Record Commissioners' Report*, XXXI, 239.

[17] Since the total amount of property remains unknown, any "poverty line" chosen from Table II would be arbitrary. Instead, estimates of poor have been calculated by adding poorhouse and unemployed figures from Table I and of near poor

sans who might dip below the minimum level of subsistence when un-employment increased, this group probably ranged from 30 to 40 per cent in 1771 and from 37 to 47 per cent in 1790.

Unemployed, old, or sick, most of the poor and their families lived outside the poorhouse. Alexander Lord, a poor laborer, had "gone broke, wife as broke"; they had a son under sixteen to share their misery. Jacob Bull, an old shoemaker, and his wife were both ill, but two other women lived in their household. And Samuel Goddard, "shoemaker, no business, poor and supported by charity," could provide his family of five with few comforts.[18] Only the very old, the totally destitute, and the terminally ill entered the poorhouse, for the social conditions there steadily declined. In 1790, the poorhouse was filthy, dark, crowded, and odoriferous. "Persons of every description and disease are lodged under the same roof and in some instances in the same or Contiguous Apartments, by which means the sick are disturbed, by the Noise of the healthy, and the infirm rendered liable to the Vices and diseases of the diseased, and profligate."[19]

The lives of the near poor were only somewhat better than those of the poor. While the number of people per dwelling declined from 9.53 in 1742 to 7.58 in 1790 (see Table V), many of the near poor lived in grossly inferior housing. The tax assessors found 90 families living in single rooms. Sixty-five of the same families were also counted by the census taker; three-quarters of this group had families of fewer than five members. Joseph Blayner, carpenter, lived with his wife and two children in a kitchen chamber while John Cartwright, cooper, his eight children, wife, and a boarder, crowded into the back of a house. Elijah Tolams, a "very poor carpenter," lived in one room with his three children, and Ebenezer Pilsbury, shoemaker, slept and worked with his six children in only two rooms.

There was a close relationship between wealth and status. Although status was not legally defined as in England, and the reputations of vari-

---

by adding the number of widows from the census to the number of persons without taxable property and of those in the lowest category of taxpayers. A fifth of the propertyless and 15% of the lowest category have been subtracted from the near poor figure to account for upward mobility. The figures, especially for 1771, are very rough, but the direction of change they indicate is accurate, and the estimates are minimal figures of the extent of poverty.

[18] "Gone broke, wife as broke," and all similar short comments are marginalia from the Tax and Rate Books, 1790.

[19] *Record Commissioners' Report*, XXXI, 239.

ous trades were unstable,[20] the order of precedence in a parade honoring President Washington in 1789 gives some indication of the prestige of various groups. The military, town and state officers, professional men, merchants and traders, and sea captains led the parade. They were followed by forty-six different artisan crafts, "alphabetically disposed, in order to give general satisfaction." No mechanical art was deemed better than the next. Sailors brought up the rear, and laborers were not included in the line of march.[21]

As Table III shows, the eleven wealthiest occupations included professional men of high status, merchants, retailers, along with several arti-

TABLE III

MEAN ASSESSED WEALTH OF SELECTED OCCUPATIONS IN BOSTON, 1790*

Rank	Occupation	Mean Assessment in Pounds	Number of Persons in Category
1	Merchant	1,707	206
2	Lawyer	846	21
3	Doctor	795	26
4	Apothecary	657	17
5	Distiller	642	47
6	Broker	622	16
7	Retailer	601	133
8	Taverner	522	26
9	Grocer	472	33
10	Chandler	347	17
11	Wharfinger	335	24
12	Tobacconist	260	17
13	Boarder-keeper	258	24
14	Printer	247	17
15	Sea Captain	240	114
16	Hatter	233	29
17	Clerk	232	28
18	Chaisemaker	188	16
19	Baker	170	64
20	Goldsmith	166	23
21	Painter	154	34

[20] Jackson Turner Main, *The Social Structure of Revolutionary America* (Princeton, 1965), *passim,* esp. 200-211.

[21] Committee to Arrange a Procession, *Procession* (Boston, 1789).

61

Rank	Occupation	Mean Assessment in Pounds	Number of Persons in Category
22	Cabinetmaker	131	15
23	Cooper	130	70
24	Founder	120	15
25	Sailmaker	112	30
26	Mason	95	44
27	Carpenter	92	140
28	Schoolmaster	89	16
29	Truckman	84	50
30	Blacksmith	83	59
31	Shipwright	78	65
32	Scribe	77	38
33	Barber	65	42
34	Blockmaker	63	16
35	Tailor	61	100
36	Caulker	53	14
37	Sea Cooper	46	16
38	Shoemaker	45	78
39	Mate	41	20
40	Ropemaker[b]	35	37
41	Duckcloth maker	25	16
42	Fisherman	15	37
43	Sailor	9	58
44	Laborer	6	157

Notes: [a] Computed from Tax and Rate Books, 1790.
      [b] Excludes 5 ropewalk owners with a mean wealth of £760.

san trades. Most of those in the economic elite—men assessed over £1,000 —were in these groups. Sea captains, with a mean wealth of £240, were lower on the list than their status might indicate. Most others whose wealth fell between £100 and £260 were artisans. Immediately below a mean of £100 were the building trades, schoolmasters, and shipwrights. Other sea artisans, and such traditionally poorer trades as tailor, shoemaker, and barber, fell between £40 and £75. Bringing up the rear were the industrial trades of ropemaker and duckcloth maker, and mariners and laborers.

An analysis of variance showed a highly significant relationship between occupation and wealth, but the magnitude of this relationship was small. Only about 19.4 per cent of the variations in the wealth of all the individuals included in Table III was accounted for by differences between occupations. The rest of the variation was within each occupation.[22] In most trades, a few men had wealth far above the group mean; a number of hatters, printers, and bakers, for example, owned large establishments. As a result, in all but three trades below chaisemaker on the table, the median wealth was fifty pounds or less. Most fishermen, sailors, and laborers had no taxable wealth at all.

Those who possessed the highest status, reputation, and wealth expected visible differences of "Equipage, Furniture, . . . and Dress" between themselves and the rest of society. They socialized mostly with each other and separated themselves from the masses by forming exclusive organizations. One of these, a dinner club that encouraged members to relax and enjoy good conversation, was open to only sixteen men, each admitted by a unanimous vote. Another, the Massachusetts Historical Society, was incorporated in 1794 by ministers, doctors, lawyers, and a scientist to diffuse historical learning. This group limited its membership to thirty.[23]

Wealthy artisans were granted substantial respect. In the parade honoring President Washington, each trade was led by a member whose wealth averaged 225 per cent more than the mean wealth of his group: the leader of the tailors, Samuel Ballard, was assessed £500; goldsmith

[22] An F test was significant at less than the .01 level. This means there is less than a 1% chance that the differences shown in Table III are random. The test is a comparison of two quantities: 1. the sum of the squared variations of each case in each occupation subtracted from the group mean; and 2. the sum of the squared variations of each group subtracted from the grand mean. Eta², calculated from the same data, tests the strength or degree of relationship. In this case, Eta² was .194, which means that about 19.4% of the difference between the means in Table III is accounted for by the differences between occupational groups. See Herbert M. Blalock, Jr., *Social Statistics* (New York, 1960), 242-252, 255-257. Stuart Blumin's calculations of Eta² on Philadelphia data from 1860 were almost identical (.17). "The Historical Study of Vertical Mobility," *Historical Methods Newsletter*, I, No. 4 (Sept. 1968), 8-10.

[23] Brissot de Warville, *New Travels*, 90; *Handbook of the Massachusetts Historical Society* (Boston, 1949), 1-3. On the continuation of deference see Josiah P. Quincy, "Social Life in Boston: From the Adoption of the Federal Constitution to the Granting of the City Charter," in Justin Winsor, ed., *The Memorial History of Boston, Including Suffolk County, Massachusetts, 1630-1880*, IV (1886), 2, 4; David Hackett Fischer, *The Revolution of American Conservatism: The Federalist Party in the Era of Jeffersonian Democracy* (New York, 1965), xiv-xv, 4-10.

Benjamin Bert, £400; shoemaker Samuel Bangs, £500; and carpenter William Crafts, £400. Nathaniel Balch, who was assessed £925, not only led his fellow hatters in the parade, but his shop was described as "the principle lounge even of the finest people in the town. Governor Hancock himself would happen into this popular resort, ready for a joke or a political discussion with Balch."[24]

While poorer groups were expected to defer to the elite, they in turn were accorded little respect. Not only did poorer artisans have less status than those who were richer, the elite tolerated insults and attacks on black men and old black women by lower-class whites. Prince Hall, leader of the black masonic lodge, nevertheless urged Boston's Negroes to ignore their white attackers and trust "men born and bred in Boston," because we "had rather suffer wrong than to do wrong, to the disturbance of the community and the disgrace of our reputation."[25]

Did the elite demonstrate any sense of social responsibility toward the poor? Noblesse oblige was practically nonexistent. The Massachusetts Humane Society, founded mainly to save people from drowning, chose to build three small huts on islands where shipwrecks were common, rather than aid the poor sailors who populated Boston's North End.[26] Men often complained to the assessors that they were poor, sick, lame, or had "little or no business." The only relief granted them was tax abatement; seventy men found on both the 1790 census and 1790 tax lists paid no taxes.

However, benevolence to widows was considered a community responsibility. A husband's death, commented one minister, "deprives a weak and helpless woman . . . of the sole instrument of her support, the guide of her children's youth, and their only earthly dependance."[27] Any charity granted by town or church went to them. The overseers of

[24] *Independent Chronicle* (Boston), Oct. 28, 1789 (I am indebted to Alfred Young for the source); Samuel Breck, *Recollections of Samuel Breck wth Passages from His Note-Books (1771-1862)* (London, 1877), 108.

[25] Prince Hall, *A Charge Delivered to the African Lodge* . . . (Boston, 1797), 10-11; and Hall, *A Charge Delivered to the Brethren of the African Lodge* . . . (Boston, 1792). About half the blacks were servants and therefore had little choice but to be respectful.

[26] M. A. DeWolfe Howe, *The Humane Society of the Commonwealth of Massachusetts: An Historical Review, 1785-1916* (Boston, 1918), Chaps. 1-2; *The Institution of the Humane Society of the Commonwealth of Massachusetts* . . . (Boston, 1788).

[27] Peter Thacher, *A Sermon, Preached in Boston,* . . . (Boston, 1795), 13.

the poor distributed minimal aid from bequests. In 1787, for example, they gave money to sixty-six different widows, most receiving nine or twelve shillings, and only fifteen women were helped more than once. The First Church, perhaps typical, collected donations for the poor quarterly and on the Sunday before Thanksgiving. Several dozen women received a pittance of two or three shillings each month from this money.[28]

Who held political office in Boston after the Revolution? In pre-Revolutionary Boston, wealthy men of high social status monopolized important positions. Minor offices went to those of less wealth and status and gave their holders a sense of belonging in the community. After the Revolution, recent research indicates, the Massachusetts legislature included more moderately wealthy men than before the war.[29] Did Boston officeholding become more widely distributed?

TABLE IV

ASSESSED WEALTH OF BOSTON OFFICEHOLDERS, 1790[a]

Office	Mean Wealth	Median Wealth	Number in Group
State Legislators	4,044	1,750	9
Overseers of Poor	3,398	1,610	12
Fire Wards	2,850	1,350	15
School Committee	1,633	1,000	9
Clerks of Market	954	875	12
Selectmen	642	500	9
Cullers of Hoops and Staves	208	175	21
Assessors, Collectors	207	200	9
Fire Companies	125	50	138
Constables	115	75	12
Surveyors of Boards	78	50	15

Note: [a] Tax and Rate Books, 1790; *Record Commissioners' Report*, XXXI, 217–224; X, 207–211. Information for a few officers could not be determined. These included 14 members of the fire companies, 4 cullers of hoops, 3 surveyors of boards, and 3 untaxed ministers who were members of the school committee. Four legislators are missing from the table: 3 were Suffolk County senators, probably residents of other parts of the county, and the other was a representative whose name was too common to identify. All other officers are included.

[28] *Record Commissioners' Report*, XXVII, 11-12, 15, 20, 25-26, 31, 33, 37, 40; First Church Poor and Sacramental Fund, First Church, Boston.
[29] Henretta, "Economic Development and Social Structure," *Wm. and Mary Qtly.*, 3d Ser., XXII (1965), 84, 89; Jackson Turner Main, "Government by the

As Table IV shows, the economic elite still dominated the most important town offices. All the state legislators from Boston were assessed over a thousand pounds and were among the wealthiest 6.8 per cent of the population. Four were merchants, two were wealthy gentlemen, one was a doctor, one a lawyer, and one a hardware store owner. Only a quarter of the firewards, who protected valuable property in case of fire, dipped below a thousand pounds; most of them were merchants, wharfingers, and wealthy shipwrights. The school committee, a newly created agency of the government, included three clergymen, three lawyers, three doctors, and two businessmen.

Probably the two most important town offices were the selectmen and the overseers of the poor. In 1790, only one of the overseers was assessed below a thousand pounds. From 1785 to 1795, eight merchants, three hardware store owners, one auctioneer, two distillers, one apothecary, one ropewalk owner, and a wealthy baker served as overseers. During the same period, selectmen included five merchants, two lawyers, the county treasurer, a captain, a retailer, an apothecary, a wharfinger, and a wealthy hatter. Five others were probably retired businessmen, whose low assessments reduced the selectmen's mean wealth.[30]

Remarkably little turnover occurred in these two time-consuming, nonpaying positions. From 1760 to 1770, the average selectman served between three and four years; there was a small rise in tenure between 1785 and 1795. Overseers served even longer terms. In the decade 1760 to 1770, the average overseer served four or five years; after the war tenures increased to from six to eight years. At annual elections, both before and after the Revolution, typically only one or two selectmen or overseers were replaced. Bostonians served longer and replaced their officials less frequently than did the citizens of many other Massachusetts towns before the Revolution.[31]

People: The American Revolution and the Democratization of the Legislatures," *Wm. and Mary Qtly.*, 3d Ser., XXIII (1966), 404; and Main, *The Upper House in Revolutionary America, 1763-1788* (Madison, Wis., 1967), 162-174.

[30] The profile of officers was drawn from sources cited in Table IV; Boston city directories, 1789 and 1796, *Record Commissioners' Report*, X, 171-296; XXXI, 53, 59-60, 65, 97, 102, 133-134, 147, 160-161, 185, 200, 217, 224, 232, 243-245, 253, 276-277, 283, 319, 349-350, 384, 391; "Assessors' Taking Books' of the Town of Boston, 1780," *Bostonian Society Publications,* 1st Ser., IX (1912), 9-59. Hereafter cited as Assessors' Books, 1780.

[31] See n. 30; Robert Francis Seybold, *The Town Officials of Colonial Boston, 1634-1775* (Cambridge, Mass., 1939), 289-305. For other Massachusetts towns before

The middling artisans, assessed between £100 and £500, were a group far larger than the economic elite, yet after the war they still held only a small percentage of major offices. Assessors and tax collectors, full-time paid officials who determined and collected taxes, were the only powerful officers of middle-class wealth. Other positions gave artisans some recognition of their special talents, but no political power. Carpenters, joiners, and cabinetmakers dominated the position of surveyor of boards; shoemakers were sealers of leather, and coopers were cullers of hoops and staves. Marine artisans formed a majority in the fire companies, the only agencies dominated by the poor and near poor. These jobs, dirty and unpaid, gave the economic elite an opportunity to share civic participation while keeping political power in its own hands.

The elite was suspicious of any attempt to organize the laboring force politically, however deferential the organizers initially were. Artisans of middle wealth, whose share of the town's taxable property had increased since 1771, founded the Mechanics Association in 1795. Only two members of the group had belonged to the economic elite in 1790, at which time the assessments of 63 per cent of those who became members fell between £100 and £500. In 1796 the group petitioned the General Court for incorporation because "the disconnected state of the mechanics of the town of Boston . . . retarded the mechanic arts of the state" whose "situation as a manufacturing country promised the greatest extension." Twenty leading merchants were personally urged to support the petition, "to patronize an institution formed for the reciprocal benefits of the merchant and mechanic." But despite the Association's broadly conceived purpose, the legislature feared the group's potential political power and three times

the Revolution, see Michael Zuckerman, *Peaceable Kingdoms: New England Towns in the Eighteenth Century* (New York, 1970), 274-276. Boston turnover and service rates were as follows:

Years	Number of Offices	Number of Officeholders	Years of Service		Rate of Turnover/Year	
			mean	median	mean	median
Selectmen						
1760–70	7	19	4.0	3.0	1.7	1.5
1785–95	9	23	4.3	4.0	2.2	1.0
Overseers of the Poor						
1760–70	12	28	4.7	4.0	1.6	1.0
1785–95	12	23	6.3	8.0	1.2	0.5

refused to grant incorporation. The Association finally succeeded in obtaining a charter in 1806.[32]

The poorer sort commanded no political resource other than ineffective deferential appeals to the wealthy. The accumulated grievances of poor mechanics were partially relieved by harassing the black population; only the middling artisans were able to organize successfully. Pressure from below on the elite was nonexistent after the Revolution, and criminal activity was rare. Between 1787 and 1790, nine men were hanged, all for robbery, while twenty-six were punished for other crimes.[33]

Boston's population steadily increased from 1630 to 1740 as the townsmen settled the entire Shawmut Peninsula, but after 1740 people migrated from eastern New England in large numbers, so that from 1742 to 1790 Boston's population grew only 8.4 per cent, a gain of 1.68 per cent per decade. (See Table V) During the same period, the American population overall expanded at the Malthusian rate of 34.7 per cent per decade. Migration patterns bypassed eastern New England; people generally traveled up the Connecticut Valley into western Massachusetts, New Hampshire, and Maine. The results may be seen in the differential population growth of areas of Massachusetts between 1765 and 1790: Massachusetts's total population increased 54.1 per cent; Boston's (based on the smaller population of 1765) 16.2 per cent; the surrounding towns of Brookline, Cambridge, Charlestown, Chelsea, and Roxbury, 18.3 per cent; and the eastern Massachusetts counties of Suffolk, Essex, Plymouth, and Middlesex, 28.5 per cent.[34] Boston's population fell after 1742 but recovered by 1771 until the British occupied the city in 1776, when people left en masse for the countryside and only slowly returned. The exodus postponed major population growth until after recovery from the effects of the war. Between

[32] Joseph H. Buckingham, *Annals of the Massachusetts Charitable Mechanics Society* (Boston, 1853), 6-10, 12-14, 57-58, 80, 94-97.

[33] Edward H. Savage, *Police Records and Recollections; or, Boston by Daylight and Gaslight* . . . (Boston, 1873), 40-42. Savage lists only punishments, not unsolved crimes.

[34] J. Potter, "The Growth of Population in America, 1700-1860," in D. V. Glass and D. E. C. Eversley, eds., *Population in History: Essays in Historical Demography* (London, 1965), 636-641; Evarts B. Greene and Virginia D. Harrington, *American Population Before the Federal Census of 1790* (New York, 1932), 21-24, 46; Herman R. Friis, *A Series of Population Maps of the Colonies and the United States, 1625-1790*, American Geographical Society Mimeographed Publication, No. 3 (New York, 1940), 16 and maps 10a, 10b, 12a, 12b.

1790 and 1820 the town's population increased at the rate of 31.3 per cent per decade.[35]

Although the population remained nearly stationary until 1790, Bostonians began to live in less settled areas. Most, however, still crowded onto about two-thirds of the peninsula. Streets in the North End and the center of town were filled with houses; yet many areas remained uninhabited, and the empty common was almost as large as the entire North End. In 1794, Boston was still "capable of great increase as many large spots of land remain vacant." Without the pressure of large population growth, there was no need to build on inaccessible areas like Beacon Hill. The relatively high population density that resulted allowed people to conduct their business with ease by walking.[36]

TABLE V

POPULATION AND DENSITY IN BOSTON, 1742 TO 1810[a]

Year	Population	Number of Houses	Number of People Per House
1742	16,528	1,719	9.53
1752	15,731	...	...
1760	15,631	...	...
1765	15,520	1,676	9.26
1771	16,540	1,803	9.12
1776	2,719	...	...
1780	10,000	...	...
1784	14,000	2,178	6.43
1790	18,038	2,376	7.58
1800	24,937	3,000	8.31
1810	33,788	3,970	8.51

Note: [a] Shattuck, *Report*, 5, 54; Greene and Harrington, *American Population*, 31; Worthington C. Ford, ed., *Writings of John Quincy Adams*, I (New York, 1913), 62; Valuation of Towns, 1768–1771: Boston, 1771, Massachusetts Archives, Statehouse, Boston, CXXXII. The 1771 figure was derived by multiplying the number of polls by 5.75, a figure suggested by the larger number of houses that year, and the large immigration between 1765 and 1771.

[35] Leo F. Schnore and Peter R. Knights, "Residence and Social Structure: Boston in the Ante-Bellum Period," in Thernstrom and Sennett, eds., *Nineteenth-Century Cities*, 250.

[36] Pemberton, "Description of Boston," Mass. Hist. Soc., *Collections*, 1st Ser., III (1794), 249-250. The North End (wards 1-5) and the West End (ward 7) were contemporary geographical areas (*ibid.*, 267). To allow analysis the South End of

Boston expanded slowly, gradually consuming her open spaces. The mean number of people per dwelling decreased from 9.53 in 1742 to 7.58 in 1790. From 1740 to 1760 few houses were built, and many were destroyed in the 1760 fire, but from 1765 to 1790 a net total of 700 new houses were constructed. A small housing boom took place between 1771 and 1790 when an average of 28.7 houses per year were built.

The new housing was probably built mostly in the open West and South Ends. As Table VI shows, these areas were gaining population. In 1742 61 per cent of the people lived in the small, crowded North End and the center of town; the remaining 39 per cent resided in the West and South Ends, about two-thirds of the town's area. Population slowly moved west and south. Ward twelve, closest to the Roxbury Neck, gained 73 per cent from 1742 to 1790; the West End gained 21 per cent; and the center of town lost population. As a result, only 43 per cent of the population lived in the North End and the center by 1790. In 1802, William Bentley, a minister from Salem, while on a walking tour, "saw the increasing wealth of the south end, so called, but the growth of West Boston by the new Bridge from Cambridge is very great. Where the popu-

TABLE VI

POPULATION OF BOSTON'S NEIGHBORHOODS, 1742 TO 1790[a]

	1742	1771	1790	Percentage of Change, 1742-1790
North End	6,229	6,165	6,331	+2
West End	1,204	1,386	1,456	+21
Center	3,843	3,796	3,304	−14
South End	5,106	5,193	6,625	+30
Other[b]	146	...	322	+120
Total	16,528	16,540	18,038	+8

Notes: [a] Shattuck, *Report*, 3-5; Valuation of Towns, Mass. Archives, CXXXII; Tax and Rate Books, 1790; *1790 Census*. For 1771, total polls in ward were multiplied by 5.75; the 1790 figure is based on name-by-name comparison of tax and census records, with interpolations where necessary.
[b] Poorhouse in 1742; poorhouse and jail in 1790.

the 1790s was divided into the center of town (wards 6, 8, and 9) and the South End (wards 10-12). Houses are drawn on Price's 1769 map reprinted as frontispiece to *Bostonian Society Publications*, 1st Ser., IX (1912).

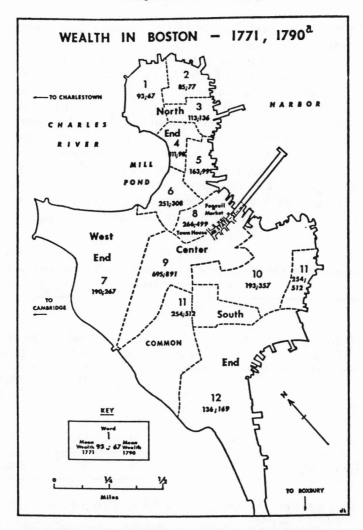

WEALTH IN BOSTON — 1771, 1790[a]

[a] Mass. Archives, CXXXII; Tax and Rate Books, 1790; *1790 Census*. The 1771 means were calculated by dividing the wealth of the ward by the number of polls; the 1790 means by dividing the ward's wealth by the number of people taxed with the addition of widows from the census. Untaxed widows were not included in the 1771 list, but the two sources are comparable because all polls (including each poll in multiple poll households and "polls not rateable") were included in the 1771 figure, but not in the 1790 figure. This seems to have underestimated the 1771 wealth.

lation was thin . . . and there were fields and marshes, are now splendid houses and crowded Streets."[37]

Boston's social geography was similar to other preindustrial towns. In those towns, wealthy merchants, lawyers, retailers, and noblemen lived on or near the main business streets. Residents of middling wealth generally lived next to them. On the outskirts, farthest away from the economic center of town, resided poor artisans and laborers.[38] In Boston, both before and after the Revolution, the farther one walked from State Street, the lower the ward's mean and median wealth became.

The center of town, with a median wealth of £125 in 1790, was the richest section. The Massachusetts Bank, the Statehouse, the market, and various retail shops were located there, mostly along State and Cornhill Streets. Families of retailers lived over their shops. Unlike

TABLE VII

RESIDENTIAL PATTERNS OF ECONOMIC AND OCCUPATIONAL GROUPS, BOSTON, 1790[a]

A. ECONOMIC GROUPS

1790 Assessment in Pounds	Percentage by Area				Number in Group
	North End	West End	Center	South End	
0	46	6	14	34	1,364
1–75	41	10	13	36	776
76–275	33	8	21	38	627
276–999	20	7	35	38	498
1000+	6	9	40	45	202
Total of All Groups	37	8	18	37	3,467

[37] William Bentley, The Diary of William Bentley, D.D., II (Gloucester, Mass., 1962 [orig. publ. 1907]), 426.

[38] Gideon Sjoberg, The Preindustrial City, Past and Present (Glencoe, Ill., 1960), 95-102; Deyon, Amiens, 247-252, 543, 566; Hoskins, Exeter, 113, 116-117; Hoskins, Provincial England, 92-93; D. V. Glass, "Notes on the Demography of London at the End of the Seventeenth Century," Daedalus, XCVII (1968), 583; Richard L. Bushman, From Puritan to Yankee: Character and Social Order in Connecticut, 1690-1765 (Cambridge, Mass., 1967), 57-58; Charles A. Beard, Economic Origins of Jeffersonian Democracy (New York, 1915), 384-386; Blumin, "Mobility and Change," in Thernstrom and Sennett, eds., Nineteenth-Century Cities, 186-190.

B. OCCUPATIONAL GROUPS

	Percentage by Area				
Occupation	North End	West End	Center	South End	Number in Group
Bakers	38	18	5	39	66
Blacksmiths	46	3	8	43	59
Building Trades	31	10	11	48	245
Coopers	70	0	3	27	70
Laborers	47	7	8	38	157
Leather Workers	33	5	10	52	108
Mariners	68	5	8	19	117
Marine Crafts[b]	72	2	6	20	193
Merchants[c]	9	12	28	51	206
Professionals	15	13	38	34	68
Retailers[d]	28	4	46	22	144
Sea Captains	46	10	16	28	114
Tailors	41	11	16	32	100
Transportation	32	4	14	50	80
Total of All Groups	40	7	16	37	1,727

Notes: [a] Tax and Rate Books, 1790. Variations in residential patterns can be seen by comparing the percentage of the total of all groups in each area with the percentage of each subgroup in the area. In Table VII A, widows from the census are included; Table VII B includes about two-thirds of all employed. A Chi Square test run on the raw data of Table VII A yielded a result that was significant at less than the .01 level. This means the probability that the distribution occurred by chance is less than 1%.
[b] Excludes ropemakers, concentrated in the West End.
[c] Includes only merchants, not other groups included under "Merchants-Traders" in Table I.
[d] Retailers and hardware store owners only.

those in the rest of the town, the buildings were predominantly brick.[39] Ward nine, on the south side of State Street, was the wealthiest in town, with a fifth of its residents assessed over a thousand pounds each, but it was closely followed by surrounding wards. The richest merchants and professional men and almost half the retailers lived in these wards, but in proportion to their numbers in the total population, fewer artisans made their homes there.

[39] Pemberton, "Description of Boston," Mass. Hist. Soc., *Collections*, 1st Ser., III (1794), 248-250.

Part of the South End was far from the center of town and quite poor, but a number of retailers and merchants, mostly of middling wealth, lived in wards ten and eleven. The area's median wealth in 1790 was only fifty pounds; but over half the people in ward twelve were assessed twenty-five pounds or less. This ward, almost as populous as the two others together, contained large numbers of laborers, truckmen, and leather workers. In 1790, the ward must still have seen intense building activity, because a third of the town's masons, carpenters, and painters resided there.

The undersettled West End, with a median wealth of twenty-five pounds, was poorer than the South End. Most of the town's ropemakers lived there, close to the ropewalks. This was the only part of town not to lose black population between 1742 and 1790; in 1790 blacks were most concentrated there. As the area became more densely settled, merchants and professional men also moved into the area; by 1790 both groups were settled there in greater proportion than throughout the town generally.

The North End was the poorest section of town in 1771, and by 1790 the wealth of its inhabitants seems to have declined. The median wealth of the area in the latter year was twenty-five pounds, but over half the people in the remote wards one and two were without taxable wealth. Most of the town's transient sailors, shipwrights, sailmakers, and other marine artisans lived there. An area dominated by marine interests, it also housed proportionately higher percentages of coopers, sea captains, laborers, tailors, and poor widows than there were in the population as a whole.

How strong was this pattern? Even though the town was small, and a few members of every economic and occupational group lived in every section, substantial economic segregation could have existed. As Table VIII shows, no group was as segregated as blacks are today.[40] There was no necessary relationship between occupation and degree of segregation. Professional men were more integrated than merchants; blacks, laborers, and tailors clustered far less than their lower-class status might indicate. Marine artisans, with their special ship-related functions, were the most segregated trade. Wealth rather than occupation determined

[40] For figures in Philadelphia see Sam Bass Warner, Jr., "If All the World Were Philadelphia: A Scaffolding for Urban History, 1774-1930," *American Historical Review*, LXXIV (1968-1969), 36-37. Figures for the index of dissimilarity for blacks in ghettos 1940-1960 run between 75 and 90. Karl E. and Alma F. Taeuber, *Negroes in Cities: Residential Segregation and Neighborhood Change* (Chicago, 1965), 37-41.

TABLE VIII

INDEX OF DISSIMILARITY OF ECONOMIC AND OCCUPATIONAL GROUPS, BOSTON, 1790[a]

Unpropertied	56.8	Marine Crafts[b]	35.5	Transportation	11.6
Assessed £1–75	26.4	Merchants	25.9	Professionals[c]	9.8
Assessed £76–275	16.7	Building Crafts	18.6	Sea Captains	8.8
Assessed £276–999	41.7	Mariners	17.3	Tailors	8.8
Assessed £1000+	28.5	Retailers	16.7	Leather Crafts	8.3
Blacks	10.4	Laborers	15.2	Bakers	6.7
Widows	19.1	Coopers	11.8	Blacksmiths	6.4

Notes: [a] Tax and Rate Books, 1790. For details on the construction of the index, which measures the average deviation within wards of the percentage of each group from its mean percentage in the total population and runs from 0 (perfect integration) to 100 (total segregation), see Taeuber and Taeuber, *Negroes in Cities*, 235–237.
[b] Excludes ropemakers, concentrated in the West End.
[c] Lawyers, doctors, an accountant, an apothecary, and an architect.

residence. Boston's propertyless residents—nearly 40 per cent of the population—were the most segregated group and mostly lived in economic ghettos at either end of town. Wealthier, and thus smaller, economic groups were less concentrated and spread more evenly across the city.

In late eighteenth-century Boston, individuals were becoming increasingly more mobile, moving from place to place and from one economic position to another, while society itself was becoming more stratified. Almost all newcomers to Boston were "warned out," officially informed that the town would not care for them if they ever needed charity.[41] Since there is no indication that warnings out were limited to the poor, they are rough measures of migration into Boston. While the scrutiny of the overseers may have increased over the period, the pattern found in Table IX is too strong to be discounted. The number of migrants remained small until 1755, then in terms both of numbers and rates, rapidly increased. After 1765, at least a tenth of Boston's residents had been in town five years or less.[42]

[41] Josiah Henry Benton, *Warning Out in New England* (Boston, 1911), 55-62; *Record Commissioners' Report*, XXV, 28, 34, 166, 212, 242.
[42] Rates for 1765-1790 were almost as great as in early modern London, but less than those in antebellum Boston. E. A. Wrigley, "A Simple Model of London's Importance in Changing English Society and Economy 1650-1750," *Past and Present*, No. 37 (July 1967), 45-49; Peter R. Knights, "Population Turnover, Persistence and

TABLE IX
WARNINGS OUT IN BOSTON, 1745 TO 1792[a]

Year	Number Warned	Number Warned/1000 Population
1745–1749	363	23.1
1750–1754	528	33.6
1755–1759	1,160	74.2
1760–1764	765	49.3
1765–1769	2,499	151.1
1770–1773	1,587	95.9
1791–1792	2,405	133.9

Note: [a] Warnings Out in Boston, 1745–1792, Records of the Overseers of the Poor of Boston, Mass., Mass. Hist. Soc. From 1745 to 1773, children and wives were listed with husbands; the 1791–1792 lists often include many entries under a single family name, but the relationships are not indicated. The 1791–1792 number/1000 population is comparable with the others; at that time a resident could be warned until he resided in the town four years. Robert W. Kelso, *The History of Public Poor Relief in Massachusetts, 1620–1920* (Boston, 1922), 59. This table represents minimum migration into Boston.

What would explain this dramatic change in the intensity of migration? Migrants in most modern societies tend to travel short distances, going from remote villages to nearby towns and from towns to more distant cities. They stop and settle at the first place where a job is offered, and travel farther only if the opportunity disappears.[43] These generalizations apply to post-Revolutionary Boston. Almost three-quarters of the migrants entering Boston in 1791 came from Massachusetts, and a third traveled ten miles or less. In point of origin, the other quarter principally divided between foreign lands and more distant American cities like New York and Philadelphia.

The migrants formed three distinct streams. Twenty-eight per cent arrived from foreign ports. The other two groups, totaling 71.2 per cent of all migrants, traveled from Massachusetts towns. Most of them,

Residential Mobility in Boston, 1830-1860," in Thernstrom and Sennett, eds., *Nineteenth-Century Cities*, 258-274.

[43] E. G. Ravenstein, "The Laws of Migration," *Journal of the Royal Statistical Society*, XLVIII (1885), 167-227, esp. 198-199; Ravenstein, "The Laws of Migration: Second Paper," *ibid.*, LII (1889), 241-305; Samuel A. Stoffer, "Intervening Opportunities: A Theory Relating Mobility and Distance," *American Sociological Review*, V (1940), 845-867; George Blackburn and Sherman L. Ricards, Jr., "A Demographic History of the West: Manistee County, Michigan, 1860," *Journal of American History*, LVII (1970), 616-617.

TABLE X

BIRTH PLACES OF THOSE WARNED OUT OF BOSTON, 1791[*]

Foreign	237	Other States	62	Massachusetts	740
England	84	Philadelphia	28	Within 10 miles of Boston	341
Ireland	52	New York City	19	Southeast of Boston	181
Scotland	31	Carolina	4	North of Boston	143
Africa	29	Maryland	3	West of Boston	75
Germany	16	New Hampshire	3		
France	14	Albany	3		
Nova Scotia	3	Hartford	2		
West Indies	8				

Total: 1,039

Note: [*] Warnings Out in Boston, Overseers of the Poor Records, Mass. Hist. Soc.

39.8 per cent of the total, migrated from nearby coastal areas such as Charlestown, Plymouth, Cape Cod, Ipswich, Salem, and Newburyport. This seaport-to-seaport stream probably brought numerous marine artisans and mariners into Boston. If the mobility of this group was as great in the 1760s, it may help to explain the number and volatility of the crowds in pre-Revolutionary Boston.[44] The final group, constituting 31.4 per cent of all migrants, came from neighboring agricultural areas that were experiencing population pressure on land. In these areas during the late eighteenth century, poverty and geographical mobility increased as the average size of landholdings fell.[45] Forced off the land and unaccustomed to urban life, these men at least temporarily joined and augmented the number of poor and near poor.

Though Boston drew many people from smaller ports, declining agricultural areas, and foreign lands, her own opportunities were limited. By 1790, 45 per cent of the taxpayers in town in 1780 had dis-

[44] Pauline Maier, "Popular Uprisings and Civil Authority in Eighteenth-Century America," Wm. and Mary Qtly., 3d Ser., XXVII (1970), 3-35.

[45] Kenneth Lockridge, "Land, Population and the Evolution of New England Society 1630-1790," Past and Present, No. 39 (Apr. 1968), 62-80; Philip J. Greven, Four Generations: Population, Land, and Family in Colonial Andover, Massachusetts (Ithaca, N. Y., 1970), 212-214; Charles S. Grant, Democracy in the Connecticut Frontier Town of Kent (New York, 1961), 94-103; Bruce E. Steiner, "New England Anglicanism: A Genteel Faith?" Wm. and Mary Qtly., 3d Ser., XXVII (1970), 122-135.

appeared from tax lists. Some had died; the rest left town. The figure is higher than that found in stable, rural communities where land is plentiful, but is low compared to nineteenth-century American cities or frontier areas.[46] Those who moved out of Boston were the poorest and least successful members of the community. As Table XI shows, only 42 per cent of those without real estate (rents) in 1780 remained in town in 1790. In Newburyport between 1850 and 1880, 41 per cent of the laborers persisted during each decade, a rate almost identical to that of the unpropertied in Boston seventy years earlier.[47] As the amount of rent reported increased, the rate of persistence rose; only one-quarter of the upper 10 per cent of those listed in 1780 had moved or died by 1790. Even if the death rates of the poor were higher, and their slippage from one list to another greater, this table suggests that a larger proportion of the poor than the rich were mobile.

TABLE XI

GEOGRAPHIC MOBILITY IN BOSTON, 1780 TO 1790[a]

Rent in Pounds in 1780	Number Reported in 1780	Number Missing in 1790	Persistence Rate
0	546	318	42
1-20	448	215	52
21-40	360	169	53
41-60	217	83	62
61-80	219	83	62
100-199	226	78	66
200+	209	54	74
Total	2,225	1,000	56

Note: [a] Assessors' Books, 1780, compared with Tax and Rate Books, 1790. The persistence rate is the percentage of the number reported in 1780 found on the 1790 list.

[46] Other rates, all expressed in terms of per cent per decade: 51% in 17th-century English towns; 22% in Dedham, Mass., 1670-1700; 56% in Boston, 1830-1860; 73% in Trempealeau Co., Wis., 1860-1880. Peter Laslett and John Harrison, "Clayworth and Cogenhoe," in H. E. Bell and R. L. Ollard, eds., Historical Essays 1600-1750, Presented to David Ogg (London, 1963), 173-177; Kenneth Lockridge, "The Population of Dedham, Massachusetts, 1636-1736," Economic History Review, 2d Ser., XIX (1966), 322-324; Knights, "Population Turnover," in Thernstrom and Sennett, eds., Nineteenth-Century Cities, 262; Curti, American Community, 68.

[47] Stephan Thernstrom, Poverty and Progress: Social Mobility in a Nineteenth Century City (Cambridge, Mass., 1964), 85.

Inward and outward mobility suggests a small, but significant, floating population of men and women at the bottom of society who moved from seaport to seaport and town to town in search of work. Many of the 278 men who were assessed for only the poll tax in 1790, but who disappeared before the census was taken, were probably among them.[48] The nature of this floating population was very similar to that in nineteenth-century Newburyport.[49] Impoverished, unemployable men dominated the wanderers in both places. The fifteen men whipped for various offenses in Boston in September 1790 were transients who had not been listed by the assessors a few months earlier.[50] Other migrants from Boston landed in the poorhouses of neighboring towns, triggering angry correspondence between their overseers and those of Boston.[51]

Uprooted, unwanted, unhealthy migrants could call no town their home. The potent identity given an individual by his community was not theirs. Thomas Seymore, an old man living off poor relief in Abington in 1805, was born and attended school in Boston, and later moved to Barnstable, Sandwich, Weymouth, and Abington, but never "gained a settlement" by paying taxes for five successive years. In his whole life, he never found a home. Similarly, Braintree demanded in 1804 that Boston "remove Stephen Randal belonging to your town." Since his arrival there in 1802, he had received relief from the town. "He has been wandering about from place to place. . . . Some part of the time chargeable. About four weeks ago he froze himself very bad in the feet and is att the Expense of two Dollars and 50 cents per week, Besides a Dollar attendance, there is no prospect of his being better very soon."[52]

After the Revolution, the old laws used to deal with migrants fell apart. Even though the state accepted responsibility for transients without legal residence anywhere in the commonwealth, the time limit for towns to present migrants with warnings out was extended from two years to three, four, and ultimately five years between 1790 and 1793.

[48] The census was taken between Aug. 2 and 22 (*Record Commissioners' Report* edition of census); when assessments were made is unknown, but assessors were elected in March and some widows of men who were taxed appear in the census.

[49] Thernstrom, *Poverty and Progress,* 84-89.

[50] *Boston Gazette* (Mass.), Sept. 20, 1790.

[51] Overseers of the Poor of Boston, Mass., Miscellaneous Papers, 1735-1855, Mass. Hist. Soc. Most letters are from the period 1800-1805; for similar examples in the 1760s see *Record Commissioners' Report,* XX, 201-202, 281-289.

[52] Overseers of the Poor, Misc. Papers, 1735-1855, Mass. Hist. Soc.

In 1794, when the state became responsible for all migrants, warnings out were finally eliminated. Instead, legal residency required payment of taxes on an assessed estate of sixty pounds for five successive years. A former apprentice who practiced his trade for five years or anyone over twenty-one years of age who lived in town for ten years and paid taxes for five became a resident. The law discouraged transients, but encouraged artisans with capital to remain.[53]

But did "expensive Living . . . [pervade] thro every Class, confounding every Distinction between the Poor and the Rich," as Samuel Adams insisted? Enough examples could be found to keep him worried. Thomas Lewis was a shoemaker assessed for £40 rent in 1780 and a wharfinger taxed on £700 in 1790; Josiah Elliot was an agent for a merchant in 1780 and owned no real estate, but in 1790 he operated a hardware store and was assessed for property worth £450; Robert Davis was a leather dresser with £30 rent in 1780, and a merchant assessed £600 in 1790.

Adams failed to see more modest gains. "Mechanics of sober character, and skilled in their trades, of almost every kind, may find employment, and wages equal to their support," wrote the Boston Immigrant Society.[54] The society was partially right. When the Mechanics Association, open only to master craftsmen, was founded in 1795, a fifth of its original members were not on the 1790 tax list; they had either been apprentices in 1790 or had entered town since that time.

A comparison of 1780 and 1790 tax lists shows that occupational mobility was very moderate and that opportunity may well have been declining. Since only those who remained in town for ten years are considered, the results are biased toward success. Only 28 per cent changed jobs, while merely 14 per cent made even minor changes in status. Changes from one artisan job to another and changes among merchants, grocers, retailers, and captains were typical—and rather trivial. Other changes resulted in new status; and about the same number rose as declined. Seventeen artisans became small shopkeepers, wharfingers, and merchants, and four advanced to professional status, while thirteen declined to laborer status. Twenty-eight tradesmen and professionals declined to artisan status, and one became a laborer.

Some new men from outlying areas probably migrated to Boston, bought tory estates, and joined the elite classes immediately after the

[53] Kelso, *Public Poor Relief*, 55-61.
[54] Immigrant Society in Boston, *Information for Immigrants to the New-England States* (Boston, 1795).

TABLE XII

OCCUPATIONAL MOBILITY IN BOSTON, 1780 TO 1790[a]

| Occupation in 1790 | Occupation in 1780 | | | | Total in 1790 |
	Pro-fessional	Tradesman	Artisan	Marine-Laborer	
Professional	42	15	4	0	61
Tradesman[b]	0	162	17	0	179
Artisan	5	23	311	9	348
Marine-Laborer	0	1	13	24	38
Total in 1780	47	201	345	33	626

Notes: [a] Assessors' Books, 1780; Tax and Rate Books, 1790. Table XII represents only about half the people who remained in Boston during the decade. Wards 5, 6, and 10 do not have occupations listed for 1780, and Negroes and widows were rarely listed. The columns are 1780, the rows 1790 (e.g., 61 professionals in 1790, 47 in 1780, 311 artisans remained artisans over the decade, 23 tradesmen became artisans). Lateral changes within the groups, which included no change in status, involved 4 professionals, 37 tradesmen, 42 artisans, 4 marine-laborers. Total changes of status: 87. Total lateral changes: 87. Total changes: 174.
[b] Retailers, merchants, businessmen.

Revolution,[55] but opportunity soon diminished and the situation became critical. As population grew, more men competed for fewer jobs; many, according to Samuel Breck, became unemployed, "so much so that several gentlemen who associated for the purpose of building three ships had solely in view the occupation of the carpenters and tradespeople."[56] Breck may not have greatly exaggerated. The percentage of laborers and other unskilled men more than doubled: between 2 and 3 per cent were in the group in 1780; the number had grown to 7.4 per cent in 1790.[57] Within the groups staying in town for the ten years, opportunities seem to have been slightly closing at the top and opening at the bottom. While ten merchants and traders became government functionaries (all

[55] Brown, "Confiscation of Loyalists' Estates," *Wm. and Mary Qtly.*, 3d Ser., XXI (1964), 546-549; Oscar and Mary F. Handlin, "Radicals and Conservatives in Massachusetts after Independence," *New England Quarterly*, XVII (1944), 352-355.
[56] Breck, *Recollections*, 178.
[57] Laborers constitute 6.1% of the people whose occupations in 1780 are known. However, the three wards from which there is no occupational data housed only 11% of the laborers in 1790. The figure of 6.1% is therefore far too high. A number of

but one in a full-time position), the total number of tradesmen declined by 11 per cent. On the other hand, the number of men in the marine-laborer category declined 12 per cent.[58]

Upward mobility among sons of artisans was somewhat greater. Jackson Main discovered that the fathers of about a quarter of the merchants sampled from the 1789 directory had been artisans such as brewers, coopers, hatters, carpenters, and tailors. Since each of these trades included a few wealthy members whose sons should have risen in the normal course of events, and Main discovered none from his sample among the wealthiest merchants, his findings, like mine, point to very modest upward mobility.[59]

While a small minority changed their status, almost two-thirds of the group changed their relative economic position in the community. Table XIII shows that 30 per cent lost and 31 per cent gained wealth. However, these figures are deceptive; probably most of those who moved during the decade feared economic decline. When geographic mobility is considered, more men lost than gained wealth. In each of the three middle categories of Table XIII, the number who fell slightly approximated the number who gained slightly. Unpropertied men who left town were probably those who could not gain a foothold in Boston, for 71 per cent of those who remained became property owners. Most made minor gains; the twenty-eight men who entered the top categories were mostly merchants who had not yet bought property in Boston in 1780. The very top category—as Sam Adams asserted—was in a state of flux; less than half the men in that group in 1780 managed to remain there in 1790, but men from the next lower category rushed to fill their places.

What all these changes meant to most workers was buying—or losing—a small piece of real estate, finding a new, somewhat different job, or receiving a small profit from one's trade. Joseph Snelling, an unpropertied joiner in 1780, gained £25 of real estate by 1790; John Scutter,

---

others in other wards have no occupations listed, and some of them may have been laborers. For a conservative estimate of the proportion of laborers, I added 30% to the number listed (38), and divided that number (50) by 2,225, the total number of males on the 1780 list. The result was 2.3%.

[58] These percentages, based on a small number of cases, must be taken as indicative only of the direction of change, not of the extent of change. It is probable that some of the difference is random. However, the figures may be minimums; Table XII probably underestimates the extent of downward mobility. See note to Table XIV.

[59] Main, *Social Structure*, 191-192.

a propertyless fisherman in 1780, was a journeyman goldsmith with £25 of real estate in 1790. Tailor Samuel Beales owned £12 10s. of real estate in 1780; by 1790, he owned property assessed at £125 and had six children and four apprentices or journeymen in his house. Small losses were equally common. John Douglass, a cooper with real estate worth £12 10s. in 1780, was a combmaker without taxable property in 1790. Samuel Clark, tailor, lost real estate worth £20 over the decade, and Richard Salter, a merchant with a rent of £180 in 1780, was a small shopkeeper with property worth only £25 in 1790.

What pattern explains these small changes? Men in some trades—merchants, professional men, builders, coopers—tended to gain wealth, while others—bakers, shoemakers, tailors—tended to lose it. Whole classes, however, neither rose nor fell; some individuals in most groups became prosperous and some poor.[60] As Table XIV illustrates, over 70 per cent of Boston's workers assumed different occupations or economic conditions over the decade. While there is a significant (and expected) ten-

TABLE XIII

PROPERTY MOBILITY IN BOSTON, 1780 TO 1790[a]

1790 Income Groups	1780 Income Groups					Total in 1790
	High 1	2	3	4	Low 5	
High 1	55	39	15	3	7	119
2	43	85	63	7	21	219
3	12	46	107	59	39	263
4	4	17	51	87	55	214
Low 5	7	14	32	71	51	175
Total in 1780	121	201	268	227	173	990

Note: [a] Assessors' Books, 1780; Tax and Rate Books, 1790. Some persons could not be ranked. Columns are 1780, rows 1790. The income groups were determined by comparing 1780 rents (hypothetically 1/6 of the real estate assessment) with total assessments in 1790. In the table, 1 is the highest and 5 the lowest group. The real figures for each group in 1780 and 1790 respectively are: 1, £200+ and £1000+; 2, £75–£199 and £276–£999; 3, £30–£74 and £76–£275; 4, £1–£29 and £1–£75; 5, £0 for both years.

[60] The problem is discussed in Blumin, "Historical Study of Mobility," Hist. Meth. Newsletter, I, No. 4 (Sept. 1968), 1-13.

TABLE XIV

OCCUPATIONAL AND PROPERTY MOBILITY IN BOSTON, 1780 TO 1790ᵃ

	Occupation Up	Occupation Same	Occupation Down	Total
Wealth Up	32	164	14	210
Wealth Same	26	186	33	245
Wealth Down	12	84	52	148
Total	70	434	99	603

Note: ᵃ Assessors' Books, 1780; Tax and Rate Books, 1790. Occupations in Table XIV are ranked as in Table III, and ranks for other occupations have been interpolated to determine direction of mobility. The occupational mobility figures are not identical to those of Table XII because of the differences in the categories of Table III; the method used here allowed inclusion of cases of lateral mobility mentioned in n. *a* to Table XII. Some cases have been lost, and several cases of men employed in 1780 and unemployed in 1790 added. Ratios of downward/downward and upward mobility in Tables XII–XIV show that Table XIV may be biased toward upward property mobility (51.7% downward/downward and upward mobility in Table XIII and only 41.3% downward in Table XIV). Since Table XIII has the larger number of cases, it should be more accurate. But with its more exact methodology, Table XIV points to a bias toward upward occupational mobility in Table XII (48.2% downward mobility in Table XII, 58% in Table XIV). Chi Square was significant at less than .01.

dency for some to rise or fall both in wealth and occupation, 74 per cent of those changing in one variable did not change the other.

Though occupational mobility had little relationship to economic mobility, age in most occupational groups was probably related to wealth.[61] A young man might begin working with little money, gain wealth, and perhaps change occupations as he grew older, lose wealth when he became an old man, and leave his widow with few worldly goods. Some impressionistic evidence supports this thesis. John Hooton followed his father's trade of oarmaker in 1780 and lived at home, but by 1790 he was a wharfinger taxed for £275. In 1780 Benjamin Jervis was a propertyless journeyman working for merchant Pascol Smith; by 1790 Jervis had set up as a merchant himself and was assessed £450. Aged Joseph Morton, propertyless in 1790, had been a taverner with a rent of £200 in 1780; John Maud, an old tailor, had a £30 rent in 1780 but was propertyless in 1790.

[61] Age and mobility were related in 19th-century Canada. Michael Katz, "The Social Structure of Hamilton, Ontario," in Thernstrom and Sennett, eds., *Nineteenth-Century Cities*, 209-244.

The social condition of the town's widows also supports this thesis. In 1790, only 76 of Boston's 575 widows owned any taxable property. Widows of very successful men managed to hold on to some property: of the widows taxed, 17 were assessed under £125, 23 from £125 to £200, 21 from £201 to £500, 10 from £500 to £1,000, and 5 over £1,000. Probably some husbands lost wealth before they died; widows quickly lost the rest. Their decline in wealth and status was steeper than almost any experienced by their husbands; the resulting loneliness and unhappiness appear in the assessor's marginal comments. Widow Gray was a "dogmatic lady," and Widow Turrell was a "talking woman." A number of widows followed callings that allowed contact with the public. Twenty-eight of them combated poverty and isolation by operating boarding houses; five others owned taverns; three managed millinery shops; and eight owned other types of retail establishments.

Inequality rapidly advanced in Boston during the Revolutionary period. Wealth was less evenly distributed than before the war, and the proportion of wealth held by the poor and middling classes declined. The growth of poverty was a major problem. As continued migration increased the numbers of poor, a surplus female population of working age was only temporarily helped by the duckcloth factory. Many citizens were able to gain economic security, but unsuccessful families lived in crowded housing or wandered from place to place in search of employment.

Rich and poor were divided by wealth, ascribed status, and segregated living patterns. Individuals could rarely breach a status barrier in fewer than two generations. While social mobility may have been relatively easy for a few immediately after the Revolution, these extraordinary opportunities tended to disappear as population returned to its pre-Revolutionary size. Since political power was monopolized by the wealthy, the poor could only deferentially appeal for aid. The economic elite socialized only among themselves, never showed visitors the semi-ghetto of the North End, and rode through the South End without seeing the poor. But increased segregation could eventually undermine deference by eliminating opportunities for the lowly to defer to their superiors.

A class system based primarily on economic divisions slowly developed. Occupation and wealth determined a man's position in the community; the few titles that survived became functional descriptions of groups, not indicators of a special status. Tax records show that "gentleman" ceased to be a social distinction, but was instead a term reserved for retired tradesmen; "esquire" was a title generally limited to lawyers and public officials. Increased wealth alone could bring higher status to tradesmen and artisans—a fact probably behind Samuel Adams's complaints.

At the same time Boston was becoming more stratified, a new political philosophy emerged. Whig theory divided society and government into three orders, democracy, aristocracy, and monarchy, and demanded that each be perpetually a check and balance on the others. After the Revolution this theory slowly gave way to a model that put the people above the entire government. They held "constituent power," enabling them to call conventions to write constitutions restraining the powers of government. Sovereignty was transferred from the king (or a branch of the legislature) to the people, and political equality was enshrined in the country's legal documents.[62]

Yet the city of Boston, increasingly democratic in theory, and increasingly stratified and divided economically and socially, managed to avoid major civil disturbances after the Revolution. Not only did social and political trends seem to run in opposite directions, but the groups of near poor who manned preindustrial crowds in Europe—apprentices, journeymen, and artisans—lived in greater profusion in Boston than in contemporary European towns.[63] What social forces kept these groups quiet after the Revolution?

Definitive answers to this question await further research, but at least some speculation is in order. Before the Revolution, crowd action was considered a legitimate means for producing social change and protecting the community. When the monarchial order seemed to deny the people their liberties, the people took to the streets. The resulting disturbances were not class conflicts, for pre-Revolutionary crowds in America were supported by the upper classes and peopled by the near poor.[64]

After the Revolution, the ideological props for violence slowly disintegrated. If the people were sovereign, if they held "constituent power," crowd action was a revolt against the people, not a conflict to

[62] Robert R. Palmer, *The Age of the Democratic Revolution: A Political History of Europe and America, 1760-1800* (Princeton, 1959), I, Chap. 8; Gordon S. Wood, *The Creation of the American Republic, 1776-1787* (Chapel Hill, 1969), Chaps. 8-9.

[63] George Rudé, *The Crowd in History: A Study of Popular Disturbances in France and England, 1730-1848* (New York, 1964), *passim*, but esp. Chap. 13; Ralf Dahrendorf, *Class and Class Conflict in Industrial Society* (Stanford, Calif., 1959), 216-218.

[64] Maier, "Popular Uprisings," *Wm. and Mary Qtly.*, 3d Ser. XXVII (1970), 3-30.

restrain one branch of government. This change did not eliminate violence, but it altered its nature.[65] Crowds would no longer be the weapons of one order, composed of elements from many economic classes, to be directed against another, but would be revolutionary instruments of class conflict.

Post-Revolutionary Boston, however, provided several structural restraints against this development. The possibility of moderate economic success and the safety valve of short-distance migrations probably limited the chance for confrontation. Unless economic disaster strikes a large number of men (and there is no evidence of this in Boston at this time), group conflict can be generated only when two organized interests compete for the same goods or power.[66] But Boston's only organized society of workers—whose members were of firm middle-class standing—willingly deferred to their social superiors.

[65] *Ibid.*, 30-33.
[66] Dahrendorf, *Class and Class Conflict*, Chaps. 5-6.

APPENDIX
OCCUPATIONS OF BOSTON MALES, 1790[c]

Occupation	Number	Occupation	Number
I. Government[b]	67	Peddler	6
Federal Officers	11	Retailer	133
Law Enforcement	10	Stationeer	5
State Officers	13	Tobacconist	17
Town Officers	33	Trader	13
		Underwriter	1
II. Professional	219	Wharfinger	24
Accountant	3		
Apothecary	17	IV. Clerical	66
Architect	1	Clerk	28
Dentist	1	Scribe	38
Doctor	26		
Lawyer	21	V. Artisans A to G	1,271
Minister	20		
Schoolmaster	16	A. Building Crafts	245
Sea Captain	114	Carpenter	140
		Glazier	12
III. Tradesmen	474		
Auctioneer	7	Mason	44
Banker	1	Painter	34
Broker	16	Joiner	5
Bookseller	2	Sawyer	7
Chandler	17	Stonecutter	3
Hardware Shop	11		
Lemondealer	10	B. Cloth Trades	289
Lumber Merchant	5	Cardmaker	24
Merchant	206	Combmaker	2

Occupation	Number	Occupation	Number
Duckcloth Maker	17	Carver	4
Furrier	3	Chairmaker	11
Hatter	29	Cooper	70
Leather Dresser	13	Turner	1
Shoemaker	78	Upholsterer	4
Shoedealer	6	Woodsealer	1
Silkdyer	3	G. Misc. Crafts	5
Tailor	100	Bookbinder	103
Tanner	10	Chaisemaker	16
Weaver	3	Huckster	4
C. Food Trades	175	Instrument Maker	3
Bacon Smoker	1	Musician	3
Baker	64	Paper-stainer	3
Bonecutter	1	Printer	17
Butcher	10	Saddler	6
Confectioneer	1	Soapboiler	6
Distiller	47	Watchmaker	8
Gingerbread Baker	2	Wheelwright	8
Grocer	33	Misc. Trades	28
Miller	4	VI. Service	183
Slop Shop	4	Barber	42
Sugar Boiler	8	Boarder-keeper	24
D. Marine Crafts	219	Carter	9
Blockmaker	16	Chaise-letter	3
Caulker	14	Coachdriver	6
Head Builder	5	Hackdriver	7
Mastmaker	7	Sexton	11
Rigger	11	Stablekeeper	3
Sailmaker	30	Taverner	26
Sea Cooper	16	Truckman	50
Oarmaker	1	VII. Mariners	117
Pumpmaker	4	Fisherman	37
Shipjoiner	7	Mate	20
Shipwright	65	Pilot	2
Staysmaker	1	Sailor	58
Ropemaker	42	VIII. Unskilled	188
E. Metal Crafts	132	Chimney Sweeper	6
Blacksmith	59	Gardener	15
Coppersmith	4	Laborer	157
Founder	15	Lightman	7
Goldsmith	23	Total Employed:	2,585
Gunsmith	1		
Ironmonger	1	Unemployed and Retired	106
Jeweler	3	Gentlemen	23
Silversmith	5	Poor (no trade)	27
Tinner	14	Poor, sick, lame	28
Whitesmith	1	Unemployed	28
Pewterer	6	Servants (white)	63
F. Woodworkers	106		
Cabinetmaker	15	Grand Total	2,754

Notes: ª Tax and Rate Books, 1790; *Record Commissioners' Report*, X. The groups are in approximate order of status. There is some unavoidable overlapping in the appendix; a few trades in parts III and VI might well be placed under the artisan category.
ᵇ Includes only those with no other listed occupation.

The European Origins of New Jersey's Eighteenth-Century Population

THOMAS L. PURVIS

ISTORIANS have long emphasized the importance of ethnic diversity in the social and cultural life of New Jersey. A wide variety of national groups has resided in the state since its founding, but statistics on the European origins of the early population are much less precise than for later periods when the United States government collected extensive documentation on immigration and nativity. Present evaluations of the national descent of New Jersey's colonial white stock derive from the opinions of William Nelson and a joint study by Howard F. Barker and Marcus L. Hansen. Nelson made the first modern estimate of ethnicity in 1909, when he calculated the percentages of different nationalities residing in the counties and the whole state in 1790.[1] His criteria were extremely limited and consisted essentially of an impressionistic survey of settlement and migration patterns. Nelson possessed an impressive knowledge of local history, but in the final analysis he produced little more than an informed guess.

The most frequently cited source detailing the national origins of white inhabitants in eighteenth-century New Jersey appeared in 1932, as part of Howard F. Barker and Marcus L. Hansen's comprehensive research into the American population's European ancestry at the time of the first census.[2] They revised Nelson's findings on the overall size of each group statewide, but made no effort to improve his figures on the counties, except for a supplemental investigation of Dutch and Swedes at the local level completed by Hansen. A significant problem with Barker and Hansen's data is that they were not obtained by the same quantitative methods they had employed in examining other states. They simply assumed that the settlers of East and West Jersey were similar in background to inhabitants of nearby New York and Pennsylvania, and then interpolated their estimates for the

Table I

PERCENTAGE DISTRIBUTION OF THE WHITE POPULATION OF NEW JERSEY BY NATIONAL DESCENT, 1790. ALL THE COUNTY ESTIMATES ARE THOSE OF NELSON, EXCEPT THE DUTCH AND SWEDISH ESTIMATES OF HANSEN IN PARENTHESES.

County	English & Welsh	Scots	Irish	Dutch (Hansen)	German	French	Swedish (Hansen)
Bergen	15	5	5	40(74.2)	20	15	5(3.0)
Burlington	85	0	10	0(6.9)	0	0	5(8.1)
Cape May	50	0	0	0(4.1)	0	0	50(8.2)
Cumberland	68	0	10	0(6.3)	10	0	12(10.0)
Essex	60	10	10	15(2.2)	0	5	0(0.3)
Gloucester	80	0	5	0(5.8)	5	0	10(14.0)
Hunterdon	30	10	10	25(10.7)	25	0	0(0.5)
Middlesex	48	20	5	20(7.6)	5	2	0(1.4)
Monmouth	75	15	5	0(30.1)	2	3	0(1.7)
Morris	55	5	10	10(4.8)	20	0	0(1.6)
Salem	83	0	10	0(2.0)	5	0	7(10.0)
Somerset[a]	50	10	3	30(79.8)	5	2	0(1.9)
Sussex	55	5	5	15(17.1)	20	0	0(0.5)
State (Nelson)[b]	58	7.7	7.1	12.7	9.2	2.1	2.9
State (Barker-Hansen)[c]	47	14.0	3.2	16.6	9.2	2.4	3.9

Source: U.S. Bureau of the Census, *A Century of Population Growth* (Washington, D.C., 1909), 119–20. The figures are derived from the text of William Nelson's letter, printed in above, which differs in some respects from the data presented in the table at the top of page 120. I have assumed that the text of Nelson's letter is correct and that the error lies in the table. [a]Plus 2.4% unknown and other. [b]Plus 0.3% unknown and other. [c]Plus 3.7% unknown and other.

mix of ethnic groups in those two states to obtain results for New Jersey.

Barker and Hansen's statistics still serve as the standard reference for European ancestry in eighteenth-century New Jersey. Nelson's research remains the most commonly cited work on the percentages of national stocks at the county level, although Hansen's conclusions regarding the number of Dutch and Swedes in different localities are generally considered more accurate for these two groups. Table I displays the findings of Nelson, and Barker and Hansen, with Hansen's revised figures on the Dutch and Swedes in parentheses. The possibility of error in all the results is quite high, since the procedures used to collect the data were inexact and often relied more on personal intuition than the application of any systematic approach.

Forrest and Helen McDonald recently demonstrated that Barker and Hansen's estimates of the proportions of different national stocks in the United States in 1790 had several deficiencies in methodology.[3] The McDonalds were able to devise more accurate testing procedures to assess the relative strengths of Celts and Englishmen living within most states, but unfortunately they did not update the earlier findings for New Jersey. Their work in updating Barker and Hansen's conclusions indicates that current data on the national descent of New Jersey's white residents could also be significantly improved. The purpose of this article is to develop more accurate statistics about the approximate size and geographical distribution of the several ethnic groups that settled New Jersey during the seventeenth and eighteenth centuries by analyzing the European-descended population of each county during the revolutionary period according to their surnames.

Barker and Hansen's estimates of the European origins of Americans in 1790 stood unchallenged for almost a half century. The fundamental premise underlying their research on ethnicity was valid, as their critics agree. Distinctive surnames known to be borne by a precise percentage of a national group can be used to calculate an arithmetic coefficient that will be sufficiently accurate to compute the proportion of people in a locality belonging to that nationality. The number of individuals bearing those same surnames within a state or county, multiplied by the appropriate numerical constant, will equal the approximate size of the group within the total population.[4] There is no other way to develop statistical measurements of ethnicity within a large population of mixed European descent than this method when no additional information is available.

The basic procedures of Barker and Hansen were sound, but their implementation suffered from several deficiencies. Forrest and Helen McDonald identified the most serious problems in their critique, and also showed how increasing the number of distinctive names used would markedly improve the methodology's exactness. The larger number of names would represent a greater percentage of the European population under investigation, and would produce a smaller, more precise, numerical constant for approximating that nationality's presence.[5] The McDonalds developed appreciably improved lists of surnames characteristic of the Scots, Irish, and Welsh peoples, and then demonstrated that the Barker–Hansen estimates for these groups and for Americans of English ancestry required substantial change.

The McDonalds did not revise their predecessors' figures for non-British stocks, nor did they update estimates of ethnicity for any states or territories whose 1790 census returns were missing. The New Jersey census rolls burned during the War of 1812, but fortunately assessment lists from every township in the state survive from the 1770s and 1780s, which identify 29,162 taxpayers.[6] Since a total of 29,779 heads of families are believed to have been enumerated in the 1790 New Jersey census, these tax rolls provide a remarkably complete substitute for the missing population schedules and enable statistics to be projected with much confidence.[7] Further examination into family nomenclature patterns among the early German, Dutch, French, and Swedish settlers in the British colonies has permitted more precise approximation of their size to replace the Barker–Hansen estimates. These sources and new techniques make it possible to undertake the first comprehensive recalculation of the European descent of eighteenth-century New Jersey inhabitants since Barker and Hansen's work appeared in 1932.

It should be understood that statistics on national origins are not the only relevant criteria for describing the early mix of peoples in the state. As Peter O. Wacker has emphasized, religious affiliation was a more important means of self-identification in eighteenth-century New Jersey than nationality.[8] Baptists and Anglicans, for example, were largely of English descent, but they had little else in common. Denominational membership and ethnicity often overlapped, as in the case of Swedes and Germans who were both Lutherans. Scots and Scots-Irish are commonly considered to have been the bedrock of the Presbyterian Church in early America, but persons of New England stock were certainly a majority of the denomination in New Jersey.[9] At the same time, ethnic groups with a history of mutual hostility sometimes found it difficult to coexist in the same church, as the split between Scottish and English Quakers during the Keithian Schism demonstrated.[10] National descent provides only one measure of cultural diversity in New Jersey during the Revolutionary era, although a very important one.

A further problem with analyzing the ancestral origins of the state's earliest white inhabitants is that many ethnic groups were amalgams of several different national stocks. Only half of the European immigrants who settled in New Netherland before 1664 came from the Dutch Netherlands, for instance.[11] The first historian of New Sweden, Israel Acrelius, likewise discovered that its inhabitants were anything but homogeneous. "Among the members of these congregations in the above list [of 1693]," he wrote of Swedes living along the Delaware River, "many Hollanders were also intermingled, inasmuch as they now regarded themselves as one people. Many others afterwards added themselves in the same manner. . . . English, Scotch, Irish, and German families, all using the Swedish language."[12] Similarly, many of the German-speaking immigrants to the British colonies were Swiss.[13] Dutch, Swedes, and even Germans in eighteenth-century America were distinguishable less by national descent than by their language, and to a large extent these non-British nationalities can be most accurately considered as linguistic groups.

The example of the Welsh can illustrate how to determine each national stock's estimated size using distinctive surnames. Approximately 15 percent of the Welsh people bear the sixteen family names of Bebb, Breese, Griffith, Howell, Humphreys, Jenkins, Lloyd, Morgan, Owen, Pritchard, Pugh, Rees, Rowlands, Tudor, Vaughan, and Wynne. The corresponding numerical constant is 6.5, but it must be reduced to compensate for the fact that 24 percent of all persons bearing the same names in Great Britain reside in England rather than Wales. Performing this calculation leaves a coefficient of 4.9.[14] The sixteen cognomens recur 217 times among taxpayers on the assessment lists from the 1770s and 1780s. Multiplying these rateables by 4.9 gives 1,063, the approximate number of taxpayers having Welsh names. Dividing this figure by the 29,162 men on the assessment rolls gives the final estimate of the Welsh stock, 3.6 percent. The percentages of all other minor stocks are similarly obtained, after which their total is subtracted from 100 percent to give the portion English.

The McDonalds' surname lists and numerical constants for the Irish and Scots have been adopted with slight variation. Three nondistinctive names (Hayes, Hughes, and Johnston), whose inclusion greatly skews the results toward a high count of Irish, were eliminated in favor of Cavanaugh, Riley, Sheehan, and Whelan, producing a multiplier of 5.[15] All the McDonalds' Scottish names were retained, except for eight that unduly exaggerate the number of Scots: Bell, Gibson, Scott, Shaw, Wallace (Wallis), Watson, Williamson, which are all numerous in England, and Kennedy, which is most common in Ireland outside Ulster. The Scottish coefficient was then changed from 4 to 3.7 by adding M'Donald, M'Kenzie, M'Kay, M'Lean, M'Leod, M'Intosh, and M'Gregor, plus their derivative forms of Donald, Donnel, Kenzie, Kay, Cloud, and Gregor.[16]

The methodology employed here is not capable of differentiating between families that had originated in Northern Ireland rather than Scotland because both held the same names. The only manner of distinguishing one group from another is to divide the total Scottish stock by a ratio representing the percentage of immigrants provided by each area during the eighteenth century. The best current research indicates that about 114,000 Ulster Scots settled in British America between 1718 and 1776, compared with approximately 62,500 Scotsmen.[17] If Northern Ireland and Scotland provided settlers to New Jersey in the same general proportion as they did to all of the American colonies, then two-thirds of all persons with Scottish names would be descended from the former rather than the latter. Arbitrarily assuming that two-thirds of all New Jersey residents with Scottish names were Scots-Irish is not a perfectly satisfactory solution to the problem of measuring the separate contributions of each to the state's population growth, but it is the only practical manner of distinguishing between the two groups now available.

Original name lists and coefficients had to be compiled for the non-British nationalities not studied by the McDonalds. Data similar to those already cited on the frequencies of surnames in Scotland, Ireland, and Wales do not exist for Germany, Holland, France, and Sweden. Such information would be of doubtful usefulness in any case, since emigration from these countries was relatively small and so not necessarily representative of the entire population. A better way to determine nomenclature patterns among such groups is to identify the most common family names borne by immigrants to Pennsylvania or New York, for it was from these provinces that most Dutch, German, and Swedish settlers came to New Jersey.

Ninety of the most common, yet distinctive, names carried by 29,758 German-speaking immigrants who arrived at Philadelphia from 1727 to 1808, accounting perhaps for 30 percent of all Germans who came to America, included 12.5 percent of the total group, giving a multiplier of 8.[18] Fourteen percent of the 1,456 male Dutch inhabitants enumerated on the earliest surviving New York tax rolls and allegiance oaths dated between 1687 and 1714 bore thirty-seven names, equal to a coefficient of 7.3.[19] A special census of Swedish inhabitants in the Delaware Valley in 1693 reveals eleven names, held by 16 percent of the population, which yields a numerical constant of 6.3.[20] The majority of French settlers in British America were Huguenots who fled to England and migrated overseas from there. Examining the baptismal registers of French Reformed churches in England reveals that 7 percent of 26,932 children born between 1581 and 1750 carried fifteen representative names, giving a coefficient of 14.[21] With these lists of national surnames and multipliers, the European ancestry of New Jersey residents in 1790 can be approximated.

The number of distinctive names for each ethnic group on the tax rolls is as follows: sixteen Welsh names, 217; fifty-four Irish names, 289; seventy-one Scottish names, 804; ninety German names, 238; thirty-seven Dutch names, 801; fifteen French names, 80; and eleven Swedish names, 49. Updated figures for each ancestral stock and the original conclusions of Barker and Hansen are shown in table II. The new and old estimates differ significantly in several regards. Barker and Hansen believed Scots

Table II

PERCENTAGE DISTRIBUTION OF THE WHITE POPULATION OF NEW JERSEY IN 1790 BY NATIONAL DESCENT: BARKER–HANSEN ESTIMATES AND REVISED FIGURES.

	Barker-Hansen	Revised Estimate	Percent Change
English[a]	47.0	50.6	+ 7.7
Welsh[a]	–	3.6	–
Scots	7.7	3.4	−42.9
Scots-Irish	6.3	6.8	+ 7.9
Irish	3.2	4.1	+28.1
Dutch	16.6	20.1	+21.1
German	9.2	6.5	−29.3
French	2.4	3.8	+58.3
Swedish	3.9	1.1	−71.8

[a]Barker and Hansen included the Welsh with the English.

Table III

PERCENTAGE DISTRIBUTION OF THE WHITE POPULATION OF
NEW JERSEY AND NEIGHBORING STATES BY NATIONAL
DESCENT IN 1790: REVISED ESTIMATES.

	N.J.	Pa.	N.Y.	Del.	U.S.
English	50.6	25.8	50.3	63.3	59.7
Welsh	3.6	3.6	3.4	5.5	4.3
Scots	3.4	7.6	4.3	4.6	5.3
Scots-Irish	6.8	15.1	8.7	9.2	10.5
Irish	4.1	7.1	4.1	8.0	5.8
Dutch	20.1	1.3	15.9	1.3	3.1
German	6.5	38.0	9.1	2.6	8.9
French	3.8	0.9	4.2	1.7	2.1
Swedish	1.1	0.6	0	3.8	0.3

to compose about 8 percent of New Jersey's white population, but revision decreases their strength to less than half this figure. The estimate of Germans drops by nearly one-third, from 9 to 6 percent, as does the number of Swedes, by almost three-quarters to a mere 1 percent. The proportion of Dutch rises to more than one-fifth of the state, while the proportion of French increases to almost 4 percent. Barker and Hansen included the Welsh with the English, and concluded that both constituted 47 percent of whites. The corrected figures show that the English alone constituted half the European population, and together with the Welsh they composed 54 percent. The only groups not to show substantial change upon revision are the Irish and Ulster Scots, who together composed about a tenth of all whites. The state's early population was approximately 70 percent British, with the High Dutch and Low Dutch constituting almost all of the remainder.

Barker and Hansen measured the major European stocks in New Jersey not by systematically analyzing distinctive surnames, but by interpolating from the ethnic mix of Pennsylvania and New York.[22] They assumed that the same groups that peopled neighboring states contributed settlers to adjacent areas of New Jersey in equal proportions, although they had no evidence for this supposition. Table III indicates that this arbitrary decision was not entirely correct, and helps explain why their results differ in many respects from those of this study, since New Jersey evidently attracted more residents from New York than from Pennsylvania.

Table III displays revised estimates for the national origins of whites in the Middle Atlantic region. The population of New Jersey strongly resembled that of New York. The estimates of English, Welsh, Irish, and French are so close that they fall within 0.5 percent of one another. The proportions of Dutch, Scots, and Scots-Irish also come within about one to four percentage points. of each other. The only significant variance between the two states was that New York lacked the equivalent of New Jersey's small Swedish community. By contrast, New Jersey's distribution of ancestral stocks differed greatly from Pennsylvania's. New Jersey's proportions of English, Scots, Scots-Irish, and Irish were approximately half those of Pennsylvania, and the percentage of Germans was only one sixth. New Jersey's numerous Dutch population had no counterpart across the Delaware River, and its percentage of French was more than four times larger. Only the Welsh formed an equal portion (3.6 percent) of both states.

The majority of postrevolutionary New Jersey's inhabitants derived from European stocks that had settled in North America during the seventeenth century: the English, Welsh, Dutch, and Swedes. Furthermore, most Scots in 1790 seem to have been descended from indentured servants or tenants recruited to colonize East Jersey during the 1680s, rather than from later immigrants. The great wave of eighteenth-century immigration from the German Palatinate and Northern Ireland that engulfed Pennsylvania and the southern backcountry essentially bypassed New Jersey. Even though the major port of entry for Germans and Ulster Scots entering America lay immediately opposite New Jersey in Philadelphia, the combined contribution of both groups to the state's population amounted to fewer than one of every seven whites by 1790.

Table IV shows projected estimates for the European origins of each county's white population. The number of rateables ranged from 426 in Cape May to 4,014 in Hunterdon, with an average of 2,200 for all thirteen counties. The accuracy of statistics on national descent can easily be distorted by small units of analysis, and so the data for individual counties are much less reliable than for the state. The data underlying table IV are not sufficiently large to guarantee complete accuracy, but the resulting figures can provide a good indication of where different groups were most numerous and give a general approximation of their size in the counties.

Table IV

PERCENTAGE DISTRIBUTION OF NEW JERSEY'S WHITE POPULATION BY NATIONAL DESCENT, 1790: REVISED EESTIMATES.

County	English	Welsh	Scots	Scots-Irish	Irish	Dutch	German	French	Swedish
Bergen	28.9	0.6	2.6	5.3	2.1	53.1	4.4	3.0	0.0
Burlington	66.8	2.5	3.3	6.6	4.6	4.0	9.7	2.0	0.5
Cape May	85.7	4.7	2.0	4.1	0.0	3.5	0.0	0.0	0.0
Cumberland	71.4	2.0	2.3	4.8	8.8	0.0	6.1	3.5	1.1
Essex	76.7	1.7	2.9	5.8	1.7	7.5	0.8	2.9	0.0
Gloucester	60.3	5.1	4.2	8.5	7.6	3.8	3.8	2.1	4.6
Hunterdon	41.4	6.0	3.1	6.3	3.4	19.1	16.1	3.8	0.8
Middlesex	46.5	3.6	9.3	4.7	4.4	27.9	1.5	2.1	0.0
Monmouth	37.9	3.6	8.3	4.1	3.2	36.5	3.1	3.3	0.0
Morris	75.1	4.5	2.1	4.3	3.3	4.8	3.1	2.8	0.0
Salem	43.9	5.9	5.2	10.5	12.3	3.5	7.9	2.9	7.9
Somerset	7.0	2.8	5.2	5.2	2.9	67.1	5.8	4.0	0.0
Sussex	54.7	2.5	3.4	6.8	2.0	8.2	17.3	4.1	1.0
State	50.6	3.6	3.4	6.8	4.1	20.1	6.5	3.8	1.1

The English and Welsh

The revised distribution of English and Welsh within the state differs significantly from Nelson's conclusions. The updated county figures fall within five percentage points of Nelson's findings only for Cumberland and Sussex, and they vary by at least fifteen points for most other counties. Northeast New Jersey was generally more Anglo-Saxon than Nelson had thought, and southern New Jersey much less so. Persons of English–Welsh descent nevertheless composed a majority, or very close to a majority, in all counties except Bergen, Somerset, and Monmouth. Two distinct concentrations of the English–Welsh stock existed in the state.[23] The first lay along the lower Delaware River, in Burlington, Gloucester, Salem, and Cumberland. The ancestors of the English population there were largely Quakers who immigrated during the seventeenth century. New England dissenters peopled the second center of English strength, Essex and Morris counties; they were also the dominant element in Cape May, whose population had more English blood than any other county in New Jersey.

The Welsh were most numerous in predominantly English areas. Providing separate figures for individuals of Welsh descent is admittedly speculative, since they invariably lived in close contact with the English without any religious or communal institutions that could transmit ethnic customs over several generations. It is doubtful that the Welsh in early New Jersey constituted a true ethnic group that would have been readily recognized by their contemporaries as distinct from the English.[24] The revised figures consequently give little more than an upper limit on the possible number of persons of Welsh extraction, as a general indication of their contribution to the state's demographic growth.

The Dutch

The Dutch were the next largest national stock, 20 percent of the state. The revised figure is much larger than Barker and Hansen's final estimate of 16.6 percent. Interestingly, it is almost identical to their initial opinion, 20.6 percent, which they rejected because it seemed too large.[25] New Jersey contained a greater percentage of Dutch than did New York, primarily because a large influx of Yankees from New England had steadily reduced the relative size of the Dutch in New York by 1790. With the exception of a very high estimate of Dutch in Bergen County, Hansen's figures on their numbers at the local level were reasonably accurate. He typically overcalculated the Dutch presence, but his margin of error was usually small. The Dutch formed a majority only in Somerset and Bergen, but they were a very substantial minority in Monmouth, Middlesex, and Hunterdon counties.

The French

French colonists were living among the Dutch in New Netherland long before the English conquest of 1664, and they may have been 7 percent of that province.[26] When the Dutch began expanding into New Jersey, many French families accompanied them. One group was sufficiently numerous to form a Huguenot congregation at Schraalenburgh in Bergen County, but most came as individuals and lived in predominantly Dutch communities.[27] These early French immigrants did not maintain a separate cultural identity, however, and assimilated into Dutch society very quickly. Later Huguenot refugees settled throughout the colony among the English-descended population, and by the 1780s they were dispersed rather evenly throughout the state.[28] By that time persons bearing French surnames probably constituted 3.8 percent of all whites. The only states with a larger proportion of French Americans in 1790 were Rhode Island (4.6 percent) and New York (4.2 percent).

The Scots

Revision greatly lowers the percentage of Scots that Nelson believed to reside in the state, from 7.7 to 3.4 percent, and reduces their proportions in most counties by at least half. Only in the central New Jersey counties of Middlesex, Monmouth, and Somerset did Scots form a sizeable portion of the local population. Ned C. Landsman, the authority on Scottish communities in New Jersey, has estimated that Scots (not counting Scots-Irish) constituted almost 10 percent of these counties in 1745. His conclusions indicate that two-thirds of all those with Scottish names in Middlesex and Monmouth were of Scottish rather than Scots-Irish background, as were half the same group in Somerset.[29] Relying on his judgment, the total projected number of Scots in these three counties has been adjusted according to those proportions. Most Scots in central Jersey derived from several hundred indentured servants and tenants transported across the Atlantic in the 1680s to work the estates of East Jersey's proprietors, most of whom were also from Scotland. The small number of Scots outside the central counties were largely the progeny of eighteenth-century emigrants who became scattered in random fashion throughout the state; they rarely formed more than 4 percent of any locality's European population.

The Ulster Scots and Irish

Ulster Scots lived primarily in the Delaware River counties opposite Pennsylvania. Emigration from Northern Ireland began accelerating after 1720 and peaked in the decade preceding the American Revolution.[30] The great majority entered the colonies through Philadelphia, from which a small number drifted to the western counties of New Jersey. Most Scots-Irish probably came as indentured servants to labor on the estates of wealthy landowners in southern Jersey, for this group was most numerous in the counties of Salem and Gloucester.

Other Irish immigrants, from the island's indigenous population, also moved to New Jersey after disembarking at Philadelphia. Their distribution followed that of the Ulster Scots, with few in East Jersey and many living along the lower Delaware. The Irish were a surprisingly large component of southern Jersey's European population, amounting to 8 percent of Gloucester, 9 percent of Cumberland, and 12 percent of Salem. Ulster Scots and other Irish settled in the same regions of New Jersey, and it is probable that their neighbors did not view them as different groups, but rather considered both simply as Irish.

The Germans

Previous estimates of the number of Germans in eighteenth-century New Jersey erred considerably regarding their overall size and distribution among the counties. Nelson and Barker both overstated their presence, undoubtedly because they relied too uncritically on John Rutherfurd's guess in 1786 that Lutherans, Mennonites, and Moravians constituted over 9 percent of the population.[31] Rutherfurd's figure was too high by almost half. Nelson's appraisal of the German component in Bergen County was also too excessive, as was his figure for Morris. It is nevertheless important to recognize that many persons of German descent (like the French) moved to New Jersey with the Dutch and intermarried with them. Perhaps one quarter of the colonists who landed in New Netherland were from Germany, but their descendants became undistinguishable from the Dutch and are counted with them in this study.[32]

John Rutherfurd wrote in 1786 that the Germans "came here late and poor, but are daily acquiring Estates, especially in the large Counties of Hunterdon and Somerset."[33] The revised figures for these areas support his assertion for Hunterdon, but indicate that few of the High Dutch were in Somerset. Sussex contained the largest proportion of Germans in any county, more than one in every six residents of this frontier region. Hunterdon and Sussex undoubtedly attracted Palatine Protestants, who arrived with little capital but had industrious spirits, because good land remained unoccupied and was relatively inexpensive. A smaller concentration of Germans lived along the lower Delaware River. Nelson greatly underestimated their strength in these counties, particularly in Burlington which seems to have been almost one tenth German. Most Germans and Swiss came to the state by way of Philadelphia, and consequently their numbers were few in East Jersey.[34]

The Swedes

Hansen significantly altered Nelson's percentages of Swedes in New Jersey, and new calculations further refine his statistics for this group. Hansen had a tendency to see Swedes everywhere, greatly exaggerating their numbers. Swedes constituted a significant part of only two counties, forming almost 5 percent of Gloucester and 8 percent of Salem. Small communities of them can be identified elsewhere along the Delaware River as far north as Sussex. Approximately 1,900 Swedes lived in New Jersey by 1790, a number equal to one-fifth of all the 9,500 persons of Swedish descent in the United States.[35]

Conclusions

Updating the conclusions of Nelson, Barker, and Hansen with more systematic research significantly alters many formerly accepted estimates of national stocks in eighteenth-century New Jersey. The numbers of English, Welsh, and Dutch were substantially higher than previously thought, while the numbers of Germans, Scots, and Swedes much lower. Basing estimates of ethnicity within the counties on quantitative methods of analysis produces numerous changes in Nelson's and Hansen's statistics for many localities. The revised data are certainly subject to an unknown degree of error, but they are as accurate as existing sources and research into nomenclature frequencies permit. As such, the new figures on national descent will improve the ability of historians to describe the contributions of different groups to population growth, frontier expansion, and numerous aspects of social life with more certainty than previous statistics have permitted.

Notes

[1] Nelson's estimates were printed in U.S. Bureau of the Census, *A Century of Population Growth, From the First Census of the United States to the Twelfth, 1790–1900* (Washington, D.C., 1909), 119–20.

[2] American Council of Learned Societies [Howard F. Barker and Marcus L. Hansen], "Report of the Committee on Linguistic and National Stocks in the Population of the United States," in American Historical Association, *Annual Report for the Year 1931* (Washington, D.C., 1932), 124. (Hereinafter, Barker and Hansen, "National Stocks")

[3] Forrest McDonald and Helen Shapiro McDonald, "The Ethnic Origins of the American People, 1790," *William and Mary Quarterly* 37 (1980):179–87.

[4] Barker and Hansen, "National Stocks", 133–63.

[5] McDonald and McDonald, "Ethnic Origins," 184–85.

[6] The tax lists for each township have been edited in *Genealogical Magazine of New Jersey* 36 (1961) to 54 (1979). They have been indexed in Kenn Stryker-Rodda, *Revolutionary Census of New Jersey* (Cottonport, La., 1972). The only township missing from the *Revolutionary Census* was Stratford in Monmouth County.

[7] U.S. Bureau of the Census, *Century of Population Growth*, 96.

[8] Peter O. Wacker, *Land and People, A Cultural Geography of Preindustrial New Jersey: Origins and Settlement Patterns* (New Brunswick, N.J., 1975), 163.

[9] Ibid., 174–76.

[10] Ned C. Landsman, "Scottish Communities in the Old and New Worlds, 1680–1760" Ph. D. diss. University of Pennsylvania, 1979, ch. 6.

[11] Davis S. Cohen, "How Dutch Were the Dutch of New Netherland?," *New York History* 62 (1981): 51–53.

[12] Israel Acrelius, *A History of New Sweden* [1759]. Translated by William M. Reynolds in *Memoirs of the Historical Society of Pennsylvania* 11 (1874), 193. As an example of the difficulty of determining the national backgrounds of Delaware River settlers who spoke Swedish, see Everett N. Strang, "The Strang Family in Southern Jersey," *Genealogical Magazine of New Jersey* 45 (1970): 111–12.

[13] Albert B. Faust estimated that as many as 25,000 Swiss may have come to America, out of an estimated 100,000 German-speaking immigrants. "Swiss Emigration to the American Colonies in the Eighteenth Century," *American Historical Review* 22 (1916): 44.

[14] The procedures used are explained in more detail in Thomas L. Purvis, "The European Ancestry of the United States Population, 1790," *William and Mary Quarterly*, 3d ser., 41 (1984), forthcoming. For the frequency of the fifteen

names, see their alphabetical listing in Henry B. Guppy, *Homes of Family Names in Great Britain* (London, 1890).

[15] The additional names and their numerical frequency in Ireland are listed in Robert E. Matheson, *Special Report on the Surnames of Ireland* (Dublin, 1909), 7–8. The other Irish names are listed in McDonald and McDonald, "Ethnic Origins," 196–97.

[16] The additional names and their frequency in Scotland are listed in Barker and Hansen, "National Stocks," 211, which are taken from the Scottish Registrar General's Sixth Annual Report of 1863. The other Scottish names are listed in McDonald and McDonald, "Ethnic Origins," 192–94.

[17] R. J. Dickson, *Ulster Emigration to Colonial America, 1718–1775* (London, 1966), 48–81; Ian C. Graham, *Colonists from Scotland: Emigration to North America, 1707–1783* (Ithaca, N.Y., 1956), 185–89.

[18] William J. Hinke, ed., *Pennsylvania German Pioneers: A Publication of the Original Lists of Arrivals in the Port of Philadelphia from 1727 to 1808* (Norristown, Pa., 1934), xxxi. The names used are Albrecht (Albright), Bachman, Baum (plus Bohm), Baumgarten, Bentz, Brunner, Christ, Conrad, Deidrich, Diehl (Deal), Dietz, Doll, Eberhart, Eckhart, Ernst, Faust, Fink, Fritz, Funk, Gebhart, Geiger, Gerber, Gerhart, Graff, Grimm, Grubb, Hartman, Hahn (Haun), Hess, Hildebrand, Hoch (Hauk), Hoff, Hoffman, Houser, Huber (Hoover), Hummel, Jaeger, Jost, Kaufman, Kesler, Keiser, Klein, Kolb (Culp), Kramer, Kraft, Krebs, Kraus, Kuhn, Kuntz, Kurtz, Lentz, Link, Ludwig, Lutz, Metz, Metzger, Meyer, Moser, Ott, Rauch, Reinhart, Rudolph, Schafer, Schaub, Schneider (Snider), Schreiner, Schutz, Schultz, Schuman, Schuster, Schwaab, Switzer, Seibert, Seitz, Seifert, Seiler, Spengler, Spiess, Stahl, Stauffer (Stover), Stumpf, Stein, Steiner, Ulrich, Vogel, Wagner, Waltz, Weigandt, Ziegler, and Zimmerman.

[19] The lists used were from Kings County (1687); Ulster County (1689); Albany County (1697); New York City (1703), which was 56 percent Dutch; Orange County (1702); Dutchess County (1714). Printed in Edmund B. O'Callahan, ed., *The Documentary History of the State of New York* (Albany, N.Y., 1849–51) 1:279–82, 366–69, 611–24, 659–61; 3:133–38; and Joel Munsell, *The Annals of Albany* (Albany, N.Y., 1850) 9:81–89. The names used are Beekman, Bogart (Bogardus), Bradt, Covenhoven, Hageman, Hendrickson, Hogeboom, Houghtling, Kipp, Outhout, Quackenboss, Rapalye, Remsen, Schuyler, Swartwout, Ten Brock, Ten Eyck, Van Buren, Van Cleef, Vandeberg, Vandeveer, Vandewater, Van Dyke, Van Horn, Van Huten, Van Husen, Van Meter, Van Ness, Van Pelt, Van Shaike, Van Slyke, Van Vleet, Van Wagonen, Van Wyck, Voorhees, Vosburgh, and Wyckoff.

[20] The Swedish census of 1693 is in *Memoirs of the Historical Society of Pennsylvania* 11:190–93. The names are Dalbo, Derickson (Derek), Justison (Justis), Matson, Paulson, Rambo, Sinickson (Sinnex, Seneca), Stalcop, Stilley, Tussey (Tossa), and Walraven.

[21] Registers of the Huguenot churches at Canterbury, Thorney, and London's Threadneedle Street, edited in Huguenot Society of London, *Publications* 5 (1891):3–409; 9 (1896):34–228; 8 (1899):70–281; 17 (1903):1–103; 23 (1916):21–241. The names are Ballou, Bodine (Bowden), Cato (Caddo), Devine, Dubois, Dumont, Dupre, Durant, Fontaine, Lamar (Delmar), Larue, LeConte, Lefevre, LeMaster, and Spain (DeSpain).

[22] Barker and Hansen, "National Stocks," 197–98.

[23] Wacker, *Land and People*, 172–84, gives a more detailed examination.

[24] Peter O. Wacker's survey of cultural groups reinforces this impression, since he found no distinctive Welsh communities (*Land and People*, 172).

[25] Barker and Hansen, "National Stocks," 210.

30 / EUROPEAN ORIGINS

26 Cohen, "How Dutch Were the Dutch of New York," 52–53.

27 Adrian C. Leiby, *The Huguenot Settlement of Schraalenburgh: The History of Bergenfield, New Jersey* (Bergenfield, N.J., 1964), 13.

28 Certain exceptionally common names held by ten or more taxpayers each in Hunterdon, Salem, and Somerset counties greatly exaggerated the percentage of French there because of the high multiplier. To obtain a more accurate figure, all such names were counted as if they occurred only three times. The original projections of French in Gloucester and Monmouth counties were so low that they were tripled to bring them into line with neighboring counties. In Monmouth County this expedient seems especially justified because of the known presence of other French families there. See Edwin Salter, "Huguenot Settlers and Landowners in Monmouth Co., N.J.," *New York Genealogical and Biographical Record* 20 (1889):30–35.

29 Draft of Appendix A, "The Scottish Population of Central New Jersey," from Ned C. Landsman's forthcoming book on Scots in New Jersey and his letter to the author of May 4, 1983, provide these estimates for Scots in central N.J. as of 1745: Middlesex, 17.9 percent; Monmouth, 6.9 percent; Somerset, 2.2 percent.

30 Dickson, *Ulster Emigration to America*, 23–64.

31 John Rutherfurd, "Notes on the State of New Jersey," [Aug. 1786] New Jersey Historical Society, *Proceedings* 2d ser., 1 (1867):88.

32 Cohen, "How Dutch Were the Dutch of New Netherland," 52–53.

33 Rutherfurd, "Notes on the State of New Jersey," 88.

34 A detailed description of German settlements is in Hubert G. Schmidt, "Germans in Colonial New Jersey," *The American German Review* (June–July 1958): 4–9.

35 On the Swedes, see Adrian C. Leiby, *The Early Dutch and Swedish Settlers of New Jersey* (Princeton, N.J., 1964), 24–33, 91–108.

Landholding, Opportunity, and Mobility in Revolutionary New Jersey

Dennis P. Ryan

A MID the current surge of scholarly interest in the social history of early America the question of the dimensions of socioeconomic change during the American Revolutionary era remains to be re-solved.[1] This deficiency is especially marked for the Middle Atlantic region in general and for New Jersey in particular.[2] The present study examines the immediate impact of the Revolution on New Jersey, focusing on the structure of landholding in East New Jersey for the years 1778-1789 and relating the distribution of land to levels of mobility and opportunity. The analysis principally concerns the 2,479 adult male inhabitants of six East Jersey

Mr. Ryan is co-editor of the Papers of William Livingston, New York University. An earlier version of this paper was presented at the Second Stony Brook Conference on Quantification in the Study of Early American History, June 1975. The author wishes to thank James A. Henretta and Carl E. Prince for their comments and criticism.

[1] The published studies of small communities, with the notable exceptions of the works of Robert A. Gross and Charles S. Grant, either terminate their analyses before 1776, leaving the effects of the American Revolution open to speculation, or do not attempt to consider the events from 1776 to 1789 as a catalyst in the evolution of pre-industrial American communities. Gross, *The Minutemen and Their World* (New York, 1976); Grant, *Democracy in the Connecticut Frontier Town of Kent* (New York, 1961).

Noteworthy articles that examine the years 1776 to 1790 include James T. Lemon and Gary B. Nash, "The Distribution of Wealth in Eighteenth-Century America: A Century of Change in Chester County, Pennsylvania, 1693-1802," *Journal of Social History*, II (1968), 1-24; Allan Kulikoff, "The Progress of Inequality in Revolutionary Boston," *William and Mary Quarterly*, 3d Ser., XXVIII (1971), 375-412; Jack P. Greene, "The Social Origins of the American Revolution: An Evaluation and an Interpretation," *Political Science Quarterly*, LXXXVIII (1973), 1-22; and Kenneth A. Lockridge, "Social Change and the Meaning of the American Revolution," *Jour. Soc. Hist.*, VI (1973), 403-439. Two unpublished studies are Arlin I. Ginsburg, "Ipswich, Massachusetts, during the American Revolution, 1763-1791" (Ph.D. diss., University of California, Riverside, 1972), and Richard J. Morris, "Revolutionary Salem: Stratification and Mobility in a Massachusetts Seaport, 1759-1799" (Ph.D. diss., New York University, 1975).

[2] Stephanie Grauman Wolf, *Urban Village: Population, Community, and Family Structure in Germantown, Pennsylvania, 1683-1800* (Princeton, N.J., 1976), is an exception.

towns—Newark, Morristown, Woodbridge, Piscataway, Shrewsbury, and Middletown—whose names appear on the tax lists of 1778-1780, the earliest available. Of that number, 1,580 still resided and paid taxes in those towns in 1789, having lived through the turmoil of the Revolutionary era.[3] Prosopographical analysis indicates that the dislocations caused by war and political independence, though severe, had little effect on the socioeconomic structure of the six communities.

Historians agree in characterizing New Jersey on the eve of the Revolution as a yeoman commonwealth whose typical citizen, the small landholder, tilled a farm averaging 75 to 100 acres, raising sufficient produce to feed his family and still provide a modest surplus for sale in New York City or Philadelphia. The farmer's life, according to one agricultural historian, was "a fairly comfortable and happy one."[4] Another scholar concludes that, despite "islands of poverty," New Jersey was "essentially middle-class" and that in 1775 it was "a land of opportunity for a man of industry and thrift. There was work for all [and] relatively easy access to land ownership."[5] New Jersey did not support a large landed aristocracy; poverty and tenancy were apparently rare. Recent studies suggest—and the present investigation tends to confirm—that this picture may be overdrawn.[6] However, all historiog-

[3] The following tax ratables were analyzed: Piscataway, May 1780, July 1784, July 1789; Shrewsbury, Feb. 1780, July 1784, July-Aug. 1789; Newark, Feb. 1779, July 1783, July-Aug. 1789; Morristown, May 1778, July 1784, July-Aug. 1789; Woodbridge, May-June 1778, Aug. 1784, Oct. 1789; Middletown, Dec. 1778, June-July 1784, June-Aug. 1789. Tax Ratables, Bureau of Archives and History, State Library, Trenton, N.J., hereafter cited as Tax Ratables. Over 400 male taxpayers were deleted from the group because they presumably had died before 1790. The sample does not include either those known to have died or those who were in their sixties by 1776 and who do not appear on any subsequent tax list. When age is unknown, it is assumed that the individual was still alive in 1790. Female taxpayers were also deleted from the total surveyed; most were widows who only briefly held a husband's land pending final disposition of the estate.

[4] Carl Raymond Woodward, Agriculture in New Jersey (New York, 1930), 38. For similar observations see Richard B. Morris, "Spotlight on the Plowmen of the Jersies," New Jersey Historical Society, Proceedings, LXVII (1949), 113, hereafter cited as Morris, "Plowmen of the Jersies"; Michael P. Riccards, "Patriots and Plunderers: Confiscation of Loyalist Lands in New Jersey, 1776-1786," New Jersey History, LXXXVI (1968), 25; Jackson Turner Main, The Social Structure of Revolutionary America (Princeton, N.J., 1965), 25; John E. Pomfret, The Province of East New Jersey, 1609-1702: The Rebellious Proprietary (Princeton, 1962), 386; Richard P. McCormick, The History of Voting in New Jersey: A Study of the Development of Election Machinery, 1664-1911 (New Brunswick, 1953), 6; Jackson Turner Main, Political Parties before the Constitution (Chapel Hill, N.C., 1973), 158; and Frank J. Urquhart, A History of the City of Newark, I (New York, 1913), 238-239.

[5] John E. Pomfret, Colonial New Jersey: A History (New York, 1973), 204-205, 217.

[6] Peter O. Wacker, The Musconetcong Valley of New Jersey: A Historical Geography (New Brunswick, 1968), and Land and People: A Cultural Geography

raphy of colonial New Jersey's social structure is impressionistic at best, because systematic analysis is severely hampered by the paucity of such records as tax lists, parish registers, and census returns, most of which were lost or destroyed during the Revolution.

The six towns under examination were primarily agrarian communities in which economic opportunity was closely related to the possession of arable land. Most East Jersey towns had easy access to markets in New York, and the growing of wheat, corn, rye, and fruit as cash crops was the region's major economic activity.[7] Subsidiary enterprises included the distilling of liquors and the raising of cattle and oxen. Although taxes were assessed on hogs, cattle, horses, and mills, a comparison of assessments for 1783-1784 in Newark and Piscataway (the least and most agrarian, respectively, of the six towns) demonstrates that land was the major factor in society's calculation of a man's material worth.[8] For the purposes of the present analysis, it is therefore essential to arrive at a reasonably accurate idea of the size of farm necessary to make its owner at least minimally "comfortable and happy"— that is to say, self-sufficient as to food—as well as the minimal size required for some commercial production.

For southeastern Pennsylvania during the eighteenth century James T. Lemon finds that "about 75 acres of cleared land would have supported an average family of five comfortably and farms larger than 75 acres would have a surplus for sale."[9] This figure can be adapted for an analysis of East Jersey, because of the similarity between the two regions in soil fertility, crop yield, technology, and types of crops. Most important, both southeastern Pennsylvania and the Hackensack, Passaic, and Raritan valleys, where the six towns were located, were agricultural hinterlands devoted to the production and processing of agricultural goods for city markets. The figure can be refined by

---

of *Preindustrial New Jersey: Origins and Settlement Patterns* (New Brunswick, 1975). Jackson Turner Main writes that New Jersey was, in general, a subsistence economy, characterized by middling farmers with small acreage and modest wealth, no well-defined upper class, and a small proportion of artisans and laborers. He finds about 30% of the people to have been without land, yet he considers Bergen, Morris, and Monmouth counties as conforming to his subsistence pattern, with the average farmer owning about 80 acres. Main, *Social Structure*, 25-28, 42-43.

[7] Only Shrewsbury contained substantial salt marshes, but these were compensated for by a broad band of fertile soil. General studies, of New Jersey agriculture and geology include Wacker, *Musconetcong Valley;* Hubert Schmidt, *Rural Hunterdon: An Agricultural History* (New Brunswick, N.J., 1946); and Albert B. Meredith and Vivian P. Hood, *Geography and History of New Jersey* (Boston, 1921).

[8] For graphs illustrating this test of the data see Dennis P. Ryan, "Six Towns: Continuity and Change in Revolutionary New Jersey, 1770-1792" (Ph.D. diss., New York University, 1974), 246-247.

[9] James T. Lemon, "Household Consumption in Eighteenth-Century America and Its Relationship to Production and Trade: The Situation among Farmers in Southeastern Pennsylvania," *Agricultural History*, XLI (1967), 68.

excluding the 20 acres of woodland in Lemon's total, for most East Jersey towns had only a small amount of such unimproved land. It is therefore safe to conclude that in New Jersey a farm of 51 acres or more, with a household size that probably averaged close to six, would have provided enough food to nourish its members.[10] Possession of a farm smaller than 51 acres would have either prompted a husbandman to rent additional land or compelled him to work in the fields of more prosperous neighbors. These alternatives would have confronted all but very young men or the elderly who had few children at home. Although the minimal acreage for self-sufficiency can be conservatively estimated at 51 acres, the ideal size for a commercial farm in the Middle Atlantic region was well over 100 acres.[11]

[10] The crops yields for rye, corn, and wheat for Morris County were, according to one contemporary estimate, slightly higher than Lemon's figure. Rayner Wickersham Kelsey, ed., [Theophile] Cazenove Journal 1794 . . . (Haverford, Pa., 1922), 4, 9. A census for Morristown in 1771-1772 shows that the average household size was 6.09. Ryan, "Six Towns," 64. Robert V. Wells finds "remarkable variation" in the size of households in West New Jersey, with an average of 6.4 for all counties (The Population of the British Colonies in America before 1776: A Survey of Census Data [Princeton, N.J., 1975], 140).

The varying but generally lower estimates of acreage necessary for self-sufficiency in New England are not applicable to New Jersey because of differences in the nature and intensity of farming. Gross, Minutemen and Their World, 214, gives a much lower estimate of 24-28 acres for a family of six. A minimum figure of 50 acres is given by Jackson Turner Main, "The Distribution of Property in Colonial Connecticut," in James Kirby Martin, ed., The Human Dimensions of Nation Making: Essays on Colonial and Revolutionary America (Madison, Wis., 1976), 58, hereafter cited as Main, "Distribution of Property in Colonial Conn." Such estimates of farm size are characterized as "fragmentary and often ambiguous" by Stephen Innes, "Land Tenancy and Social Order in Springfield, Massachusetts, 1652 to 1702," WMQ, 3d Ser., XXXV (1978), 41, n. 30. A farm of 60 acres for sale in Shrewsbury in 1784 was termed "A small Farm" (New-Jersey Gazette [Trenton], Aug. 23, 1784).

Although the tax lists include unimproved land in the aggregate figures, such acreage represented only a small amount of the land in the towns. Only in Shrewsbury, with its vast amounts of sandy soil in the southern section, was there much uncultivated and underutilized land. In 1780, 25.2% of the land fit that classification. In contrast, Piscataway and Woodbridge had no unimproved land in 1780 and 1789, respectively. Newark had less than 1% and Morristown, 15.1% in 1789, and Middletown, 7% in 1784. The figures are not skewed by the inclusion of these unimproved lands in the totals, for generally only individuals with landholdings over 100 acres held unimproved land in large tracts. These owners of unimproved land were a minority in each town.

[11] Only nine leases for tenants on four 18th-century New York manors, of a total of 504 such contracts, were for plots smaller than 50 acres. The average ranged from 106 on Livingston Manor to 237 on Cortlandt Manor. Sung Bok Kim, Landlord and Tenant in Colonial New York: Manorial Society, 1664-1775 (Chapel Hill, N.C., 1978), 188-190. The average size of farms in southeastern Pennsylvania in

Collectively, the six towns by 1778-1780 had average landholdings per taxpayer that were only slightly above the estimated level of self-sufficiency. The aggregate average was 63.9 acres for each head of household, with the individual township averages ranging from 82.7 acres in Middletown to 42.5 in Newark. By 1789, the six towns had experienced, through growing population, an aggregate decline to 54.4 acres in average landholdings. Five towns registered an increase in population from 1784 to 1790, with decennial rates of growth in the 1780s ranging from 16.0 in Middletown to 75.1 in Woodbridge. The region as a whole experienced a constant expansion of population. Rates of population growth in the four counties of Essex, Middlesex, Morris, and Monmouth ranged from 19.6 percent to 31.2 percent per decade from 1772 to 1790. Owing to this pressure, two towns, Newark and Woodbridge, had average landholdings substantially below 51 acres in 1789. By that year, in general terms, individual landholdings in the six towns were only slightly larger than those of New England.[12]

Table I shows the distribution of landholding in 1778-1780. Nearly one-third of the adult males in each town possessed farms of insufficient or "marginal" size, and another third were without land.[13] The prosperous yeomen of the Jerseys were, in fact, a minority in each town. John Dod, the Newark assessor, reported in 1779 that 395 of a total of 973 taxpayers could be classified as "poor"—those whose state tax was at the lowest rate and who, with few exceptions, owned fewer than 51 acres.[14] The proportion of those men without sufficient land varied from 55.5 percent in Piscataway to 76.2 percent in Shrewsbury. Mark E. Lender's survey of 7,500 citizens of Revolutionary New Jersey confirms these findings for many other townships in the state.[15] When it is considered that only 35.1 percent of the taxpayers in

---

1782 was 130 acres, but this average excludes individuals with small plots under 25 acres. Lemon, "Household Consumption," *Ag. Hist.*, XLI (1967), 68. The mean acreage in Chester County has been estimated at 141.6 in 1764 and 126.8 in 1791. Duane E. Ball, "Dynamics of Population and Wealth in Eighteenth-Century Chester County, Pennsylvania," *Journal of Interdisciplinary History*, VI (1976), 629. For estimates of farm sizes in New England in the 1780s see Kenneth Lockridge, "Land, Population and the Evolution of New England Society, 1630-1790," *Past and Present*, No. 39 (Apr. 1968), 67-68, and Main, "Distribution of Property in Colonial Conn.," 58, 90.

[12] Ryan, "Six Towns," 65-66, 269. The diminishing size of farms advertised for sale in 18th-century New Jersey is discussed in Wacker, *Land and People*, 400-403.

[13] On Mar. 25, 1778, the New Jersey legislature passed the first state tax bill. The Tax Ratables generally list all males and females who owned land, cattle, horses, slaves, hogs, or mills. While such items were taxed at fluctuating rates from year to year, Tax Ratables before 1790 included improved and unimproved acreage.

[14] Tax Ratables, Newark, Feb. 1779.

[15] Of those sampled by Lender, 37% were without land and another 12.5% owned fewer than 25 acres. Mark E. Lender, "The Enlisted Line: The Continental Soldier

TABLE I
LANDHOLDING, 1778 TO 1780

Category	Acreage	Total (N = 2479)		Farmer (N = 2074)	
		N	%	N	%
Commercial and Subsistent	301–500	34	1.4	26	1.3
	201–300	97	3.9	78	3.8
	151–200	108	4.4	91	4.4
	101–150	193	7.8	169	8.1
	76–100	248	10.0	219	10.6
	51–75	189	7.6	160	7.8
Totals		869	35.1	743	35.9
Marginal and Landless	26–50	350	14.1	282	13.6
	1–25	453	18.3	348	16.8
	0	807	32.5	701	33.8
Totals		1610	64.9	1331	64.2

Note: Tax ratables for this table are Piscataway, May 1780; Shrewsbury, Feb. 1780; Newark, Feb. 1779; Morristown, May 1778; Woodbridge, May–June 1778; Middletown, Dec. 1778; Tax Ratables, Bureau of Archives and History, State Library, Trenton, N.J., hereafter cited as Tax Ratables. Unimproved land was considered at one-half the acreage listed in the tax ratables. Farmers are included in the total numbers and percentages. The farmer category includes all individuals who can be identified as farmers or of indeterminate occupation. It excludes those known to be professionals, tradesmen, or laborers.

all six towns possessed more than 50 acres, it is evident that marginality and tenancy were pervasive in New Jersey after 1776.

The tax lists of 1778-1780, analyzed by age, show that a significant number of the landless or marginal men were young. (See Table II.) Over two-thirds of those under thirty-three years of age were below the level of minimal self-sufficiency by 1778-1780. Those aged thirty-three and over, however, were not necessarily able to inherit or purchase a farm of moderate size. Well over 50 percent of men aged thirty-three to forty-seven owned fewer than 51 acres. The majority of those aged forty-three to forty-seven were without sufficient land; 19.5 percent of this group owned no land. With the mean age at marriage for men in these towns estimated at twenty-five to twenty-six, and the mean number of children born at nine or more, with an average of six, the young man in his thirties probably required at least 51

of New Jersey" (Ph.D. diss., Rutgers University, 1975), 129. In southeastern Pennsylvania 30% were landless. James T. Lemon, *The Best Poor Man's Country: A Geographical Study of Early Southeastern Pennsylvania* (Baltimore, 1972), 12.

TABLE II
LANDHOLDING AND AGE, 1778 TO 1780

Age (N = 1680)	Commercial and Subsistent 51–500		Acreage 26–50		Marginal and Landless 1–25		0	
	N	%	N	%	N	%	N	%
20–22	25	21.3	15	12.8	14	12.0	63	53.8
23–27	66	21.2	38	12.2	52	16.7	155	49.8
28–32	96	33.7	36	12.6	61	21.4	92	32.3
33–37	97	41.3	40	17.0	49	20.9	49	20.9
38–42	119	48.0	47	19.0	36	14.5	46	18.5
43–47	79	46.7	28	16.6	29	17.2	33	19.5
48–52	87	63.0	16	11.6	20	14.5	15	10.9
53–62	93	52.5	31	17.5	33	18.6	20	11.3

Note: These are the exact or estimated ages in 1778. Exact dates of birth from Bible records, parish registers, and tombstone inscriptions have been found for only a minority of those in the collective profile. One-third were unidentifiable and do not appear in this table. For a full discussion of the methodology used see Dennis P. Ryan, "Six Towns: Continuity and Change in Revolutionary New Jersey, 1770–1792" (Ph.D. diss., New York University, 1974), 317–322.

acres.[16] It is clear from an analysis of the earliest available tax ratables that many men, whether young or mature, of these East Jersey towns cannot be classified as yeoman farmers in 1778-1780.[17]

The lack of opportunities in farming was responsible, in part, for the involvement of many townsmen in craft industries and part-time trades. An estimated 16.3 percent of the 1778-1780 taxpayers were principally engaged in nonfarm occupations.[18] One roster of fifty Continental dragoons from New

[16] Tabulations of data on the number of children and age of marriage of the 2,479 male inhabitants, taken from numerous parish registers, marriage bonds, genealogies, and tombstone inscriptions, are found in Ryan, "Six Towns," 69-73.

[17] Main overestimates the number of middle-class farmers, giving a figure of about one-half of the population. A consideration of marginality would have reduced his total significantly. Main, Social Structure, 25-26, 42-43. A similar pattern of declining landholding and increasing tenancy has been found in Maryland. See David Curtis Skaggs, Roots of Maryland Democracy, 1753-1776 (Westport, Conn., 1973), 53, and Gregory A. Stiverson, Poverty in a Land of Plenty: Tenancy in Eighteenth-Century Maryland (Baltimore, 1977).

[18] This percentage includes professionals, craftsmen, and artisans as well as laborers. This group was identified by an analysis of the tax lists, wills, court and church records, local histories, genealogies, and newspapers. Some individuals were assessed for little or no land but did own mills or tanyards. The tax assessor often differentiated between two individuals with the same name by recording their

Jersey shows that twenty-seven were primarily tradesmen such as nailers, masons, and tailors.[19] Extant wills from the six towns reflect the desire of fathers to have their sons learn trades. An analysis of 163 wills shows that only the mature sons, often only the eldest, could expect an adequate inherited estate. Only forty wills provided that all male heirs receive land. In thirty-nine wills fathers left only money and farm implements or craftsmen's tools to their sons.[20] The attitude of fathers is perhaps best-represented by Thomas Goodwyn, who advised his son that a career in trade and commerce was "Much Better than working at the hoe and ax."[21] The significant number of marginal farmers, day laborers, and tradesmen is evidence that the standard picture of New Jersey as a prosperous region of self-sufficient farmers requires great qualification.

The inhabitants of the six towns, caught in an economy of land scarcity, experienced additional pressures created by wartime demands for supplies and threats to physical security. No state was so deeply affected by the internal and external convulsions of those years; more military engagements occurred in New Jersey than in any other state.[22] The British forces frequently raided near their encampments for forage; the location and availability of grain and cattle were noted on maps prepared for the troops.[23] For the American forces, the procuring of grain and other foodstuffs, as well as wagons, bedding, and draught animals, from the towns of East Jersey was vital. From 1776 to 1780, when the war centered in the Middle Atlantic region, quartermasters relied on supplies from East Jersey.[24] During the

---

occupation. The figure for nonagricultural employment is about standard for the Middle Atlantic region. Main, *Social Structure,* 43. There is only an insignificant difference between the range of landholdings for this group and for farmers. Therefore, all tables include the nonfarm group in the total figures. This reemphasizes the fact that land was as important in the total wealth of a tradesman as it was in that of a farmer.

[19] Muster Roll of Second Regiment, Dragoons, Continental Army, 1780, Revolutionary War Records, no. 9907, Bur. of Archives and Hist., St. Lib., Trenton, N.J., hereafter cited as Revolutionary War Recs.

[20] Wills written from 1770 to 1785 are filed at the Bur. of Archives and Hist.

[21] Thomas Goodwyn to his son, Sept. 24, 1768, Hendrickson Papers, Box 1, Special Collections, Alexander Library, Rutgers University, New Brunswick, N.J.

[22] Howard H. Peckham, ed., *The Toll of Independence: Engagements and Battle Casualties of the American Revolution* (Chicago, 1974), 133.

[23] Map 236, British Army Maps of Sir Henry Clinton, Clinton Papers, William L. Clements Library, Ann Arbor, Mich. Inscription reads: "A Fine Foraging Country both for Cattle and Hay within six miles of Middletown Point." In order to prevent such raids, George Washington wrote to Gov. William Livingston on Apr. 1, 1777, to have him order the removal of "considerable Quantities of Grain and other provisions on or near the Coast" (Livingston Papers, Massachusetts Historical Society, Boston).

[24] Clement Biddle to Moore Furman, July 1778, Revolutionary War Recs., no. 4681.

Continental army's winter encampments at Morristown, Middlebrook, and Pompton, the region kept the army alive. Unremitting warfare, militia duty, and internal disruption created great problems for the inhabitants, who attempted to provide material support for the American army and militia. Not only was the rhythm of agriculture disturbed,[25] but those who raised a surplus were confronted with the vexing alternatives of punishment for illicit trade with the British in New York, which was their normal peacetime market, or acceptance of worthless or depreciating paper money or certificates from American commissaries.

The people of East Jersey also suffered frequent attacks upon person and property by soldiers, loyalist irregulars, patriot retaliators, and bandits and looters. Destruction of property was extensive. British troops burned many churches and schools in the six towns, destroyed saltworks and houses, and carried away bedding and other household goods. The magnitude of this damage was substantiated by the claims filed by hundreds of residents after 1781, when state appraisers took an inventory. The American forces were also guilty of destruction and theft of property, although on a smaller scale.[26] Morristown residents were victims of numerous incidents of pilferage of turkeys and cows, as well as damage to fencing. Such destruction, added to the psychological trauma of civil war, made the protracted conflict an arduous experience for the inhabitants of East Jersey.

For those who possessed little or no land, the economic chaos of war could have been mitigated by a significant redistribution of confiscated loyalist estates. It was the state's policy, however, to sell tory lands for revenue, not to ameliorate agrarian problems.[27] The sale of property was extensive and vigorous, but for those who needed land, loyalist estates were either unobtainable or subject to numerous legal entanglements. In Monmouth County, the inequity of the sales provoked a rash of complaints against the tactics of the commissioners for forfeited estates. These accusations were investigated, and the General Assembly censured the commis-

---

[25] Col. Jacob Drake, Jr., of Morris County wrote to William Livingston in early July 1776 that the harvesting of wheat had not been possible because of the emergency call-up of the East New Jersey militia when the British landed on Staten Island. Drake reported, "Our harvest is now Ripe and my men is very uneasey to think that they are Kept hear [Woodbridge] and luse what Must Seport thare children" (Jacob Drake to Livingston, July 12, 1776, Livingston Papers).

[26] "Petition of some Middletown Residents on behalf of Daniel Stevenson," 1783, Cherry Hall Papers, folder 35, Monmouth County Historical Association, Freehold, N.J. In January 1780 the British burned the Newark Academy. Damage claims for Newark, Woodbridge, and Piscataway are at the Bur. of Archives and Hist., as are "Damages by the British, Essex County," and "Damages by Americans, Morris County." Claims were never paid.

[27] Richard P. McCormick, *Experiment in Independence: New Jersey in the Critical Period, 1781-1789* (New Brunswick, 1950), 32.

115

sioners in 1779.[28] Far more disturbing were the difficulties that faced the potential purchaser. The most effective obstacle to the purchase of loyalist estates was the requirement of cash payment. This insured that poor tenants and marginal farmers could not buy land, for credit and mortgages were not available. In many cases, the tenants who rented the farms of loyalist refugees were forced to vacate, there being no preemption rights.[29] Those who did purchase estates found that their titles were legally questionable and that old debts on the estates had to be paid; tory wives claimed rights of dower, while creditors demanded payment from the new owner.[30]

In addition, although the records of the disposition of loyalist lands are too fragmentary for quantitative analysis, it is clear that only a few thousand acres in the six towns were sold and that only a small percentage of this property was of great value. Most of it was swamp, meadow, or unimproved woodland. Estates were divided and sold in small portions, but this in no way implied the democratization of landholdings, since the affluent and respected leaders of the new military and civil establishment, who were able to pay in cash, purchased the most valuable land.[31] "Genesea," writing in the Chatham newspaper in 1783, remarked, "You once had some property in your hands, forfeited to the state, by those who joined the king. . . . [I]t became as smoke in our grasp; and I believe that the public is now little the better for all that has been sold."[32] The confiscations did little to enhance the economic opportunity of most East Jersey residents.[33]

[28] "Petition of Monmouth County Commissioners for Selling Forfeited Estates," Sept. 21, 1779; "Petition of Monmouth County," May 8 and Mar. 24, 1779—all in Manuscript Collection, Box 11, Bur. of Archives and Hist. "Petition of Monmouth County," May 25, 1779, Revolutionary War Manuscripts, no. 76, Bur. of Archives and Hist.

[29] Morris, "Plowmen of the Jersies," 120; Riccards, "Patriots and Plunderers," N.J. Hist., LXXXVI (1968), 19, 25.

[30] "Petition of Dorothy Crowell," Feb. 17, 1796; "Petition of Rebekah Williams," Oct. 23, 1797; "Petition of Inhabitants of Middlesex County," Oct. 24, 1787; "Petition of Inhabitants of Monmouth County," Feb. 7, 1786; "Petition of Benjamin Stevenson," Nov. 1, 1799—all in MS Coll., Box 11, Bur. of Archives and Hist. "Petition of Major Robert Nixon of Middlesex County," n.d., New Jersey Legislative Petitions, Memorials and Addresses, Spec. Colls., Alexander Lib., Rutgers Univ.

[31] For the records referred to see Essex Commissioners' Vendue Book, 1779; "A List of the sale of certain forfeited estates lying in Woodbridge, Amboy and Piscataway sold at vendue beginning on the 22nd day of March, 1779"; "Account of sales the twenty-ninth of June 1779 sold on respective premises"; "Samuel Forman's Account," Mar. 22, 1780; and "Sale of sundry items at Public Vendue by Stillwell agent," Mar. 1784—all in Revolutionary War Recs., Forfeited Estates Box; "Accounts of notes received by John Stillwell Monmouth County, March 12, 1785," Revolutionary War Recs., Loyalists Box 2. See also Deed Book I, 239-245, and Deed Book L, 18-24, Monmouth County Courthouse, Freehold, N.J.

[32] The New-Jersey Journal (Chatham), May 21, 1783.

[33] The studies of Richard D. Brown, Robert S. Lambert, and Ruth M. Keesey confirm that the structure of society in New Jersey and elsewhere was little altered by

Debilitating conditions of deflation, debt, high taxes, and foreclosures during the Confederation era followed the dislocation of the war years. A Morristown resident commented in 1785 that "a spirit of rebellion or uneasiness subsists in the greatest part of the community."[34] In addition to the problems of repairing the material damage wrought by the war,[35] the scarcity of hard coin made fixed payments of taxes and mortgages difficult. Men who had served in the army or had materially aided the war effort were particularly affected. During the war, the certificates and promissory notes of the state had often been either accepted for payment at reduced rates or exchanged for goods. This created financial stringency for the original owner in the postwar period, when high taxes were imposed to pay off the state debt. Militia pay notes rarely remained in the hands of the men who received them; speculators used most of them to purchase confiscated estates.[36] For example, Caleb Baldwin signed over a pay certificate to Thomas Bloomfield, Jr.; this certificate eventually found its way into the hands of Benjamin Shotwell, who used it to buy a forfeited estate in Bergen County. Similarly, John Borden used a pay voucher originally issued to John Beach, a Morris County militiaman, to rent a small farm formerly owned by a loyalist in Shrewsbury.[37] Continental Line privates and noncommissioned officers from Morris County complained that they had had to part with public securities for little return and had received no pay in cash when they left the army.[38] "A Village Tenant," urging the farmers and tradesmen of the state to petition the state legislature, remarked, "Every one knows that the greatest part of them [state securities] center in a few particular hands, and that they purchased them at a large discount."[39]

---

the redistribution of loyalist land. Brown, "The Confiscation and Disposition of Loyalists' Estates in Suffolk County, Massachusetts," *WMQ*, 3d Ser., XXI (1964), 549; Lambert, "The Confiscation of Loyalist Property in Georgia, 1782-1786," *ibid.*, XX (1963), 94; Keesey, "Loyalism in Bergen County, New Jersey," *ibid.*, XVIII (1961), 568. Richard Morris calls the sales of estates in New Jersey a "windfall for insiders" ("Plowmen of the Jersies," 120).

[34] Diary of Joseph Lewis, Jan. 5, 1785, New Jersey Historical Society, Newark.

[35] J. F. D. Smyth, an English observer, noted that New Jersey towns, including Woodbridge and Newark, "have suffered extremely by the ravages of the war" (*A Tour in the United States of America* [Dublin, 1784], 250).

[36] Of 808 militia notes of the four applicable counties, only 9.9% were retained by the original owner, while 63.1% were used by the new holder to purchase a forfeited estate. Revolutionary War Recs., nos. 263-635, 852-1045, 1160-1329, 1358-1452. See also Lender, "The Enlisted Line," 268.

[37] Militia Notes, Revolutionary War Recs., nos. 861, 1362. See McCormick, *Experiment in Independence*, 215, for a discussion of speculation in certificates.

[38] "Petition of non-commissioned officers and privates of the Jersey Line residing in Morris County," n.d., Revolutionary War Recs., no. 10352; "Petition of non-commissioned officers and privates of the Jersey Line," Apr. 9, 1783, Papers of the Continental Congress, item 152, XI, National Archives.

[39] *New Brunswick Gazette, and Weekly Monitor* (New Jersey), Apr. 8, 1788.

Many complaints of indigence and financial difficulty arose from the towns in the 1780s. Remonstrances from groups of citizens flooded the state legislature. A petition signed by Morris County residents asked that taxes be permitted to be paid in certificates in lieu of gold and silver.[40] Long lists of delinquents, often for sums unpaid for five years or more, appeared in the tax rolls of Monmouth County, where collector Joseph Stillwell asked Major Joseph Seabrook of Middletown for help in gathering delinquent taxes.[41] Quakers reported the failure of members to satisfy debts.[42] Many persons lost their land through their inability to pay taxes or mortgages. Attributing his mounting debts to "the fluctuation of the times," Jonas Ward of Newark, whose land was attached and sold at sheriff's vendue, left his family of six unsupported while he languished in jail. P. Stryker of Millstone reported that farmers "cannot get the money to pay."[43] John Holmes of Middletown maintained that because of his depreciated army pay and the sale of his service certificates to speculators, "he was obliged to dispose of his property in order to support himself."[44] *The New-York Gazetteer* of March 3, 1786, noted that sixteen properties taken for debt in Morris County remained unsold for lack of cash.

The diary of Joseph Lewis, a resident of Morristown, provides a glimpse into the economic state of postwar New Jersey. Lewis cites many examples of the problems of the poor and marginal residents of Morris County and its environs. He himself often purchased foreclosed property and then either sold or leased it, sometimes to the unfortunate former owner. In some cases, more

---

See also Peter Wilson to Dirck Romeyn, June 12, 1781, Peter Wilson Papers, N.J. Hist. Soc.

[40] "Petition to the Legislative Council and General Assembly," Sept. 20, 1782, Revolutionary War Recs., no. 1339. See also "Petition of freeholders and inhabitants of Middlesex County," Oct. 29, 1784; "Petition and remonstrance of freeholders and inhabitants of Middlesex County," Jan. 24, 1783; "Representation and petition of inhabitants of Morris County," 1784; "Petition of inhabitants of Essex and Middlesex counties," n.d.—all in MS Coll., Box 6, Bur. of Archives and Hist.; "Petition of inhabitants of Essex County," Oct. 22, 1783, Revolutionary War Recs., no. 7254; and "Petition of inhabitants of Hunterdon County," Dec. 12, 1783, AM Papers, Bur. of Archives and Hist.

[41] Circuit Court Judgments, 1786-1793, Apr. 1784 and Sept. 30, 1784, Monmouth Co. Courthouse. Joseph Stillwell to Thomas Seabrook, Aug. 24, 1784, Stillwell Papers, Box 5, folder 1780-1789, New-York Historical Society, New York City.

[42] Woodbridge [Rahway] Monthly Meeting Minutes, June 16, 1784, and Shrewsbury Monthly Meeting Minutes, Dec. 4, 1786, Friends Record Center, New York City.

[43] P. Stryker to Laurence VanderVeer, June 3, 1787, VanderVeer Papers, N.J. Hist. Soc.; "Petition of Essex County residents on behalf of Jonas Ward," May 20, 1786, Insolvent Debtors, Bk. 1, Bur. of Archives and Hist.

[44] "Petition of John Holmes for benefit of act of insolvency," May 12, 1792, Revolutionary War Recs., no. 10591.

than one individual or family rented the property. Lewis noted, "The house which I had sold to Samuel Howell was on fire and in less than half an hour it was all consumed. Mr. Howell had rented the house to Abraham Hudson, who rented one room to Peter Tisha and one room to Patrick Bayles and Thomas Thompson. Hudson moved last month to New York. Patrick Bayles ran away so that there was no goods in it."[45] Joseph Lewis was able to profit by the general situation, although his brother Edward suffered greatly. On March 29, 1786, Lewis purchased Edward's land at vendue and then rented it to his brother for thirteen pounds per year.

Public reaction to deteriorating economic conditions in Morris County reached the level of active discontent by 1784. Lewis reported that a group armed with clubs stopped a vendue in Mendham at which land was to be sold for taxes. Some members of the Morristown Presbyterian Church denounced their pastor for preaching in support of payment of taxes and debts.[46] James Parker, who encountered great difficulty in collecting rents from the tenants of Sir Robert Barker, reported in 1785 that the tenants were "boisterous, licentious and abusive."[47] John Rutherfurd, a wealthy landowner and lawyer, stated in 1786 that New Jersey's economic problems were caused by "lands being broke up," poor husbandry, and "the natural encrease of the Inhabitants, without Manufactures or more Land to cultivate."[48]

By 1789, the number of adult males whose names appeared on the 1778-1780 tax lists for the six towns had been reduced by death or emigration to 1,580. Despite the disruptive experience of the war and its immediate aftermath, these persisters were somewhat better off than they had been a decade earlier. The 1789 tax assessments on land show an increase of those defined as marginal and middle-rank landholders (1-151 acres). (See Table III.) In some categories there was as much as a 20 percent decrease among the landless and tenants. From these figures one might conclude that economic opportunity increased dramatically for those at the bottom or near bottom. These columns in Table III, however, do not include younger sons and new immigrants who appeared on the tax rolls after 1780. The third

[45] Diary of Joseph Lewis, Dec. 9, 15, 1783, Feb. 4, Mar. 17, Sept. 15, 1784, Jan. 30, 1786, Jan. 26, 1787, N.J. Hist. Soc. Quotation is from the entry of Jan. 9, 1784.

[46] Ibid., Jan. 5, 23, 1785, Jan. 5, 1786. See also David A. Bernstein, ed., Minutes of the Governor's Privy Council, 1777-1789 (New Jersey Archives, 3d Ser., I [Trenton, 1974]), 261.

[47] James Parker to Sir Robert Barker, May 3, 1785, James Parker Papers, Spec. Colls., Alexander Lib., Rutgers Univ. For similar problems see Elias Boudinot to Philemon Dickinson, Jan. 11, 1790, Dickinson Papers, Historical Society of Pennsylvania, Philadelphia.

[48] John Rutherfurd, "Notes on the State of New Jersey," N.J. Hist. Soc., Procs., 2d Ser., I (1867), 81.

TABLE III
LANDHOLDING, 1789

	Original Sample (N = 1580)		Farmer (N = 1278)		All Male Taxpayers (N = 4310)	
Acreage	N	%	N	%	N	%
301–500	24	1.5	15	1.2	57	1.3
201–300	63	4.0	48	3.8	109	2.5
151–200	102	6.5	88	6.9	159	3.7
101–150	182	11.5	160	12.5	327	7.6
76–100	204	12.9	171	13.4	335	7.6
51–75	199	12.6	163	12.8	408	9.5
26–50	340	21.5	268	21.0	729	16.9
1–25	314	19.9	245	19.2	1018	23.6
0	152	9.7	120	9.4	1168	27.1

Note: Tax ratables are Piscataway, July 1789; Shrewsbury, July-Aug. 1789; Newark, July-Aug. 1789; Morristown, July-Aug. 1789; Woodbridge, Oct. 1789; Middletown, June-Aug. 1789. Unimproved land was considered at one-half the acreage listed. Farmers are included in the total numbers and percentages.

group of figures in the table, representing all taxpayers of 1789, shows that little substantial change had taken place in the distribution of property. With the landless in the total figures constituting over 27.1 percent, and those owning fewer than 51 acres making up 67.6 percent, it is evident that the landless and marginal remained the major element in the adult male population in the six towns in percentages comparable to those of the war years.[49]

The magnitude and direction of shifts in the landholding of the original group by the time of the tax assessment of 1783-1784 and that of 1789 are shown in detail in Table IV. For all categories but the landless of 1778-1780, stability, not mobility, was the primary pattern. Most stable were the marginal farmers who owned fewer than 51 acres in 1778-1780. Almost three-quarters of these men did not substantially add to their landholdings, nor did they fall into the landless group. Where there was upward mobility, it was

[49] The data and conclusions offered here agree with the findings of historians who have measured the distribution of wealth. Morris finds that in Salem, Mass., the lowest 30% owned no real estate in 1788, while the upper decile owned 55.2% of the town's land ("Revolutionary Salem," 74). Douglas Lamar Jones finds that the top decile owned 41% and 34% in Beverly and Wenham, Mass., respectively, in 1771. By 1790, this group controlled 49% and 36% of the land in those two towns. The lowest 40% owned 4-5% in the two towns in 1777 and 2% in 1790. Jones, "Geographic Mobility and Society in Eighteenth-Century Essex County, Massachusetts" (Ph.D. diss., Brandeis University, 1975), 176. For New Jersey, Lender's study of Revolutionary inhabitants in 44 towns concludes that the richest decile controlled about 45% of the wealth, while the lowest one-third owned only 10% ("The Enlisted Line," 118).

TABLE IV
ECONOMIC MOBILITY, 1778 TO 1789

Change in Landholding	1778/80 to 1783/84 (N = 2065)		1783/84 to 1789 (N = 1575)		1778/80 to 1789 (N = 1581)	
	N	%	N	%	N	%
Upper (201 acres or more)						
1. downward mobility	28	26.4	21	23.9	99	35.4
2. stability	78	73.6	67	76.1	64	64.5
Middle (101–200 acres)						
1. upward mobility	10	3.7	12	4.4	11	4.4
2. stability	187	68.5	198	72.0	160	63.7
3. downward mobility	76	27.8	65	23.6	80	31.9
Moderate (51–100 acres)						
1. upward mobility	46	9.1	47	12.4	57	18.0
2. stability	401	78.9	264	69.5	198	62.5
3. downward mobility	61	12.0	69	18.2	62	19.6
Marginal (1–50 acres)						
1. upward mobility						
a. to upper group	3	.5	0	0	3	.5
b. to middle group	20	3.0	16	2.6	24	4.4
c. to moderate group	72	10.9	62	10.4	90	16.6
2. stability	527	79.5	491	82.0	401	74.0
3. downward mobility	41	6.2	30	5.0	24	4.4
Landless						
1. upward mobility						
a. to upper group	4	.7	0	0	3	.8
b. to middle group	21	4.1	11	4.7	29	7.8
c. to moderate group	45	8.8	25	10.7	52	14.0
d. to marginal group	170	33.1	88	37.8	169	45.4
2. stability	275	53.3	109	46.8	119	32.0

Note: Table does not include numbers and percentages for emigrants.

moderate. If those owning 201 acres or more are excluded—they could only lose property to be considered mobile—over 92 percent of the persisters did not acquire enough land through purchase or inheritance to rise higher than the nearest category above them. The number of mobile taxpayers was greater during the war than during the Confederation Period.

Although 68 percent of the original landless group had acquired some property by 1789, most assumed ownership of a small farm under 51 acres. Those who made a substantial alteration from landless to self-sufficient status constituted less than 23 percent of the total group. This percentage is comparable to the upward mobility of the marginal farmers, only 21.5 percent of whom were able to add significantly to their farms by 1789 so as to achieve minimal self-sufficiency. The stability of those with small freeholds and the modest gains of the landless indicate no substantial redistribution of landed wealth and low rates of mobility in either direction.

By 1789, men who had been in their twenties and early thirties in 1778, and who still lived in their towns, found that opportunities had only slightly expanded. (See Table V.) Over 60 percent of those twenty-three to twenty-seven years of age in 1778, now aged thirty-five to thirty-nine years, remained below subsistence level. Most age groups contained a smaller percentage of the landless by 1789, but the glacial movement into the small freeholder category was probably less a function of the age of the individual than of the epoch in which he lived. All age categories still contained substantial percentages of marginal farmers and landless laborers, and most adult males under age forty-five still held fewer than 51 acres. At forty-five to forty-nine years, an age when a man usually had to support a large family, only slightly more than one-half of the persisters in the six towns owned 51 acres or more.

The large number of single men in their twenties who had been landless in 1778-1780 and had acquired some estate by 1789 tends to confirm the importance of age in relation to distribution of wealth. However, while many of the young did ultimately receive or buy small amounts of land, at no time did most gain enough to reach self-sufficiency as defined here. Increasing opportunity was limited to young men of families that were able to provide an inheritance of sufficient size or to enterprising men who earned enough money in a craft or by day labor to buy land. Only a slight majority, however, ever possessed at least 51 acres. Age therefore affords only a partial explanation of economic inequality, for a significant minority of young landless and marginal taxpayers in each town did not reach yeoman independence by maturity.[50] A further search of the tax rolls for 1796-1797 confirms that most individuals who owned fewer than 51 acres in 1789 did not significantly add to their landholdings as they became older.[51]

[50] Age as a variable in a study of landholding and economic inequality has, until recently, been neglected in the historical analysis of tax records. Recent scholarship is divided on the long-term mobility of late colonial and Revolutionary youth. John J. Waters argues that "for the vast majority of Guilford farmers a combination of kin, work, and increasing age would bring a modicum of prosperity" ("Patrimony, Succession, and Social Stability: Guilford, Connecticut, in the Eighteenth Century," *Perspectives in American History*, X [1976], 156). Although few were really well off, there was "*age inequality* rather than *wealth inequality*" (*ibid.*). Robert Gross finds, however, that in the era of the Revolution (1770-1795) "older men were holding on to their property longer than before and thereby blocking upward movement by the younger generation" (*Minutemen and Their World*, 234, n. 21). My conclusion on age contrasts with that of James A. Henretta, "Families and Farms: *Mentalité* in Pre-Industrial America," *WMQ*, 3d Ser., XXXV (1978), 7.

[51] These data were derived from Tax Ratables, Piscataway, July-Aug. 1797; Shrewsbury, June-Aug. 1797; Newark, 1796; Morristown, Sept. 1797; Woodbridge, Sept. 1797; and Middletown, 1797. A period beyond eight or nine years between tax

TABLE V
LANDHOLDING AND AGE, 1789

	Acreage						
	Commercial and Subsistent		Marginal and Landless				
Age (N = 1394)	51–500		26–50		1–25		0	
	N	%	N	%	N	%	N	%
32–34	32	41.6	17	22.1	17	22.1	11	14.3
35–39	85	38.8	56	25.6	51	23.3	27	12.3
40–44	98	49.5	46	23.2	36	18.2	18	9.1
45–49	84	51.2	38	23.2	31	18.9	11	6.7
50–54	105	57.7	40	22.0	26	14.3	11	6.0
55–59	73	54.5	26	19.4	25	18.7	10	7.5
60–64	61	62.2	20	20.4	11	11.2	6	6.1
65–74	79	55.6	26	18.3	30	21.1	7	4.9

Note: Table does not include numbers and percentages for emigrants. For sources see Table III.

The low ceiling on opportunity in East Jersey explains the exodus from their communities of a large segment of the original taxpaying group. By 1789, while 17.6 percent had increased their landholdings, and 8.1 percent held less land, 36.2 percent, or 898 individuals of the original sample, had left the towns. This rate of spatial mobility places the six towns within the parameters of other late eighteenth-century rural and urban communities that have been studied by historians. The figure is close to Jackson Turner Main's estimate of 40 percent average mobility for the new nation as a whole, though it is lower than the rate for Boston and other New England towns, as well as for southeastern Pennsylvania.[52]

lists would have significantly reduced the group by death, and infirmity and age would have reduced their landholdings. Of the 439 individuals identified, 312 (71.1%) did not add significantly to their landholdings and move out of their tenant or landless categories (0 to 50 acres). The 17% who gained enough land to be placed in a new classification were partially offset by the 6.8% who owned significantly less land by the later date. Despite the fact that all these men were adults in their forties or older by 1796-1797, only 47 (10.9%) had acquired more than 50 acres.

[52] The studies that estimate percentages of migrants who left their communities during the late 18th century give figures ranging from 36% for Beverly, Mass., 1761-1771, to 64% for Salem, Mass., 1777-1788. See Kulikoff, "Progress of Inequality in Revolutionary Boston," *WMQ*, 3d Ser., XXVIII (1971), 401-402; Philip J. Greven, Jr., *Four Generations: Population, Land, and Family in Colonial Andover, Massachusetts* (Ithaca, N.Y., 1970), 20; Jones, "Geographical Mobility and Society," 18; Morris, "Revolutionary Salem," 35; Gross, *Minutemen and Their World*, 233; Lemon, *Best Poor Man's Country*, 74-75; and Main, *Social Structure*, 193. The figure for the six towns is actually closer to Lemon's estimate, for he calculates that

The patterns of dispersion are difficult to trace. Some of the migrants appear to have moved to new land on the western and northern frontiers. In 1786, John Rutherfurd gloomily reported "great Emigrations from this State," with many going "to the other States to the southwestward, or to the western wide wilderness." Rutherfurd complained of emigrants running away when in debt.[53] In 1787 an advertisement in a New Jersey newspaper offered lands above Albany, New York, for sale "in small lots of 200 acres and upwards, very suitable for poor farmers."[54] John Cleves Symmes purchased a huge tract of land on the Miami River in Ohio. Joseph Lewis, Timothy Jones, and Thomas Kinney, leading Morristown figures, purchased shares of land, and on July 1, 1788, an unknown number of East Jersey residents set out from Morristown.[55] The movement was not simply westward, however. Some looked to New York City or to Philadelphia for more lucrative commercial opportunities or for the chance to learn or practice a trade.

The majority of migrants appear to have relocated in neighboring towns and counties in New Jersey. Many families in Monmouth County had kinsmen in the region. A list of dragoons in 1782, which notes home and place of birth, shows that only six of twenty-three soldiers still resided where they had been born. Most had moved short distances within Monmouth County or to nearby areas such as Staten Island and Morris County.[56] Local movements of individuals and families probably formed a major element of the horizontal mobility in Revolutionary New Jersey society.

The Seventh Day Baptist congregation in Shrewsbury presents an intriguing example of geographical mobility. The congregation divided in opinion between sectarian neutrality and support for independence in 1776, and disputes over bonds and debts disrupted it during the Confederation years. Without any explanation, the church records noted on September 6, 1789, "Then did the body of this Church remove from Shrosebeary in order

---

death and replacement would place his dispersal rate at 30% (*Best Poor Man's Country*, 72). The New Jersey figure eliminates those presumed or actually dead.

[53] John Rutherfurd, "A Brief Account of the State of New Jersey in America," Aug. 18, 1786, Rutherfurd Miscellaneous Collection, N.J. Hist. Soc.; Rutherfurd, "State of the United States," May 1786, *ibid.*

[54] *New-Jersey Journal and Political Intelligencer* (Elizabethtown), Jan. 10, 1787.

[55] McCormick, *Experiment in Independence*, 230-231; Andrew Sherman, *Historic Morristown, New Jersey* (Morristown, 1905), 394; Diary of Joseph Lewis, Mar. 22, 1788, N.J. Hist. Soc.

[56] Capt. John Walton's Company of Light Dragoons, Monmouth County, 1782, Revolutionary War Recs., no. 3857. Jones finds that in Chelmsford, Mass., from 1761 to 1771 over 64% of those who moved into the town came from within 10 miles ("Geographic Mobility and Society," 135). For Salem, Mass., Morris concludes that "the majority of out-migrants tended to move short distances" ("Revolutionary Salem," 54).

to Settle in the State of Verginey." Seventy-two persons, in ten families, set out for the Ohio Valley, where they formed a new church at Salem, Virginia (now West Virginia), on land that Samuel Fitz Randolph, a former resident of Piscataway, had purchased.[87]

The motivation of the Seventh Day Baptists and the many other individuals and families who left their communities can only be surmised from the data on the original taxpaying group. Whatever their reasons, it is clear that in most cases the decision to move reflected more than random whim, for breaking away was difficult. As Table VI shows, the geographically mobile group was not composed solely of young men. In most age categories there are only slight differences between migrants and the total group; those aged twenty-three to thirty-seven in 1778-1780 made up 55 percent of the migrants and 49 percent of the 2,479 male taxpayers. In fact, persons over age thirty-two in 1778 formed the majority of those who left their towns. Another hypothesis that can be dismissed is that army service broadened the horizons of the men and consequently fostered mobility after the war, for Continental soldiers and militiamen from the six towns composed only one-third of the emigrants. Privates, who were generally young and poor, were the only rank disproportionately represented.[88]

The bulk of the evidence supports the conclusion that movement from the East Jersey towns was motivated principally by the push of declining prospects, added to the attraction of new lands. As Table VII indicates, those with sufficient land rarely left. Over one-half of those on the 1778-1780 tax lists who had departed by 1783-1784 were tenants and single men at the bottom of society. From 1778-1780 to 1789, 53.9 percent of the original landless group left, as did 32.7 percent of those in the marginal category.[89] Slight improvement into a small freehold by 1784 did not prevent those with

[87] Records of the Seventh Day Baptists of Salem, West Virginia, 26, 33, 39-40, 42, Seventh Day Baptist Historical Society, Plainfield, N.J. Corliss F. Randolph, *History of the Seventh Day Baptists in West Virginia* (Plainfield, N.J., 1905), 50.

[88] Privates composed 83.3% of the total military group that migrated. Almost all officer ranks were underrepresented among the geographically mobile. Lender finds that 56.7% of the New Jersey Continental soldiers were landless and that another 12.5% owned fewer than 25 acres ("The Enlisted Line," 129).

[89] Refer to Table I for totals of landless and marginal male taxpayers in 1778-1780. Studies of other regions have reached similar conclusions. Kulikoff finds that 58% of those without property left Boston from 1780 to 1790 ("Progress of Inequality in Revolutionary Boston," *WMQ*, 3d Ser., XXVIII [1971], 402). Lemon notes that two-thirds of the lowest income group from two southeastern Pennsylvania towns disappeared between 1772 and 1782 (*Best Poor Man's Country*, 85). Morris stresses that economic opportunity was the "push" factor in migration from Salem ("Revolutionary Salem," 56). Jones finds that among the mature sons of townspeople, 51% of the migrants from 1741 to 1771 in Beverly were of the lowest 40% in real estate holdings ("Geographic Mobility and Society," 125).

TABLE VI
AGE OF MIGRANTS

Age, 1778	Number of Migrants	Percentage of Migrants	Percentage of Total Group
20–22	45	9.4	7.7
23–27	100	20.8	18.1
28–32	90	18.8	17.0
33–37	74	15.4	13.9
38–42	64	13.3	15.0
43–47	35	7.3	10.0
48–52	31	6.5	8.1
53–62	41	8.5	10.3

Note: Numbers and percentages do not reflect totals for men whose names appeared on the 1778/80 tax lists and had presumably died before 1789.

little land from leaving thereafter; during the Confederation Period most migrants came from that group. On all the tax lists for each town sampled, those owning 50 acres or less composed over 50 percent of the migrants. Economic misfortunes were mentioned as a factor in uprooting several residents in the 1780s. Major John Burrowes of Middletown went to Georgia after the war "to retrieve his fortunes."[60] David Crane, a landless resident of Morristown, left during the night of November 29, 1783, with his "family and goods."[61] Some moved and became apprentices, seeking a trade to replace the declining prospects on the farm.[62] "Genesea" surveyed the economic situation for readers of The New-Jersey Journal in 1783. Citing poor soil and little land available for purchase, he noted that "the labouring man will never be so much lost . . . as to toil for others for small wages, when, by removing a little further off, he may possess, in his own right, perhaps a better farm than any of us do at present."[63] The ability to move out, whether to another town or to a distant frontier, artificially created a degree of mobility and opportunity in New Jersey society. In this sense, Frederick Jackson Turner's "safety-valve" theory may still be valid, for the pressure and frustration caused by scarcity of land were partially dispelled, either as reality or as myth, by the opening of new lands after the Treaty of Paris in 1783.

Despite the dislocations of war and the hardships of the postwar years, no major redistribution of wealth, as measured by landholding, accompanied the

[60] Helen Fairchild, "Sketch of Major John Burrowes's Life," Revolutionary War Recs., no. 2404.
[61] Diary of Joseph Lewis, Nov. 29, 1783, N.J. Hist. Soc.
[62] Shrewsbury Monthly Meeting Minutes, Feb. 2, 1784, Friends Book Store, Philadelphia.
[63] N.-J. Jour., May 7, 1783.

TABLE VII
LANDHOLDING OF MIGRANTS

Last Rank on Tax Lists	Migrants Who Left by 1783–1784		Migrants Who Left by 1789		Total Migrants	
	N	%	N	%	N	%
Upper (201 acres or more)	25	4.6	7	1.9	32	3.6
Middle (101–200)	26	4.8	19	5.3	48	5.3
Moderate (51–100)	56	10.4	65	18.1	120	13.4
Marginal (1–50)	139	25.8	161	44.7	263	29.3
Landless	292	54.3	108	30.0	435	48.5
All taxpayers	538	21.7	360	14.5	898	36.2

Note: Those under age 60 in 1789 (unless mortality was known) whose names no longer appeared on the tax lists were presumed to be emigrants.

American Revolution in East New Jersey. Decreasing farm size and a shift to commerce and trade were evolutionary developments of a pre-industrial economy that were not significantly affected by political and military events. Confiscation of the estates of loyalist refugees provided only a brief and limited opportunity to obtain a freehold. Although there was some upward mobility through acquisition of land during the years of war and reconstruction, this partial redistribution of wealth was more than offset by the debilitating economic effects of the era on the poor and marginal. Those who were the young men of the Revolution in 1776 found themselves by war's end with only a small piece of land. The marginal rarely added to their insufficient acres. By 1797, few had substantially improved their situation. Despite the intensity of economic problems in New Jersey, the Revolution did little to alter the direction of the state's economy. In this sense, an evolutionary pattern of stability perpetuated the lack of significant economic opportunity for those on the bottom.

For the large mass at the foot of the socioeconomic ladder, the only opportunity that the Revolution presented was the chance to go elsewhere to acquire a farm or pursue a trade. By 1789, over one-half of the original single men and tenants of the 1778-1780 taxpayers had departed. In 1786, a newspaper advertisement appealed to such men to become soldiers in the Northwest Territory. "Sober prudent young men, who have no farms of their own will . . . have the best opportunity of seeing the interior parts of the country, and choosing farms where it will best suit them, and their pay will be sufficient to purchase as good a farm as any in New-Jersey," were desired.[64]

[64] N.-J. Gaz., May 1, 1786.

It is clear from an examination of tax lists, petitions and wills, and contemporary accounts of the residents of Newark, Middletown, Morristown, Woodbridge, Piscataway, and Shrewsbury that economic marginality was far more pervasive in Revolutionary New Jersey than historians have supposed. The region contained a substantial landless group, but these inhabitants were only one segment of a still larger population that was unable to realize the yeoman dream during the Revolutionary era. To those who sought to acquire sufficient land in the six towns, the first years of the new nation were far from promising and often barely endurable.

Artisans, Journeymen, and the
Transformation of Labor in
Late Eighteenth-Century Philadelphia

Sharon V. Salinger

A MERICAN historians commonly associate the emergence of capitalist labor relations in the United States with the rise of mass production in the mid-nineteenth century.[1] Long before the factory system arose, however, workers' lives had been dramatically altered, for the limitations on their material well-being often associated with industrialization had antecedents in the eighteenth century. Indeed, in Philadelphia, by the final decades of the eighteenth century, the components of a capitalist labor system had taken root: contracts between employers and workers specified more detail, worker mobility and turnover rose, and the widespread use of wage labor ushered in a period of intense job insecurity that widened the distance between masters and workers. Recent studies of material realities and their articulation in popular ideology[2] have revised our once rosy notion of automatic social mobility and the characterization of today's "journeyman as tomorrow's master."[3] Not only did capitalist labor relations precede industrialization,

Ms. Salinger is a member of the Department of History at the University of California, Riverside. She wishes to thank Kenneth Barkin, Carole Shammas, Cynthia Shelton, Charles Wetherell, and especially Steven H. Hahn and Gary B. Nash for their thoughtful criticisms of preliminary drafts. A short version of this article was presented at the December 1980 American Historical Association meeting in Washington, D.C.

[1] For notable exceptions see Alan Dawley, *Class and Community: The Industrial Revolution in Lynn* (Cambridge, Mass., 1976), and Anthony F. C. Wallace, *Rockdale: The Growth of an American Village in the Early Industrial Revolution* . . . (New York, 1978).

[2] See Gary B. Nash, *The Urban Crucible: Social Change, Political Consciousness, and the Origins of the American Revolution* (Cambridge, Mass., 1979); Billy G. Smith, "The Material Lives of Laboring Philadelphians, 1750 to 1800," *William and Mary Quarterly*, 3d Ser., XXXVIII (1981), 163-202; and John K. Alexander, "Poverty, Fear and Continuity: An Analysis of the Poor in Late Eighteenth-Century Philadelphia," in Allen F. Davis and Mark H. Haller, eds., *The Peoples of Philadelphia: A History of Ethnic Groups and Lower Class Life, 1790-1940* (Philadelphia, 1973).

[3] David Montgomery, "The Working Classes of the Pre-Industrial American City, 1780-1830," *Labor History*, IX (1968), 5.

but these new relations were a precondition of America's industrial revolution.

Labor relations changed markedly in Philadelphia during the eighteenth century. The early colonial labor market encouraged the city's master craftsmen to rely heavily on skilled bound workers, both indentured servants and slaves.[4] This coercive, paternalistic labor arrangement was at least outwardly calm.[5] Even if the interests of masters and workers differed, the goals of craft production took precedence.[6] Only three reported exceptions marred an otherwise harmonious labor history in early eighteenth-century Philadelphia. In 1707, journeymen complained about the general "Want of Employment, and Lowness of Wages occasioned by the Number of *Negroes* . . . hired out to work by the Day."[7] Twelve years later, the Common Council received several petitions from the city's carters, draymen, and porters protesting the low wages established by a recent ordinance.[8] Finally, in 1724, master carpenters separated themselves from their journeymen and combined to control labor while giving "every workman the worth of his labor."[9] Except for these minor skirmishes, Philadelphia artisans appeared united.

This outward unanimity began to collapse during the late colonial period. As the paternalistic labor system was replaced by the more consistent use of wage earners, craft organizations appeared. The pre-Revolutionary alliances assumed the form primarily of groups of master craftsmen who desired to protect their economic independence during increasingly hard times. Master mechanics sought legal controls on the

[4] Charles S. Olton, *Artisans for Independence: Philadelphia Mechanics and the American Revolution* (Syracuse, N.Y., 1975), 1; Sharon V. Salinger, "Labor and Indentured Servants in Colonial Philadelphia" (Ph.D. diss., University of California, Los Angeles, 1980), chaps. 1-3; Gary B. Nash, "Slaves and Slaveowners in Colonial Philadelphia," *WMQ*, 3d Ser., XXX (1973), 223-256.

[5] Confusion is always possible when one dares to use such ideologically laden terms as *paternalistic* when referring to labor. However, in this context, E. P. Thompson's definition seems highly appropriate. He defines paternalism as an institution that "enabled the rulers to obtain, directly or indirectly, a control over *the whole life* of the laborer." This contrasts with a labor system in which labor power is purchased ("Patrician Society, Plebeian Culture," *Journal of Social History*, VII [1974], 382).

[6] As Eric Foner explains, even if the earlier craft organizations were exclusively for masters, this did not contradict "the belief that the interests of journeymen, as the masters of tomorrow, were embraced in the 'good of the trade' " (*Tom Paine and Revolutionary America* [New York, 1976], 39).

[7] Quoted in Carl Bridenbaugh, *Cities in the Wilderness: The First Century of Urban Life in America, 1625-1742* (New York, 1938), 201.

[8] Luther A. Harr, "The Status of Labor in Colonial Pennsylvania" (M.A. thesis, Temple University, 1948); June 19, 1719, *Minutes of the Common Council of the City of Philadelphia, 1704-1776* (Philadelphia, 1847).

[9] *The Carpenters' Company of the City and County of Philadelphia. Instituted .1724* (Philadelphia, 1887).

prices of their raw materials as well as on the wages of their journeymen.[10] The Revolution disrupted these activities, however, and the unions were short-lived.[11] When mechanics met after the war, their societies bore little resemblance to their colonial predecessors. Masters continued to belong to exclusive groups, but now journeymen formed their own alliances. Two distinct types of unions emerged, and during the 1780s and 1790s unrest became endemic. For the first time, journeymen struck. Only after considerable debate were compromises reached and calm restored. Thus labor relations in Philadelphia changed perceptibly after the Revolution.

This article explores the changes. Part one traces the transformation of the city's labor system from one in which artisans depended heavily on servants and slaves to one in which employers increasingly used free labor. Although it is impossible to date precisely the point when master craftsmen departed from the consistent use of bound labor or to capture the moment when the institution ceased to be a major component in the city's labor force, the parameters of change emerge from an analysis of artisans' account books, city tax lists, runaway servant advertisements, wage rates, and servant indenture lists.

Part two describes the effects of the shift on labor relations. The organization of the post-Revolutionary artisan's shop differed greatly from that of the colonial mechanic's workplace, primarily due to the widespread use of free wage labor. Thie shift not only had important implications for the organization of production in Philadelphia but also had a profound impact on the lives of workers. As labor became almost exclusively a relationship between employers and wage earners rather than one between owners and bound laborers, the interests and goals of the groups diverged and the bonds eroded. Artisans were no longer organized around the craft, nor did they and their laborers reside under one roof.

I

For most of the colonial period bound laborers were an essential component of the Philadelphia work force. Scores of English, Scots-Irish, and German immigrants exchanged the cost of their passage to the New World for short-term bondage, and city residents eagerly purchased the contracts of these indentured servants. Slaves provided an alternative form of unfree labor, and slavery became firmly entrenched in the labor force. In the mid-eighteenth century, servants and slaves composed almost 40 percent of Philadelphia's workers. Yet by the eve of the Revolution, the city's dependence on bound labor had declined considerably; fewer

---

[10] Nash, *Urban Crucible*, 323.

[11] Olton suggests that these early craft societies failed due to the nature of the colonial marketplace (*Artisans for Independence*, 16). Nash argues more persuasively that these organizations failed because artisans had only limited power to set prices (*Urban Crucible*, 516, n. 59).

TABLE I
PHILADELPHIA ARTISANS AS SERVANT OWNERS

	Number of Servant Purchasers	Percentage of Artisan Owners
1745[a]	150	62.6
1772[b]	197	51.3
1787-1795[c]	813	28.3

[a] List of Servants Bound and Assigned before James Hamilton, Mayor of Philadelphia, 1745-1746, AM 3091.
[b] List of Servants and Apprentices Bound and Assigned before John Gibson, Mayor of Philadelphia, May 1771 to May 1773, AM 3795, Hist. Soc. Pa.
[c] Registry of Redemptioners, 1785-1831, 2 vols., AM 3791, Hist. Soc. Pa.

than one in six workers was unfree. And by 1800 bound labor had all but disappeared, making up less than 2 percent of the work force.[12]

During the mid-eighteenth century, when bound labor reached its peak in the population and accounted for almost half of the city's labor force, Philadelphia artisans relied more heavily on it than did any other occupational group. In 1745 the city's artisans composed 48 percent of the population but purchased almost 66 percent of the indentured servants (Table I).[13] By the end of the colonial period, the importance of unfree

[12] In 1751, servants and slaves accounted for approximately 38.4% of the Philadelphia work force. See Salinger, "Labor and Indentured Servants," 115, Table IV. The following table reveals the percentage of unfree labor in the pre-Revolutionary work force and is taken from Sharon V. Salinger, "Colonial Labor in Transition: The Decline of Indentured Servitude in Late Eighteenth-Century Philadelphia," Labor Hist., XXII (1981), 180, Table III.

Year	Total Servants and Slaves[a]	Approximate Free Labor Force	% Unfree Labor
1767	1083	5334	16.9
1769	1098	5626	16.3
1772	1077	6311	14.6
1773	1069	6367	14.4
1774	1126	6428	14.9
1775	1042	6989	13.0

[a] These figures include only servants and slaves of taxable ages. Slave data are from Nash, "Slaves and Slaveowners," WMQ, 3d Ser., XXX (1973), 237, Table IV. The number of slaves was reduced by 10% to exclude the township of Southwark.

After the Revolution bound labor declined from 6.4% in 1783 to only 1.0% in 1800.

[13] List of Servants and Apprentices Bound and Assigned before James Hamilton, Mayor of Philadelphia, 1745-1746, AM 3091, Historical Society of Pennsylvania, Philadelphia.

labor in Philadelphia diminished, and the artisans' share of the servant market declined. In 1767, bound labor had decreased to less than 17 percent of the work force, and artisans owned servants in roughly the same proportion as their numbers in the population (Table II). On the eve of the Revolution, unfree labor composed only 13 percent of the labor force, and while over 46 percent of the city's taxables were identified as artisans, they accounted for 40 percent of the owners of servants. The decline of artisans as servant owners was more striking after the Revolution. Artisans remained at about 50 percent of the city's taxables during the last quarter of the century, yet they accounted for only 20 percent of the servant owners in 1789 and fewer than 15 percent in 1791. In 1798 only one artisan was taxed for an indentured servant. Clearly, by the end of the century artisans no longer depended on indentured servants.

While artisans possessed fewer servants, merchants were purchasing more. In 1767 about one-fifth of the population worked in the merchant-retailing sector but owned one-third of the city's servants. The relative size of this servant-owning group continued to grow. After the Revolution, this sector owned roughly two-and-one-half times as many servants as its proportion in the population. By 1791, almost three times as many servant owners were from the merchant-retailer group than would be indicated by the city's general occupational distribution.

As artisans owned fewer servants and merchant-retailers owned more, the work roles of indentured servants changed. When the majority of them worked for artisans, they were primarily skilled laborers involved in craft production. Paul Mahoney, for example, arrived in Philadelphia in 1746 and was indentured for four years to shipwrights John Lawton and Simon Sherlock. When Mahoney absconded one year later, the ship-wrights described him in their advertisement as a sawyer—an important participant in the shipyard.[14] In 1745 tanner John Howell was apparently expanding his business, for he purchased the time of James Gardner, also a skilled tanner.[15] They probably worked side by side, performed many of the same tasks, and shared the stench of the tanyard. John Martin was indentured to a brewer; he occasionally worked as a stevedore and loaded "beer on board Captain Annis's ship."[16] As craftsmen relied less and less on bound workers, however, indentured servants were increasingly employed as unskilled or domestic workers. No doubt merchants continued to buy servants such as Antonio Askado "to be taught navigation" or William Reddel to serve as a mariner on board their ships.[17] But more and more often merchants purchased the time of unfree workers for domestic

[14] *Pennsylvania Gazette* (Philadelphia), Sept. 3, 1747.
[15] List of Servants and Apprentices, 1745-1746, AM 3091. A runaway advertisement appeared only one month after Gardner's indenture was recorded and
listed him as a skinner or leather dresser (*Pa. Gaz.*, Nov. 28, 1745).
[16] *Pa. Gaz.*, Oct. 2, 1729.
[17] Registry of Redemptioners, 1785-1831, 2 vols., AM 3791, Hist. Soc. Pa.

TABLE II

	OCCUPATIONS OF PHILADELPHIA SERVANT OWNERS (PERCENTAGES)[a]					OCCUPATIONAL STRUCTURE OF PHILADELPHIA (PERCENTAGES)[b]			
	1767	*1774*	*1789*	*1791*	*1798*	*1756*	*1774*	*1789*	*1798*
Government	.5	1.7	4.7	4.0	—	1.6	1.3	.6	1.2
Professional	3.2	4.8	9.3	6.0	—	4.1	2.7	3.3	5.2
Merchant/Retailers	33.3	37.6	48.2	60.7	—	23.7	13.9	20.9	23.6
Clerical	1.1	1.4	1.0	.7	1	.8	.8	1.9	5.5
Artisans	46.6	40.7	20.7	13.3	—	47.9	46.6	50.7	43.8
Service	12.2	10.5	6.7	8.0	—	7.6	7.2	7.7	5.8
Mariners	3.2	2.9	3.6	2.0	—	9.3	7.8	1.9	3.8
Unskilled	—	.6	—	—	—	5.1	17.6	6.5	4.6
Widows & gents	—	.8	5.7	5.3	—	—	2.2	6.5	6.4

[a] Data for 1767, 1774, 1789, 1791, and 1798 are from a count of the Philadelphia County Tax Assessment Ledgers, City Archives, Philadelphia, Pa.

[b] The occupational breakdown is derived from Allan Kulikoff, "The Progress of Inequality in Revolutionary Boston," *WMQ*, 3d Ser., XXVIII (1971), 375–412. Kulikoff divides the city into eight occupational sectors. Government workers compose one group. Professional workers include doctors, lawyers, apothecaries, ministers, and schoolmasters. Merchant/retailers are all of the people involved in buying and selling—brokers, chandlers, shopkeepers, and the largest group, merchants. Kulikoff identifies this category as tradesmen. However, an 18th-century tradesman was most likely an artisan, not a retailer. I have changed the heading to reveal wholesalers and retailers. Clerical includes workers such as notaries, scribes, and clerks. The artisan class includes seven subheadings: building crafts, cloth trades, food trades, marine crafts, metal crafts, woodworkers, and miscellaneous crafts. Those employed in the service trades include fishermen, mates, pilots, and sailors, and I also include ferrymen, shallopmen, and captains. Unskilled workers include gardeners, chimney sweeps, and laborers. The data for 1756 were provided by Billy G. Smith. The 1774 city breakdown is from Jacob M. Price, "Economic Function and the Growth of American Port Towns in the Eighteenth Century," *Perspectives in American History*, VIII (1974), 126–137. I adapted Price's data to Kulikoff's occupational scheme. The breakdown for 1789 and 1798 is from a computer printout prepared and analyzed by Billy G. Smith. The 1789 material is based on an 80% sample, and the 1798 figures are from a 60% sample. I worked these data into the occupational scheme.

TABLE III
SEXUAL COMPOSITION OF PHILADELPHIA INDENTURED SERVANTS

	Total Servants	Number of Females	Percent Female
1718-1731	193	27	14.0
1745	414	72	17.4
1772	118	36	30.5
1787-1795	841	328	39.0

See Jack and Marion Kaminkow, *A List of Emigrants from England to America, 1718-1759* (Baltimore, 1964), and sources cited in Table I.

service. The demand for domestic labor—free as well as unfree—was rising rapidly after the Revolution, when newspapers commonly carried advertisements encouraging any interested men and women, white or black, to apply for work as gentlemen's servants, waiters, or general household servants.[18]

The shifting sexual composition of Philadelphia's indentured servants provides the most striking evidence for their changing work roles. When the demand for bound labor was high, merchants implored their European agents not to send too many female servants to the colony, because they would not sell. Instead, merchants requested parcels of "stout laboring men and boys."[19] In 1745 only 17 percent of the servants destined for Pennsylvania were women (Table III). The proportion of female servants had increased to 30 percent just before the Revolution, and to almost 40 percent by 1795. Although household servants were not exclusively female, this sizable increase suggests a dramatic rise in the number of domestic laborers.

During the eighteenth century, changes in the labor market increasingly favored free over unfree labor. Early on, artisans purchased the time of indentured servants or bought slaves when wages for free laborers were high and workers were scarce. These unfree workers were a sound investment. At mid-century, employers paid free journeymen annual wages of about £35, assuming that a worker could be found.[20] By contrast, during this same period, the cost of a skilled male servant averaged about £17 for a four-year indenture payable usually in cash but sometimes in flour, with occasional short-term credit available.[21] The price of an adult male slave averaged £40-50.[22] Owners of bound workers were required to

[18] For example, *Pa. Gaz.*, June 25, Aug. 20, Nov. 5, 12, 1783, Apr. 28, June 16, 30, Dec. 22, 1784.

[19] Salinger, "Colonial Labor in Transition," *Labor Hist.*, XXII (1981), 169-172.

[20] Roger W. Moss, "Master Builders: A History of the Colonial Philadelphia Building Trades" (M.A. thesis, University of Delaware, 1972), 144.

[21] Salinger, "Labor and Indentured Servants," 177.

[22] Nash, "Slaves and Slaveowners," *WMQ*, 3d Ser., XXX (1973), 228n. The actual cost of slaves fluctuated greatly because varying rates of import duty were added to the purchase cost.

provide room and board, and had to assume the risk of illness or premature death, but barring unforeseen problems and even including the costs of provisions and bed, servants and slaves were far cheaper than free wage laborers.

By the late colonial period and especially during the years following Independence, bound labor lost its financial attractiveness. During the last three decades of the eighteenth century, its price rose to an average cost of £10 5s. for a year of a servant's time.[23] Meanwhile, wage labor became less expensive. During this same period, wages among the city's least-skilled laborers actually declined, and those of other workers barely kept pace with rising prices.[24] In 1769 the daily wage for laborers averaged a mere three shillings in Philadelphia, and in the early 1770s workers could not earn even that much.[25] Wages continued at these low levels after the Revolution. Cordwainers were paid at a stable rate during the early 1770s, but their real wages declined in 1783 and did not rise substantially until 1792.[26] Similarly, Philadelphia's tailors experienced a decline in real wages after the war, and their income did not rise perceptibly through the more prosperous decade of the 1790s.[27] Journeymen printers suffered an even more protracted slide. Their wages remained stagnant throughout the second half of the eighteenth century.[28]

Two other incentives encouraged the shift to free labor: a decreasing amount of capital for investment in bound labor and a vacillating economy that demanded a more flexible labor system. During the late colonial period economic difficulties plagued Philadelphia, and investment in unfree labor became less feasible for a substantial portion of the artisan community as well as less economical for those still in need of and able to afford additional labor. Gary B. Nash suggests that the economic contraction after the Seven Years' War diminished the capital that city master mechanics had available to invest in labor. More important, however, along with the economic incentives to switch to wage labor, was the more plentiful and reliable supply of free workers as wages decreased and mobility narrowed. Fewer Philadelphians were able to establish themselves as independent artisans but were forced instead to join the ranks of permanent wage laborers, thereby swelling considerably those ranks.[29]

[23] Registry of Redemptioners, Sept. 10, 1795, AM 3791.

[24] Nash, *Urban Crucible*, 323.

[25] *Ibid.*

[26] Smith, "Material Lives of Laboring Philadelphians," *WMQ*, 3d Ser., XXXVIII (1981), 194.

[27] *Ibid.*, 200.

[28] Rollo G. Silver, *The American Printer, 1787-1825* (Charlottesville, Va., 1967), 14.

[29] The split between masters and journeymen artisans was accompanied by economic stratification. Nash traces in elegant detail the impoverishment of a large portion of the Philadelphia population. "Penury was the lot of a growing segment of the community and economic insecurity hovered at the doors of many more."

By the 1760s, free labor best served the needs of Philadelphia's artisans. Economic instability made it far more practical to hire short-term labor than to maintain a bound labor force. Accordingly, since wage rates had fallen below the cost of unfree labor, and the uncertain economy encouraged the use of a flexible labor system at a time when the supply of wage labor was favorable, master craftsmen altered their labor practices and came to rely more consistently on free workers.

This transition brought changes in the relations between artisans and their workers even before indentured labor gave way to wage labor. The first sign was the changing contractual relationship of masters and apprentices. Although, during the colonial period, masters and apprentices signed formal agreements to specify the length of indenture and some of the apprentices' responsibilities, they relied for the most part on unwritten understanding of mutual obligations. In his study of eighteenth-century apprentice contracts, Ian M. G. Quimby found that, as the century progressed, items such as the nature and amount of work expected from the apprentice and arrangements for education and clothing were translated into monetary values and specified in greater detail.[30]

More dramatic, as wage labor rose, were changes in the character of the colonial workplace. In the colonial shop, the master craftsman labored alongside his servants or slaves, perhaps an apprentice or two, and an occasional journeyman. Stability resulted because it took four or five years for a servant to work out his indenture term and for an apprentice to learn the craft. Admittedly, servants like William Atwood, a skilled brass founder, or George Moore, a brushmaker, ran away from their owners.[31] But servants generally, and the servants of artisans in particular, seldom absconded. Newspaper advertisements suggest that at no time during the colonial period did the annual runaway rate of Pennsylvania's servants exceed 10 percent, and the vast majority of these runaways absconded from rural areas.[32] The unfree workers of the city were forced to share the

---

Nash finds many indices to support this strong statement: poor taxes rose, the number and population of institutions for the poor grew after mid-century, forced property sales and imprisonment for debt increased, and societies were formed to administer aid to the swelling ranks of the poor. During this period, master craftsmen continued to maintain economic security and in some cases added to their assets. But by 1772, 17% of Philadelphia's cordwainers were receiving some sort of poor relief, and 13% of the city's clothing workers were on the dole. Even within the better-organized building trades, about one in ten workers received some sort of aid. Nash explains that this growing poverty was caused by a number of factors. After 1760, wages failed to keep pace with costs. To compound the difficulties, unemployment rose especially in 1765-1766, 1767-1770, and 1774-1775 during the periods of nonimportation (*Urban Crucible*, 317-326).

[30] Montgomery, "Working Classes," *Labor Hist.*, IX (1968), 6; Quimby, "Apprenticeship in Colonial Philadelphia" (M.A. thesis, University of Delaware, 1963), 60.

[31] *Pa. Gaz.*, May 1, 15, 1776.

[32] Except for a brief period, 1728-1732, when only 51.7% of the runaway

workbench with their artisan owners, but the relationship was stable and, by eighteenth-century standards, long lasting.

A glimpse at some successful Philadelphia artisans illustrates the shift from bound to free labor and its impact on the work environment. Peter January began his career as a shoemaker at some point in the 1760s. When the tax assessor made his rounds in 1767, January had not yet acquired any taxable property, although both his occupational tax and his possession of two apprentices suggest that he had become a master shoemaker. This assessment placed him in the top 40 percent of the city's taxpayers. By 1775, January's business had expanded sufficiently to enable him to purchase the indentures of six servants. In addition, he hired a female servant, bringing his labor force, excluding his family, to nine—two apprentices, six bound servants, and a hired servant. January's business flourished. Five years later, having reaped the benefits of the wartime economy, he no longer considered himself a shoemaker but reported his occupation to the tax collector as a merchant. Although he had purchased one slave, indentured servants no longer appeared on his list of taxable property. If he used additional workers, he hired them. Thus, while January continued to prosper, he turned from unfree to free labor.[33]

Francis Trumble also invested heavily in bound labor, and his career demonstrates even more forcefully the transformation in labor systems. In 1756 Trumble, described by the tax assessor as a joiner and a resident of Dock Ward, placed in the top 20 percent of the city's taxables.[34] By 1772, he had moved to Southwark and purchased his own home; his personal property had increased to include three slaves and two servants.[35] In that year he purchased the time of yet another servant. Thus, in addition to his family, six bound workers resided in his household.[36] At the outbreak of the Revolution, Trumble advertised the sale of three indentured servants; each had almost four years to serve. At the same time, he sought to replace these bound laborers with wage earners, for he announced that he had

---

servants came from the rural areas of the colony, the vast majority of runaways resided outside the city. In the periods 1735-1743, 1744-1751, 1767, and 1769, 69%, 80.7%, 74.7%, and 71.2% of the runaway servants came from rural areas. Certainly, not all runaways were advertised. But one would expect a higher proportion of advertisements to come from the city rather than outlying counties. Urban residents had more convenient access to the newspapers and were more likely to have the cash to pay for the advertisements. Thus the estimates of the large difference between urban and rural runaways are probably conservative.

[33] This sketch is taken from Salinger, "Labor and Indentured Servants," 191-193.

[34] Trumble's personal property was assessed at £36 (Hannah Benner Roach, comp., "Taxables in the City of Philadelphia, 1756," *Pennsylvania Genealogical Magazine*, XXII [1961], 3-41).

[35] Philadelphia County Provincial Tax, 1772, City Archives, Philadelphia, Pa. I worked from a computer printout prepared by Gary B. Nash and Billy G. Smith.

[36] List of Servants and Apprentices Bound and Assigned before John Gibson, Mayor of Philadelphia, May 1771 to May 1773, AM 3795, Hist. Soc. Pa.

work available for four journeymen skilled in making spinning wheels.[37] Significantly, not only were Trumble's workers hired for wages and boarded apart from his household, but his house and shop were no longer contiguous. Although he still lived on Second Street in Southwark, his cabinet and chair store was located several blocks away on Front Street near Pine. Like January, Trumble had relied heavily on unfree workers during the early years of his career, but he, too, turned to hired labor as his business grew.

The transition to wage labor was no doubt far less orderly than Trumble's or January's shops would indicate. Scattered evidence from artisan shops suggests that the post-Revolutionary workplace, unlike its colonial counterpart, was characterized by high turnover. Most wage earners never stayed at one job long enough to develop a close working or personal relationship with their masters. Those who worked in Joshua Humphrey's shipyards, for example, averaged less than a few months on the job. Between 1794 and 1797, Humphrey employed over thirty-five men. Only John Grimes, Daniel McCalla, Andrew McBride, Isaac Reilly, and Thomas Cooper were counted by the foreman for at least three years of labor and were on the job more than half the working days of the average month. The majority were typified by C. Maier, who worked half a day in October 1797, and the slightly more regular Babbit, who put in an average of seven days a month during 1796.[38] Humphrey's shipyard was hardly conducive to the building of stable relationships.

The transience of journeymen was characteristic of smaller work shops as well. In 1745 Philadelphia builder Isaac Zane inherited apprentices and work contracts from a deceased friend, house carpenter James Davis.[39] But as the apprentices finished their terms, Zane switched to wage laborers and his journeymen rotated through his shop almost by the month.[40] Cabinetmaker David Evans had similar turnover rates. He employed at least seven journeymen from the time he opened his shop in 1774 until the outbreak of the Revolution. Over the course of his career he hired no fewer than seventeen workmen.[41] From 1795 to 1803,

[37] Pa. Gaz., Jan. 3, 1776.

[38] Of these journeymen, only John Grimes was located in a Philadelphia directory. It is possible that he was a master craftsman while the others were journeymen. Grimes was identified as a mast maker ([Thomas Stephens], Stephens's Philadelphia Directory, for 1796 ... [Philadelphia, 1796]).

[39] Moss, "Master Builders," 143.

[40] Ibid. By 1752, Davis's apprentices had worked out their time, and Zane replaced them with journeymen. First hired was Robert Miller, who was to be paid £27 per year plus board, but his employment with Zane lasted only one month, one week, and two days. Next Zane signed on a former Davis apprentice, William Crage, and a year later he hired Silas Engles at 4s. per day "with the journeyman supplying his own food and lodging." Two years later Zane hired an additional five journeymen. One, Jacob Austin, stayed only "3 mo. wanting five days," and a second worker died after a few months.

[41] David Hunter, "David Evans, Cabinet Maker, His Life and Work" (M.A. thesis, University of Delaware, 1954), 14-20.

cabinetmaker Samuel Ashton had five positions, yet forty-nine journeymen worked in his shop, averaging 145 days apiece. The variation in work days ranged from the 5 that David Fryer worked in 1801 to the 452 for which Ashton employed Pennel Beale between 1791 and 1792.[42] The records of these successful Philadelphia masters, regardless of their crafts, depict shops in which journeymen came and went with great frequency.[43]

Such shops resembled immigrant way stations far more than the stable settings associated with the paternalistic system. When artisans became employers, and journeymen supplanted servants and slaves, the time each worker remained in a shop decreased. Slaves were bound for life and servants' terms were fixed at four or five years, but free workers passed through fleetingly, collected their meager wages, gathered up their tools, and moved on in search of the next job. Zane's shop was unusual for the colonial period because he was one of the first to rely so heavily on free workers. By the dawn of the new century, this dizzying movement of workers characterized the artisan workplace. Such turnover not only precluded stable work relationships but helped define labor as a commodity to be hired and fired as consumer demand dictated.

Short employment periods contributed to a high rate of geographic mobility among journeymen. Sparse records prevent reliable conclusions, but the evidence suggests that workers shifted from shop to shop and frequently moved from residence to residence in the city. Journeymen also traveled from city to city, and they moved far and often. In the 1790s, advertisements in the Northampton, Massachusetts, and Charleston, South Carolina, newspapers announced the opening of cabinetmaking shops owned and operated by individuals who had labored as journeymen in Philadelphia.[44] Also suggestive of the movement out of Philadelphia is the futility of trying to locate Philadelphia journeymen among the lists of city residents. They rarely appear on tax assessment rolls or in city directories. Only three of the seventeen journeymen employed by David Evans ever paid an occupational tax in Philadelphia.[45] Although thirty-eight men worked in the Humphrey shipyard from 1794 to 1797, only

[42] Morrison H. Heckscher, "The Organization and Practice of Philadelphia Cabinetmaking Establishments, 1790-1820" (M.A. thesis, University of Delaware, 1964), 20, 24, 25.

[43] Samuel Williamson ran a modest-sized silversmithing business during the first decades of the 19th century. Williamson employed eleven craftsmen in the year 1811 alone, and the number of journeymen in his shop varied from a low of six in 1807 to a high of twelve in 1810 (Ellen Beasley, "Samuel Williamson, Philadelphia Silversmith, 1794-1813" [M.A. thesis, University of Delaware, 1964], 15).

[44] *Hampshire Gazette* (Northampton, Mass.), Apr. 8, 1795; *South-Carolina State-Gazette and Timothy and Mason's Daily Advertiser* (Charleston), Apr. 23, 1796; *Charleston Gazette*, 1796, in Charles F. Montgomery, *American Furniture: The Federal Period in the Henry Francis du Pont Winterthur Museum* (New York, 1966), 16.

[45] Nancy Ann Goyne, "Furniture Craftsmen in Philadelphia, 1760-1780: Their Role in a Mercantile Society" (M.A. thesis, University of Delaware, 1963), 27.

five can be positively located in Philadelphia directories.[46] Of Samuel Ashton's forty-nine employees, twenty-six can be found in the city directories, but most of these men were listed many years after they had worked for Ashton. Perhaps these craftsmen were omitted from the directories until they reached master status.[47] More likely, however, the elusiveness of these workers suggests that they moved often.

The boarding patterns of journeymen corroborate this picture of instability. Of those who labored for Samuel Ashton, slightly more than half (57 percent) lived with him for some period of time. However, only half of these (23 of 44) remained in his home for their full period of employment.[48] The rest boarded with him intermittently. Since workers averaged only 145 days in Ashton's employ, there must have been considerable movement in and out of his house. For example, between 1798 and 1802, Samuel Howell, a journeyman cabinetmaker, put in three stints of work for Ashton, totaling 479 work days. He resided in Ashton's house three times, even though none of his boarding periods coincided exactly with his employment periods and he stayed for only 294 days. Thomas Nap spent two months as a carver and gilder in Ashton's shop but boarded with him for only two days. Upholsterer Samuel Davis worked for Ashton for 707 days and moved into the house four different times.[49] Similarly, during the two-year period in which Thomas Janvier did cabinetwork for Daniel Trotter, he moved in and out twice. Janvier had come to Philadelphia from Maryland just before he began his time with Trotter, and he returned to the Chesapeake region soon after he left Trotter's employ.[50] Boarding was a remnant of paternalism, but, unlike the live-in arrangement typical of the servant or slave, living with one's employer did not necessarily provide security. The brevity of the stay and the constant moving about prevented journeymen from being incorporated into the shop routine, let alone the life of the family. If persistence is a measure of stability, the lives of Philadelphia's peripatetic journeymen were far from stable.

In addition to promoting labor turnover and residential mobility, the transition to free labor resulted in uncertainty of income for workers. No standard form of payment existed during this early period of wage labor. Samuel Ashton paid the typical wage, but it was often completely depleted by boarding and other expenses. He provided his workers with everything from clothes (supplied from his brother's tailoring shop) to tobacco, tools, and occasional loans. Often, at the end of a pay period, very little of the wage was left to claim. The contract drawn between Ashton and Samuel Davis implies that after everything was deducted from his pay, no cash

[46] Joshua Humphrey's Ledger and Roll Book, Hist. Soc. Pa.

[47] Heckscher, "Organization of Philadelphia Cabinetmaking," Appendix A.

[48] Ibid., 27-28.

[49] Ibid., Appendix A.

[50] "Thomas Janvier Account Book," Down Library, Photocopy 186, Henry Francis du Pont Winterthur Museum, Winterthur, Del.

changed hands. Davis's wage was fixed at twenty-five shillings for every six days "Clear of board, washing and lodging . . . to be paid in cash or clothing the balance if any there to be paid." A year later, Ashton rewrote the contract and reduced the weekly wage to twenty shillings.[51] With work and boarding periods short and remuneration small, journeymen gained neither wage security nor marketplace independence with their freedom.

In addition, no standardized wage schedule existed. Philadelphia's master mechanics paid either by the piece or by time, and each rate had its own set of risks and rewards. Employers usually controlled the form of payments, often to the disadvantage and chagrin of workers. During the early 1790s, for example, master carpenters insisted on a flat wage during the long summer days but a piece rate during the winter months when shorter days meant smaller production.[52] Typically, the different payment schedules were used sequentially. Often the youngest or newest journeyman in the shop received a piece rate.[53] More than half of Ashton's journeymen were initially hired on a piece-work basis, but only a third of them remained so.[54] Abel Hammer, for instance, was switched from a piece rate to work "by the month at the same rate he can earn at Bureaus."[55] Ashton apparently paid novice journeymen by the piece until he was satisfied that their productivity warranted time payment. Master silversmiths followed the same practice. Workers in Samuel Williamson's shop began by making inexpensive spoons and tongs on the piece rate, and progressed through more complicated forms like tumblers and cans to such valuable pieces as sugar dishes and teapots.[56] The journeymen who accepted piece-work wages were the newest employees and the least familiar with their surroundings, co-workers, and the moods of the employer; their incomes were the most vulnerable because they were based on the level of their output, tied directly to shop demand, and subject to stoppage due to inclement weather, sickness, or short supply of raw materials.

Employers made remuneration most commonly on the basis of time—

[51] Heckscher, "Organization of Philadelphia Cabinetmaking," 25-26. See also the records of Thomas Janvier who did cabinetwork for Daniel Trotter from July 1795 to Sept. 11, 1796. Janvier boarded with Trotter for only the last three months of the work period ("Janvier Account Book," Down Library, Photocopy 186).

[52] Ian M. G. Quimby, "The Cordwainers Protest: A Crisis in Labor Relations," *Winterthur Portfolio*, III (1967), 90.

[53] For examples of piece rate see Ledger of Thomas Morgan (a watchmaker of Baltimore and Philadelphia), AMB 5865, Hist. Soc. Pa.; Anne Castrodale, "Daniel Trotter, Philadelphia Cabinetmaker" (M.A. thesis, University of Delaware, 1962), 25-30; "Janvier Account Book," Down Library, Photocopy 186; and Joshua Humphrey's Ledger D, 1766-1777, Hist. Soc. Pa.

[54] Humphrey's Ledger D, 27-28.

[55] Heckscher, "Organization of Philadelphia Cabinetmaking," 34.

[56] Beasley, "Samuel Williamson," 17.

by the day, month, or year.[57] Day wages were the most risky for workers because they did not provide the informal compensation afforded by the other methods. When William Crage, a yearly contract worker, lost ten days "by a lame hand," his employer, Isaac Zane, did not dock his pay. However, Zane deducted three shillings a day from the wages of Samuel Burden, a day laborer, when "he was sick 4 days and lost a day at the fair."[58] In one instance, even the year contract did not ensure compensation for time lost due to illness. Samuel Pennock was to earn £25 a year and board, and he was to work "6 days in the week the year out, for his work and he allowing for lost time."[59] Isaac Norris, the wealthy Philadelphia merchant and urban developer, traditionally hired on a monthly basis and included subsistence. In January 1753, Benjamin Morgan agreed "to work for £3-2-5 per month on Norris's diet," and he continued to work for Norris under these terms for a year and a half.[60] At this rate he most likely earned two-and-one-half shillings per day and was guaranteed his wage if he lost work time due to illness or inclement weather. When building began on the Pennsylvania Hospital, Morgan signed on and altered his agreement to a daily rate of three-and-one-half shillings. But with this increased wage he sacrificed the security of his steady earnings. Journeymen did have some control over the style of payment, but by working for the slightly higher day wage they were vulnerable to down time. To protect their incomes when they had to stay off the job, they often had to settle for less money.

Finally, wage labor introduced job insecurity into workers' lives. Master craftsmen could let their workmen go when demand was low, leaving them to find work where they might. Under the paternalistic system, when owners were forced to sell their bound workers during hard times, the burden rested on the master not the servant. Besides the lack of job security, wage labor brought another disadvantage to the worker. If business were slow, the master probably paid the journeyman last. In 1767 a tradesman wrote to a Philadelphia newspaper describing how straitened economic conditions were affecting him. The nature of his trade, he explained, forced him to hire journeymen and three or four apprentices besides using the various members of his family. The tradesman lamented that "towards the latter end of every week, I generally make a tour amongst my employers, to collect a little money to pay my workmen, and answer some other immediate demands, but of late I meet with so little success, that I may as well stay at home . . . I no sooner return home with my small collection, than my journeymen address me for their wages, whome I am obliged to compound with the same proportion as I

[57] See, for example, Account Book of Thomas Savery, Carpenter, Philadelphia, 1782, AM 9116, Hist. Soc. Pa.; Joshua Humphrey's Ledger, 1772-1773, and Roll Book, 1794-1799, *ibid.*; and David Evans Account Book, 3 vols., AM 9115, *ibid.*

[58] Moss, "Master Builders," 144-145.

[59] *Ibid.*, 145.

[60] This entire example is taken from Nash, *Urban Crucible*, 259.

received it."[61] When capital was scarce, labor often went uncompensated. Employers gained flexibility with the advance of the system of wage labor, but employees had to worry about their next jobs and whether and how they would be paid.

II

With the rise of capitalist work relations and the widening divergence of interests between workers and employers, journeymen began to organize.[62] To a degree, masters had anticipated them in the 1760s and 1770s. In 1769 Philadelphia master cordwainers tried to convince the Pennsylvania assembly that the cost of their raw materials should be controlled in order to protect their livelihoods.[63] Also in the 1760s, Philadelphia carpenters, who had been loosely organized since 1724, joined together to attempt a rate fix.[64] And the city's master tailors combined in 1771 to control the wages of their workers as well as "to fix prices at levels that would guarantee a decent subsistence."[65] But these stirrings of craft organization do not demonstrate divisions within the crafts. They were efforts by masters to protect their profits. A possible exception was the Carpenter's Company, a virtual guild established in 1724 by wealthy

[61] *Pennsylvania Chronicle, and Universal Advertiser* (Philadelphia), May 25-June 1, 1767.

[62] A number of recent studies suggest similar disintegration of master-worker relations. Charles G. Steffen finds that alterations in the work forces of wealthier Baltimore artisans resulted in considerable journeyman unrest. In the case of Baltimore, however, the innovation by the employers was to use increasing numbers of "cheap" laborers, primarily apprentices and slaves ("Changes in the Organization of Artisan Production in Baltimore, 1790 to 1820," *WMQ*, 3d Ser., XXXVI [1979], 101-117). For Philadelphia, John K. Alexander notes that workingmen's labor organizations and political action occurred for the first time during the 1790s and that journeymen and employers clashed in economic struggles while each group pursued its own economic goals. This unrest, he claims, was the result of the continuing impoverishment of large numbers of Philadelphians. He is less concerned with the alterations in worker-employer relations or in the changing relations among workers (*Render Them Submissive: Responses to Poverty in Philadelphia, 1760-1800* [Amherst, Mass., 1980], 28). Nash relates the increasing impoverishment of the colonial urban working class to its political activism before the Revolution. His impressive study ends with the Revolution, however; the post-Revolutionary activities of the growing free wage labor class are not treated in *Urban Crucible*. Foner, in his excellent chapter on Philadelphia, also hints at the shift in employer-worker relations and the manifestations of these changes in the politics of the period. But he is not concerned with specific changes in the work environment; rather, he documents the expression of these changes in pre-Revolutionary politics (*Tom Paine*).

[63] Nash, *Urban Crucible*, 324.

[64] According to Nash, the purpose of the rate fix was to secure carpenters a decent living (*ibid.*).

[65] *Ibid.*

builder-architects. Otherwise, journeymen had not as yet identified their own interests as different from or in conflict with those of their masters.

In the post-Revolutionary period, cracks appeared in the once cohesive community of work. The first glimmerings of problems came at the time of the Federal Procession on the Fourth of July, 1788. All over America craftsmen joined to celebrate the new Federal Constitution by assembling demonstrations and floats and parading in shop garb. To all appearances, the Philadelphia procession was an orderly event with apprentices, journeymen, and masters sharing the day. "Every tradesman's boy in the procession seemed to consider himself as a principal in the business," one observer recalled. "Rank for a while forgot all its claims, and Agriculture, Commerce and Manufactures, together with the learned and mechanical Professions, seemed to acknowledge by their harmony and respect for each other, that they were all necessary to each other, and all useful in cultivated society."[66]

A close inspection of these festivities, however, reveals another side to the harmony and good cheer. This same writer hoped that these different groups would "avail themselves of their late sudden and accidental association."[67] All reporters of the event seemed delighted that harmony prevailed, that masters joined with journeymen and apprentices to celebrate this national milestone. The implications are clear: masters did not ordinarily "take counsel with journeymen or other laborers,"[68] and when they did, the gratifying convergence of these groups was cause for comment. After the festivities ended, Philadelphia residents no longer extolled the virtuous alliances between the various ranks of mechanics. On the contrary, the tenuous bonds quickly disintegrated. Journeymen organized their own groups, articulated their union with each other, and gave voice to the increasing conflicts of interest between themselves and the master artisans.

Journeymen printers organized first. In 1786 twenty-six of them banded to protest a reduction in their wages. They resolved not to work for less than six dollars a week and agreed to support any journeyman who was fired because he refused to work for less.[69] The result was Philadelphia's first labor strike, and it brought the first provisions for a union strike benefit in the country.[70] The struggle lasted for some time before

---

[66] "Observations on the Federal Procession on the Fourth of July 1788, in the City of Philadelphia, in a Letter from a Gentleman in This City to His Friend in a Neighboring State," *American Museum*, IV (1788), 76.

[67] *Ibid.*

[68] Olton, *Artisans for Independence*, 10.

[69] Silver, *American Printer*, 14.

[70] *Ibid.*; Richard B. Morris, *Government and Labor in Early America* (New York, 1946), 201. The expression of worker unrest and its relationship to politics is beyond the scope of this article. Foner suggests that many of the political disputes of the 1770s and 1780s arose from differences in the attitudes of merchants and artisans toward private property. It was not just a matter of wealth, because to the

the terms were finally accepted by the shop owners. This labor victory set the scene for other actions to follow.

Labor relations within the carpenters' trade had also changed. In 1791 the city's journeymen walked out in an unsuccessful strike against their masters.[71] *"Self-preservation,"* they cried, "has induced us to enter into *indissoluble union with each other."*[72] The sides were clearly drawn. The workers united to survive after their employers attempted to reduce their wages. What was worse, as we have seen, masters paid by time in the summer and by the piece in the winter, much to their own advantage. The journeymen resented this bitterly. They demanded that the working day be fixed from 6:00 A.M. to 6:00 P.M. regardless of the season. In order to free themselves from their current masters, the journeymen advertised that they would work for other carpenters at 25 percent less. The masters replied with ridicule—"they will work from six to six—how absurd!"—and scoffed that for journeymen to work for less pay implied that they were unqualified to work. In order to erect the buildings of the city, the trade needed responsible workers. Underneath this bravado, however, the masters worried that the actions of journeymen carpenters would ignite Philadelphia's workers in general. "If customs productive of idleness and dissipation be introduced by journeymen carpenters," they bemoaned, "the contagion will soon be communicated to other artificers."[73] The journeymen lost, but, as the masters feared, the "contagion" spread.

Organized journeymen emerged next from the city's cabinet- and chair-making trade. The prelude is unknown, but 1794 marked the beginning of a two-year battle between the craft's employers and employees.[74] On April 13, 1794, on behalf of the Federal Society of Chair Makers, three Philadelphia journeymen deposited a book of prices with the clerk of the district of Pennsylvania.[75] The masters stood firm against the demands and countered by announcing in the city's newspapers that they had positions for thirty or forty journeymen cabinetmakers who might need work.[76] Exactly what occurred over the next year is not clear, but the journeymen submitted a second edition of the Journeymen Cabinet and Chair Makers' price book in 1795. The city's master mechanics replied by distributing a handbill. Its precise contents are unknown, but some of its implications can be gleaned from the journeymen's rebuttal. The masters had apparent-

---

artisan property was "legitimate and natural only if it were the product of visible labor." Within the artisan ranks this disagreement developed because master craftsmen expanded their roles as entrepreneurs and employers while maintaining ties to their roles as laborers and craftsmen (*Tom Paine*, 39).

[71] Quimby, "Cordwainers Protest," *Winterthur Portfolio*, III (1967), 90.

[72] Quoted *ibid.*

[73] Quoted *ibid.*, 90–91.

[74] The following discussion draws heavily from Montgomery, *American Furniture*, 21.

[75] *Pa. Gaz.*, June 4, 1794.

[76] Montgomery, *American Furniture*, 21.

ly attempted to divide the journeymen by proclaiming that they "would not employ any journeymen cabinet-makers as society men, but [only] as individuals." The society of journeymen responded. They refused to work for any employer who propagated this viewpoint or alongside any journeyman "who is, or may be employed by any of the above employers, contrary to our rules."[77]

The battle raged on. In the next newspaper broadside, published on April 7, 1796, the journeymen appealed to the public for support. They argued that rapid increases of prices had left them in dire straits. Even their revised price book had been rejected, and now, they lamented, all that was left was to sever all ties with the masters. Accordingly, they announced the opening of the Ware Room on Market Street for the sale of furniture they had produced. The masters would not yield to their needs, so the journeymen struck and opened their own shop.

At the same time, they appealed to journeymen of different crafts in Philadelphia and in other American cities. Their 1796 statement graciously thanked the other societies in Philadelphia that had assisted them thus far in their struggle, "in particular the respectable and independent Societies of Hatters and Shoemakers whose general assistance has enabled us to answer the most extensive demands of the public."[78] They closed with a call for a general meeting of many mechanical societies—house carpenters, carpenters, tailors, goldsmiths, saddlers, coopers, painters, and printers—"in order to digest a plan of union, for the protection of their mutual independence."[79] Just a month before, the Philadelphia journeymen had called upon their counterparts in New York. The *Argus* published an appeal "from the working Cabinet Makers of Philadelphia, to their mechanical Fellow Citizens," to "repel any attack that has or may be made on societies of this description." The Philadelphians asked their New York brethren to declare themselves ready to assist "in a cause which will determine the independence of so useful a body as the working Citizens of America."[80] Thus, journeyman cabinetmakers did not perceive their struggle as an isolated event; they were learning that workers had to organize to secure their independence.

The details of the strike's conclusion are lost, but the outcome is clear. Both the introduction to the 1796 publication of prices and the rates stipulated in the volume reveal that the workers won their demands. The introduction to the book, signed by three "employers" and three "workmen," recounts the "great deal of trouble [that] has been occasioned between the Employers and Workmen, on account of the many late improvements in our trade."[81] With the publication of the final volume,

[77] *Ibid.*
[78] Quoted *ibid.*, 22.
[79] *Ibid.*
[80] Mar. 4, 1796, quoted *ibid.*
[81] *The Cabinet-Makers' Philadelphia and London Book of Prices* (Philadelphia, 1796), introduction, quoted *ibid.*, 24.

masters and journeymen marked a new phase in labor relations. Both parties agreed to the prices in this third edition and acknowledged that the new book represented the standard, guaranteed price for all work. In addition, the price book included an escalator clause for cost-of-living increases or decreases, so that wages would respond whenever the "necessaries of life, house-rent, &c. shall rise above what they are at present . . . [I]n like manner, the Workmen do agree to reduce the prices in the same proportion as the said necessaries lower."[82] Finally, a comparison with the prices in this edition to those in the rejected 1795 volume reveal that workmen won their price demands, since the variations are very few.[83] Thus ended the Philadelphia cabinetmakers' strike, which revealed essential differences between the visions of workers and employers. The workers' inability to support themselves on what masters were willing to pay led them to fear for their livelihoods; it also demonstrated that their basic independence was at stake. In the course of resolving the differences, the Philadelphia journeymen found allies among other journeymen craftsmen and recognized that journeymen and masters no longer shared the same interests or goals.

The activities of the city's shoemakers brought labor conflict to a crescendo. The early history of Philadelphia shoemakers, like that of other trades, was characterized by a union between ranks and a focus on craft production. During the colonial period, the craft was organized around small shops and custom work. After Independence, the city's cordwainers produced for an expanding export market.[84] The image of the master shoemaker hunched over his workbench and surrounded by a few workers faded away. Now master mechanics were more appropriately referred to as merchant capitalists, while the skilled journeyman became only part of the complex series of costs that affected the margin of the master's profits.

The early associations of shoemakers were reminiscent of other colonial craft organizations. In 1760, master cordwainers formed a fire company to provide members with fire insurance. Unlike the other unions of master mechanics of the period, the shoemakers made no attempt to control prices or wages.[85] The membership of the fire company was neither very stable nor representative of master shoemakers generally, and, like other contemporary unions, the company was short-lived. Although master cordwainers joined together after the Revolution, masters and journeymen continued to appear allied in their support of the craft. The goals of the new masters' group were geared to the regulation of business. The central provisions of their constitution prohibited membership for any master who sold his wares in the public market or resorted to public

[82] *Ibid.*
[83] *Ibid.*, 23.
[84] John R. Commons *et al.*, eds., *History of Labour in the United States*, I (New York, 1918), 6-7.
[85] I have drawn heavily from Quimby, "Cordwainers Protest," *Winterthur Portfolio*, III (1967), 86-92.

advertising of prices. The official life of this group was also brief, but it laid an important foundation for less official coalitions of masters.

In the early skirmishes within the craft, masters and journeymen acted in concert while maintaining separate identities and distinct organizations. In 1791 Peter Gordon and Nathaniel Prentice advertised in the Philadelphia papers that they had inexpensive "new patent boots" for sale.[86] Masters and journeymen both responded to protect the craft from this encroachment. Masters opposed the sale for fear that the market would be flooded with cheap goods and that their profits would suffer. They argued that these boots were hardly new, since similar footwear had been produced for more than thirty years by London cordwainers, as well as by several local craftsmen. Journeymen worried about lower wages. When Gordon and Prentice offered employment to fifty cordwainers, promised to pay them one shilling six pence above any other day wage currently available in the city, and guaranteed constant employment for one year, the journeymen were not persuaded. They accused Gordon and Prentice of misleading them. Although journeymen and masters responded independently to this threat, the interests of both groups converged in defense of the craft.

The unification of craftsmen for the good of the craft was even clearer a few years later. The Philadelphia boot and shoe industry expanded steadily throughout the late eighteenth century, and by the 1790s it included a growing export business. To encourage this trade, journeymen cordwainers consented to make shoes for export at thirty-five cents a pair less than shoes to be sold from the masters' shops. Clearly, journeymen identified the growing market with their own prosperity.

After the early 1790s, however, unity within the craft broke down. Journeymen began to feel squeezed and ever more distant from the master mechanics. In 1799 at least one hundred journeymen walked out on strike to protest an attempted wage reduction. The results were inconclusive. After a time the workers returned to their benches, although, as one disgruntled journeyman described it, "the settlement 'was near splitting the difference.' "[87] A relative calm settled over the shoemakers for the next six years, but in the fall of 1805 journeymen demanded a wage increase. The masters rejected it immediately, and the workers walked out and stayed out for over six weeks. Although they were forced to return to work at the old wage, this episode did not end the dispute.

The finale to the journeymen's actions came with the well-known conspiracy trial of 1806, which manifests in eloquent detail the increasing distance between the masters and journeymen. Tired of the constant sparring over wages, the masters took their cause to court. They accused the workmen of illegal collusion to control the price of labor. Philadelphia's most prestigious legal minds argued the case, and the results were far-reaching. For our purposes this trial provides one of the clearest

[86] *Ibid.*, 88.
[87] Quoted *ibid.*, 92.

statements about the breakdown of cohesion within the craft and the tremendous change in labor relations.

The masters and prosecutors argued that journeymen were hampering a lucrative trade. Strikes for higher wages caused business to suffer. "This is a large, encreasing, manufacturing city . . . and great sums are annually received in returns. It is then proper to support this manufacture. Will you permit men to destroy it, who have no permanent stake in the city; men who can pack up their all in a knapsack, or carry them in their pockets to New-York or Baltimore?"[88] Journeymen, the prosecution declared, were "mere birds of passage" who had only the slightest concern for the craft. Facing the prosecutors were the defendant journeymen whose lawyers declared that "labour constitutes the real wealth of the country."[89] Caesar Rodney, a defense attorney, claimed that the battle between masters and journeymen was analogous to the clash between the rich and the poor, the powerful and the destitute. The city's master cordwainers lived in large mansions and amassed great fortunes more quickly than any other profession in the city.[90] Their employees barely earned enough to subsist. While the prosecution claimed that the health of the craft was best served by the masters, Rodney argued that "the labourer [was] surely worthy of sufficient honor to enable him to live comfortably."[91] Rodney closed his defense with the observation that if radical inequalities were fair and right, and if "the labourer and journeyman enjoy too great a part of liberty," the jury should convict.[92] On the other hand, if the intent of the new Federal Constitution was to secure equality of rights without distinctions of class, the verdict should be acquittal. The jury found the journeymen guilty of "a combination to raise wages."[93]

The transition to a system of capitalist labor relations in Philadelphia was long and uneven. As the ranks of free workers swelled and unfree labor became less attractive, labor relations altered significantly. The conflicts of the 1790s were not sudden eruptions but manifestations of fundamental difficulties. Not only did the wage labor system introduce a new set of tensions within the shop, but these tensions were exacerbated by the economic constraints that limited vertical mobility. Though exploitation underlay the master-servant relationship, overt conflict was rare. As the traditional labor system broke down, masters and journeymen struggled against each other to hammer out a new system of relations. The high turnover rate in the late eighteenth-century shop may have reflected both

[88] Quoted *ibid.*, 95-96.
[89] Quoted *ibid.*, 96.
[90] *Ibid.*
[91] Leonard Bernstein, "The Working People of Philadelphia from Colonial Times to the General Strike of 1835," *Pennsylvania Magazine of History and Biography*, LXXIV (1950), 326.
[92] *Ibid.*
[93] *Ibid.*

the exploitation of labor by employers and the workers' efforts to obtain more personal independence and greater resources. In either case, the social constellation of Philadelphia had changed in an unmistakable direction long before the rise of industrialization in America.

◆◆

The Modernization of Mayo Greenleaf Patch: Land, Family, and Marginality in New England, 1766–1818

PAUL E. JOHNSON

THIS is the story of Mayo Greenleaf Patch and Abigail McIntire Patch, ordinary people who helped write a decisive chapter in American history: they were among the first New Englanders to abandon farming and take up factory labor. They did so because rural society had no room for them, and their history is a tale of progressive exclusion from an agrarian world governed by family, kinship, and inherited land. Mayo Greenleaf Patch was the youngest son of a man who owned a small farm. He inherited nothing, and in his early and middle years he improvised a living at the edges of the family economy. He grew up with an uncle and brother, combined farming and shoemaking with dependence on his wife's family in the 1790s, recruited a half-sister into schemes against his in-laws' property, then lived briefly off an inheritance from a distant relative. Finally, having used up his exploitable kin connections, he left the countryside and moved to a mill town in which his wife and children could support the family.

That is how Greenleaf[1] and Abigail Patch made the journey from farm to factory. But they experienced their troubles most intimately as members of a family; their story can be comprehended only as family history. Greenleaf Patch was a failed patriarch. His marriage to Abigail McIntire began with an early pregnancy, was punctuated by indebtedness and fre-

---

[1] The adult Mayo Greenleaf Patch went by the name of Greenleaf, the name by which his granddaughter knew him and the name that he gave the census-taker in 1790.

quent moves, and ended in alcoholism and a divorce. Along the way, a previously submissive Abigail began making decisions for the family, decisions that were shaped by an economic situation in which she but not her husband found work and by her midlife conversion into a Baptist church.

The outlines of the Patch family history are familiar, for recent scholarship on New England in the century following 1750 centers on its principle themes: the crisis of the rural social order in the eighteenth century, the beginnings of commercial and industrial society in the nineteenth, and transformations in personal and family life that occurred in transit between the two.[2] The Patches shared even the particulars of their story—disinheritance, premarital pregnancy, alcoholism, transiency, indebtedness, divorce, female religious conversion—with many of their neighbors. In short, Abigail and Greenleaf Patch lived at the center of a decisive social transformation and experienced many of its defining events.

The story of the Patches throws light on the process whereby farmers in post-Revolutionary New England became "available" for work outside of agriculture. That light, however, is dim and oblique, and we must confront two qualifications at the outset. First, the Patches were obscure people who left incomplete traces of their lives. Neither Greenleaf nor Abigail kept a diary or wrote an autobiography, their names never appeared in newspapers, and no one bothered to save their mail. Apart from one rambling and inaccurate family reminiscence,

[2] A sampling would include Kenneth A. Lockridge, "Land, Population, and the Evolution of New England Society," *Past and Present* 39 (April 1968): 62–80; Philip I. Greven, Jr., *Four Generations: Population, Land, and Family in Colonial Andover, Massachusetts* (Ithaca: Cornell University Press, 1970); Robert A. Gross, *The Minutemen and Their World* (New York: Hill and Wang, 1976); Christopher M. Jedrey, *The World of John Cleaveland: Family and Community in Eighteenth-Century New England* (New York: W. W. Norton & Co., 1979); Alan Dawley, *Class and Community: The Industrial Revolution in Lynn* (Cambridge: Harvard University Press, 1976); Paul S. Faler, *Mechanics and Manufacturers in the Early Industrial Revolution: Lynn, Massachusetts, 1780–1860* (Albany: State University of New York Press, 1981); Thomas Dublin, *Women at Work: The Transformation of Work and Community in Lowell, Massachusetts, 1826–1860* (New York: Columbia University Press, 1979). Some recent work on women and the family is cited below, note 31.

their story must be reconstructed from distant, impersonal, and fragmentary sources: wills and deeds, church records, tax lists, censuses, the minutes of town governments, court records, and histories of the towns in which they lived and the shoe and textile industries in which they worked. The results are not perfect. The broad outlines of the story can be drawn with confidence, and a few episodes emerge in fine-grained detail. But some crucial points must rest on controlled inference, others on inferences that are a little less controlled, still others on outright guesswork. Scholars who demand certainty should stay away from people like Greenleaf and Abigail Patch. But historians of ordinary individuals must learn to work with the evidence that they left behind. In part, this essay is an exploration of the possibilities and limits of such evidence.[3]

A second qualification concerns the problem of generalizing from a single case. It must be stated strongly that the Patches were not typical. No one really is. The Patches, moreover, can claim uniqueness, for they were the parents of Sam Patch, a millworker who earned national notoriety in the 1820s as a professional daredevil. The younger Patch's life was an elaborate exercise in self-destruction, and we might question the normality of the household in which he grew up.[4] Indeed the history of the Patch family is shot through with brutality and eccentricity and with a consistent sadness that is all its own. The Patches were not typical but marginal, and that is the point: it was persons who were marginal to rural society who sought jobs outside of agriculture. The number of such per-

[3] Historians' attempts to reconstruct the attitudes and actions of ordinary persons have thus far relied upon diaries and biographies, which are exceedingly rare. For the most admirable of these attempts, see Alfred F. Young, "George Robert Twelves Hewes (1742–1840): A Boston Shoemaker and the Memory of the American Revolution," *William and Mary Quarterly* 38 (October 1981): 561–623, and the biography of the immigrant Wilson Benson in Michael B. Katz's, *The People of Hamilton, Canada West: Family and Class in a Mid-Nineteenth-Century City* (Cambridge: Harvard University Press, 1975), pp. 94–111. The Patch family history, in contrast, has been excavated from materials that are available for most Massachusetts families. In large part, their story is a test of what can and cannot be done with that evidence.

[4] See Richard M. Dorson, "Sam Patch, Jumping Hero," *New York Folklore Quarterly* 1 (August 1945): 133–51.

sons grew rapidly in post-Revolutionary New England. This is the story of two of them.

I

New England men of Greenleaf Patch's generation grew up confronting two uncomfortable facts. The first was the immense value that their culture placed on the ownership of land. Freehold tenure conferred not only economic security but personal and moral independence, the ability to support and govern a family, political rights, and the respect of one's neighbors and oneself. New Englanders trusted the man who owned land; they feared and despised the man who did not. The second fact was that in the late eighteenth century increasing numbers of men owned no land. Greenleaf Patch was among them.

Like nearly everyone else in Revolutionary Massachusetts, Patch was descended from yeoman stock. His family had come to Salem in 1636, and they operated a farm in nearby Wenham for more than a century. The Patches were church members and farm owners, and their men served regularly in the militia and in town offices. Greenleaf's father, grandfather, and great-grandfather all served terms as selectmen of Wenham; his great-grandfather was that community's representative to the Massachusetts General Court; his older brother was a militiaman who fought on the first day of the American Revolution.[5]

The Patches commanded respect among their neighbors, but in the eighteenth century their future was uncertain. Like thousands of New England families, they owned small farms and had many children; by mid-century it was clear that young Patch men would not inherit the material standards enjoyed by their fathers. The farm on which Greenleaf Patch was born was an artifact of that problem. His father, Timothy Patch, Jr.,

5 William Richard Cutter, comp., *Genealogical and Personal Memoirs Relating to the Families of Boston and Eastern Massachusetts*, 4 vols. (New York: Lewis Historical Publishing Company, 1908), 1:219; *Wenham Town Records, 1730–1775* (Wenham, 1940), 1:141, 184, 2:22, 3:23, 115, 177; *Massachusetts Soldiers and Sailors of the Revolutionary War*, 17 vols. (Boston: Wright and Potter, 1903), 11:1000.

157

had inherited a house, an eighteen-acre farm, and eleven acres of outlying meadow and woodland upon his own father's death in 1751. Next door, Timothy's younger brother Samuel farmed the remaining nine acres of what had been their father's homestead. The father had known that neither Timothy nor Samuel could make a farm of what he had, and he required that they share resources. His will granted Timothy access to a shop and cider mill that lay on Samuel's land and drew the boundary between the two farms through the only barn on the property. It was the end of the line: further subdivision would make both farms unworkable.[6]

Timothy Patch's situation was precarious, and he made it worse by overextending himself, both as a landholder and as a father. Timothy was forty-three years old when he inherited his farm, and he was busy buying pieces of woodland, upland, and meadow all over Wenham. Evidently he speculated in marginal land and/or shifted from farming to livestock raising. He financed his schemes on credit, and he bought on a fairly large scale. By the early 1760s Timothy Patch held title to 114 acres, nearly all of it in small plots of poor land.

Timothy Patch may have engaged in speculation in order to provide for an impossibly large number of heirs. Timothy was the father of ten children when he inherited his farm. In succeeding years he was widowed, remarried, and sired two more daughters and a son. In all, he fathered ten children who survived to adulthood. The youngest was a son born in 1766. Timothy named him Mayo Greenleaf.[7]

Greenleaf Patch's life began badly: his father went bankrupt in the year of his birth. Timothy had transferred the house and farm to his two oldest sons in the early 1760s, possi-

[6] Will of Timothy Patch, Administration no. 20744, Essex County Court of Probate, Salem. Adult brothers shared houses and/or outbuildings with increasing frequency in the late eighteenth century. See Jedrey, *The World of John Cleaveland*, pp. 73–74, and John J. Waters, "Patrimony, Succession, and Social Stability: Guilford, Connecticut, in the Eighteenth Century," *Perspectives in American History* 10 (1976): 150.

[7] *Vital Records of Wenham, Mass., to the End of the Year 1849* (Salem: Essex Institute, 1904), pp. 65–66, 152, 214.

bly to keep the property out of the hands of creditors. Then, in 1766, the creditors began making trouble. In September Timothy relinquished twenty acres of his outlying land to satisfy a debt. By March 1767, having lost five court cases and sold all of his remaining land to pay debts and court costs, he was preparing to leave Wenham.[8] Timothy's first two sons stayed on, but both left Wenham before their deaths, and none of the other children established households in the community. After a century as substantial farmers and local leaders, the Patch family abandoned their hometown.

Greenleaf Patch was taken from his home village as an infant, and his family's wanderings after that can be traced only through his father's appearances in court. By 1770 the family had moved a few miles north and west to Andover, where Timothy was sued by yet another creditor. Nine years later Timothy Patch was in Danvers, where he went to court seven times in three years. The court cases suggest that the family experienced drastic ups and downs. Some cases involved substantial amounts of money, but in the last, Timothy was accused of stealing firewood. He then left Danvers and moved to Nottingham West, New Hampshire. There Timothy seems to have recouped his fortunes once again, for in 1782 he was a gambler-investor in an American Revolutionary privateer.[9]

That is all we know about the Patch family during the childhood of Mayo Greenleaf Patch. About the childhood itself we know nothing. Doubtless Greenleaf shared his parents' frequent moves and their bouts of good and bad luck, and from his subsequent behavior we might conclude that he inherited

[8] Records of the Essex County Court of Common Pleas, sessions of July 1764 (Dodge vs. Patch), September 1766 (Cabot vs. Patch, Jones vs. Patch, Dodge vs. Patch, Brown vs. Patch), and March 1767 (Brimblecom vs. Patch), Essex Institute, Salem; Essex County Registry of Deeds, books 123:103, 120:35, 124:64, 116:96, 123:105, 123:44, 121:132, 120:278, Essex County Courthouse, Salem. Timothy's land transfers to his sons are recorded in books 120:274 and 115:210.

[9] Essex Court of Common Pleas, July 1770 (Andrews vs. Patch), July 1779 (Gerilds vs. Patch), July 1782 (Prince vs. Patch, Putnam vs. Patch, Wilkins vs. Patch, Patch vs. Sawyer, Endicott vs. Patch), September 1782 (Prince vs. Patch), and December 1783 (Upton vs. Patch); "American Revolutionary Naval Service," *New Hampshire Genealogical Record* 5 (1908): 169.

his father's penchant for economic adventurism. He may also have spent parts of his childhood and youth in other households. Since he later named his own children after relatives in Wenham, he probably lived there in the families of his brother and uncle. We know also that during his youth he learned how to make shoes, and since his first independent appearance in the record came when he was twenty-one, we might guess that he served a formal, live-in apprenticeship. Even these points, however, rest on speculation. Only this is certain: Greenleaf Patch was the tenth and youngest child of a family that broke and scattered in the year of his birth, and he entered adulthood alone and without visible resources.

In 1787 Mayo Greenleaf Patch appeared in the Second (North) Parish of Reading, Massachusetts—fifteen miles due north of Boston. He was twenty-one years old and unmarried, and he owned almost nothing.[10] He had no relatives in Reading; indeed no one named Patch had ever lived in that town. In a world where property was inherited and where kinfolk were essential social and economic assets, young Greenleaf Patch inherited nothing and lived alone.

Greenleaf's prospects in 1787 were not promising. But he soon took steps to improve them. In July 1788 he married Abigail McIntire in Reading. He was twenty-two years old; she was seventeen and pregnant.[11] This early marriage is most easily explained as an unfortunate accident. But from the viewpoint of Greenleaf Patch it was not unfortunate at all, for it put him into a family that possessed resources that his own family had lost. For the next twelve years, Patch's livelihood and ambitions would center on the McIntires and their land.

The McIntires were Scots, descendants of highlanders who had been exiled to Maine after the Battle of Dunbar. Some had

10 Reading Town Rate Books, 1773–93, Assessor's Office, Reading Town Hall. In 1787 Patch paid a poll tax and the tax on a very small amount of personal property.

11 *Vital Records of the Town of Reading, Massachusetts, to the Year 1850* (Boston: New England Historic Genealogical Society, 1912), pp. 413, 178. Abigail gave birth seven and one-half months after the wedding.

walked south, and Philip McIntire was among those who
pioneered the North Parish in the 1650s. By the 1780s Mc-
Intire households were scattered throughout the parish. Archelaus McIntire, Abigail's father, headed the most prosperous of those households. Archelaus had been the eldest son of
a man who died without a will, and he inherited the family
farm intact. He added to the farm and by 1791 owned ninety-
seven acres in Reading and patches of meadowland in two
neighboring townships, a flock of seventeen sheep as well as
cattle and oxen and other animals, and personal property that
indicates comfort and material decency if not wealth. Of 122
taxable estates in the North Parish in 1792, Archelaus Mc-
Intire's ranked twenty-third.[12]

In 1788 Archelaus McIntire learned that his youngest
daughter was pregnant and would marry Mayo Greenleaf
Patch. No doubt he was angry, but he had seen such things
before. One in three Massachusetts women of Abigail's generation was pregnant on her wedding day, a statistic to which
the McIntires had contributed amply. Archelaus himself had
been born three months after his parents' marriage in 1729.
One of his older daughters had conceived a child at the age of
fourteen, and his only son would marry a pregnant lover in
1795.[13]

Faced with yet another early pregnancy, Archelaus McIntire
determined to make the best of a bad situation. In the winter
of 1789/90, he built a shoemaker's shop and a small house for
Greenleaf Patch and granted him use of the land on which
they sat.[14] At a stroke, Patch was endowed with family connections and economic independence.

---

12 Cutter, *Genealogical and Personal Memoirs*, 3:1155; Lilley Eaton, comp.,
Genealogical History of the Town of Reading, Mass. (Boston: A. Mudge & Son,
1874), p. 96; Will of Joseph McIntire, Administration no. 14496, Middlesex
County Court of Probate, Middlesex County Courthouse, Cambridge; Inventory
of the Estate of Archelaus McIntire, Middlesex Probate 14481; Reading Rate
Books, 1792.

13 Daniel Scott Smith and Michael Hindus, "Premarital Pregnancy in Amer-
ica, 1640–1971: An Overview and Interpretation," *Journal of Interdisciplinary
History* 5 (Spring 1975): 537–70. McIntire marriages and births are recorded in
Vital Records of Reading.

14 Record of debt in Middlesex Probate 14481.

Greenleaf Patch took his place among the farmer-shoemakers of northeastern Massachusetts in 1790. The region had been exporting shoes since before the Revolution, for it possessed the prerequisites of cottage industry in abundance: it was poor and overcrowded and had access to markets through Boston and the port towns of Essex County. With the Revolution and the protection of footwear under the first national tariffs, with the expansion of the maritime economy of which the shoe trade was a part, and with the continuing growth of rural poverty, thousands of farm families turned to the making of shoes in the 1790s.

Their workshops were not entrepreneurial ventures. Neither, if we listen to the complaints of merchants and skilled artisans about "slop work" coming out of the countryside, were they likely sources of craft traditions or occupational pride. The trade was simply the means by which farmers on small plots of worn-out land maintained their independence.[15]

The journal of Isaac Weston, a Reading shoemaker during the 1790s, suggests something of the cottage shoemaker's way of life. Weston was first and last a farmer. He spent his time worrying about the weather, working his farm, repairing his house and outbuildings, and trading farm labor with his neighbors and relatives. His tasks accomplished, he went hunting with his brothers-in-law, took frequent fishing trips to the coast at Lynn, and made an endless round of social calls in the neighborhood. The little shop at the back of Weston's house

[15] The organization of rural industry in northeastern Massachusetts is traced in Dawley, Class and Community; Faler, Mechanics and Manufacturers; and John Philip Hall, "The Gentle Craft: A Narrative of Yankee Shoe Makers" (Ph.D. diss., Columbia University, 1953). For valuable discussions of the role of cottage industry in the transition into manufacturing, see E. L. Jones, "Agricultural Origins of Industry," Past and Present 40 (July 1968): 58–71; Franklin F. Mendels, "Proto-industrialization: The First Phase of the Industrialization Process," Journal of Economic History 32 (March 1972): 241–61; Joan Thirsk, "Industries in the Countryside," in Essays in the Economic and Social History of Tudor and Stuart England, ed. F. J. Fisher (Cambridge, England: Cambridge University Press, 1961), pp. 70–88; and Hans Medick, "The Proto-industrial family economy: the structural function of household and family during the transition from peasant society to industrial capitalism," Social History 3 (October 1976): 291–315.

supplemented his earnings, and he spent extended periods of time in it only during the winter months. With his bags of finished shoes, he made regular trips to Boston, often in company with other Reading shoemakers. The larger merchants did not yet dominate the trade in country shoes, and Weston and his neighbors went from buyer to buyer bargaining as a group and came home with enough money to purchase leather, pay debts and taxes, and subsist for another year as farmers.[16]

Isaac Weston's workshop enabled him to survive as an independent proprietor. At the same time, it fostered relations of neighborly cooperation with other men. He was the head of a self-supporting household and an equal participant in neighborhood affairs; in eighteenth-century Massachusetts, those criteria constituted the definition of manhood. Mayo Greenleaf Patch received that status as a wedding present.

Greenleaf and Abigail occupied the new house and shop early in 1790, and their tax listings over the next few years reveal a rise from poverty to self-sufficiency with perhaps a little extra. In 1790, for the first time, Greenleaf paid the tax on a small piece of land. Two years later he ranked fifty-sixth among the 122 taxpayers in the North Parish.[17] Patch was not getting rich, but he enjoyed a secure place in the economy of his neighborhood. That alone was a remarkable achievement for a young stranger who had come to town with almost nothing.

With marriage and proprietorship came authority over a complex and growing household. Few rural shoemakers in the 1790s worked alone; they hired outside help and put their wives and children to work binding shoes. Isaac Weston brought in apprentices and journeymen, and Greenleaf Patch seems to have done the same. In 1790 the Patch family included Greenleaf and Abigail and their infant daughter, along with a boy under the age of sixteen and an unidentified adult

[16] John Philip Hall, "The Journal of James Weston, Cordwainer, of Reading, Massachusetts, 1788–1793," *Essex Institute Historical Collections* 92 (April 1956): 188–202.

[17] Reading Rate Books, 1790–92.

male. In 1792 Patch paid the tax on two polls, suggesting that again the household included an adult male dependent. It seems clear that Greenleaf hired outsiders and (assuming Abigail helped) regularly headed a family work team that numbered at least four persons.[18]

During the same years, Patch won the respect of the McIntires and their neighbors. When Archelaus McIntire died in 1791, his will named Patch executor of the estate. Greenleaf spent considerable effort, including two successful appearances in court, ordering his father-in-law's affairs. In 1794 he witnessed a land transaction involving his brother-in-law, again indicating that he was a trusted member of the McIntire family. That trust was shared by the neighbors. In 1793 the town built a schoolhouse near the Patch home, and in 1794 and 1795 the parish paid Greenleaf Patch for boarding the schoolmistress and for escorting her home at the end of the term.[19] Those were duties that could only have gone to a trusted neighbor who ran an orderly house.

II

Greenleaf Patch's marriage to Abigail McIntire rescued him from the shiftless and uncertain life that had been dealt to him at birth. In 1787 he was a propertyless wanderer. By the early 1790s, he was the head of a growing family, a useful member of the McIntire clan, and a familiar and trusted neighbor. Greenleaf Patch had found a home. But his gains were precarious, for they rested on the use of land that belonged not to him but to his father-in-law. When Archelaus died, the title to the McIntire properties fell to his nineteen-year-old son, Archelaus, Jr. Young Archelaus was bound out to a guardian, and

[18] U.S. Bureau of the Census, *Heads of Families at the First Census Taken in 1790: Massachusetts* (Washington, D.C.: U.S. Bureau of the Census, 1908), p. 152; Reading Rate Books, 1792.

[19] Middlesex Probate 14481; Middlesex Court of Common Pleas, September 1792, November 1793; Middlesex County Registry of Deeds, book 165:60, Middlesex County Courthouse, Cambridge; Eaton, *Genealogical History of Reading*, p. 246; Town of Reading: Orders and Receipts, 1773–93, entries for 15 September 1794 and 25 August 1795, Assessor's Office, Reading Town Hall.

Patch, as executor of the estate, began to prey openly on the resources of Abigail's family. In succeeding years bad luck and moral failings would cost him everything that he had gained.

With Archelaus McIntire dead and his son living with a guardian, the household that the senior Archelaus had headed shrank to two women: his widow and his daughter Deborah. The widow described herself as an invalid, and there may have been something wrong with Deborah as well. In the will that he wrote in 1791, Archelaus ordered that his heir take care of Deborah. His son would repeat that order ten years later, when Deborah, still unmarried and still living at home, was thirty-five years old. Shortly after the death of Archelaus McIntire (and shortly before Patch was to inventory the estate), the widow complained to authorities that "considerable of my household goods & furniture have been given to my children" and begged that she be spared "whatever household furniture that may be left which is but a bare sufficiency to keep household." At that time two of her four daughters were dead, a third lived with her, and her only son was under the care of a guardian. The "children" could have been none other than Greenleaf and Abigail Patch, whose personal property taxes mysteriously doubled between 1791 and 1792. Greenleaf Patch had entered a house occupied by helpless women and walked off with the furniture.[20]

Patch followed this with a second and more treacherous assault on the McIntires and their resources. In November 1793 Archelaus McIntire, Jr. came of age and assumed control of the estate. Greenleaf's use of McIntire land no longer rested on his relationship with his father-in-law or his role as executor but on the whim of Archelaus, Jr. Patch took steps that would tie him closely to young Archelaus and his land. Those steps involved a woman named Nancy Barker, who moved into

20 References to Deborah McIntire in the Will of Archelaus McIntire (Middlesex Probate 14481) and the Will of Archelaus McIntire, Jr. (Middlesex Probate 14483). Abigail McIntire, who was sixty-two years old at her husband's death, calls herself an invalid in a letter in his probate file. Her complaint is found there as well.

Reading sometime in 1795. Mrs. Barker had been widowed twice, the second time, apparently, by a Haverhill shoemaker who left her with his tools and scraps of leather, a few valueless sticks of furniture, and two small children. Nancy Barker, it turns out, was the half-sister of Mayo Greenleaf Patch.[21]

In November 1795 Nancy Barker married Archelaus McIntire, Jr. She was thirty-one years old. He had turned twenty-three the previous day, and his marriage was not a matter of choice: Nancy was four months pregnant. Archelaus and Nancy were an unlikely couple, and we must ask how the match came about. Archelaus had grown up with three older sisters and no brothers; his attraction and/or vulnerability to a woman nearly nine years his senior is not altogether mysterious. Nancy, of course, had sensible reasons for being attracted to Archelaus. She was a destitute widow with two children, and he was young, unmarried, and the owner of substantial property. Finally, Greenleaf Patch, who was the only known link between the two, had a vital interest in creating ties between his family and his in-law's land. It would be plausible—indeed it seems inescapable—to conclude that Nancy Barker, in collusion with her half-brother, had seduced young Archelaus McIntire and forced a marriage.[22]

[21] Nancy Barker is identified as the daughter of Patch's mother in the Will of Job Davis, Essex Probate 7278. She had lived in Wenham and had married into some branch of the Patch family; at her marriage to Jonathan Barker of Haverhill in 1786 she was "Mrs. Nancy Patch." Jonathan and Nancy Barker then show up in Haverhill as the parents of children whose names are the same as those later brought to Reading by Nancy. A shoemaker named Jonathan Barker died intestate and nearly propertyless in Haverhill in 1791. The "apparently" in the text is due to the fact that the probate file identifies that man's widow as "Anna," but vital records do not list a marriage or children for a Jonathan and Anna Barker; neither do they list the death of another Jonathan Barker. My guess is that a probate clerk simply misrecorded the name of Jonathan Barker's widow. *Vital Records of Haverhill, Massachusetts, to the End of the Year 1849*, 2 vols. (Topsfield, Mass.: Topsfield Historical Society, 1910), 2:247, 1:29; Essex Probate 1682.

[22] *Vital Records of Reading*, p. 387. This line of reasoning raises suspicions about the earlier marriage of Abigail and M. G. Patch. With one in three brides pregnant, we may safely assume that the vast majority of people experienced sexual relations before marriage. As many of them faced propertyless futures, it would be surprising if some did not realize that they could acquire property or the use of it through seduction and the hurried marriages that often resulted.

Of course, that may be nothing more than perverse speculation. Nancy and Archelaus may simply have fallen in love,
started a baby, and married. Whatever role Greenleaf Patch
played in the affair may have added to his esteem among the
McIntires and in the community. That line of reasoning,
however, must confront an unhappy fact: in 1795 the neighbors and the McIntires began to dislike Mayo Greenleaf Patch.

The first sign of trouble came in the fall of 1795, when town
officials stepped into a boundary dispute between Patch and
Deacon John Swain. Massachusetts towns encouraged neighbors to settle arguments among themselves. In all three parishes of Reading in the 1790s, only three disagreements over
boundaries came before the town government, and one of
those was settled informally. Thus Greenleaf Patch was party
to half of Reading's mediated boundary disputes in the 1790s.
The list of conflicts grew: after 1795 the schoolmistress was
moved out of the Patch household; in 1797 Patch complained
that he had been overtaxed (another rare occurrence), demanded a reassessment, and was reimbursed. Then he started
going to court. In 1798 Greenleaf Patch sued Thomas Tuttle
for nonpayment of a debt and was awarded nearly $100 when
Tuttle failed to appear. A few months earlier, Patch had been
hauled into court by William Herrick, a carpenter who
claimed that Patch owed him $480. Patch denied the charge
and hired a lawyer; the court found in his favor, but Herrick
appealed the case, and a higher court awarded him $100.52.
Six years later, Patch's lawyer was still trying to collect his
fee.[23]

There is also a question about land. In the dispute with

M. G. Patch's successes in the early 1790s may not have been a case of bad luck
turning into good; his gains may have been results of his first assault on Abigail
and her family.

[23] Records of the Town of Reading, Massachusetts, 1639–1812, 3 vols., Land
Grants and Boundaries (typescript), 3:148, Lucius Beebe Memorial Library,
Wakefield, Mass. Reading Orders and Receipts, 14 November 1797. Middlesex
Court of Common Pleas, December 1798 (Patch vs. Tuttle); Essex Court of Com-
mon Pleas, October 1798 (Herrick vs. Patch) and March 1804 (Reid vs. Patch).
See n. 28: the lawyer sold his note to another creditor.

John Swain, the description of Patch's farm matches none of the properties described in McIntire deeds. We know that Patch no longer occupied McIntire land in 1798, and town records identified him as the "tenant" of his disputed farm in 1795. Perhaps as early as 1795, Patch had been evicted from McIntire land.[24]

Finally, there is clear evidence that the authorities had stopped trusting Mayo Greenleaf Patch. Nancy Barker McIntire died in 1798 at the age of thirty-four. Archelaus remarried a year later, then died suddenly in 1801. His estate—two houses and the ninety-seven-acre farm, sixty acres of upland and meadow in Reading, and fifteen acres in the neighboring town of Lynnfield—was willed to his two children by Nancy Barker. Archelaus's second wife sold her right of dower and left town, and the property fell to girls who were four and five years of age. Their guardian would have use of the land for many years. By this time Greenleaf and Abigail Patch had moved away, but surely authorities knew their whereabouts and that they were the orphans' closest living relatives. Yet the officials passed them over and appointed a farmer from Reading as legal guardian.[25] The court, doubtless with the advice of the neighbors, had decided against placing Greenleaf Patch in a position of trust. For Patch it was a costly decision. It finally cut him off from property that he had occupied and plotted against for many years.

Each of these facts and inferences says little by itself, but together they form an unmistakable pattern: from the date of his marriage through the mid-1790s, Greenleaf Patch accumulated resources and participated in the collective life of Abigail's family and neighborhood; from 1795 onward he entered the record only when he was fighting the neighbors or being shunned by the family. The promising family man of the

[24] Records of the Town of Reading, Land Grants and Boundaries, 3:148; Federal Direct Tax of 1798: Massachusetts, New England Historic Genealogical Society, Boston, lists Archelaus, Jr. as the owner of two houses, neither of which was occupied by M. G. Patch.

[25] Middlesex Probate 14483.

early 1790s was a contentious and morally bankrupt outcast by 1798.

Late in 1799 or early in 1800 Greenleaf and Abigail and their four children left Reading and resettled in Danvers, a community of farmer-shoemakers on the outskirts of Salem. We cannot know why they selected that town, but their best connection with the place came through Abigail. Danvers was her mother's birthplace, and she had an aunt and uncle, five first cousins, and innumerable distant relatives in the town. Indeed Abigail's father had owned land in Danvers. In 1785 Archelaus McIntire, Sr. had seized seven acres from John Felton, one of his in-laws, in payment of a debt. Archelaus, Jr. sold the land back to the Feltons in 1794 but did not record the transaction until 1799.[26] Perhaps he made an arrangement whereby the Patches had use of the land. (Doubtless Archelaus was glad to be rid of Greenleaf Patch, but he may have felt some responsibility for his sister.)

Danvers was another shoemaking town, and the Patches probably rented a farm and made shoes. In 1800 the household included Greenleaf and Abigail, their children, and no one else, suggesting that they were no longer able to hire help. But this, like everything else about the family's career in Danvers, rests on inference. We know only that they were in Danvers and that they stayed three years.

Late in 1802 Greenleaf Patch received a final reprieve, again through family channels. His half-brother Job Davis (his mother's son by her first marriage) died in the fishing port of Marblehead and left Patch one-fifth of his estate. The full property included a butcher's shop at the edge of town, an unfinished new house, and what was described as a "mansion house" that needed repairs. The property, however, was mort-

26 Population Schedules of the Second Census of the United States, 1810: Essex County, Massachusetts, lists a "Mahue" G. Patch in Danvers. The sexes and ages of members of his household fit the family of Greenleaf Patch perfectly. In 1803 the recorder of a deed involving Patch spelled his name "Mayhew" (Essex Deeds, book 172:252). The McIntire-Felton transactions are recorded in Essex Deeds, books 153:95, 165:60.

gaged to the merchants William and Benjamin T. Reid. The survivors of Job Davis inherited the mortgage along with the estate.[27]

The other heirs sold to the Reids without a struggle, but Greenleaf Patch, whether from demented ambition or lack of alternatives, moved his family to Marblehead early in 1803. He finished the new house and moved into it, reopened the butcher's shop, and ran up debts. Some of the debts were old. Patch owed Ebenezer Goodale of Danvers $54. He also owed Porter Sawyer of Reading $92 and paid a part of it by laboring at 75¢ a day. Then there were debts incurred in Marblehead: $70 to the widow Sarah Dolebar; a few dollars for building materials and furnishings bought from the Reids; $50 to a farmer named Benjamin Burnham; $33 to Zachariah King of Danvers; $35 to Joseph Holt of Reading; another $35 to Caleb Totman of Hampshire County. Finally, there was the original mortgage held by the Reids.

Patch's renewed dreams of independence collapsed under the weight of his debts. In March 1803 a creditor repossessed the property up to a value of $150, and a few weeks before Christmas of the same year the sheriff seized the new house. In the following spring, Patch missed a mortgage payment, and the Reids took him to court, seized the remaining property, and sold it at auction. Still, Patch retained the right to reclaim the property by paying his debts. The story ends early in 1805, when the Reids bought Greenleaf Patch's right of redemption for $60. Patch had struggled with the Marblehead property for two years, and all had come to nothing.[28]

With this final failure, the Patches exhausted the family connections on which they had subsisted since their marriage.

[27] Will of Job Davis, Essex Probate 7278.

[28] The debts, court cases, and land transfers can be followed in Essex Court of Common Pleas, March 1803 (Sawyer vs. Patch), June 1803 (Burnham vs. Patch), December 1803 (Dolebar vs. Patch), March 1804 (Goodale vs. Patch, King vs. Patch, Sawyer vs. Patch, Reids vs. Patch), June 1804 (Totman vs. Patch, Shelden vs. Patch, Holt vs. Patch); Essex Deeds, books 172:252, 175:35, 175:186. The last entry—the purchase of Patch's right of redemption—is dated 2 February 1805.

The long stay in Reading and the moves to Danvers and Marblehead were all determined by the availability of relatives and their resources. In 1807 the Patches resettled in Pawtucket, Rhode Island, the pioneer textile milling town in the United States. It was the climactic event in their history: it marked their passage out of the family economy and into the labor market.

When the family arrived in Pawtucket early in 1807, they found four textile mills surrounding the waterfall at the center of town. The mills were small and limited to the spinning of yarn, and much of the work was done by outworkers. Children picked and cleaned raw cotton in their homes, then sent it to the mills to be carded by other children. The cotton next went to the spinning rooms, where, with the help of water-driven machinery, a few skilled men, and still more children, it was turned into yarn. Millers put the yarn out to women, many of them widows with children, who wove it into cloth. There was thus plenty of work for Abigail and her older children, and it was they who supported the family in Pawtucket. Samuel, the second son, spent his childhood in the mills, and his sisters probably did the same. It is likely that Abigail worked as a weaver; certainly the wool produced on her father's farm suggests that she knew something about that trade.[29]

That leaves only the father. Pawtucket was booming in 1807, and if Greenleaf Patch were willing and physically able, he could have found work. We know, however, that he did not work in that town. He drank, he stole the money earned by his wife and children, and he threatened them frequently with violence. Then, in 1812, he abandoned them. Abigail waited six years and divorced him in 1818. She recounted Greenleaf's drinking and his threats and his refusal to work, then revealed what for her was the determining blow: Greenleaf Patch had

[29] An excellent recent study of Pawtucket is Gary B. Kulik's "The Beginnings of the Industrial Revolution in America: Pawtucket, Rhode Island, 1672–1829 (Ph.D. diss., Brown University, 1980). On Sam Patch's career in the mills, see Dorson, "Sam Patch."

drifted back to Massachusetts and had been caught passing counterfeit money. In February 1817 he entered the Massachusetts State Prison at Charlestown. He was released the following August. Patch was fifty-two years old, and that is the last we hear of him.[30]

III

In a society that located virtue and respectability in the yeoman freeholder, Mayo Greenleaf Patch never owned land. We have seen some public consequences of that fact: his lifelong inability to attain material independence, the troubled relations with in-laws, neighbors, creditors, and legal authorities that resulted when he tried, and the personal and moral disintegration that accompanied unending economic distress.

Now we turn to private troubles, and here the story centers on Abigail McIntire Patch. Recent studies of late eighteenth- and early nineteenth-century family life have documented a decline of patriarchal authority, the creation of a separate and female-dominated domestic sphere, an increase in female religiosity, and, bound up with all three, the elevation of women's status and power within the home.[31] Most of these studies center on middle- and upper-class women, and we are left to wonder whether the conclusions can be extended to women further down the social scale. In the case of Abigail Patch, they can: her story begins with patriarchy and ends with female control. In grotesque miniature, the history of the Patches is a story of the feminization of family life.

    [30] "Petition of Abigail Patch for Divorce," Records of the Supreme Court of Providence County, September 1818–March 1819, Box 39, Providence College Archives. Convict Registers for the Charlestown State Prison, Massachusetts State Archives, Boston. A check of probate and vital records in all of the counties in which Patch or members of his family had lived turned up nothing concerning his later life.
    [31] See, esp., Nancy F. Cott, *The Bonds of Womanhood: Women's Sphere in New England, 1780–1835* (New Haven: Yale University Press, 1977); Mary Beth Norton, *Liberty's Daughters: The Revolutionary Experience of American Women, 1750–1800* (Boston: Little, Brown, 1980); Richard D. Shiels, "The Feminization of American Congregationalism, 1730–1835," *American Quarterly* 33 (Spring 1981): 46–62.

Abigail grew up in a family that, judged from available evidence, was ruled by her father. Archelaus McIntire owned a respected family name and a farm that he had inherited from his father and that he would pass on to his son; he was the steward of the family's past and future as well as its present provider. As a McIntire, he conferred status on every member of his household. As a voter he spoke for the family in town affairs; as a father and church member he led the family in daily prayers; and as a proprietor he made decisions about the allocation of family resources, handled relations with outsiders, and performed much of the heavy work.

Archelaus McIntire's wife and daughters were subordinate members of his household. He had married Abigail Felton of Danvers and had brought her to a town where she lived apart from her own family but surrounded by his; her status in Reading derived from her husband's family and not from her own. On the farm, she and her daughters spent long days cooking and cleaning, gardening, tending and milking cows, making cloth and clothing, and caring for the younger children—work that took place in and near the house and not on the farm. That work was essential, but New England men assumed that it would be done and attached no special importance to it.[32] The notion of a separate and cherished domestic sphere was slow to catch on in the countryside, and if we may judge from the spending patterns of the McIntires, it played no role in their house. Archelaus McIntire spent his money on implements of work and male sociability—horses, wagons, well-made cider barrels, a rifle—and not on the china, tea sets, and feather beds that were appearing in the towns and among the rural well-to-do. The McIntires owned a solid table and a Bible and a few other books, and there was a clock and a set of glassware as well. But the most valuable item of furniture in the house was Archelaus's desk. Insofar as the McIntires found time for quiet evenings at home, they probably spent them

32 On women's work within eighteenth-century farm households, see Norton, *Liberty's Daughters*, pp. 9–20.

173

listening to the father read his Bible (the mother was illiterate) or keeping quiet while he figured his accounts.[33]

As the fourth and youngest of Archelaus McIntire's daughters, Abigail had doubtless traded work and quiet subordination for security, for the status that went with being a female McIntire, perhaps even for peace and affection in the home. As she set up housekeeping with Mayo Greenleaf Patch, she doubtless did not expect things to change. Years later Abigail recalled that in taking a husband she wanted not a partner but "a friend and protector." For her part, Abigail spoke of her "duties" and claimed to have been an "attentive and affectionate wife."[34] It was the arrangement that she had learned as a child: husbands protected their wives and supported them, wives worked and were attentive to their husbands' needs and wishes. All available evidence suggests that those rules governed the Patch household during the years in Reading.

Abigail and Greenleaf Patch maintained neither the way of life nor the standard of living necessary for the creation of a private sphere in which Abigail could have exercised independent authority. The house was small and there was little money, and the household regularly included persons from outside the immediate family. Greenleaf's apprentices and journeymen were in and out of the house constantly. For two summers the Patches boarded the schoolmistress, and Nancy Barker may have stayed with Greenleaf and Abigail before her marriage. With these persons present in hit-and-miss records, we may assume that outsiders were normal members of the Patch household.

At work, rural shoemakers maintained a rigid division of labor based on sex and age, and Greenleaf's authority was per-

[33] The estate inventory of Archelaus McIntire and a letter that his widow signed with a mark are in Middlesex Probate 14481.

[34] "Petition of Abigail Patch for Divorce." For indications that this language was in fact Abigail's, see Nancy F. Cott's, "Eighteenth-Century Family and Social Life Revealed in Massachusetts Divorce Records," *Journal of Social History* 10 (Fall 1976): 32–33, which demonstrates widely varying marital expectations among divorcing persons.

vasive.[35] Abigail's kitchen, if indeed it was a separate room, was a busy place. There she bound shoes as a semiskilled and subordinate member of her husband's work team, cared for the children (she gave birth five times between 1789 and 1799), did the cooking, cleaning, and laundry for a large household, and stared across the table at apprentices and journeymen who symbolized her own drudgery and her husband's authority at the same time. As Abigail Patch endured her hectic and exhausting days, she may have dreamed of wallpapered parlors and privacy and quiet nights by the fire with her husband. But she must have known that such things were for others and not for her. They had played little role in her father's house, and they were totally absent from her own.

Greenleaf Patch seems to have taken his authority as head of the household seriously. Available evidence suggests that he consistently made family decisions—not just the economic choices that were indisputably his to make but decisions that shaped the texture and meaning of life within the family.

Take the naming of the children. Greenleaf Patch was separated from his own family and dependent on McIntire resources, so when children came along we would expect him and Abigail to have honored McIntire relatives. That is not what happened. The first Patch child was a daughter born in 1789. The baby was named Molly, after a daughter of Greenleaf's brother Isaac. A son came two years later, and the Patches named him Greenleaf. Another daughter, born in 1794, was given the name Nabby, after another of Isaac Patch's daughters. A second son, born in 1798, was named for Greenleaf's uncle Samuel. That child died, and a son born the following year (the daredevil Sam Patch) received the same name. The last child was born in 1803 and was named for Greenleaf's brother Isaac. None of the six children was named for Abigail or a member of her family. Instead, all of the names came from

[35] The division of labor among cottage shoemakers is described in Dawley, *Class and Community*, pp. 16–20; Faler, *Mechanics and Manufacturers*, pp. 48–51; and Elizabeth Abbott, *Women in Industry: A Study in American Economic History* (New York: D. Appleton, 1910), pp. 148–52.

the little world in Wenham—uncle Samuel's nine-acre farm, the shared barn and outbuildings, and the eighteen acres operated by brother Isaac—in which Greenleaf Patch presumably spent much of his childhood.[36]

Religion is a second and more important sphere in which Patch seems to have made choices for the family. Abigail McIntire had grown up in a religious household. Her father had joined the North Parish Congregational Church a few days after the birth of his first child in 1762. Her mother had followed two months later, and the couple baptized each of their five children. The children in their turn became churchgoers. Abigail's sisters Mary and Mehitable joined churches, and her brother Archelaus, Jr. expressed a strong interest in religion as well. Among Abigail's parents and siblings, only the questionable Deborah left no religious traces.[37]

Religious traditions in the Patch family were not as strong. Greenleaf's father and his first wife joined the Congregational church at Wenham during the sixth year of their marriage in 1736, but the family's ties to religion weakened after that. Timothy Patch, Jr. did not baptize any of his thirteen children, either the ten presented him by his first wife or the three born to Thomasine Greenleaf Davis, the nonchurchgoing widow whom he married in 1759. None of Greenleaf's brothers or sisters became full members of the church, and only his oldest brother Andrew owned the covenant, thus placing his family under the government of the church.[38]

[36] Names traced in *Vital Records of Reading* and *Vital Records of Wenham.* The naming of children was taken seriously in eighteenth-century Massachusetts. See Daniel Scott Smith, "Population, Family and Society in Hingham, Massachusetts, 1635–1880" (Ph.D. diss., University of California, 1973), pp. 340–48, and Jedrey, *The World of John Cleaveland,* pp. 78–79, 84–85.

[37] Information on Archelaus, his wife, and his daughter Mehitable is from the records of the United Church of Christ, North Reading (Mrs. Arthur Diaz, Church Clerk, personal correspondence). Abigail's sister Mary lived in Salem but baptized a child in Reading, suggesting that she was a member of a church in Salem. Archelaus, Jr. died at the age of twenty-nine without having joined a church, but his will is laden with religious language.

[38] Here and in the following paragraph, information is from the records of the First Church in Wenham, Congregational (Carol T. Rawston, Church Clerk, personal correspondence); baptisms from *Vital Records of Wenham.*

Among the Wenham Patches, however, there remained pockets of religiosity, and they centered, perhaps significantly, in the homes of Greenleaf's brother Isaac and his uncle Samuel. Uncle Samuel was a communicant of the church, and although Isaac had no formal religious ties, he married a woman who owned the covenant. The churchgoing tradition that Greenleaf Patch carried into marriage was thus ambiguous, but it almost certainly was weaker than that carried by his wife. And from his actions as an adult, we may assume that Greenleaf was not a man who would have been drawn to the religious life.

As Greenleaf and Abigail married and had children, the question of religion could not have been overlooked. The family lived near the church in which Abigail had been baptized and in which her family and her old friends spent Sunday mornings. As the wife of Greenleaf Patch, Abigail had three options: she could lead her husband into church; she could, as many women did, join the church without her husband and take the children with her; finally, she could break with the church and spend Sundays with an irreligious husband. The first two choices would assert Abigail's authority and independent rights within the family. The third would be a capitulation, and it would have painful results. It would cut her off from the religious community in which she had been born, and it would remove her young family from religious influence.

The Patches lived in Reading for twelve years and had five children there. Neither Greenleaf nor Abigail joined the church, and none of the babies was baptized. We cannot retrieve the actions and feelings that produced these facts, but this much is certain: in the crucial area of religious practice, the Patch family bore the stamp of Greenleaf Patch and not of Abigail McIntire. When Greenleaf and Abigail named a baby or chose whether to join a church or baptize a child, the decisions extended his family's history and not hers.

Abigail Patch accepted her husband's dominance in family affairs throughout the years in Reading, years in which he played, however ineptly and dishonestly, his role as "friend and protector." With his final separation from the rural economy and his humiliating failure in Marblehead, he abdicated that role. In Marblehead Abigail began to impose her will upon domestic decisions. The result, within a few years, would be a full-scale female takeover of the family.

In 1803 the sixth—and, perhaps significantly, the last—Patch child was baptized at Second Congregational Church in Marblehead. And in 1807, shortly after the move to Rhode Island, Abigail and her oldest daughter joined the First Baptist Church in Pawtucket.[39] At that date Abigail was thirty-seven years old, had been married nineteen years, and had five living children. Her daughter Molly was eighteen years old and unmarried. Neither followed the customs of the McIntire or Patch families, where women who joined churches did so within a few years after marriage. Abigail and Molly Patch presented themselves for baptism in 1807 not because they had reached predictable points in their life cycles but because they had experienced religion and had decided to join a church.

At the same time (here was feminization with a vengeance) Abigail's daughters dropped their given names and evolved new ones drawn from their mother's and not their father's side of the family. The oldest daughter joined the church not as Molly but as Polly Patch. Two years later the same woman married under the name Mary Patch.[40] Abigail's oldest sister, who had died in the year that Abigail married Greenleaf, had

[39] *Vital Records of Marblehead, Massachusetts, to the End of the Year 1849*, 3 vols. (Salem: Essex Institute, 1903), 1:380. The baptisms of Abigail and her oldest daughter were recorded in "Baptist Church of Christ, August 1805 to November 1837," 4 April 1807 and 12 April 1807, First Baptist Church, Pawtucket.

[40] "Baptist Church of Christ," 4 April 1807: "Mrs. Patch and her daughter Polly came forward...." A Mary Patch married Goodman (Edward) Jones in 1809 (James N. Arnold, *Vital Record of Rhode Island: North Providence* [Providence: Narragansett Historical Publishing Company, 1892], p. 32), and the *Manual of the First Baptist Church, Pawtucket, R.I., Organized August, 1805* (Providence: Providence Press Company, 1884), p. 28, identifies Mary Patch Jones as having joined the church in April 1807. The Molly Patch born in 1789, the Polly Patch of 1807, and the Mary Patch of 1809 were definitely the same woman.

been named Mary. The second Patch daughter, Nabby, joined the Baptist church in 1811. At that time she was calling herself Abby Patch. By 1829 she was known as Abigail.[41] The daughters of Abigail Patch, it seems, were affiliating with their mother and severing symbolic ties with their father. It should be noted that the father remained in the house while they did so.

In Pawtucket Abigail built a new family life that centered on her church and her female relatives. That life constituted a rejection not only of male dominance but of men. For five years Abigail worked and took the children to church while her husband drank, stole her money, and issued sullen threats. He ran off in 1812, and by 1820 Abigail, now officially head of the household, had rented a house and was taking in boarders.[42] Over the next few years the Patch sons left home: Samuel for New Jersey, Isaac for the Northwest, Greenleaf for parts unknown. Abigail's younger daughter married and moved to Pittsburgh. Among the Patch children only Mary (Molly, Polly) stayed in Pawtucket. In 1825 Mary was caught committing adultery. Her husband left town, and Mary began calling herself a widow. Abigail closed the boardinghouse and moved into a little house on Main Street with Mary and her children sometime before 1830.[43] She and her daughter and granddaughters would live in that house for the next quarter-century.

The neighbors remembered Abigail Patch as a quiet, steady little woman who attended the Baptist church. She did so with

[41] "Baptist Church of Christ," 12 November 1810, 31 January 1811, and 1 January 1829.

[42] Population Schedules of the Fourth Census of the United States, 1820: Providence County, Rhode Island. The household was headed by Abigail Patch and included six men between the ages of sixteen and twenty-six, all employed in manufacturing.

[43] "Baptist Church of Christ," 2 June 1825. The "widow" Mary Jones headed a household in Pawtucket in 1830 (her husband did not, and there is no record of his death or of a divorce), and a local historian states that Abigail moved into the Main Street house "about 1830." See Robert Grieve, *An Illustrated History of Pawtucket, Central Falls, and Vicinity* (Pawtucket: Gazette and Chronicle, 1897), p. 66.

all of the Patch women. Mary had joined with her in 1807, and each of Mary's daughters followed in their turn: Mary and Sarah Anne in 1829, Emily in 1841.[44] First Baptist was a grim and overwhelmingly female Calvinist church, subsidized and governed by the owners of Pawtucket's mills. The Articles of Faith insisted that most of humankind was hopelessly damned, that God chose only a few for eternal life and had in fact chosen them before the beginning of time, "and that in the flesh dwelleth no good thing."[45] It was not a cheerful message. But it struck home among the Patch women.

Apart from the church, the women spent their time in the house on Main Street. Abigail bought the house in 1842—the first land that the Patches owned—and her granddaughters Mary and Emily taught school in the front room for many years.[46] The household was self-supporting, and its membership was made up of women whose relations with men were either troubled or nonexistent. Abigail never remarried. We cannot know what preceded and surrounded the instance of adultery and the breakup of Mary's marriage, but she too remained single for the rest of her life. Sarah Anne Jones, one of the granddaughters, was thirty-six years old and unmarried when called before a church committee in 1853. Although she married a man named Kelley during the investigation, she was excommunicated "because she has given this church reason to believe she is licentious."[47] Sarah Anne's sisters, the schoolteachers Mary and Emily, were spinsters all their lives. The lives of Abigail Patch and her daughter Mary Jones had been blighted by bad relations with men; the women whom they raised either avoided men or got into trouble when they did not. Abigail Patch lived on Main Street with the other

[44] *Manual of the First Baptist Church,* p. 29.

[45] Articles of Faith in "Baptist Church of Christ." On mill-owner control, see Gary Kulik, "Pawtucket Village and the Strike of 1824: The Origins of Class Conflict in Rhode Island," *Radical History Review* 17 (Spring 1978): 15–17.

[46] North Providence Deeds and Mortgages, book 8:523, Pawtucket City Hall. On the schoolhouse, see Grieve, *Illustrated History of Pawtucket,* p. 101.

[47] "Church Meetings, January 1838 to January 1874," 29 August 1853, 30 August 1853, and 23 September 1853, First Baptist Church, Pawtucket.

women until 1854, when she died at the age of eighty-four.[48]

We know little of what went on in that house. The women lived quietly, and former pupils remembered Abigail's granddaughters with affection. But beyond the schoolroom, in rooms inhabited only by the Patch women, there was a cloistered world. Within that world, Abigail and her daughter Mary reconstructed not only themselves but the history of their family.

Pawtucket celebrated its Cotton Centennial in 1890, and a Providence newspaperman decided to write about the millworker-hero Sam Patch. He asked Emily Jones, one of Abigail's aged granddaughters, about the Patch family history.[49] Emily had been born after 1810, and her knowledge of the family's past was limited to what she had picked up from her mother and grandmother. Her response to the reporter demonstrated the selective amnesia with which any family remembers its history, but in this case the fabrications were sadly revealing.

Miss Jones told the newspaperman that her oldest uncle, Greenleaf Patch, Jr., had gone off to Salem and become a lawyer. That is demonstrably untrue. No one named Greenleaf Patch has ever been licensed to practice law in Massachusetts.[50] About her uncle Sam Patch, Emily said: in the 1820s he operated a spinning mill of his own north of Pawtucket, but failed when his partner ran off with the funds; it was only then that he moved to New Jersey and became a daredevil. That too is a fabrication. What we know about Sam Patch is that he was an alcoholic with powerful suicidal drives, and that he succeeded in killing himself at the age of thirty.[51] Miss Jones re-

[48] Grieve, *Illustrated History of Pawtucket*, p. 101.

[49] Undated clipping from the *Providence Journal*, Sam Patch Scrapbook, Rochester Public Library, Rochester, New York.

[50] Phone conversation with John Powers, Office of the Clerk of the Supreme Judicial Court for Suffolk County, Mass.

[51] A search of deeds and tax lists from the town in which Sam Patch supposedly operated a mill and a search of bankruptcy petitions in the years 1820–25 turned up nothing. Smithfield Tax Lists, Central Falls City Hall; bankruptcy petitions, Records of the Supreme Court of Providence County.

membered that her youngest uncle, Isaac, moved to Illinois and became a farmer. That was true: in 1850 Isaac Patch was farming and raising a family near Peoria.[52] It seems that Abigail Patch and Mary Patch Jones idealized the first two Patch sons by giving them successes and/or ambitions that they did not have. The third son was born in 1803 and grew up in a household dominated by Abigail and not by her dissipated husband; he became a family man. By inventing a similar ordinariness for the older sons, Abigail may have erased some of the history created by Mayo Greenleaf Patch.

Emily's memory of her grandfather provokes similar suspicions. We know that Greenleaf Patch lived in Pawtucket until 1812. But Miss Jones remembered that her grandfather had been a farmer in Massachusetts, and that he died before Abigail brought her family to Rhode Island. Greenleaf Patch, it seems, was absent from Abigail's house in more ways than one.

[52] Ronald Vern Jackson and Gary Ronald Teeples, eds., *Illinois: 1850 Census Index* (Bountiful, Utah: Accelerated Indexing Systems, 1976), p. 398.

Paul E. Johnson, *Associate Professor of History and American Studies at Yale University, is the author of* A Shopkeeper's Millennium: Society and Revivals in Rochester, New York, 1815–1837. *He is presently writing two books: a biography of Sam Patch, and a study of perceptions of Niagara Falls in the years 1790–1835.*

Notes on Disestablishment in Massachusetts, 1780-1833

John D. Cushing*

THE Congregational churches of Massachusetts during the provincial and early constitutional periods formed a system that has often been described as an "establishment." The description, while not altogether accurate, is useful if it is understood that the individual congregations were largely autonomous, that they were bound to no articles of faith by the civil authority, and that they formed a system only insofar as they shared a common historical espousal of Calvinist theology and a general acceptance of the Cambridge Platform. Of those factors only the Platform, adopted by the old Bay Colony and continuing a shadowy common-law existence under the provincial government, carried any weight in law, but since it was concerned solely with matters of church polity it was only a subsidiary factor in the maintenance of an establishment.[1]

Whatever official status the churches enjoyed was derived primarily from an act of 1692 requiring every town in the province to support by taxation of the inhabitants a system of public worship and an "able, learned orthodox minister" who, after his election at a special town meeting, became "the minister of such town."[2] Town and church did not thereby become identical bodies, but they formed what Chief Justice Lemuel Shaw many years later described as a "dual corporation."[3] The church was the ecclesiastical arm of the town, clothed

* Mr. Cushing is Librarian of the Massachusetts Historical Society, Boston. He wishes to thank Bernard Bailyn, Lyman H. Butterfield, William G. McLoughlin, and Hiller B. Zobel for reading and commenting upon this article.

[1] The Platform was adopted by the Bay Colony in 1651. N. B. Shurtleff, ed., *Records of the Governor and Company of the Massachusetts Bay in New England* (Boston, 1853-1854), II, 285; III, 70-72, 177, 204, 235, 240; IV, Pt. 1, 22, 54-57. On the common-law status of the Platform after 1692, see Edward Buck, *Ecclesiastical Law* (Boston, 1866), 77.

[2] *Acts and Resolves, Public and Private, of the Province of the Massachusetts Bay* ... (Boston, 1869-1922), I, 62-63.

[3] Luther S. Cushing, *Reports of Cases Argued and Determined in the Supreme Judicial Court of Massachusetts* (Boston, 1854-1860), VIII, 187. For Shaw's distinction between a church and a religious society, see *ibid.*, IX, 187.

with its corporate status. Until or unless a second church was formed within its geographical limits, the town managed the affairs of the parish, municipal officers were required by law to perform certain parochial duties, and few town meetings bothered to distinguish between municipal and parochial business. The result was a series of territorial parishes whose boundaries were coterminous with those of the towns, and every inhabitant of every town was also a resident of his parish, although not necessarily a member of the church.

Practical implementation of the act proved impossible from the outset and four months later it was amended by a new statute specifying that application of its terms should be restricted to new towns where no church had yet been gathered. In order to meet the needs of many older communities whose inhabitants clustered in unincorporated villages, one often remote from another, and where more than one religious society was desirable, the new law vested the responsibility for electing new ministers in the respective churches rather than in the towns. The election, however, was to be ratified by those church members who were also qualified voters of the town, and a minister so elected was to be supported by all the inhabitants residing "within such town, or part of a town, or place limited by law for upholding the publick worship of God."[4] The act securely bound every church to a corresponding legally defined geographical area. The General Court implemented its terms as occasion required by creating precincts, parishes, or special districts, each endowed with the essential powers of a municipal corporation but limited in purpose to maintaining a system of public worship.[5] Thus the terms of the act of 1692, originally

---

[4] *Acts and Resolves*, I, 103. Disputes between towns and churches were to be settled by ecclesiastical councils; when a second parish was created the remainder of the town became the first and principal parish; some towns like Rehoboth maintained two religious societies without a formal division into parishes; two parishes were sometimes merged; one parish might be created from segments of contiguous towns; or a population cluster might be attached to a parish in a neighboring town for the convenience of the worshippers. See, in order given, *ibid.*, I, 216; II, 99; XVI, 248, 338; IX, 666; III, 617. Boston churches were exceptions to the above. Towns failing to comply with the laws were subject to legal action. See *ibid.*, I, 587; II, 26-27, 275; IX, 667; Dudly Atkins Tyng, *Reports of Cases Argued and Determined in The Supreme Judicial Court of the Commonwealth of Massachusetts* (Boston, 1811-1823), V, 257. In some places the role of the town became by custom merely *pro forma*. However, see n. 50.

[5] A precinct was originally the location of a parish but the terms early became synonyms. See Theron Metcalf, *Reports of Cases Argued and Determined in the*

encompassing only entire towns, were made applicable as well to separate parishes within the towns, and no religious society formed outside some municipal corporation had any standing in law. Every resident of every parish was taxed for the support of the ministry, and none might regularly attend another church of the same denomination without first having been attached to it by the legislature. But since the provincial charter granted liberty of conscience to all subjects except Roman Catholics and since no man could be compelled to attend the church in his parish, Quakers, Baptists, Anglicans, and other minority sectarians were, in effect, dissenters from the legally established Congregational churches in their respective parishes. If they formed their own religious society it could not be described by geographical lines and the members constituted a poll parish. If they also happened to constitute a majority of the residents of a territorial parish they might, at least in theory, also become the legal parish and receive tax support.[6] Otherwise, a conscientious dissenter was required by law to support one church and by his conscience to support another.

The system continued with only minor alterations until 1727, when parish collectors were authorized to turn over to Anglican ministers the taxes paid by their communicants. The following year an outright exemption from parish rates was granted to Baptists and Quakers, much to the dismay of the regular churches whose members were suddenly faced with heavier tax burdens.[7] Both acts were temporary in nature and created as many problems as they solved. Matters soon became seriously clouded by a Baptist schism, by tax evaders who claimed suddenly to have become dissenters, and by the attempts of some collectors to evade the law. Finally, the legislature, forced to determine who was legally entitled to an exemption, required Quakers and Baptists to file certificates of church membership with town or parish clerks in order to have their parish rates abated.[8] The odious

---

Supreme Judicial Court of Massachusetts (Boston, 1841-1851), X, 515. The corporate village, unknown in Massachusetts and New Hampshire, simplified ecclesiastical jurisdiction elsewhere in New England.

[6] Trace, for example, such a struggle by the Baptists of Ashfield in *Acts and Resolves*, IV, 1015, 1036-1045, and *passim*. See also, Tyng, *Massachusetts Reports*, V, 257.

[7] *Acts and Resolves*, II, 459, 494-495, 543-544, 714-715; V, 111-113, 392-393.

[8] Evidently some assessors attempted to exclude from exemption certain kinds of property. See *ibid.*, II, 543-544. The certificate laws and related acts may be

certificate law was but one of many contributions to a makeshift system which, despite its long-range viability, was so unsatisfactory that in 1779 the architects of the new Massachusetts Constitution found ample cause to rectify its many faults.

Their work began auspiciously with the second article of the Declaration of Rights: "It is the right as well as the duty of all men . . . , publicly, and at stated seasons, to worship the SUPREME BEING, . . . and no subject shall be hurt, molested, or restrained, in his person, liberty, or estate, for worshipping GOD in the manner and season most agreeable to the dictates of his own conscience; or for his religious profession or sentiments. . . ."[9] The article was similar to the corresponding clause in the charter of 1692 and established complete religious freedom. Then the framers, anxious to minimize any possible opposition to the *entire* constitution, attempted to satisfy the conservatives, who sought security for the *status quo,* as well as the increasingly vocal advocates of a voluntary religious system. Their work resulted in a series of compromises that were enshrined in the third article of the Declaration of Rights which, at the insistence of the old order, committed the new Commonwealth to support an ecclesiastical system on the grounds that both the public welfare and the preservation of civil government "essentially depend upon piety, religion and morality." Accordingly, the General Court was vested with a mandate to require "the several towns, parishes, precincts and other bodies-politic, or religious societies, to make suitable provision, at their own expence, for the institution of the public worship of GOD, and for the support . . . of public protestant teachers of piety, religion and morality, in all cases where such provision shall not be made voluntarily."[10] Thus did the relationship between church and municipal corporation, a mere statutory matter under the provincial government, become a permanent constitutional feature of the new commonwealth.

Further compromises required all subjects to attend the instructions "of the public teachers aforesaid . . . if there be any on whose

---

traced in *ibid,* II, 494-495, 543-544, 714-715, 1022; III, 362, 644-645; IV, 67-68, 288, 420, 1036, 1045; V, 111-113. Particularly after the Great Awakening, schismatic Congregationalists were also classified as dissenters, not entitled to tax exemptions.

[9] *The Constitution or Frame of Government for the Commonwealth of Massachusetts* (Boston, 1781), 2-4.

[10] *Ibid.,* 4.

instructions they can conscientiously and conveniently attend," while the important tax clause, understood by dissenters to grant them equal status with the regular churches, provided that "all monies paid by the subject to the support of the public worship . . . shall, if he require it, be uniformly applied to the support of the public teacher . . . of his own religious sect or denomination, provided there be any upon whose instructions he attends." Other sections reserved to the people the right to elect their own ministers, prohibited the subordination of one religion to another, and guaranteed equal protection of the laws to all Christians.[11] The compromises were unfortunate. The traditionalists, disregarding the statutory evolution of religious freedoms under the provincial government, largely succeeded in enshrining the ecclesiastical *status quo* of 1779 in the constitution, thus all but precluding further evolutionary developments. The dissenters, on the other hand, had to content themselves with dispensatory concessions which they only could hope would provide equality for all religions. As a result, the third article was so laden with quasi-statutory provisions that the General Court, unlike its provincial predecessor had only the most peripheral opportunity to enact useful interpretative legislation that would meet the changing needs of the times. Moreover, the clauses of that article lacked the explicitness of statutory law and, short of a constitutional amendment, could be brought into harmony with the spirit of the second article only by adjudication.

The first significant litigation involving the third article appears to have been a suit brought by the Reverend John Murray, a Universalist minister, against the First Parish in Gloucester.[12] Behind the dispute lay Murray's doctrine of universal salvation, held by the keepers of New England's conscience to be the very antithesis of all piety, religion, and morality; the nature of his Independent Church of Christ, whose members had simply affiliated together under loose articles of association rather than under the customary church covenant; and the informality with which the congregation had merely accepted Mur-

---

[11] *Ibid.* The papers and early drafts of the committee to frame the third article disappeared shortly after the constitution was ratified.

[12] A similar case, *Balkcom* v. *Wilkerson*, was heard in 1782 by the Bristol County Court of Common Pleas, but the results were of local significance only. See Buck, *Ecclesiastical Law,* 41; and William G. McLoughlin's excellent analysis, "The Balkcom Case (1782) and the Pietistic Theory of Separation of Church and State," *William and Mary Quarterly,* XXIV (1967), 267-282.

ray as its minister without the laying on of hands and other traditional forms of ordination prescribed by the Cambridge Platform.[13] The group constituted a religious society, and could be described as a voluntary, unincorporated poll parish, but not a parish in the legal or commonly accepted sense of that term.

In 1783, a church committee attempted to take advantage of that clause of the third article allowing a dissenter to have his taxes paid to the minister of his own sect and applied to the First Parish for a tax abatement. The assessors, however, rejected the application, declaring that the Independent Church was not a religious society and its minister was not a public teacher of piety, religion, and morality as prescribed by the constitution.[14] While the outraged members pondered possible means of legal redress, the opposition seized the initiative. In December 1784, Michael Farley, sheriff of Essex County, haled Murray before the County Court of Common Pleas, declared that he was not a legally ordained minister, and invoked a 1695 statute imposing a £50 fine on anyone other than a justice of the peace or an ordained minister for performing the marriage ceremony. The mode of ordination was the point in dispute and the court awarded judgment to Farley, apparently because the Independent Church had never formally ordained its minister.[15] Had the matter been allowed to rest there, Murray would have stood legally answerable for every marriage ceremony he had performed. Therefore, almost of necessity, he entered an appeal of the judgment. At the same time he began his own suit against the First Parish to recover the taxes paid by his followers, evidently hoping that a verdict in his favor would preclude judgment for Farley upon the appeal of that action. Thus, the tax issue was brought before the courts because the establishment had taken the

---

[13] See, for example, John Cleveland, *An Attempt to Nip in the Bud, the Unscriptural Doctrine of Universal Salvation* (Salem, Mass., 1776); Andrew Croswell, *Mr. Murray Unmask'd* (Boston, 1775); and an attack by Samuel Chandler in *The Essex Gazette*, Feb. 3, 1775. The Articles of Association are in the Independent Christian Church in Gloucester, Mass.

[14] Relevant papers are in the Files of the Supreme Judicial Court of Massachusetts, case nos. 133538 and 133577, Suffolk County Court House, Boston. Hereinafter cited as Suffolk Files.

[15] Manuscript Record of the Supreme Judicial Court, hereinafter cited as Sup. Jud. Ct. Rec., 1787, f. 302, Suffolk County Court House; Suffolk Files, no. 133767. The statute of 1695 is in *Acts and Resolves*, I, 209-210.

initiative and because a dissenting minister was forced to defend himself.[16]

The case of *John Murray v. Inhabitants of the First Parish in Gloucester* was heard on appeal by the Supreme Judicial Court in June 1785. In essence, Murray contended that the constitution permitted a dissenter to have his parish taxes paid to his own religious society, provided it was not of the same sect or denomination as that of the regular parish, and that since Quakers, Baptists, and other minority religions had long enjoyed sectarian status, the Universalists, with their own views of infant baptism and eternal salvation, should be entitled to similar standing.[17] James Sullivan, Murray's attorney, attempted to rest the case on the simple premise that the Independent Church, in eschewing traditional baptismal rites, constituted a sect distinct from the Calvinist First Parish and, therefore, its minister should be entitled to receive members' taxes. When the court demanded proof that Murray was a teacher of piety, religion, and morality, Sullivan submitted evidence that he "professed to teach the Christian religion, which we thought to be a moral system, and that the persons whose taxes were in consideration attended upon him as a teacher of morality."[18]

The opposition, represented by Theophilus Parsons, charged that Murray failed to fit the constitutional prescription for a public teacher of piety, religion, and morality because, in denying the inevitability of divine retribution after death, his doctrines were opposed to morality. The court ruled that argument inadmissible in a civil tribunal but, Sullivan complained, the judges were predisposed against Murray and, "in summing up, or rather in arguing the cause, gave it as their full

[16] Murray had originally been reluctant to undertake a lawsuit for the mere purpose of collecting money and clearly it was only Farley's suit that caused him to enter the fray in earnest. See Suffolk Files, no. 133583; [Samuel Whittemore], *An Answer to a Piece Entitled "An Appeal to the Impartial Publick."* (Salem, Mass., 1785), 13; *The Life of Rev. John Murray, Written by Himself. With a Continuation by Mrs. Judith Sargent Murray* (Boston, 1870), 238.

[17] The appeal of the Farley case, to have been heard at that session, was continued to a following term. The Universalist position was stated in [Epes Sargent], *An Appeal to the Impartial Public* (Salem, Mass., 1785), discussed more fully below.

[18] James Sullivan to Rufus King, June 5, 1785, Sullivan Papers, I, Massachusetts Historical Society, Boston. Sullivan, at one time justice of the Supreme Judicial Court, and later attorney general and governor of Massachusetts, was equalled only by Levi Lincoln as an advocate of a liberal interpretation of the Constitution. The two argued most of the important religious freedoms cases of the day.

opinion that no teacher but one who was elected by a corporate society could recover the money paid by his hearers to the teacher of the parish."[19] While it had been an axiom of the provincial laws that only a corporate parish was entitled to tax support, the validity of that premise under the constitution appears to have been advanced for the first time by Justice Francis Dana in the Murray case. It soon became a standard argument for the establishment, changing the focus of all subsequent litigation on the issue. Nevertheless, the jury ignored the charge and returned a verdict for Murray, who, apparently because the legality of his ministry was still undefined, took the unusual step of entering an appeal of his own victory.[20] Then, awaiting the fall term of the court, both parties rehearsed their arguments in a number of pamphlets which, while clearly designed to enlist public sympathies for the contenders, are worthy of extensive notice here because they also amply illustrate the nature of the entire religious freedom issue as it was argued until 1833.[21]

In the course of the pamphlet debate, the First Parish charged that Murray should not be entitled to the taxes paid by his followers because he had not been legally ordained and, even if he had been, his teachings were so opposed to piety, religion, and morality that he failed to fit the constitutional prescription for a minister. Furthermore, supposing that his credentials were otherwise acceptable, the constitution excluded the ministers of unincorporated poll parishes from receiving tax support.

To the first point the Universalists replied that their minister had been ordained according to the precepts of the Cambridge Platform, which held that election to, and acceptance of, office, rather than observation of traditional ceremonies, constituted true ordination. To the second they argued that the only proper test of a minister's

---

[19] Sullivan to King, *ibid.* [Theophilus Parsons, Jr.], *Memoir of Theophilus Parsons* (Boston, 1861), 161-162.

[20] Sup. Jud. Ct. Rec., 1768, f. 245. A verdict contravening the charge from the bench left the way open for a new trial. Murray's new writ specified dissatisfaction with the monetary award as grounds for the second appeal, clearly a trumped-up reason since his original suit had been brought to establish a right rather than to recover damages. The First Parish also entered an appeal. See Suffolk Files, nos. 133577 and 133583.

[21] The issues were discussed in [Sargent], *An Appeal,* summarized in the following paragraphs. See also n. 24.

qualifications under the constitution lay in his exhorting his followers to morality, not in the substance of his teachings.[22]

On the important third charge, the First Parish argued that the first clause of the third article, requiring the support of "public protestant teachers," actually provided for the settlement of official or legal ministers, and that all subsequent references in the article to "public teachers aforesaid" referred exclusively to those ministers. Thus the clause enjoining attendance upon the "public teachers aforesaid" prescribed attendance only upon the ministrations of the legally established ministers, not upon those of voluntary sects. The clause regulating the taxes paid to support "the public teachers aforesaid" was read in the same context, and so was the guarantee that a sectarian might have his parish rate "applied to the support of the public teacher . . . of his own religious sect or denomination," although that clause did not specifically mention "teachers aforesaid."

In rejecting that construction of the tax clause, the Universalists first offered their definition of the term "sect or denomination" as it was used in the constitution, declaring that a sect was any group dissenting from an established denomination, such as the sectaries who dissented from the Church of England.[23] Admittedly, there was no similar establishment in Massachusetts from which to dissent, but the religious societies established by law constituted the legal denomination in their respective towns and parishes. Worshippers leaving one of those societies only to establish another espousing the same doctrines would not be dissenters but schismatics, who should not be entitled to tax support at the expense of the legal parish; but if they organized a society with its own forms of church discipline and its own mode of administering the ordinances, then it would qualify as a dissenting sect. The distinction had always existed in Massachusetts, and the second article of the Declaration of Rights, in providing security for the individual conscience, had implicitly recognized and

[22] "Ordination we account nothing else, but the solemn putting of a man into his . . . Office"; and, "the essence and substance of the . . . calling of an . . . Officer in the Church doth not consist in his Ordination, but in his voluntary and free Election by the Church, and in his accepting of that Election." *A Platform of Church Discipline* (London, 1653), 11. The same chapter also notes that "Church-Officers are not only to be chosen by the Church, but [are] also to be ordained by Imposition of hands and prayer."

[23] Justice Dana had declared the terms "sect" and "denomination" to be synonyms. See, [?] to Murray, n. d., *Life of Murray*, 334.

legalized dissenting sects. Under the new system, all citizens, regardless of creed, must pay a ministerial tax, but since the subordination of one religion to another was expressly forbidden, the tax clause must apply to voluntary poll parishes as well as to corporate territorial parishes.

The opposition argued, however, that only a corporate parish could be vested by the General Court with the tax power because there were no legal means to compel a voluntary sect—one not even discernible to the legislative eye—either to exercise that power or to maintain a minister. The Universalists conceded the point insofar as it applied to the collection of taxes, but reasoned that the equal protection and non-subordination clauses of the constitution prohibited applying the benefits of the system solely to corporate parishes. If the framers of the constitution intended that the legal parishes should collect the taxes from every resident within their jurisdiction, they must also have expected the collectors to distribute to the sectarian ministers the monies paid by their constituents. Otherwise, the entire clause would be superfluous because the statutes creating corporate towns and parishes implicitly exempted them from assessments by similar corporations. Another argument, holding that the Independent Church should apply to the legislature for a charter, was rejected on the grounds that once a sect became incorporated it would become as much a legal denomination as any town or parish. Since the constitution had already recognized the equality of all sects, an application for a charter was not necessary and would establish a dangerous precedent that would once more place the very existence of all sectarians at the mercy of the General Court.

While the pamphleteers thus competed for the attention of the public, including the jurors who had already been drawn for the fall term, the same end was served when the court, on its way through neighboring Middlesex County, heard a case containing similar issues.[24]

---

[24] [Whittemore], *An Answer to a Piece*, chiefly a denial of the points made in *An Appeal*, also attempted to discredit the Universalists. Murray declared it to be an "infamous collection of falsehoods" designed to influence judges and jurors, and wrote a rebuttal that would normally have appeared in the newspapers the day after court opened; "but circumstances rendered it expedient to publish it by itself" and it appeared as a broadside the day *before* the judges arrived in town. Quotations are from the Boston broadside, entitled *The Author of the Following Piece* . . . , Oct. 29, 1785.

The jury, instructed by the bench that only corporate parishes might exercise the tax power and that dissenters must file exemption certificates in order to win tax abatements, returned a verdict for the establishment, thereby contradicting, but by no means reversing, Murray's June victory.[25] That combination of events appears to have had at least a local influence on public opinion, for when Murray's appeal was called to the bar a few weeks later, the jury could not agree and the case was continued until June 1786.[26]

The points argued at that time can only be outlined here. Theophilus Parsons, holding that the constitutional mandate for a system of public worship could be implemented only by corporate bodies, based the case for the First Parish on the premise that since the third article placed the responsibility for public worship squarely upon the municipal corporations it implicitly provided for the creation of corporate parishes. Therefore, the tax clause allowed an abatement of parish rates only to incorporated societies of a denomination different from that of the legal parish.[27] In reply, Sullivan noted that the constitution required "towns, parishes, precincts, and other bodies politic or religious societies" to provide for public worship, and argued that the framers, in including "religious societies" in the list, had vested the legislature with a mandate to require unincorporated societies to maintain public worship. Furthermore, compelling a dissenter to support a corporate parish would contravene the non-subordination and equal-protection clauses of the constitution and penalize a conscientious man for his religious beliefs contrary to the liberal spirit of the framers.[28]

In giving the cause to the jury, Chief Justice William Cushing noted briefly that a proliferation of voluntary sects might leave many corporate parishes unable to fulfill the constitutional mandate to support a minister. Nevertheless, if dissenters must be incorporated in

---

[25] *Frost* v. *Cutter et al.*, Sup. Jud. Ct. Rec., June-Nov., 1785, f. 260.

[26] Sup. Jud. Ct. Rec., 1786, f. 240; *Salem Gazette,* Nov. 9, 1785. The uncertainty of even the judges on the issue is hinted in a fragment of a letter, dated Feb. 2, 1786, in Sargent's papers, suggesting the need to revise the tax clause. All members of bench and bar concerned with the Murray case had been members of the constitutional convention, and Parsons had been on the committee to draft the third article.

[27] "Notes of Cases . . . Taken by William Cushing . . . ," a manuscript notebook currently being edited for publication by the author of this article.

[28] *Ibid.*

order to derive the benefits of the constitution, their existence would be left to the discretion of the legislature which was under no obligation to charter corporations. Therefore, he reasoned, both arguments must give way to the intention of the framers to secure religious freedom for all men, to prevent the subordination of one religion to another, and to prevent inequalities because of religious beliefs. The framers had treated the subject amply, "leaving little room for construction," and had they intended the tax clause to be applied for the benefit of corporate societies alone, they would have provided a proper qualification to that effect. The chief justice also endorsed the arguments that the constitution had placed unincorporated societies under legislative control; that a sect was a group apart from "the regular establishment, if it may be so termed"; and that "sect does not mean a corporate body, but rather a division from some corporate body." Therefore, the clause allowing sectarians to have their parish rates paid to their own "religious sect or denomination" must be applied literally, provided only the dissenters be of a sect or denomination different from that of the regular parish. The associate justices concurred and the jury, after deliberating all night, returned a verdict for Murray.[29]

Again, the case defined the rights of a dissenting sect but it took no cognizance of the legal status of its minister, and any practical implications the Universalists may have found in two favorable jury verdicts were soon nullified when the long continued appeal of the Farley case was called to the bar.[30] Then, the very judges who had charged a trial jury in support of Murray's church sustained the judgment of the Common Pleas that the Independent Church, in

---

[29] *Ibid.;* Sup. Jud. Ct. Rec., 1786, f. 240; *Life of Murray,* 334. Particularly under Cushing, contending counsel were permitted to range far afield in their arguments, after which each justice charged the jury with a summary of the facts and applicable law. One charge did not necessarily agree with another and the jurors often returned verdicts based upon their own views of the law or even their own prejudices. Subsequent juries were not bound thereby and thus one verdict did not necessarily establish a firm precedent or reverse another. In cases where the general issue was pleaded, juries remained supreme until 1804. See n. 30, 41, and 48.

[30] At the Common Pleas, defense attorneys had entered a so-called plea in bar which admitted Murray had performed the marriage ceremony but asserted that he had a right to do so and, therefore, that Farley had no right to bring suit. The arguments were then a matter of law, heard by the judges without a jury, and they found that Farley did have a right to his action because Murray was not a legal minister. It was that judgment that was appealed to the justices of the Supreme Judicial Court. See Suffolk Files, no. 133767.

simply acknowledging Murray as its minister rather than ordaining him according to customary forms, had failed to ordain him at all.[81] Thus, the traditional interpretation of chapter nine of the Cambridge Platform was implicitly confirmed and the religious freedom clauses of the constitution were seriously modified. Many dissenters would long for the return of the more viable provincial system.

Murray's cause was lost and he was forced to seek temporary refuge in England. Meanwhile, a statute, passed only a few days after his victory over the First Parish, confirmed the corporate nature and function of all standing parishes, but was conspicuously silent on the matter of voluntary societies.[82] With their legal status all but undefined, sectarians became increasingly subject to harassment in the courts until 1792 when many voluntary societies, including Murray's, bowed to expediency and obtained charters of incorporation.[83] Other dissenting sects, however, preferred to stand on principle and generated such a spate of of confusing litigation that in the winter of 1799-1800, the General Court repealed all laws regulating ecclesiastical matters and replaced them with one comprehensive statute.[84]

The act of 1800 followed closely the format of the third article of the Declaration of Rights, but the original terminology was pointedly modified to stress the affiliation of church and municipal corporation to the total exclusion of voluntary societies, and to affirm that only *corporate* towns, parishes, and other bodies politic were required by law to support ministers. A tax clause, specifying that only *corporate* parishes might collect the ministerial taxes and apply them to the

[81] Sup. Jud. Ct. Rec., 1787, f. 302; Suffolk Files, no. 133767. A new trial of the Farley case, granted by the General Court upon Sullivan's petition, failed to modify the decision. *Acts and Laws of the Commonwealth of Massachusetts* [1780-1805] (Boston, 1890-1898), 1786-1787, Chap. 79, p. 712.

[82] Act of June 28, 1786, *ibid.*, 1786-1787, Chap. 10, pp. 21-24.

[83] Murray returned from England after Sullivan obtained a legislative exemption from further prosecution for prior violations of the Act of 1695. *Ibid.*, Chap. 87, p. 871. Upon his return he participated in a publicized reordination ceremony which employed quotations from the Declaration of Rights but carefully avoided all tradition. See *The Massachusetts Centinel*, Jan. 3, 1789, and the acid comments in *The Diary of William Bentley, D.D.* (Salem, Mass., 1905-1914), I, 87, 107-108, 111-112. Before seeking a charter, the church attempted to get along with a voluntary tax agreement, now displayed at the church in Gloucester. Members who filed exemption certificates are listed in "Gloucester Town Records," Book 3, 487-489, Gloucester City Hall, Gloucester, Mass. Terms of the remarkably detailed charter are in *Acts and Laws*, 1792-1793, Chap. 18, pp. 40-41.

[84] *Ibid.*, 1798-1799, Chap. 87, pp. 495-498.

support of "*any* public Teacher or Teachers aforesaid," lent some hope to sectarians, but their interests were primarily defined in two subsequent sections, one reviving the old provincial law requiring them to file certificates, another vesting assessors with the discretion to omit from their parish rolls, if they saw fit, the names of residents known to attend a church of another denomination.[35] In general, the act favored the advocates of a compulsory, tax-supported, and state-regulated system but provided sectarians with little they had not enjoyed under the old provincial government. Indeed, the Charter of 1692 had granted almost complete religious freedom. Thus, the provincial legislature had ample authority to liberalize the ecclesiastical statutes and had done so from time to time. What little hope dissenters derived from the act of 1800, however, was most tenuous since legislative authority under the constitution was limited to implementing the more restrictive terms of the third article and since any attempt by the General Court to restate the intention of the framers could be nothing more than a collective opinion which the courts might overturn.

Even before the act was engrossed a test case was in the offing. Between 1787 and 1800, the Reverend Francis Matignon, pastor of the Roman Catholic community in Boston, attempted to recover the parish taxes paid by some of his communicants to the First Parish in Newcastle, Maine, where he preached while riding circuit. James Sullivan, arguing the final appeal of the case, pointed out to the Supreme Judicial Court that the terminology of the act of 1800 permitted a sectarian to have his parish rates applied to "the public teacher of his own religious sect . . . ," rather than to "the public protestant teacher," but the judges ruled that regardless of the terminology employed by the legislature in drafting the act, the constitution provided only for the support of "public protestant teachers," a description scarcely applicable to the plaintiff.[36]

[35] *Ibid.* In towns containing only one parish, tax monies were to be deposited in the town treasury to be disbursed by the town treasurer on order from the selectmen; in multi-parish towns the same procedure was executed by corresponding officers of the corporate precinct or parish.

[36] Sup. Jud. Ct. Rec., 1800-1803, f. 125; R. H. Lord, *et al., History of the Archdiocese of Boston* (New York, 1944), I, 560, 567; and Tyng, *Massachusetts Reports*, VI, 413. For a discussion of the rights of non-protestants under the constitution, see Nathan Dane, *A General Abridgement of American Law* (Boston, 1823-1829), II, 331-333.

The Matignon case, often erroneously cited as a discriminatory judgment, is more noteworthy as the first judicial modification of the act of 1800. If it exposed one flaw in that act, sectarian antagonists soon exploited another: the failure of the statute (or any other) to define the right of a church to ordain a minister according to its own forms. Inasmuch as ministerial jurisdiction must depend in the first instance upon the legality of ordination, both factors were soon argued together in a rash of lawsuits. The inconsistent and confusing results illustrate the near chaos into which the once smoothly functioning establishment had fallen. For example, the court had refused to accept John Murray's credentials of ordination, but accepted those of the Roman Catholic Bishop of Boston, Jean Cheverus, who had been ordained a priest according to the rites of his own church rather than the forms prescribed by the Platform. Cheverus was indicted for performing the marriage ceremony while riding the circuit in Maine, but the court grudgingly admitted the validity of his ordination despite the fact that he had been ordained over no particular parish.[37] Three years later, however, when an itinerant Methodist minister, who had been ordained over an otherwise undefined "Western Circuit," attempted to collect the taxes paid by his hearers, the court flatly refused to hear his arguments *because he had been ordained over no specific parish.*[38]

With similar inconsistencies, and despite the act of 1800, litigation on the issue of incorporation continued. In 1804, a Berkshire County minister of an unincorporated religious society sued to recover the taxes paid by his followers and won a verdict, the sixth confirmation of that returned in the Murray case.[39] Three years later James Sullivan, by then governor, attempted to put an end to such costly and vexing

[37] Sullivan, as attorney general, prosecuted the bishop on the same grounds Farley had used against Murray and also charged him with acting outside his jurisdiction. The defense appears to have argued that imposition of hands, accepted in Massachusetts as validating Anglican ordinations, should also validate that of Cheverus, and once the point had been established, his jurisdiction, as pastor of the nearest Roman Catholic parish, was admitted by the court. See Lord, *History of the Archdiocese,* I, 567.

[38] *Washburn* v. *Fourth Parish in Springfield,* Tyng, *Massachusetts Reports,* I, 32. The *obiter dicta* of the court noted the impossibility of making an equitable distribution of taxes to a circuit rider. The Washburn and Cheverus cases held in common only the element of ordination. See also *Kendall* v. *Kingston, ibid.,* V, 524.

[39] *Smith* v. *Dalton,* in Dane, *Abridgement,* II, 337.

litigation by supporting a bill that would place all sects on an equal basis. Dubbed the "infidel bill," it was rejected by the General Court.[40] In the same year most dissenters gave up hope of deriving any benefits under the act of 1800 when Thomas Barnes, a Universalist minister, carried his tax suit against the First Parish in Falmouth, Maine, to the Supreme Judicial Court where Chief Justice Theophilus Parsons delivered a seventeen page opinion that became at once the classic statement of the case for the establishment.[41]

In attempting to bring order out of the admittedly chaotic judicial precedents, Parsons made a strong plea for the continued affiliation of church and commonwealth, reasoning that since it was an end of government to promote the security and happiness of the people, it was the duty of the state to compel the instruction of all men in Christian truths. In fulfilling that duty the state required the assistance of a superior power, containing a moral system upon which man might build a better society and providing "the most efficatious sanctions by bringing to life a state of future retribution."[42] Accordingly, the constitution had provided for a system of *corporate* religious societies which every resident of every parish was required to support. Dissenters had a constitutional right to maintain their own societies, but freedom of conscience, an inalienable right, was quite distinct from the power to raise money for a public purpose, and any argument to exempt a dissenter from his parish taxes "seems to mistake a man's money for his conscience." A contribution to the support of the regular churches, Parsons reasoned, was a contribution to the welfare of the state, and a man had no more right to be exempt from supporting a church he could not attend than to be free from school taxes because he had no children.

Turning to the corporate issue, the chief justice examined the clause of the constitution requiring every "town, parish, precinct and other body politic or religious society" to maintain ministers, and declared

[40] For a summary and comment upon the "Infidel Bill," see *Bentley Diary*, III, 345-346.

[41] Tyng, *Massachusetts Reports*, VI, 401-418. Arguments of contending counsel centered upon the act of 1800. The *nisi prius* system, adopted in 1804, allowed this action to be referred on a bill of exceptions from a single justice and a jury to the full bench sitting without a jury, thus affording time for Parsons to write a polished decision.

[42] Note that Parsons again voiced the objection to Universalist theology he had first advanced as an attorney in the Murray case.

that the words "or religious society," rather than being in addition to the list, simply described the corporate bodies politic mentioned in the clause as religious societies. Any other construction of the terminology would require every body politic, regardless of its purpose, to maintain ministers. He further reasoned that the constitution required the support of "public protestant teachers," and if the Matignon case had established that only *Protestant* teachers were contemplated by the constitution, then it must follow that they should also be *public* teachers, ordained over some *public* society, known in law, and formed by the public authority of the state, as opposed to private societies, voluntarily formed and privately supported.

Otherwise, Parsons followed the same reasoning he had used many years earlier in the Murray case. His opinion modified the second article of the Declaration of Rights and narrowed the equal protection and non-subordination clauses which, he declared, were mere safeguards against the erection of a state hierarchy. If the act of 1800 had made any concessions to the rights of dissenters, Parsons, convinced that the mandate of the third article could be properly implemented only through a system of corporate parishes, barred any constructive application of the act that would admit non-corporate parishes to function within that system. He noted that if a dissenting society thereby suffered undue hardship legislative melioration was available but, he warned, the legislature cannot "by any construction control the Constitution." Then, interpreting the act of 1800 according to his own understanding of the third article, he declared the two to be in perfect harmony.[43]

Barnes v. *Falmouth* marked the last significant victory for the old order. Some unincorporated societies continued to seek adjudicative relief only to find that the court stood inflexibly by the Barnes dictum, and more practical men began to seek relief through legislation.[44] Their efforts were rewarded in June 1811 with the so-called "Religious Freedoms Act."[45]

The act of 1811, the most important single statute regulating ecclesiastical affairs since 1727-1728, was justified in its preamble by

[43] Tyng, *Massachusetts Reports*, VI, 401-418. Only the few leading points in Parsons's very detailed decision have been treated here.

[44] See, for example, *Turner* v. *Brookfield* and *Lovell* v. *Byfield*, Tyng, *Massachusetts Reports*, VII, 60, 232.

[45] *Laws of the Commonwealth* [May session, 1811] (Boston, 1812), 387-389.

the non-subordination and equal protection clauses of the constitution, contrary to the solemn judicial interpretations of those clauses as mere safeguards against the erection of a state hierarchy. The act repealed all prior conflicting legislation and specifically declared the right of every man to have his ministerial taxes paid to his own religious society, corporate or not. The assessments were to be collected by the corporate towns or parishes, but the sole test of a minister's eligibility to receive the taxes of his parishioners was ordination according to the forms of his own church, regardless of whether his parochial duties were performed in one parish or several.[46] A modification of the certificate system required every person who became a member of any religious society, corporate or otherwise, to file a prescribed form with his town clerk and thus become exempt from assessments by any other religious society. The act retained the traditional relationship between church and municipal corporation, but in granting such sweeping rights to dissenters it broke with over a century of precedent. It amounted to a constructive amendment of the constitution that challenged several judicial interpretations of the religious freedom clauses. If it could be defended substantively as the will of the people it would also, if allowed to stand, eventually reduce the third article of the Declaration of Rights to a nullity.

The act worked a hardship on the corporate parishes and thus did little to abate sectarian antagonisms. The court gave some manifestation of tempering Parsons's legalistic interpretation of the third article,[47] but nearly five years elapsed before the statute was subjected to its first significant test. Daniel Adams of Rutland, a member of an unincorporated Baptist society located in neighboring Barre and served one Sunday in each month by a visiting minister, sued the Congregational assessors of Rutland for distraining his heifer in satisfaction of his parish rate. The case of *Adams* v. *Howe et al.*, clearly designed to

---

[46] No provision was made for the division of tax monies between regular and circuit clergy. (see n. 38) The act also exempted all ministers from civil taxes, a phase of the controversy beyond the scope of this article.

[47] A few months after the passage of the act, the court ruled that a part time, unordained Episcopal lay reader was a public teacher within the meaning and intent of the third article. *Sanger* v. *Roxbury*, Tyng, *Massachusetts Reports*, VIII, 265. A few days before the act had become effective, the court declared that the act of 1786 (see n. 32) was intended to comprehend poll parishes. *Minot* v. *Curtis, ibid.*, VII, 444. But subsequent expansion of that point was not immediately forthcoming. See, for example, *First Parish in Shapleigh* v. *Gilman, ibid.*, XIII, 190.

test the validity of the act of 1811, had its final hearing in September 1817 before the Supreme Judicial Court where Chief Justice Isaac Parker wrote the opinion.[48]

Parker lamented that the act was injurious to public morals and destructive of all "decency and regularity in publick worship" because it allowed any man to have his parish rate paid to any society he pleased, thus injuring the "established worship," although dissenting sects were not specifically required to maintain ministers nor were dissenters actually required by law to attend any church in order to have their taxes abated. But in examining the law within the context of the constitution, the chief justice noted that the third article of the Declaration of Rights, far from describing a religious establishment, had simply provided for freedom of conscience, asserted the right of the state to require and enforce the public worship of God, prohibited the establishment of a state hierarchy, and provided safeguards against legislative transgressions of individual rights. The actual task of implementing the article and establishing a system of worship had been left to the representatives of the people. While the framers had clearly intended and provided that the system should function within a framework of corporate parishes they had imposed no restrictions against the legislature's incorporating any number of individuals as poll parishes. Neither had they prohibited the granting of relief to sectarians, not even mentioned in the constitution, who "dissent from the established worship of the town." Furthermore, the General Court had traditionally made provisions for Quakers, Baptists, Anglicans, and others. Nor was there anything in the constitution to prohibit the legislature from conferring the rights and privileges of corporate parishes on the members of unincorporated societies.

In defense of his reasoning, Parker noted that inasmuch as the third article required the legislature to implement its terms, that body must be the sole judge of its powers under the article. If in executing their charge the members of the legislature chose to pass laws merely within the letter of the constitution, it might be an abuse of power and a neglect of duty to do so, but "this neglect does not affect

[48] *Adams* v. *Howe, ibid.,* XIV, 340-351. The case was originally heard at the Common Pleas, resulting in a special verdict that if the act of 1811 were constitutional the defendants were guilty, otherwise not guilty. Thus the judges, not a jury, made the decision, which was carried to the Supreme Judicial Court on a writ of error.

the validity of their acts." Nor was it the concern of the judiciary, whose duty it was to give effect to legislation made by proper constitutional authority, "regardless of its evil tendency." Subsequent legislatures might repeal "improvident or pernicious" statutes but until repealed they must stand as the presumed will of the people. The court could scarcely object to an act that had expanded rather than diminished personal religious freedoms, Parker observed, and although that act had probably been passed purposely in order to avoid the results of the Barnes decision its enactment was not prohibited by the constitution.[49]

In confirming the act of 1811 as a legal interpretation of the third article, Parker's decision did nothing to disturb the basic structure of the corporate parish system but confirmed that dissenting sects should function outside that structure, as Theophilus Parsons had reasoned they must. But in conferring upon them most of the rights and privileges, yet few of the responsibilities of the establishment, the decision irreparably damaged the continued functioning of the traditional system. Equally important, *Adams* v. *Howe* marked the final turning point in the nature of the struggle to define the religious freedoms clauses of the constitution. Traditionally, dissenters had complained that they were procedurally deprived of their constitutional rights by town and parish assessors, and had sought a favorable interpretation of the third article from either the judiciary or the legislature. When that objective was achieved in the Religious Freedoms Act, the Congregationalists found themselves the aggrieved party, but could complain only that the act itself was a substantive subversion of the rights of the churches established by law. There was, however, no practical remedy available to them. *Adams* v. *Howe* precluded any realistic hope of further adjudication of the issue. Meanwhile, the so-called "Unitarian schism" had so seriously divided Massachusetts Congregationalists that the concerted action necessary to secure a repeal of the act of 1811 was virtually impossible. Their cause became hopeless in October 1820, when the Supreme Judicial Court concluded the final hearings in the so-called "Dedham Case." That dispute had begun several years earlier when the people of Dedham in town meeting had

[49] *Ibid.*, 340-351. *Adams* v. *Howe* implicitly reversed the decisions in the Washburn and Kendall cases. (see n. 38) Parker expressly defended the decision in the Barnes case as comporting with the act of 1800, the then current statutory interpretation of the third article.

elected a Unitarian minister over the opposition of two-thirds of the regular Congregational society, which refused to accept the vote of the town, claimed to be the legal church, and sued the Unitarians for title to the church property. The protracted and complex litigation culminated in Parker's ruling that the constitution vested the responsibility for maintaining public worship in the towns and parishes, apart from which no church had any legal identity. Parker acknowledged that in many places custom had modified the relationship between church and municipal corporation established by the act of 1692, but that relationship had become part of the constitution to which all contrary custom and innovation must yield.[50] Therefore, the Unitarians, although a minority of the religious society, constituted the establishment in Dedham, and men who had long enjoyed membership in a church established by law suddenly found their society disestablished by the application of the very principles that had long provided support and stability for the Congregational churches of Province and Commonwealth.

Meanwhile, the dissenters who existed outside the municipal parish structure persisted in their apprehensions that the act of 1811 might be repealed. By the time of the Dedham decision they had already succeeded in focusing such widespread attention upon the religious freedom issue that it became one of the compelling reasons for assembling the Constitutional Convention of 1820.[51] That body, representing many shades of interest and presided over by the chief justice, debated the third article of the Declaration of Rights more extensively than any other single issue, but when an amendment generally comporting with the terms of the Religious Freedoms Act was finally agreed upon and submitted to the people for ratification, it was overwhelmingly rejected.[52] The act of 1811 then resumed its former im-

[50] Baker v. Fales, ibid., XVI, 488-522. Parker also cited the Platform on the matter of ordination (see esp. 512-513), and confirmed Parsons's views on the nature and the necessity of corporate parishes. See above n. 28; Avery v. Tyringham, ibid., III, 160; and Burr v. Sandwich, ibid., IX, 277.

[51] Journal of Debates . . . of the Convention . . . to Revise the Constitution of Massachusetts (Boston, 1853), vii; The Third Article of the Declaration of Rights (n.p., n.d.), 10-11, reprinted from The Spirit of the Pilgrims, IV (1831), 629-648. See also, Defence of the Third Article of the . . . Declaration of Rights (Worcester, Mass., 1820), containing a portion of Parsons's opinion in Barnes v. Falmouth, evidently republished for use at the time of the convention.

[52] Journal of the Convention, esp. 195-200, 345-349, and passim. For one analysis

portance, both to its supporters and its adversaries. One faction charged that the legislature and the courts had conspired to circumvent the constitution and to violate the intention of its framers; the opposition replied that the constitution had been intended to provide a liberal government and, unless it continued to meet the needs of the people, the liberal spirit of the framers would be nullified. The only tangible results of these and a host of other arguments was a somewhat lame legislative endorsement of the salient terms of the act of 1811.[53] Meanwhile, as the Unitarian movement gained momentum, the "Dedham Principle" was regularly applied by the courts until it became clear that neither legislation nor adjudication could any longer serve the interests of either the dispossessed Congregationalists or the traditional dissenters, who were ironically drawn together in an effort to secure the repeal of those very articles of the constitution which their once disparate interests had originally forced upon the framers. Clearly the ecclesiastical regulations suitable to the needs of 1692 or 1780 could serve no further useful or equitable purpose and, in 1833, the General Court proposed and the people ratified the eleventh amendment to the constitution which in effect repealed the troublesome third article and abolished "the churches established by law in this government."[54] Then, more than half a century after achieving political independence, Massachusetts recovered the full measure of religious freedom granted by the royal charter of 1692 but compromised in the Constitutional Convention of 1780.

---

of the ratifying vote, see J. C. Meyer, *Church and State in Massachusetts* (Cleveland, 1930), 198-200.

[53] See, for example, *Third Article of the Declaration of Rights*, 12; *Laws of the Commonwealth* [January session, 1824] (Boston, 1824), 347-348.

[54] For the enabling act, see *Laws of the Commonwealth* [January session, 1834] (Boston, 1834), 265-269. The convention of 1820 had succeeded in revising the constitution to permit the General Court, rather than cumbersome constitutional conventions, to propose amendments for popular ratification, thus indirectly facilitating the eleventh and subsequent amendments.

A CONNECTICUT SEPARATE CHURCH:
STRICT CONGREGATIONALISM
IN CORNWALL, 1780-1809

STEPHEN FOSTER

OF the many schisms that disturbed the peace of the Congregational churches of eighteenth-century Connecticut, the split in the First Church of Cornwall in 1780 was one of the least unusual. The town tired of paying its already wealthy minister his salary and tried to remove him. A contentious man, he invoked the power of the ecclesiastical establishment, the Litchfield Consociation, to help him hold his pulpit, whereupon the majority of the townspeople promptly voted themselves out of the Consociation. Failing to take over the meetinghouse and church assets by force, they set up a "Strict Congregational" Church of their own, which, after some years of lawsuits and commotion, also joined the Consociation.

Insignificant in itself, the episode typified similar upheavals in scores of other Connecticut towns. Religion itself did not cause this dispute over religious affairs. Instead, the issues changed repeatedly, although the contestants remained the Rev. Hezekiah Gold and the Litchfield Consociation on the one side, and the people of Cornwall on the other, and the object for which they fought continued to be control of the Cornwall Congregational Church. Cornwall's Congregationalists began by being surly about money, only to end by spending large sums on a crusade to overthrow ecclesiastical tyranny. When that cause finally exhausted them, they let the dispute settle itself on purely geographic lines.

The Congregationalism practiced in Connecticut in 1780 had changed greatly from the faith Thomas Hooker had brought with him from Massachusetts 150 years before, but the system still permitted enough local autonomy to insure that however widely a religious dispute might spread, each town would resolve it in its own way. Often (as in Cornwall)

309

the solutions resulted from local circumstances unconnected with theology. Not all the Connecticut towns torn by Separate church movements followed Cornwall's pattern, but they resembled that town enough to make it likely that to understand it in its moment of crisis, however undistinguished, is to begin to understand them.

I

Cornwall designates a legally incorporated area of about 30,000 acres in northwest Litchfield County near both the New York and Massachusetts state lines. Hills and a rocky soil make for a beautiful countryside, but poor farming. Isaac Stiles, the father of Ezra, wrote of Cornwall sometime before 1762:

> Nature out of her boundless Store
> Threw Rocks together and did no more.[1]

In the twentieth century the Connecticut Agricultural Experiment Station was less metrical but more specific when it described most of the area as too mountainous to be farmed easily, although "there are patches of considerable size scattered over the town which respond generously to cultivation, and are especially adapted to dairy products."[2] Cornwall was and is a good place to spend a picnic afternoon or an academic retirement, but a poor one to farm.

The first settlers, nevertheless, were farmers. The patches of considerable size attracted thirty-eight proprietors in 1740 and supported an increasing population thereafter. The number of inhabitants reached 1,021 in 1776, held steady for the course of the Revolution and then rose again, to 1,470 in 1790 and 1,614 in 1800.[3] Most of the people lived and worked on individual farms scattered over the area, separated from one

[1] Franklin B. Dexter, editor, *Extracts from the Itineraries and other Miscellanies of Ezra Stiles* (New Haven, 1916), 173.

[2] M. F. Morgan, *The Soil Characteristics of Connecticut Land Types*, quoted in Sydney K. Mitchell, *Phases of the History of Cornwall* (Canaan, Conn., n.d.), 8.

[3] Edward Comfort Starr, *A History of Cornwall, Connecticut* (New Haven, 1926), 398-399.

another by poor roads. There were clusters of people at Dud-
leytown in the south, Cornwall Hollow in the north, and at
the Center (site of the crossroads, whipping post, and meetinghouse).[4]

Bad roads and lack of nearby markets made anything other
than subsistence farming difficult but not impossible. Enterprising men like Major John Sedgwick or Captain Edward
Rogers could not make poor soil fertile or hilly land flat, but
they could build iron forges, potasheries, and sawmills, and
even, by buying up enough land, engage in commercial
agriculture on a moderate scale.[5]

Although Cornwall was never a rich town, neither was it or
any other Litchfield town the debt slave of a ruthless urban
capitalism. Most people in Litchfield County owed impressive
sums of money—but to each other, not to outsiders, and they
rarely pressed a lawsuit for nonpayment to the point where a
neighbor lost his land. Imprisonment for debt did not exist.[6]

Despite their physical isolation the residents of Cornwall
took an active part in the Revolution as early as 1774, when
they passed a resolution condemning the Boston Port Bill and
sent donations for the relief of the city.[7] Out of a total adult
male population not much over two hundred in September,
1776, seventy-three men were serving in the Continental
Army.[8] Throughout the Revolution the town met its troop
and tax quotas scrupulously; while it expressed its continuing
interest in political affairs by giving cordial approval to the
Articles of Confederation in 1778.[9]

These were a poor but honest and not a little combative folk.

[4] Starr, *A History of Cornwall* . . . , 24-25, 30.

[5] Theodore S. Gold, editor, *Historical Records of the Town of Cornwall*
(Hartford, 1904), 200-201, 205.

[6] Charles S. Grant, *Democracy in the Connecticut Frontier Town of Kent*
(New York, 1961), 74, 76-78, 80-81.

[7] Cornwall First Book (Ms. town records), 9, Office of the Town Clerk, Cornwall, Conn.

[8] "An Account of the Inhabitants of the Town of Cornwall taken first of
September, 1776," typewritten copy of Ms. census, Conn. State Library.

[9] Cornwall First Book, 19.

They fought a revolution, they agitated for a due form of civil government—and at the same time they turned their attention to their troublesome, now highly expensive gospel minister. Unfortunately, they had to deal not only with Hezekiah Gold, but with someone far more powerful and resourceful.

II

Ecclesiastical affairs in Western Connecticut in the late eighteenth century centered around one man, the Rev. Joseph Bellamy of Bethlehem. His power made and unmade the ministers of the Western Towns, and any town inclined to change its ecclesiastical arrangements would first have to reckon with him.

Bellamy combined a talent for theological controversy with the methods of a drill sergeant. Ezra Stiles thought him "a mixt character of such a Borgian Complexion as one would not wish often to appear in the Churches. His pious, ardent, turbulent and well meant zeal would at any time disturb the Peace and Tranquility of the churches. . . ." [10] For over forty years he was "Lord Bellamy" of the Litchfield Hills, the "pope" of the Western Towns, silencing, intimidating or breaking all the opponents, lay and clerical, of his system of theology, the "New Divinity."

Worked out by Bellamy, Samuel Hopkins and others, the New Divinity intensified Edwardsean theology to the point where its adherents denounced the Half-Way Covenant, denied man any role in his own salvation, and even held that the unregenerate neither could nor should pray, and ought to take joy in their own damnation if it contributed to the glory of God. The doctrine had a fatal attraction for young ministers just out of Yale, but not for their congregations, which reacted by turning to anticlericalism, deism, and "Nothingarianism." [11]

[10] Franklin B. Dexter, editor, *The Literary Diary of Ezra Stiles* (New York, 1901), III, 385.

[11] Stiles, *Itineraries*, 402, 412, 413, 414. Edmund S. Morgan, *The Gentle Puritan, A Life of Ezra Stiles* (New Haven, 1962), 172, 313-316, 410-411.

Bellamy ruled Litchfield County in 1780 through the institutions of central power, the consociation and association, but his position on the authority of those organizations had long been ambiguous. The Saybrook Platform, formulated in 1708 and enforceable at law in Connecticut until 1784, set up a semipresbyterial polity, organizing the churches of each county into consociations, their ministers into associations, but it did not clearly define the actual extent of consociational authority over local church affairs.[12] Attitudes of clerical factions towards consociational power depended mainly on who dominated the consociations. The laity could observe the bewildering (if entertaining) spectacle of groups of clergymen advocating centralized control just so long as they controlled the center, only to retreat to local autonomy once they lost their power. If Connecticut ecclesiastical history had any one theme between the First Great Awakening in 1738 and the Second at the end of the century, it was complexity and confusion. Bellamy's fifty-year career highlighted that fact.

He had been graduated from Yale in 1735, in time to become a fiery supporter of the Great Awakening when that religious revival was spreading grace and discord in about equal measure throughout New England. The opponents of the Awakening ("Old Lights"), controlled the consociations in the early 1740's, using them to keep revivalist "New Lights" out of Connecticut pulpits.[13] The New Lights called it persecution and an invasion of congregational autonomy; in Litchfield county, where Bellamy's influence grew steadily, not a single church had explicitly adopted the Saybrook Platform as late as 1762.[14]

New Lights soon gained enough support to control most of the consociations themselves. By the late 1750's many of them

12 The relevant sections of the Saybrook Platform are in Williston Walker, *The Creeds and Platforms of Congregationalism* (Boston, 1960), 503-506.

13 On the persecution of the New Lights see M. Louise Green, *The Development of Religious Liberty in Connecticut* (Boston and New York, 1905), Chap. x *passim*, especially 248-262. Also Ellen D. Larned, *History of Windham County, Connecticut* (Worcester, 1874-1880), I, 393-485.

14 Stiles, *Itineraries*, 180-182.

had changed their ideas about consociational "persecution" to the point where they were willing to try a little of their own by using the New Haven Consociation to block the ordination of Old Light ministers in Wallingford and Meriden.[15] Bellamy, however, found it expedient to remain passionately devoted to local autonomy, for outside Litchfield County the New Divinity exercised no real power. The New Light ministers controlling the other consociations favored a more "enthusiastic" ministry, but they were far too conservative to follow the New Divinity in its Edwardsean rigors and its rejection of the Half-Way Covenant (the practice of allowing members of the congregation unwilling to take communion to have their children baptized, provided the parents recited a profession of faith called "owning the covenant").[16] Throughout Connecticut, especially in the east, the men who should have supported the New Divinity broke with the consociations entirely and set up "Strict Congregational" or "Separate" churches that were neither respectable nor even legal.[17] Prudence as much as consistency dictated Bellamy's continued opposition to consociational authority, though it led him to support the ordination of Old Lights whose theology he loathed. These Old Lights for their part suddenly discovered the virtues of the congregational independence they had attacked in the years when they ran the consociations.[18]

This strange alliance proved workable but short-lived. By 1780 enough of the younger clergymen had adhered to the New Divinity to make it safe for Joseph Bellamy to champion the powers of the consociation to intervene in and decide local

[15] Charles H. Davis, *History of Wallingford, Connecticut* (Meriden, 1870), 164-209. Benjamin Trumbull, *A Complete History of Connecticut* (New London, 1898), II, 408-449. Trumbull, the New Divinity minister of North Haven, was strongly anti-Old Light.

[16] See, for example, the biographies of the Rev. Solomon Williams of Lebanon and the Rev. Samuel Bird of New Haven in Clifford K. Shipton, *Sibley's Harvard Graduates* (Boston, 1873-), VI, 354-357, XI, 359-364.

[17] C. C. Goen, *Revivalism and Separatism in New England, 1740-1800* (New Haven, 1962).

[18] The various shifts in position are summarized concisely in Morgan, *The Gentle Puritan*, 197-199.

disputes. For six years he was able to use those powers and his own influence to maintain the Rev. Hezekiah Gold in the Cornwall pulpit when most of the townspeople wanted their minister removed.

Bellamy had forced Cornwall's first minister, an Old Light named Solomon Palmer, out of the town pulpit and clear into Anglicanism in 1754.[19] When Hezekiah Gold succeeded Palmer on August 27, 1755,[20] four years after graduating from Yale, he had every reason to fear that the Pope of Bethlehem had similar plans for him. Gold was a New Light, but one of the conservative kind who favored the Half-Way Covenant and supported the consociations at a time when Bellamy still opposed them. In 1766 when Bellamy got the Litchfield Association (the county-wide organization of ministers) to condemn consociational power in the wake of the Wallingford controversy, Gold tried to convince the Cornwall church to break with the Association.[21] He failed and apparently decided to join the New Divinity. Stiles recalled in 1790:

> Dr. Bellamy when slaying and turning out Ministers in Litchfield County in his mistaken Zeal, threatened Messrs. Champion, Gould [Gold], Newel, and Smith, etc.—as well as Heaton, Palmer, Collins, Webster, Trumbul, Bartholomew, etc. The 4 first determined to stand it out—he frighted, awed and subdued Smith and made him a real convert. Gould was intimidated, submitted to the Doctor's Dictature and Haughtiness; Champion stood it out manfully . . . ; Newel sustained himself alone. . . .[22]

Gold had to abandon the Half-Way Covenant officially[23] before Bellamy would leave him in peace, but he continued to practice something very close to it. Parents not in full com-

---

19 Franklin B. Dexter, *Biographical Sketches of the Graduates of Yale College* (New York, 1885-1911), I, 387 n. T. S. Gold, *Historical Records*, 47-51.

20 Dexter, *Graduates of Yale College*, II, 242.

21 Stiles, *Itineraries*, 180, 456. John Sedgwick, *An Impartial Narrative of the Proceedings of Nine Ministers, in the Town of Cornwall; and of the Facts Which Originated their Meeting* (Hartford, 1783), 46.

22 Stiles, *Literary Diary*, III, 419.

23 T. S. Gold, *Historical Records*, 53. Starr, *History of Cornwall*, 85.

munion still owned the covenant and had their children baptized in return: as late as 1785, six of the eleven children Gold baptized were not the offspring of church members in full communion.[24]

To this theological ambivalence Gold added an unpleasant manner and a possible tendency to violence. One of his supporters admitted under oath in 1781 that the minister engaged in sharp business practices, and that there was general complaint about his worldliness and covetousness. The same witness described Gold as "a cold, dull, lifeless preacher" inattentive to his clerical duties, and added for good measure that he was generally regarded as "an obscene, ludicrous person" who acted in an "exceedingly censorious and reproachful" manner towards those who disagreed with him.[25]

Cornwall could not have been very happy with its minister. Yet with Bellamy pacified he held his pulpit without serious incident for twenty-five years and might have continued to do so in the remaining ten years of his life if the American Revolution had not broken out.

III

Like most disputes this one began over money. Connecticut law required every town to pay for the support of a learned, orthodox minister of the established Congregational church, although the individual contract between minister and town decided the actual amount of the salary. Various laws exempted Quakers, Baptists, and Anglicans from paying rates to the Congregational church if they regularly supported a minister of their own. Legally, a citizen of Connecticut could not avoid paying for the upkeep of religion, though he had some choice as to the denomination he supported.

Cornwall had no difficulty paying Gold his £64.16s.4d annually until the Revolution, when soaring state taxes and other extraordinary expenses severely strained the town's

[24] Records of the First Church of Christ in Cornwall, I, 11, photostats of the Ms. records, Conn. State Library.

[25] Affidavit of Heman Swift in Sedgwick, *An Impartial Narrative*, 46-47.

limited economy. From two pence on the pound in October, 1774 the province tax rose under the pressure of war to an alarming seventeen shillings in 1779 (though ten shillings of the total amount was payable in inflated continental currency).[26] In addition the town itself had to lay special rates to raise bounties for recruits and to pay for supplies for the army.[27]

Unlike many Connecticut towns, Cornwall made an honest effort to meet its quotas. As of May 24, 1785, it owed only £868 in back taxes, far and away the smallest amount for any of the seventy-seven towns on the arrears list. Even the neighboring towns of Kent, Canaan, Sharon, Norfolk, and Goshen, which were not much more populous, owed several times this amount.[28]

Gradually the town began to run out of money. A petition praying for tax abatements submitted to the state legislature by Andrew Young and John Sedgwick related how the residents of Cornwall "found themselves, exhausted, their stock expended and their resources at an end; the mode of levying and collecting taxes, has taken their property, and rendered their freehold burthensome and of no value. . . ." [29]

Exhausted or not the citizens of Cornwall were willing to pay for the Revolution, but not for their minister. At a time of straitened finances, he had made the mistake of taking sides in one of those inevitable feuds between two prominent families that plagued New England town life. The legislature had promoted Captain John Sedgwick over Captain Edward Rogers to the rank of major; Edward and his brother Noah Rogers allegedly attributed this to the influence of Gold, who

26 Charles J. Hoadly, editor, *Public Records of the Colony of Connecticut* (Hartford, 1850-1890), XIV, 346, 432. Leonard W. Labaree, editor, *Public Records of the State of Connecticut* (Hartford, 1894-), II, 18, 176-178, 227, 413.

27 "Extracts from Cornwall Revolutionary Records, 1774-84," 2, 7, 8, transcript of original town records, Conn. State Library.

28 Conn. Archives, Revolutionary War Papers, 1st Series, XVIII, 81.

29 Conn. Archives . . . , XXVII, Pt. 2, 238.

had been married to Sedgwick's sister. She had died in child-birth, but the family bond remained.[30]

Gold himself thought the Rogerses were the main cause of the growing dissatisfaction, but his wealth was more important. The Connecticut Assembly had excused clergymen from taxation and military service, yet Gold was rich enough to be on Ezra Stiles's list of "Wealthy Ministers in Connecticut" in 1790 with the figure "£3,000" after his name.[31] Men fighting a major war and paying heavy taxes are not always notable for sweet reasonableness; with some justice the residents of Cornwall resented their minister's exemptions.[32]

Rampant inflation accompanying the war provided the town with an opportunity to pay the ministerial rate in paper money, which daily decreased in real value. By 1779 Gold's salary had fallen over two years in arrears and a town meeting was insisting that he take it in a "Nominal Sum of Money" (paper money at face value).[33] He counterproposed that he deduct his share of the extraordinary expenses of the war from his salary and receive the remainder at full value. The towns-people rejected this offer on July 26, 1779, and then declared themselves "uneasy with, or under" Gold's "administration in the work of the Ministry." The same town meeting also recorded itself as "uneasy" with the mode of taxation in the state.[34] Tired of paying both taxes and minister, Cornwall proposed to rid itself of both.

In effect the vote ordered Gold to concur with the town in calling a council for his dismission or the town would call one on its own. Such councils were committees of the ministers and church members of nearby towns, often appointed by the

[30] Hezekiah Gold, *A True State of the Rise and Progress of the Controversy in Cornwall* (Hartford, 1783), 3-4, 12.

[31] Stiles, *Itineraries*, 405.

[32] Sedgwick wrote that the town was reluctant to pay Gold because the minister was "in very affluent circumstances." *An Impartial Narrative*, 8.

[33] Cornwall First Book, 29.

[34] Cornwall First Church Records, I, 119. Cornwall First Book, 25-26.

consociation, that ordained and dismissed ministers and mediated disputes. Before the town could legally call one, the members of the church (those townspeople in full communion) would have to pass a concurring vote. A church meeting took place on September 6, 1779, but Joseph Bellamy came down from Bethlehem to serve as moderator and dictate the proceedings. By an unstated margin the church first declined to dismiss Gold and then voted it "the duty of a christian people to make a minister's salary good as well as the wages of day labourers." [35]

The town did get a council to meet in Cornwall in November, but only to mediate the dispute. Bellamy directed this too, assisted by the Rev. Cotton Mather Smith of Sharon, his "Disciple," who "endeavored and aped an Imitation of him." [36] The council rejected the town's charges of dissatisfaction and scandal on the strictly procedural grounds that the committee presenting them had violated "gospel procedure" in failing to bring them up at a church meeting before calling in the consociation. Then, ignoring its own requirement of strict "gospel procedure," the council censured the members of the committee who were also members of the church, even though no charges had been brought against *them* at a church meeting.[37]

In protecting Gold from his congregation Bellamy found himself championing the power of the consociations to decide local disputes, a position he had condemned thirteen years before during the Wallingford dispute. But the New Divinity had not controlled the New Haven Consociation in 1766; it ruled the Litchfield Consociation in 1779. Bellamy simply chose to support central authority while it supported him, the standard tactic in Connecticut religious disputes and one the town could also use. The Cornwall dissidents had implicitly recognized consociational authority when they called on an

[35] Cornwall First Church Records, I, 120.

[36] Stiles, *Literary Diary*, III, 419.

[37] Hezekiah Gold, *A True State*, 6. Sedgwick, *An Impartial Narrative*, 8. "Gospel procedure" was based on *Matthew* 18:15-17.

ecclesiastical council to remove Gold, but once Bellamy used that authority in favor of the minister they decided to deny its validity by taking the Cornwall church out of the Litchfield Consociation.

By 1780 Gold and Bellamy together had so enraged the majority of the townspeople that they cared more about ridding themselves of the two ministers and their consociation than they did about saving money. In preparation for a local declaration of independence, a Cornwall town meeting on March 13, 1780 voted Gold full payment through 1779, £140, not in paper but at full value.[38] Then less than a month later another town meeting declared the Cornwall church "Strict Congregational" and unconnected with "the Ecclesiastical Constitution of this State," and ordered Gold "not to perform Service any more in this town." It also appointed a committee presided over by Edward Rogers to find a new minister, and another under his brother Noah to take over the meeting-house.[39] When Gold refused to surrender either pulpit or building without a concurring vote of the church, his opponents unsuccessfully tried to seize both by force. Soon after, they set up a separate Sunday service in another part of town.[40]

The committee appointed to get a new minister had better luck. After a year's search it secured the Rev. John Cornwall in June, 1781, though his services extended only to the Separates, a majority of the town, but a minority of the church. The new minister had spent most of his life working as a shoe-maker[41] and while he turned out to be a popular and effective preacher, his selection in 1781 resulted from the reluctance of any self-respecting Yale graduate to associate himself with Separatism or Strict Congregationalism. The Connecticut Gen-

[38] Cornwall Town Meetings, I, 4. Ms. record of town meetings, Office of the Town Clerk, Cornwall, Conn.

[39] Cornwall Town Meetings, I, 5.

[40] Hezekiah Gold, *A True State*, 9, 10-11. Ten of the men who tried to seize the meetinghouse suffered £5 fines. Litchfield County Court Records, VII, 40-41, 53, Conn. State Library.

[41] Edward E. Cornwall, *William Cornwall and His Descendants, A Genealogical History* (New Haven, 1901), 44. T. S. Gold, *Historical Records*, 57.

eral Assembly had legalized the movement four years before, in 1777,[42] after decades of persecution, but by then it was dying out, as most Separates either rejoined the established churches or became Baptists. The established Congregational church continued to look on Separates as schismatics or worse.

The members of the new Separate church had no quarrel with Gold's theology, for they freely tolerated doctrinal differences. When two members of the Second Church (as the Separates came to be called) declared that they wanted rebaptism by total immersion, a meeting took place to see if the church were really Baptist. The majority decided it was not, but that each member should do as he wished about baptisms, a neat solution to the most divisive religious issue in New England.[43] The church's formal statements of belief proclaimed the members' complete faith in the "Edwardean System," and Bellamy himself probably would have objected only to the one article in their creed which denied the "Civil Power" any authority in religious matters, including the power to pass laws for the support of the ministry.[44]

In fact, the so-called Separates did not think they had separated from anything or anyone besides the Consociation; they still considered themselves the lawful Church of Christ in Cornwall, the only such church, which by a majority vote had decided to dismiss its minister and renounce the Saybrook Platform. In two abortive attempts to take possession of the meetinghouse the dissidents tried to enforce this claim. Only after they failed to do so and to get an official majority of the church (as opposed to the town) to dismiss Gold did the town majority even set up the customary church organization or give Mr. Cornwall a formal call to the pulpit he already filled.[45] The town had adopted Strict Congregationalism simply be-

[42] *Public Records of the State of Conn.*, I, 232.

[43] Entry for 1787, Records of the Second Church of Christ in Cornwall, Ms. no. 9, Box H403A, Cornwall Free Library.

[44] Starr, *A History of Cornwall*, 99.

[45] Entry of Aug. 28, 1782, Second Church Records. This is two years after the original split.

cause they found that established Congregationalism worked contrary to their interests; they had meant only to take over the old church, not to set up a new one. Yet since only nine actual members of the First Church had withdrawn,[46] leaving a majority behind, there were now *two* Congregational churches in Cornwall.

Early in 1781 on Gold's request the Litchfield Association sent another committee to investigate the Cornwall dispute: Bellamy and Cotton Mather Smith came again, with the Rev. Ammi Robbins added. Aside from threatening and bullying such Separates as would still acknowledge his authority, Bellamy proposed four slanted questions to them. He never received an answer.[47]

Shortly thereafter, Gold invited himself to a meeting of the First Church and (according to John Sedgwick) blocked a new move for his dismissal. Instead, in May, the members voted themselves in "full charity" with their minister, confident he was free of scandal and heresy.[48]

Sedgwick was Gold's brother-in-law and a member of the First Church, but he thought that was going too far. Convinced that only Gold's removal could reunite the two churches, he combined with his old military rival, Edward Rogers, to bring the union about.[49] Sedgwick's reversal coincided with the start of a long, happy political career that brought him a seat in the legislature twenty-six times and a major-generalcy in the militia, but more than ambition lay behind his decision. The man who had commanded a regiment at Valley Forge had had enough of Bellamy's dictation.

Sedgwick still retained his membership in the First Church and brought a formal prosecution against Gold before the

[46] Records of the Litchfield North Consociation, II, 168-169, transcript of the original Ms., collection of the Missionary Society of Connecticut, Congregational House, Hartford.

[47] Records of the Litchfield North Consociation, II, 167, 168-169. Sedgwick, *An Impartial Narrative*, 13. The four questions are given accurately in Hezekiah Gold, *A True State*, 19.

[48] Sedgwick, *An Impartial Narrative*, 13. First Church Records, I, 121.

[49] Sedgwick, *An Impartial Narrative*, 10.

Litchfield Association on October 26, 1781.[50] Since Bellamy had just rid that organization of his last remaining clerical opponents, Abel Newell and Judah Champion,[51] it received the charges with something less than complete sympathy. Sedgwick arraigned Gold for being covetous, worldly, and more interested in business than religion; for not maintaining church discipline and allowing unqualified persons to the communion service; for violent behavior, "ludicrous, indecent and obscene language" and outright lying. The Association first refused to decide on his complaint at all, then spent three days hearing his evidence, and at the end of them refused to pass on it. Each time Sedgwick introduced proof of misbehavior the Association stated it did not approve of such conduct and asked Gold if he did. The minister's reply in the negative answered the charge. When Sedgwick objected to Bellamy he received only threats.[52]

John Sedgwick came from a family in which the title of major general was almost hereditary. His great-grandfather commanded at the siege of Jamaica in 1654, his brother was to be Speaker of the House of Representatives, and his grandson would lead a corps in the Army of the Potomac; more than most people, he did not like to be coerced. Neither did Captain Edward Rogers, his brother Noah, or Lieutenant Matthew Patterson: all of them were active men accustomed to command. None of them ranked as the richest, the most distinguished or the most educated man in Cornwall, but that only made them more sensitive about their dignity. They were willing to do a great many other things before they submitted to a clerical organization that had attempted to overawe and intimidate them.

By 1781 the quarrel in Cornwall, which had never really been about religion, had also long since ceased to be about money. The town had already paid Gold £140; it made no

50 Sedgwick, *An Impartial Narrative*, 19-20, 22-23, 39-40.
51 Dexter, *Graduates of Yale College*, II, 250-252, 262-263.
52 Sedgwick, *An Impartial Narrative*, 23-30, 35, 38.

sense for it to pay the costs of maintaining two ministers and several law suits just to keep him from getting another £89 he claimed was still due him. The Separates also wanted the meetinghouse and the parsonage fund, but they could have had both simply by paying off Gold and accepting consociational authority. The Association's opinion of October 31, 1781 had exonerated Gold, but it also advised the First Church to call a new minister if that would bring the Separates back.[53]

But the dispute had turned from an economic into a political one. The Separates no longer wanted to come back. Two years of visits by representatives of the established order had convinced most of Cornwall that outside interference was tyranny even if the tyrants were not King George and the English Parliament, but Pope Bellamy and the Litchfield Consociation. If the war for liberty from the first was a fight to the finish, the war for liberty from the second would be the same. The people of Cornwall fought the two struggles simultaneously and they presented their case accordingly. Sedgwick proceeded to write *An Impartial Narrative*, Cornwall's appeal to a candid world, and in it he attacked ministers and consociations in the same terms dozens of other Connecticut pamphleteers were currently using to challenge other institutions deemed threats to the liberties the people were struggling for in the Revolution.[54]

"A love of dominion incidental to the human heart," Sedgwick declared, and "misplaced confidence" coupled with inertia had resulted in the enslavement of nine tenths of mankind, although by nature all men were entitled to an equal share of freedom. One such enslavement was clerical power. The clergy had the same function as any other institution, that of advancing the interests of the people. Instead, left unwatched, every group of clergymen tried to transform itself into the Church of Rome, complete with a guarded mystery and despotic power:

[53] Hezekiah Gold, *A True State*, 17.

[54] Morgan, *The Gentle Puritan*, 343-344, describes the mood of the period throughout the state..

... none must be admitted but those who are qualified to support the interest of the order, and when once admitted, the same interest will induce them to support every *true son*. This at least will happen, unless the *clergy* are better than other men; and as this has not always been the case, we may probably suppose it will not always, (if so at present) continue; and it is as well the duty as the interest of every community to guard against probable evils.[55]

The ministers already had power, prestige, and organization. "Nothing is wanted but the revenues of the Romish clergy, to render the present [clergy] as formidable as those," and Connecticut law inadvertently supplied this one element needed to turn the consociations into an Inquisition with Bellamy as its Torquemada. At the same time that the law required every town to support a minister, it also enforced the consociations' claim to decide who that minister should be. "What is this, but forming in the state, offices which are uncontroulable by the law[s] and independent of them?"[56]

Nothing about this argument, not even its ferocity, distinguished it from the other crusades against closed or secret organizations with which Connecticut occupied itself throughout the 1780's.[57] Cornwall had not been the only town to suffer the consociations' displeasure during the Revolution: the Rev. Isaac Foster accused the Hartford Consociation in 1780 of using the Saybrook Platform to introduce "a tyranny more intolerable on the people than that from which they are trying to free themselves."[58] The people resented any kind of tyranny, domestic or foreign, and democratic hostility combined with anticlericalism forced all mention of the Platform out of the revised code of state laws in 1784, though the Congrega-

[55] *An Impartial Narrative*, iii-vi.

[56] *An Impartial Narrative*, v-vi.

[57] Cf. the resolutions of a Torington town meeting printed in *Connecticut Courant*, July 29, 1783, which all but advocate armed resistance to the payment of officers' pensions.

[58] Quoted in M. Louise Green, *The Development of Religious Liberty in Connecticut*, 338.

tional establishment managed to keep some legal privileges.[59]

Sedgwick's pamphlet also closely resembled the brief that many other writers were preparing against the Society of the Cincinnati and "commutation" (a commuted pension for officers of the Continental Army) at just the time he was attacking the clergy. When the army officers organized the Cincinnati, an hereditary benevolent society, in 1783, the citizens of Connecticut promptly denounced it as "a new and dangerous order of men" who aspired to form an hereditary nobility by creating a prestigious and exclusive organization with a fixed public revenue (the commuted pension).[60]

Hezekiah Gold could not match his brother-in-law's revolutionary rhetoric. His ill-tempered reply, *A True State of the Rise and Progress of the Controversy in Cornwall,* could do no better than to accuse Sedgwick of being *non compos mentis.*[61] But in the law courts the minister had considerably greater success. A series of suits and counter suits ultimately ended in his favor in 1783, and he got his £89.[62] He also stayed on as minister of those townspeople who had remained loyal to the First Church, while the Second continued on its Separate way under John Cornwall.

This financial settlement differed only slightly from the one Gold had proposed to a town meeting in 1779.[63] Four years of schism, tumult, and law suits had not saved Cornwall a penny,

[59] Green, *The Development of Religious Liberty . . .* , 339-341.

[60] Resolutions of the Middletown Convention printed in *Connecticut Courant,* March 30, 1784. Cf. the letters of "A Convention Man" and "AZ" in *Connecticut Courant,* Feb. 3, 1784, Feb. 10, 1784.

[61] 11-12.

[62] The legal battles can be traced in Cornwall Town Meetings, I, 14, 16, 27, 28, 29-30 and in the Litchfield County Court Records, VIII, 20. Although the town announced its intention of appealing to the Litchfield Superior Court and the Assembly a search of the Superior Court dockets for 1783 in the Conn. State Library and of the Conn. Archives failed to turn up any record of such an appeal.

[63] He deducted his share of the extraordinary expenses of the war and received the rest of his money in silver or its equivalent as full payment for the period between Jan. 1, 1780 and Oct., 1782, the date the Second Church became legally entitled to exemption from the ministerial rate for the established church.

but by 1783 liberty not money concerned the townspeople. In fact, they no longer limited their conception of liberty and equality simply to freedom from the Litchfield Consociation; now they wanted an end to all exclusive organizations and all inequalities.

When the Middletown Convention met in the fall of 1783 to agitate for the overthrow of both the Cincinnati and commutation, Cornwall naturally approved of the meeting and sent as its representative Captain Edward Rogers.[64] The Second Church, the center of anticonsociational feeling, grew so enthusiastic it sent the Rev. John Cornwall as its own delegate in addition to the representative of the town.[65]

The same egalitarian spirit continued in Cornwall and in Connecticut in the latter part of the decade. When Peter Bulkley of Colchester introduced a "tendry act" into the Assembly on June 11, 1787 to relieve debtors, advocates of the bill proudly declared it would lead to a relatively equal distribution of property among the people, an essential of popular government. Their opponents, more conservative, accepted the need for a near equal distribution of property, but felt existing inheritance laws already provided for it.[66]

The bill failed by a lopsided margin, but the voting anticipated the struggle over ratification of the federal constitution in the following December. It also indicated the extreme to which some Litchfield men carried their concept of equality. In Litchfield County the towns supporting the Bulkley bill with its radical egalitarianism opposed the Constitution, which outlawed bills of its type, and towns opposing the bill supported the Constitution,[67] yet the county's debtors were not

<hr/>

[64] Cornwall Town Meetings, I, 30.

[65] Entry of Sept. 9, 1783, Second Church Records.

[66] *Connecticut Courant*, June 11, 1787.

[67] The six towns one or more of whose representatives voted for the Bulkley bill cast seven "no" and four "yes" votes at the ratifying convention; the thirteen towns one or more of whose representatives voted against the bill cast nineteen "yes" and four "no" votes at the convention. The convention as a whole voted 128 to 40 in favor of ratification. *Public Records of the State of Connecticut*, VI, 549-552.

suffering from the kind of oppression Bulkley sought to end. His preamble announced that suits for debts were increasing, and his supporters claimed his act "put it out of the power of creditors to torment poor debtors" and abolished imprisonment for debt. In point of fact, suits for debt in Litchfield County were declining markedly in number, while only one man in the history of the county had been imprisoned for debt since 1752. In all of Cornwall, Kent, Sharon, and Salisbury in the same period only 145 attachments on land for nonpayment had been granted, and the lands of absentee speculators accounted for most of them.[68] The Litchfield County representatives were bitter-end egalitarians indeed, fighting the good fight in a place where there was no one to fight it for. Among them, voting both for the bill and against the Constitution, stood Cornwall's representative, Lieutenant Matthew Patterson, an active leader of the Separates.

Cornwall did not send Sedgwick to the constitutional convention though he had represented the town in the Assembly for most of the preceding five years. Experience had made him gloomy and he would probably have voted for ratification. By 1787 he no longer talked of institutions of government with quite the same contempt as in 1783. In May, 1787 he wrote that he was convinced "a national Revolution is approaching in America for want of the necessary powers of Government . . . had every state given Congress the power this has, I apprehend it might have been sufficient." He had not lost faith in democracy, he only apprehended "that Democratical Governments depend on a due Execution of the law, and the laws for regulating the Militia, are the first, and only effectual support of all others." [69]

Sedgwick was tired, and perhaps Cornwall was growing tired as well. The church settlement of 1783 had only been a truce; the opposing parties continued sporadic feuding, but after 1787 the intensity of the controversy fell off. The quarrel

[68] Grant, *Kent*, 69, 80-82.
[69] Conn. Archives, Rev. War, 1st Series, XXXVI, Pt. 1, 20.

dragged slowly on towards a solution based neither on finance nor on liberty.

IV

The two churches made one last effort to unite when the Rev. Medad Rogers began to assist John Cornwall at the Second Church in 1785 and also to preach occasionally at the First Church. Rogers was the ideal compromise. After graduating from Yale in 1777, he studied divinity for two years with the Rev. Benjamin Trumbull, a New Divinity stalwart.[70] His theology made him acceptable to Bellamy (more acceptable than Gold in fact), while he was also the brother of Dr. Timothy Rogers, the town physician and a sympathizer of the Second Church. In contrast to Gold, whose worldliness and general bad temper gained him few supporters, the new minister was humble and committed. He liked to talk about "the moral character of God, proved from the works of creation" and avoided deeper and more dangerous topics.[71] Modest, troubled and in dead earnest, nothing about Rogers could offend anyone. Altogether, he seems one of the few New England clergymen of the eighteenth century who might have made a success in the same profession in the twentieth.

Rogers bore abuse from Gold patiently for months while the two churches negotiated terms for reunion. The Second Church insisted that the reunited organization have no connection with the Consociation, a condition the First was reluctant to grant. Finally, on March 8, 1786, the First Church voted to dismiss its minister.[72]

Gold denied the validity of the vote and called in the Consociation once again. Under Bellamy's direction a full meeting of the Consociation held in Cornwall on April 25, 1786, re-

---

70 Dexter, *Graduates of Yale College*, III, 703-704.

71 Rogers, Oct. 30, 1781, to Benjamin Trumbull, Benjamin Trumbull Mss., Beinecke Library, Yale University. Rogers repeatedly had trouble expounding even the most basic elements of Calvinist theology, as he reported to Trumbull in a letter of March 17, 1780, Trumbull Mss., and recorded on March 1, 1786 in his Ms. diary, also in the possession of the Beinecke Library.

72 Entries of Feb. 15, 1786, Feb. 27, 1786, March 1, 1786, March 6, 1786, March 8, 1786, Rogers Ms. diary.

fused to dismiss Gold and then voted to meet again in June "in order to prosecute the general Design of the present Mutiny."[73] That proved unnecessary, for in May Gold and his church came to an agreement. By the terms of a highly peculiar settlement Gold relinquished his salary and all ministerial authority over the church and promised not to hinder the choice of a new minister. In return, since a Congregational minister put his clerical status in doubt if he did not serve a specific church, the First Church did not officially dismiss him. Thus Gold retained "the Rights of an ordained Minister in other Churches," the right to conduct marriages (and collect the attendant fees) and all other privileges and exemptions state law granted to ministers.[74]

The Consociation agreed to this "Predicament"; Cornwall and Hezekiah Gold had parted at last. Four years later in May, 1790, he died of influenza. The great engine of discord, Joseph Bellamy, also passed away that year, and Litchfield County was a little quieter.

A good point for a happy ending, except that the split did not end. When two churches could not agree on Rogers' salary, he moved on to New Fairfield in October, 1786. Two years later John Cornwall also left, joining a general exodus of Litchfield men to Dutchess County, New York.[75]

Both churches found new ministers (the First the Rev. Hercules Weston, the Second the Rev. Israel Holley), but all hope of unity left with Rogers. The Second Church voted to build itself a meetinghouse and the First to replace its old one.[76] No one any longer thought of seeing both congregations under one roof on a Sunday morning.

The Second Church erected its building at the Center, but the First Church moved its new meetinghouse well over a mile southward to the Plain, where the present village of Corn-

[73] Records of the Litchfield North Consociation, II, 63-64.

[74] Records of the Litchfield North Consociation, II, 64-66.

[75] T. S. Gold, *Historical Records*, 58. Dexter, *Graduates of Yale College*, III, 704. Edward E. Cornwall, *William Cornwall and his Descendants*, 44.

[76] T. S. Gold, *Historical Records*, 128 n.

wall stands. They would have moved it farther south still if the subscribers to the new building had not insisted on its construction at the Plain.[77]

The new location intensified an already existing geographical aspect of the split: most of the Separates lived in the northern half of Cornwall and most of the adherents of the First Church in the southern, so that the two groups were also known as the Northern and Southern Societies. Only a little more than a mile separated the two meetinghouses, but it was a very hilly mile with no road over it. Members of the Northern Society had to ride up to five miles over bad roads to get to their meetinghouse as it was, and they hesitated to push beyond that over rough country to the Plain.

At the same time the older motives for division were dying out. The records of the Second Church show an altercation with the First as late as 1801, but it became harder and harder to maintain the old crusade against consociational oppression as time passed and the Litchfield Consociation grew less oppressive. New settlers to whom the traditional feuds meant nothing came in, while some old residents moved on to Vermont, New York, and Ohio. The return of John Sedgwick to the First Church in 1793 registered the lessening tension.[78]

In 1797 the North Society, the old Separate Church, petitioned the Assembly to regularize the status quo by dividing Cornwall along an east-west line into two legally incorporated ecclesiastical societies. The inhabitants to the south of the line would adhere to the First Church and the inhabitants to the north to the Second.[79]

A "society" was simply the legally designated geographical territory of any given established church. The law deemed every resident of a society a member of its Congregational church and required him to pay for the support of its minister unless and until he filed a certificate showing that he con-

77 Starr, *History of Cornwall*, 87-88. First Church Records, IV, 1-9.

78 First Church Records, quoted in Starr, *History of Cornwall*, 89.

79 Copy of petition in Box H403A, Cornwall Free Library. The original is not in the Conn. Archives.

tributed to the support of a church of another denomination. Only one legally established society existed in Cornwall, coterminal with the town's boundaries, and it was that of the First Church. Every new settler became a supporter of that church unless he said otherwise. In petitioning the Assembly to divide this society and assign the northern half to it, the Second Church in effect had asked to return to the establishment and to have its rival's legal advantage in securing new members canceled.

The inhabitants of northern Cornwall had to petition again in 1799, 1803, and 1804 before the Assembly acted. The petition of April 21, 1804 pointed out that by dividing the existing ecclesiastical society the Assembly would only be giving the force of law to existing conditions. Of the 121 families attending worship at the Second Church, 117 lived north of the proposed line, while 106 of the 121 families supporting the First Church lived south of it. Taxable property of the two groups was almost equal in value. Reunion between the two societies, the petitioners related, had been attempted, had failed, and was no longer possible. The only reason given: simple distance. Because of the state of the roads the petitioners found it inconvenient to attend services in the meetinghouse of the First Church.[80]

The Assembly granted the petition after a fashion. Instead of dividing the existing society, it set up a second society without any fixed boundaries. The signers of the petition and anyone else who claimed the privilege by December 1, 1804, would become members of this new society, while new residents had one year to enroll themselves with the clerk of the Second Society or they automatically became members of the First.[81] The petitioners had hoped for more, but at least they had legal recognition once again after twenty-four years without it.

Rehabilitation of the Second Church with the Litchfield Consociation took a little longer. The Church had dropped the designation "Strict Congregationalist" in 1803, and after

[80] Conn. Archives, Ecclesiastical Affairs, 2nd Series, I, 150, 152, 154.
[81] Conn. Archives . . . , I, 156ab.

the departure of the unorthodox Israel Holley (who had no formal education and a long history of ministering to Separate churches) it replaced him with the more respectable Rev. Josiah Hawes. Hawes was the standard "godly, learned gospel minister," having graduated from Williams College and then studied divinity with the Rev. Charles Backus of Somers. The Litchfield Association had licensed him to preach and the Consociation regularly ordained him at Cornwall on March 14, 1805. Finally in 1809, the Second Church formally rejoined the Litchfield Consociation and a permanent settlement was almost at hand.[82]

Almost—one symbolic event remained to complete the story. On September 23, 1816, thirty-six years after the original separation and less than two years before the total disestablishment of the Congregational church in Connecticut, a resident of Cornwall petitioned the Assembly on an ecclesiastical matter. He was legally registered as a member of the First Society, but asked the Assembly to transfer him to the Second because "his local situation in Said Town is such that it is very inconvenient for him to attend Public Worship at the usual place of the Said first society." He lived in northern Cornwall, much closer to the meetinghouse of the Second Society.[83] Petition granted. The name of the petitioner was Hezekiah Gold: he was the son of the late minister and the nephew of John Sedgwick. What had started as a quarrel over money and became a struggle for liberty ended as a question of geography.

[82] T. S. Gold, *Historical Records*, 66-69. Starr, *History of Cornwall,* 99-100, 313, 315. *Contributions to the Ecclesiastical History of Connecticut* (New Haven, 1861), 449.

[83] Conn. Archives, Ecclesiastical Affairs, 2nd Series, I, 157-158.

Evangelicals Triumphant: The Baptists' Assault on the Virginia Glebes, 1786-1801

Thomas E. Buckley, S.J.

ONE spring day in 1787, John Waller, a Baptist preacher, boldly approached the distinguished Episcopal vestrymen of Berkeley Parish in Spotsylvania County and invited them to sign a petition to the Virginia legislature for the sale of the parish farm lands. Like many former parishes of the Church of England after the Revolution, Berkeley lacked an incumbent minister. Waller informed the vestry of his intentions not only for the Berkeley glebe but for selling "all the Vacant Glebes, and Continue Selling as they became Vacant." Accused of attempting to eliminate the Episcopal clergy, Waller retorted, "If they were true Ministers of the Gospel they would preach as well without Glebes." A vestryman reported that the interview "ended at Last with my telling him that I would Neither Sign for nor against it; that I believed the assembly was very full of it and needed no further information, and, whatever they did I Should Submit to."[1]

Waller, whose nickname had been "Swearing Jack" before he got religion, served regularly on the General Committee, the central organization for Virginia Baptists. When Virginia's General Assembly met in the fall of 1787, his petition was among several urging the sale of the glebes. Another from Lyttleton Parish in Cumberland County asked also that the church building there be opened to all denominations and attacked the pretensions of incumbent minister Christopher McRae, "who, exercising a power given by the law which was in force before the Revolution, conceives, that he alone may lock the door and that he alone has a right to keep the key." To a legislature bone weary of religious bickering, the Baptists pointed out that "feudes and jealousies" were created by a preferential system that "tends only to sow seeds of Discord and crumble us into parties."[2] Alerted to the threat, Episcopalians countered with

Fr. Buckley is a member of the Department of History at Loyola Marymount University, Los Angeles. A version of this article was presented at a symposium at the Institute of Early American History and Culture in April 1983. The author wishes to thank Richard Beeman, Angus Hawkins, Donald G. Mathews, Thad W. Tate, and Joseph Tiedemann for their criticism and encouragement.

[1] Joseph Herndon to [James] Stephenson, Apr. 8, 1787, typescript, Letters of Joseph Herndon, Alderman Library, University of Virginia, Charlottesville.

[2] The other petitions that year favoring the sale came from Buckingham, Chesterfield, Cumberland, and Orange counties (Religious Petitions, 1774-1802, Presented to the General Assembly of Virginia, Oct. 6, 17, Nov. 20, 1787,

petitions decrying any "Act of Violence" against their property, and from Waller's county the Berkeley vestry announced that they planned to hire "an orthodox Minister" and desired no further "oppression or Molestation" from anyone.[3]

As the confrontation between Waller and the vestrymen demonstrates, the passage in 1786 of Thomas Jefferson's bill establishing religious liberty did not end church-state controversy or remove religion from the realm of politics. In fact, the episode exemplifies the continuing struggle pitting educated Episcopal clergy and gentry against middling- and lower-sort evangelical challengers that had agitated Virginia for the previous quarter century.[4] At issue was the property held by what had been the established Church of England: the churches and chapels, the communion plate and liturgical books, and the glebe lands, homes, barns, and slaves set aside for the ministers' use. Colonial legislation had provided for such property, and over the years it accrued from public sources and private donations in all of the almost one hundred Anglican parishes formed before 1776.[5] East of the Blue Ridge, these holdings were often extensive and sometimes quite valuable.[6] The eventual seizure of this property was the most radical step

microfilm, Virginia State Library, Richmond); they were also signed by Baptist clergy in those areas. The names of the Baptist ministers and preachers are in John Asplund, *The Annual Register of the Baptist Denomination, in North-America; to the First of November, 1790 . . .* ([Richmond, Va., 1791]), 23-34.

[3] Religious Petitions, Cumberland Co., Nov. 6, Spotsylvania Co., Nov. 10, 22, 1787. Two years later the vestry was finally successful in hiring Hugh Corran Boggs, a newly ordained minister who served as rector of Berkeley Parish until his death in 1828 (G. MacLaren Brydon, "A List of Clergy of the Protestant Episcopal Church Ordained after the American Revolution, Who Served in Virginia between 1785 and 1814, and a List of Virginia Parishes and Their Rectors for the Same Period," *William and Mary Quarterly*, 2d Ser., XIX [1939], 399).

[4] For an excellent study of this conflict see Richard R. Beeman and Rhys Isaac, "Cultural Conflict and Social Change in the Revolutionary South: Lunenburg County, Virginia," *Journal of Southern History*, XLVI (1980), 525-550.

[5] Two fine articles dealing with the Anglican minister and his parish are Arthur Pierce Middleton, "The Colonial Virginia Parson," *WMQ*, 3d Ser., XXVI (1969), 425-440, and "The Colonial Virginia Parish," *Historical Magazine of the Protestant Episcopal Church*, XL (1971), 431-446.

[6] The extent and value of this property are attested by various sources. Newspaper advertisements for clergymen invariably describe the glebe and houses and sometimes give the acreage. For example: Elizabeth City Parish (Elizabeth City County), "house of brick with four rooms and a passage above, and as many below stairs, all convenient and necessary out houses, the land very good, and contains 200 acres, with plenty of rail timber," and 24 slaves (*Virginia Independent Chronicle* [Richmond], Sept. 17, 1788); Hungar's Parish (Northampton County), "1600 acres of land . . . a good old fashioned brick dwelling house, with all necessary out-houses, in good repair." It included gardens, orchards, and 12 slaves, and the vestry stated that the land produced "handsome profits." It had come to the parish by private donation (*Virginia Gazette and General Advertiser* [Richmond], Aug. 3, 1803). Vestry books occasionally state the parish holding. For example, the

taken in the aftermath of the Revolution against any religious body or against the property rights of any individual or group in any state.

Despite this fact, historians have paid little attention to the fight over the church's property in Virginia. Most treat it briefly as a postscript to the passage of Jefferson's statute rather than as an important incident in its own right.[7] Political historians in particular have misinterpreted it, most often by attributing the repeal of the glebe laws to party politics and to the intervention of Jefferson's close political associate James Madison.[8] However, there is no evidence that Madison became involved or that Republican-Federalist rivalries caused the final result. The struggle over the glebe lands ended as it did because Baptist religious leaders developed the political skills and gained sufficient support from evangelicals and others across the state to force the legislature to undo a major social-political compromise of the Revolution.

Most important, the larger significance for the nation of the fight over the glebes in Virginia has been completely overlooked. The contest demonstrates the practical effect of the Statute for Religious Freedom. That act did not rigidly separate church and state. Instead, by guaranteeing complete freedom of religious belief and expression, it encouraged Baptist churchmen to engage in the political arena in pursuit of further legislative goals. Success in the glebe contest trained them to compete on their own and helped lay the foundation for an organized evangelical bloc ready to impose, by legislation if necessary, its values and culture on the American body politic. Coming just before the Second Great Awakening swelled the pietistic camp, the triumph of Baptist-led forces in the glebe struggle in Virginia foreshadowed this critical development of evangelical politics in America. As the largest, most populous state and a center of Baptist strength and influence, Virginia set the pace for what would follow throughout much of the nation. Church-state interaction in the Old Dominion in the years immediately following the guarantees of religious

---

Henrico Parish (Henrico County) vestry estimated the worth of their 196 acres at £1,000 in 1791. It was rented out for £40 a year (St. John's Vestry Book, Apr. 25, 1791, Virginia Historical Society, Richmond). The personal property and land tax records at the Virginia State Library give further indications of the worth of this property.

[7] For example, H. J. Eckenrode, *Separation of Church and State in Virginia: A Study in the Development of the Revolution* (Richmond, Va., 1910). Denominational historians have provided the best coverage. See George MacLaren Brydon, *Virginia's Mother Church and the Political Conditions under Which It Grew* (Philadelphia, 1952), II, 474-535; Charles F. James, *Documentary History of the Struggle for Religious Liberty in Virginia* (Lynchburg, Va., 1900); Garnett Ryland, *The Baptists of Virginia, 1699-1926* (Richmond, Va., 1926); and Reuben Edward Alley, *A History of Baptists in Virginia* (Richmond, Va., 1973).

[8] See, for example, Richard R. Beeman, *The Old Dominion and the New Nation, 1788-1801* (Lexington, Ky., 1972), 93-95, 198-199, and Norman K. Risjord, *Chesapeake Politics, 1781-1800* (New York, 1978), 487-489.

liberty in Jefferson's statute is a paradigm for the entanglement of religion and politics in American history.

This study, first, examines the debate in the legislature and the Virginia countryside that culminated in the repeal of the laws granting property to the Episcopal church; second, proposes reasons for the Baptists' eventual triumph; and, third, offers an explanation for the collapse of Episcopalian opposition.

ACTIONS AFFECTING CHURCH-STATE RELATIONS
VIRGINIA, 1776-1802

1776   Virginia Declaration of Rights: Sixteenth article guarantees freedom of conscience.
        Assembly exempts dissenters from taxation for the established church, suspends taxes for church members, and affirms the church's property title.
1779   Jefferson presents Statute for Religious Freedom.
        Assembly ends all religious taxation.
1784   Baptists organize General Committee.
        Assembly grants Incorporation Act to Protestant Episcopal
   ·   Church and reaffirms property title.
        Assembly debates but postpones General Assessment.
1785   Statewide discussion of General Assessment proposal.
        Episcopalians hold first church convention.
1786   Assembly passes Statute for Religious Freedom.
1787   Incorporation Act repealed.
1799   Glebe laws repealed.
1802   Assembly provides for sale of glebe lands.

The ownership and control of Episcopalian property had supposedly been settled at the outset of the Revolution. In 1776 Virginia's Declaration of Rights guaranteed freedom of conscience, and that autumn the assembly effectively ended religious taxation. However, in what Episcopalians later termed a "compact," the law exempting dissenters from church taxes also provided that "in all time coming" the glebes and all other church property were to be "reserved to the use of the church by law established."[9] Nonetheless, the Revolution severely crippled the Church of England in Virginia; it not only lost public financial support and suffered a shortage of clergy, but it was unable to reorganize without legislative authorization. The last factor was the most critical in the 1780s. Episcopalians, particularly lay communicants, could not envision acting without government approval. Nor did the assembly demonstrate a desire to abdicate control, then or for many years thereafter. The state had

[9] The complete text of the law is in William Waller Hening [ed.], *The Statutes at Large: Being a Collection of All the Laws of Virginia, from the First Session of the Legislature, in the Year 1619* (Richmond, Va., and Philadelphia, 1809-1823), IX, 164-167, hereafter cited as Hening, *Statutes at Large.*

dominated the church too long. Although the legislature passed an incorporation act in 1784 for a renamed Protestant Episcopal Church in Virginia, this law did not free the church from legislative control. While reconfirming the church's title to its property, this act made ecclesiastical polity a matter of civil law. Since it smacked of legislative interference in internal church matters and evinced special concern for the Episcopalians, the act enraged the recently emancipated evangelicals.[10]

Even before it passed, Presbyterians expressed their resentment at the "unjust preeminence" and "substantial advantages" that the legislature had accorded the Episcopalians. A major complaint was that "an Estate . . . worth several hundred thousand pounds in Churches, Glebes, and derived from the pockets of all religious societies" had been awarded to one church "without compensation or restitution to the rest,. who in many places formed a large majority of the Inhabitants."[11] Then the same assembly that approved the incorporation act almost passed a general assessment tax to support "Teachers of the Christian Religion." Evangelicals saw this as yet another stratagem to help the Episcopal church revive and joined Madison and his allies in a vigorous campaign against it. After an extraordinary public debate in 1784-1785, the lawmakers rejected the assessment and enacted the guarantees embodied in Jefferson's statute.[12]

Flushed with victory in the assessment contest, Presbyterians and Baptists then attacked the incorporation act and the right of the Episcopal church to the glebes and church buildings. Baptists seized the offensive in the legislative session of 1786-1787. During the earlier church-state contests they had organized a General Committee composed of representatives from the district associations in Virginia to oversee matters of general interest, particularly "political grievances." Despite a distrust of hierarchical or centralized church government, the ministers recognized the need for concerted action in the highly volatile political climate of the time. Reuben Ford and John Leland, two of Virginia's most influential Baptist leaders, were delegated to represent the committee's view to the assembly.

Their petition was a carefully worded, highly emotional document that blasted the legislature for betraying Virginia's Declaration of Rights, joining "Church and State" in the incorporation act, laying "the founda-

[10] Thomas E. Buckley, S.J., *Church and State in Revolutionary Virginia, 1776-1787* (Charlottesville, Va., 1977), 87-170, *passim*. For the text of the incorporation act see Hening, *Statutes at Large*, XI, 532-537. This civil law established a church convention with lay and clerical delegates as the governing body of the church and fixed conditions and times for elections, vestry meetings, etc.

[11] Religious Petitions, May 26, 1784.

[12] The passage of Jefferson's bill has been treated in numerous studies. Important documents from this church-state settlement may be found in Eckenrode, *Separation of Church and State*. Buckley, *Church and State*, is a legislative history. The social dimensions of this controversy are best explained by Rhys Isaac, *The Transformation of Virginia, 1740-1790* (Chapel Hill, N.C., 1982).

tion for Ecclesiastical Tyranny," and taking "the first step towards an Inquisition."[13] In the next weeks this petition was joined by almost thirty others, mainly from tidewater and piedmont counties where Baptists were numerous. Following a strategy used successfully to pass Jefferson's statute, the committee had circulated county petitions for repeal of incorporation, sale of the "public property" held by the Episcopalians, and application of the resulting funds to "public use." These memorials laid bare the anger and stored-up antagonism of previous decades. While varying in style and language, they advanced a common historical perspective and interpretation of the Declaration of Rights. From the petitioners' viewpoint the church property had originally been wrested by force from their colonial forebears and given to the established church. Instead of returning it to the people at the Revolution, the assembly had transferred it to one religious group that not only bore no intrinsic connection to the now defunct colonial church but departed from it in name, laws, and forms of worship. Baptists saw this as oppression pure and simple. "Tyranny is not the better," one petition complained, "for being on this side of the Atlantic."[14]

The fourth article of the Declaration of Rights had stated "that no man, or set of men, are entitled to exclusive or separate emoluments or privileges from the community, but in consideration of publick services." Yet, in granting the Episcopalians exclusive use of the property that had belonged to the Church of England, the legislature had done precisely that.[15] "Good God," another memorial exclaimed, "can this be equal for a man that has five or six children, to will fi[f]ty or a hundred thousand pounds to one; and not one English Shilling to the rest of his Children; when all the Children Labour'd alike to Raise that hundred thousand pounds?"[16] The Episcopalians had been taken into the "Lap of the Legislature" and had been made the assembly's "favourite" and the "Church of the state." An Albemarle County petition bluntly reminded the assembly of another constituency with political power: "our whish [sic] is this, that our own delegates ... should be as free giving their own Sentiments as the Water that Runeth down the Brook: [but] if this Our

[13] Religious Petitions, Nov. 1, 1786.

[14] Robert B. Semple, *A History of the Rise and Progress of the Baptists in Virginia* (Richmond, Va., 1810), 69-71; Religious Petitions, Chesterfield Co., Nov. 24, 1786. Baptists argued that the renamed Protestant Episcopal Church in Virginia with its new church canons and revised liturgy was not the same as the former Church of England in Virginia.

[15] The most comprehensive treatment of this article is in A. E. Dick Howard, *Commentaries on the Constitution of Virginia* (Charlottesville, Va., 1974), I, 77-81. The Baptist petitions that quoted the article left off the second half, which continued: "which not being descendible, neither ought the offices of magistrate, legislator, or judge to be hereditary." The Revolutionary convention of 1776 never intended to apply this article to the established church (Buckley, *Church and State*, 18-19).

[16] Religious Petitions, Albemarle Co., Nov. 24, 1786.

Petition should meet with any Opposition and it comes to be debated in the house, pray Gentlemen be so kind as to let us see the ayes and noes."[17] The Baptists expected results from the legislature.[18]

Episcopalians fought back. Aware of the Baptist campaign, in May a convention had appointed a standing committee to look after the church's interests in Richmond, drafted a petition not to "be deprived of those conveniences" provided by incorporation, and urged parishes to submit memorials on the church's behalf.[19] In the greatest postwar display of Episcopalian unity, at least thirty-six congregations responded. They likewise advanced a common historical perspective, pointing out that most of the churches were built, and the glebes purchased, when virtually everyone belonged to the established church and "there was scarce any such thing as a Baptist" or any other kind of dissenter in Virginia. When the break with England came, Episcopalians had favored the Revolution and "cheerfully" accepted disestablishment, even though their number "far exceeded that of the Dissenters." Moreover, "as a compact" for accepting an end to state financial support, the 1776 legislature had guaranteed the security of their church property, not as a fresh grant but as a confirmation of what they already owned.[20] This compact theory was not new. In 1781 the Baptist John Leland had applied to the father of James Madison to use a church in St. Thomas Parish in Orange County. Denying the request, the senior Madison pointed to the 1776 act and noted that the dissenters had accepted the reservation of "the glebes, churches, books, plate, ornaments, donations" to the established church in exchange for the "privilege" of exemption from supporting it.[21]

Episcopalians also rejected the Baptist interpretation of the fourth article of the Declaration of Rights. It did not refer to churches or glebes, they insisted, but to hereditary offices inconsistent with republican

[17] *Ibid.*, Louisa Co., Oct. 31, 1786; Chesterfield Co., Nov. 24, 1786; Henrico Co., Oct. 31, 1786; Albemarle Co., Nov. 24, 1786.

[18] Neither Hanover nor Lexington presbyteries mention this issue in their minutes for 1786 (Records of the Proceedings of Hanover Presbytery, 1786-1814, Minutes of Lexington Presbytery, 1786-1792, Union Theological Seminary, Richmond). Only one memorial came from the largely Presbyterian counties across the Blue Ridge (Religious Petitions, Rockbridge Co., Nov. 2, 1786), and none from Prince Edward, the Presbyterians' piedmont center.

[19] *Journal of a Convention of the Protestant Episcopal Church in Virginia ... 1786,* in Francis L. Hawks, *Contributions to the Ecclesiastical History of the United States of America,* I (New York, 1836-1839), app. 13-17. Religious Petitions, Nov. 10, 1786.

[20] Religious Petitions, Stafford and King George counties, Nov. 24, Elizabeth City Co., Dec. 4, Caroline Co., Dec. 4, 1786.

[21] [William] Meade, *Old Churches, Ministers, and Families of Virginia* (Philadelphia, 1891), II, 87. County petitions had also made this point before (see, for example, Religious Petitions, Amelia Co., Nov. 8, 1784). For Leland's role as an advocate for religious freedom see L. H. Butterfield, "Elder John Leland, Jeffersonian Itinerant," American Antiquarian Society, *Proceedings,* LXII (1952), 155-242.

principles. Apart from history or legislation, they based their case on the rights of private property. If the legislature could seize the glebes and churches, then no one's property was secure, "for with equal propriety, and with the same justice, all grants for Lands under the Kings of England, now held under those grants; and all Donations, from any former Assembly, may by this, or any succeeding Assembly be declared null and void." The Episcopal standing committee warned that the "Violence" that took away their property would have a catastrophic effect on public confidence in government.[22]

As with the Baptist memorials, beneath the reasoned Episcopalian arguments the emotional currents of hurt, anger, and resentment ran deep. David Griffith, bishop-elect for Virginia, commented grimly: "It would seem that nothing will satisfy these people but the entire destruction of the Episcopal Church."[23] The petitions depicted the horrible effects of the seizure of Episcopalian property: churches converted into barns and stables, ministers driven off their lands and abandoned, and the old mother church reduced to wreckage. They also questioned the motives of the opposition, men of "envious disposition" whose "levelling Principles" were unfriendly to good order and the peace of society.[24] Coming from a broad spectrum of counties and signed by some of the most respected state leaders, the Episcopalians' memorials provided a strong counter to those of the Baptists. Madison, a member of the House of Delegates, wrote Jefferson that the property issue "involved the Legislature in some embarrassment."[25] The hyperbolic rhetoric of both sides betrayed the deep hostilities that had been building between Baptists and Episcopalians for over a generation.

Realizing that any decision they made would offend a sizable element of Virginia's population, the politicians compromised. A brief bill authorized all religious societies to appoint trustees to hold and manage their property and repealed the incorporation act as well as any other acts that inhibited the Episcopal church from regulating its own affairs.[26] It was a

[22] Religious Petitions, Elizabeth City Co., Dec. 4, 1786; Miscellaneous Petition, Dec. 5, 1786.
[23] Griffith to William White, Oct. 20, 1786, William White Papers, Church Historical Society, Austin, Tex.
[24] Religious Petitions, Stafford Co., Nov. 24, 1786; Miscellaneous Petition, Dec. 4, 1786.
[25] Madison to Thomas Jefferson, Feb. 15, 1787, in Julian P. Boyd et al., eds., The Papers of Thomas Jefferson (Princeton, N.J., 1950-   ), XI, 153. Although the vote on the church property was not recorded, Madison evidently voted against the seizure of the glebes and churches (Benjamin Johnson to Madison, Jan. 19, 1789, in William T. Hutchinson et al., eds., The Papers of James Madison [Chicago and Charlottesville, Va., 1962-   ], XI, 424).
[26] Hening, Statutes at Large, XII, 266-267. The initial draft of the bill opened all Episcopal churches to "common use" and authorized the sale of the glebes in parishes where no Episcopalians resided or where the majority of inhabitants, under certain restrictions, desired it. This entire section was eliminated during the

significant step, but not sufficient to satisfy the Baptists. The government removed itself from the business of "spirituals," as Baptists wanted, but the property was not touched, for in effect the lawmakers confirmed the "compact" of 1776. Repeal of incorporation in 1787 gave evangelicals the smaller portion of the loaf.[27]

The next year's legislature confirmed that decision. Despite the Baptists' petitions as well as a memorial from a convention of Presbyterians in the Shenandoah Valley, a limited resolution to sell those lands "in which there is no Episcopalian minister" on the condition that "a majority of the parishioners agreed to the sale" was defeated by a vote of 62 to 45. George Mason, James Monroe, George Nicholas, and other key figures who had supported Jefferson's statute now deserted their former allies.[28] Their position may have been eased by the fact that the Baptist General Committee had that year accepted, though by a margin of only one vote, the proposition that the glebes and churches were "public property". and so submitted no petition to the assembly.[29]

The legislators who opposed selling the vacant glebes in 1788 may have shared Madison's concern about the potential danger of majority tyranny. Writing to Jefferson the next fall, Madison warned of "the danger of oppression" from majority rule. "The invasion of private rights is *chiefly* to be apprehended," he wrote, "from acts in which the Government is the mere instrument of the major number of the constituents." And he warned Jefferson "that if a majority of the people were now of one sect," a religious establishment "would still take place and on narrower ground" than had been proposed by the assessment bill.[30] Madison's closest associates in the assembly evidently agreed with him. The will of the majority did not necessarily spell justice. Evangelicals who wanted the

---

debate ("A bill to impower certain societies to hold lands and for other purposes," Sessions of 1786/87, Box 10, Rough House Bills, Va. State Lib.). Madison, along with John Page, a member of the Episcopal standing committee, and Zachariah Johnston, a Presbyterian leader, had served on the ten-member drafting committee (*Journals of the House of Delegates of Virginia* [Richmond, 1827-1828], Dec. 23, 1786, 120).

[27] Griffith thought repeal had put the Episcopalians "in a very embarrassing situation," probably because it revoked their church polity. However, the 1787 Episcopal convention simply passed legislation providing for their own internal government and reenacted the canons of 1785 (David Griffith to William White, Apr. 28, 1797, White Papers; *Journal of a Convention ... 1787*, in Hawks, *Contributions*, I, app. 18-25).

[28] The Presbyterian petition came from Lexington Presbytery in Augusta County, Religious Petitions, Oct. 31, 1787; *Jours. House of Delegates*, Dec. 4, 1787, 82.

[29] Semple, *Baptists in Virginia*, 74. Even some Baptists acknowledged the existence of a compromise in 1776. See Benjamin Johnson to James Madison, Jan. 19, 1789, in Hutchinson *et al.*, eds., *Madison Papers*, XI, 424.

[30] Madison to Jefferson, Oct. 17, 1788, in Boyd *et al.*, eds., *Jefferson Papers*, XIV, 19.

lawmakers to reverse the direction taken by previous legislatures and to seize the glebes and churches could not count on support from their old allies in the campaign for Jefferson's statute. To the Virginia gentry, private property was sacrosanct. Though the Episcopal church no longer had any special standing in law, its right to the glebe lands and church buildings appeared secure.

Although they were losing votes in Richmond, Baptists were gaining them across the state. Virginia was experiencing a full-scale religious revival, the first since before the Revolution; by the time it ended two years later the ranks of Baptists, Methodists, and Presbyterians were swelled with renewed and enthusiastic adherents.[31] Numbers tell the story. The *Baptist Register* for 1790 listed 204 churches in Virginia with 262 ordained ministers or licensed preachers and 20,443 baptized members. "There are more people who attend the Baptist worship, than any kind of worship in the state," John Leland asserted. That same summer Isaac Backus noted in his diary that the Episcopal church was "now fallen into contempt . . . and the Baptists are in the best credit with their rulers of any denomination in Virginia."[32] Baptist leaders reported to their New England brethren that Virginia was fast becoming "a Goshen for Israel to dwell in."[33]

By gathering large numbers into the evangelical fold, this awakening profoundly influenced the politics of church property. The impact was felt first in the congressional elections. Alarmed by the failure of the new Federal Constitution to provide "sufficient provision for the secure enjoyment of religious liberty," Baptist ministers and congregations became heavily involved in the 1788 elections. Recognizing their importance to his campaign for a seat in the House of Representatives, Madison penned a carefully crafted letter to George Eve, pastor of Blue Run Church in Orange County, stating his support for amendments and "particularly the rights of Conscience in the fullest latitude."[34] Madison had already gone out of his way to meet with Leland, whose pastorate fell within his district. Remembering Madison's role in the passage of Jefferson's bill, both Eve and Leland supported his election. Evidently they

[31] For the general revival of 1787-1789 see Wesley M. Gewehr, *The Great Awakening in Virginia, 1740-1790* (Durham, N.C., 1930), 167-186, and John B. Boles, *The Great Revival, 1787-1805: The Origins of the Southern Evangelical Mind* (Lexington, Ky., 1972), 7-8.

[32] Asplund, *Register of the Baptist Denomination*, 47; L. F. Greene, ed., *The Writings of the Late Elder John Leland* . . . (New York, 1845), 117; William G. McLoughlin, ed., *The Diary of Isaac Backus* (Providence, R.I., 1979), III, 1273.

[33] The General Committee . . . to . . . the Several Baptist Associations in the Northern States, Mar. 8, 1788, Warren Association Papers, Andover Newton Theological School Library, Newton Centre, Mass.

[34] Semple, *Baptists in Virginia*, 77; Madison to Eve, Jan. 2, 1789, in Hutchinson *et al.*, eds., *Madison Papers*, XI, 405.

made a difference. As one supporter assured Madison in December, "the Baptist Interest seems every where to prevail."[35]

Aware of their communion's growing numbers and electoral influence, the 1789 General Committee prepared a long petition dealing with church property and added two arguments that would carry increased weight in the next decade.[36] The ministers first pointed out that glebes were "not such inchanted Places" that previous legislatures had refused to sell them; they had been sold before, "and if they *can* be sold for one good Purpose we hope they *will* be for a better." Second, they argued that the basis for land claims was "Social Right," not "Nature" or "Grace." In a free government the majority decided what should be done. Therefore, "if a Majority of Voices, governed by the Principle of *Right*, say, that the Episcopal Church ought to have all the Property," then "said church is entitled to it; otherwise the Law by which they hold it, may be as easily repealed as any other Law whatever." The Baptist leaders' case came perilously close to might makes right, but they claimed to represent a majority of Virginians who wanted the church property laws revoked.[37]

Numbers, however, did not translate into votes. Majority support, if indeed it was present, was not enough to persuade the assembly. Legislative supporters of the Baptist position proposed that the assembly refer the matter to the people by printing the General Committee's memorial and soliciting popular opinion. This strategy had defeated the assessment, but defenders of the Episcopal church fought back from the high ground of private property, and the legislature voted to postpone the whole business.[38] Determined to impress the assembly with the Baptists' numerical strength, the General Committee made an even stronger effort in 1790 to arouse public support, but, despite an outpouring of petitions, the assembly turned down a resolution for the sale by a crushing vote of 52 to 89.[39] The ministers would not give up the issue. Instead they shifted

[35] Both Madison and James Monroe had voted against the sale of the church property, so that could not have been the major issue, though Monroe had apparently promised to support the Baptist cause only to reverse himself in the legislature. Benjamin Johnson to James Madison, Jan. 19, 1789, in Hutchinson *et al.*, eds., *Madison Papers*, XI, 424. Leland congratulated Madison on his election and stated, "One thing I shall expect; that if religious Liberty is anywise threatened, that I shall receive the earliest Intelligence" (Leland to Madison, c. Feb. 15, 1789, *ibid.*, 442-443).

[36] This time the committee appears to have united in its opposition to the Episcopal church's retention of title to the glebe lands. A factor was the bill passed by the 1788 assembly reconfirming to the newly constituted trustees of the Protestant Episcopal Church all the powers formerly held by the vestries. Whenever the legislature seemed to be cultivating the church, the General Committee reacted (Hening, *Statutes at Large*, XII, 705-706).

[37] Religious Petitions, Nov. 14, 1789.

[38] *Jours. House of Delegates*, Nov. 27, Dec. 9, 1789, 83-84, 113. The vote was 69 to 58.

[39] The number of ministers' signatures suggests that the petitions must have circulated at church meetings; most were well subscribed (Religious Petitions, Oct.

strategies during the next five years, searching for weaknesses in their adversaries' position.[40] In one major change the General Committee in 1794, possibly to circumvent scruples about evicting incumbent ministers or seizing church buildings and plate, decided no longer to request immediate sale of church property but simply to ask for repeal of all legislation assigning it to the Episcopal church. However, the assembly defeated a resolution to repeal the glebe laws by a vote of 52 to 80.[41]

In refusing the Baptist petition, the lawmakers drew upon two critical considerations: the property rights of corporations and the role and powers of the judiciary. Thomas Evans, a delegate from Accomac County, explained the "principle" that the assembly followed in upholding the church's title to the property: if "they are private rights vested in bodies corporate capable of holding such rights, it is beyond the power of the legislature to divest them, or if, as is questioned they be not held by bodies capable in law, that is a judicial question and pertains not to us, and the Commonwealth cannot take notice of its rights to property heretofore held by others, till an inquest of office found in our favour." Evans decried the efforts of some petitioners to make judges out of legislators or give them "an absolute power over the rights of property."[42] In order to prevail, the General Committee and its supporters would have to counter the property argument and champion legislative supremacy.

The Baptists, however, did win a precedent-setting assembly battle in 1794. Buckingham County petitions, probably sponsored by Baptist churches, had requested the sale of the Tillotson Parish glebe. In calm, dispassionate tones they depicted an Episcopal church in collapse. Al-

---

30, Oct. 30–Nov. 15, 1790, *passim*). *Jours. House of Delegates*, Nov. 19, 1790, 73-74.

[40] Their first success came in 1792, when the House of Delegates passed by one vote a resolution to permit the sale of the glebes in those parishes where the majority of freeholders wished it, provided that incumbent ministers retained their rights to the lands. But the draft bill was rejected on first reading (Religious Petitions, Miscellaneous Petition, Oct. 10, 1792; *Jours. House of Delegates*, Dec. 8, 17, 1792, 177, 192; a "bill authorizing the sale of glebe lands," Dec. 17, 1792, in House of Delegates Bills, Resolutions, Etc., Box 14, Rough Bills, Oct. 1792). The vote to reject the draft was not recorded.

[41] Religious Petitions, Nov. 25, 1794; *Jours. House of Delegates*, Nov. 28, 1794, 48-49. At a June meeting in 1790, the Roanoke Association, an important Southside grouping of more than 30 churches and 2,100 members, had disagreed with the General Committee's circular letter. Although accepting that report's "spirit and intent," these ministers believed that "Compassion" required them to leave incumbent clergymen and their families alone. All the churches should be opened, but only vacant glebes should be sold, and they would endorse no petition that said otherwise. No memorials were submitted that fall from counties in the Roanoke Association (Roanoke Baptist Association, Records, 1789-1831, June, 1790, photostat, Virginia Baptist Historical Society, Richmond).

[42] Thomas Evans to John Cropper, Nov. 30, 1794, John Cropper Papers, Va. Hist. Soc.

though the people had been taxed to buy a glebe and construct a residence, the last minister had died and not been replaced. Before the buildings decayed completely, the petitioners wanted the property sold and the money applied to reduce parish taxes.[43] Though the Episcopal convention had known trouble was brewing in Buckingham and authorized the parish to elect a vestry, none had been elected and no counterpetition was presented from Tillotson Episcopalians.[44] The Baptists' case carried the legislature. A few days after refusing to repeal the glebe laws, the assembly completed work on a bill appointing commissioners to sell the Tillotson glebe. Legislative support for Episcopal church property was eroding.[45]

The act approving this sale only expanded government intervention in church affairs, for state regulation had never really ended. Even after the passage of the 1787 bill authorizing Episcopalians to manage their own affairs, the assembly went on approving requests from parish trustees to sell glebes and purchase new ones.[46] Aware of potential problems, the church leadership had endeavored to assert its authority. The 1790 Episcopal convention asserted that it was the "exclusive owner" of the property and that the legislature had no right to sell or dispose of it "to any other purpose," and it forbade vestries or trustees to do so "without the consent of a Convention."[47] But that same winter, in response to county petitions, the lawmakers in Richmond took it upon themselves to divide

[43] Three hundred twenty-seven people signed these five identical petitions, including several Baptist ministers (Religious Petitions, Nov. 15, 1794). The Episcopal minister had been William Peasley, who had served throughout the Revolution and either died or retired in 1787. No one replaced him, and no vestry seems to have been selected after 1785 (Brydon, "List of the Clergy," *WMQ*, 2d Ser., XIX [1939], 425).

[44] *Journal of a Convention . . . 1794*, in Hawks, *Contributions*, I, app. 66.

[45] *Jours. House of Delegates*, Nov. 22, 27, 28, Dec. 1, 2, 1794, 30, 45, 47-48, 54, 57. The text of the bill is in Samuel Shepherd, ed., *The Statutes at Large of Virginia, 1792-1806: Being a Continuation of Hening* (Richmond, 1835-1836), I, 311. The final House vote was 68 to 58. In the vote switching between the resolution for repeal of the glebe laws and the final vote on the sale of Tillotson glebe, 17 delegates who had disapproved of the Baptist petition later approved the glebe sale and 16 others either abstained or were absent. In contrast, only 3 votes shifted on the other side and only half as many absented themselves. From the start of the church property contest, the tidewater delegates had been a bulwark against encroachments on the Episcopal church's property. In 1794, 29 tidewater delegates (74.4%) opposed the Baptist resolution and the rest abstained or were absent, but on the Tillotson issue, 10 of these 29 either switched and voted to sell the glebe or abstained. Similar shifts occurred in the piedmont and Southside.

[46] For this legislation of 1787 and 1788 see Hening, *Statutes at Large*, XII, 627, 720.

[47] *Journal of a Convention . . . 1790*, in Hawks, *Contributions*, I, app. 31, 33. This convention also authorized the trustees of Bruton Parish to sell the glebe if they judged that it would benefit the parish. This is the first example of a convention asserting its authority in this way (*ibid.*, 31).

a parish and create a new one, to order the Episcopalians to elect trustees for both parishes, and to give instructions for the disposition of glebe lands in the old parish and the purchase of new ones.⁴⁸ In the matter of its property, the church remained under the assembly's thumb.

This situation became even more apparent two years later in the case of St. Patrick's Parish in Prince Edward County. A county petition from this Presbyterian stronghold pointed out that the parish had neither an Episcopal vestry nor "any people that call themselves Episcopalians." Some years earlier, money had been raised by the sale of the glebe, church furniture, and plate. The petitioners asked that the money be spent "for some public use." After two months of intermittent discussions, votes, and amendments, the assembly passed an enabling law.⁴⁹ If this could be done with parish funds, a case could be made for selling other church property and using the money, particularly in places where few if any Episcopalians lived or that lacked incumbent ministers. In authorizing the sale of the Tillotson glebe, the 1794 legislature accepted this argument. By both state and church law the Episcopal vestry owned and managed all church property, but at least in parishes without vestries the assembly had filled the vacuum and challenged the church's control of the property.

The next fall the Baptists seized upon this precedent. Baptist residents in four parishes, two of them with incumbent ministers, requested the sale of church property, and a Halifax County petition elaborated an argument designed to meet objections to repeal of the glebe laws raised in the 1794 legislature. This petition maintained that the vestries of the old established church had been corporations, but when the Revolution dissolved them, the property reverted to "the original Donors," the people of the state. The assembly's donation of this property to the Episcopal church was a "usurpation."⁵⁰ Episcopalians fought back with memorials defending their property.⁵¹ Caught between the opposing religious forces and immersed

⁴⁸ Hening, *Statutes at Large*, XIII, 189-191.
⁴⁹ Religious Petitions, Oct. 4, 1792; *Jours. House of Delegates*, Oct. 4, 24, 25, 29, Nov. 30, Dec. 1, 1792, 10, 73, 75, 85, 154, 156. Hening, *Statutes at Large*, XIII, 555-556. Confusion over jurisdiction continued through these years. The legislature received requests to authorize the sale of church property, while some parish vestries, drawing upon previous acts of the legislature and the newly formed Episcopal church canons, bypassed the assembly and asked permission of the church convention (*Journal of a Convention ... 1793*, and *Journal of a Convention ... 1796*, in Hawks, *Contributions*, I, app. 59, 68).
⁵⁰ Religious Petitions, Halifax Co., Nov. 16, Powhatan (Southam Parish) Co., Powhatan and Chesterfield (King William Parish) counties, Nov. 24, 1795. The Louisa County petition is only in *Jours. House of Delegates*, Nov. 17, 1795, 22-23. Alexander Hay was the minister in Antrim Parish (Halifax), and John Hyde Saunders was in Southam Parish (Brydon, "List of the Clergy," *WMQ*, 2d Ser., XIX [1939], 428, 432).
⁵¹ Religious Petitions, Halifax Co., Nov. 17, Powhatan Co., Powhatan and Chesterfield counties, Nov. 24, 1795. These Episcopalian petitions mustered about 200 signatures, while over 1,000 names were appended to the memorials advocating the sale. Lest the legislature miss the point, the pro-sale petitions

in the politics of the Jay Treaty, the legislature temporized; in the end, a resolution of support for the Baptist petition was defeated by the slender margin of seven votes.[52]

Alarmed by the erosion of support in the legislature, a well-attended Episcopal convention in May 1796 devoted much discussion to the glebe issue and produced a memorial that the assembly referred, together with the annual Baptist petition, to the Committee for the Courts of Justice, the body responsible for questions of property and constitutionality. The committee report was a forceful defense of the church's historic title to the glebes and churches. They "were vested in the respective parishes as members of the church of England, and not as professors of any other religious persuasion." The legislature of 1776 had promised that the property would continue to be held by the Church of England, and the Protestant Episcopal Church "is the same in its rights" with that church. It mattered not how the property had been acquired; if the state had granted it in 1776, it was now private property like any other grant. To settle the dispute permanently, the committee recommended that the assembly issue a declaration guaranteeing nonintervention in the church's property.[53]

Legislative supporters of the Baptist position were prepared to meet the private property issue directly and proposed an amendment to replace the committee report. The central point, they argued, was whether the glebes had in fact been "invested in the parishes as members of the church of

---

carefully totaled names for each column and put the grand total at the end. At least nine Baptist ministers signed them, including Reuben Pickett and George Smith, two of the leaders of the General Committee.

[52] *Jours. House of Delegates*, Nov. 27, 1795, 47-48. The vote was 63 to 70. A geographical shift was taking place with ominous implications for the Episcopal church. Fourteen (42%) of the piedmont delegates in 1794 voted for the repeal resolution, while 13 (39%) opposed it. This roughly equal division had been present from the beginning of the contest. But now 21 (64%) were supporters of the Baptist position and only 5 (15%) voted against it. Later in the session the legislature voted by the wide margin of 69 to 35 to postpone discussion on the petitions to sell the individual glebes, but here again the piedmont most strongly opposed the motion (*ibid.*, Dec. 16, 1795, 101-102). Thus by the end of 1795 the piedmont even more than the west offered solid regional backing for the Baptist cause.

[53] *Journal of a Convention ... 1796*, in Hawks, *Contributions*, I, app. 67-69. Religious Petitions, Nov. 17, 22, 1796. The Episcopalian petition argued that the parishes had originally received the property not from the legislature, which had only directed that land be set aside for the church's use, but by purchase or gift. *Jours. House of Delegates*, Nov. 17, 22, Dec. 14, 1796, 23, 35, 77. For the functions of this committee see Thomas Evans to John Cropper, Nov. 30, 1794, Cropper Papers. The assignment of these petitions is significant. In the past they had always gone either to the Committee for Religion or to the Committee of the Whole House. The committee's report was presented by Robert Andrews, the Williamsburg delegate and a former Episcopal minister who had served as secretary to his church's convention that year.

England." An analysis of Virginia's colonial laws dealing with vestries, ministers, and glebes showed that the parishes had never been incorporated. A parish "defines a demarcation of limits and is not technically used as a designation of persons." Although the colonial vestries "had been incorporated in each parish," they were never "invested with any species of property, personal or fiduciary in the glebes," and although the vestries could buy glebes and present ministers to the governor for induction, once that had taken place ministers held the property "independent of all persons." But a minister was not free to dispose of the glebe acting either alone or with the vestry and parish. Therefore, the real trustees had never been the vestries but "the original grantees." When the object of the trust, the established church, ended at the Revolution, all church property reverted to those "original grantees." Since the people were sovereign in Virginia, they, together with the heirs of private donors, were entitled to the property. It was an ingenious argument calculated to turn the Episcopalians' claim to "private property" on its head; for if the property had reverted to the state (that is, the people), the Baptist case that the legislature had acted improperly in giving it to one religious group was immeasurably strengthened.[54]

After reviewing the disestablishment legislation since 1776, pointing out the limitations inherent in the laws incorporating the Episcopal church, and endowing its vestries with control over the church's property, the amendment shrewdly noted that over the past ten years the legislature had approved bills disposing of glebes. Clearly, the assembly had exercised "legislative right" and shown "the insufficiency of any private title." Therefore, in awarding the property to the Episcopal church, the lawmakers had "either violated private property . . . or devoted public property to the exclusive use of a particular sect." The advocates of the Baptist memorial proposed three resolutions: that the legislature should repeal the church property laws, that incumbent ministers should retain their glebes for their lifetimes, and that vacant glebes should be sold and the money applied to the education of "poor children."[55] This sweeping rejoinder to the Episcopalian position left the House at an impasse, and the matter was later postponed until the next session. But the Baptists and their allies had finally offered the legislature a plausible case to justify the repeal of the glebe laws, and the delegates ordered two thousand copies of the committee report with proposed amendments to be printed and circulated for a full discussion by Virginians.[56]

Baptist leaders predicted victory. "The Business was put in such a

[54] *Jour. House of Delegates,* Dec. 14, 1796, 77-79.
[55] An amendment was added at this point in the third resolution on Dec. 23. It struck out the words appropriating the money to education and substituted "to such purposes as the persons resident within the bonds of the parish wherein any glebe may be situated, or a majority of them, may approve" (*ibid.,* Dec. 23, 1796, 95).
[56] *Ibid.,* Dec. 23, 1796, 96.

Train," David Barrow wrote Isaac Backus early in 1797, "that it is more than probable, it will be effected the next session."[57] The assembly had referred the glebe issue to the people, and although overshadowed by reaction to the Jay Treaty, it was warmly canvassed in at least some of the spring elections.[58] Anticipating the argument of the Episcopalians, an eventually victorious candidate in Fairfax County declared that the glebe laws probably violated the Declaration of Rights but that was for the legislature, not the courts, to decide. "Acts of the Assembly," he wrote, "are to be repealed or interfered with in any form by no other power but the Assembly itself."[59] Legislative supremacy was crucial to the Baptist position because supporters of the Episcopal church dominated the bench.

Preachers and politicians alike prepared for the assembly session of 1797-1798, but a petition war did not break out across the state. The Baptist ministers drafted their regular memorial, a brief document that lacked the passion of earlier petitions.[60] Perhaps they realized they had already won. Nor did the Episcopalians deluge the legislature with memorials, though one prominent layman, Edmund Pendleton, suggested a petition campaign. Drawing upon his legal background and legislative experience, Pendleton drafted an elaborate defense of the church property laws. As president of the convention that had approved both the state constitution and the Declaration of Rights, and as Speaker of the House of Delegates in the fall of 1776, he wrote with unique authority of the intention of Virginia's founding fathers. Reviewing the work of the first assembly, he stated that an understanding had existed that "by common consent, and with a view to avoid all future contest," the same act that ended religious taxes had reserved the property to the Episcopal church. Further, the assembly had been "declaring a subsisting right and not creating a new one." Property rights were "sacred."[61]

[57] Barrow to Backus, Jan. 27, 1797, Backus Papers, Andover Newton Theol. School Lib. Barrow was a leader in the Portsmouth Association and General Committee (James B. Taylor, *Lives of Virginia Baptist Ministers* [New York], 1860, 161-163).

[58] For one participant's comment on the involvement of state politics in national affairs see John Marshall to Charles Lee, Apr. 20, 1797, in Charles T. Cullen *et al.*, eds., *The Papers of John Marshall* (Chapel Hill, N.C., 1974), III, 70-71.

[59] The victor was Augustine Smith, the incumbent. He had been challenged by John Hunter, who argued that the glebe issue belonged in the Court of Appeals. *Columbian Mirror and Alexandria Gazette*, Mar. 23, Apr. 4, 1797. The newspaper for Apr. 18 shows the initial results of the poll: Roger West, 155; Aug. J. Smith, 127; John C. Hunter, 79. West and Smith eventually won, but the vote for Smith may not have been based on his views about church property. In the assembly West would vote against the Baptist position and Smith for it.

[60] Only one county petition for repeal was submitted (Religious Petitions, Fauquier Co., Dec. 9, 20, 1797).

[61] David John Mays, ed., *The Letters and Papers of Edmund Pendleton, 1734-1803* (Charlottesville, Va., 1967), II, 638-646, 642. For Pendleton's work on behalf of

Pendleton proposed that, for the sake of "uniformity," the church circulate a memorial in the parishes for signatures, but Episcopal leaders had determined on a different strategy.[62] Rather than hold the usual May convention that year, they would meet in Richmond at the start of the assembly session in December and lobby directly for their cause. The legislature convened on December 4, and two days later thirty-one clerical and forty lay delegates met in the capitol. The distinguished assemblage included Gov. James Wood, three state senators, and thirteen members of the House of Delegates. At the outset Bishop James Madison produced a letter from three of Virginia's most noted lawyers: Bushrod Washington, Edmund Randolph, and John Wickham. The church was "the exclusive owner" of its property, they asserted. Its title stood "upon the same grounds with the rights of private property," and a property issue could be decided "by the judiciary, and the judiciary alone." This judgment, together with Pendleton's defense, formed the basis for the convention's resolutions and memorial to the assembly. The Episcopalians appointed a committee to present their petition and to propose that the assembly submit the issue to "a proper tribunal of justice."[63]

When the matter was discussed in January, the House rejected the Episcopalian position by an overwhelming vote of 97 to 52 and by the same margin passed a resolution for repeal of the glebe laws. A comparison of Table I with Table II illustrates the dramatic shift in votes from earlier years. For example, in 1789 the tidewater and Northern Neck voted heavily against the Baptist memorial, while the piedmont was closely divided. But in the 1797 vote to repeal the laws, Episcopalian support in the Northern Neck and tidewater eroded significantly, and the piedmont was practically unanimous in support of the Baptist petition.

Table III provides a profile of the members of the House of Delegates for the sessions of 1797 and 1798. Baptist supporters tended to be middling planters, evangelical or possibly Episcopalian in religion, of a younger age, and less experienced in government but with a good political future. For example, 61 percent of those who voted to repeal the glebe laws in 1797 were under forty years old, while 49 percent of their opponents fell in that age bracket. Delegates with seniority and wealth

---

his church in 1776 see David John Mays, *Edmund Pendleton, 1721-1803: A Biography* (Cambridge, Mass., 1952), II, 129, 133-137.

[62] Pendleton to [Bishop James Madison], Sept. 25, 1797, in Mays, ed., *Letters of Pendleton*, II, 642. Only two petitions opposed repeal that year—one in Pendleton's own hand from his parish in Caroline, the other from neighboring Spotsylvania (Religious Petitions, Dec. 18, 1797).

[63] *Journal of a Convention . . . 1797*, in Hawks, *Contributions*, I, app. 69-72. For Washington and Wickham see *Dictionary of American Biography*. Randolph's part in the controversy is ably told in John J. Reardon, *Edmund Randolph: A Biography* (New York, 1974), 348-353. The five members were Ludwell Lee from the Senate, and Robert Andrews, James Breckenridge, John Page, and George K. Taylor from the House of Delegates.

TABLE I
1789 VOTE TO POSTPONE THE BAPTIST PETITION, BY REGION

	Yes		No		Abstain	
	N	%	N	%	N	%
Northern Neck	14	53.8	3	11.5	9	34.6
Tidewater	28	75.7	1	2.7	8	21.6
Southside	13	39.4	8	24.2	12	36.4
Piedmont	11	35.5	14	45.2	6	19.4
Shenandoah Valley	1	10.0	8	80.0	1	10.0
West	2	5.6	24	66.7	10	27.8
Totals	69	39.9	58	33.5	46	26.6

Sources: *Journals of the House of Delegates of Virginia* (Richmond, 1827-1828), Session of 1789/90, *passim*; Earl Gregg Swem, comp., *A Register of the General Assembly of Virginia, 1776-1918, and of the Constitutional Conventions* (Richmond, 1918), 30-31.

tended to favor the Episcopalian position. Forty-two (43 percent) of the Baptists' friends had no previous service in the House of Delegates, while only fifteen (29 percent) of the Episcopalians' supporters were in that category. More than a quarter of the opponents of repeal but only 10 percent of its advocates had served five or more terms in the House. Two-thirds of those backing the Episcopal church were major or wealthy planters, but only 42 percent of the Baptist supporters belonged in these categories. The church's supporters were also the largest slaveholders. More than half (58 percent) had ten or more slaves, as contrasted with only 38 percent of the proponents of repeal. In other respects, such as education, marriage, and Revolutionary War service, the backgrounds of

TABLE II
1797 VOTE TO REPEAL GLEBE LAWS, BY REGION

	Yes		No		Abstain	
	N	%	N	%	N	%
Northern Neck	10	38.5	12	46.2	4	15.4
Tidewater	5	12.8	22	56.4	12	30.8
Southside	25	67.6	8	21.6	4	10.8
Piedmont	28	84.8	3	9.1	2	6.1
Shenandoah Valley	7	70.0	2	20.0	1	10.0
West	22	68.8	5	15.6	5	15.6
Totals	97	54.8	52	29.4	28	15.8

Sources: *Jours. House of Delegates*, Session of 1797/98, *passim*; Swem, comp., *Register of the General Assembly*, 48-49.

TABLE III
COMPOSITION OF VIRGINIA'S HOUSE OF DELEGATES, 1797-1798

	N	%		N	%
Residence			*House Tenure in 1798*		
Northern Neck	36	13.9	No previous terms	119	45.9
Tidewater	60	23.2	1 term	37	14.3
Southside	54	20.8	2-4 terms	66	25.5
Piedmont	45	17.4	5-7 terms	23	8.9
Shenandoah Valley	14	5.4	8-10 terms	9	3.5
West	50	19.3	More than 10 terms	5	1.9
Age			*Non-Agricultural Occupation*		
Under 30	39	15.1	Artisan	1	0.4
30-39	62	23.9	Minister	2	0.8
40-49	41	15.9	Doctor	6	2.3
50-59	25	9.6	Lawyer	38	14.7
60 and over	8	3.1	Inn/Tavernkeeper	3	1.2
Unknown	84	32.4	Merchant/Trader	9	3.5
			Other professional	6	2.3
Religion			Unknown/none	194	74.9
Episcopalian	78	30.1			
Methodist	11	4.2	*Agricultural Status*		
Presbyterian	39	15.1	Farmer	7	2.7
Baptist	16	6.2	Lesser planter	91	35.1
Lutheran	5	1.9	Major planter	93	35.9
Quaker	1	0.4	Wealthy planter/son	26	10.1
Unknown	109	42.1	Unknown/none	42	16.2
Education			*Slaveholding*		
William and Mary	23	8.9	None	16	6.2
Other college	17	6.6	1-4	47	18.1
Unknown/no college	219	84.6	5-9	66	25.5
			10-19	69	26.6
			20-49	31	12.0
Marital Status			50-99	7	2.7
Single	32	12.4	Over 100	1	0.4
Married	165	63.7	Unknown	22	8.5
Unknown	62	23.9			
Political Affiliation			*Service in Revolutionary War*		
Federalist	96	37.1	Service	95	36.7
Republican	156	60.2	No Service	78	30.1
Unknown	7	2.7	Unknown	86	33.2
Previous Political Experience			*Future Political Career*		
Local/county	33	12.7	Local/county	9	3.5
House of Delegates	107	41.3	State legislature	124	47.9
State judge, senator	20	7.7	Va. Convention	11	4.2
Other state office	6	2.3	Federal office	5	1.9
Federal office	24	9.3	None/unknown	93	35.9
None/unknown	86	33.2			

supporters and opponents are strikingly similar. The lawyers in the House split narrowly, 12 to 10, for the Baptist position.

Several days after this vote a bill was presented *"to repeal certain acts, declaring the construction of the Bill of Rights and Constitution concerning Religion, and directing the disposition of Glebes and Churches."* At this stage the bill contained a preamble and two sections. The preamble stated that, since 1776, assemblies had approved a series of acts "inconsistent with the principles of the Constitution, and of Religious Freedom," and leading "to the reestablishment of a National Church." To prevent this, the first section repealed all such acts and declared that the "true exposition of the principles of the Bill of Rights and Constitution" was to be found in Jefferson's statute for religious freedom. The second section dealt with the disposition of the church property. In parishes without incumbent ministers, a majority of the inhabitants could elect commissioners to sell the property for "the general benefit" or "the education of poor children"; however, they could not "dispossess any minister now in actual possession, of any Glebe or other parish property." By requiring a majority of the parish to vote, the bill left a loophole for parishes where Episcopalians might be numerous to retain the property indefinitely. This second section must have been a subject of much debate and disagreement, for when the engrossed bill was presented for a final vote in the House, it had been dropped and the bill's title rewritten to omit any reference to glebes and churches.[64] Reporting to his constituents, Gideon Spencer reflected the exhaustion many delegates felt: "I hope it will meet with no opposition in the Senate and that we shall at length get rid of a subject that has cost the state such an immensity of money both from its being so often agitated and from the lengthy debates which it has occasioned."[65]

Only the preamble and repeal section went to the Senate, which could not initiate legislation but could amend or reject measures passed by the lower house. Senators tended to be older, wealthier, and more conservative, and their Speaker, Ludwell Lee, had attended the Episcopal convention. The House of Delegates was probably not surprised when the Senate returned the bill with two substantial amendments. The first coupled repeal of the laws with a commission to the state's attorney general to take the question to the courts. Until it be settled there, parishes, vestries, and incumbent ministers retained all property. Second, the Senate wanted a declaration that the bill did not imply "a legislative opinion upon the subject of the owners of the said property." The House

[64] The printed version with handwritten amendments is available: Jan. 21, 1798, House of Delegates Bills, Resolutions, Etc., Box 16, Rough Bills, Jan. 1798. *Jours. House of Delegates*, Jan. 2, 4, 5, 8, 13, 15, 1798, 73, 78, 80, 85, 94, 96.

[65] Gideon Spencer [printed letter concerning action of the General Assembly], Jan. 15, 1798, Va. Hist. Soc. The discussion already had consumed three full days, and more would come when the Senate proposed amendments.

defeated these amendments, but when the Senate demurred, the bill failed to pass.[66]

For Episcopalians, defeat had only been postponed. From the Baptists' General Committee that spring one association's delegates reported "that love and harmony Appeared amongst them and that they hope they shall obtain their request from our Legislature Next Session." In the winter of 1798, the Alien and Sedition Acts provoked major political battles, and it was not until the assembly had almost finished the session that the annual Baptist petition was discussed. There were no counterpetitions. The bill approved by the lower house the year before was reintroduced and moved easily through the legislature. A single amendment declaring that the ownership question should be decided by the judiciary was defeated 57 to 86. The House divided along the same socioeconomic lines at the 1797 session.[67] Opposition had collapsed.

Although this act only repealed laws and did not sell a single piece of property, a movement in that direction was inevitable. Three years later, after numerous petitions for the sale of individual glebes, the assembly passed an act "concerning the glebe lands and churches within this commonwealth." This act had a long and tangled history as it was repeatedly amended in both House and Senate. The final law provided that glebes and their buildings could be sold by the overseers of the poor in any vacant parish or whenever an incumbent minister resigned or died. The proceeds were to be spent as the majority of parish freeholders desired, but not for "any religious purpose whatsoever." At Senate insistence, churches, churchyards, books, and communion plate were specifically excluded from sale; by implication these remained the property of the Episcopalians.[68] Despite this compro mise, the preamble demonstrated that the Baptist interpretation carried the day: "All property formerly belonging to the [Episcopal] church, of every description, devolved on the good people of this commonwealth, on the dissolution of the British government here. . . . And although the general assembly

[66] The first amendment failed 36 to 79 (*Jours. House of Delegates*, Jan. 20, 22, 1798; 105-106, 108).

[67] Records of the Strawberry Baptist Association, 1787-1822, May 1798, 101, photostat, Va. Baptist Hist. Soc. Delegates who wanted to refer the glebe issue to the courts tended to be younger and have less legislative experience. The lawyers voted 13 to 9 to hand the matter over to the judges. *Jours. House of Delegates*, Dec. 15, 1798, Jan. 18, 21, 23, 25, 1799, 24, 84, 86, 97, 98, 100. Cynthia A. Miller, ed., *Journal of the Senate of Virginia, Session of 1798/99* (Richmond, Va., 1977), Jan. 23, 24, 1799, 96-97, 100-101. The text of the bill is in Shepherd, ed., *Statutes at Large*, II, 149.

[68] In the session of 1812 a bill "concerning churches, church plate and property" was introduced in the legislature that authorized the "overseers of the poor" in each county "to demand, receive, sue for and recover, . . . the plate and other property belonging or attached to the several churches," and to sell the churches at public auction "whereever the majority of the parish inhabitants wish it." The bill passed several readings before it was rejected (House of Delegates Bills, Resolutions, Etc., Box 27, Rough Bills, Oct. 1812).

possesses the right of authorizing a sale of all such property indiscriminately, yet being desirous to reconcile all the good people of this commonwealth, it is deemed inexpedient at this time to disturb the possession of the present incumbents." The bill passed its final reading in the lower house by a vote of 126 to 39. Only a diehard remnant remained to defend the property claims of the Episcopal church. On January 29, 1802, the Speaker of the House of Delegates signed the engrossed bill.[69] The Baptists had won a decisive victory.

In passing the repeal legislation and the bill to sell the glebes, the General Assembly repudiated the judgment of virtually every assembly since the Revolution and of some of the Old Dominion's finest legal minds. No other state acted in this fashion. The governments of Maryland and the Carolinas, where the Church of England had also been established and the glebes and church buildings had been transferred to the Episcopalians, never seized the church's property. That it happened in Virginia was due principally to the Baptist General Committee—to its shrewd political intelligence, organizational ability, willingness to search out allies wherever they might be found, and untiring persistence despite numerous rebuffs.

The political skill of the Baptist leaders was essential to the outcome. Almost every year the legislature could expect a memorial from the General Committee complaining of the property laws. These appeals were not simple repetitions. The ministers varied their arguments and demands, probed for weaknesses in their opponents' case, and responded ingeniously to every defense offered by supporters of the Episcopal position. The fact that evangelicals—Baptists, Methodists, and Presbyterians—had gained adherents while Episcopalians lost them was not in itself sufficient to turn the tide on the glebe issue. The major shift toward the Baptist position in the assembly occurred only after evangelicals presented a plausible rebuttal to the Episcopalian argument for the rights of private property. Conservative legislators could then jump off the fence without fear that they were setting a dangerous precedent.

The adroit verbal maneuvering in Richmond was matched by a carefully orchestrated public appeal throughout the state. County petitions were

[69] *Jours. House of Delegates,* session of 1801/02, *passim.* The draft texts and amendments will be found in "A Bill concerning the Glebe Lands and Churches of this Commonwealth," Dec. 11, 1801, House of Delegates Bills, Resolutions, Etc., Box 18, Rough Bills, Dec. 1801. The engrossed text and amendments are in Box 20, *ibid.* The final text is in Shepherd, ed., *Statutes at Large,* II, 314-316. For the passage of the bill through the legislature and some reflections on its legality see William Brockenbrough to Joseph C. Cabell, June 18, 1801, Cabell Family Papers, Accession #8-111, Alderman Lib., Univ. of Va.; Nicholas Faulcon to John Hartwell Cocke, Jan. 17, 1802, John Hartwell Cocke Papers, Accession #1480, *ibid.;* and William Brockenbrough to Spencer Roane, Sept. 5 [1802], Harrison Family Papers, 1756-1893, Va. Hist. Soc.

creatively developed and generally well subscribed, apparently at church meetings.[70] Handbills were published and reprinted in the press reiterating the arguments against the glebe laws, expressing the ministers' frustration at the assembly's repeated refusals to repeal them, and urging popular opposition at the next legislative session.[71] Thus Baptist leaders, operating particularly through the General Committee, mastered techniques of effective lobbying and developed mass support.

Nor did it hurt their cause that ministers and congregations embraced the majority party of Republicans in Virginia. Like most Virginians, Baptists naturally gravitated to a party whose emphasis on political simplicity, decentralized government, and social equality harmonized with their own style of polity and worship. Republicanism embodied that egalitarianism that formed the central theme of so many of their petitions to the assembly. A major purpose of their struggle, in the words of one Baptist leader, was that the repeal of the glebe laws would set "all sects . . . upon a level."[72] For them, as for other religious groups who had once been called dissenters, the hope for "equal religious liberty" had been a crucial factor in their support for Jefferson's statute. Repeal of the glebe laws was necessary to fulfill the implicit promise of that act. The laws regarding glebe lands and church buildings were the last remnant of the old establishment—a continuous reminder of a colonial past when "through the adulterous connection between Church and State, the impositions of king craft and priest craft . . . cherish'd and supported each other." Allowing the Episcopal church to retain the glebe property implied that within Virginia there still existed "a *favorite Church* in a *Republican Government*," an intolerable denial of the freedom and equality secured by the Revolution.[73]

Baptists openly identified with Republican viewpoints. In the 1790s, policies of the Federalist administration, particularly Washington's proclamation of neutrality in the war between Britain and France and the use of force against the Whiskey rebels, provoked strong negative reactions in Virginia. Then the appointment of John Jay as American negotiator with Britain and the resulting treaty of 1795 heightened partisan tensions. Throughout these conflicts, the Republican friends of Jefferson dominated

[70] For example, a circular letter from the General Committee, drafted by Leland, stated that the ministers would "make a vigorous exertion, for the sale of the glebes, and free occupation of the churches by all religious societies," and asked local churches to send in petitions with "as many subscribers" as possible (*Minutes of the Baptist General Committee, at Their Yearly Meeting, Held in the City of Richmond, May 8th, 1790* [Richmond, Va. (1790)], 4-8).

[71] Henry Toler to Isaac Backus, May [?], 1795, Backus Papers. "An Address to the Public," *Columbian Mirror and Alexandria Gaz.*, June 23, 1795.

[72] John Leland, *A Storke at the Branch. Containing Remarks on Times and Things* (Hartford, Conn., 1801), 19. For other examples of this issue see Religious Petitions, Nov. 20, 1787, Aug. 14, 1789, Oct. 30, 1790.

[73] Religious Petitions, Nov. 24, 1795, Nov. 5, 1790, Richmond Co., Oct. 30, 1790.

state politics, while Federalists remained a distinct minority.[74] Baptist churches and ministers did not hide their political affiliation. A church in Caroline County deplored the Jay Treaty's tendency "to draw us smoothly, swiftly and dreadfully into the whirlpool of oppression— oppression Civil and Religious"; and the Goshen Association appointed a day of fasting and prayer "for a deliverance from the dangers we apprehend in consequence of [the] late [Jay] Treaty."[75] "I am strongly convinced," wrote one Baptist minister, "that the people of Virginia are unanimously in favour of the French Republic." From his perspective, a war against France would destroy "our liberties and union."[76]

The General Committee's petition in 1795 reflected the charged political atmosphere. The ministers' chief argument now became the clash between the inequities of the glebe laws and the "grand leading Principles of Republicanism," and they attacked the glebe laws as "inconsistent with the dignified Character which true Republicans ought to sustain." [77] Now that the church property issue was thrust into politics, it was politically astute for the ministers to emphasize their political connection and concentrate their pressure on Republican delegates from counties where evangelicals were numerically powerful. Some Republicans undoubtedly swung to the Baptist cause in order to strengthen their own political position; some Federalists, too, probably changed their views in response to pressure from evangelical constituents. One contemporary historian claimed that Baptists in some counties were able to decide the election and place "a worthy and useful member" in the legislature.[78] The political efforts of the Baptists were well rewarded.

But despite the political campaign, the glebe fight, like church-state issues in earlier years, was not decided along partisan lines. When the 1797 repeal bill passed the House of Delegates, thirty-two Federalists and sixty-four Republicans supported it, while twenty-five Federalists and twenty-seven Republicans were in opposition. In 1798, when the assembly rejected the amendment to refer the glebe issue to the courts, thirty Federalists and twenty-seven Republicans supported that Episcopalian position, while eighteen Federalists and sixty-eight Republicans rejected it. The Federalists' conservative instincts, as well as their concentration in older counties where Anglicanism had been strong, may have induced a higher proportion of them to support the Episcopal church's position. In

---

[74] For the developing politics of the period see Beeman, *Old Dominion and New Nation*, 119-137, 140-144, and Risjord, *Chesapeake Politics*, 424-460.

[75] Religious Petitions, Nov. 17, 1795; Burruss's Baptist Church to Goshen Association, Sept. 1795, Miscellaneous Manuscripts, Va. Baptist Hist. Soc.; *Minutes of the Goshen Baptist Association Holden at Glensoe's Meeting House, N. Fork, Pamunkey, in Orange County ... 1795* (Richmond, Va., 1795), 5.

[76] Elisha Purrington to Isaac Backus, Louisa [Co.], Mar. 31, 1797, Backus Papers.

[77] Religious Petitions, Miscellaneous Petition, Nov. 17, 1795.

[78] William Fristoe, *A Concise History of the Ketocton Baptist Association ...* (Staunton, Va., 1808), 90.

a letter to Jefferson toward the close of the 1797 session, James Madison clearly stated that the glebe issue was not a party contest.[79] Some of the staunchest advocates of the church's property rights were Republicans devoted to the political fortunes of Jefferson, but both he and Madison sensibly stayed away from the battle.

The Baptist General Committee also mobilized popular support among other evangelicals across Virginia and even attempted a formal alliance with Methodists and Presbyterians. The latter were the most likely prospects, since each of Virginia's two presbyteries had at one time or another discussed the issue and drafted petitions. In the Shenandoah Valley, the ministers and lay elders of Lexington Presbytery drafted an elaborate memorial in 1787 against the "exclusive appropriation of the glebes and churches" by what was an "infant church." Three years later, in 1790, the Baptist General Committee sent agents to enlist Hanover Presbytery. Although the presbytery, while declaring the Baptist proposal "reasonable and just," declined the invitation "on Account of some Circumstances," the very next year it passed a motion to "concur with the Baptist Church in a remonstrance and petition to the General Assembly ... to sell the Glebes and open the Church Doors." A committee was appointed to draft a memorial and present it to the legislature but failed to do so. When the issue came before the Hanover Presbytery again in 1792, the committee presented a petition that was initially approved, yet two

[79] Madison to Jefferson, Jan. 21, 1798: "You will have seen in the newspapers the proceedings on the Amherst Memorial, on the Glebes and Churches, and on the proposition for reviewing the Constitution. The first was the only test of party strength, and so far deceptive, as it confounds scrupulous Republicans with their adversaries in the votes against a Legislative censure on the Grand Jury" (James Madison, *Letters and Other Writings of James Madison, Fourth President of the United States* [Philadelphia, 1867], II, 122, and Papers of James Madison, Ser. I, reel 5, microfilm, Library of Congress). See also *Jours. House of Delegates*, Dec. 19, 28, 1797, 40-41, 61-64).

Madison was referring to a petition from Amherst and other piedmont counties that attacked the Richmond grand jury, composed mainly of Federalists, for its presentment against Samuel Jordan Cabell, a Republican congressman who had criticized the Adams administration. This was the major political issue of the session and serves to identify Federalists and Republicans in the assembly. But Madison did not take a position in this letter or elsewhere on the church property issue. He was not required to do so, and there were important Virginia Republicans on both sides of the question. Unfortunately, historians have been confused by an inaccurate quotation of a portion of the above letter in Stanislaus Murray Hamilton's edition of Monroe's writings. Dropping the comma after "Memorial," he quoted Madison as writing "the Amherst Memorial on the Glebes and Churches"; thus linked, the glebe question becomes "a test of party strength." Not this year or at any time in the 1790s did Amherst send a petition concerning the glebes (see Hamilton, ed., *The Writings of James Monroe, Including a Collection of His Public and Private Papers and Correspondence* ... [New York, 1898-1903], II, 97n). For examples of the problem created by this inaccuracy see Beeman, *Old Dominion and New Nation*, 198, and Risjord, *Chesapeake Politics*, 488, 671, n. 16.

days later, "after deliberating fully," the presbytery rejected it. Hanover Presbytery did not discuss the issue again, nor did Lexington Presbytery or the Synod of Virginia.[80]

The Hanover Presbytery minutes do not explain the "Circumstances" of 1790 or its refusals to openly support the sale of the glebes, but the reasons were probably related to other petitions to the legislature. Throughout this period, the two Presbyterian colleges in Virginia, Hampden-Sydney and Liberty Hall, sought help from the legislature. So also did various Presbyterian congregations. In 1789 the assembly gave land to the Presbyterians in Lexington for a church building and the next year authorized lotteries to build Presbyterian churches in Alexandria and Shepherd's Town.[81] The presbyteries could hardly petition for the seizure of Episcopalian property while asking the assembly for financial assistance and other favors for themselves.

The Baptist General Committee also reached out to their biggest rivals in the business of salvation, the Methodists. In numbers, Methodists were right behind Baptists with more than 15,000 members in twenty-three circuits located entirely or mainly within the commonwealth.[82] Two Baptist emissaries presented their case to the Methodist conference of preachers at Petersburg in June 1790 but failed to gain any declared support. The Methodists may have been too deeply preoccupied with their own problems and internal divisions.[83] But even if the preachers considered the Baptist proposal, it is unlikely that they would have cooperated. Methodist conferences avoided church-state disputes and particularly any activity directed against the Episcopal church. For some the old ties of affection lingered. Devereux Jarratt, the evangelical Episcopal minister who had welcomed Methodist preachers, remained a

[80] Religious Petitions, Augusta Co., Oct. 31, 1787; *Minutes of the Baptist General Committee . . . 1790*, 4-8; Records of Hanover Presbytery, July 10, 1790, Aug. 1, Oct. 29, 1791, May 12, July 28, 30, 1792, 29, 45, 50, 56, 58, 59.

[81] *Jours. House of Delegates*, Nov. 14, 27, 28, 30, Dec. 1, 3, 1789, 59, 86, 88, 89-90, 92, 98. Religious Petitions, Berkeley Co., Nov. 13, 1790, Alexandria Town, Nov. 16, 1790; Hening, *Statutes at Large*, XIII, 85, 174-175.

[82] *Minutes of the Methodist Conferences, Annually Held in America, from 1773 to 1794, Inclusive* (Philadelphia, 1795), 144-148.

[83] There is no record of the Methodist Conference's reaction to the Baptist proposal, but Baptist representatives did attend the meeting in 1791 (*Minutes of the Baptist General Committee, Held at Nuckols's Meeting House, in the County of Goochland, May 1791* [Richmond, Va., 1791], 6), and there are references in pro-Episcopal petitions to the conference's refusal to cooperate with the Baptist committee (Religious Petitions, Amelia Co., Nov. 4, 1790, Lunenburg Co., Nov. 19, 1790). For Bishop Francis Asbury's reflections on the Petersburg meeting see Elmer T. Clark *et al.*, eds., *The Journal and Letters of Francis Asbury* (Nashville, Tenn., 1958), I, 642. James O'Kelly, an influential minister in Southside Virginia, was opposing Asbury's authority and would soon break with the church and organize the Republican Methodists. For the O'Kelly schism see Charles Franklin Kilgore, *The James O'Kelly Schism in the Methodist Episcopal Church* (Mexico City, 1963).

friend,[84] and the status of religious freedom after the passage of Jefferson's statute satisfied Methodist leaders. Writing from Virginia to an English correspondent in 1788, Bishop Francis Asbury probably reflected the sentiments of his coreligionists: "We enjoy real liberty here, no denomination hath any preeminence over another, and I hope never will have. I wish we may all stand on equal ground."[85] In some respects, an alliance with Baptists would have been unnatural for the Methodists, since the two churches were in direct competition. Isaac Backus is a case in point. The New England Baptist toured Virginia for five months in early 1789, preaching over one hundred sermons. In a letter to his wife explaining his delay in returning to Connecticut, he emphasized the "zeal" of the Methodists, their assaults on the "most essential doctrine of the gospel," and his responsibility "to hold up light against their errors." Backus regarded his trip as a great success, but he had not advanced ecumenical cooperation.[86]

Yet the Baptist position aroused popular support among both Presbyterians and Methodists. Although church bodies did not take a public stand, individual Presbyterian clergy and laity supported the seizure of the church property.[87] Areas in the Southside and the Shenandoah Valley where Presbyterians were numerous consistently favored the sale of the glebes, and where it counted most, in the assembly, Presbyterians voted 19 to 1 to repeal the glebe laws in 1797.[88] Rank-and-file Methodists also circulated petitions against the glebe laws and sided with the Baptists in the assembly.[89] Thus the Baptist General Committee successfully drew other evangelicals to enlist in their cause.

[84] Bishop Thomas Coke, the other Methodist bishop in America with Asbury, and Bishop James Madison both expressed desire for reunion between Episcopalians and Methodists (William White, *Memoirs of the Protestant Episcopal Church in the United States of America* ... , 3d ed. [New York, 1880], 195-196). See also Coke to White, Apr. 24, 1791, *ibid.*, 408-412.

[85] Asbury to Jasper Winscom, Aug. 15, 1788, in Clark *et al.*, eds., *Journals and Letters of Asbury*, III, 64.

[86] For Virginia Methodism in the early period see William W. Bennett, *Memorials of Methodism in Virginia, from its Introduction into the State, in the Year 1772, to the Year 1829* (Richmond, Va., 1871); William Warren Sweet, *Virginia Methodism: A History* (Richmond, Va., 1955); Gewehr, *Great Awakening*, 138-166; and Frank Baker, *From Wesley to Asbury: Studies in Early American Methodism* (Durham, N.C., 1976).

Isaac Backus to William Rogers, Oct. 21, 1789, Backus to [Susanna Mason Backus], Mar. 9, 1789, Backus Papers.

[87] Even though the presbyteries did not submit petitions, ministers regularly signed county memorials. For example, Religious Petitions, Prince Edward Co., Oct. 4, 1792, contained the signatures of Archibald McRoberts and Drury Lacy, two leaders of Hanover Presbytery.

[88] Of 23 Presbyterians identified in that session, only 2 abstained or were absent for that vote.

[89] Edmund Pendleton to [Bishop James Madison], Sept. 25, 1797, Mays, ed., *Letters of Pendleton*, II, 642; *Virginia Argus* (Richmond), Oct. 17, 1797. Seven

Throughout the struggle, the tenacity of the Baptists was as important as their political acumen. Their "unreasonable and unparalleled Obstinacy," as Episcopalians saw it,[90] is particularly striking since for the first eight years of the campaign the assembly easily and overwhelmingly rejected their petitions. Nevertheless, the preachers refused to drop the issue. Such persistence requires explanation. On one level the church property issue was important to their organization and unity as a religious denomination in the 1790s. Unity had finally been achieved in 1787 when conflicting groups of Regular and Separate Baptists came together first in the General Committee and then in the General Association.[91] But the next year this association was dissolved, and the General Committee was left as the only representative body for all Virginia Baptists precisely at a time when revivals were enlarging their ranks. Composed of the most influential ministers, the committee functioned well as a central organization responding to issues and questions arising from the associations.

Not all congregations or preachers were comfortable with this arrangement because Baptists were wary of anything that threatened the "liberties of the Churches."[92] But major resistance surfaced only after the committee condemned slavery in 1790.[93] The storm of opposition provoked by that action seriously threatened the committee's existence. In a circular letter the following year, the committee explained: "We desire you to view us, only as your political mouth, to speak your cause to the State Legislature, to promote the interests of the Baptists at large, and endeavour the removal of every vestige of oppression."[94] Though the ministers renounced any intention of interfering in slavery, which was not then a political issue, some Baptists still questioned the legitimacy of a General Committee. Two years later the ministers protested that their sole concern was the *external* interest" of Baptists and denied any "power over the *liberty* and *independence* of the Churches."[95] Some committee members disliked this limitation on their discussions, but the glebe issue was the only matter that they negotiated successfully after 1792, and following the repeal of the glebe acts the group dissolved.[96] Thus, for

---

Methodists have been identified in the 1797 assembly; five voted for repeal, one opposed, and one abstained or was absent.

[90] Religious Petitions, Amelia Co., Nov. 4, 1790.

[91] For the complex history of the various Baptist groups see *Encyclopedia of Southern Baptists*, s.v. "Virginia, Baptist General Association of."

[92] See, for example, *Minutes of the Ketocton Baptist Association, Held at Long-Branch, in Fauquier County, August, 1792* ([n.p., n.d.]), Aug. 18, 1792, 4, and "Records of the Strawberry Baptist Association, 1787-1822," Oct. 1792, 50-51.

[93] *Minutes of the Baptist General Committee . . . 1790*, 6-7.

[94] *Minutes of the Baptist General Committee, 1791*, 8.

[95] *Minutes of the Baptist General Committee, Holden at Muddy-Creek Meeting-House: Powhatan County, Virginia* (Richmond, Va., 1793), May 13, 1793, 4, 7. The majority of ministers voted "that the subject be dismissed from this committee, as believing it belongs to the legislative body."

[96] *Minutes of the Baptist General Committee Held at Waller's Meeting-House, in*

those ministers to whom the survival of the General Committee was important for Baptist unity and organization, the church property question was extremely useful. It justified the committee's continued existence.

A more compelling reason for pursuing the glebe issue was the jealousy and bitterness that marked the historic relationship between Baptists and the old establishment. Charged by Episcopalians with an "exclusive self-love," Baptist leaders felt obliged to justify their cause.⁹⁷ To the public at large they explained in 1795 that they were moved not by "impure motives" but by concern for "principle." Their petitions, however, betrayed deep antagonism and resentment. Baptists blamed Episcopalians for the oppression they had experienced before the Revolution. One imprisoned minister later wrote that every "persecution" invariably had "a priest at the end of it, and received the hearty concurrence of their parishioners."⁹⁸ An Episcopalian responded in kind: "actuated by the malicious and revengeful spirit of Haman who erected a gallows in his own house to hang Mordecai thereon, [Baptists] have also erected in [their] imaginations one on which we too are to swing."⁹⁹ Baptists knew that Episcopalians tended to look down on them as a lower class of people and often ridiculed their religious enthusiasm. As Bishop James Madison, cousin to James Madison the politician, had written in 1790: "Ignorance and Enthusiasm are Hydras which require a powerful Arm to oppose them."¹⁰⁰ Baptists reciprocated with an intense dislike that sometimes bordered on hatred. To Baptist William Price, Episcopalians were "too aristocratic and overbearing," possessed of "English airs" and "arrogance of demeanor among neighbors." "Such a Church," he wrote, "is not suited to a liberty loving people."¹⁰¹

The Baptists were also aware of their own growth and development. Their ministers were no longer, if they ever had been, poor or crude. Though to the unconverted they might appear as stump ranters, they held land and slaves like any other comfortably fixed middling sort of citizens in the commonwealth.¹⁰² Yet in spite of their status, or perhaps because

---

Spottsylvania County (Richmond, Va. [1799]), 4. The committee also recommended that the association consider "the expediency of instituting, and continuing a general annual meeting . . . for promoting the cause of Religion, and for preserving union and harmony amongst the churches." The next year Virginia Baptists instituted the General Meeting of Correspondence to meet this need.

⁹⁷ Religious Petitions, Lunenberg Co., Nov. 19, 1790.

⁹⁸ James Ireland, *The Life of the Rev. James Ireland, Who Was, for Many Years, Pastor of the Baptist Church at Buck Marsh, Waterlick and Happy Creek, in Frederick and Shenandoah Counties, Virginia* (Winchester, Va., 1819), 182.

⁹⁹ *Va. Argus,* Oct. 17, 1797.

¹⁰⁰ Madison to William White, Dec. 19, 1790, White Papers.

¹⁰¹ William Price to Edward Payne, Dec. 20, 1787, and Price to Luke Allen, Dec. 23, 1787, in Richard E. Coe, ed., "Price's Priceless Pen," *Flintlock and Powderhorn: Magazine of the Sons of the Revolution,* I (1976), 12-13.

¹⁰² Asplund lists all the Baptist ministers and licensed preachers in Virginia in

of it, anxiety over their place in society pervaded their petitions. The slightest sign of legislative concern or preference for the old establishment inevitably provoked a strong reaction. Baptists deeply resented an assembly that spent time "brooding over this Egg of Priest-craft" while discriminating against them and disregarding their repeated memorials.[103] They had never willingly tolerated "oppressions," and they would not do so now when they represented, in the words of one legislative draft, "a numerous and respectable part of this Community."[104] Conscious of their status as a significant religious body, they were galled that a "Deaf" assembly treated Episcopalians as "a *favorite Church*."[105]

Thus the Baptists stayed with the church property fight until they prevailed, and it was this persistence, together with their political acumen, effective organization, and popular support from other evangelicals, that persuaded the legislature to resolve the issue in their favor.

If strong, determined, and coherent leadership was noteworthy among the Baptists, its conspicuous absence on the Episcopalian side was also crucial to the result. The church had been in decline since the Revolution, and its problems accelerated in the 1790s. Perhaps the most serious difficulty Episcopalians faced was an acute shortage of competent clergy, yet even a zealous minister such as Jarratt wrote discouragingly in 1794: "In my own parish also, I have the mortification to behold those, who were once my near and dear friends, yea my children in the gospel, fall off from me, and join with my most notorious enemies."[106]

They were not necessarily going over to the evangelicals. When an Episcopalian condemned the "gross, destructive and heathenist infidelity"

1790 by county (*Register of the Baptist Denomination,* 24-32). Checking these data against the personal property and land tax books in the Virginia State Library, I was able to locate 198 (74%) of the 267 men listed by Asplund. Of these, 135 (68%) had one or more slaves above 12 years of age. The property holdings of 119 ministers averaged 406 acres. In contrast, both Episcopal and Presbyterian clergy ranked above them. For the Episcopalians see Brydon, "The Wealth of the Clergy," *Hist. Mag. Protestant Episcopal Church,* XII (1953), 91-98. Of 19 Presbyterian ministers located in the personal property and land tax books, 14 had a total of 75 slaves of tithable age. Their land holdings equaled those of the Episcopalians.

[103] "An Address to the Public," *Columbian Mirror and Alexandria Gaz.,* June 23, 1795; Religious Petitions, Miscellaneous Petition, Nov. 17, 1795.

[104] See a "bill authorizing the sale of glebe lands," Dec. 17, 1792, in House of Delegates Bills, Resolutions, Etc., Box 14, Rough Bills, Oct. 1792.

[105] Religious Petitions, Chesterfield Co., Nov. 13, 1790, Richmond Co., Oct. 30, 1790.

[106] Devereux Jarratt, *The Life of the Reverend Devereux Jarratt, Rector of Bath Parish, Written by Himself in a Series of Letters Addressed to the Rev. John Coleman* (Baltimore, 1806), 123. For Bishop Madison's concern over the clergy see Madison to William Peachy, Aug. 1, 1794, in Meade, *Old Churches,* II, 175.

abounding in Virginia, he echoed the evangelical lament of the 1790s.[107] The revivals had ended by 1791, and clergy of all churches anguished over the spiritual torpor of congregations and the coldness of their preachers' sermons. "Religion is at the lowest ebb that ever it has been among us," one Baptist leader reported to Backus, and his witness was confirmed by other ministers. The enemies were deism and infidelity. Thomas Paine's *Age of Reason* had become the "Bible" of the "ungodly"; across Virginia "error and vice" displayed a "Brazen face." "With what boldness they blaspheme," another Baptist complained. "Even the very children appear to ketch it from their Parents."[108] When a traveling businessman attended church services in Richmond one Sunday, he was disgusted by the "levity" and "indecorum" of young men and women in the congregation, particularly when the minister spoke of the "depravity of human nature." Friends told him that this was typical behavior, deliberately intended to display "contempt of religion." Working as a tutor in Richmond in 1798, the future Unitarian leader William Ellery Channing noted the neglect of Scripture and the growth of "infidelity." Frustrated by his failure to find anyone with whom to discuss religious topics, he complained that "religion is in a deplorable state. Many of the people have wondered how I could embrace such an *unprofitable* profession as the ministry."[109] The times were not propitious for churchmen.

Weakened by its losses to evangelicals as well as to the growing forces of irreligion, the Episcopal church split over the glebe issue in the 1790s. The solidarity so noticeable a decade earlier collapsed before the Baptist assault. The challenge to the glebe laws on the grounds of republican liberties and equalitarian values moved even some Episcopalians to vote against their church. Of fifty-nine House members identifiable as Episcopalians in the 1797 session, only twenty-nine (49 percent) opposed the repeal of the glebe laws in 1797, while nineteen (32 percent) supported it. The next year, when church leaders were hoping for an appeal to the courts, only twenty-seven (50 percent) of the Episcopalians in the legislature backed that position, while nineteen (35 percent) rejected it.

Bishop Madison's leadership left much to be desired. Shortly after his consecration in 1790, he had promised Bishop William White of Philadelphia: "Much indeed is necessary to be done in this State. I will not be deficient on my Part, as far as my feeble Exertions may extend."[110] But his feebleness increased with the passing years, matching the decline of his

[107] *Va. Argus*, Oct. 17, 1797.
[108] Eleazar Clay to Isaac Backus, May 23, 1795, William Brown to Isaac Backus, Feb. 20, 1797, George Smith to Isaac Backus, Mar. 15, 1797, Backus Papers.
[109] "Viator," *Virginia Gazette, and General Advertiser* (Richmond), Mar. 22, 1797; William Ellery Channing, *Memoir of William Ellery Channing, with Extracts from His Correspondence and Manuscripts*, 4th ed. (Boston, 1850), I, 126.
[110] Madison to William White, Dec. 19, 1790, White Papers. The best study of Madison is Charles Crowe, "Bishop James Madison and the Republic of Virtue," *Jour. So. Hist.*, XXX (1964), 58-70. See also the sketch by G. MacLaren Brydon in *DAB*, XII, 182-184.

church. His convention strategy of 1797 failed utterly, as we have seen, and after 1797 Madison made no efforts to organize resistance to the repeal of the property laws. No convention assembled in 1798, nor did individual parishes follow the tactics Pendleton suggested and send legislative petitions. A well-organized campaign might conceivably have prevented church support from hemorrhaging. Episcopalians had rallied before. But this would have required vigorous leadership and persuasive politicking in 1798, and the bishop had no heart for such activities. The House vote reflected the internal division. The church was of two minds, as was its bishop.[111]

Madison's difficulties in rallying support may have stemmed, at least in part, from the fact that many post-Revolutionary Virginians thought bishops out of place in the new nation. As "the creatures of Kings" and unfriendly to republican forms of government, they belonged with an established church in a royal realm.[112] In 1795 a satirical newspaper article, commenting on a monument to be erected at the Halifax County courthouse, described the principal figure as "a *Republican Bishop* . . . He has the head of an *ass*, the feet of a *Bull*, and the tail of a Monkey." And the attack on episcopacy continued in verse: "Lo! a Bishop without a King! / Poor lifeless, senseless, Popish thing."[113] Even devout Episcopalians were leery of lodging bishops in Virginia. After almost two centuries without a resident episcopate, some found it unnatural and unnecessary. The old system had worked well enough to suit their tastes, and they did not appreciate the need for a hierarchy to complete church polity. The first bishop-elect, David Griffith, chosen in 1785 by the church's first convention, was never consecrated because he could not raise sufficient funds for the trip to London. Madison had presided at the conventions of 1785 and 1786, but he apparently refused to be a candidate for the episcopal office. He may have belonged to the faction that did not think bishops necessary, for Griffith considered him a major factor in stalling his consecration. After Griffith's death, however, Madison accepted the nomination and quickly raised sufficient funds to sail to England for consecration—a feat which, as chairman of the standing committee of the diocese, he had been unable or unwilling to accomplish for Griffith.[114] Madison himself was

[111] For an example of one Episcopalian's reasoning in favor of the glebe sale see Meade, *Old Churches*, I, 187-188.

[112] "The Petersburg Monitor," *Virginia Gazette and Petersburg Intelligencer*, Dec. 14, 1786. The conflict over a Virginia episcopate before the Revolution is covered in Brydon, *Virginia's Mother Church*, II, 341-359, and Carl Bridenbaugh, *Mitre and Sceptre: Transatlantic Faiths, Ideas, Personalities, and Politics, 1689-1775* (New York, 1962), 316-332.

[113] *Richmond and Manchester Advertiser*, Aug. 20, 1795.

[114] There were three candidates for bishop in 1786. Griffith, rector at Fairfax Parish in Alexandria, received 32 votes; John Bracken, rector at Bruton Parish in Williamsburg, 10 votes; and Samuel Shield, rector at York Hampton Parish, 7 votes. Madison was chosen to chair the standing committee. The powers of this group were extensive and made them the ruling body of the church between

never completely accepted by the people he was commissioned to serve. John Tyler expressed sentiments shared by many in the gentry class: "when I speak of the Bishop I feel the highest veneration for his character as a Man, but I like him not the better for his canonicals, they will not let men be enough of Republicans—besides he went to *Great Britain* for the exaulted station. Now who wou'd ever be sent to Heaven by such a People?"[115] Madison evidently wondered that himself. He often betrayed an ambivalence toward his calling, particularly when the church was under pressure. Although his public exhortations in conventions and his private correspondence with Bishop White display a pious concern for the church's welfare, church matters did not intrude into his letters to public figures who might have offered political advice or support in the legislative battles.[116] While lambasting "immorality" and "impiety" at church meetings, he presided over the College of William and Mary, which became notorious for those qualities.[117] And despite the limitations placed upon the bishop by the Virginia canons, Madison neglected even basic responsibilities. He did not make the prescribed parish visitations on a regular basis, nor did he attend the triennial General Convention of the Episcopal church after 1795.[118] He also dallied repeatedly with the idea of resigning.

---

conventions. Madison did not give up his position as chairman when he was nominated as bishop (*Journal of a Convention . . . 1786*, in Hawks, *Contributions*, I, app. 14, 15, 17; *Journal of a Convention . . . 1790, ibid.*, app. 30, 31). For Griffith's difficulties with the standing committee in general and Madison in particular see his letters to William White for Sept. 26, Oct. 20, 26, 1786, May 28, Aug. 16, 1787, White Papers. The best studies of his career are G. MacLaren Brydon, "David Griffith, 1742-1789: First Bishop Elect of Virginia," *Hist. Mag. Protestant Episcopal Church*, IX (1940), 194-230, and William Sydnor, "Doctor Griffith of Virginia: Emergence of a Church Leader, March 1779–June 3, 1786," *ibid.*, XLV (1976), 5-24, and "Doctor Griffith of Virginia: The Breaking of a Church Leader, September 1786–August 3, 1789," *ibid.*, XLV (1976), 113-132.

[115] Tyler to St. George Tucker, July 10, 1795, John Tyler Papers, microfilm, Lib. Cong.

[116] Madison to White, July 12, Dec. 19, 1790, White Papers. For his public statements see *Journal of a Convention* for 1791, 1793, and 1799. in Hawks, *Contributions*, I, app. 37-45, 55-59, 78-83. For his private correspondence see, for example, his letters to Henry Tazewell for the period 1795 to 1798, James Madison Papers, Duke University Library, Durham, N.C. Despite the pressure the church was under in Virginia during this time, Madison does not mention church problems to Tazewell, a devout Episcopalian. In fact, he defended the legislature against Tazewell's criticism. Of the 1797 session, the bishop wrote, "I cannot however accord with all your observation upon the last House of Delegates. Their Conduct ought to be exposed in Defense of pure and genuine Republicanism" (Feb. 4, 1798, *ibid.*).

[117] *Journal of a Convention . . . 1799*, in Hawks, *Contributions*, I, app. 81; Joseph C. Cabell to David Watson, Mar. 4, 1798, David Watson Papers, Lib. Cong.

[118] Madison's last report of a visitation was made to the 1796 convention (*Journal of a Convention . . . 1796*, in Hawks, *Contributions*, I, app. 68). He attended the General Conventions of 1792 and 1795 but absented himself thereafter (William

He wrote his cousin James Madison in 1794 that he had been considering "retiring to some comfortable little Farm in a healthy Part of the Country." In the spring of 1798 at the height of the crisis over the church's property, a correspondent in Kentucky informed one of Madison's neighbors that the bishop "proposes to visit Kentucky in the fall with a view of procuring a farm for his future residence." Finally, in 1801 Madison again expressed interest in relocating and was also weighing the advantages of becoming a candidate for the presidency of a college in New York. In none of these letters did he mention his episcopal responsibilities.[119]

Although clerical chores awakened little interest in Madison, he threw himself enthusiastically into Republican politics. As the Baptists were launching their final assaults against the glebes in 1797, the bishop called a meeting of freeholders to protest the policies of the Adams administration, and the following spring he drafted a special prayer to be used throughout his diocese against the possible war with France.[120] But the bishop's passion for Jeffersonian Republicanism was not matched by an equivalent commitment to the cause of his church. Although his intervention might not have affected the outcome of the church property struggle, his apparent indifference outside of convention did not rally support, particularly when the church was already divided and apathetic. Only two more state conventions were held between 1798 and Madison's death in 1812. Both urged the bishop and standing committee to "pursue to the end" the defense of the church's right to the glebes. Madison expressed confidence in 1799 that the courts would prove a "shield against every attack."[121]

His hopes were misplaced. A case involving the vacant glebe lands of

Stevens Perry, ed., *Journals of the General Conventions of the Protestant Episcopal Church, in the United States of America, from A.D. 1785 to A.D. 1853, Inclusive* (Claremont, N.H., 1874), I, 161, 199. In 1798, John Braken and Robert Andrews were deputed to attend, but there were no representatives from Virginia in 1801, 1804, 1808, or 1811. At the Baltimore meeting of 1808, the General Convention expressed the fear that the Virginia church was on the verge of "total ruin, unless great exertions . . . are employed to raise her" (*ibid.*, I, 380-381). Long before this, Bishop Madison had evidently stopped writing to Bishop White.

[119] Madison to Madison, Nov. 12, 1794, in Hutchinson *et al.*, eds., *Madison Papers*, XV, 374; David Meade to Judge [Joseph] Prentis, Apr. 30, 1798, Webb-Prentis Papers, Accession #4136, Alderman Lib., Univ. Va.; Madison to James Madison, Feb. 23, 1801, Madison Papers, Ser. 1, reel 6, microfilm, Lib. Cong. The college in New York was probably Columbia. The presidency had been vacant since the summer of 1800 and was only filled in May 1801 by the election of another Episcopal clergyman, Charles H. Wharton, of New Jersey ([Brander Matthews *et al.*], *A History of Columbia University, 1754-1904* [New York, 1904], 81-82).

[120] Crowe, "Madison and the Republic of Virtue," *Jour. So. Hist.*, XXX (1964), 61.

[121] *Journal of a Convention . . . 1799*, and *1805*, in Hawks, *Contributions*, I, app. 73, 79, 85.

Manchester Parish in Chesterfield County, *Turpin et al.* v. *Locket et al.*, was ultimately heard by the state's Court of Appeals. In a split decision the judges upheld the constitutionality of the act providing for the sale of the church lands. The Baptists stayed with their cause to the end. After the case had turned out to their satisfaction, the Virginia associations formed a committee to "declare our respect" to the lawyers who had argued for the sale.[122]

With the issue of the church property successfully concluded, Baptist leaders enjoyed a sense of personal achievement not present after the passage of the Virginia Statute for Religious Freedom a dozen years before. Then the applause had gone to Jefferson and Madison and their rationalist allies. Now the victory belonged to a Baptist-led evangelical coalition, not the Republican party. Baptists relished their moment of triumph. As one minister informed Isaac Backus, they had finally realized "liberty and equality with all religious societies."[123] In achieving that position over a quarter century and in the glebe fight in particular, the Baptists mastered the skills and developed the organization needed to engage in the competitive politics of a pluralistic society. They also found individuals in other religious bodies who shared their goals and supported their cause. As a result of their enormously effective lobbying efforts, a major social-political compromise of the Revolution, the guarantee of the church property to the Episcopalians in 1776, was undone.

The contest over the church property was the first opportunity for Virginia to test its justly heralded Statute for Religious Freedom. While recognizing the right of each person to freedom of belief and worship and eliminating the possibility of financial support of the churches by the state, it did not disentangle religion from politics or sever relations between church and state. Nor did Virginians understand Jefferson's statute to require that separation. The repeal of the glebe laws that concluded the struggle for religious freedom meant that all churches were now able to compete on a completely equal basis. They were eager to do so, especially against the forces of deism and irreligion. In fact, as the repeal bill reached its final form, Baptists and other evangelicals were already moving on to a new agenda. The glebe struggle had given them a new awareness of their political leverage in the state. They pushed bills to toughen the antigaming laws, outlaw dueling, and close theaters. In the 1798 assembly, for example, 70 percent of those voting to suppress stage plays also supported

[122] Mays, *Edmund Pendleton*, II, 340-342; Brydon, *Virginia's Mother Church*, II, 503-505; Margaret Virginia Nelson, *A Study of Judicial Review in Virginia, 1789-1928* (New York, 1947), 66; *Minutes of the Baptist Middle District Association, Holden at Rice's Meeting House, in Prince Edward County, the Second Saturday in October, 1804* (Richmond, Va. [1804]), 4.

[123] Absolom Waller to Isaac Backus, Apr. 24, 1799, Backus Papers. Other letters to Backus in the same collection from other Baptist ministers indicate similar sentiments (John Courtney to Backus, Apr. 15, 1799, and Henry Toler to Backus, Apr. 21, 1799).

the Baptist position on the glebes.[124] The years ahead would see one move after another to embody evangelical values in the laws of Virginia, the other states, and ultimately the Union.

Thus the glebe issue points beyond Virginia to the interaction of religion and politics present throughout American history. During the next century and into the twentieth, like-minded evangelicals would organize what William Lee Miller has called "pan-Protestant alliances." Through churches, voluntary societies, and civil government they worked to transform America into a Christian country.[125] The successful fight to repeal the church property laws in Virginia and to force the sale of the glebes anticipated the development of politically skilled religious leaders eager to serve as moral stewards and willing to impose their religious values and culture upon American society.[126] As Alexis de Tocqueville later wrote, by preaching a common morality and "regulating domestic life" religion served as the principal support for democratic society. He thus identified religion as "the first of the political institutions" in the republic.[127] With the Baptist triumph in Virginia, the interaction of church and state, religion and politics, had only just begun in the new United States.

[124] *Jours. House of Delegates,* Dec. 27, 29, 1798, 45, 53, Jan. 13, 1802, 67. The vote to suppress theatrical performances failed, 51 to 71. The Richmond theater had burned down the previous January, which inspired a lively exchange in the press about the role of God and the quality of the performances (*Va. Gaz. and General Advertiser,* Jan. 31, Feb. 7, 14, 21, 1798).

[125] William Lee Miller, *The First Liberty: Religion and the American Republic* (New York, 1986), 233.

[126] Some useful studies of this development are Mark DeWolfe Howe, *The Garden and the Wilderness: Religion and Government in American Constitutional History* (Chicago, 1965); Elwyn A. Smith, "The Voluntary Establishment of Religion," in Smith, ed., *The Religion of the Republic* (Philadelphia, 1971), 154-182; Robert T. Handy, *A Christian America: Protestant Hopes and Historical Realities* (New York, 1971); Cushing Strout, *The New Heavens and New Earth: Political Religion in America* (New York, 1974); John F. Wilson, *Public Religion in American Culture* (Philadelphia, 1979); and Miller, *First Liberty,* esp. 227-353. For more recent developments see Robert Booth Fowler, *A New Engagement: Evangelical Political Thought, 1966-1976* (Grand Rapids, Mich., 1982), and Richard V. Pierard, "The New Religious Right: A Formidable Force in American Politics," *Choice,* XIX (1982), 863-879.

[127] Alexis de Tocqueville, *Democracy in America* (1835), ed. J. P. Mayer, trans. George Lawrence (Garden City, N.Y., 1969), 290-292.

A VERY WINTRY SEASON

Virginia Baptists and Slavery, 1785-1797

by James David Essig*

In 1798 David Barrow concluded a distinguished ministry among the Baptists of Virginia. As a gifted preacher and organizer, Barrow had watched the Virginia Baptists grow from a despised, embattled minority to a respectable denomination. But the Baptists had disappointed Barrow in one important respect: they had failed to share his convictions about the iniquity of holding slaves. Finding no way to support a family in Virginia without the use of slave labor, Barrow settled his affairs, bid his friends farewell, and sought out a new home on the rich lands of Kentucky.[1]

Barrow's departure marked the end of a brief but significant period during which Virginia Baptists deliberated the rightfulness of holding blacks in bondage. Historians have noted that between the years 1785 and 1797 the Baptists of Virginia expressed uneasiness about slavery, encountered resistance toward further discussion, and then fell silent on the matter.[2] The historians have furnished enough quotations to convince us that such a discussion took place, but they have not explained why slaveholding emerged as a pressing issue during those years.

An examination of the religious context of the discussion establishes a connection between the sudden concern about slavery and a spiritual crisis that the Baptists suffered at the time. The early Baptists of Virginia cultivated a style of spirituality emphasizing primitive Christian simplicity and a renunciation of the world and its charms. In the decades before the American Revolution, the social and legal realities of the Old Dominion permitted the Baptists to view themselves as the despised, the lowly, and the outcasts of fashionable society. The early experience of the Baptists, which greatly enhanced their style of spirituality, also fostered values and attitudes that carried an inherent antislavery potential. The postwar era, however, presented Virginia Baptists with developments that threatened to

---

*Mr. Essig is an instructor in history at Yale University, New Haven, Connecticut.

[1] Carlos R. Allen, Jr., "David Barrow's Circular Letter of 1798," *William and Mary Quarterly*, 3rd ser., XX (July 1963), 440-451.

[2] For a survey of Baptist opinion on slavery, see Reuben E. Alley, *A History of Baptists in Virginia* (Richmond, 1974), pp. 125-127; W. Harrison Daniel, "Virginia Baptists and the Negro in the Early Republic," *Virginia Magazine of History and Biography*, LXXX (January 1972), 60-69; Garnett Ryland, *The Baptists of Virginia: 1699-1926* (Richmond, 1955), pp. 150-155; H. Shelton Smith, *In His Image But . .: Racism in Southern Religion, 1780-1910* (Durham, 1972), pp. 47-48; and Robert G. Torbet, *A History of the Baptists* (Valley Forge, 1950), p. 282ff.

destroy their identity as a separated people by eroding their carefully preserved distinctions between church and world, Christ and culture. In this context, the short-lived concern about slavery can be viewed as part of a Baptist attempt to deal with the unsettling disparity between profession and practice.

In an effort to account for the brief existence of Baptist antislavery feeling, we shall first explore the Virginia Baptist experience for attitudes and values which could issue in an aversion to slaveholding. Next we shall analyze the nature of the spiritual malaise that overtook Virginia Baptists in the early national period. Finally, we shall relate the colloquy on slave- holding to the doubts that the Baptists expressed about themselves and their religious situation.

I

The Baptists of Virginia, a young plantation tutor observed, were "Gen- erally accounted troublesome" by the civil and ecclesiastical authorities of the colony.[3] As exponents of what H. Richard Niebuhr termed the "Christ against culture" viewpoint, the Virginia Baptists defined themselves in opposition to the dominant structures of power and social prestige.[4] Their rejection of the Anglican Church, their simple lifestyle, and their demand for religious freedom set the Baptists apart as a disaffected group in colonial Virginia. Schooled in the experience of dissent, the Virginia Baptists applied some of their more memorable lessons to interpret the meaning of slavery.

Those Virginians who professed Baptist beliefs in the years before the American Revolution fell under suspicion as subversives. Their insistence on adult rather than infant baptism, later regarded as a harmless religious preference, reminded many eighteenth-century Protestants of the radicalism of the sixteenth-century German Anabaptists. In 1534 the German Ana- baptists staged a bloody uprising at Münster, leaving a reputation for fanaticism that subsequent Baptist groups found difficult to live down. The Virginia Baptists found themselves accused of plotting sedition and all

---

[3] Hunter Dickinson Farish, editor, *Journal and Letters of Philip Vickers Fithian: A Plantation Tutor of the Old Dominion, 1773-1774* (Charlottesville, 1968), p. 72.

[4] H. Richard Niebuhr, *Christ and Culture* (New York, 1951), pp. 45-82. Rhys Isaac has offered a splendid treatment of the "struggle for allegiance" between the social worlds of the Baptists and the gentry in "Evangelical Revolt: The Nature of the Baptists' Challenge to the Traditional Order in Virginia, 1765-1775," *William and Mary Quarterly*, 3d ser., XXXI (July 1974), 345-368. See also his "Preachers and Patriots: Popular Culture and the Revolution in Virginia," in Alfred F. Young, editor, *The American Revolution: Essays in the History of American Radicalism* (DeKalb, 1976), pp. 127-156.

manner of unspeakable crimes against society. "What evil has not been reported of us?" David Thomas demanded to know in a forceful defense of his fellow Baptists. "Yea, what attrocious villa[i]ny can be mentioned, that has not been laid to our charge?"[5] As reputed public enemies, the early Baptists of Virginia enjoyed no intimacy with the governing authorities or the self-appointed guardians of peace and good order.

Though they were not the social incendiaries that their detractors pictured them to be, the Baptists did constitute a disruptive element in the religious life of the Old Dominion, and as such they became a matter of concern for the civil authorities. Regarding the Church of England as a scripturally unsound institution, the Baptists organized their own churches in Virginia. Unlike the Church of England, the Baptist churches had no official standing in the eyes of the civil government and received no financial support from it. The Act of Toleration, passed by the English Parliament in 1689, granted nonconformists in Virginia a limited toleration, provided that they obtained licenses from the government to preach and hold meetings. Bureaucratic obstacles in Virginia, however, made licenses difficult to come by, while many Baptist preachers rejected the idea that the call of the Spirit had to be authorized by the state. In the first half of the eighteenth century, the colonial authorities managed to overlook the irregularities of the Baptists as long as they kept a low profile and posed no serious threat to the Established Church. A flurry of organizational activity that occurred at the middle of the century made the Baptists more conspicuous and, from the authorities' point of view, more irksome.[6]

The mid-century surge of activity gathered force with the arrival of the Separate Baptists. When Shubal Stearns entered the colony in 1754 to begin his energetic labors, he imported a religious fervor that had already swept through New England during the Great Awakening. At that time, a desire for a clearer separation between church and world led some New Englanders to leave their churches and form new ones where only those adults who could demonstrate conversion were baptized and admitted as members.[7] It was this Separate, or "New Light," brand of Baptist belief that Stearns brought to Virginia. Stearns and his Yankee associates travelled widely through Virginia and North Carolina, earning the name "strollers"

---

[5] David Thomas, *The Virginian Baptist: A View and Defence of the Christian Religion as it is Professed by the Baptists of Virginia* (Baltimore, 1774), p. 6.

[6] For the information in this paragraph I have relied on William L. Lumpkin, *Baptist Foundations in the South: Tracing through the Separates the Influence of the Great Awakening, 1754-1787* (Nashville, 1961), pp. 105-113.

[7] C. C. Goen provides a detailed account of the Separate Baptists of New England in *Revivalism and Separatism in New England, 1740-1800* (New Haven, 1962).

for their itinerant mode of preaching and encouraging other Baptists to expand their own evangelistic efforts.[8] Preaching the necessity of the new birth in Christ, the evangelical Baptists of the mid-eighteenth century carried on an aggressive and successful work.

In addition to the necessity of the new birth, the roving Baptist exhorters also preached the necessity of guarding against a "worldly spirit," for an overfond regard for the vanities of this world, they believed, would rob evangelical religion of its vitality. Thus Henry Toler could wish, "O that God would deliver me from Pride, and as much as possible from all this World."[9] To demonstrate their rejection of the world, the Baptists refused to conform to the tastes and conventions of polite society. As one gentleman told it, this meant that the Baptists were "quite destroying pleasure in the country; for they encourage ardent Pray'r; strong & constant faith, & an entire Banishment of *Gaming, Dancing,* and Sabbath-Day Diversions."[10] Moreover, no pleasantries, rhetorical graces, or verbal conceits adorned the Baptist proclamation of the gospel. David Thomas found "our present gravity" more suitable for preaching than the jesting and bantering demanded by the "polite airs" of the world.[11] A lack of gentility could even be a spiritual asset. Robert Semple, an early historian of the Virginia Baptists, celebrated the era when Baptist ministers, "unrefined in their manners and awkward in their address," turned these shortcomings to advantage and reaped a harvest of souls.[12]

The Virginia Baptists further demonstrated the depth of their spirituality through the way they dressed. Semple believed that God blessed the labors of the early itinerants because they were "very plain in their dress," while "pampered" Anglican ministers lay "rolling on the bed of luxury."[13] The Separates refused to unite with another group of Baptists in 1772, suspecting them of indulging their members in "superfluity of apparel."[14] John Leland, a Baptist preacher from New England who was certainly no fop when it came to clothes, found himself in violation of the Virginia Baptist dress code by adhering to the custom of his region, "each one putting on such apparel

---

[8] Lumpkin, *Baptist Foundations in the South,* p. 68.
[9] Henry Toler, Diary, 1782-1784, July 12, 1783, typed copy at the Virginia Baptist Historical Society, University of Richmond. I would like to thank members of the staff at the Society for making this and other documents available to me.
[10] Farish, *Journal and Letters of Philip Vickers Fithian,* p. 72.
[11] Thomas, *Virginian Baptist,* p. 60.
[12] Robert Semple, *A History of the Rise and Progress of the Baptists in Virginia* (Richmond, 1810), p. 26.
[13] *Ibid.*
[14] Lemuel Burkitt and Jesse Read, *A Concise History of the Kehukee Baptist Association* (Halifax, 1803), p. 38.

as suited his fancy." [15] This casual attitude toward one's personal appearance simply would not do among people who advertised their separation from the world by means of a stylized simplicity. Plain dress, plain talk, and plain manners ranked high in the Baptist scheme of values and kept them a safe distance from the vanities of "the glittering world." [16]

One class of citizens provided Virginia Baptists with a living illustration of the perils that the "glittering world" presented to the godly life. Only rarely did members of the gentry interest themselves in New Light religion, which they generally regarded as a crude and joyless fanaticism. Between the Blue Ridge and the Chesapeake Bay, James Ireland found that few of the "politest part of the people" had any concern for the state of their souls.[17] This fact did not surprise Ireland or his colleagues. Where the "pride of life" has been predominant, William Fristoe explained, one should not expect deep religious commitment, for "it is impossible to court popularity and the friendship of the carnal world, and enjoy communion with God at the same time." [18] A failure to interest the gentry therefore gave the Baptists indirect assurance about their own godliness.

The Baptists drew yet another lesson from the social make-up of their religious body. Just as in the days of the apostles, they believed, God had chosen the despised and lowly to confound the wisdom of the mighty. "The truth is," David Thomas asserted, "poverty, the want of erudition, and the malice of an ungodly world, are just so many more likely characters of God's election, than of the contrary." [19] William Fristoe declared that the shortage of rich converts "gave clearer proof of the genuine quality of religion among us," for in the early Christian era it was the "common people" who received the word with gladness. Not that poverty placed the Almighty under obligation to bestow grace, as Fristoe quickly pointed out, but it permitted Christians to escape "a gaudy, superfluous appearance, a stream whose rapid current has swept the polite world away." [20]

When he described the factors that hindered the rich man's entry into the Kingdom of God, Fristoe touched on one aspect of the gentry's lifestyle that provided the foundation for the prodigal habits of that class. Early in childhood, as Fristoe had it, the children of the planters contracted sinful habits because they were "freed from hard labor, by having slaves to labor

---

[15] Semple, *History of the Rise and Progress of the Baptists*, p. 177.
[16] William Fristoe, *A Concise History of the Ketocton Baptist Association* (Staunton, 1808), p. 149.
[17] James Ireland, *The Life of James Ireland* (Winchester, Va., 1819), p. 182.
[18] Fristoe, *Concise History of the Ketocton Baptist Association*, p. 151.
[19] Thomas, *Virginian Baptist*, p. 55.
[20] Fristoe, *Concise History of the Ketocton Baptist Association*, p. 153.

for them," an exemption that allowed them time to indulge in sports, balls, and other diversions of the "high life." [21] According to this interpretation, slavery gave the planters leisure, and leisure led to sinful pastimes; hence there was something vaguely unwholesome about the use of slave labor. A similar impression struck David Barrow, that tough-minded antislavery figure who would carry his convictions into Kentucky. He cited the example of Christ himself, who "had no *slaves*, but it seems *wrought* for his *livelihood* . . . at the *business* of a carpenter." [22] On one level, then, slavery intruded upon the Baptist consciousness as the means by which the planters enjoyed their fashionable but godless lifestyle.

Doubts about slavery arose for the Baptists in another manner. Out of their struggle for religious liberty, the Baptists derived the ability to identify with limited aspects of the slave's experience, an identification that the gentry facilitated by resisting Baptist efforts to convert the slaves.

As embodiments of the worldly spirit, members of the gentry fulfilled Baptist expectations by attempting to suppress their evangelistic activities. In addition to the legal disabilities that they suffered as dissenters, the Baptists encountered less official forms of harassment ranging from catcalls to physical abuse. The local gentry of Virginia took an active role in both kinds of persecution. Sometimes they acted in an official capacity, as when the sheriff whipped John Waller for disturbing the peace, while at others they indulged themselves in malicious amusement, as when the "gang of well-dressed men" nearly drowned David Barrow in a mock baptism. [23] The Baptists thrived on the enmity of "the learned, the wealthy, and those of great parentage," [24] testing their mettle and developing an identity as an "oppressed people" [25] in the process.

When they took the gospel to the slaves, the Baptists met with victims of another kind of oppression, and there directing it stood a class of familiar antagonists. Itinerant preaching disturbed the peace, but in the eyes of Virginia's large slaveholders, evangelistic work among the slaves disrupted the self-contained world [26] of the eighteenth-century plantation. Colonel Landon Carter, a planter of strong opinions and little patience, registered

---

[21] *Ibid.*, p. 151.

[22] David Barrow, *Involuntary, Unmerited, Perpetual, Absolute, Hereditary Slavery, Examined on the Principles of Nature, Reason, Justice, Policy, and Scripture* (Lexington, Ky., 1808), p. 38.

[23] Elder John Williams, Journal, 1771, p. 3, copy in the Virginia Baptist Historical Society; David Benedict, *A General History of the Baptist Denomination in America, and Other Parts of the World* (Boston, 1813), II, 249n.

[24] Fristoe, *Concise History of the Ketocton Baptist Association*, p. 64.

[25] *Ibid.*, p. 90.

[26] Gerald W. Mullin has so depicted the eighteenth-century plantation in *Flight and Rebellion: Slave Resistance in Eighteenth-Century Virginia* (New York, 1972), p. 7ff.

disgust when one of his slaves showed evidence of the "new light" persuasion. "I believe it is from some inculcated doctrine of those rascals [i.e., the New Lights] that the slaves in this Colony are grown so much worse," he wrote in his diary in 1770.[27] To compound his frustrations, one of Carter's overseers joined the Baptists and informed his employer that "he cannot serve God and Mammon, has just been made a Christian by dipping, and would not continue in my business but to convert my people." Singularly unimpressed by this proposal, Carter deemed such "religious villains" to be as unsatisfactory as "horrid hellish rogues" when it came to the effective management of slaves.[28] Another critic of the Baptists charged that, by breaking up families and drawing "Slaves from the Obedience of their Masters," the Baptists brought Virginia to the brink of social chaos: "the very Heartstrings of those little Societies which form the greater are torn in sunder, and all their Peace destroyed."[29]

The Baptists, for their part, protested that their only concern was with the souls of black folk, but the evangelistic imperative generated a militance that could not be so easily contained. Even as he tried to refute the charge that Baptists divided slaves from their masters, David Thomas struck a menacing posture towards those who would obstruct the work of spiritual liberation:

When the LORD JESUS displays the banners of his love, and his gospel trumpet sounds proclaiming liberty to the captives; Beelzebub will not fail making an horrible uproar, we may be sure. . . . The war is most just, and it must be carried on, whatever outcries the usurper, or his confederates, may think proper to make. The strong holds must be demolished, the prison doors broken down, and the iron fetters dissolved, let who will gainsay it. The elect slaves must be redeemed, though others choose to hug their chains and even curse their best friends, who offer to set them free.[30]

Such rhetoric, though it fell far short of a revolutionary manifesto, did nothing to allay gentry suspicions about the social consequences of the New Light, while in the evangelical mind it fostered an association between spiritual and temporal bondage.

By unfurling the banner of religious liberty on the plantation, the Baptists discovered that they held some common ground with the slaves. While

---

[27] Jack P. Greene, editor, *The Diary of Colonel Landon Carter of Sabine Hall, 1752-1778* (Charlottesville, 1965), I, 378.

[28] *Ibid.*, II, 1056-1057.

[29] "An Address to the Anabaptists Imprisoned in Caroline County, August 8, 1771," quoted in Lewis Peyton Little, *Imprisoned Preachers and Religious Liberty in Virginia* (Lynchburg, 1938), p. 259.

[30] Thomas, *Virginian Baptist*, pp. 58-59.

preaching in Culpeper County, James Ireland recoiled with astonishment as members of a slave patrol broke up a gathering by beating blacks in the congregation, "being urged thereto by the enemies and opposers of religion."[31] Ireland's own experience of persecution led him to interpret the violence as a skirmish in the ongoing struggle for religious liberty, not as an effort to maintain slave discipline. In a similar fashion, John Leland depicted the injustice of slavery in categories familiar to the Baptists. "Liberty of conscience, in matters of religion, is the right of slaves beyond contradiction," he announced in *The Virginia Chronicle,* "and yet many masters and overseers will whip and torture the poor creatures for going to meeting, even at night, when the labor of the day is over."[32] Eventually Leland came to understand slaveholding and religious persecution as two expressions of the same oppressive spirit. After religious freedom had been obtained in Virginia in 1785, he could declare that "As personal slavery exists chiefly in the southern states, so religious slavery abounds exclusively in three or four of the New England states."[33] Before 1785, however, both forms of oppression existed side by side in Virginia, and the slaveholding, persecuting gentleman brought them both into focus for the Baptists.

None of the foregoing attitudes had an inevitable tendency to produce convictions against holding blacks in bondage. In Baptist circles, antislavery sentiment could serve as a vehicle for hostility toward members of the gentry, either because of their lifestyle or because of the part they played in religious persecution: "anti-slavery" could mean "anti-gentry" or "anti-religious oppression." These associations, which made an inquiry into the rightfulness of slavery possible, did not by themselves necessitate that such an inquiry take place. It took a mood of apprehension to bring out the antislavery possibilities embedded in the Virginia Baptist experience. That mood descended over the Baptists in the late 1780s.

II

By December of 1785 the Baptists of Virginia had every reason to rejoice about their prospects as a denomination. The successful conclusion of the war with Britain had secured the civil liberties of these ardent patriots, while an act of the Virginia legislature, passed late in 1785, guaranteed their religious freedom. But how would the Baptists adjust to a

---

[31] Ireland, *Life of James Ireland*, p. 135.
[32] L. F. Greene, editor, *The Writings of the Late Elder John Leland* (New York, 1845), p. 95.
[33] *Ibid.*, p. 268.

situation which no longer required persecution for righteousness' sake, one which no longer provided a test for one's spiritual mettle? Having fought the good fight and won, how would they maintain morale, discipline, and group identity?

Several Baptist spokesmen agreed that success had a debilitating effect on the piety of their brothers and sisters. Danger signals appeared as early as 1783, when Richard Dozier recorded his dismay at seeing believers who imagined that "they have taken themselves out of the world, and at the same time following the world."[34] Virginia Baptists succumbed as readily as the rest of their countrymen to the rage for imported finery that flooded American ports after the war. Dozier issued a warning to those whose new taste in clothes smacked more of "proud profanity" than the "humble religion" of the lowly Jesus: "Your boots and spurs and half gloves too, look too much like what worldlings do."[35]

As Baptist elders looked back on it, the enactment of religious liberty brought mixed blessings in its train as well. The normally jocose Leland saw little to cheer him in the behavior of his fellow Baptists. "The ways of Zion mourned," he observed. "They obtained their hearts' desire, (freedom,) but had leanness in their souls." Far from inaugurating an era of religious prosperity, the legislature's enactment ushered in a time when "iniquity did abound, and the love of many waxed cold."[36] Robert Semple followed Leland in relating the Baptists' spiritual depression to their unaccustomed status before the law. "As if persecution was more favorable to vital piety, than unrestrained liberty," he wrote, "they seem to have abated in their zeal, upon being unshackled from their manacles."[37]

Even a local revival lasting from 1785 to 1792 could not lift Baptist morale; in fact, this awakening further eroded the social basis of the Virginia Baptist identity. Numerical growth added respectability to the Baptist cause in the eyes of the world, Semple reported, and "This could not but influence their manners and spirit more or less." As a result of the revival, "great changes took place among the Baptists, some for the better, and others for the worse."[38] Acquiring a taste for respectability with unbecoming ease, Baptist preachers discarded their "odd tones, disgusting whoops and awkward gestures" in favor of a more "correct" style of address. Furthermore, the Baptists "were joined by persons of much greater weight, in

---

[34] Richard Dozier, Text Book, September 21, 1783, Virginia Baptist Historical Society.
[35] *Ibid.*
[36] Greene, *Writings of the Late John Leland*, pp. 112-113.
[37] Semple, *History of the Rise and Progress of the Baptists*, p. 35.
[38] *Ibid.*, pp. 38-39.

civil society." Although Semple recorded this development with pride, a note of wistfulness crept into his appraisal of the changes wrought by having so many of the better sort within the Baptist fold. He concluded that "a great deal of that simplicity and plainness, that rigid scrupulosity about little matters, which so happily tends to keep us at a distance from greater follies, was laid aside." [39] All things considered, the postwar era was, as Semple put it, "a very wintry season" for the Baptists of Virginia. [40]

A chill had settled into the marrow of Baptist piety, and denominational leaders blamed worldliness for the decline in fervor. As early as 1789, the Roanoke Association of Baptists reminded its member churches of the need for "pious deportments" to counteract the luxury and extravagance of the times, but within a few years they began to look among themselves for offending evils. [41] At a meeting of the Kehukee Association in 1790, David Barrow took Luke 12:15 as his text and warned his brethren to beware of covetousness, that inordinate desire for material possessions. [42] The Middle District's Circular Letter of 1791 named covetousness as "one great reason, why we are so languid in vital religion." [43] Letters from twenty member churches gave delegates to the 1793 meeting of the Strawberry Association "an account of Zion's leanness in general, which calls aloud for lamentation." When lamentations alone produced no reformation, the Strawberry Association provided Baptists with a list of soul-searching questions in 1794, one of which recalled a neglected style of spirituality: "Do I live a life of self-denial and mortification[?]" [44] The fact that such a question had to be asked at all reveals how far the Baptists had departed from the ideal of apostolic simplicity.

In postwar Virginia the godly hankered after riches, and the rich displayed a new-found desire for godliness. Virginia Baptists lost their bearings when these two trends combined to erase the familiar boundary between church and world, Christ and culture. Disoriented by success, bewildered by the unforeseen effects of prosperity, the Virginia Baptists advanced a

---

[39] *Ibid.*, p. 39. Wesley M. Gewehr pointed to the Baptist successes on the Northern Neck as one reason for the increased numbers of gentle folk in the denomination (*The Great Awakening in Virginia, 1740-1790* [Durham, N. C., 1930], pp. 173, 177).

[40] Semple, *History of the Rise and Progress of the Baptists*, p. 36.

[41] Roanoke Association, Minute Book, 1789-1831, Circular Letter of 1789, p. 17; Circular Letter of 1794, p. 105, photocopy of original at Virginia Baptist Historical Society.

[42] Burkitt and Read, *Concise History of the Kehukee Baptist Association*, pp. 102-103. The Kehukee Association at this time included churches in Virginia.

[43] Semple, *History of the Rise and Progress of the Baptists*, p. 196.

[44] Strawberry Association, Minute Book, 1787-1822, Circular Letter of 1793, p. 63; Circular Letter of 1794, p. 78, photocopy of original at Virginia Baptist Historical Society.

short distance toward an antislavery position in an attempt to recover some sense of direction and purpose.

III

During the period of religious depression, which lasted from about 1785 to the onset of the Second Great Awakening, the Virginia Baptists turned their attention to slavery. Within the context of the postwar concern over worldliness, the practice of holding slaves loomed before Baptists as evidence of the unholy desire for prestige and affluence. In *The Annual Register* of 1790, John Asplund asked his readers to consider seven "inconsistencies" within the entire denomination, each a contradiction to Christ's teaching and "our holy profession." [45] Quite significantly, Asplund listed slaveholding as the first item requiring attention. Next came the complaint that fathers had failed to provide enough religious instruction to make their children "at least useful members of society," an indication that young Baptists, like the children of the gentry, were frittering their time away in vain pursuits. After this Asplund named "Extravagance or superfluity, not only in eating or drinking, but especially in dress, that we may not be conformed to the sinful customs of this world; but be a separate people, denying all ungodliness and worldly lust, &c." [46] By liberating their slaves, by supervising their children's pastimes, and by returning to their former simplicity, the Baptists might maintain their "holy profession" and shore up their deteriorating religious identity.

John Leland, who had firsthand knowledge of the Virginia Baptists, went one step further than Asplund by linking slaveholding with the desire for worldly advancement. "The custom of the country is such," he explained in *The Virginia Chronicle*, "that, without slaves, a man's children stand but a poor chance to marry in reputation." Leland discerned that this widely held belief represented "one of the great difficulties that prevent the liberation of the slaves among the common sort." [47] And the "common sort," as Leland well knew, formed the backbone of the Virginia Baptists. These observations led him to detect the "voice of covetousness" [48] in reasoned pleas for caution and moderation in handling the matter of slavery.

---

[45] John Asplund, *The Annual Register of the Baptist Denomination, in North America; To the First of November, 1790* (Philadelphia, 1792), p. 56. The other four items requiring attention were contributions for the poor and ministers, attendance at worship, the encouragement of ministers, and the constitution of churches (p. 57). Asplund wrote the preface from Southampton County, Virginia.
[46] *Ibid.*, pp. 56-57.
[47] Greene, *Writings of the Late John Leland*, p. 97.
[48] *Ibid.*

Delegates to the 1796 meeting of the Portsmouth Association shared Leland's perception of a link between slaveholding and covetousness. When the delegates, with David Barrow as moderator, asked themselves the cause of these "present and distressing times," they came up with an unequivocal answer: *"We believe covetousness is the source."* Covetousness distracted ministers from their duties and made laymen tightfisted in their contributions to the poor, they stated. The delegates went on to declare that

Covetousness, leads Christians, with the people of this country in general, to hold and retain in *abject slavery*, a set of our poor fellow creatures, *contrary to the laws of God and nature:*—for these, and on account of that *detested conformity* to the wicked *ways* and *customs* "of this present evil world;" and for the *abominations* practiced among the citizens in common, we think the *Church* and *Land mourns.*[49]

The Baptist concern over slaveholding represented an extension of an older concern about maintaining a godly distance from an ungodly world.

Between 1785 and 1797, when the problem of worldliness assumed a new urgency, the Virginia Baptists held their short-lived discussion about slavery. The General Committee, a council created by the district associations to administer Virginia Baptist affairs, opened the discussion in 1785 by declaring "hereditary slavery to be contrary to the word of God."[50] By and large, however, the body of churches ignored this resolution, with only the Black Creek Church deciding that slavery "is unrighteous."[51] The Ketocton Association attempted to formulate a plan of gradual emancipation in 1787, but this proposal excited such a "tumult" that the Association dropped it.[52]

Matters stood unchanged until the 1790 meeting of the General Committee, where delegates debated the "equity, of Hereditary Slavery" for a "considerable time."[53] The minutes of this meeting unfortunately do not include a record of the arguments employed by the opponents of slavery, but they do establish the fact that David Barrow and John Leland were present. Their voices almost certainly made significant contributions to the proceedings. When a group which included Barrow failed to come up with a satisfactory resolution on slavery, the task fell to Leland. His resolution, quoted fondly and frequently by subsequent Baptist historians, blended

---

[49] *Minutes of the Portsmouth Association . . . 1796* (n. p., n. d.), p. 5.

[50] *Minutes of the Baptist General Committee . . . May 1791* (Richmond, 1791), p. 5. The records of this session contain the only reference to the resolution of 1785.

[51] Quoted in Daniel, "Virginia Baptists," *VMHB*, LXXX, 66.

[52] Semple, *History of the Rise and Progress of the Baptists*, pp. 303-304.

[53] *Minutes of the Baptist General Committee . . . 1790* (Richmond, 1790), p. 5.

republican and biblical rhetoric into an antislavery declaration: slavery was "a violent deprivation of the rights of nature" and "inconsistent" with a republican government; Baptists should use "every legal measure to extirpate this horrid evil from the land"; and they should pray to the Almighty that the legislature would "proclaim the great Jubilee" in a manner "consistent with the principles of good policy."[54]

Though Leland's resolution had enough support to pass at the General Committee's meeting, it met with a cool reception at a local level. The unenthusiastic response of the associations revealed the limits of antislavery efforts within the Baptist denomination. Throughout the long struggle for toleration, the Baptists championed liberty of conscience against the forces of "oppression," those who would suppress a diversity of opinion on religious matters. Having won that contest, individual Baptists had no intention of relinquishing their consciences to a new episcopacy of Baptist elders. The high value placed on liberty, which had once permitted white evangelicals to identify with the victims of physical oppression, also prohibited the General Committee from making emancipation a uniform, binding policy for all Baptists.

The Baptist response to Leland's resolution can therefore be explained in part as resistance to ecclesiasticism rather than antislavery itself. Members of the Roanoke Association, for example, reported that "we are not unanimously clear" about the rightfulness of slavery, but they were certain that "neither the general committee nor any other Religious Society whatever has the least right to concern therein as a society, but leave every individual to act at discretion, in order to keep a good conscience before God."[55] Believing that members of the General Committee had overreached their authority, the Strawberry Association entered a terse formulation into its records: "we advise them not to interfere with it."[56] To be sure, the appeal to conscience could disguise less principled objections to further debate, perhaps even from those who made the appeal most fervently. But whether it proceeded from highminded devotion to principle or self-interest, the appeal successfully enervated the antislavery activity of the Committee. Faced with indifference or disapproval from the member associations, the General Committee voted in 1793 "that the subject be dismissed from this committee, as believing it belongs to the legislative body."[57] By "legislative body" the Committee meant, of course, the Virginia

---

[54] Ibid., p. 7.
[55] Roanoke Association, Minutes, June 1790, pp. 39-40.
[56] Strawberry Association, Minutes, May 1792, p. 45.
[57] Minutes of the Baptist General Committee . . . 1793 (Richmond, 1793), p. 4.

General Assembly. The Committee's action amounted to an admission that the Virginia Baptists, as a religious body, would do nothing about slavery. Realizing its impotence to do anything more than pass resolutions, the Committee referred the problem to individual consciences and the secular authorities. Individual Baptists might petition the General Assembly to effect a gradual emancipation, as the Dover Association advised them to do in 1797.[58] But by defining slavery as a legislative problem, the Committee handed other Baptists an excuse for inaction. If slavery was a legislative problem, then responsibility for emancipation fell upon the lawmakers. Until such time as they saw fit to act, the Baptist churches should withhold comment and tend to their spiritual affairs, among which slaveholding no longer had a place. John Leland recognized this readiness to dissociate slavery from the legitimate concerns of the churches. In his valedictory address, he had to preface his remarks on slavery with the assurance that he did not intend to "drop the ministerial vest, and assume the politician's garb to-day."[59] In 1796 the Ketocton Association confirmed a tendency of Baptists to excuse themselves from responsibility on the grounds that it was none of their business. When the Happy Creek Church sent that Association an inquiry on the righteousness of slaveholding, the Association refused to answer, "considering it an improper subject of investigation in a Baptist Association, whose only business is to give advice to the Churches respecting religious matters; and considering the subject of this query to be the business of government."[60] As a political problem, slaveholding simply did not constitute a soul-endangering sin.

Some Virginia Baptists detected casuistry where their brothers and sisters professed conviction. David Barrow and Carter Tarrant, who continued the antislavery struggle in Kentucky, laid bare the evasions and inconsistencies in the Baptist position on slaveholding, and they did it as only Baptists could. Refusing to regard slaveholding as a political problem, Barrow continued to denounce it as a "fashionable" sin: "I believe, the main objections against emancipation are never brought in sight—which I presume are the following, viz. 'The love of money,' which is covetousness, self-aggrandizement, and self-ease."[61] Tarrant blamed worldliness for the defective moral vision of the Baptists. "Blinded by covetousness and intoxication with the

---

[58] Dover Association, Minutes, 1797, Virginia Baptist Historical Society.
[59] Greene, *Writings of the Late John Leland*, p. 174.
[60] Quoted in Ryland, *Baptists of Virginia*, p. 154.
[61] Barrow, *Slavery*, pp. 41, 45.

cup of Babylon, they call evil good and good evil," he declared.[62] As for the excuse that the civil government allowed slavery, "What is this in fact," Barrow asked, "but saying the policy of a nation supercedes the law of God?"[63] Tarrant scored a direct hit when he taunted, "Some will plead our civil government, as if the church was beholden to the world for assistance in matters of religion, and had no king nor constitution of her own."[64] In their stance against worldliness and their refusal to let the civil government determine matters of conscience, Barrow, Tarrant, and other unknown antislavery spokesmen faithfully preserved two features of Baptist spirituality. By the early years of the nineteenth century, however, they had become prophets without honor in southern Baptist circles.

The majority of Virginia Baptists stopped worrying about slavery when they stopped worrying about themselves. As the Second Great Awakening made its invigorating influence felt in the opening years of the nineteenth century, the winter of their discontent passed into a vernal season of assurance and renewal. No longer troubled about the rightfulness of slaveholding, they contented themselves with the task of disciplining masters for excessive cruelty toward their slaves.[65] Though the subject requires further study, it appears as though the Second Great Awakening hastened the decline of antislavery sentiment among southern evangelicals by demonstrating, to their satisfaction, the compatibility of slaveholding with godliness. After all, if slaves could be redeemed from sin, and masters could be similarly redeemed, then perhaps the institution of slavery itself could be redeemed if all the individuals involved were converted. Pious masters instructing their slaves in godliness, pious slaves serving their masters with Christian humility[66]—in the warm glow of such a vision, the former associations between slaveholding, persecution, and a sinful lifestyle melted away. While the southern evangelicals of the early nineteenth century had not yet developed this line of thought into a defense of slavery as a positive good, they anticipated a later generation's view of the planta-

---

[62] William Warren Sweet, *Religion on the American Frontier: The Baptists* (New York, 1931), p. 569.

[63] Barrow, *Slavery*, p. 47n.

[64] Sweet, *Religion on the American Frontier*, p. 568.

[65] See, for example, Minutes of the Roanoke Association, June 1790, pp. 39-40; Minutes of the Dover Association, 1796.

[66] I have reconstructed this outlook from a number of evangelical sources, including, Henry Pattillo, *The Plain Planter's Family Assistant* (Wilmington, 1787), pp. 25, 46-51; *Virginia Religious Magazine* (May and June 1807), pp. 161-170; James Hall, *A Narrative of a Most Extraordinary Work of God in North Carolina. . . .* (Philadelphia, 1802), p. 21; and Edmund Botsford, *Sambo and Toney: A Dialogue Between Two Servants* (New York, n. d.), originally published in 1808.

tion as a school where benighted heathen might learn the rudiments of Christianity and civilization.

With the spread of evangelical Christianity, the world had become a more hospitable place for the Virginia Baptists than it had been for their predecessors. The world, however, had obtained concessions from the Baptists, as an old woman revealed when in the early 1800s she told a Baptist minister, "Your society are much more like other folks now than they were when I was young."[67] The Baptist attitude toward slavery was a case in point. More deeply committed to the preservation of the social order than their forebears, more closely identified with its ruling interests, white Baptists of Virginia removed slaveholding from the agenda for reform.

---

[67] David Benedict, *Fifty Years Among the Baptists* (New York, 1860), p. 93.

Eighteenth-Century American Women
in Peace and War:
The Case of the Loyalists

Mary Beth Norton

I n recent years historians have come to recognize the central role of the family in the shaping of American society. Especially in the eighteenth century, when "household" and "family" were synonymous terms, and when household manufactures constituted a major contribution to the economy, the person who ran the household—the wife and mother—occupied a position of crucial significance. Yet those who have studied eighteenth-century women have usually chosen to focus on a few outstanding, perhaps unrepresentative individuals, such as Eliza Lucas Pinckney, Abigail Smith Adams, and Mercy Otis Warren. They have also emphasized the activities of women outside the home and have concentrated on the prescriptive literature of the day. Little has been done to examine in depth the lives actually led by the majority of colonial women or to assess the impact of the Revolution upon them.[1]

Such a study can illuminate a number of important topics. Demographic scholars are beginning to discover the dimensions of eighteenth-century households, but a knowledge of size alone means little without a delineation of roles filled by husband and wife within those households.[2] Historians of

Ms. Norton is a member of the Department of History, Cornell University. She wishes to thank Carol Berkin, Carl Kaestle, Pauline Maier, Robert Wells, and Peter Wood for their comments on an earlier version of this article. A portion of it was read at the Second Berkshire Conference on the History of Women, held at Radcliffe College, Oct. 1974.

[1] See, for example, such works as Mary Sumner Benson, *Women in Eighteenth-Century America: A Study of Opinion and Social Usage* (New York, 1935); Elisabeth Anthony Dexter, *Colonial Women of Affairs*, 2d ed. (New York, 1931); and Joan Hoff Wilson, "Dancing Dogs of the Colonial Period: Women Scientists," *Early American Literature*, VII (1973), 225-235. Notable exceptions are Julia Cherry Spruill, *Women's Life and Work in the Southern Colonies* (Chapel Hill, N.C., 1938), and Eugenie Andruss Leonard, *The Dear-Bought Heritage* (Philadelphia, 1965). On the importance of the early American family see David Rothman, "A Note on the Study of the Colonial Family," *William and Mary Quarterly*, 3d Ser., XXIII (1966), 627-634.

[2] Two recent works that deal with family size, among other topics, are Robert V. Wells, "Household Size and Composition in the British Colonies in America, 1675-1775," *Journal of Interdisciplinary History*, IV (1974), 543-570, and Daniel Scott

nineteenth-century American women have analyzed the ideology which has been termed the "cult of true womanhood" or the "cult of domesticity," but the relationship of these ideas to the lives of women in the preceding century remains largely unexplored.[3] And although some historians of the Revolution now view the war as a socially disruptive phenomenon, they have not yet applied that insight specifically to the study of the family.[4]

Fortunately, at least one set of documents contains material relevant to an investigation of all these aspects of late eighteenth-century American family life: the 281 volumes of the loyalist claims, housed at the Public Record Office in London. Although these manuscripts have been used extensively for political and economic studies of loyalism, they have only once before been utilized for an examination of colonial society.[5] What makes the loyalist

Smith, "Population, Family and Society in Hingham, Massachusetts, 1635-1880" (Ph.D. diss., University of California, Berkeley, 1973). Internal household relationships in 17th-century New England have been analyzed by Edmund S. Morgan, *The Puritan Family: Religion & Domestic Relations in Seventeenth-Century New England* (Boston, 1944), and John Demos, *A Little Commonwealth: Family Life in Plymouth Colony* (New York, 1970).

[3] Barbara Welter, "The Cult of True Womanhood, 1820-1860," *American Quarterly*, XVII (1966), 151-174, was the first to outline the dimensions of this ideology. For writings dealing with some of the implications of the "cult of domesticity" see Carroll Smith-Rosenberg, "The Hysterical Woman: Sex Roles and Role Conflict in 19th-Century America," *Social Research*, XXXIX (1972), 652-678; Ann Douglas Wood, "Mrs. Sigourney and the Sensibility of the Inner Space," *New England Quarterly*, XLV (1972), 163-181; Kathryn Kish Sklar, *Catharine Beecher: A Study in American Domesticity* (New Haven, Conn., 1973); and Nancy Falik Cott, "In the Bonds of Womanhood: Perspectives on Female Experience and Consciousness in New England, 1780-1830" (Ph.D. diss., Brandeis University, 1974), esp. chap. 6. An explicit assertion that women were better off in 18th-century America than they were later is found in Dexter, *Colonial Women of Affairs*, vii, 189-192, and in Page Smith, *Daughters of the Promised Land* (Boston, 1970), 37-76. But two European historians have appropriately warned that it may be dangerous to assume the existence of a "golden, preindustrial age" for women, noting that the "goldenness is seen almost exclusively in terms of women's work and its presumed relationship to family power, not in terms of other vital aspects of their lives, including the physical burdens of work and child bearing." Patricia Branca and Peter N. Stearns, "On the History of Modern Women, a Research Note," *AHA Newsletter*, XII (Sept. 1974), 6.

[4] For example, John Shy, "The American Revolution: The Military Conflict Considered as a Revolutionary War," in Stephen G. Kurtz and James H. Hutson, eds., *Essays on the American Revolution* (Chapel Hill, N.C., 1973), 121-156; John Shy, "The Loyalist Problem in the Lower Hudson Valley: The British Perspective," in Robert A. East and Jacob Judd, eds., *The Loyalist Americans: A Focus on Greater New York* (Tarrytown, N.Y., 1975), 3-13; and Ronald Hoffman, *A Spirit of Dissension: Economics, Politics, and the Revolution in Maryland* (Baltimore, 1973), esp. chaps. 6, 8.

[5] Catherine S. Crary, "The Humble Immigrant and the American Dream: Some

claims uniquely useful is the fact that they contain information not only about the personal wartime experiences of thousands of Americans but also about the modes of life the war disrupted.

Among the 3,225 loyalists who presented claims to the British government after the war were 468 American refugee women. The analysis that follows is based upon an examination of the documents—formal memorials, loss schedules, and private letters—submitted by these women to the loyalist claims commission, and on the commission's nearly verbatim records of the women's personal appearances before them.[6] These women cannot be said to compose a statistically reliable sample of American womanhood. It is entirely possible that loyalist families differed demographically and economically, as well as politically, from their revolutionary neighbors, and it is highly probable that the refugee claimants did not accurately represent even the loyalist population, much less that of the colonies as a whole.[7] Nonetheless, the 468 claimants included white women of all descriptions, from every colony and all social and economic levels: they were educated and illiterate; married, widowed, single, and deserted; rural and urban; wealthy, middling, and poverty-stricken. Accordingly, used with care, the loyalist claims can tell us much about the varieties of female experience in America in the third quarter of the eighteenth century.[8]

Case Histories, 1746-1776," *Mississippi Valley Historical Review*, XLVI (1959), 46-66.

[6] For a detailed examination of the claims process see Mary Beth Norton, *The British-Americans: The Loyalist Exiles in England, 1774-1789* (Boston, 1972), 185-222. More than 468 women appear in the claims documents; excluded from the sample selected for this article are all female children, all English women who never lived in America (but who were eligible for compensation as heirs of loyalists), and all American women who did not personally pursue a claim (that is, whose husbands took the entire responsibility for presenting the family's claims). In addition to those requesting reimbursement for property losses, the sample includes a number of women—mostly the very poor, who had lost only a small amount of property, if any—who applied solely for the subsistence pensions which were also awarded by the claims commissioners. On the allowance system see *ibid.*, 52-61, 111-121, and 225-229.

[7] On the statistical biases of the loyalist claims see Eugene Fingerhut, "Uses and Abuses of the American Loyalists' Claims: A Critique of Quantitative Analyses," *WMQ*, 3d Ser., XXV (1968), 245-258.

[8] This approach to women in the Revolutionary era differs from the traditional focus on their public contributions to the war effort. See, for example, Elizabeth F. Ellet, *The Women of the American Revolution* (New York, 1848-1850); Walter Hart Blumenthal, *Women Camp Followers of the American Revolution* (Philadelphia, 1952); Elizabeth Cometti, "Women in the American Revolution," *NEQ*, XX (1947), 329-346; and Linda Grant DePauw, *Four Traditions: Women of New York during the American Revolution* (Albany, 1974).

One aspect of prewar family life that is systematically revealed in the claims documents is the economic relationship of husband and wife within the household. All claimants, male and female alike, had to supply the commission with detailed estimates of property losses. Given the circumstances of the war, documentary evidence such as deeds, bills of sale, and wills was rarely available in complete form, and the commission therefore relied extensively upon the sworn testimony of the claimants and their witnesses in assessing losses. The claimants had nothing to gain by withholding information, because the amount of compensation they received depended in large part on their ability to describe their losses. Consequently, it may be assumed that what the loyalists told the commission, both orally and in writing, represented the full extent of their knowledge of their families' income and property.[9] The women's claims thus make it possible to determine the nature of their participation in the financial affairs of their households.

Strikingly, although male loyalists consistently supplied detailed assessments of the worth of their holdings, many women were unable to place precise valuations on the property for which they claimed compensation. Time after time similar phrases appear in the records of oral testimony before the commission: "She cant say what the Houses cost or what they woud have sold for" (the widow of a Norfolk merchant); "Says she is much a Stranger to the state of Her Husband's Concerns" (the widow of a storekeeper from Ninety-Six, South Carolina); "It was meadow Land, she cannot speak of the Value" (a New Jersey farmer's widow); "Her husband was a Trader and had many Debts owing to him She does not know how much they amounted to" (a widow from Ninety-Six); "She can't speak to the Value of the Stock in Trade" (a Rhode Island merchant's widow); "It was a good Tract but does not know how to value it" (the widow of a Crown Point farmer).[10]

[9] Only if they intended to commit fraud could loyalists gain by withholding information from the commission; two refugees, for example, requested compensation for property they had already sold during the war. But the commissioners found deliberately fraudulent only 10 of the claims submitted to them, and although they disallowed others for "gross prevarication," none of the claims falling into either category were submitted by women. See Norton, *British-Americans*, 217-219, on the incidence of fraud, and 203-205, 216-217, on the importance of accurate testimony.

[10] Joyce Dawson, testimony, May 5, 1787, A.O. 12/56, 330, Public Record Office; Isabella McLaurin, testimony, Nov. 27, 1784, A.O. 12/47, 233; Margaret Hutchinson, testimony, Aug. 10, 1786, A.O. 12/16, 34; Margaret Reynolds, testimony, Dec. 9, 1783, A.O. 12/46, 168; case of Mrs. Bowers, Feb. 24, 1783, A.O. 12/99, 48; Elizabeth Campbell, testimony, n.d., A.O. 12/26, 267. For other similar statements see A.O. 12/10, 254, A.O. 12/48, 233, A.O. 12/50, 390-391, and A.O. 13/68, pt. 1, 183.

Even when women submitted detailed loss schedules in writing, they frequently revealed at their oral examinations that they had relied on male relatives or friends, or even on vaguely recalled statements made by their dead husbands, in arriving at the apparently knowledgeable estimates they had initially given to the commission. For example, a New Jersey woman, questioned about her husband's annual income, referred the commissioners to her father and other male witnesses, admitting that she did not know the amount he had earned. Similarly, the widow of a Charleston saddler told the commissioners that "she does not know the Amount of Her husband's Property, but she remembers to have heard him say in the year 1777 that he was worth £2,000 sterling clear of all Debts." Such statements abound in the claims records: "She is unable to speak to the value of the Plantn herself, but refers to Mr. Cassills"; "Says she cannot speak to the Value—the Valuatn was made by Capt McDonald and Major Munro"; "Says her Son in Law Capt Douglas is better acquainted with the particulars of her property than herself and she refers to him for an Account thereof."[11]

Although many female claimants thus lacked specific knowledge of their families' finances, there were substantial variations within the general pattern. The very wealthiest women—like Isabella Logan of Virginia (who could say only that she and her husband had lived in "a new Elegant, large double Brick House with two wings all finish'd in the best taste with Articles from London") and Mrs. Egerton Leigh of South Carolina (who gave it as her opinion that her husband had "a considerable real Estate as well as personal property . . . worth more than £10,000 . . . tho' she cannot herself speak to it with accuracy")—also tended to be the ones most incapable of describing their husbands' business affairs.[12] Yet some wealthy, well-educated women were conversant with nearly every detail of the family finances. For the most part, this latter group was composed of women who had brought the property they described to their husbands at marriage or who had been widowed before the war and had served as executrixes of the estates in question for some time. A case in point is that of Sarah Gould Troutbeck, daughter, executrix, and primary heir of John Gould, a prosperous Boston merchant. Her husband John, an Anglican clergyman, died in 1778, and so

[11] Frances Dongan, testimony, Dec. 6, 1784, A.O. 12/13, 267-272; case of Charlotte Pollock, June 27, 1783, A.O. 12/99, 336; Mary Ann Balfour, testimony, Mar. 13, 1786, A.O. 12/48, 242; Janet Murchison, testimony, July 26, 1786, A.O. 12/34, 405; Mary Kearsley, testimony, Apr. 28, 1785, A.O. 12/38, 282. Cf. Mrs. Kearsley's testimony with her written memorial, A.O. 13/102, 324-329. And see, for other examples, A.O. 12/4, 220, A.O. 12/14, 265, A.O. 12/47, 239, A.O. 13/63, 342, and A.O. 13/94, 318-326.

[12] Isabella Logan, loss schedule, Feb. 17, 1784, A.O. 13/32, 129; case of Lady Leigh, July 1, 1783, A.O. 12/99, 313. See also the claim of Mary Auchmuty, A.O. 12/24, 114-117, 264-266, and A.O. 13/63, 133-140.

she carried the full burden of presenting the family's claim to the commission. Although she deprecatingly described herself to the board as "a poor weak Woman unused to business," she supplied the commissioners with detailed evidence of her losses and unrelentingly pursued her debtors. "Your not hearing from me for so long a time may induce you to think I have relinquishd my claim to the intrest due on your note," she informed one man in 1788. "If you realy entertain any such thoughts I must beg leave to undeceive you." In addition, she did what few loyalists of either sex had the courage to attempt—return to the United States to try to recover her property. When she arrived in 1785, she found her estates "in the greatest confusion" but nevertheless managed within several months to repossess one house and to collect some debts. In the end she apparently won restoration of most of her holdings.[13]

Yet not all the female loyalists who had inherited property in their own right were as familiar with it as was Sarah Troutbeck. Another Massachusetts woman admitted to the commissioners that she did not know the value of the 550 acres left her by a relative, or even how much of the land was cultivated. "Her Brother managed everything for her and gave her what Money she wanted," she explained. In the same vein, a New Yorker was aware that her father had left her some property in his will, but "she does not know what property." A Charleston resident who had owned a house jointly with her brother commented that "it was a good House," but the commission noted, "she does not know the Value of it." And twice-widowed Jane Gibbes, claiming for the farms owned by her back-country South Carolina husbands, told the commission that she had relied on neighbors to assess the worth of the property, for "she can't speak positively to the value of her Lands herself."[14]

But if Jane Gibbes could not precisely evaluate the farms she had lived on, she still knew a good deal about them. She described the total acreage, the amount of land under cultivation, the crops planted, and the livestock

[13] Sarah Troutbeck to commissioners, June 5, 1787, A.O. 13/49, pt. 2, 565; Troutbeck to Samuel Peters, May 22, 1788, Peters Papers, III, fol. 83 (microfilm), New-York Historical Society, New York City; Troutbeck to commissioners, Jan. 3, 1785, A.O. 13/137, 609. Her total claim covers fols. 539-590 in A.O. 13/49, pt. 2, and fols. 726-740 in A.O. 13/74. On the recovery of her property see A.O. 12/81, 47. For other examples of well-to-do women with a good knowledge of the family property see A.O. 13/134, 571-574, and A.O. 12/54, 61-71 (Mary Rothery), A.O. 13/64, 81-99, and A.O. 13/97, 344-348 (Henrietta Colden), and A.O. 12/13, 311-314 (Mary Poynton). Mary Winslow knew her own property in detail but was not so familiar with her husband's (A.O. 13/79, 757-758).

[14] Case of Mrs. Dumaresq, Mar. 31, 1783, A.O. 12/99, 134; case of Margaret Smithies, Nov. 13, 1783, A.O. 12/100, 66; case of Barbara Mergath, May 8, 1783, A.O. 12/99, 234; Jane Gibbes, testimony, Dec. 15, 1783, A.O. 12/46, 245-247.

that had been lost. In this she was representative of most rural female loyalists with claims that were not complicated by the existence of mortgages or outstanding debts. Although they did not always know the exact value of the land for which they requested reimbursement, they could supply the commission with many important details about the family property: the number of cattle, horses, sheep, and hogs; the types of tools used; the acreage planted, and with what crops; the amounts of grain and other foodstuffs stored for the winter; and the value of such unusual possessions as beehives or a "Covering Horse." It was when they were asked about property on which they had not lived, about debts owed by their husbands, or about details of wills or mortgages that they most often admitted ignorance.[16]

A good example is Mary McAlpin, who had settled with her husband on a farm near Saratoga, New York, in 1767. She did not know what her husband had paid for some unimproved lands, or the acreage of another farm he had purchased, but she was well acquainted with the property on which they had lived. The farm, she told the commissioners, "had been wholly cleared and Improved and was in the most perfect State of Cultivation." There were two "Log Houses plaistered and floored," one for them and one for their hired laborers, and sufficient materials on hand to build "a large and Commodious Brick House." Her husband had planted wheat, rye, peas, oats, barley, corn, turnips, potatoes, and melons; and "the Meadows had been laid down or sown with Clover and Timothy Grass, the two kind of Grass Seeds most Valued in that Country." The McAlpins had had a kitchen garden that produced "in great abundance every Vegitable usually cultivated in that part of America." Moreover, the farm was "well Provided" with such utensils as "a Team waggon, Carts sledges Carwls [sic] Wheels for Waggons, Wheels for Carts, Wheelbarrows, drags for Timber Ploughs, Harrows Hay Sythes Brush Sythes Grubbling Harrows, and all sorts of Carpenters Tools Shoemakers Tools Shovels, Spades, Axes Iron Crow Barrs etc."

After offering all these details, however, Mrs. McAlpin proved unable to assess the value of the property accurately. She gave the commission a total claim of £6,000, clearly an estimate, and when asked to break down a particular item on her schedule into its component parts she could not do so, saying that "She valued the Whole in the Lump in that Sum." Moreover,

[16] Jane Gibbes, testimony, Dec. 16, 1783, A.O. 12/46, 247-249; Widow Boyce, loss schedule, Oct. 16, 1783, A.O. 13/90, 181; Elizabeth Hogal, loss schedule, n.d., A.O. 12/27, 37. Typical examples of claims submitted by rural women may be found in A.O. 13/56, 91-93, A.O. 13/138, 475, A.O. 12/4, 72-74, A.O. 12/20, 270-271, A.O. 12/26, 14-16, and A.O. 12/29, 79. Cf. claims from rural men in A.O. 13/79, 73-77, 211-216. For a claim involving property owned elsewhere see that of Elinor Maybee, A.O. 12/28, 343-346, and A.O. 12/64, 1; for one involving both a mortgage and a misread will see that of Margaret Hutchinson, A.O. 12/16, 33-37, and A.O. 12/63, 61.

she proved ignorant of the terms of her husband's will, confusedly telling the commissioners that he had "left his real personal Estate to his Son—This she supposes was his Lands" (the board's secretary noted carefully, "This is her own Expression"), when in fact she had been left a life interest in the real estate plus half the personal estate.[16] In short, Mary McAlpin typifies the rural female claimant, though her husband's property was substantially larger than average. She knew what he had owned, but she did not know exactly how much it was worth. She was well acquainted with the day-to-day operations of the farm but understood very little about the general family finances. And she knew nothing at all about legal or business terminology.

The pattern for urban dwellers was more varied. In the first place, included in their number were most of the wealthy women mentioned earlier, both those who knew little or nothing about their husbands' estates and those who, like Sarah Troutbeck, were conversant with the family holdings. Secondly, a higher percentage of urban women engaged directly in business. Among the 468 female claimants there were forty-three who declared either that they had earned money on their own or that they had assisted their husbands in some way. Only three of these forty-three can be described as rural: a tavernkeeper's wife from Ticonderoga, a small shopkeeper from Niagara, and the housekeeper for the family of Col. Guy Johnson. All the other working women came from cities such as Boston, Philadelphia, Charleston, and New York, or from smaller but substantial towns like Williamsburg, Wilmington, N.C., and Baltimore. The urban women's occupations were as varied as the urban centers in which they resided. There were ten who took lodgers, eighteen shopkeepers and merchants of various sorts, five tavernkeepers, four milliners, two mantua makers, a seamstress, a midwife, an owner of a coffeehouse, a schoolteacher, a printer, one who did not specify an occupation, and two prostitutes who described themselves as owners of a small shop and declared that their house had been "always open" to British officers needing "aid and attention."[17]

As might be expected, the women who had managed businesses or assisted their husbands (one wrote that she was "truly his Partner" in a "steady Course of painfull Industry") were best informed about the value of their property. Those who had been grocers or milliners could usually list in

---

[16] Mary McAlpin, loss schedule, n.d., A.O. 13/131, 10-11, and testimony, Nov. 14, 1785, A.O. 12/21, 51-65.

[17] The list totals more than 40 because some women listed two enterprises. The women divided as follows: 10 each from New York City and Charleston, 7 each from Boston and Philadelphia, 2 from Baltimore, and 1 each from Savannah, Williamsburg, Wilmington, N.C., and St. Augustine. Twenty-eight were long-time widows or single, or were married but operated businesses independently of their husbands; 8 assisted their husbands; and 7 took over businesses after the death or incapacitation of their husbands.

detail the stock they had lost; the midwife had witnesses to support her claim to a high annual income from her profession; the boardinghouse keepers knew what they had spent for furniture and supplies; and the printer could readily value her shop's equipment.[18] But even these working women could not give a full report on all aspects of their husbands' holdings: the widow of a Boston storekeeper, for example, could accurately list their stock in trade but admitted ignorance of the value of the property her husband had inherited from his father, and although the widow of another Boston merchant had carried on the business after her husband was wounded at Bunker Hill, she was not familiar with the overall value of their property.[19]

It is therefore not surprising that women claimants on the average received a smaller return on their claims than did their male counterparts. Since the commissioners reimbursed only for fully proven losses, the amounts awarded are a crude indicator of the relative ability of individual refugees to describe their losses and to muster written and oral evidence on their own behalf. If women had known as much as their husbands about the family estates, there would have been little or no difference between the average amounts granted to each sex. But of the claims heard in England for which complete information is available, 660 loyalist men received an average return of 39.5 percent, while for 71 women the figure was 34.1 percent. And this calculation does not take into account the large number of women's claims, including some submitted by businesswomen, which were entirely disallowed for lack of proof.[20]

In the absence of data for other time periods and populations, it is difficult to assess the significance of the figures that show that slightly less than 10 percent (9.2 percent, to be exact) of the loyalist refugee women worked outside the home. Historians have tended to stress the widespread participation of colonial women in economic enterprise, usually as a means of

[18] The quotation is from Rachel Wetmore, claims memorial, Mar. 25, 1786, A.O. 13/16, 271. For a milliner's claim see Margaret Hutchinson's, A.O. 13/96, 601-602; for a grocer and boardinghouse keeper's see Sarah Simpson's, A.O. 12/25, 25-28. The midwife, Janet Cumming, claimed to have made £400 sterling annually, and her witnesses confirmed that estimate (A.O. 12/50, 347-348). See also Margaret Draper's original and revised loss estimates, A.O. 13/44, 342-344, 387, and Mary Airey's schedule, A.O. 12/24, 79.

[19] Hannah Pollard, claims memorial and testimony, A.O. 13/49, pt. 1, 158-159, 166; testimony re: claim of Mary Campbell, Oct. 24, 1786, A.O. 12/50, 103-105. The detailed schedule presented by the tavernkeeper Rachel Brain had been prepared by her husband before his death; see A.O. 12/26, 308-310.

[20] For a general discussion of claims receipts see Norton, *British-Americans*, 216-220. Property claims submitted by 10 of the businesswomen were disallowed, and at least another 10 of them apparently did not pursue a claim for lost property. (Because of the destruction and disappearance of some of the claims records it is impossible to be more precise.)

distinguishing them from their reputedly more confined nineteenth-century counterparts.[21] The claims documents demonstrate that some women engaged in business, either alone or with their husbands, but 9.2 percent may be either a large or a small proportion of the total female population, depending on how one looks at it. The figures themselves must remain somewhat ambiguous, at least until additional data are obtained.[22] What is not at all ambiguous, however, is the distinctive pattern of the female claimants' knowledge.

For regardless of whether they came from rural or urban areas, and regardless of their background or degree of participation in business, the loyalist women testified almost exclusively on the basis of their knowledge of those parts of the family property with which their own lives brought them into regular contact. What they uniformly lacked were those pieces of information about business matters that could have been supplied only by their husbands. Evidently, late eighteenth-century American men, at least those who became loyalists, did not systematically discuss matters of family finances with their wives. From that fact it may be inferred that the men—and their wives as well, perhaps—accepted the dictum that woman's place was in the home. After all, that was where more than 90 percent of the loyalist women stayed, and their ignorance of the broader aspects of their families' economic circumstances indicates that their interest in such affairs was either minimal or else deliberately thwarted by their husbands.[23]

It would therefore appear that the 9 percent figure for working women is

[21] This emphasis appears to have resulted from the influence of Dexter's *Colonial Women of Affairs*. Although she was careful to explain that she had searched only for examples of women who worked outside the home, and although she did not attempt to estimate the percentage of such women in the female population as a whole, historians who draw upon her book invariably stress the wide-ranging economic interests of colonial women. See, for example, Gerda Lerner, *The Woman in American History* (Reading, Mass., 1971), 15-19, and Carol Ruth Berkin, *Within the Conjuror's Circle: Women in Colonial America* (Morristown, N.J., 1974), 8-10.

[22] If anything, the loyalist claimants tended to be more urban than other loyalists and the rest of the American population, and therefore would presumably over-represent working women. See the analysis in Norton, *British-Americans*, 37-39, and Fingerhut, "Uses and Abuses of Loyalists' Claims," *WMQ*, 3d Ser., XXV (1968), 245-258. Further, the method of choosing the sample—including only those women who themselves submitted claims and pension applications—would also tend to bias the result in favor of working women, since they would be the most likely to act on their own.

[23] The failure of 18th-century men to discuss finances with their wives is also revealed in such letters as that of Jane Robbins to her daughter Hannah Gilman, Sept. 1799, Gilman Papers, Massachusetts Historical Society, Boston. Mrs. Robbins declared that, although her husband had made his will some years before, "I never saw it till after his death." Further, she informed her daughter, on his deathbed he told her, "I should have many debts to pay that I knew nothing about."

evidence not of a climate favorable to feminine enterprise but rather of the opposite: women were expected to remain largely within the home unless forced by necessity, such as the illness or death of their husbands, to do otherwise. The fact that fewer than one-half (seventeen, to be precise) of the working women enumerated earlier had healthy, living husbands at the time they engaged in business leads toward the same conclusion. The implication is that in mid-eighteenth-century America woman's sphere was rigidly defined at all levels of society, not merely in the wealthy households in which this phenomenon has been recognized.[24]

This tentative conclusion is supported by evidence drawn from another aspect of the claims, for a concomitant of the contention that colonial women often engaged in business endeavors has been the assertion that colonial men, as the theoretical and legal heads of household, frequently assumed a large share of domestic responsibilities.[25] Yet if men had been deeply involved in running their households—in keeping accounts and making purchases, even if not in doing day-to-day chores—they should have described household furnishings in much the same detail as their wives used. But just as female claimants were unable to delineate their husbands' business dealings accurately, so men separated from their wives—regardless of their social status—failed to submit specific lists of lost household items like furniture, dishes, or kitchen utensils. One such refugee observed to the commission in 1788, "As Household Furniture consists of a Variety of Articles, at this distance of time I cannot sufficiently recollect them so as to fix a Value on them to the Satisfaction of my mind."[26] It is impossible to imagine a loyalist woman making a comparable statement. For her, what to a man was simply "a Variety of Articles" resolved itself into such familiar and cherished objects as "1 Compleat set blue and white Tea and Table China," "a Large new Goose feather Bed, bolster Pillows and Bedstead," "a Small painted Book Case and Desk," "1 Japan Tea Board," "2 smoothing Irons," and "1 old brass Coffee Pott." Moreover, although men usually noted losses of clothing in a general way, by listing a single undifferentiated sum, women frequently claimed for specific articles of jewelry and apparel. For example, Mary Swords of Saratoga disclosed that she had lost to rebel plunderers a "Long Scarlet Cloak" and a "Velvet Muff and Tippett," in addition to "One pair of Ear

[24] Berkin, *Conjuror's Circle*, 12-14, and Nancy F. Cott, ed., *Root of Bitterness: Documents of the Social History of American Women* (New York, 1972), 8-10, link sex role differentiation specifically to the upper classes that were emerging in the process which has been called "Europeanization" or "Anglicization."
[25] See, for example, Spruill, *Women's Life and Work*, 78-79.
[26] David Ingersoll to commissioners, July 30, 1788, A.O. 13/74, 288. For rare cases of men who did list household furnishings see A.O. 13/98, 431-432, and A.O. 13/73, 140-155.

Rings French paste set in Gold," "One small pair of Ear Rings Garnets," and "one Gold Broatch with a small diamond Top."[27]

The significance of such lists lies not only in the fact that they indicate what kinds of property the claimants knew well enough to describe accurately and in detail, but also in the insight they provide into the possessions which claimants thought were sufficiently important to mention individually. For example, a rural New York woman left no doubt about her pride in "a fine large new stove"; a resident of Manhattan carefully noted that one of her lost beds was covered in "Red Damask"; and a Rhode Islander called attention to the closets in her "large new dwelling house."[28] The differentiated contents of men's and women's claims thus take on more importance, since the contrasting lists not only suggest the extent of the claimants' knowledge but also reveal their assessments of the relative importance of their possessions. To men, furniture, dishes, and clothing could easily be lumped together under general headings; to women, such possessions had to be carefully enumerated and described.

In the end, all of the evidence that can be drawn from the loyalist claims points to the conclusion that the lives of the vast majority of women in the Revolutionary era revolved around their immediate households to a notable degree. The economic function of those households in relation to the family property largely determined the extent of their knowledge of that property. In rural areas, where women's household chores included caring for the stock and perhaps occasionally working in the fields, women were conversant with a greater proportion of the family estates than were urban women, whose knowledge was for the most part confined to the furnishings of the houses in which they lived, unless they had been widowed before the war or had worked outside the home. The wealth of the family was thus a less significant determinant of the woman's role than was the nature of the household. To be sure, at the extreme ends of the economic scale, wealth and education, or the lack of them, affected a woman's comprehension of her family's property, but what the women displayed were relative degrees of ignorance. If the loyalist claimants are at all representative, very few married colonial women were familiar with the broader aspects of their families' financial affairs. Regardless of where they lived, they were largely insulated from the agricultural and business worlds in which their husbands engaged daily. As a result, the

[27] Martha Leslie, loss schedule, Mar. 25, 1784, A.O. 13/91, 2-3; Frances Dongan, inventory, [Nov. 1, 1783], A.O. 13/109, 45; Catherine Bowles, loss schedule, May 10, 1783, A.O. 13/90, 175-176; Mary Swords, "Things Plundered from me by the Rebels," n.d., A.O. 13/67, 311.
[28] Mary Gibbins, loss schedule, n.d., A.O. 13/80, 167; "Estimate of Losses sustained at New York by Hannah Foy in the year 1775" [1782], A.O. 13/54, 431; Elizabeth Bowers, loss schedule, n.d., A.O. 13/68, pt. 1, 64.

Revolutionary War, which deprived female loyalists of the households in which they had lived and worked, and which at the same time forced them to confront directly the wider worlds of which they had had little previous knowledge, was for them an undeniably traumatic experience.

At the outbreak of the war, loyalist women expected that "their Sex and the Humanity of a civilized People" would protect them from "disrespectfull Indignities." Most of them soon learned otherwise. Rebel men may have paid lip service to the ideal that women and children should be treated as noncombatants, but in practice they consigned female loyalists to much the same fate as their male relatives. Left behind by their fleeing husbands (either because of the anticipated difficulties of a journey to the British lines or in the hope that the family property might thereby be preserved), loyalist wives, with their children, frequently found themselves "stripped of every Thing" by American troops who, as one woman put it, "not contented with possessing themselves of her property were disposed to visit severity upon her person and Those of her friends."[29] Female loyalists were often verbally abused, imprisoned, and threatened with bodily harm even when they had not taken an active role in opposing the rebel cause.[30]

When they had assisted the British—and many aided prisoners or gathered intelligence—their fate was far worse. For example, the New Yorker Lorenda Holmes, who carried letters through the lines in 1776, was stripped by an angry band of committeemen and dragged "to the Drawing Room Window . . . exposing her to many Thousands of People Naked." On this occasion Mrs. Holmes admitted that she "received no wounds or bruises from them only shame and horror of the Mind," but a few months later, after she had shown some refugees the way to the British camp, an American officer came to her house and held her "right foot upon the Coals until he had burnt it in a most shocking manner," telling her "he would learn her to carry off Loyalists to the British Army."[31]

[29] Sarah Stuart, memorial to Lords of Treasury, Jan. 22, 1786, A.O. 13/135, 702; Elizabeth Phillips, affidavit, Oct. 9, 1788, A.O. 13/67, 303; Phebe Stevens, claims memorial, Mar. 23, 1784, A.O. 13/83, 580. For accounts of rebel looting see, for example, A.O. 12/56, 326-327, A.O. 13/73, 485, A.O. 13/91, 190, A.O. 13/93, 556, A.O. 13/102, 1278, A.O. 13/109, 43, A.O. 13/121, 478, and A.O. 13/126, 589.

[30] See, for example, A.O. 12/21, 53-54, A.O. 13/110, 351, A.O. 13/112, 55, A.O. 13/123, 240-241, A.O. 13/128, 7, and A.O. 13/135, 698. Two women said they suffered miscarriages as a result of scuffles with Revolutionary troops (A.O. 13/81, 59, and A.O. 13/64, 76-77), and a third was raped by a rebel soldier. The latter incident is discussed in Thomas Goldthwait to his daughter Catherine, Aug. 20, 1779, J. M. Robbins Papers, Mass. Hist. Soc.

[31] Lorenda Holmes, claims memorial, n.d., A.O. 13/65, 529-530. Similar though less graphic tales were recounted by other women whose assistance to the British was also discovered by the Revolutionaries. See A.O. 12/49, 56-58, A.O. 12/102, 80,

As can readily be imagined, the women did not come through such experiences emotionally unscathed. One Massachusetts mother reported that her twelve-year-old daughter suffered from "nervous Fits" as a result of "the usage she met with from the Mobs"; and another New England woman, the wife of a merchant who was an early target of the local committee because he resisted the nonimportation movement, described to a female friend her reaction to a threatening letter they had received: "I have never injoyed one hours real Sattisfaction since the receipt of that Dreadfull Letter my mind is in continual agitation and the very rustling of the Trees alarms me." Some time later the same woman was unfortunate enough to be abused by a rebel militiaman. After that incident, she reported, "I did not recover from my fright for several days. The sound of drum or the sight of a gun put me into such a tremor that I could not command myself."[32] It was only natural for these women to look forward with longing to the day when they could escape to Canada or, better still, to England, "a land of peace, liberty and plenty." It seemed to them that their troubles would end when they finally left America. But, as one wrote later with the benefit of hindsight, their "severest trials were just begun."[33]

Male and female refugees alike confronted difficult problems in England and Canada—finding housing, obtaining financial support, settling into a new environment. For women, especially widows with families, the difficulties were compounded. The Bostonian Hannah Winslow found the right words: it was a "cruell" truth, she told her sister-in-law, that "when a woman with a family, and Particularly a large one, looses her Husband and Protector People are afraid to keep up the Acquaintance least they may ask favrs."[34] Many of the men quickly reestablished their American friendship

---

A.O. 13/45, 530, A.O. 13/67, 192, A.O. 13/68, 125, A.O. 13/96, 263, and A.O. 13/102, 1107.

[32] Mary Serjeant, loss schedule, Feb. 19, 1783, A.O. 13/49, pt. 1, 285; Christian Barnes to Elizabeth Smith, July 13-28, 1770, Christian Barnes Letterbook, Library of Congress; Barnes to Elizabeth Smith Inman, Apr. [2]9, [1775], in Nina Moore Tiffany, ed., Letters of James Murray, Loyalist (Boston, 1901), 187-188.

[33] Louisa Susannah Wells Aikman, The Journal of a Voyage from Charlestown, S.C., to London undertaken during the American Revolution... (New York, 1906), 52; Catherine Goldthwait to Elizabeth [Inman], Mar. 27, 1780, Robbins Papers, Mass. Hist. Soc. For a discussion of the loyalists' initial optimism and subsequent disillusionment see Mary Beth Norton, "The Loyalists' Image of England: Ideal and Reality," Albion, III (1971), 62-71.

[34] Hannah Winslow to [a sister-in-law], June 27, 1779, Winslow Papers, Mass. Hist. Soc. See also Rebecca Dolbeare to John Dolbeare, Aug. 30, 1780, Dolbeare Papers, Mass. Hist. Soc.; Polly Dibblee to William Jarvis, Nov. 1787, A.O. 13/41, 248. For a general discussion of the exiles' financial problems see Norton, British-Americans, 49-61. For another similar observation by a single woman see Louisa Oliver to Andrew Spooner, Mar. 1, 1788, Hutchinson-Oliver Papers, Mass. Hist. Soc.

networks through the coffeehouses and refugee organizations; the women were deprived not only of the companionship such associations provided but also of the information about pensions and claims that was transmitted along the male networks. As a result, a higher proportion of female than male loyalists made errors in their applications for government assistance, by directing the memorials to the wrong officials and failing to meet deadlines, often because they learned too late about compensation programs. Their standard excuses—that they "had nobody to advise with" and that they "did not know how to do it"—were greeted with skepticism by the claims commission, but they were undoubtedly true.[35]

On the whole, female loyalists appear to have fared worse in England than their male counterparts, and for two major reasons. In the first place, the commissioners usually gave women annual pensions that were from £10 to £20 lower than those received by men, apparently because they believed that the women had fewer expenses, but also because in most cases the women could not claim the extra merit of having actively served the royal cause.[36] Second, fewer women than men found work to supplement the sums they received from the government. To the wealthier female refugees work seemed so automatically foreclosed as an option that only a small number thought it necessary to explain to the commission why they could not contribute to their own support. Mary Serjeant, the widow of a Massachusetts clergyman, even regarded her former affluence as a sufficient reason in itself for her failure to seek employment. In 1782 she told the commissioners, "Educated as a Gentlewoman myself and brought up to no business I submit it to your [torn], Gentlemen, how very scanty must be the Subsistence which

[35] The quotation is from the case of Mary Hind, Feb. 1783, A.O. 12/99, 35. For examples of other women who claimed ignorance of proper forms and application procedures see A.O. 12/46, 165, A.O. 12/99, 238, A.O. 13/24, 284, A.O. 13/26, 63, 199, 282, 360, A.O. 13/113, 88, A.O. 13/131, 65, and A.O. 13/137, 150. Of course, a few men also made similar claims; see, for example, A.O. 12/43, 322-325, 328-331, and A.O. 12/46, 63. On the male networks see Norton, British Americans, 63-79, 162-164, 186-196, 206-216. The memorials submitted by women were not only more prone to error but also more informal, less likely to be written in the third person, less likely to contain the sorts of ritualistic phrases and arguments used by the men, and consequently more likely to be personally revealing.

[36] Norton, British-Americans, 52-61, 111-121, discusses the bases for pension decisions. It was standard practice for the commission to lower a family's allotment immediately after the death of the husband, regardless of the fact that the widow usually had to meet medical and funeral expenses at exactly that time. The pension records (A.O. 12/99-105, and T. 50/11ff, Public Record Office) show that women's pensions were normally smaller than men's. In addition, T. 50/11 reveals a clear case of discrimination: in 1789 the Charleston midwife Janet Cumming (see note 18 above) was, under the commission's rules, entitled to an annual pension of £200 for loss of profession (she was the only woman to qualify for one in her own right); instead, she was granted only a £50 widow's allowance.

my Own Industry [can] procure us." Those who did try to earn additional income (many of whom had also worked outside the home in America) usually took in needlework or hired out as servants or housekeepers, but even they had trouble making ends meet. One orphaned young woman reported, "I can support myself with my needle: but not my two Sisters and infant Brother"; and another, who had learned the trade of mantua making, commented, "I now got Work for my self [sic]—but being oblidged to give long credit and haveing no Money of my one [sic] to go on with, I lived Cheifly upon tea which with night working brought me almost into the last stadge of a Consumtion so that when I rec'd my Money for work it went almost [all] to dockters."[37]

Many of the loyalist women displayed a good deal of resilience. Some managed to support themselves, among them the Wells sisters of Charleston, who in 1789 opened a London boardinghouse for young ladies whose parents wished them to have a "suitable" introduction to society. Others survived what might seem an overwhelming series of setbacks—for example, Susannah Marshall of Maryland, who, after running taverns in Baltimore and Head of Elk and trying but failing to join Lord Dunmore off Norfolk in 1776, finally left the United States by sea the following year, only to have her chartered ship captured first by the Americans and then by the British. In the process she lost all the goods she had managed to salvage from her earlier moves, and when she arrived in England she not only learned of her husband's death but was unsuccessful in her application for a subsistence pension. Refusing to give up, she went to work as a nurse to support her children, and although she described herself to the commission in 1785 as "very Old and feeble," she lived long enough to be granted a permanent annual allowance of £20 in 1789.[38]

Susannah Marshall, though, had years of experience as a tavernkeeper

[37] Mary Serjeant to John Wilmot and Daniel P. Coke, Dec. 1, 1782, A.O. 13/49, pt. 1, 283; Ann Asby to commissioners, Apr. 14, 1788, A.O. 13/43, 147; Susanna Sandys, memorial, n.d., A.O. 13/84, 613. (Sandys was English, though the daughter of a refugee, and is quoted here because of the detailed nature of her comments.) For a statement similar to Mrs. Serjeant's see Margaret Smythies to Lords of Treasury, Jan. 23, 1782, A.O. 13/67, 230. For two women who did explain why they could not work see A.O. 13/75, 627, and A.O. 13/53, 193. Information about nearly all the loyalist women who worked in England may be located in the following documents: A.O. 12/30, 230, A.O. 12/99, 50, 244, 264, A.O. 12/101, 137, A.O. 12/102, 87, 136, 164, 165, 175, 187, A.O. 13/43, 661, A.O. 13/44, 427, A.O. 13/71, 156, and A.O. 13/131, 359.

[38] On the Wells sisters' enterprise see Steuart Papers, 5041, fol. 123, National Library of Scotland, Edinburgh; Ann Elmsley to James Parker [1789?], Parker Papers, Pt. IV, no. 15, Liverpool Record Office, England; and Aikman, *Journal of a Voyage*, 71. Susannah Marshall's story may be traced in A.O. 13/62, 4, 7, A.O. 12/6, 257-263, and A.O. 12/99, 244.

behind her and was thus more capable of coping with her myriad difficulties than were women whose prewar experience had been restricted to their households. Such women recognized that they were "less able than many who never knew happier days to bear hardships and struggle with adversity." These women, especially those who had been, as one of them put it, *"born to better expectations"* in America, spoke despairingly of encounters with "difficultys of which she had no experience in her former life," of "Adversities which not many years before she scarcely thought it possible, that in any situation, she should ever experience."[39]

For women like these, exile in England or Canada was one long nightmare. Their relief requests have a desperate, supplicating tone that is largely absent from those submitted by men. One bewailed the impending birth of her third child, asking, "What can I do in my Condishtion deprived of helth with out Friends or mony with a helpless family to suffer with me?" Another begged the commission's secretary for assistance "with all humility" because "the merciless man I lodge with, threatens to sell the two or three trifling articles I have and put a Padlock on the Room unless I pay him the Rent amounting to near a Pound." By contrast, when a man prepared a memorial for the exceptionally distressed Mrs. Sarah Baker, he coolly told the commissioners that they should assist her because her children "as Soldiers or Sailors in his Majesty's Service may in future compensate the present Expence of saving them."[40]

The straits to which some of the female refugees were driven were dramatically illustrated in early 1783 when a South Carolina woman appeared before the commission "in Rags," explaining that she had been "obliged to pawn her Goods." It was but the first incident of many. Time and again women revealed that they had sold or pawned their clothes—which were usually their most valuable possessions—to buy food for themselves and their children. One was literally "reduced to the last shift" when she testified before the commission; another, the New Yorker Alicia Young, pawned so much that "the want of our apparel made our situation very deplorable"

---

[39] Harriet, Mary, Sarah, and Elizabeth Dawson and Ann Dawson Murray to commissioners, n.d., A. O. 13/113, 195; Mary Muirson to Lords of Treasury, May 28, 1784, A.O. 13/56, 342; Isabella Logan, claims memorial, Feb. 17, 1784, A.O. 13/32, 126; Patience Johnston, claims memorial, Dec. 21, 1785, A.O. 13/26, 196. For similar statements see A.O. 13/40, 93, A.O. 13/75, 354, 603, A.O. 13/132, 257, and A.O. 13/134, 504.

[40] Mary Lowry to [Samuel Remnant], n.d., A.O. 13/31, 202; Mary Curtain to Charles Monro, July 7, 1789, A.O. 13/137, 98; Samuel Peters to Daniel P. Coke, Nov. 20, 1784, A.O. 13/43, 352. Cf. the statements in the text with those of men; for example, Samuel Porter to Lords of Treasury, Feb. 23, 1776, T. 1/520, 27; Thomas Banks to Lords of Treasury, Feb. 9, 1779, T. 1/552, 3; John Saunders to Lords of Treasury, Mar. 31, 1785, F.O. 4/1, 248, Public Record Office.

until friends helped her to redeem some of her possessions. Strikingly, no man ever told the commission stories like these. Either male refugees were able to find alternatives to pawning their clothes, or, if they did not, they were too ashamed to admit it.[41]

Such hardships took a terrible mental as well as physical toll. Evidence of extreme mental stress permeates the female loyalists' petitions and letters, while it is largely absent from the memorials of male exiles. The women speak constantly of their "Fear, Fatigue and Anxiety of Mind," their "lowness of Spirit," their "inexpressable" distress, their "accumulated anguish." They repeatedly describe themselves as "desolate and distressed," as "disconsolate, Distressed and helpless . . . with a broken Spirit Ruined health and Constitution," as "Oppressed in body and distressed in mind."[42] "I am overwhelm'd with misfortunes," wrote one. Poverty "distracts and terrifies me," said another; and a third begged "that she may not be left a Prey to Poverty, and her constant companons [sic], Calamity and Sorrow." "My pen is unable to describe the horrors of My Mind—or the deploreable Situation of Myself and Infant family," Alicia Young told a member of the commission. "Judge then Dr Sir what is to become of me, or what we are to exist upon—I have no kind of resource. . . . oh Sir the horrors of my Situation is almost too much for me to bear." Most revealing of all was the wife of a Connecticut refugee: "Nature it self languishes," Mary Taylor wrote, "the hours that I should rest, I awake in such an aggitation of mind, as though I had to suffer for sins, that I neaver committed, I allmost shudder when I approache the Doone [doom?]—as every thing appears to be conspired against me, the Baker, and Bucher, seams to be weary of serving me oh porvity what is its Crime, may some have Compassion on those who feeals its power—for I can doo nothing—but baith my infant with my tears—while seeing my Husbands sinking under the waight of his misfortuens, unable to afford me any release."[43]

[41] Case of Margaret Reynolds, Mar. 26, 1783, A.O. 12/99, 116; Charlotte Mayne to—[Aug. 1783], H.O. 42/3, Public Record Office; Alicia Young to Robert Mackenzie, June 3, 1789, A.O. 13/67, 641. Mrs. Young gave the commissioners a detailed list of the items she had pawned (A.O. 13/67, 646). For other similar accounts of women pawning or selling their goods see A.O. 12/99, 13, 56, 60, A.O. 12/101, 196, 364, A.O. 13/43, 350, A.O. 13/64, 76, and A.O. 13/135, 81, 426.

[42] "Mrs Derbage's Narrative," Mar. 1789, A.O. 13/34, 298; Penelope Nicoll, deposition, July 6, 1787, A.O. 13/68, 267; Mary Broadhead to commissioners, Nov. 12, 1788, A.O. 13/125, 626; Margaret Draper to John Robinson, June 27, 1777, A.O. 13/44, 345; Rose Brailsford to Lords of Treasury, Dec. 29, 1779, A.O. 13/125, 580; Joyce Dawson to Lord Dunmore, July 24, 1781, A.O. 13/28, 220; Charlotte Pollock to Lords of Treasury, n.d., A.O. 13/133, 442.

[43] Lucy Necks to Lady North, Aug. 14, 1781, A.O. 13/32, 155; Elizabeth Barkesdale to commissioners, Nov. 24, 1786, A.O. 13/125, 402; Lydia Doty to Lords of Treasury, May 8, 1782, A.O. 13/113, 328; Alicia Young to Robert Mackenzie,

Even taking into account the likelihood that it was more socially accept-able for women to reveal their emotions, the divergence between men's and women's memorials is too marked to be explained by that factor alone. It is necessary to probe more deeply and to examine men's and women's varying uses of language in order to delineate the full dimensions of the difference.[44] As C. Wright Mills pointed out in an influential article some years ago, actions or motives and the vocabularies utilized to describe them cannot be wholly separated, and commonly used adjectives can therefore reveal the limitations placed on one's actions by one's social role. Mills asserted that "the 'Real Attitude or Motive' is not something different in kind from the verbalization or the 'opinion,'" and that "the long acting out of a role, with its appropriate motives, will often induce a man [or, one is compelled to add, a woman] to become what at first he merely sought to appear." Furthermore, Mills noted, people perceive situations in terms of specific, "delimited" vocabularies, and thus adjectives can themselves promote or deter certain actions. When adjectives are "typical and relatively unquestioned accom-paniments of typal situations," he concluded, "such words often function as directives and incentives by virtue of their being the judgements of others as anticipated by the actor."[45]

In this theoretical context the specific words used by female loyalists may be analyzed as a means of understanding the ways in which they perceived themselves and their circumstances. Their very phraseology—and the man-ner in which it differs from that of their male counterparts—can provide insights into the matrix of attitudes that helped to shape the way they thought and acted. If Mills is correct, the question whether the women were deliberately telling the commission what they thought it wanted to hear

---

June 6, 1789, A.O. 13/67, 643; Mary Taylor to commissioners, Apr. 12, 1783, A.O. 13/42, 590. In sharp contrast to such statements, Andrew Allen, a male refugee, wrote in Feb. 1783, "Notwithstanding what has happened I have the Satisfaction to feel my Spirits unbroken and my Mind prepared to look forwards without Despon-dency." Allen to James Hamilton, Feb. 3, 1783, Dreer Collection, Historical Society of Pennsylvania, Philadelphia.

[44] Recent articles by linguists raise provocative questions about sex differences in speech. Most of them are concerned with 20th-century oral expression, however, and it is difficult to determine how accurately they apply to 18th-century documents. Among the most interesting are Nancy Faires Conklin, "Toward a Feminist Analysis of Linguistic Behavior," *University of Michigan Papers in Women's Studies*, I (1974), 51-73; Mary Ritchie Key, "Linguistic Behavior of Male and Female," *Linguistics: An International Review*, LXXXVIII (1972), 15-31; Cheris Kramer, "Women's Speech: Separate but Unequal?," *The Quarterly Journal of Speech*, LX (1974), 14-24; and Robin Lakoff, "Language and Woman's Place," *Language in Society*, II (1974), 45-79.

[45] C. Wright Mills, "Situated Actions and Vocabularies of Motive," *American Sociological Review*, V (1940), 904-913, esp. 906-909.

becomes irrelevant: it is enough to say that they were acting in accordance with a prescribed role, and that that role helped to determine how they acted.[46]

With these observations in mind, the fact that the women refugees displayed an intense awareness of their own femininity assumes a crucial significance. The phrases permeate the pages of the petitions from rich and poor alike: "Though a Woman"; "perhaps no Woman in America in equal Circumstances"; "being done by a Woman"; "being a poor lame and infirm Woman." In short, in the female loyalists' minds their actions and abilities were to a certain extent defined by their sex. Femininity was the constant point of reference in measuring their achievements and making their self-assessments. Moreover, the fact of their womanhood was used in a deprecating sense. In their own eyes, they gained merit by not acting like women. Her services were "allmost Matchless, (being done by a Woman)," wrote one; "tho' a Woman, she was the first that went out of the Gates to welcome the Royal Army," declared another. Femininity also provided a ready and plausible excuse for failures of action or of knowledge. A South Carolinian said she had not signed the address to the king in Charleston in 1780 because "it was not posable for a woman to come near the office." A Pennsylvanian apologized for any errors in her loss estimate with the comment, "as far as a Woman can know, she believes the contents to be true." A Nova Scotian said she had not submitted a claim by the deadline because of "being a lone Woman in her Husband's Absence and not having any person to Advise with." A Vermonter made the ultimate argument: "had she been a man, Instead, of a poor helpless woman—should not have faild of being in the British Servace."[47]

The pervasive implication is one of perceived inferiority, and this implication is enhanced by the word women used most often to describe them-

---

[46] The only woman claimant who appears to have manipulatively assumed a "feminine" role was Sarah Troutbeck. It is also difficult to determine, first, what it was that the commission "wanted" to hear from female loyalists and, second, how the women would know what the commission wanted, given their isolation from the male information networks. It could perhaps be argued that every 18th-century woman "knew" what every 18th-century man expected of her, but the fact is that the women claimants had a great deal to gain by displaying a very "unfeminine" knowledge of their husband's estates and by demonstrating their competence to the commission. See, for example, A.O. 12/101, 186, A.O. 12/40, 40-44, and A.O. 12/66, 6.

[47] The long quotations: Margaret Hutchinson, claims memorial, Feb. 23, 1784, A.O. 13/96, 601; Eleanor Lestor, claims memorial, n.d., A.O. 12/48, 359; Elizabeth Thompson to John Forster, Dec. 21, 1785, A.O. 13/136, 8; Mary Kearsley, testimony, Apr. 28, 1785, A.O. 12/38, 282; Mary Williams, affidavit, Dec. 21, 1785, A.O. 13/26, 535; Catherine Chilsom, claims memorial, Mar. 11, 1786, A.O. 13/24, 90. The shorter phrases: A.O. 13/16, 271, A.O. 13/24, 357, A.O. 13/26, 357.

selves: "helpless." "Being a Poor helpless Widow"; "she is left a helpless Widow"; "a helpless woman advanced in life"; "being a helpless woman": such phrases appear again and again in the claims memorials.[48] Male loyalists might term themselves "very unhappy," "wretched," "extremely distressed," or "exceedingly embarrassed," but *never* were they "helpless." For them, the most characteristic self-description was "unfortunate," a word that carried entirely different, even contrary, connotations.[49] Male loyalists can be said to have seen their circumstances as not of their own making, as even being reversible with luck. The condition of women, however, was inherent in themselves; nothing they could do could change their circumstances. By definition, indeed, they were incapable of helping themselves.

It should be stressed here that, although women commonly described themselves as "helpless," their use of that word did not necessarily mean that they were in fact helpless. It indicates rather that they perceived themselves thus, and that that perception in turn perhaps affected the way they acted (for example, in seeking charitable support instead of looking for work). Similarly, the fact that men failed to utilize the adjective "helpless" to refer to themselves does not mean that they were not helpless, for some of them surely were; it merely shows that—however incorrectly—they did think that they could change their circumstances. These two words, with all their connotations, encapsulate much of the divergence between male and female self-perceptions in late eighteenth-century America, even if they do not necessarily indicate much about the realities of male-female relationships in the colonies.[50]

There was, of course, more to the difference in sex roles than the sex-related ways in which colonial Americans looked at themselves. The claims documents also suggest that women and men placed varying emphases on

[48] A.O. 13/118, 488, A.O. 13/67, 234, A.O. 13/73, 586, A.O. 13/81, 59. Men also described women in the same terms; for examples see A.O. 13/28, 215, and A.O. 12/101, 235. The widows of Revolutionary soldiers also called themselves "helpless"; see, for example, Papers of the Continental Congress, V, 16 (M-41), Roll 50, V, 37, 122 (M-42), Roll 55, National Archives.

[49] T. 1/612, 157, A.O. 13/53, 62, A.O. 13/137, 574, A.O. 12/8, 124. For a few "unfortunate" men see A.O. 12/46, 104, A.O. 12/51, 208, A.O. 12/13, 188, and A.O. 12/42, 132.

[50] The women who were most definitely not helpless (for example, Susannah Marshall, Janet Cumming, and Sarah Troutbeck) did not use that word to describe themselves. Consequently, it appears that the term was not simply a formulaic one utilized by all women indiscriminately, but rather that it represented a real self-perception of those who did use it. At least one 18th-century woman recognized the sex-typed usage of the word "helpless." In her book of essays, Judith Sargent Murray noted that she hoped that "the term, *helpless widow*, might be rendered as unfrequent and inapplicable as that of *helpless widower*." See Judith Sargent Murray, *The Gleaner*, III (Boston, 1789), 223.

familial ties. For women, such relationships seemed to take on a special order of magnitude. Specifically, men never said, as several women did, that after their spouses' deaths they were so "inconsolable" that they were unable to function. One woman declared that after her husband's execution by the rebels she was "bereft of her reason for near three months," and another described herself as "rendred almost totally incapable of Even writing my own Name or any assistance in any Shape that Could have the least Tendency to getting my Bread."[51] Furthermore, although loyalist men expressed concern over the plight of the children they could not support adequately, women were much more emotionally involved in the fate of their offspring. "Your goodness will easily conceive, what I must feel for My *Children*," Alicia Young told a claims commissioner; "for myself—I care not—Misfortunes and distress have long since made me totally indifferent to everything in the World but *Them*—they have no provision—no provider—no protector—but God—and me." Women noted that their "Sorrows" were increased by the knowledge that their children were "Partners in this Scene of Indigence." Margaret Draper, widow of a Boston printer, explained that although she had been ill and suffering from a "disorderd Mind," "what adds to my affliction is, my fears for my Daughter, who may soon be left a Stranger and friendless." In the same vein, a New Jersey woman commented that she had "the inexpressible mortification of seeing my Children in want of many necessaries and conveniencies. . . . and what still more distresses me, is to think that I am obliged by partaking of it, to lessen even the small portion they have."[52]

The women's emphasis on their families is entirely compatible with the earlier observation concerning the importance of their households in their lives. If their menfolk were preoccupied with the monetary consequences of adhering to the crown, the women were more aware of the human tragedy brought about by the war. They saw their plight and that of their children in much more personal terms than did their husbands. Likewise, they personalized the fact of their exile in a way that male loyalists did not, by almost invariably commenting that they were "left friendless in a strange Country."

[51] Isabella Logan, claims memorial, Feb. 17, 1784, A.O. 13/32, 126; Jane Hilding, claims memorial, July 30, 1788, A.O. 13/46, 315; Joyce Dawson to Lord Dunmore, July 24, 1781, A.O. 13/28, 220. Also of interest is Jane Constable to Lords of Treasury, n.d., A.O. 13/73, 374.

[52] Alicia Young to Robert Mackenzie, June 6, 1789, A.O. 13/67, 643; Jane Roberts, claims memorial, Mar. 17, 1784, A.O. 13/71, 245; Margaret Draper to Lord ——, Oct. 15, 1782, A.O. 13/44, 349; Elizabeth Skinner to commissioners, Aug. 28, 1786, A.O. 13/112, 61. Mrs. Draper lived to see her daughter well married (Margaret Draper to the Misses Byles, June 21, 1784, Byles Papers, I, 134, Mass. Hist. Soc.). Cf. men's attitudes toward their children and other dependents in A.O. 13/75, 556, A.O. 12/105, 115, A.O. 13/131, 399, and A.O. 13/137, 2.

Refugee men, though they might call themselves "strangers," rarely noted a lack of friends, perhaps because of the coffeehouse networks. To women, by contrast, the fact that they were not surrounded by friends and neighbors seemed calamitous. "I am without Friends or Money," declared one; I am "a friendless, forlorn Woman . . . a Stranger to this Country, and surrounded by evils," said another. She is "far from her native Country, and numerous Friends and Relations where she formerly lived, much respected," wrote a third of her own condition.[53]

When the female refugees talked of settling elsewhere or of returning to the United States, they spoke chiefly of the friends and relatives they would find at their intended destinations. Indeed, it appears from the claims that at least six women went into exile solely because their friends and relatives did. A loyalist woman who remained in the United States after the war explained that she did so because she chose "to reside near my relations [rather] than to carry my family to a strange Country where in case of my death they would be at the mercy of strangers." And Mary Serjeant's description of her situation in America as it would have been had her husband not been a loyalist carried the implication that she wished she too had stayed at home: "His poor Children and disconsolate Widow would now have had a House of their own and some Land adjoining to it And instead of being almost destitute in a Land of Strangers would have remained among some Relatives."[54]

In sum, evidence drawn from the loyalist claims strongly suggests that late-eighteenth-century women had fully internalized the roles laid out for them in the polite literature of the day. Their experience was largely confined

[53] Elizabeth Putnam to Thomas Dundas, Nov. 7, 1789, A.O. 13/75, 309; Elizabeth Dumaresq to Lord Shelburne, Sept. 14, 1782, A.O. 13/44, 429; Elizabeth Barkesdale to commissioners, Nov. 24, 1786, A.O. 13/125, 402, Rachel Wetmore, claims memorial, Mar. 25, 1786, A.O. 13/16, 272. Other comments on neighbors and relatives may be found in A.O. 12/3, 231, A.O. 12/56, 339, A.O. 13/25, 275, A.O. 13/32, 595, A.O. 13/44, 345, A.O. 13/75, 544, 641, and A.O. 13/107, 271. Mr. and Mrs. James Parker had an interesting exchange of letters on the subject of whether she would join him in England, in which her ties to her American friends figured strongly. "Tho I would not hesitate one moment to go with you my Dearest friend to any place on earth, yet I cannot think of parting forever with my Dear and valuable friends on this side the atlantick, without many a heart felt sigh," she wrote on July 24, 1783. His response (Mar. 5, 1784) recognized her concern: "I realy sympathize with you on this trying scene of leaving of your Country and all our friends." Parker Papers, Pt. VIII, nos. 26, 31, Liverpool Record Office.

[54] Elizabeth Macnair to John Hamilton, Dec. 27, 1789, A.O. 13/131, 400; Mary Serjeant to John Wilmot and Daniel P. Coke, Dec. 1, 1782, A.O. 13/49, pt. 1, 283. See also A.O. 13/34, 471, and A.O. 13/70B, 145, on resettlement. For women who followed friends and relatives into exile see A.O. 13/116, 468, A.O. 13/114, 662, A.O. 12/102, 24, and A.O. 13/37, 3.

to their households, either because they chose that course or because they were forced into it. They perceived themselves as "helpless"—even if at times their actions showed that they were not—and they strongly valued ties with family and friends. When the Revolution tore them from the familiar patterns of their lives in America, they felt abandoned and adrift, far more so than did their male relatives, for whom the human contacts cherished by the women seemed to mean less or at least were more easily replaced by those friendships that persisted into exile.

The picture of the late-eighteenth-century woman that emerges from the loyalist claims, therefore, is of one who was almost wholly domestic, in the sense that that word would be used in the nineteenth-century United States. But at the same time the colonial woman's image of herself lacked the positive attributes with which her nineteenth-century counterpart could presumably console herself. The eighteenth-century American woman was primarily a wife and a mother, but America had not yet developed an ideology that would proclaim the social value of motherhood. That was to come with republicanism—and loyalist women, by a final irony, were excluded by their political allegiance from that republican assurance.[55]

[55] On the development of republican ideology pertaining to women see Linda K. Kerber, "Daughters of Columbia: Educating Women for the Republic, 1787-1805," in Stanley Elkins and Eric McKitrick, eds., The Hofstadter Aegis (New York, 1974), 36-59.

WOMEN IN THE ERA OF THE
AMERICAN REVOLUTION:
THE CASE OF NORWICH, CONNECTICUT

BARBARA E. LACEY

WAS the condition of women in eighteenth-century America improving or deteriorating? Did the Revolution change women's status? One answer emphasizes patriotic activities, contrasting them to worsening legal and household oppression; another is that women's domestic drudgery was lessening and the ideology of the Revolution was a liberating influence.[1] These questions, and their one-sided answers, remain unresolved. This essay documents the principal trends in women's condition in a single community, Norwich, the second largest Connecticut town at midcentury, where women were benefiting in some aspects of domestic and economic life and suffering in others. While the Revolution accelerated changes which had been in progress for decades, it also contributed to a new self-awareness of women as a group. Rather than "improving" or "deteriorating," the lives of women in Connecticut were growing more complex.

A study of eighteenth-century American women begins with the household, the focal point of most women's lives. Mehetabel Coit of Norwich, for example, records in her journal family events—the births of her children, visits of friends, and various domestic recipes.[2] The composition of the colonial household—age, sex, and number of members—

---

[1] The debate is outlined by James H. Hutson, "Women in the Era of the American Revolution: The Historian as Suffragist," *The Quarterly Journal of the Library of Congress*, XXXII, 290-303 (Oct., 1975). Hutson supports the view that the Revolution was liberating. Joan Wilson presents the case for the oppression of women in this era in a thorough survey of relevant studies, "The Illusion of Change: Women and the American Revolution," in *The American Revolution: Explorations in the History of American Radicalism*, Editor, Alfred F. Young (DeKalb, 1976), pp. 383-445.

[2] Mehetabel Chandler Coit, *Her Book, 1714* (Norwich, 1895). Similarly, Catherine Fennelly, in *Connecticut Women in the Revolutionary Era* (Chester, Ct., 1975), devotes much of her study to descriptions of women's homes, dress, health, and social life.

has been a subject of inquiry since Arthur Calhoun stated that Puritan "girls often married at sixteen or under," and "families of ten and twelve children were very common."[3] These generalizations have been largely disproved by analyses of such Massachusetts communities as Andover and Hingham.[4] Genealogical data available for Norwich reveal that Calhoun exaggerates the case for Connecticut. By analyzing records for a sample of Norwich families, it is possible to estimate size of family, age at marriage, and numbers never marrying.[5]

Family size in Norwich, as in Massachusetts towns, declined unevenly through the eighteenth century. The change was

TABLE 1. SIZE OF FAMILY

Generation	No. of Sibling Groups	Average No. of Siblings
III (Born 1660-1715)	7	8.1
IV (Born 1682-1761)	28	6.4
V (Born 1714-1794)	64	5.9
VI (Born 1744-1802)	60	6.3

expressed in one woman's diary as a new family ideal: "Fine Children I[de] have,—three or four/ They should have wisdom in great store."[6] Larger families occurred with regularity, but the average of six children was smaller than Calhoun believed.

[3] Arthur W. Calhoun, *A Social History of the American Family From Colonial Times to the Present* (Cleveland, 1917), I, 67, 87.

[4] Philip J. Greven, Jr., *Four Generations: Population, Land and Family in Colonial Andover, Massachusetts* (Ithaca, 1970), and Daniel Smith, "Population, Family and Society in Hingham, Massachusetts, 1635-1880," Diss. University of California, Berkeley, 1973.

[5] Family trends were determined from the genealogical work of Mary Perkins, *Old Families of Norwich, Connecticut, Genealogies, 1660-1800* (Cambridge, 1900), using Part I of Volume I, the published portion of Perkins' manuscript data. The lineage of five Norwich families—Adgate, Backus, John Baldwin, Henry Baldwin, and Bingham—was traced for seven generations, including the original settlers who moved to Norwich in 1660 and are identified as Generation I. Only figures for Generations III to VI are included in the tables below.

[6] Abigail Reynold (Mrs. Giles L'Hommedieu) of Norwich, Diary, 1794-1809, 23, MS in the Connecticut State Library, Hartford, hereafter called CSL.

In contrast, age at marriage for Norwich men and women did not alter radically during the century. There was a slight rise, from 24 to 26 years, in the age of marriage for men, and a recurring age of 23 for women. Norwich women married in their early twenties, which seems old compared to Calhoun's

TABLE 2. AVERAGE AGE AT FIRST MARRIAGE

Generation	Males No. of Indivs.	Av. Age	Females No. of Indivs.	Av. Age
III	18	24.2 yrs.	18	24.1 yrs.
IV	62	25.1	39	24.1
V	84	24.2	68	22.3
VI	50	26.7	37	23.7

teen-age brides, but the data do not depart significantly from findings for Andover and Hingham. It is also consistent with the colonial demographic pattern in which female age at marriage was high in the eighteenth compared to the seventeenth century.[7]

Statistics on age at marriage should be supplemented with data on those who never married. The proportion of single women in Norwich was growing rapidly, reaching 20 percent

TABLE 3. NEVER MARRYING

Gen.	No. of Males Mar.	Never Mar.	No. of Females Mar.	Never Mar.	Percentage Never Marrying Male	Female
III	22	1	21	1	4.3%	4.5%
IV	66	5	40	2	7.0	4.7
V	94	8	70	13	7.8	15.6
VI	54	3	38	10	5.2	20.8

of the marriageable female population by the end of the century. At the Revolution, women were waiting to marry, and many remaining single.

7 Robert V. Wells, "Quaker Marriage Patterns in a Colonial Perspective," *William and Mary Quarterly*, xxix, 415-442 (July, 1972).

An explanation for this phenomenon involves the sex ratio, which, as census figures will show, was growing more disproportionate as the town sent men to new settlements, resulting in a surplus of women. A partial explanation of the trend toward late marriage and celibacy also may have involved new attitudes about marriage, observable in the *Norwich Packet*. This newspaper, on January 29, 1794, contained "An Address to Maids" suggesting ways to encourage marital unions, including bounties on marriage and taxes on celibacy. On the one hand, the writer claimed women had refused to enter matrimony: "Whenever you have been questioned with respect to your intention of marriage, you have uniformly pleaded the war prevented you"; yet he hoped that his suggestions for correcting the situation would be welcomed. Whether voluntarily or forced by circumstances, an increasing number of women were not marrying, and contemporaries were aware of it.

Census data for 1774 give some indication of the sex distribution of the Norwich population.[8] Males outnumbered females under the age of 20, while females predominated in the older age groups. For example, between 10 and 20 years of age, there were 916 males and 749 females, while between 20 and 70 years, there were 1,468 males and 1,574 females. The total population did not change appreciably by 1790. The number of inhabitants included 7,578 in 1790, compared to 7,321 in 1774. Frances Caulkins believes this "slight variation" from the earlier figure was due to "the war of the Revolution and repeated emigrations."[9] Since these factors would tend to diminish the male population, the ratio between men and women probably increased between 1774 and 1790.

Evidence of the distribution of this population into house-

[8] *Norwich Packet*, April 21-28, 1774.

[9] Caulkins, *History of Norwich, Connecticut: From Its Possession by the Indians, to the Year 1866* (Hartford, 1866; rep. Chester, Ct., 1976), p. 522. The growth in population and wealth of eastern Connecticut at mid-century is described by Richard Bushman, *From Puritan to Yankee, Character and the Social Order in Connecticut, 1690-1765* (New York, 1967), pp. 122-134.

holds suggests that the conjugal family did not always live alone.[10] The 1774 census lists persons, families, and dwelling houses by church district or society. The First Society included 1,978 persons, 317 families, and 283 houses, while the East Society had 1,100 persons, 76 families, 69 houses. These figures indicate that in 1774 there was more than one family per dwelling, and the older parts of the town had more families per house than did the newer societies.

A fragment of census data exists for a slightly later period in Norwich. An agricultural return for the East Society in 1779 includes 200 families and 1,153 persons. The total of persons in 1779, 1,153, is close to that of 1,100 for the East Society in 1774, but the total of families, 200, is considerably more than the earlier 76. The definition of a "family" may have varied from one census to another. However, if the number of dwelling houses can be presumed not to have radically changed by 1779 from the 69 noted in the 1774 census, it is evident, whether from the 1774 or 1779 census, that 76 to 201 families were occupying 69 households in one section of late eighteenth-century Norwich.[11] The existence of similarly extended households throughout the town is also documented by probate records. Extended households imply for women a sharing of domestic responsibilities with other women, and possible conflict over the use of the kitchen, disciplining of children, and division of household tasks. The role of a woman in the house may not always have been clear or satisfying.

The changing position of women in Norwich families is also revealed in eighteenth-century wills. Although probate

10 Census data indicating a norm of nuclear families in Rhode Island are presented by John Demos, "Families in Colonial Bristol, Rhode Island: An Exercise in Historical Demography," *William and Mary Quarterly*, XXV, 40-57 (Jan., 1968). However, since Demos has no data on the number of dwellings which housed these families, his argument against the existence of extended households is flawed. Fortunately, census data for Norwich include information about numbers of houses as well as numbers of families and their members.

11 An Account of the Names of the Families and Persons...in the East Society in Norwich the 29th of April AD 1779, MS at CSL. Data for the First Society in 1779, in Caulkins, p. 356, indicate 367 families were occupying the 283 houses counted in 1774.

records are a reliable source of information, since women wrote wills and received bequests, they have been relatively neglected in studies of American women. Inheritances by women are usually described as being in moveable property rather than real estate.[12] On the contrary, women took part in land inheritance during the colonial period, and bequests to women in money and bills of credit took on a new meaning as the colonial economy grew more complex. In European rural society, through partible inheritance, women increasingly came into control of land, and the attachment of property to women for the purpose of making a match was important in the maintenance of class structure and monogamous institutions.[13] Norwich probate records indicate comparably significant aspects of family organization and the economic role of women in eighteenth-century Connecticut.[14] Wills and inventories tell about widows and daughters: the amounts of real and personal estate they received; provisions for their use of the house; and their maintenance by sons.

The condition of widowhood is illuminated by an examination of colonial wills. A widow was entitled by Connecticut intestate law to a dower of a one-third portion of her deceased husband's real estate for life, and also to one-third of his personal property. At her death, the real property of her deceased husband which she had been using would be disposed of by his descendants "according to the will of the Deceased; and where there is no will, according to law"; the personal prop-

---

[12] See Linda Auwers, "Fathers, Sons, and Wealth in Colonial Windsor, Connecticut," *Journal of Family History*, III, 142 (Summer, 1978). In Norwich, the land inheritance of women was not always mentioned in wills because daughters sometimes received their portions when they married rather than when their fathers died; occasionally wills confirmed these previous land settlements.

[13] Jack Goody, "Inheritance, property and women: some comparative considerations," in Jack Goody, Joan Thirsk, and E. P. Thompson, *Family and Inheritance, Rural Society in Western Europe, 1200-1800* (New York, 1976), pp. 10-36.

[14] A sample of 170 Norwich probate records was taken at random, utilizing at least 40 percent of all known wills in each of five twenty-year periods, from the New London Probate Court Record Books, 1697-1748, vols. A-E, and Norwich Probate Court Record Books, 1748-1799, vols. 1-9, MS on microfilm at CSL.

erty was at her own disposal.[15] Many Norwich men left their widows more than their legal due. About 50 percent of the men studied in each of five twenty-year periods gave their wives more than her thirds, either in personal or real property, or both. There was no appreciable variation over time or between economic groups. Nearly every will provided the wife with use of the house during her widowhood. Frequently, responsibility for maintenance of the widow by the son was also specified, but this stipulation steadily declined in frequency over the century.

At midcentury, a typical will gave to the wife the use and improvement of the east room of the house, one half of the cellar, a garden spot, a cow, and a horse; the sons, as a condition of their inheritance, were to provide the wife yearly with cords of wood, bushels of Indian corn, and a barrel of cider, but only "as long as she is my widow." A quarter of a century later, maintenance of widows changed slightly; one man indicated that his widow was not to improve her thirds in the land herself, but "should Annually Let out the Same to my Son for a Reasonable Yearly Rent." While such provisions decreased as the century progressed, it was increasingly the practice for probate courts to assign definite portions of the house, barn, and orchard to the widow; specification in wills may no longer have been deemed necessary.

Nevertheless, other records indicate a decline in family support of the widow. One in 1777 was "put out" to her son in Norwich by New London selectmen, who stated that "whenever he Chuses to Send her Back We Shall be Holden & Ready to accept her again & Support her." One-third of the individuals, from 1770 to 1790, who received certificates to reside in Norwich were widows who apparently no longer had certain means of support in their communities. Two-thirds of those on the poor list in 1785 were widows maintained by the town.[16] By 1800, Norwich widows seem to have had increasing

15 *Acts and Laws of His Majesties Colony of Connecticut in New England, 1702* (Boston, 1702; rep. Hartford, 1901), pp. 28-29.

16 Norwich Records of Town Votes, IV, 145-146, title page; V, 35-36. Photocopy of MS at City Clerk's Office, City Hall, Norwich.

problems and uncertain status within the family and the community.[17]

Probate records also describe the role of the daughter in the eighteenth-century family. Under partible inheritance in Connecticut, daughters inherited equally with sons, although the eldest son was entitled to a double portion; where there were no sons, daughters could share the entire estate. Moreover, the provision by which land descending to married daughters became the property of their husbands was changed as early as 1723; married women's real estate could not be alienated or disposed of without their consent.[18]

Daughters in Norwich were recipients of personal or moveable property in nearly every case. They also inherited land and money, but these tendencies changed over time. Money bequests, sometimes nominal, increased through the century, except for a drop at the end of the period. Land bequests to daughters, made in 50 percent of the wills at the beginning of the century, grew unevenly to 65 percent of the wills by 1800. Women were gaining control over significant amounts of property, particularly in land.

Wills provided for use of the house, and in some instances, for maintenance of daughters by sons; from 1760 to 1799, one-quarter of the wills included such stipulations. Joshua Calkin, in his will dated 1770, gave to his daughter the north end of the house "where I now live (where I expect my wife live with her)." Another man of the same period provided that his "daughter Sarah shall be Comfortably maintained by my five sons . . . by an equal Proportion During her Natural Life." More frequently, the daughters were provided with support "if they do not marry." Other female relatives, including mothers, aunts, and sisters, were also given use of the house or maintenance.

---

[17] A comparable situation in Woburn has been analyzed by Alexander Keyssar, "Widowhood in Eighteenth-Century Massachusetts: A Problem in the History of the Family," *Perspectives in American History*, VIII, 83-122 (1974).

[18] *Acts and Laws*, 61; *The Public Records of the Colony of Connecticut* (Hartford, 1850-1890), VI, 425.

Wills give the impression of a surplus female population which families were attempting to provide for and incorporate. Daughters were gaining control over significant forms of property at the same time that they were increasing their dependence on kin. The burden of responsibility was frequently on the son, who often had to pay legacies to female relatives out of his inheritance and share the house with them. The effect on daughters may have been to make them feel "troublesome." Increases in money and land bequests may indicate some effort by men to make their daughters either more independent or more desirable as marriage partners.

The wills of women provide an interesting case apart. Written by widows and single women, in all economic categories, they predominate in the middle and lower ranges. Some disposed of limited amounts of property: one woman referred to "all my estate, it being only Personal estate." Others had extensive holdings: one widow had land, buildings, and slaves which she had held "in Partnership and in Common" with her deceased husband.

Women bequeathed their property in various ways. Eight left goods to brothers and sisters; two gave double portions to their eldest sons; thirteen stipulated that they were leaving equal amounts to their children; and four left gifts to female friends outside the family. Many left token bequests to grandchildren. Rather than favoring the eldest son, which would have been the case had they died intestate, women usually treated their children equally.

Perhaps what is most significant about women's wills is simply their existence. There were twenty-eight such wills; one appeared in the first quarter century, a few at midcentury, and eighteen were probated after 1770. Wills may reflect a new sense of self-worth on the part of women, who chose to take the disposal of their worldly goods into their own hands. The gift of a calico gown or a brass kettle to a female friend, however modest in value, may have expressed ties of friendship between women outside the family which were being acknowledged and increasing in importance.

Divorce records are an added source of information about the changing condition of women. Divorce was possible in Connecticut on grounds of "Adultery, or fraudulent Contract, or wilful Desertion for Three Years with total Neglect of Duty; or in the Case of Seven Years absence of one Party not heard of."[19] The law on divorce differed from that in England, as well as "more liberal and reasonable."[20] Indeed, it was considered "indulgent" by Sarah Kemble Knight, an acute contemporary observer of Connecticut society.[21]

TABLE 4. DIVORCE PETITIONS

	1710-19	'20-29	'30-39	'40-49	'50-59	'60-69	'70-79	'80-89	'90-99
New London Co.									
Men	0	2	4	2	3	5	5	10	8
Women	2	11	9	15	15	14	24	18	27
Norwich									
Men	0	0	1	1	1	2	1	1	0
Women	0	0	1	3	1	7	10	6	8

Norwich divorce papers in the New London County Superior Court records, and data on county divorces offer a useful comparison for trends in the town.[22] There was an overall rise in the number of divorces in most categories. However, Norwich men were infrequent applicants for divorce—only seven suits by men, compared to thirty-six by Norwich women, during the century. Norwich women, like New London County women, increasingly and successfully petitioned for

[19] *Acts and Laws,* 28.

[20] Zephaniah Swift, *A Digest of the Laws of the State of Connecticut* (New Haven, 1822), I, 23.

[21] Sarah Kemble Knight, *The Journal of Madam Knight* (Boston, 1972), p. 22. Nancy Cott, "Divorce and the Changing Status of Women in Eighteenth-Century Massachusetts," *William and Mary Quarterly,* XXXIII, 592 (Oct., 1976), finds 216 petitions in Massachusetts between 1715 and 1786. In New London County alone at least 137 petitions were made between 1720 and 1789 to the Superior Court; the General Assembly also received requests for divorce.

[22] New London County, Superior Court, Divorce Papers, 1719-1875, MS at CSL.

divorce, naming desertion and adultery as the principal grounds. Claims of desertion, or nonsupport, predominated.

The divorce rate rose critically during the war years, and some petitions cited war-related circumstances. One Norwich woman testified in 1782 that her husband was "taken by the British Enemy and Voluntarily Joined Said Enemy in their Service Against the United States of America." Another complained in 1783 that her husband had deserted her and "joined a British ship in Caroline." Similar stories prevail in New London County divorce records; on one occasion it was the wife who abandoned her husband for a British refugee. A noteworthy case during the Revolutionary period may involve its liberating ideology; a mulatto woman, sued for divorce by a Norwich "servant for life," explained to the court that she deserted her husband because she did not want her children, if they had any, to follow in the same "condition."

It is difficult to evaluate the significance of increasing rates of divorce. The growing number of female petitioners could have been a response to the spirit of independence, and to the republican emphasis on private as well as public virtue. Nancy Cott suggests that this was the case in Massachusetts, where most petitions were based on the grievance of adultery. However, since two-thirds of the petitions by Norwich women were on charges of desertion, the intent of Connecticut female petitioners may have been primarily to achieve the economic rights of *feme sole* status, enabling women better to support themselves.

While divorce records show that the Revolution increased the stress on some marriages, town and state records indicate that the war served to consolidate and strengthen the ties of other families. The outbreak of hostilities caused several Boston families to seek refuge in Norwich until Boston was evacuated; some stayed with their Norwich connections for most of the war.[23] Apparently the political allegiance of these families was in question; in May, 1775, the town voted to

23 Caulkins, p. 379.

admit none "Inimical to the Common Cause of America," and required the Boston residents to be informed of "the Sentiments of the Town that they May Govern them Selves accordingly."[24] Other families came from Newport, New York, and New London to wait out the troubled times.[25]

Norwich also received several families from Long Island after the British occupation. These refugees had a difficult time in Connecticut, being required to pay military and poll taxes, but not allowed to vote. Connecticut residents, according to one Long Islander, either "could not or would not" help them. Many families, after exhausting their resources, petitioned the Assembly for permission to return to their homes, even though their lands and houses had been devastated by the British.[26]

The Long Island families made an effort to settle in Norwich, while the Boston families intended only a temporary stay. Both found unreceptive conditions. Kinship ties, whether in Boston or on Long Island, proved strong and were not permanently disrupted by the war.

The Revolution also affected the lives of women in Norwich families.[27] Women were urged to boycott British goods and wear homespun clothes,[28] and had difficulties in finding tea, flax, and wool at a "Constitutional Price."[29] Some of them boarded prisoners and soldiers, occasionally with fatal results; one woman died of smallpox contracted from inoculated soldiers who lodged in her house.[30]

The Revolution also encouraged women to act as a group.

[24] Norwich Records of Town Votes, IV, 130.

[25] Caulkins, p. 380.

[26] Frederic Mather, The Refugees of 1776 from Long Island to Connecticut (Albany, 1913; rep. Baltimore, 1972), pp. 187-194.

[27] Some activities of Norwich women during the war are included in Joan Nafie, To the Beat of a Drum: A History of Norwich, Connecticut, During the American Revolution (Norwich, 1975), pp. 107-108.

[28] Norwich Packet, Nov. 24-Dec. 1, 1774.

[29] Letters dated May 7 and 21, 1776, in W. D. McCrackan, Editor, The Huntington Letters, in the Possession of Julia Chester Wells (New York, 1897), pp. 26-27, 31.

[30] Norwich Packet, April 21-28, 1777.

Numbers of Norwich women joined to bring in the harvest while men were away at battle:

Norwich, North Part of East Society. In this distressing Time of gathering in the Harvest, the Men being universally gone, the Burden being so heavy on Those who are left, that they could not accomplish it without much Difficulty, a Number of Young Women, willing to support the Cause which the Men are engag'd in, on the 3rd inst. having short Notice, assembled together at the House of Captain Stephen Johnson, between the Hours of one and two o'clock, and husked out near two Hundred Bushels of corn, partook of an elegant Supper and returned to their respective Dwellings by Day light. On the 10th inst. fifty young Women with a few young Men, met at the House of Capt. Ambrose Blunt, and husked about five Hundred Bushels of Corn for him, and after having regaled themselves, they returned to their respective Homes. We hope this laudable Example may be followed.[31]

Women also met to help a wife whose husband was a war prisoner:

The benevolent disposition of the people of Chelsea is truly worthy of imitation—Mrs. Corning (wife of Mr. Joseph Corning, now a prisoner with the enemy) being under low circumstances, and destitute of necessary cloathing for her children, a number of respectable ladies of the first character appointed a day on which they assembled, and spent the same in spinning; after which they presented her with the yarn to a considerable amount. —If acts of this kind were more practiced, of what advantage would it be to the community, and how much to the honor of the FEMALE SEX?[32]

Formations of such groups were spontaneous responses to the trials of war; they may, however, have had lasting effect on women's behavior in later years.

After the war, women continued to take successful action in a number of areas. In court, widows were given increased control over their deceased husbands' estates: three Norwich

31 *Norwich Packet*, Oct. 7-14, 1776.
32 *Norwich Packet*, March 21, 1780.

widows were permitted by the Assembly to sell land belonging to their husbands' heirs, and the widow of a Norwich Loyalist successfully petitioned from London to receive the value of her husband's confiscated estate.[33] Church membership by women was increasing relative to that of men, and formed the basis for participation in missionary and charitable societies in the early nineteenth century.[34] Women were taking a new interest in their own education.

The writings of several women at the end of the century reveal the importance of education. Nancy Hyde of Norwich observed that formerly women had been confined to "the narrow circle of domestic concerns," but "the present era, has rescued women from the shackles of ignorance, . . . and allowed her such various privileges" as "the acquisition of knowledge."[35] Lydia Sigourney wrote about a woman of property who had been her benefactor in Norwich shortly after the Revolution.[36] Judith Murray acknowledged that the "Door of Science" was barred to women but, believing the "Page of Revelation" had opened before her, published a theological study at Norwich in 1782.[37]

These new interests and a nascent self-consciousness were expressed in a "sisterly covenant" in Norwich in 1790. Thirty-nine members of the Chelsea Congregational Church formed a society to "help each other in our Christian course," agreeing to meet each week to read Scripture, pray, and sing hymns.[38]

[33] The Public Records of the State of Connecticut (Hartford, 1894-1967), VII, 153, 533; IX, 374; Connecticut Archives, Revolutionary War, 1st. Ser., XXIX, 13-15, MS at CSL.

[34] Numbers of men and women taken into full communion were tallied by decade from the Records of Baptisms, Marriages, Deaths and Church Admissions of the Fifth Church of Norwich, from 1737 to 1824, MS at CSL.

[35] The Writings of Nancy Maria Hyde of Norwich, Connecticut, Connected With a Sketch of Her Life, [Editor, Lydia Huntley Sigourney] (Norwich, 1816), pp. 154-155.

[36] [Lydia Huntley Sigourney], Sketch of Connecticut, Forty Years Since (Hartford, 1824).

[37] [Judith Sargent Murray], Some Deductions from the System Promulgated in the Page of Divine Revelation, Ranged in the Order and Form of a Catechism (Norwich, 1782).

[38] A form of Sisterly Covenant made in The Year 1790, photocopy of MS at CSL.

The objectives were reformulated in 1800; thereafter the Ladies' Literary Society gathered "for the Special Purpose of Enlightening our Understanding, expanding our Ideas, and promoting useful Knowledge among our Sex."[39] The group spent its time commenting on the Bible, historical works, and selections from magazines. The society's minutes indicate how Norwich women felt about themselves at the turn of the century.

The women were aware of a common bond. They read selections from the Old Testament about Abigail and Deborah, which showed "there are seasons when it is by a woman's wisdom a people are saved." They discussed an "Address to Females" in the *Massachusetts Magazine,* which pointed out "the influence [women's] maners and examples have on society" to reclaim "the profligate (of the other sex)." They read from Ramsey's *History of the American Revolution,* and noted the contributions women made by abstaining from foreign manufactures, dressing in homemade garments, and inspiring men at war "to perform the most glorious actions." Ramsey's account of the surrender of Burgoyne prompted a spirited response: "We I mean females are of importance in the scale of beings—let us then enquire what we can do toward securing those rights & priviledges we have so nobly gained."[40]

Women in the society were aware that men could be critical of their endeavors, and they were uncertain in their replies. One woman expressed confidence in her activities. She read a letter on the "Insensability of men to the Charms of a female mind Cultivated with polite and solid literature," and felt "the pleasure resulting from an informed understanding is itself a recompence worth the pursuit." Another woman, however, questioned the society's activities. She read about the "impropriety of Females arrogating to themselves those pursuits & employments which are more suitable to the other sex." Another commented ambiguously on this composition, noting that "the author did not mean to exclude the acquisi-

[39] Minutes of Ladies' Society, 1800-1805, 1, MS at Connecticut Historical Society, Hartford.

[40] Minutes, pp. 19, 254, 49.

tion of useful knowledge only that our pursuits should be truly feminine, ever remembering that 'woman shines best in her proper sphere.'"[41] Others justified their educational program by observing that it would help make them better wives and mothers. The society lasted until 1805, when several members died from "a dreadful malady" in Chelsea, and meetings were discontinued. The minutes comment poignantly that death had severed "the bonds of sisterhood."[42]

Overall, the records for Norwich relating to women indicate a change of role. At the beginning of the century, most women married, had children, and spent their days with their families. As time wore on, more women were not marrying; families were smaller; not every wife had a home of her own; divorce was increasing; widows were no longer sure of places to live. Moreover, women were increasing their property holdings, undertaking outside interests in church and educational activities, and developing friendship with other women. Participation in the Revolution increased women's self-awareness.

Social and economic developments had made women more independent, forcing them to respond positively to new, uncertain positions, and to reevaluate their role. On the one hand, marriage and family continued as a desirable goal, even though a satisfying union was increasingly difficult to achieve. Most women were at one with society in accepting this incipient Victorian ideal. On the other hand, women were no longer divided into separate households, but began to unite in their own organizations. Shared experiences in the outside world must have given some women the courage to reevaluate their lives, and formed a basis for the future women's rights movement.

The Revolution may have neglected certain female rights, but it was not an era that produced merely an "illusion of change." The lives of Norwich women changed measurably throughout the eighteenth century with respect to household

41 Minutes, pp. 112, 35.
42 Minutes, p. 246.

size and composition, numbers never marrying, inheritance, divorce, education, and group activities. While these facts can be evaluated, it is a dubious undertaking to list such phenomena under the simplistic dichotomy of improvement or decline. Historical investigation increasingly seeks to discover the nature and extent of change and continuity in the past—to clarify how the status of women was different in 1800 compared to 1750—but the findings cannot be neatly fitted into a conception of progress or its antithesis.

"The Living Mother of a Living Child":
Midwifery and Mortality in
Post-Revolutionary New England

Laurel Thatcher Ulrich

FORTY-ONE years ago, Richard Harrison Shryock could summarize the history of early American midwifery in a few sentences. "The history of obstetrics and of pediatrics," he wrote, "affords other illustrations of the way in which inadequate medical science affected the public health. Maternity cases were left, in English-speaking lands, almost entirely to midwives. . . . And since midwives lacked any scientific training, obstetrics proceeded on the level of folk practice, and with consequences which may be easily imagined."[1] The consequences could be imagined because few persons in 1948 doubted the superiority of medical science over folk practice.

The advent of "natural" childbirth, culminating in recent years in the revival of lay midwifery, has changed historical judgments as well as obstetrics. In revisionist histories of childbirth, the pleasant story of scientific progress has been replaced by a darker tale of medical competitiveness and misplaced confidence in an imperfect science. Medical science did not on the whole increase women's chances of surviving childbirth until well into the twentieth century, the new histories argue, and may actually have increased the dangers. As Richard W. and Dorothy C. Wertz explain, puerperal fever, the dreaded infection that killed so many women in the nineteenth century, "is probably the classic example of iatrogenic disease—that is, disease caused by medical treatment itself."[2]

Ms. Ulrich is a member of the Department of History, University of New Hampshire. Versions of this article were presented at meetings of the Benjamin Waterhouse Medical Society (Boston University), the Maine Society for the History of Medicine, the American Antiquarian Society Seminar in Political and Social History, and the comparative history seminar at the University of New Hampshire. Acknowledgments: I am grateful to those groups and to Worth Estes, Judith Walzer Leavitt, Janet Polasky, and Cornelia Dayton for helpful comments. Some parts of this essay will appear in my forthcoming book on the diary of Martha Moore Ballard.

[1] Shryock, *The Development of Modern Medicine: An Interpretation of the Social and Scientific Factors Involved*, rev. ed. (London, 1948), 77-78.

[2] Judith Walzer Leavitt, *Brought to Bed: Childbearing in America, 1750 to 1950* (New York, 1986), 56-57, and "'Science' Enters the Birthing Room: Obstetrics in America since the Eighteenth Century," *Journal of American History*, LXX (1983),

Although historians trace to the eighteenth century the gradual supplanting of midwives by physicians, most detailed studies have concentrated on the nineteenth century or later. The few discussions of childbirth in early America have dealt with urban centers and with the work of prominent physicians such as William Shippen of Philadelphia.[3] Almost nothing is known about rural obstetrics or about the activities and attitudes of midwives. This essay begins to fill that gap. Its central document is the manuscript diary of a Maine midwife, Martha Moore Ballard, who lived at Augusta (then part of Hallowell) from 1778 to 1812. It also uses English obstetrical literature, scattered physicians' and midwives' records from Maine and New Hampshire, and the papers of Dr. Jeremiah Barker of Gorham, Maine.

Martha Ballard performed her first delivery in 1778, though her diary does not begin until six years later. Between 1785 and 1812 she recorded 814 deliveries. The expansiveness of her record is unusual not only among midwives (few of whom left any written evidence of their practice) but among country physicians as well. Yet the diary has received little scholarly attention. Historians who have used it have relied on an abridged version published in Charles Elventon Nash's *History of Augusta*. For most, the details of Ballard's practice have seemed less important than her symbolic image as a "traditional" midwife. One work portrays her as an untrained, intensely religious, and poorly paid practitioner, who nevertheless shared some of the attitudes of contemporary physicians. Another associates her with nineteenth-century controversies between midwives and physicians, emphasizing her helplessness when accused by a local physician of "meddling by giving her opinion of a disease."[4]

Serious study of the entire diary shatters such stereotypes. Although physicians were delivering babies in Hallowell as early as 1785, Martha Ballard was clearly the most important practitioner in her town. Because her record documents traditional midwifery at a moment of strength, it allows us to shift the focus of inquiry from the eventual triumphs of medical science to the immediate relations of doctors and midwives in an era of transition. What is most apparent on close examination is the *success* of Ballard's practice, measured on its own terms or against contemporary medical literature. Although elements of the new obstetrics had begun to

---

281-304; Wertz and Wertz, *Lying-In: A History of Childbirth in America* (New York, 1977), xi, x, 128.

[3] Catherine M. Scholten, "'On the Importance of the Obstetrick Art': Changing Customs of Childbirth in America, 1760 to 1825," *William and Mary Quarterly*, 3d Ser., XXXIV (1977), 429-431, and *Childbearing in American Society, 1650-1850* (New York, 1985), chap. 2; Wertz and Wertz, *Lying-In*, chap. 2; Leavitt, *Brought to Bed*, 36-44, 263-265.

[4] Nash, *The History of Augusta: First Settlements and Early Days as a Town, Including the Diary of Mrs. Martha Moore Ballard (1785-1812)* (Augusta, Me., 1904); Wertz and Wertz, *Lying-In*, 9-10; quotation from Scholten, *Childbearing*, 45; Leavitt, *Brought to Bed*, 37.

filter into the region, the old rituals of childbirth remained powerful. In her record, it is the physicians—particularly the young physicians— who appear insecure and uncomfortable.

The diary also extends and deepens recent discussions concerning eighteenth-century modes of delivery. A number of historians have argued that English innovations, such as William Smellie's improved forceps, encouraged an interventionist obstetrics that eventually displaced the gentler practices of midwives. Edward Shorter has countered that eighteenth-century English midwives were themselves "wildly interventionist" and that physicians, not midwives, introduced the notion of "natural" childbirth. This new obstetrics, he argues, was in part a response to general cultural trends—a medical reflection of Enlightenment respect for nature—and also a consequence of the work of pioneering physicians like Charles White, whose textbook published in London in 1773 was the first example of a fully noninterventionist obstetrics.[5]

By shifting the balance of attention from obstetrical prescriptions to obstetrical results, Ballard's diary provides a new vantage point for assessing this controversy. Although it reveals little about the particulars of Ballard's methods (we do not know, for example, whether she applied hog's grease to the perineum or manually dilated the cervix), it offers compelling evidence of her skill. Maternal and fetal mortality rates extracted from the diary compare favorably with those for physicians in both England and America, countering the horror stories of eighteenth-century literature as well as the casual assumptions of twentieth-century historians. The consequences of Ballard's practice need not be imagined.

In most respects Martha Ballard's is a typical eighteenth-century rural diary—a laconic record of weather, sermon texts, family activities, and visits to and from neighbors. Obstetrical and general medical entries are interwoven with this larger accounting of ordinary life, although she gave birth records a special significance by summarizing them in the margins, numbering each year's births from January to December. Each delivery entry gives the father's name, the child's sex, the time of birth, the condition of mother and infant, and the fee collected. Many also include the time of the midwife's arrival and departure, the names of the attendants who assisted her, and the arrival of the "afternurse," who cared for the woman during lying-in (the week or two following delivery). Succeeding entries record follow-up visits or hearsay reports about the mother and child.

The account of Tabitha Sewall's delivery on November 12-13, 1790, is typical:

[5] Wertz and Wertz, *Lying-In*, 34-43; Scholten, *Childbearing*, 34-36; Leavitt, *Brought to Bed*, 38-40; Shorter, "The Management of Normal Deliveries and the Generation of William Hunter," in W. F. Bynum and Roy Porter, eds., *William Hunter and the Eighteenth-Century Medical World* (Cambridge, 1985), 371-383.

I was Calld by Colonel Sewall to see his Lady who was in Labour. Shee was not so ill as to Call in other assistance this day. I slept with her till about 1 hour morn when shee calld her Neighbours to her assistance. Mrs Sewal was ill till 3 hour pm when shee was thro divine asistance made the Living Mother of a Living Son her 3d Child. Mrs Brooks, Belcher, Colman, Pollard & Voce assisted us . . . Colonel Sewall gave me 6/8 as a reward. Conducted me over the river.

The only unusual thing about this account is the reference to "divine asistance," suggesting that Mrs. Sewall or her midwife encountered some difficulty along the way. Everything else about the description is routine. The father or a near neighbor summoned the midwife. The woman remained "ill" for several hours. Just before the birth she called her female neighbors. The child was delivered—safely. The father paid the midwife and escorted her home. In the eight deliveries Martha Ballard performed for Tabitha Sewall, the description of one differs very little from another. Mrs. Sewall "was safe delivered at 7 hour morn of a fine Daughter and is Cleverly," Ballard wrote, or "Mrs Suall Delivard at 1 this morn of a son & is Cleverly."[6]

Ballard performed her first delivery at the age of forty-three shortly after moving to the District of Maine from Oxford, Massachusetts. Although she had no doubt assisted in many births in Oxford (she was herself the mother of nine children), she seems not to have practiced alone until she came to Hallowell. Demographics may explain her entry into the profession. In Oxford she had been surrounded by older women; her maternal grandmother was still alive in 1777. In Hallowell she was one of the older women in a young and rapidly growing town. The diary opens in January 1785, the year she turned fifty. It ends with her death in May 1812, just ten days after she performed her last delivery at the age of seventy-seven.

The diary tells us nothing of how she acquired her skills, though genealogical data suggest that her family had something of a medical bent. Two of her sisters married doctors; a maternal uncle was a physician. Certainly, her family demonstrated an unusual commitment to education. Her uncle Abijah Moore was Oxford's first college graduate. Her younger brother, Jonathan, was the second.[7] She probably learned midwifery in the

---

[6] Martha Moore Ballard Diary, 2 vols., Maine State Library, Augusta, Me., Apr. 2, 1788, Dec. 31, 1786. According to the *Oxford English Dictionary*, "cleverly" means "well" or "in health" in some dialects. This is obviously the meaning Ballard intended. Henry Sewall, Tabitha's husband, also kept a diary. He mentioned Martha Ballard's presence on only four of the eight occasions, never recorded paying a fee, and only twice mentioned the presence of other birth attendants. Henry Sewall Diary, Massachusetts Historical Society, Boston, Mass.

[7] The medical tradition continued into the 19th century. Ballard's diary was inherited and preserved by her great-granddaughter, Dr. Mary Hobart, who practiced obstetrics at New England Hospital in Boston. Clara Barton, the Civil War nurse and founder of the American Red Cross, was Ballard's grandniece.

same way her husband, Ephraim, learned milling or surveying—by practice, by observation, and by working alongside someone who knew more than she.

Ballard's assurance as a midwife is the best evidence we have of her training. In almost 1,000 births she did not lose a single mother at delivery, and only five women died in the lying-in period. Infant deaths were also rare. The diary lists fourteen stillbirths in 814 deliveries and five infant deaths within an hour or two of birth. When Mrs. Claton and her infant both died in the autumn of 1787, a week after delivery, Ballard noted the singularity of the event: "I asisted to Lay her out, her infant Laid in her arms, the first such instance I ever saw & the first woman that died in Child bed which I delivered."[8] The sight was as unusual as it was affecting. Under Martha Ballard's care, a woman could expect to become "the living mother of a living child."[9]

By twentieth-century standards, of course, both maternal and infant mortality were high. The diary records one maternal death for every 200 births. Today the rate for the United States is one per 10,000. But as Judith Walzer Leavitt has demonstrated, such dramatic gains in obstetrical safety have come in the past fifty years; as late as 1930 there was one maternal death for every 150 births in the United States. A recent study of early twentieth-century births in a Portsmouth, New Hampshire, hospital gives stillbirth rates five times as high as Ballard's. The turning point for fetal as well as maternal deaths was the 1940s.[10]

The appropriate question is how Martha Ballard's record compared with those of her contemporaries, particularly with New England physicians who began the regular practice of obstetrics in the eighteenth and early nineteenth centuries. Direct comparisons are difficult, in part because physicians' records tend to be organized much differently from hers. Most

[8] Ballard Diary, Aug. 16, 20, 1787. Since the first fatality occurred during the diary period, I have included the 177 pre-diary births in arriving at the total of 991 births.

[9] The phrase was conventional, and it persisted into the 19th century. Leavitt, for example, quotes a woman who gave thanks for having become "the living mother of a living and perfect child" (Brought to Bed, 34). Ballard's version of the statement was usually gender specific, as in "the living mother of a living son" or "the living mother of a fine Daughter" (Ballard Diary, Dec. 30, 1789).

[10] Leavitt, Brought to Bed, 23-26; Helen M. Wallace, Edwin M. Gold, and Edward F. Lis, eds., Maternal and Child Health Practices: Problems, Resources, and Methods of Delivery (Springfield, Ill., 1973), 185; J. Worth Estes and David M. Goodman, The Changing Humors of Portsmouth: The Medical Biography of an American Town, 1623-1983 (Boston, 1986), 298. In 2.3% of Ballard's deliveries the child was stillborn or died in the first 24 hours of life. For Portsmouth Hospital the figures were 11.4% (1915-1917), 4.8% (1925-1941), 1.2% (1954-1957), and 0.8% (1971-1983). Because methods of compiling statistics vary markedly over time, these numbers must be considered approximations. Stillbirth ratios, for example, might be affected by abortions, spontaneous or induced. On the development of obstetrical record keeping in general see James H. Cassedy, American Medicine and Statistical Thinking, 1800-1860 (Cambridge, Mass., 1984), 80-83.

are simply a record of fees collected. Some doctors kept notes on unusual cases; a few compiled mortality tables for their towns. Account books, obstetrical case notes, and mortality tables seldom overlap, however, so that we know the numbers of deliveries performed by one physician but not the results, the management of extraordinary cases by another but not the overall caseload, and the incidence of stillbirths for a given town but not the numbers of maternal deaths or the names of practitioners. Comparison with midwives' registers is easier, since midwives typically listed all births, live as well as stillbirths, chronologically from the beginning to the end of their careers. Few such lists survive, however, and none that I have found offers the kind of narrative detail available in the Ballard diary.

Despite the difficulties, it is nevertheless possible to construct some comparisons. Table I gives stillbirth ratios derived from Ballard's diary, two physicians' records, two midwives' registers, and several published mortality tables. At first glance it is the success of Ballard's practice that stands out. Whether her record is compared to that of Hall Jackson, a prominent eighteenth-century physician, or to Lydia Baldwin's, a contemporary Vermont midwife, it is eminent.[11] Yet none of the mortality ratios is as high as impressionistic accounts would lead us to believe, nor are there clear differences between midwives and physicians.

Most obstetrical treatises published in the first three-quarters of the eighteenth century emphasized the terrors of obstructed birth. Even authors who mistrusted "man-midwifery" and the use of forceps acknowledged the problems. Sarah Stone, an English midwife writing in 1737, described a breech delivery in which it took her an hour and a half to turn and extract the fetus. When she reached for the child, it "suck'd my fingers in the Womb, which concern'd me, fearing it impossible for the poor Infant to be born alive." Writing two decades later, Dr. Edmund Chapman, an English physician, included more gruesome tales. Among cautionary examples he cited one ignorant doctor who, not knowing "the Method of *Turning* a Child, made frequent use of the *Hook* and the *Knife*, and several other shocking and barbarous instruments, even while the Child was *Living*." Dr. William Smellie, the London physician whose improved forceps supposedly solved such problems as these, included vivid case studies in his published works, evenhandedly distributing the blame for mismanaged deliveries among superstitious midwives and

[11] The lack of detail in the other sources makes it difficult to know whether the data are precisely comparable. Ballard's diary distinguishes between stillbirths and deaths within a few minutes or hours of birth. If other records melded those two categories, her record would look better by comparison. Still, adding the five very early deaths in her practice to stillbirths results in a ratio of only 2.3, almost identical with Jackson's and slightly lower than Baldwin's. Jennet Boardman's register includes three categories: "born dead," "died," and "died at age ——— or on ———." I list all those infants described as "dead" or "born dead" as stillborn, but exclude the "died" entries, some of which deaths may have occurred immediately after birth.

TABLE I
COMPARATIVE STILLBIRTH RATES

	Total Births	Total Stillbirths	Stillbirths per 100 Live Births
Martha Ballard Augusta, Maine 1785-1812	814	14	1.8
Hall Jackson Portsmouth, N.H. 1775-1794	511	12	2.4
Lydia Baldwin Bradford, Vt. 1768-1819	926	26	2.9
James Farrington Rochester, N.H. 1824-1859	1,233	36	3.0
Jennet Boardman Hartford, Conn. 1815-1849	1,113	36	3.3
Portsmouth, N.H. 1809-1810	541	14	2.7
Marblehead, Mass. 1808	222	7	3.3
Exeter, N.H. 1809	53	1	1.9
United States* 1942			2.0

* Fetal death ratio, defined as fetal deaths of 28 weeks or more gestation per 1,000 live births.

Sources: Martha Moore Ballard Diary, 2 vols., Maine State Library, Augusta, Maine; J. Worth Estes, *Hall Jackson and the Purple Foxglove: Medical Practice and Research In Revolutionary America, 1760-1820* (Hanover, N.H., 1979), 120; A Copy of Records from an Original Memorandum Kept by Mrs. Lydia (Peters) Baldwin, typescript, Baker Library, Dartmouth College, Hanover, N.H.; James Farrington Medical Record Books, 1824-1859, Special Collections, Dimond Library, University of New Hampshire, Durham; "Midwife Records, 1815-1849, Kept by Mrs. Jennet Boardman of Hartford," Connecticut Historical Society, *Bulletin*, XXXIII (1968), 64-69; Lyman Spalding, *Bill of Mortality for Portsmouth*, Broadside (Portsmouth, N.H., 1809, 1810); John Drury, *Bill of Mortality for Marblehead, 1808*, Broadside (Marblehead, Mass., 1809); Joseph Tilton, M.D., *Bill of Mortality for Exeter, New Hampshire*, Broadside ([Exeter, N.H., 1809]); Helen M. Wallace, "Factors Associated with Perinatal Mortality and Morbidity," in Helen M. Wallace, Edwin M. Gold, Edward F. Lis, eds., *Maternal and Child Health Practices: Problems, Resources, and Methods of Delivery* (Springfield, Ill., 1973), 507.

poorly trained physicians. In comparison, Ballard's delivery descriptions are remarkably bland: "the foet[u]s was in an unnatural posetion but I Brot it into a proper direction and shee was safe delivered." Usually she said even less: "removed obstructions" or "used means."[12]

Just as striking, given the tenor of the prescriptive literature, is her independence of Hallowell's physicians. Although the English authors agreed that midwives were capable of handling routine deliveries, authorities differed on the question of their ability to negotiate emergencies. Most publishing physicians argued that the sign of a good midwife was her willingness to call for help when needed. As Brudenell Exton put it, "the more knowledge they have, the readier they are to send for timely Assistance in Cases of Danger." Sarah Stone, the English midwife, disagreed, as did Nicholas Culpeper, a seventeenth-century herbalist and astrologer whose books were still being reprinted in New England in the early nineteenth century. Culpeper told the "Grave Matrons" who followed his advice that "the Lord will build you Houses as he did the Midwives of the *Hebrews*, when *Pharaoh* kept their Bodies in as great bondage as *Physitians* of our times do your Understandings." Both authors believed that experienced midwives were better equipped to handle difficult deliveries than officious but poorly prepared physicians.[13]

Ballard's philosophy was closer to Culpeper's than to Exton's. Although she had cordial relations with Hallowell's physicians, several of whom occasionally officiated at routine births, she seldom needed their help. A handful of her patients called *both* a doctor and a midwife at the onset of labor, but even in those cases she usually handled the delivery. Only twice in her entire career did she summon a doctor in an emergency, once in 1785 and again in 1792. She was not herself responsible for the first emergency. Arriving late, she found the patient "greatly ingered by some mishap," though the midwife or neighbor who had delivered the child did "not allow that shee was sencible of it." Calling the doctor may have been

[12] Stone, *A Complete Practice of Midwifery* . . . (London, 1737), 76-77; Chapman, *A Treatise on the Improvement of Midwifery, Chiefly with Regard to the Operation* . . . , 3d ed. (London, 1759), xiv; Smellie, *A Collection of Cases and Observations in Midwifery*, 3d ed., III (London, 1764), for example, 1-69, 416-427; Ballard Diary, Aug. 29, 1797, July 19, 1794, Feb. 18, 1799.

[13] Nich[olas] Culpeper, *A Directory for Midwives; or, A Guide for Women, in Their Conception, Bearing, and Suckling Their Children* . . . (London, 1651), "Epistle Dedicatory"; Stone, *Complete Practice*, ix; Henry Bracken, *The Midwife's Companion; or, A Treatise of Midwifery, Wherein the Whole Art Is Explained* . . . (London, 1737), 146; Chapman, *Improvement of Midwifery*, vii-xiii; Brudenell Exton, *A New and General System of Midwifery* . . . (London, 1751), 11. The library of the College of Physicians and Surgeons, Philadelphia, has an autographed and annotated copy of Exton owned by Dr. John McKechnie, who emigrated from Scotland to Maine in 1755 and apparently practiced medicine until his death in 1782. Martha Ballard may have known him; three of his married daughters were among her patients (James W. North, *The History of Augusta* [Augusta, Maine, 1870], 913-914).

Ballard's way of resolving a disagreement over the severity of the injury.[14]

In the other case she described her feelings in vivid language, though characteristically she offered little obstetrical detail:

> My patients illness Came on at 8 hour morning. Her women were Calld, her Case was Lingering till 7 p.m. I removd difuculties & waited for Natures opperations till then, when shee was more severly atackt with obstructions which alarmed me much. I desird Doct Hubard might be sent for which request was Complid with, but by Divine assistance I performed the oppration, which was blisst with the preservation of the lives off mother and infant. The life of the latter I dispard off for some time.

In the margin of the day's entry she added, "The most perelous sien I Ever past thro in the Course of my practice. Blessed be God for his goodness."[15] Whether Dr. Hubbard's emergency skills included the forceps delivery of a living child or only the dismembership of a dead one, we do not know. Fortunately, in this case as in all the others, Ballard and her patient got along without him.

In difficult deliveries, she typically gave God the credit for her success. The phrases are formulaic: "Her illness was very sever a short space but Blessed be God it terminated in Safety and the infant is numbered among the living," or "She had a Laborious illness but Blessed be God it terminated in safety. May shee and I ascribe the prais to the Great Parent of the universe."[16] One should not assume from such language, however, that Ballard lacked confidence in her own ability or that she relied on faith to the exclusion of skill. She knew that God worked through her hands.

Her confidence may actually have increased with the arrival of Dr. Benjamin Page in Hallowell in 1791. Page is remembered in local history as an extraordinarily successful physician. When he died in 1844, after more than fifty years of practice, the *Boston Medical and Surgical Journal* published an eleven-page biography proclaiming his skills as a general practitioner, surgeon, and gentleman. According to the anonymous author, Page was also "unequalled in the success of his obstetric practice. . . . [H]e attended upwards of *three thousand females in their confinement, without the loss of a single life from the first year of his practice!* This is almost miraculous, and may challenge the professional records of Europe or America for anything to compare with it."[17]

This is not the picture of Page preserved in Ballard's diary. Her first encounter with the young doctor was at the delivery of his near neighbor, Mrs. Benjamin Poor, the wife of a printer newly arrived in the town.

[14] Ballard Diary, Nov. 11, 1785.
[15] *Ibid.*, May 19, 1792.
[16] *Ibid.*, June 30, 1807, Mar. 31, 1800.
[17] "Memoir of Benjamin Page, M.D.," *Boston Medical and Surgical Journal*, XXXIII (1845), 9, 173.

Perhaps the woman intended medical delivery; perhaps she was simply worried that her midwife would not arrive in time. "I Extracted the child," Ballard wrote. "He Chose to close the Loin." The language is opaque here, suggesting either a friendly division of duties or an officious take-over by the doctor. The second encounter was more troublesome. Ballard had been sitting up all night with twenty-year-old Hannah Sewall, who had recently arrived in Hallowell from the town of York. "They were intimidated," she wrote, "& Calld Dr. Page who gave my patient 20 drops of Laudanum which put her into such a stupor her pains (which were regular & promising) in a manner stopt till near night when she pukt & they returned & shee delivered at 7 hour Evening of a son her first Born."[18] Hannah Sewall's intimidation, so called, may have had something to do with the fact that she had grown up in an elite family in a coastal town and was already familiar with medical delivery. As for Ballard, she was openly annoyed. Thereafter she was unmerciful in reporting Page's mistakes.

"Sally Cocks went to see Mrs. Kimball," she wrote. "Shee was delivered of a dead daughter on the morning of the 9th instant, the operation performed by Ben Page. The infants limbs were much dislocated as I am informed." She even questioned the doctor's judgment on nonobstetrical matters. Called to treat an infant's rupture, she recommended the application of brandy. "They inform me that Dr. Page says it must be opined [opened], which I should think improper from present appearance," she added. In June 1798, while she was engaged in another delivery, the doctor again delivered a stillborn child. Her report of the event was blunt: "Dr Page was operator. Poor unfortunate man in the practice."[19]

Page was unfortunate, but in eighteenth-century terms he was also ill prepared, as his administration of laudanum at Hannah Sewall's delivery suggests. The prescriptive literature recommended the use of opiates for *false* pains but not for genuine labor; Page was apparently having difficulty telling one from the other. Experience was the issue here as in so many other aspects of midwifery. Ballard had sat through enough lingering labors to know promising pains from false ones. Her reference to the doctor's dislocation of an infant's limbs also suggests lack of familiarity with the difficult manual operation required in breech births. The English midwife Sarah Stone had warned against doctors like him, "boyish Pretenders," who having attended a few dissections and read a few books professed to understand the manipulative arts so important to midwifery. Even Henry Bracken, an author who insisted that midwives should call in

[18] Ballard Diary, Nov. 17, 1793, Oct. 9-10, 1794. For additional detail on relations between midwives and physicians in Hallowell see Laurel Thatcher Ulrich, "Martha Moore Ballard and the Medical Challenge to Midwifery," in James Leamon and Charles Clark, eds., *From Revolution to Statehood: Maine in the Early Republic, 1783-1820* (Hanover, N.H., 1988), 165-183.
[19] Ballard Diary, July 8, Aug. 14, 1796, June 14, 1798.

a doctor in difficult births, cautioned, "I would never advise any one to employ a *young* physician."[20]

After 1800, Page's misadventures disappear from the diary. Presumably, he eventually learned the obstetrical art in the way Ballard did—by experience.

Extracting the child was only part of the problem. Toward the end of the eighteenth century, English writers began to give as much attention to the dangers of the lying-in period, particularly the problem of childbed fever, as to delivery itself. Puerperal fever may in fact have been rare in England in the early years of the eighteenth century; obstetrical treatises published before 1760 rarely comment on its treatment.[21] Thomas Denman's *Essays on the Puerperal Fever* appeared in London in 1768. Four years later, Charles White appended a detailed account of puerperal mortality in British hospitals to his *Treatise on the Management of Pregnant and Lying-In Women*.[22]

Puerperal fever is a wound infection caused by bacterial invasion of the uterine cavity. The infectiousness of the disorder was first suggested in the 1840s by Dr. Oliver Wendell Holmes in the United States and Dr. Ignaz Semmelwis in Austria, though the bacteriology of the disease was not settled until the 1880s, when Louis Pasteur demonstrated the presence of what is now known as streptococcus in patients suffering from the affliction. The symptoms—elevated temperature, headache, malaise, and pelvic pain—usually do not appear until several days after delivery. With certain strains of bacteria there is a profuse and foul-smelling discharge.[23]

At least one of Martha Ballard's patients probably died of puerperal infection. Mrs. Craig was "safe Deliverd of a very fine Daughter" on March 31, 1790, but after five days finding her "not so well as I could wish," Ballard administered a "Clister [enema] of milk, water, & salt" and applied an "ointment & a Bath of Tansy, mugwort, Cammomile & Hysop which gave Mrs. Cragg great relief." A week later the woman was still "Exceeding ill." Someone (perhaps a physician) prescribed rhubarb and Peruvian bark but without effect. A day or two later Dr. Cony "plainly told the famely Mrs. Cragg must die." She expired that night. Ballard helped

[20] Thomas Denman, *An Introduction to the Practice of Midwifery* (New York, 1802 [orig. London, 1794, 1795]), 179; Stone, *Complete Practice*, 76-77, xiv; Bracken, *Midwife's Companion*, 194.

[21] Exton, for example, gives no more attention to childbed fever than to afterpains (*System of Midwifery*, 150). In addition to the English works cited above, I have read the Worcester, 1794, edition of Alexander Hamilton, *Outlines of the Theory and Practice of Midwifery*, first published in Edinburgh in 1784. It also ignores the problem.

[22] White, *A Treatise on the Management of Pregnant and Lying-In Women* ... (London, 1772).

[23] Erna Ziegel and Carolyn Conant Van Blarcom, *Obstetric Nursing*, 6th ed. (New York, 1972), 522-526; Wertz and Wertz, *Lying-In*, 119-128; Leavitt, *Brought to Bed*, 154-155.

dress her body for burial. "The Corps were Coffined & sett in the west room," she wrote. "Purge & smell very ofensive." Meanwhile, neighbors came by turns to "give the infant suck."[24]

Although Ballard attempted no diagnosis in this case, the symptoms fit the clinical description of puerperal fever. Perhaps one or two others among the five maternal deaths in her practice can also be attributed to infection. One woman was "safe delivered," fell ill a few days later, and died two weeks after delivery. Another died four days after giving birth at a time when scarlet fever, a form of streptococcus infection, was present in the town. In the two remaining maternal deaths, however, other symptoms were apparent. One woman was suffering from measles.[25] The other was in convulsions when delivered of a stillborn daughter and was still experiencing "fitts" four days later when she died. She was no doubt a victim of eclampsia, the most severe stage of an acute toxemia of pregnancy, a condition that is still considered one of the gravest complications of childbirth today.[26]

The Ballard diary suggests that puerperal infection was present in late eighteenth-century Maine, but the random appearance of the disease shows why it was seldom identified and discussed. In contrast, contemporary English physicians were encountering a truly alarming phenomenon. Charles White reported mortality rates for several London and Dublin hospitals that at midcentury were losing one out of every thirty or forty patients to puerperal fever. In 1770, in one London hospital, one of every four women died, most from infection. (See Table II.) White was astonished that two hospitals that had been established at the same time, were an equal distance from the center of London, were directed by eminent physicians, and treated the same number of patients should have markedly different death rates. In true Enlightenment fashion he concluded that one hospital smothered patients with an artificial regimen, while the more successful one was not only less crowded and closer to fields and fresh air but obliged patients to do more for themselves.

White believed that bad habits led to childbed fevers. "Violence used either by instruments or by the hand, in the extraction of the child or the placenta," might bring on an inflammation of the womb, a condition made worse by the custom of pampering women in childbed. A woman should not be delivered in a hot room, or have her child or placenta dragged from her, or lie in a horizontal position in a warm bed drinking warm liquids for a week after delivery. Physicians and midwives were both to blame for practices that all too frequently led to maternal death. He suspected that lower-class women, who could not afford pampering, did better in childbirth than their more affluent neighbors, and he cited christening and

[24] Ballard Diary, Mar. 31, Apr. 4, 5, 10, 11, 12, 13, 15, 16, 1790.
[25] Ibid., Oct. 18, 21, 24-29, 1802.
[26] Ibid., Feb. 26, 27, Mar. 1, 2, 4, 1789; Ziegel and Van Blarcom, Obstetric Nursing, 208-213.

TABLE II
COMPARATIVE MATERNAL MORTALITY RATES

Place	Total Births	Maternal Deaths	Deaths per 1,000 Births
London A			
1767-1772	653	18	27.5
1770	63	14	222.2
London B			
1749-1770	9,108	196	21.5
1770	890	35	39.3
London C			
1747-"present"	4,758	93	19.5
1771	282	10	35.4
London D	790	6	7.5
Dublin A			
1745-1754	3,206	29	9.0
Dublin B			
1757-1775	10,726	152	14.1
1768	633	17	26.8
1770	616	5	8.1
Martha Ballard			
1777-1812	998	5	5.0
1785-1812	814	5	6.1
United States			
1930			6.7
1935			5.8
1940			3.8
1945			2.1

Sources: Charles White, *A Treatise on the Management of Pregnant and Lying-In Women* (Worcester, Mass., 1793 [orig. publ. London, 1772]); Ballard Diary; Wallace, Gold, and Lis, eds., *Maternal and Child Health Practices*, 285.

death ratios from London and Manchester parish records to prove his point.[27]

Had White known about Martha Ballard, he would have had a ready explanation for her success: she practiced among frontier women who lived close to nature. In fact, Ballard was probably guilty of one of the practices White deplored—using hot drinks laced with alcohol. Still, there

[27] White, *A Treatise on the Management of Pregnant and Lying-In Women* (Worcester, Mass., 1793 [orig. publ. London, 1772]), 17-31, 219, 236-240. White's estimates for London and Manchester work out to maternal mortality rates of 13/1000 and 6/1000 respectively. For a modern effort to compute maternal mortality ratios from parish christening and death records, see B. M. Willmott Dobbie, "An Attempt to Estimate the True Rate of Maternal Mortality, Sixteenth to Eighteenth Centuries," *Medical History*, XXVI (1982), 79-90. Dobbie believes that maternal mortality in England may have been as high as 29/1000, as compared with earlier estimates of 10-15/1000.

is plenty of evidence in the diary of the kind of vigor he admired. Ballard's patients were not all as sturdy as Mrs. Walker, who was "sprigh about house till 11 [and] was safe delivrd at 12," or as courageous (or foolhardy) as Mrs. Herriman, who "wrode in a sleigh 13 miles after her illness was on her"; but few Hallowell women could afford to lie in bed.[28] Ballard's own daughter, Dolly Lambert, was "so well as to be helpt up and sett at table for breakfast" twenty-four hours after giving birth to her fourth child. Ballard generally left her patients in the care of an afternurse a few hours after delivery, but when she stayed overnight she helped to get the woman out of bed in the morning. "Got my patient up, Changd her Lining and came home," she wrote (in this case, twelve hours after delivery), and "help[ed] Mrs Williams up & maid her Bed and returned home" (twenty-four hours after birth).[29]

Modern epidemiology confirms Charles White's belief that environment affected mortality, though, of course, the theoretical explanations differ from his.[30] Because Ballard was a part-time practitioner who delivered women at home and shared their postpartum care with nurses and family members, she had little opportunity to spread puerperal infection from one patient to another. The opposite conditions existed in the London hospitals, where as White himself suspected, the use of instruments in delivery probably increased the lacerations and tears that encouraged septicemia. Higher incidence of venereal disease in London may also have been a factor.[31]

That childbearing was safer in rural Maine than in London hospitals hardly seems surprising. The more interesting question for our purposes is how the literature emanating from those hospitals affected obstetrical practice in country places. Here the writings of Dr. Jeremiah Barker of Gorham, Maine, are particularly revealing. In February 1785 Barker initiated a discussion in the *Falmouth [Maine] Gazette* over the causes of an unusual "mortality among child-bed women, which has prevailed of late." Dr. Nathaniel Coffin, whose practice was in Falmouth (now Portland), submitted an angry response that was published in the next issue of the paper. Yes, several women had died in childbed in and about the town, but since the cause was unknown there was nothing that could have been done to save them. He denied that there was an epidemic, and he accused Barker of awakening "all those fears and apprehensions, which are but too

[28] Ballard Diary, Mar. 11, 1790, Jan. 19, 1800.

[29] *Ibid.*, Apr. 17, 1801, May 31, 1799, Nov. 28, 1787; see also *ibid.*, June 30, 1794, June 3, 1795, Aug. 10-11, 1799.

[30] Some 19th-century Americans debating the causes of childbed fever used the same environmental argument, anticipating the conclusions but not the logic of 20th-century historians (Charles E. Rosenberg, *The Care of Strangers: The Rise of America's Hospital System* [New York, 1987], 124-126, 376, n. 10, n. 11).

[31] Dorothy I. Lansing, W. Robert Penman, and Dorland J. Davis, "Puerperal Fever and the Group B Beta Hemolytic Streptococcus," *Bulletin of the History of Medicine*, LVII (1983), 70-80. On the complexities of the puerperal fever debate in the 19th and early 20th centuries see Leavitt, *Brought to Bed*, chap. 6.

often cherished by the sex." The debate continued through four issues of the newspaper, Barker insisting that an excess of bile characterized all the cases of puerperal fever he had studied, Coffin retorting that Barker had misread the symptoms.[32]

Barker included additional detail on the puerperal fever controversy in "History of Diseases in the District of Maine," a manuscript that he wrote after his retirement from active practice in 1818. Taken together, the newspaper stories and the "History" tell us a great deal about how medical reforms, initiated in London, were received in America. In his letters to the *Falmouth Gazette* Barker appears as a bold empiric asserting the power of direct experimentation against the dated theories of academic physicians. In his manuscript he reveals that the source of his ideas was a work by Thomas Denman, presumably his 1768 essays on puerperal infection.[33]

According to Barker's history, the puerperal fever outbreak began at the same time as an equally troubling rash of wound infections. In the spring of 1784, he recalled, "some unusual appearances took place in wounds & bruises, even trivial ones, which baffled the skill of the Surgeon, and issued in the death of the patient. . . . Local inflammations chiefly from injuries were more frequent and untractable during the year than I ever knew them to be before or since. The subjects of these complaints were chiefly males and apparently of good constitutions."[34] At the same time, several women in Gorham, Falmouth, and adjoining towns contracted puerperal fever. Although Barker made no connection between the two phenomena, it is difficult for a twentieth-century reader to avoid doing so.

Since Barker gave no statistics on the number of men who died from infected wounds or of women who suffered from childbed fever, and since birth and death records for the region are incomplete, it is impossible to know how serious the problem really was. Barker simply tells us that few women who suffered childbed fever survived, and that he attended autopsies in three different towns. Yet his description confirms the rarity of the disorder in the region. "The ill success which attended my practice," he wrote, "induced me to write to several aged & experienced physicians in different portions of Massachusetts, for advice, as puerperal fever had never appeared among us excepting in a few sporadic cases, which yielded to common means." His correspondents had never seen such an epidemic themselves, but they referred him to the works of Denman and other unnamed British authors. It was from Denman's book, apparently, that Barker got his notions about bile and the use of "the bark" (quinine) as a remedy. He also wrote to Dr. Ammi Ruhamah Cutter of Portsmouth, New Hampshire, who had reportedly experienced high mortality from

[32] *Falmouth Gazette and Weekly Advertiser*, Feb. 12, 26, Mar. 5, 12, 1785.
[33] Jeremiah Barker, "History of Diseases in the History of Maine," chap. 3, Barker Papers, Maine Historical Society, Portland.
[34] *Ibid.*

childbed fever. Cutter suggested applying "fermenting cataplasms to the abdomen composed of flower & yeast."[35]

Barker credited none of these sources in his 1785 newspaper letters, however, nor did he elaborate on the problems in his own practice. Alluding to an unusual childbed mortality, "especially in the town of Falmouth" (where Nathaniel Coffin practiced), he offered his remedies as a disinterested effort to "secure the happiness of mankind." Although he claimed to have "taken the opinion of the Massachusetts Medical Society," he gave no names.[36] Whom was he addressing? Surely not his fellow doctors. If that had been his intent, he would have limited himself to the private correspondence he had already begun. Instead he reached beyond the medical fraternity to the literate public of his region. The very form of his argument suggests that some part of his intended audience was female.

When Barker asserted that his patients could testify to the effectiveness of his methods, Coffin countered, "I am sorry the Dr. is obliged to have recourse to the female sex for a vindication of them." He suggested that the young doctor read "Astruc, Brooks, and others" to correct his faulty diagnosis. Barker retorted that the proposed authors were not only "Obsolete" but "esteemed of less consequence, in many respects, than the opinion of some of the female sex, founded on experience, in this more enlightened age."[37] The reliance on experience was, of course, a staple of Enlightenment medicine. Whereas earlier physicians had relied on theoretical learning, English reformers like William Smellie had emphasized the necessity for practical training in the manual arts of midwifery. Ironically, the obstetrical Enlightenment encouraged physicians to assume women's work in the very act of celebrating its importance. As Thomas Denman expressed it, "A natural labour was the last thing well understood in the practice of midwifery, because scientific men, not being formerly employed in the management of common labours, had no opportunity of making observations upon them."[38]

Barker's regard for female experience was conditional. He praised enlightened women who sought his care but mistrusted traditional midwives and nurses. His case notes from 1774 describe his efforts to deliver a woman with an imperforate vagina after the ministrations of her "friends" had failed. "I found that nothing could be done but to dilate the Perineum for the egress of the Child," he wrote, "and 'tho the operation is simple, yet fearing the sensure of the Vulgar (if any misfortune should befall the patient, afterwards) advised to send for Dr. Savage as an

[35] Ibid.

[36] Falmouth Gaz., Feb. 12, 1785.

[37] Ibid., Feb. 26, Mar. 5, 12, 1785. Coffin was perhaps referring to Richard Brookes, The General Dispensatory . . . (London, 1753), or The General Practice of Physic . . . (London, 1754) and to Jean Astruc, A Treatise of the Diseases of Women . . . , 2 vols. (London, 1762), or Elements of Midwifery, containing the Most Modern and Successful Method of Practice in Every Kind of Labor . . . (London, 1766). Astruc's works were translated from the French.

[38] Smellie, Collection, III, 533-543; Denman, Introduction, I, 171.

assistant." As it happened, the dead fetus was delivered before the second physician arrived.[39] Barker's concern about the censure of "the Vulgar" suggests the difficulties many physicians had in establishing credibility in the region, not only in obstetrical but in general medical cases. One young man entering practice in Waterville, Maine, in the 1790s even signed contracts with prospective patients, promising not to charge them if his remedies failed.[40]

Like Benjamin Page of Hallowell, Barker had begun his medical career after a brief apprenticeship with a Massachusetts physician. In 1774 he was twenty-two and in his second year of practice. The newspaper debate suggests that, ten years later, he had grown tired of his practice in Gorham and adjoining towns, and perhaps hoped to attract the attention of prosperous families in the port of Falmouth.[41] Jeremiah Barker knew that women, whether vulgar or enlightened, were guardians of a doctor's reputation.

For his part, Coffin was furious at Barker for questioning the skills of other physicians. He was also dismayed that the younger doctor should invoke the authority of the Massachusetts Medical Society, even though he was not a member. When Coffin wrote to the society in 1803 recommending a number of new members from Maine, he explicitly excluded Barker, partly on the basis of the 1785 affair, which still rankled. (The society ignored his advice and elected Barker anyway.)[42] Thus a young physician moving into obstetrical practice in the 1780s and 1790s had two obstacles to overcome—folk reliance on traditional midwifery and the mistrust of older, more conservative physicians.

For our purposes, however, the more important issue is the way in

[39] Jeremiah Barker, Medical Cases, 1771-1796, Barker Papers.

[40] Loose paper dated Apr. 29, 1802, Moses Appleton Papers, Waterville Historical Society, Waterville, Me. On the larger question of lay resistance see William G. Rothstein, *American Physicians in the Nineteenth Century: From Sects to Science* (Baltimore, 1972), 128-138, and Joseph F. Kett, *The Formation of the American Medical Profession: The Role of Institutions, 1780-1860* (New Haven, Conn., 1968), 101-107.

[41] Barker was born in Scituate, Mass., began his practice in Gorham, Me., in 1772, removed to Barnstable on Cape Cod after a year, returned to Gorham in 1779, and finally went to the Stroudwater section of Falmouth in 1796 (James Alfred Spalding, *Jeremiah Barker, M.D., Gorham and Falmouth, Maine, 1752-1835*, reprinted from *Bulletin of the American Academy of Medicine*, X ([1909], 1-2). Barker had an indirect link to British medicine. In mid-career his mentor, Dr. Bela Lincoln of Hingham, Mass., had spent a year studying in London hospitals and acquiring an M.D. from King's College, Aberdeen. Spalding, *Barker*, 1-2; Clifford K. Shipton, *Sibley's Harvard Graduates: Biographical Sketches of Those Who Attended Harvard College*, XIII (Boston, 1965), 456.

[42] Nathaniel Coffin to Massachusetts Medical Society, May 8, 1803, and Jeremiah Barker to Joseph Whipple, July 12, 1803, Countway Medical Library, Boston. In the long run, Barker may have been more forgiving than Coffin. His manuscript history describes Coffin as a physician "who commanded an extensive practice in physic, surgery and obstetrics, with good success" ("History," chap. 2).

which the puerperal fever incident of 1784-1785 began to shape Barker's practice. All of the cases of childbed fever described in his history came from that outbreak, yet he used them to support a long, detailed discussion of the cure and prevention of the disorder. Even by his own account, puerperal fever cannot have been a serious problem in the region. Most of the physicians to whom he wrote had seen only scattered cases; all of them referred him to British authors for an understanding of the subject. Coffin even doubted that the deaths could be attributed to a single disease, and he questioned whether he or any other physician could have done anything to prevent them. In Barker's own practice the trouble also faded away. There were additional cases during the winter of 1784-1785, he wrote, yet the disease showed "decreasing malignancy and mortality. Since which it has not appeared among us, excepting in a few sporadic cases, which seldom proved fatal."[43] Yet by 1818 his interpretation of the 1784-1785 cases had expanded to encompass citations from medical literature published as late as 1817.[44] Barker measured his entire career against that single early disaster. Since it was never repeated, he assumed that his preventative practices were successful.

Barker combined the noninterventionist prescriptions of the late eighteenth century—better ventilation, lighter food, avoidance of alcohol—with more heroic measures. "The means of prevention may be reduced to two," he argued. First, the physician should treat the patient during labor as though she were already a victim of the disease, drawing blood, administering emetics and cathartics, debarring her "entirely from spirits," and keeping her "on a low diet, without any animal food, in a well ventilated apartment without any curtains, on a mattress or straw bed." The second method involved "facilitating or rather hastening, by artificial means, the termination of labour."[45] Presumably, this meant using forceps and possibly ergot, a powerful and dangerous drug that, when given orally, stimulates uterine contractions.[46] In this, Barker departed from the advice of his 1784 mentor, Thomas Denman, who, like Charles White, believed that forceps should be used rarely and that hastening labor led to postpartum complications.[47]

What we have, then, is a clear example of the way in which medical literature in combination with local experience came to define a practice.

[43] Barker, "History," chap. 2.

[44] *Ibid.* The citations on puerperal fever are, as he gave them, "Dr. Terriere, 1789; Dr. Biskell, *Medical Papers*, v. 2, 1798; *London Medical Repository*, May 1815; *New England Journal*, v. 4, 5; Dr. Channing, *New England Journal*, vol. 6, 1817; *Medical Repository*, vol. II."

[45] Barker, "History," chap. 2.

[46] Leavitt, *Brought to Bed*, 144-145.

[47] On some things Denman had changed his own mind by 1794. Although he continued to oppose intervention in labor, he did accept bloodletting as a cure for puerperal fever, something he had dismissed in his earlier treatise, as had Barker in his *Falmouth Gaz.* letters. Denman, *Introduction*, I, 184-190, II, 253-254; *Falmouth Gaz.*, Feb. 26, 1785.

Barker's need to differentiate himself from other practitioners, as well as his desire to apply the latest in scientific knowledge to the management of his practice, made it impossible for him to see the 1784-1785 outbreak as an anomaly. Thereafter, he was convinced that it was his own intervention that had prevented a similar disaster from occurring. In contrast, Martha Ballard's nonscientific, even providential interpretation of events enabled her to treat each case on its own terms. For every patient, she did what she knew how to do and let God determine the outcome. This is not to say that she was incapable of experimentation or that she never wondered why one infant died and another lived. It is simply to argue that her craft was oriented toward practical results rather than theoretical explanation. The death of Mrs. Claton or Mrs. Craig did not destroy her confidence in the soundness of her methods. Hers was not an approach that encouraged innovation, but neither did it promote ill-considered intervention.

Adrian Wilson has estimated that, in nature, 96 percent of births occur spontaneously. Approximately 4 percent involve serious obstruction of some kind and cannot be delivered without intervention. An additional 1 percent, though spontaneous, result in complications—minor ones such as fainting, vomiting, and tearing of the perineum, or major events like hemorrhaging or convulsions.[48] Martha Ballard's records fit Wilson's typology well. Approximately 95 percent of her entries simply say "delivered" or "safe delivered." In the remaining 5 percent, some sort of complication is indicated, by explicit reference to obstructions, an oblique comment on the severity of the labor, or simply an acknowledgment that the delivery was accomplished through the mercy of God. Her records thus attest to the relative safety of childbearing as well as to her skill in managing difficult labors. Her ministrations no doubt improved the conditions of birth, but, perhaps even more important, she did little to augment the dangers.

In this regard it is interesting to compare her records with those of James Farrington of Rochester, New Hampshire, a nineteenth-century physician whose caseload was similar to hers and whose records, unlike those of his eighteenth-century predecessors, are extraordinarily complete. Dr. Farrington began the study of medicine in 1814, two years after Ballard's death. His manuscript records include a systematic register of 1,233 deliveries performed between 1824 and 1859. At first glance, his stillbirth and mortality ratios confirm the conclusions of revisionist histories—that childbirth became more dangerous in the nineteenth century. Farrington's stillbirth ratios are higher than any of the eighteenth-century practitioners and closer to those of the nineteenth-century midwife Jennet Boardman. (See Table I.) Even more striking is the number of maternal deaths at delivery. That he was occasionally called to complete someone else's mismanaged delivery is certain, though those few cases that include extended descriptions suggest that, regardless of

[48] Adrian Wilson, "William Hunter and the Varieties of Man-midwifery," in Bynum and Porter, eds., *William Hunter*, 344-345.

practitioner, nineteenth-century obstetrical practice added new dangers to the old problems of obstructed birth. Curiously, there is no indication of puerperal fever in Farrington's records. One might have expected at least a few cases of infection over such a long career. Since his tightly organized accounts, with one exception, list deliveries *only*, it is possible that such cases, usually arising a week or so after delivery, appeared in another set of more general medical records.[49]

Farrington recorded five maternal deaths. One woman, he wrote, was "enfeebled by intemperance." Another had a severe cold and "spoke but few words after delivery, but sunk away without a groan." The most dramatic case had been abandoned by another physician. Farrington described it as "preternatural labor requiring in the end the dissection of the infant," adding details that might have come from English obstetrical literature a hundred years before: "the external parts of generation much lacerated and mangled by *hooks, pincers, and knives.*" The woman survived Farrington's extraction of the dismembered fetus but died five days later. A fourth woman died of bleeding after an unidentified attendant failed to extract the placenta. The fifth woman suffered a ruptured uterus: "in a few minutes the whole child could be felt expelled from the Uterus within the abdominal cavity." The woman lived about an hour.[50]

The numbers are small, however, and, without more detail on postpartum infection, inconclusive. The most striking contrast between Farrington's and Ballard's records is not in mortality rates themselves but in their characterizations of delivery. The process of labor was biologically the same, yet their descriptions differ markedly. Whereas Ballard thought in terms of the general outcome ("left mother and child cleverly"), Farrington focused on theoretical categories. Labors were "natural," "tedious," "premature," "preternatural," "complicated," or, after 1838, "instrumental," regardless of whether the mother and child survived.[51] Twenty percent of the deliveries in his records are listed as something other than "natural."[52]

[49] Franklin McDuffie, *History of the Town of Rochester, New Hampshire, from 1722 to 1890*, ed. Silvanus Hayward (Manchester, N.H., 1892), I, 345-346; James Farrington Medical Record Books, 1824-1859, Special Collections, Dimond Library, University of New Hampshire, Durham. Farrington added an entry about the woman dying five days after delivery in different colored ink at the end of his delivery record. On the general pattern of listing childbed deaths under other causes see Wertz and Wertz, *Lying-In*, 125-126.

[50] Farrington, Medical Record, Case #451, Sept. 9, 1835, #118, Feb. 24, 1825, #442, May 28, 1835, #292, Jan. 30, 1831.

[51] Farrington used forceps before 1833; he just did not have a separate category to cover instrumental labors.

[52] Joan M. Jensen's analysis of 109 deliveries by an early 19th-century Chester, Pa., physician shows no maternal deaths at delivery, 7% stillbirths, and 30% difficult labors (*Loosening the Bonds: Mid-Atlantic Farm Women, 1750-1850* [New Haven, Conn., 1986], 30-33). The low caseload of this physician, roughly 14

Here the telltale category may be his 102 cases of "tedious" labor, defined in the medical literature as lasting longer than twenty-four hours. In one case, which terminated safely at twenty-six hours, Farrington reported taking blood from the woman's arm, then giving an opiate. Four hours before the birth he gave her "Ergot in Infusion" and was pleased when he was able to deliver the child "without Instruments though for several hours no alteration was made by the force of the Pains."[53] Reading such an account, one finds it difficult not to think of Ben Page's administration of laudanum at the delivery of Hannah Sewall. Ironically, the remedy that so dismayed Martha Ballard was by now a standard part of the physician's arsenal. The three remedies—laudanum, ergot, and forceps—went together, accomplishing, as the physicians and perhaps many of their patients thought, an artificial hastening of labor.[54]

Judith Walzer Leavitt has argued that women chose medical intervention. Sally Drinker Downing, for example, sought out the services of the Philadelphia physician William Shippen, who administered opium during her 1795, 1797, and 1799 deliveries. Leavitt concludes that "the prospect of a difficult birth, which all women fearfully anticipated, and the knowledge that physicians' remedies could provide relief and successful outcomes led women to seek out practitioners whose obstetric armamentarium included drugs and instruments."[55] Leavitt may be right about Downing, yet Martha Ballard's diary adds a new dimension to the question of choice. At ten o'clock on the evening of October 21, 1794, she was summoned to the house of Chandler Robbins, a Harvard graduate and new resident of Hallowell. "Doctor Parker was call'd," she wrote, "but shee did not wish to see him when he Came & he returnd home. Shee was safe delivered of a son her first Born at 10 hour 30 minutes Evening"— that is, twenty-four and one-half hours after summoning the midwife. Ballard's reward for officiating at this "tedious labor" was eighteen shillings and the satisfaction of knowing that God and the parents were pleased.

This brief survey of Martha Ballard's diary and related documents supports the reformist point that birth is a natural process rather than a life-threatening event. It suggests that rural midwives were capable of managing difficult as well as routine births, that the need for medical intervention was by no means obvious, and that puerperal infection, though present, was still only a random problem in the last years of the eighteenth century. For midwives like Martha Ballard or Lydia Baldwin, experience defined competence, yet in the years following the Revolution a number of brash young men with more confidence than experience took

---

deliveries a year, suggests the presence of other practitioners, probably including midwives.
[53] Denman, *Introduction*, 171; Farrington, Medical Record, Case #539, Aug. 8, 1839.
[54] Leavitt, *Brought to Bed*, 43-44.
[55] *Ibid.*, 40.

up the practice of delivering babies. Not content with the more restrained role of older doctors, they consulted British literature and sought advice from other physicians to solve their problems and validate their skills. That they gravitated toward works that emphasized the necessity of intervention is hardly surprising. In a competitive environment no bright young physician could embrace Charles White's advice that the less done in childbirth the better. Employing forceps, letting blood, administering opiates and ergot, they set themselves apart from the manual skills and the providential faith of the midwives.

During the earlier years of Martha Ballard's midwifery in Hallowell, however, the success of such physicians was by no means assured. In 1800, when age, ill health, and a move to a more distant part of the town forced her to cut back her practice, she was the single most important practitioner in her town, and she knew it.

Between Slavery and Freedom: Virginia Blacks in the American Revolution

By Sylvia R. Frey

The American Revolution was a social and economic upheaval of cataclysmic proportions. Its disruptive and destructive effects were more profoundly felt in the South than anywhere else in the country.[1] In part this was due to prolonged conventional operations there, but it was also due to the ferocious fratricidal war that distinguished the Revolution in the South. In states such as Virginia, with a high concentration of enslaved people, the disorder endemic to the war awakened chronic white fears of a general servile uprising. Although slave unrest was widespread, no revolt by force of arms occurred. The fact that North American slaves were less "conspicuously rebellious" in the Revolutionary era than were slaves in the British Caribbean has concerned a number of historians. One scholar views the absence of any massive revolt as the result of changes in the southern labor force during the first half of the eighteenth century: the shift from free, independent labor to slave labor; from a free, depressed lower class of potentially armed and dangerous men to a totally oppressed, permanently enslaved labor force with "no hope, no rising expectations, and no arms."[2] A more recent study contends that the North American plantation organization, with the dominating presence of the master, inhibited the development of the tribal cohesiveness that characterized the islands' plantation organization

---

[1] Two recent essays which make this point are Mary Beth Norton, "'What an Alarming Crisis Is This': Southern Women and the American Revolution," in Jeffrey J. Crow and Larry E. Tise, eds., *The Southern Experience in the American Revolution* (Chapel Hill, 1978), 203–34; Ronald Hoffman, "The 'Disaffected' in the Revolutionary South," in Alfred F. Young, ed., *The American Revolution: Explorations in the History of American Radicalism* (DeKalb, Ill., 1976), 273–316.

[2] Edmund S. Morgan, "Conflict and Consensus in the American Revolution," in Stephen G. Kurtz and James H. Hutson, eds., *Essays on the American Revolution* (Chapel Hill, 1973), 295.

Ms. Frey is associate professor of history at Newcomb College, Tulane University.

The Journal of Southern History
Vol. XLIX, No. 3, August 1983

and produced widespread violence against whites by black guerrilla bands.[3]

The purpose of this essay is first to suggest that the absence of any major slave revolts in Virginia and elsewhere in the South during the Revolutionary era should not obscure the high degree of resistance to slavery that existed there. Secondly, it is to argue that to a far greater extent than is generally recognized the actions of both belligerents discouraged large-scale insurrections. In his classic work *The Negro in the American Revolution* Benjamin Quarles maintains that "The number of Negroes who fled to the British ran into the tens of thousands."[4] Contemporary estimates of total slave losses in the South ran as high as 55,000,[5] although estimates of individual state losses taken together are considerably higher even than that. The Revolutionary War's historian, David Ramsay, for example, claimed that South Carolina alone lost 25,000 slaves.[6] Jefferson calculated Virginia's fugitives to be "30,000 in the one year of 1778."[7] The lack of hard statistics makes it impossible to ascertain precisely how many Virginia slaves "voted with their feet" by defecting to the British. But Virginia's slave population of about one-quarter million was concentrated in the Tidewater section of the state most ravaged by war. Good evidence from widely scattered sources, both British and American, strongly suggests that Jefferson's estimates of slave losses might in fact be reliable.

Long before the British tendered their help, blacks began defecting to them in the mistaken belief that the British view of slavery was substantially different from that of most Virginia planters. Late in 1774, for example, "a few of those unhappy wretches" met together and selected a leader "who was to conduct them when the English troops should arrive." According to James Madison, who reported the conspiracy to William Bradford, the slaves expected freedom in exchange for their defection. Their plans were, however, "discovered and proper precautions taken to prevent the Infection." Fearing its disruptive effect, Madison closed with a warning that "It is prudent such things should be concealed as well as suppressed."[8]

[3] Michael Mullin, "British Caribbean and North American Slaves in an Era of War and Revolution, 1775–1807," in Crow and Tise, eds., *The Southern Experience in the American Revolution*, 235–67.

[4] Quarles, *The Negro in the American Revolution* (Chapel Hill, 1961), 119.

[5] Quoted in Jeffrey J. Crow, "Slave Rebelliousness and Social Conflict in North Carolina, 1775 to 1802," *William and Mary Quarterly*, 3d Ser., XXXVII (January 1980), 89.

[6] Ramsay, *History of South Carolina from Its First Settlement in 1670 to the Year 1808* (2 vols., Newberry, S. C., 1858), I, 272.

[7] Thad W. Tate, *The Negro in Eighteenth-Century Williamsburg* (Williamsburg, Va., 1965), 219.

[8] To William Bradford, November 26, 1774, William T. Hutchinson, William M. Rachal, *et*

But blacks continued to flock to the British. The arrival in Norfolk in July 1775 of British troops from St. Augustine produced "exceeding bad effects" upon the blacks in the area.[9] Disturbed over the "elopement" of their slaves to the men of war, a deputation from the borough of Norfolk waited upon Captain John McCartney, commanding officer of the *Mercury,* and Matthew Squire, commanding the *Otter.*[10] Despite repeated assurances from both officers that no encouragement would be given runaways, numbers of slaves, individually and in pairs, fled to the war craft and were welcomed on board. Inhabitants near Elizabeth City County were particularly incensed at Captain Squire for harboring and employing the slaves who came to him while the *Otter* lay in the York River. By September it was painfully clear to the inhabitants of Norfolk and Elizabeth City counties that the British naval force had not only welcomed slaves who came to them, but in some instances had seized and carried away several free blacks.[11]

Moreover, although Governor John Murray, fourth Earl of Dunmore, had not as yet openly invited a slave rebellion, he had secret plans to do so. The suspicions held by the rebellious planters that the governor was "tampering with the Slaves and that he has it in contemplation to make great use of them in case of a civil war in this province,"[12] were in fact well founded. In a letter to the Earl of Dartmouth written in March reporting on the gunpowder affair Dunmore announced his intention to "arm all my own Negroes and receive all others that will come to me whom I shall declare free." Properly armed, he boasted, his force would soon "reduce the refractory people of this Colony to obedience."[13]

In August the officers of the American volunteer companies in Williamsburg informed the Virginia convention that "The Governor's Cutter has carried off a number of Slaves belonging to private gentlemen[.]"[14] Moved perhaps by the officers' urgings that it was "high

---

al., eds., *The Papers of James Madison* (13 vols. to date, Chicago, London, and Charlottesville, 1962-), I, 129-30.

[9] Norfolk Borough Committee to Peyton Randolph, July 31, 1775, Robert L. Scribner and Brent Tarter, eds., *Revolutionary Virginia. The Road to Independence* (6 vols. to date, Charlottesville, 1973-), III, 378.

[10] *Virginia Gazette* (Dixon and Hunter), August 5, 1775.

[11] Norfolk Borough Committee to Randolph, July 31, 1775; Virginia Committee of Safety at Williamsburg, October 24, 1775, Scribner and Tarter, eds., *Revolutionary Virginia*, III, 378; IV, 269.

[12] To William Bradford, June 19, 1775, Hutchinson, Rachal, *et al.,* eds., *Papers of James Madison*, I, 153.

[13] Dunmore to Dartmouth, March 1, 1775, Colonial Office Papers, Class 5/1373 (Public Record Office, London, Eng.); hereinafter cited as C.O. 5 with appropriate numbers.

[14] Officers to the President and Gentlemen of the Convention, Scribner and Tarter, eds., *Revolutionary Virginia*, III, 385.

[time] to establish the doctrine of repraisal [*sic*] & to take immediate possession (if possible of his person) at all events of his property,"[15] the Virginia Committee of Safety ordered Colonel William Woodford to lead his own regiment and five companies of minutemen to Norfolk to protect and defend "the persons and properties of all friends to the cause of America."[16] Dunmore's military operations in Virginia in the following months have been so frequently described and at such length that a detailed account here is unnecessary. For nearly a year he led or ordered spoiling operations along Virginia's waterways, causing considerably more fear than havoc. After several minor clashes with militiamen, Dunmore declared martial law on November 7, 1775. Shortly afterwards he issued his famous proclamation from on board the *William*, which he had seized from local merchants and fitted out for war. Directed principally at "all indented Servants, Negroes, or others, (appertaining to Rebels,) . . . that are able and willing to bear Arms,"[17] Dunmore's proclamation was designed to encourage the defection of useful blacks without provoking a general rebellion.

It has been estimated that no more than eight hundred slaves were able to reach Dunmore. That figure is probably low. For nearly a year Dunmore's small tenders plied Virginia's rivers, "Plundering plantations and using every Art to seduce the Negroes."[18] Small bands of his soldiers, most of them black, made frequent sorties on shore to liberate or to seize fellow blacks.[19] Although most of the slaves who deserted to Dunmore fled as individuals or in small groups, there were instances of successful desertion by a plantation's entire slave force. For example, all eighty-seven of John Willoughby's slaves fled his plantation in Norfolk County to join Dunmore.[20] Despite heavy losses by death and by capture, when Dunmore abandoned Gwynne's Island in June 1776 he left tents "capable of containing about 700 or 800 men,"[21] which suggests substantial augmentation by runaways.

After Dunmore's expulsion in August 1776 Virginia was not invaded again for several years, although the Chesapeake was regularly raided by British barges and by privateers. In a coastal raid in

[15] *Ibid.*
[16] Orders for Colonel William Woodford, *ibid.*, IV, 270.
[17] Dunmore's Proclamation, November 7, 1775, *ibid.*, IV, 334.
[18] Quarles, *Negro in the American Revolution*, 31; Robert Carter Nicholas to the Virginia Delegates in Congress, November 25, 1775, Julian Boyd *et al.*, eds., *The Papers of Thomas Jefferson* (18 vols. to date, Princeton, 1950–), I, 266–68 (quotation on p. 267).
[19] *Virginia Gazette* (Dixon and Hunter), December 2, 1775.
[20] "Petitions and Letters to the Convention, Governor or House of Delegates Praying for Relief, 1775–1783," *Richmond College Historical Papers* (2 vols., Richmond, 1915), II, 342.
[21] From John Page, July 12, 1776, "Lee Papers," New-York Historical Society, *Collections*, V (New York, 1873), 134.

February 1777, for example, "British ships in the Bay . . . [took] on board" approximately three hundred blacks from Northumberland, Gloucester, and Lancaster.[22] British operations in the bay during the summer of 1777 also stirred up considerable black unrest. In an effort to execute the British strategy of securing the middle colonies by capturing Philadelphia, General Sir William Howe proceeded to the Quaker City by way of Chesapeake Bay. Blacks flocked "down from the interior parts of the country,"[23] enticed by British promises of "fine cloaths and other inducements."[24] As the British fleet advanced up the bay to Head of Elk in Maryland, eight or ten privateers followed in its wake. ". . . they purpose to lie behind the fleet," an observer in Annapolis wrote, ". . . and then run along shore, and into the unguarded rivers, and plunder the inhabitants. Negroes are their chief object, whom they intend to sell in the West Indies."[25]

But it was the area of sprawling plantations and extensive slaveholding, situated between the Rappahannock and James rivers, that suffered the most severe losses. In their erratic progress back and forth through the low country British armies commanded by Benedict Arnold, William Phillips, and Charles Cornwallis, second Earl Cornwallis, wreaked economic havoc along the lower James and York rivers and on the shores of the Chesapeake and Potomac. In each of these extended operations the state lost heavily in tobacco, horses, and slaves.[26] General Henry Clinton sent an expedition to Virginia from New York in May 1779. Led by Admiral Sir George Collier and General Edward Matthews, this was the first of several water expeditions into the deeply indented Virginia shore. Meeting no opposition at Portsmouth, the two-thousand-man force remained in the area for ten or twelve days, destroying public stores and plundering the inhabitants of livestock and slaves. Using Portsmouth as a center, they sent out raiding parties, one of which burned the town of Suffolk and destroyed thousands of barrels of pork and great quantities of naval stores. After filling twenty-eight transports with an estimated three thousand hogsheads of tobacco, several thousand head of cattle and horses, and one thousand slaves, they hoisted sail and put to sea.[27]

[22] Quarles, *Negro in the American Revolution*, 117.
[23] William Paca to Governor Johnson, September 26, 1777, Maryland State Papers, Rainbow Series: Red Books, 4562-1 (Maryland Hall of Records, Annapolis, Md.).
[24] Benjamin Rumsey to Governor Johnson, August 27, 1777, *ibid.*, 4561-69.
[25] *Virginia Gazette* (Purdie), September 26, 1777.
[26] Lewis C. Gray, *History of Agriculture in the Southern United States to 1860* (2 vols., Washington, 1933), II, 589-92, 602-608, 615-17.
[27] Robert Honeyman Diary, June 1, 1779 (Manuscript Division, Library of Congress, Washington, D. C.). Honeyman, a Hanover County physician and planter, was a neutral during most of the war. His account of events was apparently gathered from newspapers, rumors, and personal experience but is generally a reliable source. See also *Virginia Gazette* (Dixon

When, later in August, Matthews left Virginia to rejoin Clinton in New York he took with him 518 more blacks, 256 of them men, 135 of them women, and 127 children.[28] Simultaneously with Matthews's operations, British privateers roamed the Potomac, burned the tobacco warehouse and several vessels loaded with tobacco at Wicomico, and carried off a number of slaves and livestock.[29]

Near the end of October a British fleet commanded by General Alexander Leslie entered the capes of Virginia and landed about three thousand men at Portsmouth. Apparently ordered by Clinton to penetrate the Chesapeake Bay to prevent Virginia and Maryland from sending military supplies and troop reinforcements to Horatio Gates's army after the Battle of Camden,[30] the expedition lay quietly for three or four weeks in the Portsmouth area, venturing out only as far as Hampton to collect livestock. American observers, by now accustomed to seeing their slaves taken, noted in astonishment that they "behaved with great moderation . . . took nothing but provisions; prohibited all plundering; dismissed the Negroes who came to join them and even gave up some vessels they took in Portsmouth harbour."[31] Finding "something Mysterious in their leaving their Slaves on shore . . . ," Edmund Pendleton speculated that the fleet lacked either the room or the manpower to accommodate them, or else that they had "designs of further Hostility."[32] In fact, the Patriot victory at King's Mountain, which forced Cornwallis to retreat from Charlotte to Winnsboro, and the rapid build-up of Virginia militia to oppose Leslie led to the decision to withdraw Leslie's troops, which were needed to reinforce Cornwallis, and forced Leslie to turn away the slaves who fled to him.[33]

Leslie's fleet had hardly cleared the bay before another fleet entered the Virginia capes on December 30 and soon afterwards sailed up Hampton Roads. Commanded by Benedict Arnold, the 1,600-man force was sent by Clinton to conduct harassing raids. The object of the operation was to aid Cornwallis in North Carolina by burning the Virginia stores that supplied Nathanael Greene and by perhaps forcing Greene to divert some of his troops away from North

---

and Nicolson), May 29, 1779; Hon. Whit. Hill to Hon. Thomas Burke, Executive Letter Book, 1779, William L. Saunders and Walter Clark, eds., *The Colonial and State Records of North Carolina* (30 vols., Raleigh and other cities, 1886–1914), XIV, 1–4.

[28] Quarles, *Negro in the American Revolution*, 115.

[29] Honeyman Diary, June 28, 1779.

[30] Hutchinson, Rachal, *et al.*, eds., *Papers of James Madison*, II, 156, n. 1.

[31] Honeyman Diary, December 2, 1780.

[32] From Edmund Pendleton, November 27, 1780, Hutchinson, Rachal, *et al.*, eds., *Papers of James Madison*, II, 208.

[33] *Ibid.*, 156n1.

Carolina toward Virginia.[34] Reinforced by two thousand men, Arnold began the systematic raiding that devastated James River communities all the way up to Richmond. The primary objective of the expedition was destruction of public stores: rum, tobacco, and arms and ammunition at the foundry at Westover. The secondary objective of Arnold's Virginia operations was plunder.

With no army to oppose it, this small British force seized and destroyed much of the state's resources and carried away a vast amount of booty: flour, leather, war materiel of every description including brigantines, sloops, and schooners loaded with goods of a great value. The area also lost heavily through the flight or seizure of slaves: "The families within ye Sphere of his Action," the Reverend James Madison wrote to his son, "have suffered greatly. Some have lost 40, others 30, every one a considerable Part of their Slaves."[35] In March Major General William Phillips brought another 2,500 men to Virginia to join Arnold's force for a new invasion projected from Portsmouth. The combined force now commanded by Phillips conducted raids of exceptional severity in the low country. Pursuing a policy of systematic devastation, the Phillips-led troops reportedly seized or burned eight thousand hogsheads of tobacco at Petersburg, Osborne, Manchester, and Blandford, greatly disturbing the industry. To fill their need for cavalry and wagon horses, they seized hundreds of horses, producing a desperate scarcity that continued for some time after the war.[36]

As the army advanced up the James River, numbers of slaves, perceiving that freedom was at hand, "flocked to the enemy from all quarters, even from very remote parts . . . ."[37] Looking on with a sense of incredulity, Edmund Pendleton observed "so infatuated are these wretches that they continue to go to them, notwithstanding many who have escaped inform others of their ill treatment, those who are not sent off to the West Indies being kept at hard labour upon very short allowance, so as to perish daily."[38] Except for a few

[34] Franklin and Mary Wickwire, *Cornwallis: The American Adventure* (Boston, 1970), 252.

[35] From the Rev. James Madison, January 18, 1781, Hutchinson, Rachal, *et al.*, eds., *Papers of James Madison*, II, 293.

[36] Descriptions of the raids can be found in Samuel Graham, "An English Officer's Account of His Services in America—1779–1781," *Historical Magazine*, 1st Ser., IX (August 1865), 246–48; John G. Simcoe, *Simcoe's Military Journal. A History of the Operations of a Partisan Corps, Called the Queen's Rangers* . . . (New York, 1844), 194; Banastre Tarleton, *A History of the Campaigns of 1780 and 1781 in the Southern Provinces of North America* (London, 1787), 335–40; Frederick Mackenzie, *Diary of Frederick Mackenzie, Giving a Daily Narrative of His Military Service as an Officer of the Regiment of Royal Welsh Fusiliers During the Years 1775–1781* . . . , edited by A. French (2 vols., Cambridge, 1930), II, 522.

[37] Honeyman Diary, May 11, 1781.

[38] From Edmund Pendleton, May 7, 1781, Hutchinson, Rachal, *et al.*, eds., *Papers of James Madison*, III, 111.

planters who managed to remove their slaves "up the country," most of those who lived along the river's edge lost heavily: "Some lost 30, 40, 50, 60 or 70 Negroes besides their stocks of cattle, sheep and horses."[39] At the end of the war several prominent men from Princess Anne and Norfolk counties submitted a memorial to Commander-in-Chief Guy Carleton requesting his aid in recovering "at least 300 negroes" taken by the army in its operation there.[40] Raids carried on simultaneously in the Potomac up to Alexandria also did considerable damage as the British landed troops on both sides of the river to burn houses, destroy shipping, and steal or entice slaves.[41]

On May 6 Phillips received word from Cornwallis informing him of the earl's intention to abandon North Carolina and inaugurate a campaign in Virginia. Phillips immediately marched to Petersburg to await Cornwallis there but died of a fever five days before the earl arrived.[42] Late in May Cornwallis began the long campaign that ended in Yorktown. Leading a disciplined and mobile army, he covered vast distances, interrupted only by a number of engagements. From Petersburg to Hanover Courthouse, to Old Albemarle Courthouse, north to Richmond, south again to Williamsburg, Jamestown, Suffolk, and Portsmouth, he finally reached Yorktown on August 2.

Faced with the grim prospect of losing all their slaves, white families along the route of Cornwallis's army hastily removed them and their livestock to safer ground.[43] Failure to do so proved for many to be a costly mistake. After the army passed Mattoax near Petersburg William Withers reported to St. George Tucker that Tucker's wife's plantation had lost its work force: "Not any of your Negroes at Mattoax have appeared at Suppy. Your overseer has now only two Hands able to work and one Horse." Worried about bringing in the crops, Withers advised Tucker that "if you have any such as will not go off to the Enemy, I wou'd advise your sending him those . . . ."[44] Assessing the situation later in August, Withers described conditions as still "greatly distressed" by sickness and desertion among the slaves.[45] In his own cryptic shorthand he told how losses in crops, livestock, and labor were for many planters compounded by "the treachery of the Negroes beyond expectation, often where concealed discover their Masters and their Propty at Petersburg sd. to be some thouds."[46]

[39] Honeyman Diary, May 11, 1781.
[40] Hutchinson, Rachal, et al., eds., Papers of James Madison, VII, 6, n. 3.
[41] George Mason to Virginia Delegates, April 3, 1781, ibid., III, 55; Honeyman Diary, April 30, 1781.
[42] Wickwire and Wickwire, Cornwallis, 319, 326.
[43] William Withers to St. George Tucker, May 20, 1781, Tucker-Coleman Papers (Earl Gregg Swem Library, College of William and Mary, Williamsburg, Va.).
[44] Ibid.
[45] Ibid., August 10, 1781.
[46] Ibid., May 20, 1781.

Although Cornwallis's army "did not compel any" slaves to go with them, "wherever they had an opportunity the soldiers and inferior officers likewise, enticed and flattered the Negroes and prevailed on vast numbers to go along with them . . . ."[47] Urged by Virginia authorities to release captured slaves, Cornwallis readily conceded that "great numbers have come to us from different parts of the country." How many cannot be precisely ascertained, but Clinton observed that on the day he took command in Virginia, Cornwallis had "above 7,000 men," and "I have always understood thousands of poor blacks." When he surrendered at Yorktown, Cornwallis had, according to Clinton, some 5,000 sailors and blacks, in addition to 4,000 regular troops. Since only about 800 of the 5,000 were "man of war sailors," the rest were apparently runaways.[48]

In the absence of full statistics on slave losses, isolated figures such as those presented here are highly suggestive if not definitive. The conclusion is inescapable that the volume of runaways was large—so large as to threaten the stability of slave society and create a severe shortage of slave laborers. By 1780 inflation and British raids had driven the price of "common planting Negroes" to over £4,000 and of "boys and girls" to £3,000 in terms of current money.[49] It is very possible that the demand for slave labor, which continued into the postwar years, inhibited rather than inspired the movement for emancipation.

Virginia authorities, faced with the loss of the work force and haunted by the consuming fear of an organized slave rising, imposed a rigorous system of controls to minimize the possibilities for mass escapes and reduce the opportunities even for individual defections. Citizen patrols were increased to maintain constant surveillance of blacks. Since Virginia slaves traditionally escaped through the web of waterways that interlaced the Tidewater region,[50] whenever British barges were known to be in an area the militia was sent out to remove all small craft moored at landings in coves on the numerous creeks and rivers.[51] Laws that were both co-optive and repressive were quickly enacted by the Virginia Convention. To discourage defections, the convention offered pardons to all fugitives who voluntarily

[47] Honeyman Diary, May 27, 1781.

[48] Cornwallis to Gov. Thomas Nelson, Jr., July 1781, Cornwallis Papers PRO 30/11/5, ff. 155–62 (Public Record Office); cited hereinafter as PRO 30/11. Benjamin F. Stevens, ed., *The Campaign in Virginia, 1781. An Exact Reprint of Six Rare Pamphlets on the Clinton-Cornwallis Controversy, with Very Numerous Important Unpublished Manuscript Notes by Sir Henry Clinton* . . . (2 vols., London, 1888), I, 76, 1a, 2d.

[49] Honeyman Diary; the entry carries no specific date but is with the material for the beginning of 1780.

[50] See Gerald W. Mullin, *Flight and Rebellion: Slave Resistance in Eighteenth-Century Virginia* (New York, 1972), for a thorough discussion of the problem through the entire century.

[51] From Lt. Col. Read, April 7, 1776, "Lee Papers," IV, 390.

returned within ten days and approved the death penalty for those captured from the British.[52] Another law decreed that slaves taken in arms would be transported and sold in the West Indies.[53]

Because it was thought to have an immediate and enduring impact, swift exemplary punishment was sometimes employed. One slave, the property of William Smith, was shot and killed after refusing to surrender to Virginia troops.[54] Two runaways, mistaking an American armed vessel in the James River for a British tender, declared their desire to serve Lord Dunmore and were promptly arrested, tried, and sentenced to death "as an example to others."[55] Shortly after Dunmore's Proclamation nine blacks, two of them women, were taken in an open boat trying to reach Norfolk. Two were wounded; the rest, the *Virginia Gazette* ominously predicted, "will soon be made examples of."[56]

Since, however, the state was responsible for compensating the owners of executed slaves[57] and because runaways were often the most skilled and therefore the most valuable slaves Virginians frequently resorted to more practical forms of punishment in order to protect costly investments in human chattel. In a typical case, four Northampton County slaves were captured while attempting to reach Dunmore: two of them were sentenced to be hanged, the other two each to have one ear cut off, to be given thirty-nine lashes on the bare back, and then to be placed in the pillory.[58] But the owners of the four slaves, Thomas Parramore and John Bowdoin, Jr., both prominent Northampton County planters, pleaded that "these deluded Wretches" were persuaded by an unidentified white man of the "extraordinary good treatment" of blacks by Dunmore and so endeavored to escape to him.[59] The Virginia Committee of Safety ordered a letter written to Northampton County officials recommending them to delay the execution of the slaves until the convention could rule on the matter. The Virginia Convention ultimately granted a reprieve

---

[52] *The Proceedings of the Convention of Delegates . . . on the 20th of March, 1775* (Richmond, 1816), 66.

[53] William W. Hening, ed., *The Statutes at Large; Being a Collection of All the Laws of Virginia from the First Session of the Legislature in the Year 1619* (13 vols., Richmond, New York, and Philadelphia, 1819–1823), IX, 106.

[54] *The Proceedings of the Convention of Delegates on Monday . . . the 6th of May, 1776* (Richmond, 1816), 10.

[55] *Virginia Gazette* (Dixon and Hunter), April 13, 1776.

[56] *Ibid.*, December 2, 1775.

[57] A 1705 statute impowered justices to value condemned slaves; public funds were used to compensate the owner once the assembly was satisfied of the claim. Tate, *Negro in Eighteenth-Century Williamsburg*, 178–79.

[58] Scribner and Tarter, eds., *Revolutionary Virginia*, VI, 305, 485.

[59] *Ibid.*, 449–50. Two of the four slaves in question were valued at £76 5s which perhaps influenced their owners. *Ibid.*, 485.

and ordered the prisoners sent to work in the lead mines in Fincastle County instead.[60]

Hard labor in remote Fincastle or Montgomery county mines had the clear advantage over execution of removing potential trouble-makers without substantial cost to the state. At the same time it provided a work force to produce lead for cartridges, of which the state was "in *extreme want*."[61] Throughout the Revolution numbers of slaves, some of them "merely suspected of a design to . . . escape" to the British, were escorted under heavy guard to the mountainous western region of the state to labor in the lead mines. Others were put to work making saltpeter, so they could perform useful service without causing further trouble.[62]

Transportation and incarceration, though they contributed nothing to the expansion of the state's industrial base, also militated against a servile rising. At the urging of some inhabitants of Norfolk and Princess Anne counties[63] the Virginia Convention invoked the law allowing transportation and sale to rid the state of troublesome blacks. In January 1776, for example, the convention ordered thirty-two blacks taken prisoner at Great Bridge to be "properly valued" and then to be transported for sale in the West Indies or the Bay of Honduras, the profits after expenses to be paid to their respective owners. Nine others apprehended as runaways but, not being suspected of bearing arms against the state, were ordered restored to their owners if claimed; if unclaimed they were to be sold at public auction.[64] The black crews of several vessels "supposed to be British property" were also ordered sold at public auction by the convention, with the proceeds paid to the state.[65]

Yet another means of handling captured fugitives was to incarcerate them in the public gaol at Williamsburg. Although some of the prisoners were put to labor on public-works projects, many of them languished and died while awaiting trial. After several slaves died in the Williamsburg jail[66] their owners petitioned the convention to investigate conditions there. Since the state was liable for their deaths the convention appointed a committee to the task. The com-

[60] *Proceedings of the Convention of Delegates . . . on Monday, the 6th of May, 1776*, p. 26.

[61] To Samuel Huntington, March 21, 1781, Boyd *et al.*, eds., *Papers of Thomas Jefferson*, V, 199.

[62] *Proceedings of the Convention of Delegates . . . on Monday, the 6th of May, 1776*, pp. 17, 29, 36, 37.

[63] *The Proceedings of the Convention of Delegates . . . on Friday, the 1st of December, 1775* (Richmond, 1816), 94–95.

[64] *Ibid.*, 99–100.

[65] *Proceedings of the Convention of Delegates . . . on Monday the 6th of May, 1776*, pp. 65–66.

[66] *Ibid.*, 10, 25.

mittee reported that the "jail, being badly planned and situated for the purpose of admitting a free air . . ." was also greatly overcrowded. The rooms which contained the black prisoners "abound with filth . . . owing to the want of necessary hands to assist in providing for so large and unusual a number of prisoners . . . ." The committee recommended that windows be cut in the walls of the jail and that the rooms be cleaned with vinegar and fumigated with burning tar to eliminate the "offensive smell, which . . . would be injurious to the most robust health . . . ." Fearful of an epidemic of putrid fever, the convention approved the measures.[67]

The apparatus of suppression was designed to intercept those slaves bold enough to try to join the British. The psychology of fear was meant to intimidate those who dreamed of doing so. Mixing persuasion with threats, the *Virginia Gazette* printed grim warnings to its readers, including one addressed directly to their slaves. Professing a desire "to give them a just view of what they are to expect, should they be so weak and wicked as to comply with what lord Dunmore requires," the subscriber predicted that the British, once their ends were served, would "either give up the offending negroes to the *rigour* of the laws they have broken, or sell them in the West Indies, where every year they sell many thousands of their miserable brethren to perish either by the inclemency of the weather, or the cruelty of barbarous masters." After noting that Dunmore's Proclamation did not extend to the aged, the infirm, or to women and children, he reminded those contemplating defection that their defenseless families would be left "at the mercy of an enraged and injured people." If that cruel prospect did not deter them, he urged would-be runaways to consider the difficulties of escaping and "what they must expect to suffer if they fall into the hands of the Americans. . . . whether we suffer or not," he concluded, "if you desert us you most certainly will."[68]

Running away by slaves had been defined as a criminal act in Virginia since 1680.[69] The chances of being caught by the county militia or by a local patrol and of being punished by death, transportation, or hard labor were good, particularly during the war years when white fears of a servile rising were abnormally high. Under these conditions running away was a desperate measure to escape bondage.

[67] *Ibid.*, 36-37.

[68] *Virginia Gazette* (Pinkney), November 23, 1775, quoted in Scribner and Tarter, eds., *Revolutionary Virginia*, IV, 459-62; first quotation on p. 460, second on p. 462, third on p. 461, fourth on pp. 461-62. The editors identify the writer of the piece as John Page, vice-president of the Virginia Committee of Safety. It was entitled "A Few Anonymous Remarks on Lord Dunmore's Proclamation." *Ibid.*, 464, n. 21.

[69] Tate, *Negro in Eighteenth-Century Williamsburg*, 164-65.

Although in the anarchic conditions created by war many slaves eluded both belligerents, the majority fled to the British army, perceiving that it offered them the best prospects for freedom.

In keeping with the promise of freedom given first by Dunmore to Virginia slaves and then made general by Clinton in 1779 the British army received, if it did not always welcome, the runaways. Inhibited by inherited racial attitudes still intrinsic to British society,[70] the army was never genuinely committed to a policy of liberation. Although his proclamation cast Dunmore in the role of liberator, it was by no means a general emancipation. At best, it was a selective offer of freedom, directed principally at "all indented Servants, Negroes, or others, (appertaining to Rebels,) . . . that are able and willing to bear Arms . . . ."[71] Despite his ambitious plans to organize a black army and to use it to discipline the rebellious Virginians, Dunmore was no champion of emancipation. A slaveowner himself, he persistently invited slave defections without, however, freeing his own slaves or unleashing the black violence feared by the horror-stricken proprietor class—a fact that escaped neither the Patriot press nor Virginia slaves. When, for example, two of Dunmore's slaves passed through Fredericksburg en route to his Berkeley plantation the *Virginia Gazette* pointedly noted that "his lordship has not been so very generous to his own bondsmen as he wished to be to those who were the property of others . . . ."[72] Some blacks were equally suspicious of Dunmore's motives. On being asked his opinion of Dunmore's offer of freedom, Caesar, "the famous barber of York," replied "that he did not know any one foolish enough to believe him, for if he intended to do so, he ought first to set his own free."[73] Although Clinton's proclamation promised freedom to those blacks who voluntarily joined the British, it threatened seizure and sale of those taken in arms against the British, the proceeds to be used "for the benefit of their captors."[74]

Selective and limited, British army policy was designed first to meet Britain's special manpower needs: to provide pioneers and military laborers in North America, and to satisfy the perennial shortage of recruits for service in the West Indies, where European troops

---

[70] Sylvia R. Frey, "The British and the Black: A New Perspective," *Historian*, XXXVIII (February 1976), 225-38.

[71] Dunmore's Proclamation, November 7, 1775, Scribner and Tarter, eds., *Revolutionary Virginia*, IV, 334.

[72] *Virginia Gazette* (Purdie), December 9, 1775; January 12, 1776 (quotation).

[73] *Ibid.* (Pinkney), December 9, 1775.

[74] Proclamation, June 30, 1779, British Headquarters Papers (Microfilm, Howard Tilton Library, Tulane University, New Orleans, La.); cited hereinafter as British Headquarters Papers.

were regularly and rapidly destroyed by the climate. The narrow limits of the policy were, moreover, purposely and unashamedly designed to accommodate the army's time-honored practice of taking spoils of war. Military expediency joined to the practice of despoiling the enemy produced a policy of ambivalence that both contradicted and invalidated even their limited and selective offer of freedom. Thus, even while the army acted as the essential catalyst to black resistance to slavery, army priorities, which conflicted with those surrounding emancipation, effectively discouraged slave rebellions of the type found in the West Indies and doomed black resistance in America to the largely individual form of defection to the British.

The army's employment of the former bondsmen lays bare its motives in inviting their defection and reflects the deeply entrenched racial attitudes that imbued it. Although the British stood to gain significant military advantage from their black allies, they made only limited use of blacks in combat. The garrison posted by Dunmore at Great Bridge in Norfolk County was defended by twenty-five privates of the 14th Regiment, some volunteers, and "a good many Negroes."[75] In the encounters preceding the major action at Great Bridge and in the battle of Great Bridge itself Dunmore's black soldiers were in the middle of the action. American forces, in a skirmish on December 4, reported killing sixteen blacks and five whites.[76] The following day an American party that fell in with a guard of about thirty mostly black troops, killed two and took two prisoners.[77] In the action at Great Bridge on December 9 Dunmore's black troops, led by Captain Samuel Leslie, brought up the rear ranks while the elite grenadiers led the advance upon the bridge.[78] Although the action lasted only twenty-five minutes, Americans counted 65 dead and wounded and estimated British losses at 102.[79]

Dunmore's use of armed troops on land was, however, exceptional. Generally, the British preferred to restrict the use of armed blacks to actions at sea. British barges manned by black and white crews plied Virginia's rivers throughout the war. In the summer of 1781, for example, a "felonious corps of negroes and mulattoes," serving on the *Surprise* commanded by a Captain Ross, plundered homes on the

[75] Charles Fordyce to James Urquart, December 1, 1775; Samuel Leslie to General Gage, December 1, 1775, Vol. I, 355, 433, Miscellaneous Papers, Item 51, Intercepted Letters, 1775–81, Records of the Continental and Confederation Congresses, Record Group 360 (National Archives, Washington, D. C.).

[76] *Virginia Gazette* (Pinkney), December 9, 1775.

[77] *Ibid.*

[78] *Ibid.* (Purdie), December 15, 1775.

[79] *Ibid.* (Pinkney), December 13, 1775.

Rappahannock and the Piankatank rivers, "deluded" some slaves to join them, and seized by force those who would not.[80] A Captain Robinson with four barges manned by a hundred mostly black crewmen conducted marauding expeditions through the summer and fall of 1781, leading a harassed resident of the Accomack shore to complain to the commissioner of war that "We have had most alarming times this Summer, all along shore, from a sett of Barges manned mostly by our own negroes who have run off." Eventually, Robinson himself was captured.[81]

The military's reluctance to arm slaves reveals the dilemma inherent in its self-interested policy of emancipation: how to woo slaves belonging to rebels without attracting those belonging to Loyalists; how to induce fear in defiant white southerners without incurring their permanent hostility; how to inspire enough black resistance to satisfy British military needs without inciting rebellion. It was on the rock of this dilemma that British slave policy foundered. Instead of calling slaves to arms, the British army summoned them to serve. Although nominally free once they entered British lines, the majority of blacks continued to be employed in a servile capacity. Several hundred served Cornwallis's army as batmen or body servants, performing duties consistent with servile status in a slave society. Regulations issued by Cornwallis at Petersburg allowed each infantry field officer to keep two blacks; captains, subalterns, staff and quartermaster sergeants, and sergeant majors were each permitted to have one black servant. Frequent reminders in the general orders, however, indicate that the regulations were routinely ignored by officers and that even common soldiers "harboured" black servants.[82]

The great majority of black fugitives worked as military laborers, performing the menial and often the most rigorous and hazardous jobs. Dunmore's black soldiers apparently did all of the drudgery, "acting as scullions, &c. on board the fleet";[83] during emergencies they were "kept constantly employed in digging entrenchments in wet ground, till at length the severity of their labour forced many of them to fly."[84] To spare his white soldiers from an unwholesome climate and

[80] The Humble Petition of Sundry Persons . . . to the Governor of Virginia . . . September 8, 1781, William Palmer et al., eds., *Calendar of Virginia State Papers and Other Manuscripts, 1652-1781, Preserved at the Capitol in Richmond* (11 vols., Richmond, 1875–1893), II, 404–405.

[81] Colonel George Corbin to Colonel William Davies, August 18, 1781; Levin Joynes to Colonel Davies, September 10, 1781, *ibid.*, 340, 411 (quotation).

[82] Regulations Regarding the Number of Negroes and Horses, May 21, 1781, June 18, 1781, Orderly Books, British General and Brigade Orders, Lord Cornwallis, Virginia and Yorktown, May 23–October 22, 1781 (Manuscript Division, Library of Congress); cited hereinafter as General and Brigade Orders.

[83] *Virginia Gazette* (Purdie), March 22, 1776.

[84] *Ibid.* (Pinkney), November 30, 1775.

a severe work schedule General Phillips organized 250 black defectors into a company of pioneers and put them to work erecting fortifications in the sandy soil at Portsmouth. Led by a white officer, the black pioneers were, Phillips reported to Clinton, "of the greatest use" in the various departments of the army and in the construction of works and dams to raise the waters of the creeks.[85] While he remained at Portsmouth, Cornwallis employed over a thousand blacks "to cut wood [and to] work on the trenches . . . ."[86] Later upon his arrival there in August Cornwallis began fortifying Yorktown and Gloucester on the opposite shore. But the construction of earthworks, "carried forward day and night . . . ," took a heavy toll of British troops.[87] Reflecting the common assumption that because of their dark skins and equatorial origins blacks were better able to withstand heat, Cornwallis ordered army blacks to do the heavy labor, observing that "the heat is too great to admit of the soldiers doing it."[88] All of "the other drudgeries," such as burying offal at the cattle pens or clearing the streets of filth and rubbish or digging new and filling in old latrines, were assigned to the black troops to conserve the European troops.[89]

Whereas southern slaveowners often recognized the potential hazards of overexertion and exposure and eased their slaves' tasks at certain times of the year, the British army, driven by the dangers and necessities of war, made excessive demands on its military laborers. At the same time, it failed to provide either adequate food and clothing or effective protective and curative therapy for them. Although all eighteenth-century armies suffered high disease rates, the incidence of disease among army blacks was conspicuously higher than it was among white troops. Hundreds of Dunmore's blacks died of disease, which army doctors attributed to overcrowding and lack of clothing.[90] Deserters from his service complained of "Hungry bellies, naked backs, and no fuel; besides, in other respects, the most cruel and inhuman treatment."[91]

What they probably referred to were the shortages of food and clothing and the overcrowding aboard the tenders, which led to an outbreak of jail fever, forcing Dunmore to land at Tucker's Mills on

[85] Phillips to Clinton, April 3, 1781, PRO 30/11/5, ff. 155–62.
[86] Joseph G. Rosengarten, ed., "Popp's Journal, 1775–1783," *Pennsylvania Magazine of History and Biography*, XXVI (No. 1, 1902), 38.
[87] "The Doehla Journal," translated by Robert J. Tilden, *William and Mary Quarterly*, 2d Ser., XXII (July 1942), 241, 243 (quotation), 244.
[88] Cornwallis to O'Hara, August 4, 1781, PRO 30/11/89, ff. 1–2.
[89] Clinton to Cornwallis, August 30, 1781, Sir Henry Clinton Papers, 1750–1812 (William L. Clements Library, Ann Arbor, Mich.).
[90] Dunmore to Germain, March 30, 1776, C.O. 5/1353, f. 378.
[91] *Virginia Gazette* (Pinkney), December 13, 1775.

the west side of the Elizabeth River.[92] But, prevented by American forces under Lieutenant Colonel Frank Eppes from making incursions into the countryside for food,[93] Dunmore departed the Elizabeth River, leaving behind 150 dead blacks.[94] Late in June he landed some eight hundred, mostly black, troops on Gwynne's Island at the mouth of the Piankatank River. In an effort to contain the spread of smallpox then ravaging his force he inoculated the healthy and sent the infected to hospitals built on the opposite side of the island. Still the disease spread, killing, Dunmore reported to his superiors, "an incredible number of our people, especially the blacks."[95] Daily nearby Virginia troops witnessed the horrible evidence of that mortality: bodies, decimated by disease, floated down the river into which they had been thrown in haste in lieu of burial.[96]

When finally routed by American forces the British vessels slipped their cables and fled Gwynne's Island, abandoning cannon, cattle, horses, furniture, tents for seven to eight hundred men, and several hundred sick, dying, and dead blacks. An American officer, part of the two-hundred-man landing force, recoiled at the "scene of misery, distress, and cruelty, [such as] my eyes never beheld . . .": a child sucking at the breast of its dead mother; adults, still gasping for life, stretched out near the river's edge, where they had crawled to find water and to escape the intolerable stench of the dead bodies that lay uncovered in open fields or sprawled together in shallow, mass graves.[97] Although the total number of the dead cannot be ascertained, one American officer counted 130 graves, "or rather holes," as he put it. In the seven-week occupation of Gwynne's Island, American sources estimated that five hundred of Dunmore's people died, most of them blacks.[98] Twenty years later, "the shocking remembrance of thousands of miserable negroes who had perished there with hunger and disease" still remained. As he traveled along the Elizabeth River, Benjamin Henry Latrobe, architect and engineer, recorded in his journal that "Many Waggon loads of bones of Men women and children . . . covered the sand for a most considerable length. . . . The remnants of decaying rags still point to the skeletons

---

[92] Dunmore to Germain, March 30, 1776, C.O. 5/1353, f. 378.
[93] From Eppes, April 6, 1776, "Lee Papers," New-York Historical Society, *Collections*, IV (New York, 1872), 384.
[94] Honeyman Diary, March 17, 1776.
[95] Dunmore to Germain, June 26, 1776, C.O. 5/1353, f. 386.
[96] From Andrew Lewis, June 12, 1776, "Lee Papers," V, 65.
[97] The source of the first quotation is *Virginia Gazette* (Purdie), July 19, 1776; the description of the child sucking at its mother's breast and the following details are from *ibid*. (Dixon and Hunter), July 20, 1776.
[98] For reports of the scene at Gwynne's Island see From John Page, July 12, 1776, "Lee Papers," V, 134; *Virginia Gazette* (Purdie), July 19, 1776 (quotation).

of many of these miserable victims . . . ."[99]

In February a "contagious Distemper" struck the blacks who had joined Arnold in 1779. Aggravated by severe shortages of provisions that left even the "horses starving for want of Forage,"[100] the disease "raged among the Negroes . . . [and] swept off great numbers of them,"[101] including thirteen to fourteen of Jefferson's runaways.[102] Although blacks are no more or less immune to smallpox than are whites, all other factors being equal,[103] a disproportionately high percentage of black followers of the British army were ravaged by that disease. Inoculation had been the accepted prophylaxis against smallpox since early in the century. Perhaps because the operation was expensive,[104] its use was generally confined to white troops during the Revolution. In June the disease infected the blacks with Cornwallis in Richmond. To impede the contagion inoculation was recommended. It was apparently not universally practiced, however, since a later order urged "such men as never had such disorder to avoid communicating with the nigros, untill a proper oppertunity shall be found to have them inoculated."[105] Perhaps because the prophylactic procedure was confined to only a few, the disease spread rapidly. In July it broke out among the black refugees with Leslie at Portsmouth. Overwhelmed by its pervasiveness, Leslie ordered over seven hundred stricken blacks distributed "about the rebel plantations."[106] Leslie perhaps hoped that as valuable property they would be cared for by whites in the area, but Virginians viewed "their diabolical Practice . . . of sending out amongst us Persons infected with the Small Pox," as a callous attempt to spread one of the most vicious and fatal diseases of the day.[107]

Through the rest of the British presence in Virginia, the virulence and pervasiveness of the disease went unchecked among black followers of the army. On August 5 General Charles O'Hara, who

[99] Edward C. Carter et al., eds., The Virginia Journals of Benjamin Henry Latrobe, 1795-1798 (2 vols., New Haven and London, 1977), I, 83.

[100] Col. James Innes to Jefferson, March 6, 1781, Palmer et al., eds., Calendar of Virginia State Papers, I, 557.

[101] From David Jameson, March 10, 1781, Hutchinson, Rachal, et al., eds., Papers of James Madison, III, 16.

[102] Jefferson's Statement of Losses to the British at His Cumberland Plantations in 1781, January 27, 1783, Boyd et al., eds., Papers of Thomas Jefferson, VI, 224-25.

[103] See Todd L. Savitt, Medicine and Slavery: The Diseases and Health Care of Blacks in Antebellum Virginia (Urbana, Chicago, and London, 1978), for a thorough discussion.

[104] Thomas McKeown and R. G. Brown, "Medical Evidence Related to English Population Changes in the Eighteenth Century," in D. V. Glass and D. E. C. Eversley, eds., Population in History: Essays in Historical Demography (London, 1965), 292.

[105] June 18, 1781, General and Brigade Orders.

[106] Leslie to Cornwallis, July 13, 1781, PRO 30/11/6, ff. 280-81.

[107] Col. John Page to Gov. Nelson, August 7, 1781, Palmer et al., eds., Calendar of Virginia State Papers, II, 300.

replaced Leslie when the latter was ordered to Charleston, wrote to ask Cornwallis's advice about the rapidly worsening situation: "What will you have done with the hundreds of infected Negroes, that are dying by scores every day?"[108] Although humanitarian concern was present in Cornwallis's reply, it was the threat of impending outbreaks of pestilence in the ranks that clearly occupied his attention: "It is shocking to think of the state of the Negroes, but we cannot bring a number of Sick and useless ones to this place; some place must be left for them and some person of the Country appointed to take charge of them to prevent their perishing."[109]

For the time being at least O'Hara ignored Cornwallis's instructions: "Unless I receive orders to the contrary from you," he wrote in reply, "I will continue to victual the sick Negroes, above 1,000 in number. They would inevitably perish," he warned, "if our support was withdrawn. The people of this country are more inclined to fire upon than receive and protect a Negro whose complaint is the smallpox — the abandoning of these unfortunate beings to disease and famine, and what is worse than either, the resentment of their enraged master, I should conceive ought not to be done."[110] Cornwallis's final word on the subject made it clear that the preservation of the more valuable lives of white soldiers was the first priority of his command: "I leave it to your humanity to do the best you can for the poor Negroes, but on your arrival here we must adopt some plan to prevent an Evil which not only destroys a great quantity of Provisions, but will certainly produce some fatal distemper in the Army."[111]

A week later, when the evacuation of Portsmouth began, O'Hara, on Cornwallis's advice, gave military success the highest priority. After promising his superior officer "not [to] leave behind me any thing I conceive to be of smallest service, . . ." O'Hara sent to Cornwallis at Yorktown four hundred fit blacks to meet his pressing need for laborers.[112] As for the sick blacks, "We shall be obliged to leave near 400 wretched Negroes; I have passed them all over to the Norfolk side, which is the most friendly quarter in our neighborhood and have begged of the people of Princess Ann and Norfolk counties to take them." Noting that he had left the sick blacks provisions for forty-five days, O'Hara concluded that such time "will either kill or cure the greatest number of them . . . ."[113]

---

[108] O'Hara to Cornwallis, August 5, 1781, PRO 30/11/70, ff. 12–13.

[109] Cornwallis to O'Hara, August 7, 1781, Charles Cornwallis Papers (microfilm in Alderman Library, University of Virginia, Charlottesville, Va.); the originals are in the Public Record Office, PRO 30/8.

[110] O'Hara to Cornwallis, August 9, 1781, PRO 30/11/71, ff. 16–17.

[111] Cornwallis to O'Hara, August 10, 1781, Cornwallis Papers.

[112] O'Hara to Cornwallis, August 15, 17, 1781, PRO 30/11/70, ff. 20–21, 22–23.

[113] *Ibid.*, August 17, 1781, PRO 30/11/70, ff. 22–23.

Perhaps communicated by the blacks sent by O'Hara from Portsmouth, smallpox broke out among the black troops at Yorktown in August. To make matters worse, the "great number of refugees" from Norfolk, Suffolk, and Princess Anne counties who arrived with O'Hara on August 22[114] led to the rapid consumption of provisions.[115] As supplies dwindled, rations for blacks were the first to be cut. On September 4 orders were given to issue peas instead of flour to the Negroes. Within a week all of the food was bad, and the garrison was forced to eat "putrid ships meat and wormy biscuits that have spoiled on the ships." But when even contaminated rations became scarce, portions allotted to the blacks were surreptitiously withheld. After noting that "Great abuses have been committed in victualling the Negroes," the general orders for September 15 instructed the deputy quartermaster general to collect returns of the blacks with the various departments and to appoint someone to supervise the issuance of their rations.[116]

On October 1 the town of York was completely invested by Franco-American forces. By October 7 the British, forced to abandon several outworks, were confined to a narrow area within the town. Many of the garrison were sick with dysentery and bloody flux or smallpox.[117] On that day an eyewitness reported that the British "have turned several hundred Negroes out of the town in a most deplorable condition, perishing with famine and disease."[118] At the surrender an American account described the tragic conclusion of the black flight to freedom with Cornwallis: "An immense number of Negroes have died, in the most miserable Manner in York."[119]

The maintenance of racial distinctions such as these clearly point up the ambiguities that suffused British policy toward American slaves. So too did the British tendency to view blacks as marketable commodities. White Virginians frequently complained of the British practice of selling captured slaves in the West Indies. Rumors of the transportation and sale of black defectors began soon after Dunmore issued his proclamation and persisted until he abandoned the state. On his departure, for example, it was speculated that the destination of the thirty-five southbound vessels was the sugar islands, where the

---

[114] Cornwallis to Clinton, August 22, 1781, Charles C. Cornwallis, *An Answer to that Part of the Narrative of Lieutenant General Sir Henry Clinton, K. B., Which Relates to the Conduct of Lieutenant General Earl Cornwallis, During the Campaign in North-America in the Year 1781* (London, 1783), 187.

[115] Cornwallis to Clinton, August 22, 1781, PRO 30/11/74, ff. 74–75.

[116] September 15, 1781, General and Brigade Orders.

[117] "Doehla Journal," 245.

[118] Honeyman Diary, October 7, 1781.

[119] Edward M. Riley, ed., "St. George Tucker's Journal of the Siege of Yorktown, 1781," *William and Mary Quarterly*, 3d Ser., V (July 1948), 387.

black troops would be offered for sale.[120] During the Phillips-Arnold raids, it was reported that in one shipment from Yorktown 360 captured blacks were removed for sale.[121]

Whether these charges are true cannot at this point be established. Undoubtedly, many Virginia slaves ended up in military service in the West Indies. A declining white population and an unsuitable climate for Europeans that produced an appallingly high death rate among troops stationed there and created a chronic need for manpower led colonial nations to adopt the practice of recruiting slaves for military service in the Caribbean.[122] During the American Revolution, when the British need for troops there became desperate, the employment of black laborers to conserve the strength of British regulars was accelerated. Several shiploads of "English Negroes," apparently the unclaimed property of Loyalists, were ordered by General Sir John Vaughan to the public service in St. Lucia in 1780.[123] "In 1779 . . . the Black Carolina Corps was raised from among loyalists and free Negroes. After the British surrender at Yorktown this corps was distributed among several British islands . . . ."[124] Upon the evacuation of South Carolina in 1782 General Leslie organized a black corps from among the protected blacks with the army and designated them for service in the West Indies.[125] On Cornwallis's orders Leslie sent two hundred Carolina blacks to St. Lucia to work as military laborers in order to conserve the strength of white troops.[126] In anticipation of an attack by French and Spanish forces the crown late in 1782 authorized the raising of three corps – one of them in America – for the defense of Jamaica.[127]

There is no conclusive evidence, however, that the army engaged in slave traffic. The British record is certainly not above suspicion. The army freed no slaves when such action would seriously hamper the

[120] Peter Minor to Garrett Minor, August 9, 1776, Garrett Minor and David Watson Correspondence (Manuscript Division, Library of Congress). Peter Minor was with the 5th Regiment, which was ordered to defend against a Dunmore landing. Like many other Patriots he reported that half of Dunmore's vessels were departing for the West Indies to sell blacks there. Actually, the thirty-five ships sailed for St. Augustine in East Florida. The blacks aboard were, Governor Patrick Tonyn explained to the Secretary of State, "sent here to be kept in custody," Tonyn to Germain, October 10, 1776, C.O. 5/557, ff.3, 193.

[121] From Edmund Pendleton, May 7, 1781, Hutchinson, Rachal, *et al.*, eds., *Papers of James Madison*, III, 111.

[122] Roger N. Buckley, *Slaves in Red Coats: The British West India Regiments, 1795–1815* (New Haven and London, 1979), 1–4.

[123] A. St. Leger to Sir John Vaughan, December 17, 18, 1780, Sir John Vaughan Papers, 1779–1781 (William L. Clements Library).

[124] Buckley, *Slaves in Red Coats*, 4.

[125] Leslie to Carleton, July 19, 1782, Alexander Leslie Letter Book, Emmet Collection 15628 (New York Public Library, New York City).

[126] Carleton to Leslie, September 10, 1782, British Headquarters Papers.

[127] Archibald Campbell to Carleton, December 6, 1782, PRO 30/55, f. 56.

successful prosecution of the war. On more than one occasion military commanders sacrificed morality to expediency by restoring runaways to their owners. Unable to accommodate all those who claimed his protection, Dunmore disarmed the black soldiers least fit for service and abandoned them to the mercy of their former owners.[128] Despite his obligation to them, Dunmore forced many black defectors to return to their owners who had taken the oath of allegiance to Britain.[129] At Governor Thomas Nelson's request Cornwallis agreed to allow white owners to search for their slaves in British encampments and to take those who were willing to return, provided the former master was neither in the military nor a public official and provided he gave his parole not to act contrary to British interests in the future.[130] Slaves seized from farms on the Rappahannock and the Piankatank rivers by the British privateer *Surprise* were promptly returned from New York and restored to their owners when it was discovered that they were the property of Virginia Loyalists.[131] When, desperate for supplies, the army requested and obtained leave from Virginia authorities to restore kidnapped slaves and other plunder in exchange for provisions, they quickly perverted the flag-of-truce vessels for partisan purposes. Only the slaves belonging to Loyalists or to passive citizens were restored; those belonging to active Patriots were retained.[132]

By these and by related actions the British army demonstrated clearly that what was singularly important to it was military success. Almost equally high among military priorities was the collection and sale of spoils of war. It was the view of the army that captured enemy property could be disposed of in any way the captor deemed proper, and slaves were property.[133] Counterpoised to Clinton's offer of freedom to those blacks who voluntarily joined the British was the threat that all those taken in arms would be "purchased for the public service and sold for the benefit of their captors."[134] A quiet agreement between military and civil officials allowed the sale of spoils to

[128] John R. Sellers, "The Virginia Continental Line, 1775–1780" (unpublished Ph.D. dissertation, Tulane University, 1968), 102.
[129] *Virginia Gazette* (Pinkney), November 30, 1775.
[130] Cornwallis to Nelson, August 6, 1781, PRO 30/11/90, ff. 19–20.
[131] Account of the Capture of a Schooner Called the "Hero's Revenge" . . . , Palmer *et al.*, eds., *Calendar of Virginia State Papers*, II, 170; General James Robertson to Cornwallis, August 22, 1781, PRO 30/11/6, ff. 367–68.
[132] Gov. Jefferson to Mr. James Hunter, January 10, 1781; Gov. Jefferson to Baron Steuben, February 20, 1781; Gov. Jefferson to Mrs. William Byrd, March 1, 1781; Gov. Jefferson to Baron Steuben, March 10, 1781; Gov. Jefferson to Colonel John S. Wells, May 9, 1781, H. R. McIlwaine, ed., *Official Letters of the Governors of the State of Virginia* (3 vols., Richmond, 1926–1929), II, 269–70, 363–64, 381–82, 397–99, 509.
[133] Negroes, September, 1819, PRO 30/8/344, ff. 109–11.
[134] Proclamation, June 30, 1779, British Headquarters Papers.

enrich the officers who led the expeditions and to reward the impoverished soldiers who served in them. After the military operations that devastated the Chesapeake in 1779 General Edward Matthews and Sir George Collier, who led the naval forces, "divided one-eighth of the total prize money between themselves," the rest between the army and navy.[135] Similar arrangements were made between Arnold and Captain Thomas Symonds, commanding officer of the *Charon*, before the Virginia expedition. En route to Virginia the two officers agreed to an equal division of the spoils between the services. Soon, however, dissension wrecked the accord, and the case was remanded to the New York vice-admiralty court.[136] The court awarded half the proceeds to the 280 sailors, but retained the other half pending the king's pleasure. Finally, in March 1782, after Clinton personally interceded with the crown on behalf of the army,[137] the king ruled that one-eighth of the amount remaining should be paid to Arnold, the rest to be divided among the officers and soldiers "as had been done on former occasions."[138]

Evidence of a market in slaves is not conclusive, but it is suggestive. When in June, a little more than a month after Cornwallis took command in Virginia, Arnold, with Cornwallis's approval, left Virginia for New York, Cornwallis explained his departure as due to "his present indispositions." But, perhaps to vindicate himself from any charges Arnold might make that he was receiving a disproportionately large share of the plunder, "especially the negro and tobacco traffic," Cornwallis added a careful demurrer: "He will represent the horrid enormities which are committed by our privateers in Chesapeake-bay; and I must join my earnest wish, that some remedy may be applied to an evil which is so very prejudicial to his Majesty's service."[139] The most revealing evidence linking the army to slave traffic is Leslie's expression of concern that the smallpox epidemic at Portsmouth "will ruin our market, which was bad enough before."[140]

Although the system of surveillance set up by the Patriots reduced the physical opportunities for slaves to run away and made mass escapes difficult, in and of themselves surveillance and exemplary punishment were not enough to prevent rebellion, given the fierce desire for freedom exhibited by Virginia slaves. But the ambivalence

[135] Williard M. Wallace, *Traitorous Hero: The Life and Fortunes of Benedict Arnold* (New York, 1954), 277–78.
[136] Col. James Innes to Jefferson, March 6, 1781, Palmer *et al.*, eds., *Calendar of Virginia State Papers*, I, 557; From David Jameson, March 10, 1781, Hutchinson, Rachal, *et al.*, eds., *Papers of James Madison*, III, 15.
[137] C.O. 5/106, f. 42.
[138] Wallace, *Traitorous Hero*, 277–78.
[139] Stevens, ed., *Campaign in Virginia*, I, 487.
[140] Leslie to Cornwallis, July 13, 1781, PRO 30/11/6, ff. 280–81.

and contradictions inherent in British policy made it clear to blacks, if not to their frightened white owners, that the British call to arms against their masters was aimed at winning the war, not at promoting social change. Promised freedom, the great majority of blacks who offered themselves to the British as willing soldiers were assigned instead to servile status. Unarmed, overworked, underfed, discarded when rendered useless by disease, they found little hope or encouragement for rebellion with the army, which used them as a tool instead of as a weapon. Thus discouraged, most Virginia slaves sensibly chose the relative security of the farm or plantation over the uncertainties of army life. Thousands of others, however, risked the perils of running away and the terrible realities of army life because they perceived in that course the best prospects for freedom. The fact that so many made that hazardous choice is compelling evidence of the depth of black resistance to slavery in eighteenth-century Virginia and indeed throughout the Revolutionary War South.

Slave Rebelliousness and Social Conflict in North Carolina, 1775 to 1802

Jeffrey J. Crow

QUILLO, a slave of James Hunt of Granville County, North Carolina, has not been remembered as a Revolutionary patriot or prominent political figure, but to local whites he must surely have seemed a troublesome symbol of the American Revolution gone awry. In April 1794, Granville County authorities accused Quillo of plotting a slave insurrection. Slaves who testified against him disclosed some striking attitudes and ideas among blacks. Quillo, they said, had "intended to give a large treat at Craggs Branch to the black people." While serving cider and brandy, he planned to hold an "election" in which slaves would choose burgesses, justices of the peace, and sheriffs "in order to have equal Justice distributed so that a weak person might collect his debts, as well as a Strong one." Not only had Quillo asked several slaves to stand as candidates, but the bondsmen expected these black representatives to employ force "in collecting the monies due them." In his defense Quillo asserted that the idea for an election had come from Tom, a mulatto slave. The election had been called off or postponed because someone had broken into a white man's cellar and stolen liquor. If the election had been held, the slaves who attended could have been charged with the theft of that liquor. According to the slave deponents, Quillo had also been in touch with a Negro in neighboring Person County who had heard that a band of Negroes intended to march toward Granville. One slave charged that after the election Quillo and "his associates were to proceed to inlist what forces they could to join the said party from Person and with them to force their way wherever they choosed, and to murder all who stood in their way, or opposed them." Quillo had supposedly vowed to "clear . . . out" the whites if they tried to interfere.[1]

Quillo's "election" may have been a ruse for some deeper scheme, but

Mr. Crow is head of the General Publications Branch, Historical Publications Section, of the North Carolina Division of Archives and History, Raleigh. He wishes to thank Robert M. Calhoon, Robert F. Durden, Paul D. Escott, Raymond Gavins, Marvin L. Michael Kay, Marc W. Kruman, William S. Price, Jr., and Peter H. Wood for their many helpful suggestions during the preparation of this article. Mr. Crow and Mr. Kay plan to analyze the evolution of class and caste structures in North Carolina, 1740-1810, in a future study.

[1]Trial of Quillo, Apr. 1794, Granville County Papers, North Carolina Division of Archives and History, Raleigh.

the manner in which he organized his polls with a "treat," like a country squire, could not have escaped Granville County whites. Something unsettling to whites was happening when slaves could speak of "equal justice" and contemplate the democratic election of a shadow government. The contagion of liberty that had been released by the American Revolution was dangerously spreading to the "wrong" people.

Slave rebelliousness was a familiar reality in eighteenth-century America. This may explain why most historians who have studied blacks in the colonial and Revolutionary periods have never been drawn into the debate over the creation of docile Sambos that absorbed scholars of nineteenth-century slavery for so long.[2] Students of the subject now agree that most slaves were never reconciled to, or broken by, the system. Though few organized or participated in rebellions, many engaged in other acts of resistance such as running away, arson, poisoning, destruction of property, sabotage, and assault.[3] Benjamin Quarles's classic study of the Negro in the Revolution provided the first comprehensive view of black engagement in and response to the War for Independence. Quarles found that blacks were far from passive; they fought for both sides, provided significant manpower to the British and American armies, and took active steps to achieve their freedom. Since the appearance of Quarles's book, Winthrop D. Jordan, Gerald (Michael) W. Mullin, and Peter H. Wood have added to our knowledge of slave rebelliousness in the eighteenth century with their perceptive and sensitive treatments of black life and white attitudes.[4]

Yet the link connecting slave rebelliousness to the Revolution or to the social turmoil that attended the Revolutionary War remains tenuous. The bondsmen's attitudes toward the Revolution are not revealed directly in a corpus of writings but must be inferred from their behavior in response to social, political, cultural, and military pressures. The American Revolution provides dramatic evidence to suggest that those pressures were immense.

[2] Stanley M. Elkins, *Slavery: A Problem in American Institutional and Intellectual Life* (Chicago, 1959); Ann J. Lane, ed., *The Debate over Slavery: Stanley Elkins and His Critics* (Urbana, Ill., 1971).

[3] See especially Kenneth M. Stampp, "Rebels and Sambos: The Search for the Negro's Personality in Slavery," *Journal of Southern History*, XXXVII (1971), 367-392; John W. Blassingame, *The Slave Community: Plantation Life in the Antebellum South* (New York, 1972), 184-216; and Paul D. Escott, *Slavery Remembered: A Record of Twentieth-Century Slave Narratives* (Chapel Hill, N.C., 1979), 71-94.

[4] Benjamin Quarles, *The Negro in the American Revolution* (Chapel Hill, N.C., 1961); Winthrop D. Jordan, *White over Black: American Attitudes toward the Negro, 1550-1812* (Chapel Hill, N.C., 1968); Gerald W. Mullin, *Flight and Rebellion: Slave Resistance in Eighteenth-Century Virginia* (New York, 1972); Peter H. Wood, *Black Majority: Negroes in Colonial South Carolina from 1670 through the Stono Rebellion* (New York, 1974). See also Wood's excellent historiographical analysis, " 'I Did the Best I Could for My Day': The Study of Early Black History during the Second Reconstruction, 1960 to 1976," *William and Mary Quarterly*, 3d Ser., XXXV (1978), 185-225.

As John Shy has argued, the Revolutionary War was a "political education conducted by military means" for thousands of Americans—black as well as white, he might have added.[5] In the South, that education took place amidst great social chaos, approaching anarchy, that had been set off by the war but continued long after hostilities ended in 1783.

North Carolina was particularly vulnerable to the devastating effects of the war. Cherokee raids in the west, British raids along the coast, and a loyalist uprising of Scottish Highlanders at the Battle of Moore's Creek Bridge confronted the North Carolinians at the outset of the conflict. Though the British did not invade North Carolina until 1780, loyalism plagued the new state government, and a major tory plot was uncovered and quashed in 1777. In the later stages of the war North Carolina became the battleground of Nathanael Greene and Lord Cornwallis, spawning a fierce internecine warfare between whigs and tories that lasted well into 1782. War-weary North Carolinians learned to their sorrow that the patriot militia treated them no better than marauding loyalists did.[6]

The peace treaty of 1783 did not magically restore order to North Carolina's social, economic, and political life. Commerce was at a standstill and the currency was virtually worthless. Not one newspaper was being published in the state. Courts met sporadically. In the wake of British occupation and the "Tory War," needy families in the lower Cape Fear counties were even exempted from paying taxes. Bitter antagonisms still divided the people, and loyalists continued to suffer social ostracism, legal sanctions, and political discrimination.[7] Such distressed circumstances greatly affected public and private life. When William Hooper, one of North Carolina's signers of the Declaration of Independence, was elected to the General Assembly in 1782, he spoke of contributing his "mite towards relief of this wretched state from its present anarchy and gloomy expectations."[8] More than a year later Moravian leader Friedric Wilhelm Marshall still found North Carolina's prognosis poor: "It cannot be denied that this country is in the condition of a patient convalescing from fever, who begins to be conscious of his weakness and still needs medicine and care. The land itself, the people of property, commerce, public and private credit, the currency in circulation, all are laid waste and ruined."[9]

It is the thesis of this article that the Revolution generated powerful

[5]John Shy, "The American Revolution: The Military Conflict Considered as a Revolutionary War," in Stephen G. Kurtz and James H. Hutson, eds., *Essays on the American Revolution* (Chapel Hill, N.C., 1973), 121-156, quotation on p. 147.

[6]Jeffrey J. Crow, "Tory Plots and Anglican Loyalty: The Llewelyn Conspiracy of 1777," *North Carolina Historical Review*, LV (1978), 1-17; Carole Watterson Troxler, *The Loyalist Experience in North Carolina* (Raleigh, 1976); Robert O. DeMond, *The Loyalists in North Carolina during the Revolution* (Durham, 1940).

[7]Samuel A'Court Ashe, *History of North Carolina*, II (Raleigh, 1925), 1-22.

[8]William Hooper to James Iredell, Apr. 8, 1782, in Don Higginbotham, ed., *The Papers of James Iredell* (Raleigh, N.C., 1976), II, 336.

[9]F. W. Marshall to Unity's Vorsteher Collegium, Oct. 28, 1783, in Adelaide L. Fries, ed., *Records of the Moravians in North Carolina*, IV (Raleigh, 1930), 1921.

internal tensions that racially destabilized southern society, particularly in North Carolina. The social conflict and disorder endemic to the Revolutionary War and its aftermath weakened stratified systems of caste. It has often been noted that clashes between ethnic groups intensify when the social structure lacks definition. Disorders occur in precisely those situations that are characterized by uncertainty over the color line and its breakdown. Demographic changes that disrupt old social patterns, major catastrophes such as war, and the transformation of values when new ideas are introduced generate tension and misunderstanding.[10] Between the outbreak of the Revolution and the turn of the nineteenth century acute tensions, which frequently erupted into violence, existed between blacks and whites in the South. Racial conflict polarized both groups but also promoted collective responses from each. For Afro-Americans, unstable racial patterns forged new hopes of freedom and a growing sense of cohesiveness that helped mold a black community. For whites, fluid racial patterns produced unsettling fears and a lack of social cohesiveness as blacks became increasingly assertive and white dissenters attempted to ameliorate slavery or abolish it completely. White fears of slave insurrection, heightened by instances of black unrest, culiminated in the widespread slave revolt scares of 1800-1802. The brutal subjugation of a small number of slave conspirators and the terrorization of countless other bondsmen restored white solidarity. The reassertion of the dominant white group's authority erased questions about caste and about the social position of blacks that had vexed southern whites since the Revolution. The color line was once more powerfully reinforced.

In focusing on North Carolina in the crucial years between 1775 and 1802, the present analysis pursues three lines of inquiry: how the actions of Afro-Americans contributed to the social trauma of the Revolution; how whites responded to the realization that their movement for Independence was unavoidably affecting the institution of slavery and the behavior of their black bondsmen; and, finally, how the conflicting perceptions of blacks and whites collided to produce the slave insurrection scares of 1800-1802.

The tremendous upheaval in the South that the Revolution brought about is only beginning to be explored. The Revolution occasioned a breakdown of the normal cohesive elements in southern society that sanctioned existing power relationships, thereby allowing economically and politically dispossessed groups to challenge the authority of the ruling class. This challenge came not only from tories and the "disaffected," but

[10]Lewis A. Coser, *Continuities in the Study of Social Conflict* (New York, 1967), 59, 96; Coser, "Some Sociological Aspects of Conflict," in Gary T. Marx, ed., *Racial Conflict: Tension and Change in American Society* (Boston, 1971), 14-16; Tamotsu Shibutani and Kian M. Kwan, "Changes in Life Conditions Conducive to Interracial Conflict," *ibid.*, 135, 138-141; Joseph S. Himes, "The Functions of Racial Conflict," *ibid.*, 456-460.

also from slaves.[11] Slave rebelliousness manifested itself in two ways: open revolt by force of arms, and defection to the British. Southern Revolutionaries accused the British crown of stirring up the slaves with promises of freedom. The North Carolina whig James Iredell, writing in 1776, cited Britain's "diabolical purpose of exciting our own Domestics (Domestics they forced upon us) to cut our throats, and involve Men, Women, and Children in one universal Massacre."[12] But the slave unrest that accompanied the opening stages of the war was too widespread to have been the work of a single British conspiracy, though royal governors and military observers had often commented on the potential for a massive slave insurrection in the southern colonies. From the Chesapeake to the Georgia coast, black insurgents sprang into action even before the British tendered their help. Mindful of that threat, North Carolina whigs had been closely monitoring their slaves long before Lord Dunmore of Virginia offered freedom to slaves who enlisted in the service of the crown.

The town of Wilmington was especially sensitive to the danger of insurrection because of its large black populace. Located at the mouth of the Cape Fear River, Wilmington was the chief entrepôt for North Carolina's growing naval stores industry and for the rice that the province's coastal planters produced. Consequently, surrounding New Hanover County had one of the largest and most concentrated Negro populations in the colony. Negroes constituted over 60 percent of the taxables in the county.[13] In June 1775 the Wilmington Committee of Safety, enforcing a 1753 statute that ostensibly limited the bearing of arms to those slaves whose masters had posted bond for them, disarmed all blacks to keep them "in order." It also instituted "Patroles to search & take from Negroes all kinds of Arms whatsoever." The situation, warned Wilmington Revolutionaries on July 13, was "truly alarming, the Governor collecting men, provisions, warlike stores of every kind, spiriting up the back counties, & perhaps the Slaves." The Revolutionaries charged that the British commander of Fort Johnston, guarding the entrance to Cape Fear, "had given Encouragement

---

[11]Three recent essays that explore slave unrest and social disorder during the Revolution are Ronald Hoffman, "The 'Disaffected' in the Revolutionary South," in Alfred F. Young, ed., *The American Revolution: Explorations in the History of American Radicalism* (DeKalb, Ill., 1976), 273-316; Michael Mullin, "British Caribbean and North American Slaves in an Era of War and Revolution, 1775-1807," in Jeffrey J. Crow and Larry E. Tise, eds., *The Southern Experience in the American Revolution* (Chapel Hill, N.C., 1978), 235-267; and Peter H. Wood, " Taking Care of Business' in Revolutionary South Carolina: Republicanism and the Slave Society," *ibid.*, 268-293.

[12]["Causes of the American Revolution"], June 1776, in Higginbotham, ed., *Iredell Papers*, I, 409.

[13]H. Roy Merrens, *Colonial North Carolina in the Eighteenth Century: A Study in Historical Geography* (Chapel Hill, 1964), 77-79; James M. Clifton, "Golden Grains of White: Rice Planting on the Lower Cape Fear," *N.C. Hist. Rev.*, L (1973), 365-369. The General Assembly of 1715 defined all slaves over 12 years of age as taxables.

to Negroes to Elope from their Masters & they [the British] promised to protect them."[14] Janet Schaw, a Scottish gentlewoman then visiting the lower Cape Fear, observed the mounting hysteria. The Revolutionaries, she wrote, claimed that the crown had promised "every Negro that would murder his Master and family that he should have his Master's plantation. This last Artifice they may pay for, as the Negroes have got it amongst them and believe it to be true. Tis ten to one they may try the experiment, and in that case friends and foes will be all one."[15] When Schaw traveled to Wilmington in July 1775, the slaves accompanying her "were seized and taken into custody till I was ready to return with them." An insurrection was expected hourly. "There had been a great number of them [blacks] discovered in the adjoining woods the night before," she explained, "most of them with arms, and a fellow belonging to Doctor [Thomas] Cobham was actually killed. All parties are now united against the common enemies." Patrols regularly searched Negro houses, and authorities imposed a curfew on all blacks. Decidedly loyalist in her views, Schaw talked to the commander of the midnight patrol and found that he thought the Revolutionaries' agitation about a slave revolt "a trick intended in the first place to inflame the minds of the populace, and in the next place to get those who had not before taken up arms to do it now and form an association for the safety of the town." In other words, the commander was convinced that the Wilmington patriots were preying upon white fears of slave rebellion to unite the white populace behind the Revolutionary cause. He believed the death of Cobham's slave an unconscionable act because "it was a fact well known" that the slave regularly met his black "Mistress every night in the opposite wood." The slave "wench" was forced "to carry on the intrigue with her black lover with great secrecy" because her master was so strict. Plotting a tryst, not an insurrection, had cost the slave his life. Even so, Schaw concluded, "My hypothesis is . . . the Negroes will revolt."[16]

Schaw's assessment of the situation proved correct, for the rumors of a slave insurrection that spread across the Carolinas in the summer of 1775 were not unfounded.[17] The alarm first sounded across the Tar River basin—Beaufort, Pitt, and Craven counties—in July 1775. On July 1 the Pitt

[14]Committee Minutes, June 21, 1775, Leora H. McEachern and Isabel M. Williams, eds., *Wilmington—New Hanover Safety Committee Minutes, 1774-1776* (Wilmington, N.C., 1974), 30; Wilmington Safety Committee to Samuel Johnston, July 13, 1775, *ibid.*, 43; Committee Minutes, July 21, 1775, *ibid.*, 45, 47. See also Proceedings of the Safety Committee at Wilmington, July 7, 1775, in William L. Saunders, Walter Clark, and Stephen B. Weeks, eds., *The Colonial Records of North Carolina* (Raleigh, Winston, Goldsboro, and Charlotte, 1886-1914), X, 72, hereafter cited as *N.C. Recs.*

[15]Janet Schaw, *Journal of a Lady of Quality* . . . , ed. Evangeline Walker Andrews and Charles M. Andrews (New Haven, Conn., 1921), 199.

[16]*Ibid.*, 199-200, 201.

[17]In South Carolina a Charles Town merchant, Josiah Smith, Jr., stated that "our Province at present is in a ticklish Situation, on account of our numerous Domesticks, who have been unhappily deluded by some villainous Persons into the no-

County Committee of Safety, acting on a tip from a slave informant, alerted patrollers to the possibility of an insurrection. One week later the committee ordered the patrollers to "shoot one or any number of Negroes who are armed and doth not willingly surrender their arms," and gave them "Discretionary Power, to shoot any Number of Negroes above four, who are off their Masters Plantations, and will not submit." The insurrection was termed a "deep laid Horrid Tragick Plan laid for destroying the inhabitants of this province without respect of persons, age or sex." A posse of some one hundred men apprehended the "suspected heads" of the plot until over forty blacks had been jailed. The movers behind the scheme were said to be a white sea captain and "Merrick, a negro man slave who formerly Belonged to Major Clark a Pilot at Okacock but now to Capt[ain] Nath Blinn of Bath Town." For two days the safety committee sat in judgment of the suspected conspirators and ordered approximately ten (the exact number is indeterminable) to be whipped with "80 lashes each." Several others had their ears cropped, but the remainder were evidently released.[18]

No sooner had these blacks been punished than word came of other Negroes "being in arms on the line of Craven and Pitt." To meet this threat whites "posted guards upon the roads for several miles that night." Another report alleged that a band of 250 slaves had been pursued for several days "but none taken nor seen tho' they were several times fired

---

tion of being all set free on the Arrival of . . . new Gov[erno]r Lord W[illia]m Campbell[;] it is their common Talk throughout the Province, and has occasioned impertinent behaviour in many of them, insomuch that our Provincial Congress now sitting hath voted the immediate raising of Two Thousand Men Horse and food, to keep those mistaken creatures in awe, as well as to oppose any Troops that may be sent among us with coercive Orders" (Smith to James Poyas, May 18, 1775, and to George Appleby, June 16, 1775, in Josiah Smith, Jr., Letter Book, Southern Historical Collection, University of North Carolina at Chapel Hill).

[18]Proceedings of the Safety Committee in Pitt County, July 8, 1775, N.C. Recs., X, 87; John Simpson to Richard Cogdell, July 15, 1775, ibid., 94-95. Merrick's role in the plot raises interesting questions about the activities of Negro pilots at the beginning of the Revolution. Tensions between Negro and white pilots had erupted in 1773 when white watermen petitioned the legislature to deny licenses to free Negroes and slaves who were guiding vessels up and down the province's rivers "to the Great prejudice and Injury of your Petitioners." The white pilots also condemned "the Insolent and Turbilent disposition and behaviour of such Free negroes and Slaves" (To His Excellency Josiah Martin . . . , N.C. Recs., IX, 803-804). In Charles Town in Aug. 1775, Revolutionaries executed Thomas Jeremiah, a free Negro pilot and reputed loyalist who had allegedly incited slaves to revolt. On this episode see Wood, " 'Taking Care of Business,' " in Crow and Tise, eds., Southern Experience, 282-287. A Negro pilot steered Sir Peter Parker's fleet into Charles Town harbor for the British assault in June 1776 (Virginia Gazette [Purdie], July 12, 1776). Such well-traveled slaves as pilots may have been the first to join the British and offer their especially valuable skills. The relative freedom they enjoyed by performing such a critical function in the coastal trade appears to have made them a rebellious lot, particularly resistant to white control.

at." Negroes who were captured revealed that a group of slaves planned to rise on the night of July 8 and "to fall on and destroy the family where they lived, then to proceed from House to House (Burning as they went) until they arrived in the Back Country where they were to be received with open arms by a number of Persons there appointed and armed by Government for their Protection, and as a further reward they were to be settled in a free government of their own." Unlike the purported plot in Wilmington, the Tar River conspiracy seems to have been a genuine threat. The chairman of the Pitt County safety committee noted that "in disarming the negroes we found considerable ammunition."[19]

Violence between master and slave was only one measure of the tensions afflicting southern society. Defection to the British was a powerful political statement in itself, and those slaves who chose this course vastly outnumbered those who took up arms. In North Carolina numerous slaves from as far inland as 150 miles escaped to the British fleet as soon as the warships dropped anchor off the mouth of the Cape Fear River in March 1776. Captain George Martin, under Sir Henry Clinton's command, organized the runaways into a company of Black Pioneers, support troops who relieved British soldiers of such onerous duties as building fortifications, laundering clothes, cooking, and managing horses and wagons. The Negro unit, numbering fifty-four at the outset, provided valuable intelligence on the roads and waterways of North Carolina, South Carolina, and Georgia. One ex-slave, for example, was from Town Creek, North Carolina, and knew the road as far as Cross Creek (present-day Fayetteville) "and above that the road from Virg[inia] to Charlestown." Another worked on the Wilmington ferry and was familiar with the road as far north as New Bern and as far south as Georgia. One runaway, named River, had fled from Charles Town. His owner was Arthur Middleton, who would soon sign the Declaration of Independence for South Carolina.[20] River had already declared his own independence.

The admiralty muster rolls of the ships off Cape Fear in the spring of 1776 frequently recorded the names of Negroes who "deserted from the Rebels" or "fled for Protection." H.M.S. *Scorpion*, for instance, listed thirty-six defectors on March 3, 1776. At least eleven and probably twelve women were among this group. Fifteen of these blacks, including one woman, joined Sir Peter Parker's fleet on May 21 for service in the Royal Navy.[21] Some of these runaways may have been refugees from a grisly

[19]Simpson to Cogdell, July 15, 1775, *N.C. Recs.*, X, 94-95.

[20]"List of the Names of the Negroes belonging to Capt. Martin's Company, who they belonged to and the respective places they lived at," copy from the Sir Henry Clinton Papers, Clements Library, University of Michigan–Ann Arbor, held by the N.C. St. Arch.

[21]North Carolina Colonial Records Project, British Records Collection, Adm. 36/8377, N.C. St. Arch. Several black refugees who boarded H.M.S. *St. Lawrence* in Apr. 1776 later joined the British army at Staten Island in New York (*ibid.*, Adm. 36/8434).

mission that South Carolina Revolutionaries had conducted against Sullivan's Island in Charles Town harbor in December 1775. Many slaves had fled to the island, and the Council of Safety ordered William Moultrie to destroy their encampment. Under cover of darkness Moultrie and fifty or sixty raiders "early in the Morning sett Fire to the Pest house, took some Negroes & Sailors Prisoners, killed 50 of the former that would not be taken, and unfortunately lost near 20 that were unseen by them till taken off the Beach by the Men Warrs Boats."[22]

Slaves defected from tories as well as from whigs. Lieutenant Isaac DuBois, submitting a loyalist claim for compensation after the war, declared that his slave London, a baker, had "joined the Kings Troops at Cape Fear in North Carolina, was taken into the Service by Order of Sir Henry Clinton, and inrolled in a Company of Black Pioneers under the command of Captain George Martin, by which Service the said Slave became intitled to his Freedom."[23] Similarly, John Provey, a free black, evidently had no trouble deciding which side proffered the best hope of freedom. He gave up his small North Carolina farm "at the Commencement of the late unfortunate Troubles in North America" and "took the first Opportunity of joining His Majesty's troops under the Command of Sir Henry Clinton at Cape Fear, leaving all his Property behind him, and remained with the Army till its arrival at New York in 1776, when he was regularly Inlisted into a Company stiled the Black Pioneers, with which he bore arms until the End of the War."[24]

Throughout the war, blacks capitalized on the unsettled conditions brought on by civil strife, roving armies, and the weakened mechanisms of control to seek their freedom. Wherever the British army marched, slaves followed. What had been a trickle of runaways in 1775-1776 became a flood after the British inaugurated their southern offensive in late 1778. Charles Stedman, Cornwallis's commissary, recalled simply that "the negroes in general followed the British army." Whitmel Hill, one of North Carolina's largest slave owners and a leading Revolutionary, excoriated the British for "carrying off large droves of Slaves," but blacks needed no encouragement from the redcoats to flee their masters. Despite misgivings on Clinton's part, Cornwallis was forced to devise careful plans to utilize the bonanza of manpower available to him. In 1780 he appointed John Cruden, a Wilmington loyalist and merchant, commissioner of sequestered estates in South Carolina and subsequently in North Carolina. Cruden was eventually responsible for over 5,000 blacks on an estimated 400

[22]Josiah Smith, Jr., to James Poyas, Jan. 10, 1776, in Josiah Smith, Jr., Letter Book; "Journal of the Council of Safety," Dec. 7, 9, 10, 1775, South Carolina Historical Society, *Collections*, III (Charleston [1859]), 64-65, 73, 75. Smith reported that the *Scorpion*, cruising the coastal waters with North Carolina royal Gov. Josiah Martin in Jan. 1776, had on board "Forty of our Negros." These may have been survivors of the Sullivan's Island raid.

[23]Loyalist Claim by Isaac DuBois, 1789, Brit. Recs. Coll., A.O. 12/73.

[24]Loyalist Claim by John Provey, 1784, *ibid.*, A.O. 13/123.

whig plantations, where provisions for the British army were to be grown.[25]

Many runaway slaves accompanied Cornwallis's army as it drove through North Carolina. The British general turned these camp followers into an army of foragers despite "great Complaints . . . of Negroes Stragling from the Line of March, plund[e]r[in]g & Using Violence to the Inhabitants[.] It is Lord Cornwallis possitive Orders that no Negroe shall be Suffred to Carry Arms on any pretence." In time he ordered an end to the "Shameful Marauding" and "Scandalous Crimes" of his Negro legions, but he never ceased using them.[26]

A stronger image of social revolution could hardly have existed in the South than a band of black foragers swooping down on a small farm and stripping it of foodstuffs and livestock. Some fear-struck North Carolina slaveholders fled to Virginia "with their Negroes and Effects."[27] Black Carolinians, meanwhile, closely observed the progress of the British army, hung on rumors, generated a few themselves, and waited for the right moment to bolt for freedom. Mrs. Jean Blair, who had moved her household inland from Edenton to Windsor as the war had drawn closer, wrote in January 1781 that "the Negroes bring Strange storys. They say people are getting ready to run again and the English are to be in Edenton by Saturday." Once Cornwallis came near, the flight began. "All my Brothers Negroes at Booth except two fellows are determined to go to them, even old Affra," Mrs. Blair sadly conceded. "W[hitmel] Hill lost twenty in two nights." Mrs. Blair also feared the black foragers. "It is said they have no Arms," she declared, "but what they find in the houses they plunder. When they applyed for arms they were told they had no occasion for any as they were not to go any place where any number of Rebels were collected. It is said there are two thousand of them out in different Partys."[28] Another slaveholder reported the loss of "60 prime slaves," while one

[25]Stedman, The History Of The Origin, Progress, And Termination Of The American War, II (London, 1794), 217n.; N.C. Recs., XIV, 2. Lt. Col. Hardy Murfree informed North Carolina republican Gov. Abner Nash in 1780 that "a great many Negroes goes to the Enemy" (Murfree to Nash, Nov. 1, 1780, ibid., XV, 138). On Cruden's activities see Loyalist Claim by James Cruden (brother of the late John Cruden), 1788, Brit. Recs. Coll., A.O. 12/37, A.O. 13/28; Franklin and Mary Wickwire, Cornwallis: The American Adventure (Boston, 1970), 142-143; and Sylvia R. Frey, "The British and the Black: A New Perspective," The Historian, XXXVIII (1976), 229-230, 232.

[26]A. R. Newsome, ed., "A British Orderly Book, 1780-1781," N.C. Hist. Rev., LX (1932), 276, 280, 287, 296, 297, 370, quotation on p. 296.

[27]Turnbull to Lord Rawdon, Oct. 23, 1780, Cornwallis Papers, P.R.O. 30/11/3, 263-264, Library of Congress.

[28]Jean Blair to Helen Blair, Jan. 4, 1781, in Higginbotham, ed., Iredell Papers, II, 203; Blair to Hannah Iredell, May 10, 19, June 5, 1781, ibid., 239, 245, 257; Blair to James Iredell, July 21, 1781, ibid., 266.

whig predicted that if Cornwallis could arm them, he could raise an Army of "500 Negroes" in Wilmington alone.[29]

The chaos of the war forced Afro-Americans to make difficult decisions. William Hooper identified the personal conflicts, created by the war, that made one slave a rebel and another a loyal servant. During the British evacuation of Wilmington in November 1781, three of Hooper's bondsmen went "off with the British"; another was seized by the patriot militia; and five others died of smallpox. His house servant John, however, resisted British bribes. He was offered everything—clothes, money, freedom— "to attach him to the service of the British. . . . He pretended to acquiesce, and affected a perfect satisfaction at this change of situation; but in the evening of the day after Mrs. Hooper left the town, he stole through the British sentries, and without a pass, accompanied by a wench of Mrs. Allen's, he followed Mrs. Hooper seventy miles on foot, and overtook her, to the great joy of himself and my family." John's sister Lavinia "pursued a different conduct. She went on board the fleet after the evacuation of the town, and much against her will was forced ashore by some of my friends and returned to me."[30]

Lavinia's actions symbolized Afro-Americans' rising expectations, which were swelled by the war. Her freedom ship had sailed away, but the desire for freedom burned hotter than ever among slaves who, like her, stayed behind. The Revolution was a great liberating experience for thousands of slaves. Contemporaries estimated that the South lost as many as 55,000 bondsmen. Many evacuated with the British or were emancipated. Others simply attempted to pass as free blacks.[31] But the whites who forced Lavinia to return to bondage also symbolized an inescapable truth about postwar southern society: the white community would not give up slavery. Thus the racial conflict that the tumultuous events of 1775 had sharpened did not subside in the war's aftermath but deepened as the opposing interests of blacks and whites collided.

The South's weakened social structure after the war made the region fertile ground for racial conflict. Free blacks were no longer predominantly light-skinned mulattoes, and this change made caste distinctions based on color difficult to enforce. Slaves had learned during the war that collective action, particularly defection to the British, offered the chance for freedom. In postwar North Carolina, collective resistance to slavery became more prevalent and purposive. Bands of runaways in the

---

[29]Nathan Bryan to Gov. Thomas Burke, Sept. 6, 1781, N.C. Recs., XV, 634-635; William Caswell to Burke, Sept. 4, 1781, ibid., XXII, 593. See also Loyalist Claim by Samuel Marshall, 1789, Brit. Recs. Coll., A.O. 12/74.

[30]Hooper to James Iredell, Feb. 17, 1782, in Higginbotham, ed., Iredell Papers, II, 328, 329.

[31]Historian David Ramsay estimated that South Carolina alone lost 25,000 slaves in the Revolution (Ramsay's History of South Carolina, from its First Settlement

Great Dismal Swamp or near towns such as New Bern and Wilmington had occasionally sent tremors through colonial North Carolina, to be sure, but those rebels were often African newcomers, unlikely candidates to organize a full-scale slave revolt. They had been content to remain isolated and insulated in their lowland fastnesses.[32] Rebel slaves after the war had decidedly different objectives. At the same time whites had to contend with a bewildering maze of social conditions in which slaves agitated for freedom, free blacks proliferated, and troublesome dissenters raised questions about slavery and its humanity. This instability fostered deep anxieties, social stress, and mounting tensions.

Among those North Carolinians who sought to ameliorate slavery was William Hooper. Born and educated in Boston, Hooper had led a successful fight in 1773-1774 to pass a law that made it a crime to kill a slave.[33] In 1784 he introduced a bill in the state's House of Commons that might be termed a "slave bill of rights." The bill passed one reading in the lower house before being sent to the Senate, where it was evidently buried. It would have provided slaves with limited protection from arbitrary treatment by their masters. Hooper's bill stated that slaves constituted "a very large part of the property of the good Citizens of this State" and were needed as a labor force. Thus for reasons of "humanity and the policy and interest" of the slave owners, slavery must be rendered "as little burdensome and distressing as possible." Declaring that "justice should be duly administered to those of our fellow Creatures who are consigned to

in 1670 to the year 1808, I [Newberry, 1858], 178-179, 270-272). See also Mary Beth Norton, " 'What an Alarming Crisis Is This': Southern Women and the American Revolution," in Crow and Tise, eds., Southern Experience, 215, 223, 233, n. 38, and Ira Berlin, Slaves without Masters: The Free Negro in the Antebellum South (New York, 1974), 15-50.

[32]During the constitutional convention of 1835, William Gaston, justice of the North Carolina Supreme Court, noted "that previous to the Revolution there were scarcely any emancipated Slaves in this State; and that the few free men of color that were here at that time, were chiefly Mulattoes, the children of white women, and therefore unquestionably free, because their mothers were so" (Proceedings and Debates of the Convention of North-Carolina Called to Amend the Constitution of the State [Raleigh, 1836], 351). Ira Berlin substantiates the large number of mixed bloods among free Negroes (as early as 1755 in Maryland) in Slaves without Masters, 3-4, 6-7, 177-181. Marvin L. Michael Kay and Lorin Lee Cary in their paper "Albion's Fatal Tree Transplanted: Crime, Society, and Slavery in North Carolina, 1748-1772," delivered at the 1978 meeting of the Southern Historical Association in St. Louis, Mo., estimate that at least 25% of the runaways they surveyed were "unmistakably African." See also Jeffrey J. Crow, The Black Experience in Revolutionary North Carolina (Raleigh, 1977), 41-45, and Alan D. Watson, "Impulse toward Independence: Resistance and Rebellion among North Carolina Slaves, 1750-1775," Journal of Negro History, LXIII (1978), 317-328.

[33]Crow, Black Experience in North Carolina, 25; Don Higginbotham and William S. Price, Jr., "Was It Murder for a White Man to Kill a Slave?: Chief Justice Martin Howard Condemns North Carolina's Peculiar Institution," WMQ, 3d Ser., XXXVI (1979), 593-601.

such servitude," the bill enjoined slaveholders to provide "wholesome and competent diet and Cloathing," and limited whippings to twenty-five lashes, since "immoderate correction is a dishonour to a free Country and a disgrace to humanity." It also promised slaves the same punishments as whites. For example, a slave who committed a crime for which a white man would hang could not be put to death in any other manner.[34]

The humanitarian movement to ameliorate slavery, like Hooper's bill, made little headway in North Carolina. North Carolina Quakers took a determined stand against slavery, but their efforts were only modestly successful. In 1775 the Standing Committee of the Yearly Meeting in North Carolina debated the issue of slavery and the following year advised Friends "to Cleanse their Hands" of slave ownership. By 1777 Quakers had manumitted at least forty slaves in North Carolina, prompting a troubled General Assembly to enact a law to "prevent domestic Insurrections." The lawmakers denounced the "evil and pernicious Practice of freeing Slaves . . . . at this alarming and critical Time." They authorized county sheriffs to apprehend and auction off any slaves freed illegally. This same law was reenacted in 1788 and again in 1796.[35]

During the war and until the nineteenth century sheriffs rounded up recently freed blacks and sold them at public auctions. Quaker attorneys attempted various defenses to prevent reenslavement. They argued, for example, that the 1777 statute was an ex post facto law. When that failed, they turned to the natural rights philosophy that had been so central to the Revolution's ideology. A lawyer defending the Negro Judy before the Perquimans County court during the 1790s asserted that "the taking, apprehending and dragging of Negroes (as confessedly done in the Case) living quietly and peaceably with their masters from their houses, is arbitrary and illegal." He contended that such action was "unjust & incompatible with liberty," that it violated the Bill of Rights, and that "all

---

[34]Legislative Papers (House of Commons), Box 52, May-June 1784, N.C. St. Arch.; Journal of the House of Commons, May 1784, *N.C. Recs.*, XIX, 637. For other forms of social control and punishment of blacks, including castration and burning, see Marvin L. Michael Kay and Lorin Lee Cary, " 'The Planters Suffer Little or Nothing': North Carolina Compensations for Executed Slaves, 1748-1772," *Science and Society*, XL (1976), 288-306, and Crow, *Black Experience in Revolutionary North Carolina*, 19-33, 38-39.

[35]Manuscript Minutes of the Yearly Meeting of Friends in North Carolina, Quaker Collection, I, 132, Guilford College Library, quoted in Peter Kent Opper, "North Carolina Quakers: Reluctant Slaveholders," *N.C. Hist. Rev.*, LII (1975), 37; Laws of North Carolina, 1777, *N.C. Recs.*, XXIV, 14-15, quotations on p. 14; David Brion Davis, *The Problem of Slavery in the Age of Revolution, 1770-1823* (Ithaca, N.Y., 1975), 198-199. Documents illustrating Quaker antislavery convictions are printed in Robert M. Calhoon, *Religion and the American Revolution in North Carolina* (Raleigh, 1976), 41-49.

[36]Case of Negro Judy, n.d., Perquimans County Slave Papers, 1759-1864, N.C. St. Arch. See also Case of Harry, Dinah, and Patt, Apr. 5, 1785, and Account of sales of Negroes, Oct. 1788, *ibid.*

Men possess certain natural & unalienable rights to life Liberty & property," even Negroes.[36]

The Quakers' activities greatly alarmed other whites and magnified their anxieties. In 1795 a Pasquotank County grand jury bitterly chided the Friends for promoting slave unrest and endangering the white populace. The grand jurors asserted that Quakers were subjecting the state to "great perril." The "idea of emancipation, amonghts Slaves is publicly held out to them, and incouraged by the Conduct of the Quakers," the jurors charged. "The Minds of the Slaves, are not only greatly corrupted and allienated from the Service of Their Masters . . . But runaways are protected, harbored, and incourag'd by them—Arsons are even committed, without a possibility of discovery." The Quakers persisted in this behavior, the jurors complained, despite the "miserable havock and massacres which have taken place in the West Indies, in consequence of emancipation; Knowing the opinion of the Northern States; of the many thousand Slaves around them; and of the infatuated enthusiasm of Men calling themselves religious."[37]

The white backlash against manumission—invariably led by slaveholders—overwhelmed the humanitarian gestures of the Quakers and other freethinkers. This opposition manifested itself in several ways. When a Nova Scotian ship, manned by Negro seamen and auxiliaries, sailed into New Bern in 1785, the legislature urged the governor to seize the black crew as the property of United States citizens. The blacks, nine men and two women, had allegedly left with the British at the end of the war. Their freedom was short-lived, for Governor Richard Caswell complied with the lawmakers' request.[38] Similarly, the General Assembly overturned the will of Mark Newby, who had intended that his slaves be freed at age twenty-one. Only six of the assemblymen protested the reenslavement of the blacks as "tyrannic and unconstitutional."[39] By 1790 North Carolina was the only southern state in which manumission was not the prerogative of the slave owner. A 1741 act stipulated that only the county court could free slaves after determining their worthiness by virtue of "meritorious services."[40]

Why was this so? North Carolina had a reputation during the eighteenth century as a haven for fugitive slaves, and Tar Heel slaveholders were not eager to embellish that reputation. The Great Dismal Swamp, trackless and virtually impenetrable, in particular served as a sanctuary for runa-

[37]Grand Jury Presentment, Dec. 1795, Pasquotank County Slave Papers, 1734-1860, N.C. St. Arch.

[38]Jour. House of Commons, Dec. 1785, N.C. Recs., XVII, 385, 389; Caswell to John C. Bryan, Dec. 30, 1785, Mar. 12, May 24, 27, June 23, July 10, 1786, ibid., 595-596, XVIII, 571-572, 623, 625, 663, 680-681; Caswell to John W. Stanley, May 27, 1786, ibid., XVIII, 624-625; Caswell to Abner Neale, June 23, 1786, ibid., 662-663.

[39]Journal of the State Senate, Nov. 1790, ibid., XXI, 762-763; Jour. House of Commons, Dec. 1790, ibid., 1004, 1019-1020, quotation on p. 1020.

[40]Berlin, Slaves without Masters, 29.

ways.[41] North Carolina's repressive laws reflected the unstable conditions that alarmed slaveholders; easing manumission would only flood society with more free blacks. Because skin color was no longer strictly emblematic of caste, the General Assembly in 1785 finally resorted to badges to distinguish free Negroes from slaves. Henceforth, free blacks in Wilmington, Washington, Edenton, and Fayetteville had to register with the town commissioners, pay a fee, and wear a "badge of cloth . . . to be fixed on the left shoulder, and to have thereon wrought in legible capital letters the word FREE."[42]

In spite of such repressive strictures the white community could not maintain absolute control over the bondsmen's lives or eradicate their hopes for freedom. Black assertiveness in postwar North Carolina revealed a greater collective consciousness among slaves and an increasing willingness to use violence to liberate not only individuals but groups of slaves. In 1783 the Chowan County court tried the slave Grainge for the "atrocious Crime of endeavouring to Stir up Slaves for the Diabolical purpose of Murdering their Masters and Mistresses." He was found guilty and sentenced to "have Both his Ears Cut off & have two hundred Stripes well Laid on his Bare Back." William Bryan of Craven County received £50 from the General Assembly in 1783 "for a negro man slave killed in suppressing of Rebel Slaves." Two years later the Chowan County court found the Negro Titus guilty of "breaking open the Public Goal (sic) . . . and letting out several [black?] Prisoners therein Confined."[43]

Fears of collective resistance to slavery proliferated during the 1790s after news arrived of major slave revolts in the West Indies, especially Saint Domingue. A report from New Bern in 1792 asserted that "the negroes in this town and neighbourhood, have stirred a rumour of their having in contemplation to rise against their masters and to procure themselves their liberty; the inhabitants have been alarmed and keep a strict watch to prevent their procuring arms; should it become serious, which I don't think, the worst that could befal us, would be their setting the town on fire. It is very absurd of the blacks, to suppose they could accomplish their views." In the summer of 1795 Wilmington suffered sporadic attacks by a "number of runaway Negroes, who in the daytime secrete themselves in the swamps and woods" and at night commit "various depredations on the neighboring plantations." They fatally ambushed at least one white overseer and wounded another. Posses eventually killed five of the rene-

---

[41]Mullin, *Flight and Rebellion*, 110-112.

[42]Laws of North Carolina, 1785, *N.C. Recs.*, XXIV, 725-730, quotation on p. 728. Statutes should not be mistaken for actual behavior; they reflected instead the type of ideal behavior the legislators hoped to elicit. In effect, laws were a response to a perceived social disorder. On this point see Jordan, *White over Black*, 587-588, and William M. Wiecek, "The Statutory Law of Slavery and Race in the Thirteen Mainland Colonies of British America," *WMQ*, 3d Ser., XXXIV (1977), 258-280.

[43]The Chowan County court cases are in C.R.X. (County Records X), Box 4, N.C. St. Arch. For Bryan's compensation claim see *N.C. Recs.*, XIX, 258.

gades, including their leader, the "General of the Swamps."[44] In Bertie County in 1798 three black men were accused of heading a conspiracy of 150 slaves, armed with "Guns, clubs, Swords, and Knives." Evidently, the blacks "did attack, pursue, knock down and lay prostrate the patrollers," but the only casualty was a horse. Consequently, the three leaders were convicted of a high misdemeanor against "the laws and dignity of the state," instead of rebellion, and were punished with thirty-nine lashes and cropped ears.[45]

The fear that slave insurrections might spread from the West Indies to North America enveloped the South. In 1795, North Carolina barred the entry of all West Indian slaves over the age of fifteen, traditionally the age at which white boys were considered fit for military service. Later that year, when French refugees fleeing the racial wars of the Caribbean sailed into Wilmington with thirty or forty of their slaves, residents prevented their landing for fear that the blacks might incite revolt. In 1798, Governor Samuel Ashe went so far as to issue a proclamation that urged citizens to block the landing of any Negroes from the islands, slave or free. Ashe called on all civil and military officers on the coast to enforce the slave trade laws stringently.[46]

The conflict between master and slave, the anxieties of whites caused by slave restiveness, the frustration of blacks as avenues to freedom were continually blocked, and the crisscrossing social tensions among various groups, white and black, in post-Revolutionary North Carolina society culminated in a major slave insurrection scare in 1802. This event came in the midst of the Second Great Awakening and in the wake of the Gabriel Prosser revolt in Richmond two years earlier. Quakers continued to agitate for emancipation and flout the manumission laws, and the bitter presidential campaign of 1800 had just been fought. These conflicts fragmented the white community severely, and slaves displayed acumen and shrewd political judgment in seizing such a moment to revolt.[47]

[44]The New Bern situation was reported in the *Boston Gazette, and the Country Journal,* Sept. 3, 1792, and reports about Wilmington in 1795 appeared in the *Wilmington Chronicle: and North-Carolina Weekly Advertiser,* July 3, 10, 17, 1795, and the *City Gazette & Daily Advertiser* (Charleston), July 18, 23, 1795, all as quoted in Herbert Aptheker, *American Negro Slave Revolts* (New York, 1943), 213, 217.

[45]Trial of three Negro men, May 31, 1798, Bertie County Slave Papers, 1744-1815, N.C. St. Arch.

[46]P. Manyeon to Benjamin Smith, Dec. 2, 1795, Slavery Papers, Miscellaneous Collection, N.C. St. Arch.; R. H. Taylor, "Slave Conspiracies in North Carolina," *N.C. Hist. Rev.,* V (1928), 25. A petition from citizens of Wilmington to Congress in 1803 precipitated a national debate on the importation of blacks and mulattoes from the West Indies and the passage of legislation to counter the menace (Jordan, *White over Black,* 382-383).

[47]Particularly trenchant discussions linking social tensions among whites with slave rebelliousness are Jordan, *White over Black,* 115-121; Wood, " Taking Care of Business,' " in Crow and Tise, eds., *Southern Experience,* 268-293; and Eugene

The Great Revival in particular produced new tensions in the social order. The interracial camp meetings, the democratic appeal of the Methodist and Baptist services, the abolitionist impulse of Methodism in its fledgling years, and the phenomenon of black preachers exhorting racially mixed congregations differed sharply from previous modes of religious expression and custom.[48] These conditions helped nurture the flowering of the black church, which quickly became a locus of collective resistance to slavery. As an institution independent of the ruling elite, the black church attracted the loyalty of an oppressed group, selected its own leadership, and—to the extent that it provided a structure for social solidarity—served a fundamental political purpose in challenging the elite's power.[49]

When translated into political terms, black religion and the egalitarianism of evangelical Protestantism had explosive results. Indeed, the fear that conversion might foster rebellion greatly exercised the slaveholding South in the eighteenth century.[50] After Prosser's revolt in 1800, St. George Tucker, one of the nation's most perceptive opponents of slavery, concluded that the "love of freedom" among Negroes was ineluctable. "Fanaticism is spreading fast among the Negroes of this country," he cautioned, "and may form in time the connecting link between the black religionists and the white. . . . It certainly would not be a novelty, in the history of the world, if Religion were made to sanctify plots and conspiracies."[51] The specter of black jacobinism infused with religion, raised by Federalists against Jeffersonians in 1800, led a Virginian to observe after

---

D. Genovese, *Roll, Jordan, Roll: The World the Slaves Made* (New York, 1974), 587-597. See also David Barry Gaspar, "The Antigua Slave Conspiracy of 1736: A Case Study of the Origins of Collective Resistance," *WMQ*, 3d Ser., XXXV (1978), 308-323.

[48]Rhys Isaac, "Evangelical Revolt: The Nature of the Baptists' Challenge to the Traditional Order in Virginia, 1765 to 1775," *WMQ*, 3d Ser., XXXI (1974), 345-368; Donald G. Mathews, *Slavery and Methodism: A Chapter in American Morality, 1780-1845* (Princeton, N.J., 1965), 3-29; W. Harrison Daniel, "Virginia Baptists and the Negro in the Early Republic," *Virginia Magazine of History and Biography*, LXXX (1972), 60-69.

[49]Donald G. Mathews, *Religion in the Old South* (Chicago, 1977), 185-236; Vincent Harding, "Religion and Resistance among Antebellum Negroes, 1800-1860," in August Meier and Elliott Rudwick, eds., *The Making of Black America: Essays in Negro Life and History*, I (New York, 1969), 179-197.

[50]During the first Great Awakening, George Whitefield was blamed for inciting Negro plots in places such as New York and South Carolina (Jordan, *White over Black*, 181). Landon Carter commented that his slaves had "grown so much worse" since the quickening of the religious pulse (Jack P. Greene, ed., *The Diary of Colonel Landon Carter Sabine Hall, 1752-1778*, I [Charlottesville, Va., 1965], 378).

[51][St. George Tucker], *Letter To A Member Of The General Assembly Of Virginia On The Subject Of The Late Conspiracy Of The Slaves; With A Proposal For Their Colonization* (Baltimore, 1801), 11-12.

the near-cataclysm at Richmond, "This doctrine, in this country, and in every country like this (as the horrors of St. Domingo have already proved) cannot fail of producing either a general insurrection, or a general emancipation. It has been most imprudently propagated at many of our tables, while our servants have been standing behind our chairs, for several years past. It has been, and is still preached by the Methodists, Baptists and others, from the pulpit, without any sort of reserve. What else then could we expect than what has happened?"[52]

Beginning in Kentucky, the Great Revival swept eastward and arrived in North Carolina in the fall of 1801.[53] By early 1802 blacks and whites were attending camp meetings, where impassioned religious services often induced hysterical responses. The Reverend Samuel McCorkle described how "as if by an electric shock, a large number in every direction, men, women, children, white and black, fell and cried for mercy."[54] But more than religious conversion was taking place at these gatherings. The revival offered an opportunity for, and was an instrument of, Negro rebellion. At the same time that religion stirred the souls of North Carolinians, not coincidentally rumors of a black slave insurrection spread through the eastern counties of Camden, Bertie, Currituck, Martin, Halifax, Pasquotank, Hertford, Washington, and Warren.

Former Governor William R. Davie raised the initial alarm in February 1802. Writing to Governor Benjamin Williams from Halifax County, Davie reported a suspected Negro plot originating in Southampton County, Virginia, and extending down the Roanoke River valley into North Carolina. A Negro organizing the revolt had allegedly written a letter addressed to the "Representative of the Roanoak Company." In language reminiscent of both the political and spiritual revolutions of the eighteenth century this letter stated that once the "conflagration" began, whites would "acknowledge liberty & equality" and be "glad to purchase their lives at any price." Whites must learn that "the breath of liberty is as free for us as for themselves." The letter was signed a "true friend in liberty or death." Davie nervously compared the situation with Saint Domingue, where the murder of several thousand whites had stained "the whole Colony."[55]

---

[52]*Virginia Herald* (Fredericksburg), Sept. 23, 1800, as quoted in Jordan, *White over Black*, 396.

[53]The standard work on this social phenomenon, though it does not pay much attention to Afro-Americans, is John B. Boles, *The Great Revival, 1787-1805: The Origins of the Southern Evangelical Mind* (Lexington, Ky., 1972).

[54]Samuel McCorkle to John Langdon, Jan. 8, June 4-8, 1802, in William Henry Foote, *Sketches of North Carolina, Historical and Biographical* ... (New York, 1846), 392, 402-403.

[55]Correspondence between William R. Davie and Benajmin Williams, Feb. 1802, is in the Governor's Letter Book [Benjamin Williams], 542, 552, 556, 560, 565, N.C. St. Arch. Other correspondents in the letter book discussed rumors of slave unrest in other counties but generally discounted the existence of any plot, especially in Camden County. From Halifax County came a petition to pardon the

The fires of slave rebellion ignited not in Halifax County, however, but in an area farther down the Roanoke River, near its confluence with Albemarle Sound. As in Prosser's conspiracy, a few of the plotters in North Carolina could read and write and thus pass information and messages. They were acculturated slaves with freedom of movement that enabled them to reach numerous bondsmen on the widely scattered plantations. The interconnecting waterways of eastern North Carolina evidently made the transmission of information not only feasible but unstoppable. The insurgents used social occasions in the slave quarters—in one instance a dance or "Ball"—to map out their strategy. But at the core of the plot may have been the black preacher.

Dr. Joe, a slave preacher, apparently served the North Carolina conspiracy in much the same way that Martin Prosser, a preacher, served his brother Gabriel's plot in Richmond. In May 1802 the Pasquotank County court tried Dr. Joe for conspiring with Tom Copper "to Rebel and make insurrections." Tom Copper was a black guerrilla whose camp was hidden in the swamps near Elizabeth City. Styling himself the "General to command this county in a plot to kill the white people," Copper staged a daring raid on Elizabeth City's jail with "six stout negroes, mounted on horseback" to liberate the slaves held there on a conspiracy charge. Four of the marauders were captured, but two escaped.[56] The Pasquotank County court found Dr. Joe innocent of any complicity with Copper, but his master had to post a bond of £200 for his release plus two sureties of £250 each to guarantee his good behavior. Moreover, the court enjoined the preacher not to "Assemble or hold any Meeting, Congregation or other Assembly of Slaves or other people of Colour upon or under any pretence Whatsoever."[57]

Suspicions about the activities of Dr. Joe and other slave preachers were well founded. The black conspirators used religious meetings to plot their uprising. At one sermon the slave Charles angrily told another slave that "there were a great many whites there ... [and] that they ought to be killed." One slaveholder, a Baptist elder, gave his slave Virginia permission "to hold a night Meeting on Monday Night," that is, a religious service, at which plans for the revolt were subsequently discussed. The slave Moses admitted that "Joe preached with a pistol in his pocket." Another slave had observed several conspirators "talking low" and "while at preaching saw [a] number of Negroes standing talking two & two during the sermon." The slave Frank, one of the ringleaders ultimately executed, had been seen at a "quarterly Meeting at Wiccacon." The conspirators

---

slave Toney, who had been convicted of plotting an insurrection. Williams pardoned him.

[56]*Raleigh Register and North-Carolina State Gazette*, June 1, 1802; Aptheker, *Slave Revolts*, 231-232.

[57]Trial of Dr. Joe, May 22, 1802, Pasquotank County Court Minutes, 1799-1802, N.C. St. Arch.; Calhoon, *Religion and the Revolution*, 66-68.

planned to coordinate the rising on June 10, 1802, to coincide with the quarterly meetings of several Kehukee Baptist associations, when the whites would be most vulnerable. One insurgent stated succinctly that "they were to begin at the Quarterly Meeting."[58]

Accumulated tensions, unbearable grievances and frustrations, and the example of Prosser's revolt helped propel these blacks toward rebellion. A few conspirators apparently associated the plot with a class revolt, for they anticipated reinforcements from Tuscarora Indians and from "a number of poor people (white which they expected would Join them)." Caesar, one of the leaders or "captains" of the cabal, told Moses that he foresaw "a Warm Winter, a dry Spring & a Bloody Summer, & that he expected the Negroes were going to Rise." Dave, another leader ultimately executed, confided to Sam that he was "very tired & weary" because "the Damn'd White people plagued him so bad they ought all to be killed & shall . . . if he could get a great many to join him." Peter "had fallen out with his overseer & had been whipped & Damn him he ought to be killed & all the rest." Peter had also attended "a logg roling & the Overseer had been whipping two of the negroes," which reinforced his determination to revolt. Sam told Harry "that them guns we heard was in Virginia & that the Negroes was then fighting the White people." Indeed, Dave insisted that the conspirators "could get encouragement from Virginia. The head negroes in Virginia lives about Richmond." These men spoke not as solitary rebels who sought personal liberty but as individuals who identified with an oppressed group and were willing to use violence against the system that enslaved them.

In May, patrollers in Bertie County had been unable to uncover any evidence of the slave plot. Then on June 2, 1802, while searching Negro houses in Colerain, they found a small piece of paper that listed the names of fourteen black men. The Negro woman in whose house the paper was discovered confessed that the slave Fed had left it with her that morning and said that he was carrying it from Sumner's Frank to Brown's King. The communication began, "*Captain Frank Sumner is to command* (and then names of the men and the 10th of June was the time) *you are to get as many men as you can—To Capt. King, Brown, &c.*"[59] During the ensuing week the Negroes named in the letter were apprehended and confined at Windsor. On June 10 the Bertie County court convened. The court consisted of some of the county's most prominent slaveholders, including United States Senator David Stone. The justices grimly undertook the business of trying the suspected conspirators. Six plotters, including Sumner's Frank

---

[58]The sources for this plot, especially depositions, are too numerous to cite for each quotation. The information, unless specified, has been culled from the Slavery Papers, Misc. Coll.; Perquimans County Slave Papers, 1759-1864; Bertie County Slave Papers, 1744-1815; and the *Raleigh Reg.*, May-Aug. 1802. The bulk of the depositions relating to the slave plot is in the Bertie County Slave Papers.

[59]*Raleigh Reg.*, July 6, 1802. See also Guion Griffis Johnson, *Ante-Bellum North Carolina: A Social History* (Chapel Hill, 1937), 510-513.

and Senator Stone's Bob, were hanged with ruthless dispatch. Though the court prescribed the punishments and performed the executions, the whole process had the aspect of lynch law. The Bertie court hanged eleven blacks, deported six more who offered testimony, and whipped and cropped perhaps two dozen others.

The Colerain letter had evidently circulated through several northeastern counties. The Negro Dennis, owned by Thomas Fitts of Bertie County, confessed that Jacob of Perquimans County "gave a letter to Mr. Browns Frank[.] They all knew of This letter, he saw Jacob of Edenton [Chowan County] & he told his depon[en]t he Gave a letter to Frank, to be Carried to King who was to Carry it to Dave, Mr. Browns Hestor read the letter, & Said to Dave, Mr. Fitt & Mr. Brown was To be first Killed, as they were Supposed to be the head Men on The river."⁶⁰ The imprisoned slaves testified that the plot had been in the works for several weeks, and its leaders had planned to rendezvous in Plymouth the night of June 9. There "they expected to receive considerable reinforcements from up and down the [Roanoke] river. . . . Some were offered county money to join, other[s] clothes and arms to go to Virginia to help the blacks there to fight the whites." In Washington County on the south side of Albemarle Sound a "rumpus" resulted in the shooting of "6 or 7 blacks . . . on their way to Williamston," also on the Roanoke. As reconstructed by white interrogators, the plot included caching guns and ammunition in the swamps, and crafting other weapons such as clubs with nails driven through them. On the night of the uprising the insurgents were to form into companies under their captains, "go to every man's house, set fire to it, kill the men and boys over 6 or 7 years of age; the women over a certain age, both black and white were to share the same fate; the young and handsome of the whites they were to keep for themselves, and the young ones of their own colour were to be spared for waiters." The slave Bob explained that the rebels had intended to divide up the lands among themselves. Moses, who asserted "he would be no mans Slave," had pledged to take one particular white girl as his "wife." Thomas Blount, a former congressman and leading slaveholder, understood "that when all the white men were killed the Black men were to take their places, have their wives, &c. &c."⁶¹

One could easily overstate the insurgents' plans to take white wives, to murder all women (black and white) over a certain age, and to spare a few black women as servants. White fantasies about Negro sexuality were of-

⁶⁰A letter, supposedly written by a Negro conspirator, is in the Bertie County Slave Papers, 1744-1815. The letter, though badly faded, is obviously the one cited in the *Raleigh Reg.*'s account of the insurrection.

⁶¹*Raleigh Reg.*, June 22, July 27, 1802; Charles Pettigrew to Ebenezer Pettigrew, June 21, 1802, in Sarah McCulloh Lemmon, ed., *The Pettigrew Papers*, I (Raleigh, N.C., 1971), 287-288; Thomas Blount to John Gray Blount, June 28, 1802, in William H. Masterson, ed., *The John Gray Blount Papers*, III (Raleigh, N.C., 1965), 516-517. See also Nathaniel Blount to Charles Pettigrew, May 4, 1802, in Lemmon, ed., *Pettigrew Papers*, I, 283.

ten at the center of insurrection scares. The image of sexually aggressive Negroes reflected white anxiety and guilt about the treatment of black women. In times of interracial crisis white men were quick to impute to others their own sexual aggressiveness. Despite numerous rumors to the contrary in North America and the West Indies throughout the eighteenth century, there is no evidence of rebel slaves seizing white women for their own use.[62] In the North Carolina plot, blacks expressly stated that they were fighting "against the white people to obtain their liberty." Moreover, black women played key roles in the conspiracy, from organizing meetings to passing messages, so it seems unlikely that they would have agreed to their own systematic extermination or reenslavement.

Even so, it is always difficult to separate black intentions from white hysteria in such situations. There is little doubt that an insurrection plot, centered in Bertie County, existed. The plot was certainly known to blacks in adjoining counties such as Hertford and Martin, but how well coordinated the conspiracy was beyond those boundaries is impossible to determine. It is clear, however, that an insurrection mania possessed whites. Besides the eleven slaves hanged in Bertie, the toll in other counties included four in Camden, two in Currituck, two in Martin, and one each in Perquimans, Hertford, Washington, Edgecombe, and Halifax. Another two dozen slaves were executed in Virginia, where a similar insurrection scare existed in 1802. By all accounts, eastern North Carolina was in an uproar during the spring and summer. The county militias were out in force, visiting plantations, keeping "nearly every negro man . . . under guard," and seizing suspected rebels (especially those who could read and write) against their masters' wishes. More than one hundred Negroes were jailed in Martin County alone. One episode illustrates particularly well the hysteria engulfing eastern North Carolina. A rumor swept Winton in Hertford County that Windsor in Bertie County had been attacked and burned by rebelling slaves. The town council dispatched a messenger to ascertain the truth of the report. On the way he met a rider from Windsor who had been sent to Winton for the same purpose.[63]

In Martin County the white hysteria that led to the incarceration of over one hundred blacks subsided as cooler heads prevailed. Dispassionate ob-

---

[62]Jordan, *White over Black*, 150-153; Allan Kulikoff, "The Origins of Afro-American Society in Tidewater Maryland and Virginia, 1700 to 1790," *WMQ*, 3d Ser., XXXV (1978), 239-240.

[63]*Raleigh Reg.*, July 6, 1802. Two companion papers on the North Carolina and Virginia slave insurrection scares were delivered at the 1977 meeting of the Organization of American Historians in Atlanta, Ga. Scott Strickland in "The 'Great Revival' and Insurrectionary Fears: North Carolina, 1801-1802," focused on the white community's reaction to the religious revival and its impact on race relations. Bertram Wyatt-Brown in "Slave Insurrection Scares as Southern Witchhunts: The Case of Virginia, 1802," totally discounted any revolt in the Old Dominion. Both viewed the insurrection scares as a means of solidifying the white community and setting boundaries for permissible slave behavior. See also Thomas C. Parramore, "The Great Slave Conspiracy," *The State*, XXXIX (Aug. 15, 1971), 7-10, 19.

servers like "J.R." admitted that some people had credited the wildest reports of slave insurgency while others dismissed the most sober evidence. He hinted that some planters did not want their slaves implicated in the plot for financial reasons. He also reported that Martin County magistrates kept compliant and militant slaves in separate jails. A county committee of inquiry then examined the suspects individually, beginning with the youngest. The interrogators told the younger slaves that they had been implicated and that they would receive lenient treatment if they confessed. In this way some twenty-five or thirty were questioned without the lash. However, the "old ones and chiefs amongst them, were true and faithful to their trust; not one of them would acknowledge at first that he knew anything of the plot." Tight-lipped rebels would give "no information until whiped." The coerced confessions "agreed perfectly with the evidence of the others, that never received a stroke." Ultimately, only two of the conspirators in Martin County were hanged. The others "received a very severe reprimand, and were made sensible to the folly and danger of their attempt; after which every one was chastised, more or less, according to his previous bad or good conduct, and ordered home."[64]

The fear of Negro insurgencies in the eighteenth century, as in other periods of southern history, provided the impetus for reasserting social control and unifying the white populace. In such instances, racial conflict resolved certain tensions and reestablished stability by eliminating causes of fragmentation among whites. Antagonists in one setting (politics, religion, economics) became allies in another.[65] Janet Schaw had witnessed the same phenomenon in Wilmington in 1775 when loyalists joined whigs to suppress an expected slave insurrection.

The insurrection scare of 1802 in North Carolina climaxed three decades of heightening conflict between blacks and whites. The Revolutionary War, with its severe strains and disruptive impact on society, left a legacy of unstable racial patterns in which blacks and whites struggled to define their places and roles in postwar society. Afro-Americans, buoyed by rising hopes of freedom, developed a greater cohesiveness and took collective measures to oppose the slaveholders' regime. Whites attempted to maintain their authority in the face of restive slaves, religious egalitarians, and a few slaveholders who wished to improve the slave's lot even as they perpetuated slavery. Violence between blacks and whites signaled society's internal tensions, but it also served a political function—as a form of resistance among blacks and as a means of social control among whites.

Slave rebelliousness had always carried within it the seeds of political protest, but the Revolution provided the social and ideological conditions necessary to galvanize blacks into collective resistance and to create a new

---

[64] A letter by "J.R." appeared in the *Raleigh Reg.*, July 27, 1802.
[65] A cogent article examining this process in another time and place is Dan T. Carter, "The Anatomy of Fear: The Christmas Day Insurrection Scare of 1865," *Jour. So. Hist.*, XLII (1976), 345-364.
[66] [Tucker], *Letter . . . On The Subject Of The Late Conspiracy*, 7.

sense of community among slaves. St. George Tucker recognized this revolutionary process when he identified the difference between those slaves who ran off to the British in 1775 and those who joined Gabriel Prosser in 1800. At the beginning of the Revolution, he observed, slaves had "fought [for] freedom merely as a good; now they also claim it as a right."[66]

David Ross and the Oxford Iron Works:
A Study of Industrial Slavery in the
Early Nineteenth-Century South

Charles B. Dew*

HISTORIANS have documented the extensive use of slave labor in southern iron manufacturing during the colonial, Revolutionary, and early national periods, but a lack of detailed information on the operations of southern blast furnaces and forges during these years has prevented scholars from learning very much about the day-to-day functioning of this important phase of the South's industrial slave system.[1] The recent uncovering of a substantial portion of a letterbook kept by David Ross, a prominent Virginia merchant, planter, and the principal owner and developer of one of the largest iron works in the Revolutionary and post-Revolutionary South, provides a rare opportunity to examine the life of the black iron worker in the early nineteenth century.[2] The Ross Letterbook, which deals with operations at his Oxford

* Mr. Dew is a member of the Department of History, University of Missouri—Columbia. He wishes to thank the National Endowment for the Humanities for a summer stipend which enabled him to complete the research for this article and to express his gratitude for a summer residency fellowship at the Robert S. Starobin Memorial Library, Hancock, Mass., where this article was written. He is also grateful for the generous financial aid granted in support of his residency at the Starobin Library by the American Council of Learned Societies and the Research Council of the University of Missouri—Columbia.

[1] The employment of slave labor in early southern iron works is mentioned in Kathleen Bruce, *Virginia Iron Manufacture in the Slave Era* (New York, 1931), 11-13, 15, 48n, 55-58, 129-130, 231-232; Samuel Sydney Bradford, "The Ante-Bellum Charcoal Iron Industry of Virginia" (Ph.D. diss., Columbia University, 1958), and in an article drawn from this study, "The Negro Ironworker in Ante Bellum Virginia," *Journal of Southern History*, XXV (1959), 194-196; Gerald W. Mullin, *Flight and Rebellion: Slave Resistance in Eighteenth-Century Virginia* (New York, 1972), 85, 87-88; Lester J. Cappon, "Iron-Making—A Forgotten Industry of North Carolina," *North Carolina Historical Review*, IX (1932), 340; Ernest M. Lander, Jr., "The Iron Industry in Ante-Bellum South Carolina," *Jour. So. Hist.*, XX (1954), 350. The outstanding work on Virginia slavery in the post-Revolutionary era, Robert McColley, *Slavery and Jeffersonian Virginia* (Urbana, Ill., 1964), does not discuss the use of slave labor in the state's iron industry.

[2] David Ross Letterbook, 1812-1813, Virginia Historical Society, Richmond. This

Iron Works in Campbell County, Virginia, during 1812 and 1813, gives a remarkably full picture of slave working and living conditions at this installation and offers insight into a number of key topics, including the status of the black family in this industrial setting, the nature of the relationship between the ironmaster and his bondsmen, and the application and effectiveness of the employer's various disciplinary and incentive techniques.

For a man who was probably "the richest of all planters" in Virginia in the 1780s, surprisingly little is known about Ross.[3] He was born in Scotland about 1739 and immigrated to the American colonies in the mid-1750s.[4] By the time of the Revolution he had established himself as a leading Richmond and Petersburg tobacco merchant and shipowner and worked a large plantation at Point of Fork, the junction of the James and Rivanna rivers some forty-five miles west of Richmond. As part of his business activities Ross regularly offered land, indentured servants, and slaves for sale, and he had begun acquiring a black labor force which would eventually place him among the largest slaveowners in Virginia. By the late 1780s, when Ross's wealth was probably at its zenith, he had amassed over 100,000 acres of land scattered across twelve counties in Virginia; he owned more horses than anyone else in the state, 254; his cattle holdings, 806, ranked second only to those of Charles Carter; and his ownership of 400 slaves made him the fifth largest slaveholder in the Old Dominion.[5] If he was not the wealthiest planter in the state during this

---

letterbook has been in the Society's collections for many years, but until 1972 a sizable portion of the letters could not be read because someone, evidently in the 1820s, had used the volume as a scrapbook for newspaper clippings. I wish to thank the manuscript curators at the Society for their kindness is skillfully removing the clippings and allowing me to examine the Ross letters which had previously been obscured. Unfortunately some pages in the letterbook are missing; those that remain are numbered 83-88, 93-161, 178-181, 190-191, 210-243, 256-257, and 274-397. I have maintained Ross's orthography intact in quotations from this source, while inserting bracketed interpolations where necessary.

[3] Jackson T. Main, "The One Hundred," *William and Mary Quarterly*, 3d Ser., XI (1954), 363. Ross's neglect by historians can undoubtedly be explained by the lack of any sizable body of Ross manuscripts.

[4] In two letters written in 1813 Ross gave his age as 74 and stated that he had been in America almost 60 years; Ross to William C. Williams, July 1, 1813, and to Mrs. Ross, Sept. 1818, Ross Letterbook. The *Virginia Patriot* (Richmond), May 5, 1817, noted that Ross was "in the 77th year of his age" when he died on May 4, 1817. A biographical note on Ross in William T. Hutchinson and William M. E. Rachal, eds., *The Papers of James Madison* (Chicago, 1962-), III, 60n, gives the year of his birth as ca. 1736 as well as other pertinent information.

[5] Thomas S. Berry, "The Rise of Flour Milling in Richmond," *Virginia Magazine of History and Biography*, LXXVIII (1970), 393; Edmund Berkeley, Jr., "Prophet

decade, he must have been very nearly so.

Ross's Revolutionary career began with accusations of disloyalty to the patriot cause and ended with a term of vital and, for Ross, financially expensive service to the state. In 1776 and 1777 he was forced to defend himself against charges of toryism on two separate occasions, but in both instances he was able to convince Virginia officials that the accusations were groundless.[6] In late 1780 he began acting as commercial agent for the state, with primary responsibility for supplying Virginia troops with clothing, ordnance, lead, and other important military stores.[7] During his tenure as commercial agent Ross drew heavily on his own financial resources to help sustain the credit of the state and apparently worked with great energy to meet the needs of the Virginia forces. He resigned as commercial agent in April 1782 in order to take a seat in the General Assembly as a delegate from Fluvanna County. He served in the two legislative sessions of 1782 and was reelected in 1783, but continued to transact a considerable amount of business for the state after leaving his post as commercial agent. Although by his wartime activities Ross ended speculation about where his loyalty lay in the struggle with Great Britain, he did so at a price. In 1787 he was still seeking reimbursement from the state for advances made during the Revolution.[8] As Ross's property hold-

---

Without Honor: Christopher McPherson, Free Person of Color," *ibid.*, LXXVII (1969), 180-181. On Ross's activities as a seller of land and indentured and slave laborers see his numerous advertisements in Purdie and Dixon's *Virginia Gazette* (Williamsburg), Sept. 17, 1767; Mar. 3, Nov. 10, 1768; Jan. 26, 1769; Aug. 16, Oct. 18, 1770; Jan. 10, 31, May 9, July 4, 1771. See *ibid.*, May 12, 1768; May 18, June 29, 1769; Nov. 14, 1771, for Ross's ownership of slaves prior to the Revolution, as indicated by his advertisements for runaways. The information on Ross's wealth in the 1780s is from Main, "One Hundred," *WMQ*, 3d Ser., XI (1954), 363, 368-383. Those who held more slaves than Ross were Charles Carter (785), William Allen (700), Robert Beverly (592), and Robert Carter (445). George Washington, with 390 slaves, ranked just below Ross. Main's figures are based on the manuscript county tax lists for 1787 and 1788 at the Virginia State Library, Richmond.

[6] The charges came from Pittsylvania County, where Ross was accused of issuing a commission to another man to lead an Indian attack on the area, and from Dinwiddie County, where unspecified charges of disloyalty were leveled against him; Dixon's *Va. Gaz.*, Oct. 18, 1776, and Purdie's *Va. Gaz.*, Feb. 14, 1777.

[7] Gov. Thomas Jefferson sent Ross his commission as commercial agent on Feb. 2, 1781; Ross, however, had been exercising the duties of that office since Dec. 27, 1780, and had been acting as a commissary officer for the state for over a year before his appointment as commercial agent; Julian P. Boyd, ed., *The Papers of Thomas Jefferson* (Princeton, N. J., 1950-), IV, 228n, 475n. Ross's responsibilities as commercial agent included supervising the state's lead mines and ordnance-casting facilities; see Jefferson to Ross, Mar. 20, 1781, *ibid.*, V, 191-192, and Ross to John Staples, June 3, 1813, Ross Letterbook.

[8] Benjamin Harrison to the Virginia Delegates, Feb. 9, 1782, in Hutchinson and

ings in the 1780s indicate, however, his sacrifices for the commonwealth certainly did not cripple him financially, and in the postwar years he expanded his range of investments dramatically both inside and outside Virginia.[9] He also retained and developed the most important industrial property he had acquired during the war years, the Oxford Iron Works, a major manufacturing enterprise located on the south side of the James River some eight miles southeast of Lynchburg.[10]

Some confusion exists over exactly when Ross acquired the Oxford property, but he clearly was in control of the works by the fall of 1776 and was soon in a position to exploit the wartime demand for iron. At the outset of Ross's ownership the Oxford works consisted of a well-timbered 6,000-acre tract with several banks of iron ore and a forge and bloomery for refining pig metal into bars and other semifinished iron products. Water power was supplied by Beaver Creek, a tributary of the James.[11] Oxford lacked a blast furnace which could convert the ore into

---

Rachal, eds., *Madison Papers*, IV, 60; V, 126n, 206n, and *Calendar of Virginia State Papers and Other Manuscripts* . . . (Richmond, Va., 1875-1893), III, 118. As a member of the Assembly Ross could not officially hold another state appointment.

[9] Among Ross's most important postwar investments were substantial interests in Richmond coal mining and flour and grist milling enterprises, ownership of a pioneer western iron works, the Holston Iron Works in Tennessee, and major participation in Georgia and Mississippi land speculations through the Virginia Yazoo Company; see James Currie to Jefferson, Oct. 17, 1785, in Boyd, ed., *Jefferson Papers*, VIII, 643; Berry, "Flour Milling in Richmond," *VMHB*, LXXVIII (1970), 393-395; Samuel C. Williams, "Early Iron Works in the Tennessee Country," *Tennessee Historical Quarterly*, VI (1947), 39-41; Robert Douthat Meade, *Patrick Henry*. II: *Practical Revolutionary* (Philadelphia, 1969), 423; Ross to Seaton Grantland, June 27, 1812, Ross Letterbook. Ross also continued to play a role in public life as a Virginia delegate to the Annapolis Convention in 1786 and as a director of, and major investor in, the James River Company, which was seeking to develop the transportation potential of the James. Ross had earlier served as a trustee of a similar project to improve the Potomac; see Currie to Jefferson, Aug. 5, 1785, and Ross to Jefferson, Oct. 22, 1785, in Boyd, ed., *Jefferson Papers*, VIII, 343, 660; Hutchinson and Rachal, eds., *Madison Papers*, VIII, 471; "Education in Colonial Virginia," *WMQ*, 1st Ser., VII (1898-1899), 4; Purdie and Dixon's *Va. Gaz.*, Nov. 3, 1774.

[10] J. P. Lesley, *The Iron Manufacturer's Guide to the Furnaces, Forges and Rolling Mills of the United States* . . . (New York, 1859), 64. The works lay in a section of Bedford County that became part of Campbell County when that jurisdiction was created in 1781. The site of the Oxford furnace is now a wayside on U.S. Route 460 about eight miles east of Lynchburg.

[11] R. H. Early, *Campbell Chronicles and Family Sketches, Embracing the History of Campbell County, Virginia, 1782-1926* (Lynchburg, Va., 1927), 148-149, dates Ross's acquisition of the Oxford property in 1787, but his land purchases in that year were clearly an expansion of his original holdings. Ross was writing letters from "Oxford" in November 1776, and in 1812 he noted that the Oxford estate had been settled for 36 years, which would confirm 1776 as the original date

pig iron, however, and Ross moved promptly to correct this deficiency. By 1779 a blast furnace had been completed, and Ross negotiated a contract with Virginia to supply the state-owned Westham Foundry with a substantial quantity of high-quality pig iron suitable for casting ordnance.[12] Over two hundred pieces of ordnance were cast at Westham out of Oxford iron during the war, and Ross claimed in later years that not one failed to pass "double Proof," a test firing with twice the normal powder charge.[13] In addition, the Oxford works furnished shot and shell, bar iron, nail rods, camp kettles, horseshoes, and other iron supplies to state quartermasters in Virginia and North Carolina and to the forces fighting in the South under General Nathanael Greene.[14] Ross undoubtedly profited also from a brisk private demand for American-made iron during the war. Thomas Jefferson estimated in the early 1780s that Oxford was producing more pig iron, 1,600 tons, than any other blast furnace in Virginia, and he praised the "remarkable" strength of Ross's cast iron. "Pots and other utensils, cast thinner than usual, of this iron, may be safely thrown into, or out of the wagons in which they are transported,"

---

of purchase; see Ross to John Hook, Nov. 30, 1776, David Ross Papers, Va. State Library, and Ross, "Memorandum for Mr. Robert Richardson" (Dec. 1812), Ross Letterbook. The Oxford property as it probably existed at the time of Ross's purchase is described in a 1772 advertisement offering the works for sale; Rind's Va. Gaz., Oct. 22, 1772. See also Lesley, Iron Manufacturer's Guide, 64.

[12] The tonnage called for in Ross's state contract is in some doubt. Most contemporary sources give the figure as 250 tons, but Ross claimed in 1813 that his contract called for 1,000 tons, of which 380 tons were delivered before British forces destroyed the Westham Foundry in Jan. 1781; see Jas. Innes, Wm. Nelson, and Geo. Lyne to Jefferson, Nov. 16, 1779, and Jefferson to the Board of Trade, Dec. 10, 1779, in Boyd, ed., Jefferson Papers, III, 188-189, 214; Ross to the governor, Oct. 23, 1792, Cal. Va. State Papers, VI, 108; Ross to John Staples, Sept. 14, 1813, Ross Letterbook.

[13] Ross told the superintendent of the Virginia State Armory in June 1813 that 210 cannon, all of which had passed double proof, had been cast from Oxford pig at Westham during the war, but in a subsequent letter he gave the figure as 250 pieces; Ross to John Staples, June 3, Sept. 14, 1813, Ross Letterbook. The high quality of Ross's iron and of the ordnance cast from it was confirmed by former Gov. Patrick Henry, who wrote in 1786 that "Virginia was indebted to Mr. Ross alone, for the excellent Cannons that were made here during the war of his Iron." Henry to Gov. Richard Caswell, Nov. 21, 1786, in Walter Clark, ed., The Colonial and State Records of North Carolina (Raleigh and Goldsboro, N. C., 1886-1914), XVIII, 787.

[14] Bruce, Virginia Iron Manufacture, 64; George Muter to Jefferson, Jan. 14, 1781, in Boyd, ed., Jefferson Papers, IV, 354; Nicholas Long to Jefferson, Mar. 29, 1781, ibid., V, 281; Ross to the executive, Feb. 24, 1783, in Cal. Va. State Papers, III, 447; Proceedings of the Board of War, Sept. 3, 5, 1780, in Clark, ed., N. C. Recs., XIV, 377-378; Ross to Gov. Thomas Burke, Aug. 24, 1781, ibid., XXII, 574-575; Henry to Gov. Caswell, Nov. 21, 1786, ibid., XVIII, 787.

Jefferson claimed. "Salt pans made of the same, and no longer wanted for that purpose, cannot be broken up, in order to be melted again, unless previously drilled in many parts."[15] The Oxford works remained in production after the Revolution ended, and Ross concentrated on blacksmith work and on the manufacture of merchant bars (standard-sized bar iron for the plantation and blacksmith trades), and pots, kettles, and assorted cast iron hollow ware for domestic use.[16]

By the early nineteenth century, the Oxford "estate," as Ross usually referred to the iron works property, had grown well beyond its original dimensions and capabilities. Additional land purchases had expanded the estate to some 24,000 acres, and the manufacturing facilities consisted of a blast furnace, a refinery forge of four fires and two hammers with a productive capacity of four tons of bar iron per week, and a chaffery forge of one fire and one hammer for the manufacture of wrought iron blooms. In the Oxford smith shop, a force of ten to twelve blacksmiths turned out a wide assortment of tools, plows, wagon irons, horseshoes, and the like, while an equal number of potters ladled molten iron directly from the open-hearth blast furnace and cast the hollow ware that Jefferson found so impressive. Elsewhere on the estate wood choppers cut timber, colliers converted it into charcoal, and miners dug the iron ore and limestone needed to feed the blast furnace. The product of all this labor—bars, castings, smith's work, and excess pig iron—was floated down the James River by three Oxford boat crews and sold either to customers along the river or in Richmond. The Oxford property also embraced a large grist mill and four plantations which produced much of the grain and fodder needed to sustain both the labor force and the large number of draft animals engaged in working the estate.[17] The varied and fre-

---

[15] Thomas Jefferson, *Notes on the State of Virginia*, ed. Thomas Perkins Abernethy (New York, 1964), 24-25. Jefferson ascribed the same qualities to cast iron produced at Isaac Zane's Marlboro Iron Works in Frederick County. Bruce, *Virginia Iron Manufacture*, 64n, suggests that Jefferson's tonnage estimate of Oxford pig iron production may be inflated, but Oxford's position as the largest single producer of pig iron in the state during this era is not in question. Jefferson put Ross's bar iron production at approximately 150 tons per year.

[16] Ross to Samuel Dyer, Jr., Dec. 3, 1812, Ross Letterbook.

[17] The best description of the Oxford property is contained in an advertisement written by Ross offering the estate for lease, Sept. 3, 1811, a copy of which is in the William Bolling Papers, Duke University Library, Durham, N. C. See also the testimony of William Mewburn in *Granberry & Hancock* v. *Ross,* Mar. 20, 1811, copy, *ibid.*, Ross, "Memorandum for Robert Richardson" (Dec. 1812), Ross to Dyer, Dec. 3, 1812, to William J. Dunn, May 7, 1813, to Mr. Whaites, June 2, 1813, and to John Staples, Aug. 9, Sept. 16, 20, 1813, Ross Letterbook.

quently complex tasks involved in the operations at Oxford were performed almost entirely by slave men, women, and children belonging to Ross.

The range of skills possessed by the black workers at Oxford made them one of the most remarkable industrial slave labor forces ever assembled in the antebellum South. The founder, who had full responsibility for the highly technical and demanding day-to-day management of the blast furnace, was a slave named Abram who had been raised at Oxford. The four furnace keepers, who were the founder's principal assistants and who directed furnace operations in his absence, were also slaves, as were the fillers, whose job was to dump measured amounts of ore, charcoal, and limestone into the furnace day and night when it was in blast.[18] The blacksmiths, potters, refinery men, hammermen, miners, colliers, teamsters, and general furnace hands were all slave workers. The crops were planted, cultivated, and harvested by "about thirty four plantation servants and four overseers belonging to the Estate," Ross wrote in 1811, which indicates that he was using slave supervision for agricultural as well as industrial work.[19] This is also borne out by instructions Ross gave his white manager at Oxford concerning the hiring of two men to oversee plantations where Ross felt it necessary to have a white man present. "I found overseers in general the most worthless set of men and their wives still worse," Ross commented. "I have an utter aversion to them after long experience, [but] there must be a white overseer at Cars [plantation], also at Johns[;] the plantation at Cars is so near the [iron] works that one of our people will not be able to keep his authority over the waggoners etc."[20] Ross was obviously reluctant to use white men on the estate in any capacity if he could possibly avoid doing so.

"With the exception of a white hired carpenter a miller and myself, every person upon the Oxford Iron Works Estate is a slave and the property of David Ross Esqr," wrote the manager in overall charge of operations in 1811. "The total number of slaves is upwards of two hundred and twenty."[21] A listing of the Oxford slaves made in the same year pro-

---

[18] Ross to Mr. Douglas, Feb. 7, 1812, Ross Letterbook, and testimony of Mewburn, Bolling Papers. For an excellent discussion of the skills required of the founder, keepers, and fillers see Joseph E. Walker, *Hopewell Village: A Social and Economic History of an Iron-Making Community* (Philadelphia, 1966), 231-236.

[19] Ross, advertisement to lease Oxford Iron Works, Sept. 3, 1811, Bolling Papers.

[20] Ross to William J. Dunn, Aug. 1813, Ross Letterbook.

[21] Testimony of Mewburn, Bolling Papers.

TABLE I
SLAVES AT THE OXFORD IRON WORKS
JANUARY 15, 1811

	Men[a]	Boys[b]	Women[a]	Girls[b]	Total
Furnace and Forges	19	1	10	1	31
Blacksmiths	5	4			9
Coaling Grounds	13	7	3	1	24
Ore Banks	3	2	1	2	8
Carpenters	6	2			8
Wagoners	6				6
Odd Hands	3				3
Plantation Hands	7	3	14	1	25
House Servants	___	1	1	1	3
Total Work Force	62	20	29	6	117
Old People[c] and Children	7	41	14	41	103
Total Slave Force	69	61	43	47	220

Notes and Sources:
[a] Slaves were classed as adult men and women after they reached 18.
[b] With the exception of one 11-year-old boy who worked at the coaling ground, all of the boys and girls in the labor force were between 14 and 17.
[c] The "Old People" classification was used to designate slaves who were unable to work either because of old age or chronic illness. The seven men in this category ranged in age from 65 to 90. The 14 women listed as "Old People" included six who were under 60 (their ages were 16, 36, 50, and 54, and two were 42); the remaining eight nonworking women were between 60 and 80.
The source for this table is "List of Slaves at the Oxford Iron Works in Families and Their Employment, Taken 15 January 1811," in the William Bolling Papers, Duke University Library, Durham, N. C.

vides a detailed occupational breakdown of the labor force (Table I). These figures may well underestimate the number of effective workers at Oxford, however, since the list does not include Ross's three crews of black boatmen and gives only twenty-five plantation hands instead of the thirty-four workers and four overseers mentioned by Ross later in 1811. He noted in November 1812 that "we can muster 140 or 150 men, women, boys and girls fit for service" (as opposed to the 117 slaves listed as employed in Table I).[22]

The raw figures in Table I also fail to convey the versatility and self-sufficiency of the Oxford slave force. In a letter to his son in 1813 Ross described with obvious pride the range of skills possessed by some of his black workers: "Many of my servants at Oxford have double trades some of them treble, most of my Blacksmiths are also potters, and part of them go into the pot houses when the furnace is in blast [;] last Augt at the Commencement of the blast, Nat Senr, King, Alexander and Jack resumed their potting business, their strikers [helpers] were very little inferior to themselves, some of them had been 7 years at the trade, and I promoted four of them to fill the place of the four potters."[23] In addition, as many as one hundred laborers would be shifted from industrial to agricultural tasks when the furnace blew out and extra hands were needed on the plantations.[24] From all appearances, Ross was not exaggerating in the slightest in 1811 when he outlined the industrial capabilities of his Oxford workers: "The Servants belonging to the Estate are sufficient in number, well qualified by experience and practice and properly arranged to the various departments of the business, to execute every branch without the assistance of any other mechanic either in making Bar Iron, or common moulded Iron—repairing or rebuilding any of the machinery of the Forges Furnaces or Mills—Mining or Coaling—and besides the Blacksmithery competent to the uses of the Estate, there are four Smiths and strikers with Tools complete for manufacturing new work for sale."[25]

The 1811 enumeration that forms the basis for Table I reveals that the number of women and children employed at Oxford almost equaled the number of men, and that of the eighty-nine slaves who were engaged in various aspects of iron manufacturing thirty-four were women, boys, or girls. As a general rule, children do not appear to have been placed in the work force until they were fourteen years old. Between the ages of eight and thirteen most of them were assigned the job of tending

---

[22] Ross to Robert Richardson, Nov. 10, 1812, Ross Letterbook.
[23] Ross to David Ross, Jr., July 25, 1813, *ibid.*
[24] Ross to Thomas Evans, Aug. 10, 1813, *ibid.*
[25] Ross, advertisement to lease Oxford Iron Works, Bolling Papers.

the younger children. At least one child in this age bracket, eleven-year-old Champion, was working, however, as a wood hauler at the coaling grounds in 1811, together with six other boys, whose ages ranged from fourteen to seventeen. All these boys except Champion, whose father mined limestone, were the sons or grandsons of colliers and were thus working alongside close relatives. The same general pattern held true for the three women and one girl who were employed in coaling. All four raked leaves, which were used with dirt to cover smoldering wood while it was being converted into charcoal; three of the leaf rakers, Kitsey (age twenty-five), Jenny (eighteen), and Mary (fifteen), were the daughters of colliers, and the fourth, Molly Bland (fifty-five), was married to a collier. Children, and some of the "superanuated people" on the estate, were also used to clean sand off finished castings at the pot houses.[26]

The exact nature of the duties and physical demands placed on the women working at the blast furnace and the ore banks is unclear. One task that can be identified was the assignment given the one woman and two girls who were part of the mining operation; they were responsible, at least in part, for cleaning and picking over the ore so that it would be as free as possible from impurities before it went to the furnace. These three workers were Betty (age twenty-two), the wife of one of the miners, and two unmarried girls, Phillis (eighteen), whose father was a blacksmith, and Judy (seventeen, described as having "sore eyes"), the daughter of a skilled refinery hand.[27] Some of the female furnace and mining laborers must have been engaged in occupations that required physical strength, for Ross noted in 1813 that "no less than seven women at the Furnace and Ore Banks" were "so far advanced in pregnancy that they can't do their duty[;] indeed some are delivered [and] others confined," and as a result "all the stoutest spinning girls" on the plantations had "been drawn out to supply their place."[28] On at least one occasion a woman was temporarily placed at one of the most physically taxing jobs at the works, as Ross noted in 1813: "Susan [a weaver at an Oxford plantation] . . . who was for sometime promising to improve took retrograde course and fell off [;]

[26] "List of Slaves at the Oxford Iron Works in Families and Their Employment, Taken 15 January 1811," Bolling Papers, and Ross to George Beverley and Miles Todd [Apr. 1813], Ross Letterbook.

[27] "List of Slaves at Oxford Iron Works," Bolling Papers, and Ross to William J. Dunn, June 1, 1813, Ross Letterbook.

[28] Ross to John Duffield, Jan. 9, 1813, Ross Letterbook.

I sent her to the mines by way of an agreeable change and improvement—I understand she has returned [to her weaving] and that the digging of iron ore and raking it, has greatly enlightened her weaving talents."[29] Generally, however, Ross seems to have attempted to match the physical abilities of his workers with the tasks given to them and to have deviated from this practice only for disciplinary purposes.[30] As in the case of most of the women and children engaged in other phases of iron manufacturing, the blast furnace personnel drawn from these two groups tended to be the wives and children of men working with or near them. For example, Delphia, a twenty-two-year-old furnace worker, was the daughter of Abram the founder (age fifty-two) and was married to one of her father's chief assistants, Simon (twenty-seven), a keeper at the blast furnace. The only young girl listed as a furnace laborer in 1811, Molly (fifteen years old), was the child of a furnace wagoner named Arthur (fifty-five) and his wife Juno (forty-four), who also worked at the furnace.[31]

The nucleus of the slave force that operated the Oxford works in the first decades of the nineteenth century was apparently on the estate when Ross purchased it, but he wasted little time in attempting to acquire additional black workers.[32] He was attending slave sales in the fall of 1776, and in February 1777 he advertised that he wished "to hire 50 stout NEGRO MEN" for his iron works and that he would give "*ready money* for twenty YOUNG NEGRO FELLOWS from 16 to 20 years of age."[33] Later that year he again offered to buy "likely young Negroes from 15 to 20 Years of Age" and to hire "50 or 60 Negro men for one, two, or three Years." He promised to pay "an advanced Price for Carpenters and Wheelwrights" but warned that he would "not be

[29] *Ibid.*
[30] When Ross wanted some unimproved land on one of his Oxford plantations cleared, he wrote the overseer, "I expect some more strong hands must be added that they may be clearing and mauling while the weaker hands are ploughing and harrowing the winter and spring crops." Ross to Tarlton Rice, Sept. 25, 1813, *ibid.* See also Ross, "Memorandum for Richardson," *ibid.*
[31] "List of Slaves at Oxford Iron Works," Bolling Papers.
[32] Ross wrote from Oxford in 1776 asking a business partner to purchase ten gallons of "strong whiskey" and five gallons "of good brandy if you can procure it cheap" because "there has been so much idleness here that my people must now work all weather and I wish to give them spirits when wel"; Ross to John Hook, Nov. 30, 1776, Ross Papers. In 1812 Ross noted that "Abram . . . my founder at Oxford—has been raised there from childhood"; Ross to Mr. Douglas, Feb. 7, 1812, Ross Letterbook.
[33] Ross to John Hook, Oct. 30, 1776, Ross Papers, and Purdie's *Va. Gaz.*, Feb. 14, 1777.

concerned with any that are noted Runaways." "The situation of the Works is very healthy," he assured slaveowners, "the Labour of the slaves moderate, and they shall have a plentiful Diet."[34] Ross's rather effusive Virginia advertisements evidently did not bring in as many slaves as he desired. In 1781, when he was considering expanding the capacity of his works, he estimated that he would need almost one hundred additional workers, and he asked the governor of North Carolina if there were "any Public Slaves in your State that could be hired or purchased."[35] Ross obviously preferred to buy rather than hire slave workers, and ultimately he was able to purchase the hands he needed. By the time of the second war with Great Britain he could boast that "every branch of the business is carried on by the Servants belonging to the Estate, [and] we have no hirelings above the rank of a wood cutter."[36]

From Ross's point of view, the almost total exclusion of white artisans from his iron works was a distinct advantage. He claimed that "nothing affords me more delight than to make 'the lower son of labour smile,' " but his professed benevolence toward the working class clearly did not embrace free white mechanics.[37] Because they were relatively scarce in Virginia and their skills were in constant demand, Ross maintained that white artisans could get exorbitant wages and then strike and halt production whenever it suited their fancy. He was willing to use white craftsmen on a temporary basis for construction work if his slave hands were too busy to do the job, and he would employ a few white tradesmen in noncritical positions—a harnessmaker, a tanner, a weaver, a stonemason—if he needed a specific skill at a particular time.[38] Ross would

[34] Dixon's *Va. Gaz.*, Nov. 7, 1777. Mullin, *Flight and Rebellion*, 185, n. 30, states that "more slaves ran off from iron foundries than from any other nonagricultural industry" in 18th-century Virginia.
[35] Ross to Gov. Burke, Aug. 24, 1781, in Clark, ed., *N. C. Recs.*, XXII, 574.
[36] Ross to John Staples, Sept. 16, 1813, Ross Letterbook. Both Bradford, "Negro Ironworker," *Jour. So. Hist.*, XXV (1959), 195, and Mullin, *Flight and Rebellion*, 87-88, claim that the labor demands of the Revolutionary era brought about a shift from slave ownership to slave hiring at Virginia iron works. If such a shift occurred at Ross's works during the war, and his advertisements indicate that it may well have, the change was clearly a temporary one.
[37] Ross to Julia, Aug. 3, 1813, Ross Letterbook. The quotation is a rough rendition of lines from the British poet James Thomson's "Britannia," published in 1729; the lines actually read
    ". . . bid Industry rejoice
    And the rough sons of lowest Labour smile."
[38] Ross, "Memorandum for Richardson," and Ross to John Henderson, Aug. 1, 1813, to Laurence Huron, Aug. 15, 1813, to Richard Netherland, Aug. 17, 1813, and to Tarlton Rice, Sept. 25, 1813, *ibid.*

employ a white mechanic, however, only as a youthful apprentice, apparently to be trained for elevation to a supervisory post, and he severely limited their number. In 1813 he wrote that he wanted two young boys not over fourteen or fifteen, of "sound health" and raised by parents of "fair and honest character," bound to the works until they were of age, but he warned that " 'twould be imprudent in the parents as in myself to introduce a dull Clod headed lad, who after labouring through his apprenticeship could not be promoted."[39] Some white management was needed on the estate, however, and in 1812 and 1813 during Ross's frequent absences from the works, operations were directed by three "superintending clerks," as he called them, all of whom appear to have been related to Ross: William J. Dunn, Robert Richardson, and Ross's son-in-law John Duffield.[40]

Ross's attitude toward his slave workers was much more complex than the incident involving Susan, the weaver who was sent to the ore bank, would indicate. Ross could write of "the inborn depravity of the African," but then add in the same sentence that "it would be as ungenerous as painful to think or to say that" this "depravity" could "not be eradicated in the third or fourth generation" of "our own native born people."[41] He warned his white clerks at Oxford to be alert at slaughtering time because "the slaves feel nearly as great a temptation to steal the offall of hoggs as if it was so many dollars scattered on the ground," but at the same time he believed that white wagoners coming onto the estate had stolen most of the hollow ware that had disappeared over the years.[42] He could be a stern master when he thought circumstances warranted strong discipline, but he combined with this trait what appears to have been a genuine respect for many of the black people under his control and a concern for their welfare that transcended the obvious necessity of protecting the health and well-being of his very valuable chattels. On balance his actions show that when he referred to his slaves as "poor unfortunate people . . . placed under the authority of temporary masters who have command over them altho' less understanding and sometimes less integrity than those poor blacks," he was doing more than indulging in a bit of hypocritical humility.[43] Indeed, Ross seems

---

[39] Ross to George Revelly, Sept. 8, 1813, *ibid*.
[40] Ross to William J. Dunn, [July] 5, [1813], and to Staples, Sept. 13, 1813, *ibid*.
[41] Ross to Robert Richardson, Jan. 19, 1813, *ibid*.
[42] Ross to William J. Dunn, Jan. 9, 1813, and to Robert Richardson, Nov. 28, 1812, *ibid*.
[43] Ross to Robert Richardson, Jan. 1813, *ibid*.

to have had serious doubts about the propriety of owning slaves, but, like so many other Virginians of the Jeffersonian era, he was willing to let the next generation solve the problem of slavery. He hoped if he "lived to see his [son Frederick's] education perfected, that he would never have any inclination to hold his fellow men in Slavery," Ross wrote in 1813.[44] In the meantime he would do what he could to be a kind, but not overindulgent, master.

Ross's feelings toward his skilled slave artisans are most clearly revealed in his relationship with Abram, the Oxford founder. Ross considered Abram an exceptionally able iron worker, but his regard for him seems to have gone beyond simply an admiration of his abilities. In 1812 when Ross was considering making some changes in his blast furnace machinery, he sent Abram to secure the services of a mechanic at another Virginia furnace who understood the contemplated improvements. Abram carried a letter of introduction from Ross to the furnace manager outlining his mission and explaining that neither Ross nor his clerks were free to come. "I have said this much, to apologize for sending upon this business, a man of colour," Ross informed the manager, "but this can be no objection to a man of sense." Ross then proceeded to describe Abram's extraordinary qualities:

I have ... committed to the bearer Abram, my instructions as to engaging a mechanic, which he will show you—he is my founder at Oxford— has been raised there from childhood, and supports an unblemished character, for his integrity, good understanding, and talents from his infancy to his gray hairs—the utmost confidence may be given to his communications—his honor and integrity [are] untarnished, and unexceptional— he will deliver this letter to you on his arrival, and will not speak a word to any person on the estate, without your permission—I want no people of any description, except a mechanic for the purposes before mentioned, and if you'll have the goodness to recommend Abram to a suitable person, you'll much oblige me.[45]

It clearly required "a man of sense" to supervise all of the operations for which Abram had responsibility. In addition to managing the furnace when it was in blast, he had the task of making all furnace repairs and processing the ore before the furnace was blown in. On one occasion when Abram was absent from Oxford for a brief time prior to

---

[44] Ross to John Duffield, Jan. 9, 1813, *ibid.*
[45] Ross to Mr. Douglas, Feb. 7, 1812, *ibid.*

going into blast, Ross told one of his white superintendents to keep an eye on the preparation of the ore "untill Abram returns."[46] If Ross wanted experiments conducted to determine the productivity of the furnace, the richness of the ore, or the efficiency of the workers, he charged Abram with prime responsibility for the tests. If Ross wanted a carefully selected sample of pig iron sent to a potentially large buyer, Abram chose the pigs.[47] In short, Ross apparently considered his founder the most valuable man, black or white, on the estate. In 1812 when a white plantation overseer at Oxford charged Ross with comparing him unfavorably to Abram, Ross replied that he had never made such a comparison, but if the overseer wanted one made, Ross would be glad to oblige him. "Your occupations [are] perfectly different," Ross observed: "you are a farmer, he works in iron—and no man in your line of business could obtain half as much as he could were he permitted to hire himself to any of the large works to the North [,] South and West."[48]

Ross's pride in his slave force extended to a number of other workers as well. The teamsters on the estate "can and will make any horse work," Ross bragged, and when he sent a white purchasing agent north to buy mules he wanted "Wagonner Ned" to accompany the agent and make the actual selections.[49] An incident which occurred in 1813 revealed Ross's attitude toward another key group of Oxford workers. "The Blacksmiths have continued to support their character," Ross wrote in January of that year; "they have finished (6 weeks ago) two iron doors and frames for the Lynchburg Bank vaults which met not only with approbation but admiration, at the handsome workmanship and the unquestionable security."[50] When the bank directors balked at the price of the work, however, and insisted on calling in outside arbitrators for an appraisal, Ross was enraged. "I shall not trust a decision to the ignorant makers of Grubbing Hoes," he answered. "The Oxford Smiths have served a long and severe apprenticeship to their Trade and I will never disgrace them."[51] The dispute was settled only after Ross agreed

[46] Ross to William J. Dunn, June 1, 19, Sept. 16, 1813, *ibid.* If Ross wanted to give Abram specific instructions prior to a blast, he sometimes bypassed his white clerks and wrote directly to him; see abstract of letter "to Abram the founder at Oxford Works," Mar. 15, 1813, *ibid.*

[47] Ross, "Memorandum for Richardson," and Ross to William J. Dunn, June 1, Aug. [?] 17, 1813, *ibid.*

[48] Ross to John Pierce, [Feb.] 3, 1812, *ibid.*

[49] Ross to Robert Wright, Aug. 22, 1813, and to William Mewburn, Aug. 1, 1813, *ibid.*

[50] Ross to John Duffield, Jan. 9, 1813, *ibid.*

[51] Ross to Davidson Bradfute, Jan. 14, 1813, and to Robert Richardson, Jan. 19, 1813, *ibid.*

that two highly skilled Richmond artisans were qualified to determine a fair price for the job.[52] Ross boasted on another occasion that his blacksmiths were "famous" for their mill irons, "being in the practice of making a great many," and that the tools turned out in his smith shop were of superior quality. "Tis not practicable for the country smiths to work either so reasonable or so well," he claimed, "because my Smiths make one or two hundred axes at a time without changing to other articles and so on."[53]

"You may tell Abram and other faithful servants that they are not forgotten and I shall soon be with them," Ross told one of his white managers in 1813, "and you may with the utmost candor assure the rascally part of our servants that they may rely with certainty that they shall not be forgotten."[54] As this statement indicates, Ross discriminated between what he considered the good and bad performance of his slaves, and his techniques for disciplining and motivating them reflected this differentiation. "I have confidence in the integrity of the Founder and his keepers and fillers," Ross noted in November 1812, and "the Potters also seem to do their duty," but "there has been much waste, much plundering and great idleness at the Forges." Although his "Swaggering Forge men" were "spoiled servants" whose work would have to improve, Ross warned his clerks that the situation had to "be corrected by degrees" because it had "been of long continuance."[55] He realized, as did many industrial employers of slave labor in the late eighteenth and early nineteenth centuries, that skilled slave artisans would not perform satisfactorily if compulsion were the only prod to their labor and that there were definite limits on what slaves could be forced to do.[56] The most valuable vein of iron ore at Oxford had to be abandoned, for example, because Ross's slaves simply refused to work in the deep, narrow pit after a large rock fell some 150 feet from the

[52] Ross to Davidson Bradfute, Apr. 10, 24, May 10, 1813, *ibid.*

[53] Ross to William Bodkin, June 29, 1813, and to Samuel Dyer, Jr., Dec. 3, 1812, *ibid.* The "mill irons" Ross mentioned were for grist mills, saw mills, and the like.

[54] Ross to Robert Richardson, Jan. 5, 181[3], *ibid.*

[55] Ross to Richardson, Nov. 10, 1812, *ibid.*

[56] Robert S. Starobin, *Industrial Slavery in the Old South* (New York, 1970), 101, documents the use of incentive payments in the iron industry as far back as the 1790s.

top of the mine and killed three black miners.[57] Similarly Ross was forced to use a white miller at Oxford because his best slave miller, Billy Bacon, insisted on being hired out in Richmond. "If I could have prevailed on him to have gone to my mill at the Iron Works I would not have taken forty pounds a year" for him, Ross told Bacon's employer.[58] When Ross proposed a change in the work rules for his slave hands, he ordered his white superintendents to "consult with the most sensible" bondsmen in the affected job categories, and he professed himself willing to modify his instructions if the workers convinced him of "anything unreasonable" in his proposals.[59] Even when slaves were willing or could be made to work at the task assigned them, however, it took more than force to make them work well. Positive incentives were also needed, and the most critical and difficult day-to-day managerial problem that faced Ross, and indeed all employers of slave labor in the Old South, was to find a balance between coercion and reward that would maximize the work of the slave force and minimize the cost to the employer.

In trying to achieve this balance Ross seems to have depended more on incentive than on force. Physical punishment was apparently inflicted only when he felt that circumstances clearly demanded it, but this did not mean that his white managers should tolerate slipshod work, as he informed them in 1812. "'Tis an essential part of duty never to withhold censure from bad worksmanship," he advised; "there ought to be no indulgence on this point [;] 'tis injurious to the workman and disgraceful to the business."[60] Censure could take many forms. It could be verbal; it could consist of denying a slave a new issue of clothing; it could take the form of a transfer to a more arduous job; it could involve the whip. A severe chastisement occurred in 1813 when the apparent negligence of two of Ross's boatmen resulted in the loss of a valuable cargo of slave clothing. "Upon the receipt of this letter I have to request that you . . . and some of the most respectable black people seize upon Aaron and Lewis, carry them with ropes round their necks to the boat landing where the load was lost and there have them stript naked and 39 stripes inflicted well placed on the bare backs of each of those scoundrels," Ross ordered his clerks. He added in a postscript that "you are to give some of my trusty servants half a dollar for whipping each of those rascals provided they do their duty." "I shall be well pleased

---

[57] Ross to John Staples, June 3, 1813, Ross Letterbook.
[58] Ross to John J. Werth, Jan. 5, 1812, *ibid.*
[59] Ross to John Duffield, Nov. 13, 1812, *ibid.*
[60] Ross, "Memorandum for Richardson," *ibid.*

if you can sell them both to the Carolina Hogg drivers," Ross continued in another angry letter. "Such scoundrels are not fit companions for honest servants."[61] Ross must have regained control of his temper shortly afterward, however, since there is no indication that the two men were sold and this is the only mention of a whipping in the surviving pages of Ross's letterbook for 1812 and 1813.[62] In addition to any humanitarian considerations, Ross undoubtedly knew that the constant use of force could well lead to a deterioration rather than an improvement of conditions. It was much more judicious to maintain good performance by the careful use of incentives and rewards, Ross believed, and even when performance fell off, as in the case of his "Swaggering Forge men," the master's purposes would generally be better served if the correction took place "by degrees" and with a minimal use of physical coercion.

The ultimate incentive was the prospect of eventual freedom in return for satisfactory service, but Ross used this only on one occasion that can be documented, and this instance did not involve his Oxford slaves.[63] He attempted to obtain steady labor from his iron workers and his plantation hands by means that fell short of promised emancipation, but the techniques he employed still touched the lives of the black men, women, and children on the estate in a number of fundamental ways.

At their basic level these incentives involved the food supplied to the Oxford hands. "The male Laborers are all allowed a double Quantity of Bread and an equal quantity of meat as the Common rations allowed to a Soldier or a Sailor," Ross stated in 1811, "and the females in due proportion." He reinforced this point in 1813 when he told his managers, "You may be assured that nothing will be lost by feeding the people well." Financial reverses temporarily forced Ross to abandon

[61] Ross to Robert Richardson, Jan. 14, 1813, and to William J. Dunn, Jan. 1813, *ibid.*

[62] Ross did, however, state in 1813 that if a blacksmith "named Humphry belonging to Mrs. Ross that . . . has given over working for his Mrs. and chooses to work for himself" refused to execute an order for plows, he, Ross, would "hire him and carry him to the Iron Works where he shall be compelled to make them." Ross to Tarlton Rice, Sept. 25, 1813, *ibid.*

[63] Berkeley, "Prophet Without Honor," *VMHB*, LXXVII (1969), 180-190, describes the extraordinary career of one black man emancipated by Ross. The slave, Christopher McPherson, was the son of a black woman named Clarinda and a Scots merchant, Charles McPherson, who was undoubtedly a friend of Ross. Charles McPherson persuaded Christopher's original owner to sell the boy to Ross, and Ross provided Christopher with an education and later freed him. According to McPherson's own account, while still a slave he acted as the clerk and "Principal Storekeeper" at a Fluvanna County store owned by Ross and in this capacity had "8 to 10 white Gentlemen . . . under my directions" (181). McPherson continued to work for Ross for seven years following his emancipation in 1792.

issuing double rations in 1812 and 1813, but he made extensive purchases of cattle and hogs in the latter year in an effort to reinstitute the practice, in part because his slaves had come to view the larger quota "as their legal right."[64]

Clothing was another simple but important item that Ross employed in his efforts to motivate, and occasionally discipline, his workers. His instructions regarding the apportioning of winter cloth among his workers in 1813 reveal how he tried to use the allocation of clothing to reward the most skilled and diligent slaves as well as to provide for those most in need:

I direct the distribution as followeth—I shall begin with infants— each infant is allowed by me 1½ yds white Flannel, the same may be given to pregnant women and where the infants are advanced some months give them 2 yds—I direct to all the females, a jacket of Cotton with long sleeves, to shelter their arms from cold and frost—The Waggoners are to have coats, vests and pantaloons of cotton—all the Colliers and Miners the same—The blue cloth is of good quality and I allot it to the furnace people first and potters, Smiths next and forgemen next— a coat of blue cloth and waistcoat of scarlet flannel with sleeves— Edmund [a potter] to be particularly attended to—give him pantalloons also of blue cloth—as to the distribution of the Blankets, the first object is to supply women with young children and next such cases as you may think proper according to the best of your judgment—So far as I am able to judge the Watermen are the most unfaithful people attached to the estate—you'll give them nothing.[65]

The more elaborate clothing provided certain groups of slaves was clearly meant to acknowledge the good performance of the hardest workers and to give the most accomplished artisans a conspicuous badge that would mark them as superior craftsmen and men of elevated status at the works.

On several occasions Ross gave his managers specific directions about Edmund, the potter singled out for special attention in the distribution of clothing, and these orders show another of Ross's approaches to the complex problem of motivating unfree labor. Edmund, who was seventeen years old in 1813, was one of the more valuable young potters

[64] Ross, advertisement to lease Oxford Iron Works, Bolling Papers; Ross to William J. Dunn, Aug. 1813, and to Thomas Hopkins, Aug. 15, 25, 1813, Ross Letterbook.
[65] Ross to William J. Dunn, Jan. 1813, Ross Letterbook.

on the estate since he specialized in casting "small pots, Bowls, Stewpots and the like" which "if well made will provide double price for the iron." "The thrifty housewives like to do a great deal of their cookery in their own chamber by a little servant under their own eye while they are not interrupted by other avocations," Ross explained; "hence the small ware will always meet a good market." Ross wanted "Edmund to be employed exclusively in small ware—'tis best fitted for his strength and years and best calculated to make him a good workman." In addition, Ross thought his clerks might "rouse his ambition by giving him a Stamp to distinguish his workmanship that I may know it from the others[;] he has great ambition which is a very laudable virtue when properly guided."[66] Ross evidently placed considerable faith in the power of encouragement and commendation. Following a trial of Oxford pig iron at the Virginia State Armory in 1813, the Armory superintendent praised the high quality of the metal, and Ross promptly forwarded a copy of the complimentary appraisal to the works. "You have my permission to communicate this information to Abram and such of the Workmen as you think it will have a good effect upon," he instructed his clerks.[67] From Ross's point of view, such things as hallmarks for young slaves and encouraging words for key artisans had an added advantage in that they cost him nothing, but he was not always able to get off so cheaply.

Like most employers of industrial slaves in the antebellum South, Ross paid his bondsmen in various ways for doing more than they were required to do. Compensation for labor over and above the assigned task ("overwork," as it was usually called) took several forms, but most commonly it consisted of payment in either cash or goods for exceeding daily or weekly production quotas, working on Sundays or holidays, or rendering some extraordinary service to the master. The slaves were also permitted to raise hogs and cultivate their own crops in their spare time.[68] Ross believed that the relatively small amount of resources allocated to these incentives produced much more work than could be

[66] Ross, "Memorandum for Richardson," and Ross to William J. Dunn [Apr. 1813], *ibid*.

[67] Ross to William J. Dunn, June 1, 1813, *ibid*.

[68] Ross to Charles W. Beard, Jan. 18, 1812, to Reuben Smith, Mar. 27, 1812, and to William J. Dunn, Nov. 13, 1812, *ibid*. The best general discussion of the industrial overwork system is in Starobin, *Industrial Slavery*, 99-104. See also Charles B. Dew, "Disciplining Slave Ironworkers in the Antebellum South: Coercion, Conciliation, and Accommodation," scheduled for publication in *American Historical Review*, Apr. 1974.

done using several times as much money to pay the wages of free laborers. A letter addressed to a white plantation overseer at Oxford illustrates Ross's firm belief in both the effectiveness and the economic benefits of using slaves in any and all positions, including most supervisory posts. This letter, which Ross wrote after learning that the overseer had taken on a young white assistant, also conveys the flavor of much of his correspondence touching on money matters:

Your assistant when fixed in a house and home in six months [will] get a wife and her relations to be maintained—in three months more, he would get a mare and colt and in six months more, he would get a Studd horse, all to be maintained out of my corn—if your honesty and character compelled you to take notice of such abuses this young rascal would be ready to gouge out your eyes [;] you may find, or already know, that all I have described has actually happened within a short distance of your house—Take I say again and again one of my most faith[ful] servants[,] give him some encouragement or fourth part of what you must give to a white lad [and] take my word for it you'll find him ten times better than any you can hire—he will labour day by day[,] he has ten time[s] more experience, and [is] a much honester man, he will receive your instructions with patience and humility and if a reprimand becomes necessary he will receive it without putting out your eyes.[69]

An incident that threatened a slave woman with a severe beating showed another of Ross's approaches to the question of discipline and motivation. In the summer of 1813 the overseer who had earlier charged Ross with comparing him unfavorably to Abram got into a brawl with one of the white managers at the iron works. The fight ended when Patsey, a slave who worked on one of the Oxford plantations, stepped between the two men, separated them, and prevented them from renewing the fray. The overseer's response to Patsey's action was to go to Lynchburg and obtain a constable—"the lowest officer of Executive Justice known in our Government," snorted Ross—who took Patsey into the city in order to administer a public whipping as punishment for engaging in a fight with a white man. The clerks at Oxford learned what had happened, however, and they reached Lynchburg before the whipping occurred and brought Patsey back to the works with them.[70]

[69] Ross to Reuben Smith, Mar. 27, 1812, Ross Letterbook.
[70] Ross to John Pearce, Aug. 25, 1813, and to John Duffield, Sept. 26, 1813, *ibid.*

Ross's response was to reward Patsey with a shawl "for her good conduct . . . and as compensation for [her] trouble in being carried to Lynchburg." "My servants must remain dutifull and obedient to their Superiors that I have placed over them," Ross explained, "but there may happen times and occasions, which calls for different exertions, and out of the usual line of daily labour, [and] when such occassions offers, to do good and prevent evil in a judicious manner, and without intended violence, further than self preservation, their conduct will meet my approbation."[71] When the overseer protested that Ross had no business rewarding the black woman, Ross replied by asking him "if such conduct [as Patsey's] would have been meritorious in a white man or a white woman, was it not still more so in a slave"? Ross answered his own question by firing the overseer.[72]

Of all the techniques of incentive and reward employed by Ross, probably none was more important than his policy toward the family arrangements of the slaves on the Oxford estate. It seems significant that the detailed 1811 slave enumeration lists the work force by family units, with the father, mother, children, and sometimes aged in-laws grouped together, along with the age and occupation of each slave. Ross insisted that children under ten be kept with their parents, and the listing indicates that older sons and daughters usually remained in the family until they married.[73] As mentioned earlier, members of the same family frequently worked in close physical proximity to each other, and there was a strong tendency for slave artisans to pass their skills on to their sons. To cite one typical example, three children and a grandchild of Big Abram, a sixty-year-old collier, were employed at raking leaves and hauling wood at the coaling grounds in 1811, and one of Big Abram's sons, Nickie, nineteen, had evidently mastered the art of making charcoal by that date since he is given the same occupational designation as his father. A similar working relationship existed between four other slave colliers and their children and was characteristic of most other phases of the Oxford operation. Little Nat, eighteen, was working at the refinery forge with his father, Ben Gilmore, forty-eight. Under the guidance of his father, Billy Goochland, twenty-six (who was married to Patsey, the slave woman who broke up the fight in 1813), had become a capable wheelwright. Two blacksmiths, Shop Phill, fifty,

[71] Ross to Robert Richardson, July 1, 1813, *ibid.*
[72] Ross to John Pearce, Aug. 25, Sept. 15, 1813, *ibid.*
[73] "List of Slaves at Oxford Iron Works," Bolling Papers, and Ross, advertisement to lease Oxford Iron Works, *ibid.*

and Sharper, forty-five, were training their teenage boys to be smiths, and the two sons of Ned Gordon, a sixty-eight-year-old carpenter, were both qualified woodworkers in 1811.[74]

An apparent attempt by a slave women to kill her newborn baby in 1812 prompted an outraged Ross to outline at length his attitude toward slave marriage, family life, parental authority, prenatal care, and religion. Little Fanny, thirty-two years old and a daughter of Big Abram, the collier, had five children in 1811 but according to the enumeration did not have a husband. After the birth of her sixth child the next year she evidently abandoned the infant in the woods, an act which she apparently tried to justify on the basis of her religious convictions. Details are sketchy and are contained in a letter which Ross addressed to one of his clerks after he was informed of the attempt. Because all that can be learned about this incident is contained in this one document and because of the wealth of information it reveals about Ross's views on related subjects, it merits rather full quotation:

I cannot lose a minute in expressing my surprise and indignation at the extravagant conduct of little Fanny. Tis happy for her and pleasing to me, that the infant has been preserved, 'tis particularly pleasing, because had the innocent child perished I would have prosecuted her unto the ignominious death of the Gallows, the laws of humanity and the laws of the land must not be prosterated to the wild ravings of fanatisism. Tis well known that I demand moderate labour from the servants, as a compensation for my benevolence towards them (you know how small the compensation I have received) in other respects, I have in a great measure left them free only under such controul as was most congenial to their happiness. I have never laid any restrictions on their worshipping the deity agreeably to their own minds (so far as rational) in any manner they please—as to their amorous connections (perfectly natural) I have not been merely passive, but have upon more occasion than one or two declared my sentiments, that the young people might connect themselves in marriage, to their own liking, with consent of their parents who were the best judges[;] 'tis true I have discouraged connections out of the estate and particularly with free people of colour, because I was certain, 'twould be injurious to my people, but I have used no violence to prevent those connections for tis well known that now they exist upon my estate and have not been expelled but no longer attend—Tis very much my wish that my servants should connect themselves in a decent manner and behave as a religious people ought

[74] "List of Slaves at Oxford Iron Works," *ibid.*

to do—human nature is frail and apt to err—Fanny was under no restraint as to a husband whom so ever she might choose—What then could induce her to such an inhuman act. She had little to fear from her earthly master and still less to fear from heaven—two wrongs can never make any point right—because when united the two makes it a much worse matter—her going astray was most certainly wrong, but an attempt to destroy the most innocent infant was horrid damnable— as to Fanny's tale of being delivered in the woods, [it] is not to be credited. My conduct to pregnant women requires no comment, you know that no pregnant women is put to labour within some weeks of her delivery, and as long afterwards—Tis not my desire to make this poor woman unhappy quite otherwise, but 'tis my earnest wish that this hapless innocent may be taken the utmost care of and that nothing may be wanting to the preservation of this exposed child that my estate can furnish—
P S   You will please me and I hope to be pleased yourself in exposing such an abominable conduct [,] the disgrace of all religion and most abominable to me as the master.[75]

Ross repeated his concern about the care and treatment given pregnant women on his estate in a letter written in 1813 after he learned that one of his weavers had suffered a miscarriage. The woman, Jeany, had "absented herself from weaving perhaps a fortnight before I left you," Ross remarked; "I had indeed some suspicion of her real complaint and winked at her absence." Her miscarriage occurred after she stopped work. "Similar accidents to her's is the natural lot of humanity—but it sometimes proceeds from abuses—too severe labour—imprudent punishments [,] accidental hurts—falling down or violent alarms," he continued. "I cannot think the first two causes were ever felt—as to accidents 'tis impossible for me to prevent accidents—her trade was weaving which is the usual employment of a great number of white females, and if it be injurious to pregnant women, I never was informed of it—I hope," he added, "she is doing well."[76]

Slave parents at Oxford clearly played a significant role in their children's lives. Except in extraordinary cases like Little Fanny's, they had almost complete responsibility for raising their children, and their normal prerogatives included the right to approve or disapprove a proposed marriage. Fathers frequently trained their sons to follow their trades, and both boys and girls usually worked close to their parents. Ross undoubt-

---

[75] Ross to Robert Richardson, Apr. 30, 1812, Ross Letterbook.
[76] Ross to Robert Richardson, Jan. 5, 181[3], *ibid.*

edly thought that a large delegation of authority to slave parents was the only decent way for a master to behave toward his servants, but he also recognized that it was good business. There was no better way to insure that a new generation of skilled artisans would be available when needed, and stable family arrangements helped immeasurably with the difficult job of maintaining discipline and deterring runaways. When the breakup of a plantation adjoining Oxford threatened to separate James Noble, one of Ross's best carpenters, from his wife and two small children, Ross purchased the, woman and the infants even though he considered the price exorbitant. "The woman and children would be of no consequence was it not for James Nobles comfort," Ross admitted, and when some difficulty developed over the transaction he noted, "I cannot relinquish my claim to the family on account of her husband."[77] Ross precipitated a similar situation in 1812 when he broke up a plantation in Botetourt County and moved the slaves who had been working there to Oxford. One of the men, Solomon, an agricultural worker in his mid-fifties, immediately ran back to Botetourt to join his wife. Realizing that he would be inviting trouble if he tried to force the man to stay at one of the Oxford plantations, Ross first hired him out in the vicinity of his wife's home and then sold him to a planter in the same neighborhood. "My intention was to leave the man where he seemed desirous of living," Ross explained.[78]

In addition to acting as a check against runaways, happy slave marriages allowed Ross to avoid some other potentially damaging disciplinary problems. In 1812 Jenny, an unmarried Oxford slave, and her young child obtained a pass from one of Ross's clerks and took the stage to a Richmond suburb, where she and the child spent several days at the home of a white widower named William Mewburn who had previously managed the estate. Ross was furious when he found out what had happened, particularly after a conversation with his founder revealed that Mewburn planned to keep Jenny and the child for an extended visit:

Abram casually mentioned your wishes that Jenny might remain 8 or 10

---

[77] Ross to Robert Richardson, Feb. 11, 1812, Sept. 25, 1813, and to William Bailey, Sept. 24, 1813, *ibid.* See also Ross to William J. Dunn, Aug. [?] 28, 1813, and to Thomas Bottler, Dec. 29, 1812, *ibid.*

[78] Ross to John Cole, Nov. 28, 1812, to Edmond Sherman, Feb. 8, 9, Mar. 17, Nov. 28, 1812, June 22, July 21, Aug. 10, 19, Sept. 8, 13, 1813, and to Robert Wright, Aug. 22, 1813, *ibid.;* statement of William Mewburn concerning the hire of Solomon, Oct. 26, 1812, Bolling Papers.

days and then go home in your gigg[.] [T]his would by no means answer and would countenance a repetition of a similar conduct in herself and perhaps yours. I hesitated some time as to the propriety of a conveyance by the stage and causing her to walk home for contuminious conduct but believing her partly innocent [and] the child perfectly so I concluded the stage the most prudent conveyance—the plan of the gigg [is] inadmissible for many reasons[;] in the first place 'would hold out a temptation for repeating the same impropriety as well by herself and others. I am well informed that five or six more are ready for a similar expedition if this suceeds to their wishes— . . . I expect her to be returned by the stage in such a manner as may best insure safety to herself and [the] child and I promise or rather shall endeavor to pass this improper conduct over as to the woman but no farther.[79]

The real point of the affair as far as Ross was concerned seems to have been the threat it posed to discipline and domestic tranquillity on the estate. He was thoroughly indignant over the moral breach involved, which he termed "so disgraceful as no man of sentiments could [countenance]," but he saved his full anger for the clerk at Oxford who had jeopardized operations there by giving Jenny the pass. For one of the superintendents to have committed "a violation of . . . duty" that so endangered his employer's interests could only be explained, Ross concluded, "as an act of a man of unsound mind."[80]

Evidence of the effectiveness of the twin prods of force and incentive employed by Ross is largely indirect, but it does indicate that he achieved some measure of success in his attempts to obtain a satisfactory amount of labor without undue reliance on physical coercion. As noted earlier, there is only one mention of a whipping in the Ross Letterbook, and Solomon, the slave who returned to Botetourt County to be with his wife, is the only runaway discussed in the extant letters.[81] Given Ross's pro-

---

[79] Ross to William Mewburn, Jan. 23, 1812, Ross Letterbook. Jenny is described in the 1811 list as a 21-year-old mulatto furnace worker; "List of Slaves at Oxford Iron Works," Bolling Papers. See also Ross to Robert Richardson, Jan. 26, 1812, Ross Letterbook.

[80] Ross to Robert Richardson, Feb. 5, 20, 1812, Ross Letterbook.

[81] The only suggestion that the potential for grave disciplinary problems existed at Oxford during Ross's ownership is contained in the testimony of a slave who was supposedly involved in Gabriel's rebellion in 1800. According to the confession of Gilbert, a slave who lived in the Richmond area, a slave by the name of Sam Byrd, Jr., had informed him, Gilbert, that he, Byrd, had been told by a black post rider who carried mail to Charlottesville "that he [the post rider] had conveyed the intelligence respecting the Insurrection as far as Mr. Ross's Iron Works." See

clivity for detailed review of the shortcomings of the Oxford operation, it seems unlikely that he would have ignored additional instances of either of these difficulties if they had occurred. Indications do exist, however, that his system of compensating slave workers for exceeding their required tasks enabled some of the Oxford slaves to earn fairly impressive amounts for themselves. After visiting one of his outlying plantations in 1812, Ross wrote that he had found the manager "in a wretched situation" with "nothing for himself and consequently nothing for me. I am convinced that any one of fifty slaves at Oxford could honestly [have] entertained me better than this manager."[82] In a similar vein he told an overseer on his Pittsylvania County plantations that "the quantity of pork you talk of is the most disgraceful that I could have imagined—there are some of the negroes at the iron works that will kill nearly as much as your plantations."[83] Ross's pride in his Oxford artisans has already been mentioned, and it seems unlikely that this pride rested totally on an excessively charitable assessment of their abilities and performance. Charity does not appear to have been one of Ross's most keenly developed character traits.

At the same time, however, Ross was deeply distressed over the heavy indebtedness of the Oxford estate and placed part of the blame on his slave workers. "I believe Oxford is the most scandalous establishment in America concerning their debts," Ross fumed in 1813. "We have no credit[,] no one will indeed no one ought to trust us because we dont pay" our bills. "I have assisted the Estate for the last ten years with considerable sums more than I received," he complained to his clerks; "how ... does it happen that we are the servants of servants, disgraced, involved in distress and mortifications . . . [?] How does this ruinous state of things happen?" The answer lay partially, but only partially, in the indifference and relative ignorance of some of his Oxford workers, particularly the "Swaggering Forge men." "If the forges were workt as they ought to be there could be no difficulty in paying the debts," Ross believed, "but our ruin is that the labourers [do] not labor." " 'Tis mortifying that we remain allways in a state of primitive ignorance and that in thirty years we have not gained one week on the scale of improvement,"

"Information from Jno. Foster respecting the intended Insurrection, Sept. 23d 1800," Executive Papers, Va. State Library. This third-hand report is the only indication that the Oxford slaves might have known in advance about the proposed uprising, and there is no evidence of their participation in the planning or attempted execution of the abortive rebellion.
[82] Ross to Reuben Smith, Mar. 27, 1812, Ross Letterbook.
[83] Ross to Charles W. Beard, Jan. 18, 1812, *ibid.*

he added on another occasion.[84] Ross realized, however, that the relatively poor labor situation at several places on the estate was not totally the fault of his workmen, as he explained in a particularly revealing letter to one of his Oxford managers in 1812:

I am of opinion that if the smiths are kept at faithful and steady labour you'll find it the most productive [department] on the estate . . . however I believe every smith here [in Richmond] black and white works twice as much as our Smiths and I really believe the Wheelwrights do three times as much as our people. My nearest neighbours are two worthy men in partnership [,] wheelwrights with two or three Journeymen—tis astonishing the quantity of work they do [;] they hire two negro Smiths who seem to do their work well—Upon examining the wheelwright work here tis twice as strong as ours. . . . No part of Virginia requires stronger work than our ground. . . . I wish you to read this to old Ned and his sons—they are good people but have never seen any other workmen than at the Oxford estate—they have no chance for improvement—there is no emulation—the father and son joggs on in the old way [.] I wonder they do so well.[85]

The same situation existed at the Oxford forges. "I dare say you are correct as to my Forgemen," Ross admitted to a friend in 1812; "they were as good workmen 20 years ago as they are now—they have had no chance to improve—they have not [had] an opportunity of travelling to see other works and the annual improvements [made there]." Ross did not permit his "Iron Works people . . . to stop so that my people in every branch have remained as it were stationary." Although he had hoped "to give them a better chance in a short time," he failed to explain how this would be done.[86]

In the absence of detailed bookkeeping and production records, it is exceedingly difficult to assess the role which slave labor may have played in the continuing financial difficulties of the Oxford estate. Ross berated his white clerks more often than his black workmen in his frequent speculations on the causes of Oxford's declining fortunes. "Those that ought to represent the master are not unfrequently inferior to the Servant," he complained in a memorandum to one of his managers. "The

[84] Ross, fragment of a letter to an Oxford clerk [Feb. 1813], to Robert Richardson, Nov. 10, 1812, Feb. 19, 1813, and to William J. Dunn [Apr. 1813], June 17, 1813, ibid.
[85] Ross to Robert Richardson, Nov. 10, 1812, ibid.
[86] Ross to Thomas Evans, June 24, 1812, ibid.

true cause" of Oxford's failure to earn an adequate return "will be found in the want of talents and want of sobriety in the manager and clerks," he charged; "for ten years this reduced the estate into distress and ruin from which it will be difficult, perhaps impossible to relieve it." The extravagant debts incurred on behalf of the estate by one former manager, William Mewburn, amounted to "not less than 20,000$." Trying to give advice to another former superintendent named Gilchrist was like "cutting a block of marble with a razor," Ross remarked, and this employee had unfortunately trained one of Ross's relatives who still held a supervisory post at the works. "Will you never forget the habits you acquired under Gilchrists administration[?]" Ross asked. "He had no notion of the beauties and pleasures of order, regularity and punctuality[;] his plan, if he ever had any plan, . . . was to conduct his business without order, in a manner that rendered confusion still more confused, he had no system, he was like a certain species of fish, that delight in muddy water."[87] The present batch of clerks was no better, Ross bluntly informed them, and he passed along some wisdom he had recently acquired on the problem of obtaining adequate management: "There has long been a contrariety of opinions . . . whether is it most dangerous to employ an active sensible scoundrel or an honest simple indolent man—about two years ago in a large company of gentlemen where I was a guest this subject was agitated. 'Twas determined that the first character was safest provided the employer was apprized of it, because he was capable of exertions and [his] employer would be on his guard—as to the other character 'twas more dangerous[;] confidence was placed in his honesty and he ruined or injured by his apathy or folly."[88] Ross considered it his great misfortune to be constantly burdened with the second class of employee. He felt that the proof of his analysis of Oxford's financial difficulties came in late 1812 when a series of experiments carried out by his slaves demonstrated both the richness of the ore on the property and the skill of his artisans in converting it into high quality iron products. "I hope you are convinced," Ross told his clerks at the end of the tests, "that all the distress and mortifications of the Oxford estate is founded in the bad management of the business alone and not in the poverty of the estate or the imbecillity of the mechanicks or labourers

[87] Ross, "Memorandum for Richardson," and Ross to Robert Richardson, Nov. 14, 1812, Aug. 18, 1813, and to John Duffield, Jan. 9, 1813, *ibid.*
[88] Ross to Robert Richardson, Feb. 19, 1813, *ibid.*

or of any materials."[89]

Ross was obviously a demanding employer, but his low estimate of the capabilities of the three superintending clerks seems at least partially justified. A critically important blast had to be halted during the War of 1812 because they had not had the foresight to build up an adequate supply of ore and charcoal, despite a warning from Abram that the shortages would force him to stop the furnace. "You boldly volunteered yourself to keep the furnace in blast and said I might rest satisfied it should be done [but] to be candid I never put the smallest confidence in this vapour," Ross informed one of his clerks; "almost since I left Oxford you have been in a state of stupefaction not natural indeed but more criminal because it was artificial and done by yourself."[90]

Ross was even more enraged by his managers' subsequent mishandling of a major repair job at the works. Ross had ordered repairs to the forge dam in June 1813, but he was startled to learn the next month that his superintendents had undertaken to build an entirely new dam.[91] What disturbed him even more, however, was that the first news he received of this project came in a letter from the black workmen who were attempting to build the dam:

We wish you were here to see the present situation of the dam we are about, it appears we shall never get it done, the water is so deep where the foundation is to be cleared out, little or nothing can be done towards a good foundation. . . . We do little or nothing under our present arrangements, and management, our only object is to apprise you of our situation that we may not be blamed for what we cannot help. We wish you to come up imidiately that you may see with your own eyes and judge by your own understanding. When so great a Jobb as this was set about, it might well be expected that it was seriously thought of, wisely planed, and the utmost foresight used to have every thing prepared, this is not the case, and it seems intended that the whole blame of delay and perhaps of miscarriage and ruin must fall upon innocent men. We can do the Work which belongs to us to do. We have no authority to command wagons, to force provisions, or to provide the materials absolutely necessary, this is the duty of our Superiors.

Carpenter George for himself and others.[92]

[89] Ross to Robert Richardson, Oct. 30, Nov. 10, Dec. 1812, Jan. 5, 181[3], *ibid.*
[90] Ross to Robert Richardson, Feb. 19, 1813, *ibid.*
[91] Ross to William J. Dunn, June 19, 1813, *ibid.*
[92] Carpenter George for himself and others to Ross, June 24, 1813, *ibid.*

Since Ross was confined at that time by "the bite of a large vicious dog" and could not go up to the works, he immediately ordered Carpenter George to come to Richmond. "In order to obtain any satisfactory information respecting my affairs, I am obliged to send for the most confidential servants at a heavy expense of time[,] labour and money," Ross complained,[93] and he criticized sharply the managers' handling of the entire project: "Everything is to be accomplished by the main strength of the servants, they are compelled by the folly of their conductors to work up hill constantly and what little they accomplish is by treble labour. . . . although you could not be ignorant that your talents were limited and your experience very small, yet you enter upon a very heavy piece of work without consulting your employer or even informing him what you were about . . . it appears to be an undertaking without a plan, without foresight, without Judgemt trusting no doubt as your predecessors have done before you that the main strength, blood and sweat of the servants would do the work and draw a veil over your misconduct."[94] Ross's anger over this affair did not entirely subside until the dam was completed in the fall.[95]

Although Ross was occasionally dissatisfied with the work of his slaves and was frequently disgusted with the performance of his clerks, he himself must bear primary responsibility for what was probably the most important single factor in the financial difficulties at Oxford. The forge dam was only a small part of a much larger and more critical problem. Because Beaver Creek, the stream that supplied power to the works, lacked an adequate supply of water for as much as three to five months out of the year, production was constantly being interrupted.[96] "When there was water, there was no iron, and when there was water and iron there was no coals and thus debts accumulated from time to time until all credit was lost," Ross lamented in 1813.[97] But Ross did not make a significant attempt to correct the power deficiency, which he acknowledged was "worse than ruinous," until 1813, when the prospect of high wartime profits held out the hope of an adequate return on the substantial capital investment required to move his operations to the

[93] Ross to [Thomas Hopkins], [June 1813], to William J. Dunn [July 2, 1813], and to Robert Richardson, July 5, 1813, ibid.
[94] Ross to William J. Dunn, July 4, 1813, ibid.
[95] Ross to William J. Dunn, Aug., Sept. 16, 1813, ibid.
[96] Ross to William J. Dunn, Aug. 1813, and to Juliana Ross, Aug. 27, 1813, ibid.
[97] Ross to William J. Dunn, Aug. 17, 1813, ibid.

nearby James River.[98]

Ross's inability to deal with the crippling lack of water power at Oxford prior to the War of 1812 was the result of a series of financial crises that threatened to engulf him during the post-Revolutionary era. "Mr. Ross has unlimited credit in this place," James Madison wrote from Philadelphia in 1782,[99] but three years later one of Jefferson's correspondents described quite a different situation in London. "You will be surprized when I tell you that Ross' Credit here is absolutely wrecked, his Debts selling at a considerable Discount in the Hands of Trustees," reported William Short. "This is another Paradox," he continued. "I am told he could not be trusted for a Shilling and yet I think he must still be rich."[100] A series of suits brought by both his British and American creditors in the late eighteenth and early nineteenth centuries resulted in a number of judgments against Ross involving hundreds of thousands of dollars and the temporary loss of the income produced by most of his lands and slaves in the upper South. In 1793 a consortium of Ross's domestic and foreign creditors was awarded control for ten years of all of his agricultural and industrial holdings in Virginia and Tennessee and the approximately 450 slaves engaged in working these properties; included in this settlement were the Oxford works and the entire Oxford slave force.[101] In 1807, three years after he regained control of the estate, he mortgaged the Oxford slaves in order to raise money to meet other heavy financial obligations.[102] The War of 1812 offered Ross an exceptional opportunity to increase sharply the net income of the Oxford estate, undertake major improvements at the works, and perhaps extricate himself and his slaves from the perilous situation in which his overextended investments and mercantile losses had placed them.[103]

---

[98] Ross to Thomas Evans, Aug. 10, 1813, to Richard Netherland, Aug. 17, 1813, and to William J. Dunn, Aug. 1813, *ibid.*

[99] Madison to Edmund Randolph, Sept. 3, 1782, in Hutchinson and Rachal, eds., *Madison Papers*, V, 105.

[100] Short to Jefferson, Aug. 7, 1785, in Boyd, ed., *Jefferson Papers*, VIII, 358.

[101] Indenture between David Ross and James Currie, Duncan McLauchlan, William Pasteur, and William Ross, Nov. 30, 1793, John Hook Papers, Duke University Library.

[102] *Bond* v. *Ross,* 3 Fed. Cas. 842 (1815).

[103] On Ross's post-Revolutionary investments, see n. 9 above. Some of Ross's mercantile difficulties are described in a pamphlet entitled *The Case of John Hook vs. David Ross in the Court of Appeals* (Richmond, Va., 1802), a copy of which is in the Va. Hist. Soc.'s rare book collection. See also Berry, "Flour Milling in Richmond," *VMHB,* LXXVIII (1970), 395. Main, "One Hundred," *WMQ,* 3d Ser., XI (1954), 363, notes that Ross "eventually lost much of his wealth."

Ross obviously wanted no repetition of the charges of toryism which had plagued him during the first war with Great Britain. " 'Tis true my age seventy four might well excuse my arm from manly feats of strife," he told an acquaintance in 1813; "nevertheless I can probably render some services, and I wish it known that I am ready to stand or fall for my adopted country [;] my wounds [the dog bite] are getting better," he added, "and in three days I can march to any part of the City, I hope."[104] To members of his immediate family, however, Ross expressed quite a different view. " 'Tis an unnecessary and unnatural war," he confided to his daughter; "when the European nations were struggling to get free from the grasp of an usurper and tyrant who could imagine that America would have taken up arms in favour of France[?]"[105] But Ross was not about to let such considerations stand in the way of his efforts to repair the fortunes of the Oxford works. "The present flattering prospects accasioned by the war . . . will vanish on the return of Peace," he warned his managers as he urged them to make every effort to reach full production as quickly as possible.[106] He pressed for military contracts for blacksmith's work and pig and bar iron wherever the opportunity for sales existed.[107] Enough orders came in to convince Ross that the estate could clear $20,000 on iron sales in 1813,[108] and his estimate would have been even larger, he noted ruefully, if his "worthy confidential Clerks" had not bungled at a critical moment: "Who could have imagined that I should have lost the sale of the Smiths work, because I could not procure in ten weeks 'an inventory of what was on hand of Chain traces etc. ['], the Governor and Council have supplied themselves from other quarters more worthy of respect. . . . if it were ask't how my worthy confidential Clerks were employed, when they could not do an hours work in ten weeks, and by this negligence lost me the sale of all the Smith's work on hand, and perhaps all that could have been made for two months, an answer will be found in the poor servants honest reply, 'do not accuse us' look to your managing Clerks for the evils of the Estate 'We do our duty but cannot do theirs.' "[109] Both military and private sales were up enough,

[104] Ross to William C. Williams, July 1, 1813, Ross Letterbook.
[105] Ross to Eliza, July 14, 1813, *ibid.*
[106] Ross to William J. Dunn, Aug. 17, 1813, *ibid.*
[107] Ross to Mr. Whaites, June 2, 1813, to George Williamson, June 2, 1813, to John Staples, June 3, Aug. 9, 1813, to William Wardlaw, Aug. 10, 1813, to Gen. Taylor, Sept. 11, 1813, and to William J. Dunn, Aug. 17, 1813, *ibid.*
[108] Ross to William J. Dunn, Aug. 17, 1813, *ibid.*
[109] Ross to William J. Dunn, Aug. 1813, *ibid.*

however, to convince Ross that the time had come to make plans for a major expansion of his works that would shift the location of most of the manufacturing operations from Beaver Creek to the James River. As soon as some of his seemingly interminable litigation was decided in his favor, Ross remarked in August 1813, he would begin building a new "Forge, slitting and rolling mill, . . . trip and tilt hamr and a large manufacturing mill." Construction would take three years, he predicted, and like almost everything else at Oxford the work would be initiated and carried to completion by his "Black people principally."[110]

Ross's hopes for an expanded Oxford on the James were never realized. Continuing financial difficulties, adverse court decisions, wartime competition from newer blast furnaces in the Shenandoah Valley, the coming of peace, and his failing health combined to defeat his ambitious plans.[111] "I have been infirm for two years," Ross told Jefferson in 1813, but, he added, "Surely we can not complain of decaying vigour, when we reflect since we were in action how many fabricks bound by wood and Iron have mouldered away and long [been] forgotten."[112] Ross died on May 4, 1817; his will directed that his two sons each receive "36 slaves in fair families" and that the remainder of his estate be divided equally among the two sons and his two daughters.[113] The provisions of the will and the necessity of settling the debts of the estate were undoubtedly the prime factors behind the breakup of the Oxford slave force, which apparently occurred in 1819.[114]

The probable fate of many of Ross's artisans is indicated in a letter written in 1828 by David S. Garland to William Weaver, a prominent

[110] Ross to Thomas Evans, Aug. 10, 1813, and to Richard Netherland, Aug. 17, 1813, *ibid.*

[111] Ross to John Staples, Sept. 14, 20, 1813, *ibid.*, and *Bond* v. *Ross.*

[112] Ross to Jefferson, Aug. 7, 1813, Ross Letterbook.

[113] *Virginia Patriot* (Richmond), May 5, 1817; *Richmond Enquirer*, May 6, 1817; "Last Will and Testament of David Ross," Apr. 24, 1817, copy, Va. State Library.

[114] The year in which a substantial portion of the Oxford slaves appear to have been sold is suggested by the following entries in the Campbell County tax lists, taken from the Campbell County Personal Property Tax Books, Va. State Library:

Year	Name	Slaves over 16	Slaves over 12
1816	David Ross	145	50
1817	David Ross	125	19
1818	David Ross	100	30
1819	David Ross Estate	25	15

Lesley, *Iron Manufacturer's Guide*, 64, stated in 1859 that Oxford "was abandoned about 1837 and has disappeared." If Oxford was in production as late as the 1830s, however, it clearly was not manned by Ross's slaves; see n. 115.

Valley ironmaster with works in Rockbridge and Botetourt counties:

I have recd your esteemed favour of the 19th Inst. in which you inform me that you would be pleased to purchase my man Billy Goochland that formerly belong'd to Ross's Estate.

It being Holiday times the fellow has concluded to visit his friends owned by you and to see you also, in order that he may make up his mind how far he wou'd be pleased with an Exchange of residence— He is an exceedingly valuable man and was appraised the highest of any negro in Ross's Estate except one. He has been brought up to the wheel wright and mill-right trade and is a good workman at either. He is an excellent hand at stocking plows making Harrows . . . etc. and a good common carpenter. In addition to these qualifications, He is Honest, sober and industrious and punctual in the observance of orders, and very attentive to his business in the absence of his master. Upon the whole I regard him to be one of the most valuable negroes that I was ever acquainted with. But still my want of money makes me willing to sell him, and nothing short of a fair liberal offer will get him.[115]

The shift of the Virginia iron industry to the richer mineral area west of the Blue Ridge Mountains in the early nineteenth century seems to have drawn at least some of the Oxford hands into the Valley, where they may well have trained many of the black iron workers who manned Virginia's furnaces and forges in the late antebellum years. And just as these men brought their skills into the Valley, such Valley ironmasters as Weaver took up the incentive schemes practiced by Ross on the Oxford estate. Compensation for overwork and recognition of the family and its vital role in training, disciplining, and motivating slave workers were to

---

[115] David S. Garland to William Weaver, May 23, 1828, William Weaver Papers, Duke University Library. Garland was a resident of the town of Glasgow in Rockbridge County. The letter makes no mention of Patsey, Billy Goochland's wife while the two slaves were working at Oxford. Weaver's correspondence contains specific references to at least three other slaves who had belonged to Ross. In 1828 an agent of Weaver wrote from Lynchburg that he had recently talked to a former Oxford smith, Blacksmith Phill, about the whereabouts of Aron, a highly skilled iron worker who had previously helped man the Oxford chaffery forge. Blacksmith Phill reported that Aron had gone "to the Western country" but that another Oxford artisan, Ben Gilmore, was "in the neighborhood and is a stout old man sufficiently strong to draw Iron pretty well." J. W. Schoolfield to Weaver, Feb. 28, 1828, *ibid.* Weaver subsequently purchased Gilmore and employed him, probably at his Buffalo Forge in Rockbridge County, until 1830, when he gave Gilmore permission to return to the Lynchburg area and purchase himself. Wm. C. McAllister to Weaver, Feb. 22, 1830, *ibid.*

become central features in the functioning of slavery in the iron industry not only in Virginia but throughout the entire antebellum South.[116]

[116] See Dew, "Disciplining Slave Ironworkers," *AHR*, forthcoming, Apr. 1974.

A Tale of Two Plantations:
Slave Life at Mesopotamia in Jamaica
and Mount Airy in Virginia, 1799 to 1828

Richard S. Dunn

O N January 1, 1809, John Tayloe, one of Virginia's leading planters, took a detailed census of the 384 slaves on his Mount Airy estate, listing each man, woman, and child by name, age, occupation, and monetary value. On the same day the overseer for a big Jamaican absentee planter, Joseph Foster Barham, was taking a similar census of the 322 slaves on Barham's Mesopotamia estate in which he listed each person by name, age, occupation, and physical condition. Thousands of other North American and West Indian slave inventories survive, especially in probate records, but what gives the Mount Airy and Mesopotamia lists special value is that the owners of these estates made a systematic practice of cataloguing their slave gangs annually over a long time span. The Barhams at Mesopotamia kept annual inventories from 1751 to 1832; seventy-five of these lists survive.[1] The Tayloes at Mount Airy kept annual inventories from 1808 to 1855, and forty-five of these lists survive.[2] Setting the two lists of 1809 against each other, we

Mr. Dunn is a member of the Department of History, University of Pennsylvania. He wishes to thank the American Philosophical Society for supporting his research at Oxford and London, and the National Endowment for the Humanities for supporting his research in Virginia. He drafted the article while a visiting member of the Institute for Advanced Study in Princeton, and benefited greatly from comments offered by colleagues at an Institute seminar and at a University of Pennsylvania history workshop.

[1] The Mesopotamia slave lists are filed in the Clarendon Manuscript Deposit, Barham Papers, Boxes b. 34, 35, and 36, Bodleian Library, Oxford University. The lists run in a broken series covering the years 1736, 1743-1744, 1751-1752, 1754-1769, 1771-1776, 1778, 1780-1781, 1784-1785, 1790-1806, 1808-1819, 1822-1832. From 1762 onward the lists are especially valuable because they give the age as well as the name, occupation, and condition of each slave. I wish to thank the earl of Clarendon for permitting me to use the Barham Papers, and Stanley L. Engerman both for pointing out data in this collection which I otherwise would have overlooked and for making helpful criticisms.

[2] The Mount Airy slave lists are found in four inventory books in the Tayloe Papers, Virginia Historical Society, Richmond. The earliest of these books, kept by John Tayloe III, contains slave lists for 1808-1823 and 1825-1828 (MSS 1 T2118d538). The other three, kept by his son William Henry Tayloe, contain slave lists for 1829-

can compare the structure of a Virginia plantation with a Jamaica plantation at a particular moment—just as the slave trade was closing in the United States and the British West Indies. Setting the two series of inventories against each other, we can make a running comparison between the two estates over a considerable stretch of years, and get a sense of two distinctly different slave communities in action.

Two bricks do not make a house, and it cannot be claimed that Mount Airy was representative of all Chesapeake plantations or Mesopotamia of all Caribbean estates. Still, microcosmic case studies have their utility, especially for studying such a topic as slave life, where the macrocosmic work of the cliometricians has stirred such controversy. Quantification itself is surely not at issue; the historian who wishes to interpret slave records çannot get very far without employing techniques of aggregative analysis. What is at issue is the cliometricians' habit of counterfactual hypothesis, their manipulation of synthetic figures extrapolated from mathematical models, and their certitude that by such tactics they can "correct" the "errors" of previous interpreters.[3] Quite apart from the question of the historical accuracy of the cliometricians' findings, their abstract mode of computation tends to rob men and women of individual personality, strips communities of local variety, and turns both people and places into digits in a data bank. The present essay attempts a more intimate picture of slave life. The Mesopotamia and Mount Airy inventories are so richly detailed that one can tease from them a sense of time and motion. The inventories generate statistical information about a considerable number of people—1,400 slaves owned by the Barhams and 1,100 slaves owned by the Tayloes—but the strength of the documentation lies more in its quality than in its quantity. Close examination of conditions on

---

1836 (MSS 1 T2118d13410); for 1837-1838 (MSS 1 T2118d13424); and for 1840-1847 and 1849-1855 (MSS 1 T2118a13). Probably the series began well before 1808 and continued after 1855, but other inventory books seem not to have survived. I wish to thank the Virginia Historical Society for permitting me to use the Tayloe Papers.

[3] This is not the place to detail the bulky polemical literature concerning the cliometric approach to the history of slavery. A good way to enter the debate is to compare Robert William Fogel and Stanley L. Engerman, *Time on the Cross: The Economics of American Negro Slavery*, 2 vols. (Boston, 1974), with Herbert G. Gutman's sharply critical review essay, "The World Two Cliometricians Made," *Journal of Negro History*, LX (1975), 54–227. For examples of cliometric work based more on hypothesis than on historical evidence see the essays by Richard Sutch, Jack Ericson Eblen, and Claudia Dale Goldin in Stanley L. Engerman and Eugene D. Genovese, eds., *Race and Slavery in the Western Hemisphere* (Princeton, N.J., 1975). It should be added that both the quantitative and the nonquantitative students of U.S. slavery have concentrated overwhelmingly on the years 1830-1860 because documentation for this period is much richer than for the colonial and early national periods. The Tayloe slave lists have extra value because they permit close investigation of slave life before 1830.

these two estates suggests that slave life—like any other variety of human experience—defies precise statistical formulation. Three-dimensional people emerge with variegated life histories and complex communal roles.[4]

In 1809 the slave gangs at Mesopotamia and Mount Airy were about equal in size. The 322 slaves at Mesopotamia constituted a fairly typical Jamaican plantation labor force, for the island was completely dominated by the estates of a few hundred sugar planters, and Mesopotamia was only slightly above average in strength for a Jamaican sugar estate. By Virginia standards, on the other hand, the 384 slaves at Mount Airy constituted a production force of exceptional size, for in Virginia only a few planters owned large gangs, and the great majority of slaves were distributed among middling and small farmers. Furthermore, while Mesopotamia was situated in Jamaica's richest sugar-growing district, Mount Airy lay in a tidewater region of declining agricultural importance, where the planters had switched from tobacco to wheat and corn in search of a viable product. The slaves at Mesopotamia were engaged in a labor-intensive enterprise, partly agricultural and partly industrial, that required a large, coordinated work force. The slaves at Mount Airy were doing much the same work as small free farmers elsewhere in the United States. Sugar production was the sole concern at Mesopotamia and the sole rationale for the organization of the slave force there. At Mount Airy commercial agriculture was less vitally important, and the slaves on this estate spent considerably less than half their labor in the production of cash crops.

The owners of the two estates, the Barhams and the Tayloes, had been large landholders and slaveholders in Jamaica and Virginia respectively for four generations. As big planters, they reflected in their contrasting life styles some of the basic differences between the two societies. The Tayloes lived in

[4] The Mesopotamia and Mount Airy slave lists form two of the longest series presently known. Amother long series of 27 lists from Worthy Park estate in Jamaica, spanning the years 1784-1838, is analyzed by Michael Craton and Garry Greenland, *Searching for the Invisible Man*, forthcoming. I am much indebted to Mr. Craton for letting me read his manuscript and for fruitful discussion comparing Worthy Park with Mesopotamia. For background information on Jamaica in the early 19th century see Edward Braithwaite, *The Development of Creole Society in Jamaica, 1770-1820* (Oxford, 1971), and Orlando Patterson, *The Sociology of Slavery: An Analysis of the Origins, Development and Structure of Negro Slave Society in Jamaica* (Rutherford, N.J., 1969). The closest equivalent studies for Virginia are Robert McColley, *Slavery and Jeffersonian Virginia*, 2d ed. (Urbana, Ill., 1973), and Gerald W. Mullin, *Flight and Rebellion: Slave Resistance in Eighteenth-Century Virginia* (New York, 1972). For full discussion of a Jamaican estate comparable to Mesopotamia see Michael Craton and James Walvin, *A Jamaican Plantation: A History of Worthy Park, 1670-1970* (Toronto, 1970); and for discussion of a Northern Neck Virginia slaveholder comparable to Tayloe see Louis Morton, *Robert Carter of Nomini Hall: A Virginia Planter of the Eighteenth Century* (Williamsburg, Va., 1941).

the Northern Neck, tracing their property back to Col. William Tayloe (d. 1710), who laid out a tobacco farm on the Rappahannock River, manned at the time of his death by twenty-one slaves. His son John Tayloe I (1687-1747), the chief architect of the family fortune, established an ironworks on the upper Rappahannock, opened up new farms in four Virginia counties and in Maryland, obtained a seat on the Virginia Council, and left his heirs a force of 328 Negroes, one of the grandest mid-eighteenth-century slave gangs in the Chesapeake region. In the next generation John Tayloe II (1721-1779) played the role of leisured gentleman. At Mount Airy, overlooking the Rappahannock, he built an imposing mansion and laid out a mile-long race course. Though he sat on the council, John II was better at horse breeding than at politics, and though he accumulated further property, much of it was lost during the Revolutionary War. His son John Tayloe III (1771-1828)— the owner of Mount Airy in our period—spent his youth in England at Eton and Cambridge as though no Revolution had taken place. The 1787 tax lists credit him with 11,200 acres and 290 slaves in four counties—less property than his grandfather had possessed. Still, John III remained one of the chief slaveholders in the state and by far the largest property holder in Richmond County. As his family grew (he had seven sons and five daughters to provide for), he picked up additional property in Virginia, Maryland, the District of Columbia, and Kentucky. He built the elegant Octagon House as his town residence in Washington, and founded the Tappahannock Jockey Club to promote horse breeding and racing. On his death, he left the fifth generation of Tayloes a rich legacy of twenty-three farms, three ironworks, city houses in Washington, and some 700 slaves.[5]

By contrast, the Barhams, like most big Jamaica planters, had become absentees. They traced their island holdings back to Col. Thomas Foster, who started a sugar estate in the western parish of St. Elizabeth in the 1670s, and to his son Col. John Foster (1681-1731), who opened additional sugar estates. John Foster's widow married a Jamaica physician, Dr. Henry Barham (1692-1746), and in 1736 they retired to England, well able to afford the luxury of absenteeism, since their six Jamaican properties produced a gross income of around £20,000 per year. John Foster's youngest son, Joseph Foster (1729-1789), took the name Joseph Foster Barham and inherited from

---

[5] For a biographical sketch of the Tayloe family see *Virginia Magazine of History and Biography*, XVII (1909), 369n-375n. Col. William Tayloe's estate was inventoried at his death in Richmond County Wills and Inventories, 1709-1717; John Tayloe I's will and inventory are *ibid.*, 1725-1753; John Tayloe II's will is in the Richmond County Will Book, 1767-1787—all in the Virginia State Library, Richmond. John Tayloe III's will, dated Dec. 1827, is in the Tayloe Papers, MSS 1 T2118d539-545. His property holdings for 1787-1788 have been calculated by Jackson T. Main, "The One Hundred," *William and Mary Quarterly*, 3d Ser., XI (1954), 383-384.

his stepfather the Mesopotamia estate in the fertile Westmoreland plain on the southwestern tip of the island. Though he lived as an absentee proprietor in Shropshire, Barham took unusual interest in the spiritual welfare of his slaves. He urged Moravian missionaries to come to Jamaica, where they established a station at Mesopotamia. In 1768, during the early days of this mission, eighty-four of Barham's slaves were baptized, and in 1816, when the Gothic novelist "Monk" Lewis visited Mesopotamia, he found the Moravians still at work, though only fifty slaves now belonged to their church. The owner of Mesopotamia in our period was Joseph Foster Barham II (1759-1832), of Stratford Place, Middlesex. This gentleman lived on an even handsomer scale than his Virginian counterpart John Tayloe III, was rich enough to marry an earl's daughter, and sat in Parliament. During his twenty-seven years in the House of Commons Barham worked actively for the sugar lobby, but he also voted in the 1790s to abolish the slave trade, and he published a pamphlet in 1823 favoring gradual emancipation of the slaves—on condition that the West Indian proprietors be handsomely compensated for their loss.[6]

In 1809 the Tayloes' Mount Airy estate and the Barhams' Mesopotamia estate, roughly equal in scale, were quite different in arrangement. The Tayloes' Mount Airy Department, or Rappahannock Farms, consisted of nine separate but interdependent units, each managed by its own overseer, strung a distance of thirty miles along both sides of the river. Six of these units were in Richmond County on the north bank, one was in Essex County on the south bank, and two were in King George County farther up the north bank. Perhaps forty whites lived on the whole estate; Tayloe himself had a family of eleven in this year, and most of his overseers seem to have had wives and children. The central unit, Mount Airy proper, was the home plantation where Tayloe resided for half of each year, from April to October; he took his family to Washington for the winter months. No farming was done at Mount Airy. The 106 slaves who lived there in 1809 were employed as domestic servants or craft workers. The other eight units—Old House (where the first Tayloe mansion had stood), Doctors Hall, Forkland, Mask-

---

[6] For information on Joseph Foster Barham see *Gentlemen's Magazine: and Historical Chronicle* (London, 1832), Pt. I, 102, Pt. II, 573, and Joseph Foster Barham, *Considerations on the Abolition of Negro Slavery* (London, 1823). The Barham holdings in Jamaica in 1739 can be traced via Edward Long's list of 428 sugar plantations for that year, Additional Manuscripts, 12, 434, 1-12, British Museum. Their holdings in 1754 can be traced via the quitrent list of Jamaican landholders, C.O. 142/31, Public Record Office. For the Moravians see M. G. Lewis, *Journal of a West India Proprietor, 1815-1817*, ed. Mona Wilson (Boston, 1929 [orig. publ. London, 1834]), 152-153. I am much indebted to Althea Silvera, West India Reference Library, Institute of Jamaica, Kingston, for additional information on the Barhams.

field, Menokin, Gwinfield, Hopyard, and Oakenbrow—were all farms, with a total of 8,000 acres. The 278 slaves who lived on these eight quarters in 1809 produced about 7,000 bushels of wheat and 14,000 bushels of corn for Tayloe to sell.[7] In the eighteenth century the Tayloes had grown tobacco on the Rappahannock, but no tobacco was cultivated in 1809.

Mesopotamia was differently organized, with all 322 slaves grouped into a single sugar production unit of 2,448 acres. Four hundred acres were planted in cane, and the rest of the land was used for cattle pens, pasture, and slave provision grounds, or was left uncultivated. Like all the big Jamaican sugar estates, Mesopotamia had its own mill for grinding the cane, a boiling house and a curing house for converting the cane juice into sugar, and a distillery for converting the sugar by-products into rum. The Mesopotamia workers produced about 250 hogsheads of sugar and 120 puncheons of rum for sale in 1809.[8] As at Mount Airy, they were divided into agricultural laborers, craft workers, and domestics, but they all lived together in a single village. To manage this work force Joseph Foster Barham II employed a small and highly transitory staff of whites. The overseer and five or six bookkeepers and artisans lived on the estate, and another two or three whites lived six miles away at the Barham storehouse in the port town of Savanna la Mar. Occasionally this staff included married men with wives and children, but most were single males, and few stayed on the Barham payroll for more than a year or two.[9] Thus the blacks at Mesopotamia outnumbered the whites by a ratio of 50:1, whereas at Mount Airy the ratio was closer to 10:1.

Today the Virginia Tayloes still live at Mount Airy in their sandstone mansion of Italianate design built in 1755. From this house, standing on a hill above the river, one can easily recapture the scene in 1809: the terraces, gardens, orangery, bowling green, and deer park, and down below the site of the old race course and the farmland where the Tayloe slaves once grew wheat and corn. But at Mesopotamia there are few tangible reminders of the Barhams' presence. Sugarcane is now cultivated at this estate by the Barham Sugar Workers Co-operative, a new experiment in which the cane workers own and operate their farm communally. The Barham Farm cane is processed at a giant modern factory several miles away. The old Mesopotamia

[7] No Mount Airy production figures survive for 1809, but in 1811 Tayloe's Rappahannock farms produced 8,664 bu. of wheat, of which 7,003 were sold, and the corn crop totaled 14,119 bu., with another 2,906 bu. in rent from Tayloe's tenants. See John Tayloe's Minute Book, 1811-1812, Tayloe Papers, MSS 1 T2118a10.

[8] No Mesopotamia production figures survive for 1809, but in 1817 the estate produced 254 hogsheads of sugar, of which 248 were sold, and 120 puncheons of rum, of which 113 were sold. Expense accounts, 1816-1817, Barham Papers, Box b. 33.

[9] There are lists of the white staff at Mesopotamia for the years 1789-1798 and 1816-1817, *ibid.*, Boxes b. 33, 36.

sugar works are in ruins, the old plantation house has been torn down, and only a pair of stone gate pillars and a few Barham and Moravian missionary gravestones recall the bygone activities of the slave-owning sugar magnates.[10]

What can be learned about slave life on these two estates from the Mount Airy and Mesopotamia inventories? Since space does not permit analysis of all 2,500 slaves owned by the Tayloes and Barhams during the 104 years covered by the two sets of inventories, we shall focus on the 668 slaves who lived at Mount Airy during a twenty-year span, 1809-1828, and the 548 slaves who lived at Mesopotamia during an equivalent and overlapping period, 1799-1818.[11] Tracing the individual histories of these 1,216 people, we can compare demographic trends, family structure, and labor patterns in the two slave gangs, as well as the managerial policies of the two owners.

Unfortunately, it is impossible to convey in brief compass the richly detailed biographical information in these inventories about hundreds of Mount Airy and Mesopotamia slaves. To illustrate, let us follow the careers of two people, chosen at random from the top of the alphabet—a woman named Agga at Mount Airy and a man named Augustus at Mesopotamia. In 1808 Agga was a thirty-one-year-old spinner valued at £70, which was slightly above the standard adult female price at Mount Airy. Her father had been a gardener; both parents were dead or gone by 1808. Her husband, Carpenter Harry, was forty-two in that year. Agga and Harry had four young children: ten-year-old John, who was put in a field gang for the first time in 1808 and sold in 1819; eight-year-old Michael, who entered the work force as a carpenter in 1812; three-year-old Kitty, who was sent to the Tayloes' house in Washington as a domestic in 1815; and one-year-old Caroline, who was sold in 1818. Agga had four more children in 1808, 1810, 1813, and 1818. Her two younger boys, Tom and George, became carpenters like their father and brother, and her two younger girls, Georgina and Ibby, became field hands.

[10] I wish to thank H. Gwynne Tayloe for generously showing me his family house at Mount Airy. The house is described by Thomas Tileston Waterman and John A. Barrows, *Domestic Colonial Architecture of Tidewater Virginia* (New York, 1968), 126-137. Mesopotamia is described by Paul F. White and Philip Wright, *Exploring Jamaica* (New York, 1969), 166-167; and the *Jamaica Daily News*, Feb. 19, 1975, has an article on the Barham Sugar Workers Co-operative.

[11] The dates chosen for Mesopotamia are a decade earlier than for Mount Airy because of an awkward three-year gap (1819-1821) in the Mesopotamia records, during which time Barham imported about 110 slaves from Springfield estate. This short gap may seem trifling, but the missing birth and death lists obscure the demographic data, and the 110 new Springfield slaves who first appear in 1822 are not identified as family groups, hence making more difficult the already formidable task of analyzing family structure. Since Mesopotamia's records are complete for the years 1799-1818, this equivalent span has been substituted.

Agga was forty-one years old when her last baby was born, and fifty-two when her husband died. In 1844, when the most detailed of the Mount Airy lists was taken, she was sixty-seven and in failing health, but still employed as a spinner. One son lived with her in 1844; two daughters and seven grandchildren lived on neighboring Rappahannock farms; the other five children and five traceable grandchildren had moved away or died.

In the Mesopotamia list Augustus is recorded as an invalid in 1809, having retired from the work force at age sixty-seven. One can trace Augustus through almost his entire long career via fifty-seven Mesopotamia inventories. He first appears on a crude list dated April 18, 1743, before the Mesopotamia managers began keeping annual records or listing the slaves by age. At this time Augustus was about three years old; his name appears toward the bottom of the boys' group with half a dozen other children who in later lists turn out to be the same age. Eight lists later, in 1756, he is promoted from the boys' to the men's group; he was then about sixteen years old and valued at £75, the price of an able adult working man at that date. In 1762, when the Mesopotamia lists become much more detailed, Augustus is described as twenty-two years old, in good health, and employed as a distiller, a post he held for the next forty years. In 1768 he was baptized into the Moravian church with the name of Peter (though he remains Augustus on the slave lists) and recovered from the smallpox without ill effect. He began to decline in health in his early forties, being characterized as "sickly" for the first time in 1781. By 1785 he was spitting blood. Nevertheless, he kept working in the still house until 1802, when he was transferred to the easier job of head watchman. In 1809, when he was retired to invalid status, he was probably two years older than his then stated age of sixty-seven, and he died at seventy-two on February 16, 1812.

As is evident from these two examples, the Mount Airy and Mesopotamia inventories are more precise and systematic documents than most population counts or census returns, including modern ones, because they were reworked annually over a long period, and because they report at least four variables per year for each slave. Thus they surmount the problem of record linkage, which is so bothersome in attempting to compare any two census lists compiled at ten-year intervals. In the Mesopotamia list for 1809 there are nine males with the name of John, and on the corresponding Mount Airy list there are twelve Johns; but each of these individuals can be distinguished from the others by maternal lineage, occupation, state of health, and especially by age. Reporting of age is seriously defective in most forms of census taking. Demographers put little credence in the stated ages of elderly people, and develop compensatory techniques to combat obvious tendencies toward age heaping—overreporting of age in even digits and in multiples of five and ten—or such more subtle problems as the under-reporting of females aged ten to nineteen and the overreporting of females aged twenty-five to thirty-four.[12]

If such defects are built into current census taking, it is obvious that age statements for slaves on most eighteenth- and nineteenth-century documents are mere guesswork. But the ages of the Mesopotamia and Mount Airy slaves can usually be accurately established. Neither set of lists shows significant age heaping or other signs of gross distortion. At Mesopotamia the Barhams kept birth registers after 1773, so that the exact ages of most slaves born on the estate during our period are recorded. The Tayloes did not keep birth registers, but the birth years for nearly half the Mount Airy slaves can be established. In compiling their lists, the census takers sometimes carelessly repeated last year's age or capriciously added ten years when a person looked old or sick. The stated ages of some elderly slaves cannot be verified and are doubtless inflated, but most other errors can be corrected. Since a great many of the slaves who were brought into the two estates arrived as children, the initial age estimates for these people are probably not wildly wrong, and the census takers endeavored to correct errors. For instance, an African girl named Matura, who arrived at Mesopotamia in 1792, was classified at first as eleven years old, but the next year her age was advanced to fourteen. Four years later, at the (corrected) age of eighteen, Matura had her first child— and as we shall see, this was early for motherhood in Mesopotamia. Thus the two series stand up under close inspection as consistent and reliable; their greatest shortcoming is that they generally identify only the mothers, not the fathers, of slave children, and thus preclude full analysis of family structure.

Table I compares demographic trends on the two estates. As is well known, over a span of two centuries the Virginia slave population experienced marked natural increase while the Jamaican slave population experienced marked natural decrease. Virginia planters imported fewer than 150,000 slaves between 1609 and 1808, and the black population of the state in 1809 was about 415,000. Jamaican planters imported something like 750,000 slaves between 1655 and 1808, yet the black population on the island in 1809 was only about 350,000.[13] As Table I demonstrates, Mount Airy and Mesopotamia reflected these demographic conditions. The most basic contrast between the two slave communities was that Tayloe's slaves increased and multiplied, whereas Barham had to keep restocking Mesopotamia with fresh purchases. The Mount Airy totals in Table I are partly conjectural,

[12] Ansley J. Coale and Paul Demeny, *Methods of Estimating Basic Demographic Measures from Incomplete Data* (New York, 1967), 19-21.

[13] For slave import and black population estimates see Philip D. Curtin, *The Atlantic Slave Trade: A Census* (Madison, Wis., 1969), 52-59, 71-74, 136-145; U.S. Bureau of the Census, *Negro Population, 1790-1915* (Washington, D.C., 1918), 45-57; George W. Roberts, *The Population of Jamaica* (Cambridge, 1957), 35-43, 65; and Braithwaite, *Development of Creole Society*, 152, 168, 207.

TABLE I
SLAVE POPULATION CHANGES OVER TWENTY YEARS

	Mount Airy, Virginia, 1809-1828			Mesopotamia, Jamaica, 1799-1818		
	Male	Female	Total	Male	Female	Total
Population at outset	219	165	384	190	174	364
Increase:						
Born	131	116	247	61	63	124
Purchased	3	0	3	28	32	60
Moved in[a]	17	17	34	0	0	0
	151	133	284	89	95	184
Decrease:						
Died	45	43 ⎫		132	101	233
Est. died	27	13 ⎭ 128				
Sold	8	29 ⎫		0	0	0
Est. sold	5	10 ⎭ 52				
Moved out[b]	53	31 ⎫		0	0	0
Est. moved out	32	9 ⎭ 125				
Freed	1	0	1	2	4	6
	171	135	306	134	105	239
Population at close	199	163	362	145	164	309
Recorded Birth rate	39.83 per 1000			18.89 per 1000		
Recorded Death rate	20.64 per 1000			35.49 per 1000		

Notes: [a] From other outlying Tayloe estates.
[b] To other outlying Tayloe estates.

because John Tayloe III was constantly switching slaves from one quarter to another, or handing over farms (with slaves attached) to his sons, or opening new farms, or selling surplus slaves, without leaving adequate record. It is thus impossible to tell which of the thirty-four slaves who moved into the Rappahannock farms during this period were bought, and which were transferred from outlying Tayloe estates. Likewise, it is impossible to tell what happened to ninety-six of the 306 slaves who dropped off the Tayloe lists. But inspection of the 209 known deaths, sales, and transfers during this period reveals a persistent pattern: those Mount Airy slaves who were sold or transferred were generally in their 'teens or twenties, whereas Mount Airy slaves who died were almost always younger or older than this—under ten or over thirty.[14] The Mount Airy estimates in Table I assume that the ninety-six unidentifiable deaths, sales, and transfers follow exactly the same pattern as the 209 that are known.

The vital rates in Table I pose an interpretive problem. The demographers Ansley Coale and Paul Demeny have published 192 model life tables and nearly 5,000 stable population tables, derived mainly from twentieth-century European vital statistics and census returns, so as to estimate the full range of population parameters in various regions of the world. Historians interested in slave demography have employed these tables to project birth rates for eighteenth- and nineteenth-century slave populations at around 50 per 1,000 with death rates in the low to mid-thirties.[15] But this assumes that past slave populations experienced the same range of fertility and mortality levels as current nonenslaved populations. The demographic patterns for Mount Airy slaves do indeed seem compatible with Coale and Demeny's schedules. Tayloe kept no vital registers; hence his inventories clearly under-report infant births and deaths. Furthermore, he moved many slaves off the estate, thus depressing the fertility and obscuring the mortality of his population. But Mesopotamia's vital rates appear to be more accurate. Barham's bookkeepers kept birth and death registers that report the deaths of newborn infants. Quite possibly they failed to note many other infant births and deaths; but even if the reported vital rates are far too low, the Mesopotamia data on age composition, longevity, and rate of natural decrease make a very poor fit with all of Coale and Demeny's tables. Clearly, the demographic pattern at Mesopotamia differed radically from Mount Airy's; I believe that it also differed from all observed modern populations.

[14] Of the 88 Mount Airy slaves whose deaths are recorded between 1809 and 1828, 48% were children under 10, only 9% were in their 'teens or 20s, and 43% were adults over 30. Of the 121 slaves recorded as sold or transferred, 25% were children under 10, 55% were in their 'teens or 20s, and only 20% were over 30.

[15] The model tables are published in Ansley J. Coale and Paul Demeny, *Regional Model Life Tables and Stable Populations* (Princeton, N.J., 1966); their "West" family of tables—the only set to encompass non-European demographic experience—draws no data from slave populations. Jack Eblen uses these tables to postulate natural increase and high birth rates among the Cuban and Jamaican slaves. Eblen, "On the Natural Increase of Slave Populations," in Engerman and Genovese, eds., *Race and Slavery*, 244-247. However, Michael Craton's analysis of demographic evidence at Worthy Park estate, Jamaica, supports my findings.

The striking feature of the Mesopotamia vital records is the feeble birth rate. In an average year seventy-five women of child-bearing age lived on the estate, yet they produced only six recorded live births. Whether or not these figures are correct, 109 more slaves died than were born, 1799-1818, and Barham sustained his work force only by importing sixty new slaves. These new slaves came mainly in a single transaction from Cairncurran estate in Jamaica, rather than from Africa. No Mesopotamia slaves had been bought from African traders since 1792, with the result that by 1809 only 19 percent of the slave force had come straight from Africa, another 19 percent had been bought from other Jamaican plantations, and 60 percent were born at Mesopotamia.[16] Those coming from Africa had arrived at Mesopotamia in small lots of ten or a dozen; most commonly they had been teenage boys. The "seasoned" slaves acquired from neighboring plantations came in much larger groups—40 from Three Mile River estate in 1786, 61 from Southfield in 1791, 56 from Cairncurran in 1814, and about 110 from Springfield around 1820. Obviously, these people knew each other already, and they came in family groups, parents with children, the very old and the very young, and almost as many females as males. Thus while in the mid-eighteenth-century Mesopotamian slave life had been marked by ethnic diversity, with Negroes coming from various regions of West and Central Africa, speaking different languages and holding conflicting values, with the passage of time the estate became far more homogeneous, not to say inbred. Table I suggests the extremely immobile character·of slave life on this estate. Negroes born at Mesopotamia almost invariably spent their entire lives there. Negroes bought from an African trader or from another planter were almost never sold again. Between 1751 and 1818 only four Mesopotamia slaves were sold, ten were manumitted, and five ran away. None were transferred to Joseph Foster Barham's other sugar estate, the Island, in neighboring St. Elizabeth parish.

Everything was different at Mount Airy. There were twice as many recorded births as deaths on this estate, few new slaves were imported, and the slight population decline between 1809 and 1828 is explained by a massive exodus of slaves—approximately 177 in twenty years. At least thirty-nine Rappahannock slaves—predominantly young males—were sent 180 miles west to the Tayloes' Cloverdale ironworks in Botetourt County beyond the Blue Ridge in 1811-1814. Another twenty-two went to Windsor Farm in King George County in 1820-1821. When John Tayloe III bought Deogg Farm in King George County in 1824, he staffed it entirely with slaves drawn from his neighboring Rappahannock farms. John III stated in his will that he disliked separating slave families, and the inventories show that he generally did sell mothers with their young children. But not always. In 1816 Forkland

[16] The origins of the remaining 2%—mainly old people who had been living on the estate since the 1740s—cannot be traced.

Cate was sold without her four-year-old son Alfred, and Gwinfield Rachel was sold without her six-year-old son Billy. A number of girls were separated from their mothers and sold at about age nine, and by the time they reached their early 'teens boys and girls were at the prime age for transfer to a new quarter or for sale off the estate. For example, a boy named John, after spending the first decade of his life with his mother at Doctors Hall, was put in the field gang at Forkland at age eleven, was then switched to Old House at age fifteen, and was sold at age eighteen. Almost all of these Negroes must have been native Virginians. Back in the early eighteenth century the Tayloes had established their slave force with Africans, but John III had no need for the slave trade and small need for slave purchases. Only three of the 668 slaves on the Mount Airy lists for 1809-1828 are identified as "newly purchased." Starting as he did in the late 1770s with about 200 Negroes, Tayloe could, through the process of natural increase alone, come close to building up his force to the point where, fifty years later, he had 700 slaves to distribute among his seven sons.[17]

Examination of the shifting population on one Rappahannock farm, the Hopyard quarter, shows how Tayloe's system worked. This farm had a slave force of forty-six in 1809, of whom twenty-six were classified as working field hands. During the next twenty years thirty slaves were born at Hopyard, three grown slaves moved in, and thirty-nine dropped off the lists. Five of these thirty-nine were moved to other Rappahannock farms, four were moved to Cloverdale, nine died, and eleven were sold—ten of them in a single year, 1816, when two women, Kesiah and Patty, were sold together with eight of their young children. Ten of those who disappeared from the Hopyard lists cannot be traced, but judging by their ages, five of them probably died and five were probably transferred out of the Rappahannock district. Thus Hopyard—a comparatively small population unit—produced some twenty-five slaves for sale or transfer in twenty years. By 1828 the Hopyard gang had dropped to forty, but since twenty-seven of these were classified as working hands, the farm was as strongly staffed as in 1809. Only

[17] My figures on the total size of John Tayloe's slave force are only approximate. I have tried to trace his holdings from 1787 onward through the annual county personal property tax lists in the Va. State Lib., but this is hard to do, since he and his sons held slaves in many counties and the tax assessors frequently confused their slaves with slaves held by planters named Taylor. The process followed by John Tayloe III is easier to trace in the records of a contemporary South Carolina cotton planter, Peter Gaillard, who inherited his property in 1784 and retired from business in 1825. Gaillard started with 134 slaves, bought 125 more (mainly in the 1800s in order to set up his three elder sons), and sold 35. During his 40 years of plantership his slave force doubled through natural increase: 456 births as against 237 deaths. Thus by 1825 he was able to give 433 slaves to his eight children and still have 10 left to attend him in his old age. See Peter Gaillard's Account and Memorandum Book, Gaillard Papers, South Carolina Historical Society, Charleston.

nineteen of the forty-six slaves who were there in 1809 were still there twenty years later. But some families remained largely intact. Four men and four women, very probably married couples, and nineteen of the four women's children and grandchildren accounted for most of the Hopyard population in 1828.

At Mount Airy, as at Mesopotamia, the age profile of the slave population fluctuated considerably from year to year. In Table II age distribution within the two slave gangs has been averaged out over a twenty-year period to show basic differences between the proportions of males and females, young and old, on the two estates. Several obvious and important differences emerge. Mount Airy had a much higher proportion of children—naturally enough, since the recorded birth rate was greater. Mount Airy had a much younger population, with the median age at twenty, as against twenty-seven in Mesopotamia. Mount Airy had a higher proportion of males, including young adult males of prime working age (20-34). Mesopotamia had a higher proportion of females in every age group above fourteen, most particularly young women of prime child-bearing age (20-29). This makes the low Mesopotamia birth rate especially puzzling. Mesopotamia also had a higher proportion of relatively old people, with nearly 20 percent of the population beyond the age of forty-five, and a higher percentage than at Mount Airy beyond the age of sixty.

At Mesopotamia, as was generally the case on West Indian sugar estates, the females proved tougher than the males and better able to survive the trauma of slavery. In the eighteenth century, when the Barhams kept restocking from African slave traders, they maintained a pronounced male

TABLE II
AGE DISTRIBUTION OVER TWENTY YEARS

	Mount Airy 1809-1828		Mesopotamia 1799-1818	
	Percent of Total Pop.		Percent of Total Pop.	
Age	Males	Females	Males	Females
0-14	22.1	17.9	14.7	14.4
15-19	6.1	4.0	4.6	5.0
20-24	5.5	3.8	3.8	4.0
25-29	3.9	3.4	4.5	4.1
30-34	4.1	2.8	3.1	3.4
35-39	3.2	2.9	5.7	4.3
40-44	3.3	2.5	5.0	3.7
45-	7.5	7.0	8.9	10.8
Totals	55.7	44.3	50.3	49.7

majority—as high as 148 males for every 100 females in 1772, for example. But between 1799 and 1818 this male preponderance disappeared, and by 1818 the females were in a decided majority (88/100). The significance of this shift in the sex ratio becomes clearer if we focus attention on those Mesopo- tamia slaves of prime working age, between seventeen and forty years old, who were categorized as "able bodied" rather than sickly, weak, or diseased. The number of healthy slaves of prime age at Mesopotamia was always strikingly small—ranging from one-fourth to one-third of the total slave force. During the 1799-1818 span 52 percent of the healthy prime-aged slaves at Mesopotamia were women. Thus much of the heavy labor at Mesopo- tamia had to be performed by females who—especially since they produced few children—occupied a role radically different from that taken by women in most western societies.

At Mount Airy the women remained a minority. Part of the explanation is demographic, for, as Table I shows, there was a surplus of male births between 1809 and 1828. But the sex ratio was also powerfully affected by the Tayloes' transfer of slaves from Mount Airy. Clearly, the Tayloes valued women well below men, as shown by the inventory of 1809, where the females are priced at an average of £53 6s. 2d. apiece as against £64 2s. 2d. for the males.[18] About two-thirds of the slaves transferred from the Rappa- hannock district to other family farms were males—thus helping to build a solid majority of men on the Tayloe work gangs. Enough females stayed at Mount Airy to perform domestic tasks and to assure a healthy rate of natural increase. The rest were sold.

About three-quarters of the Mount Airy slaves sold between 1809 and 1828 were female. Of the twenty-nine female sales for which we have definite record, four were small children, all sold with their mothers. Sixteen were girls aged nine to seventeen; of these, eleven were sold separately from their kin and none had babies of their own. The remaining nine were mature women, of whom seven were mothers, sold in combination with thirteen of their young children. From a practical standpoint it was doubtless sensible to sell slave girls at the preadolescent/adolescent stage of life, when they com- manded a price that amply repaid the cost of their upbringing and when they were old enough to work for a new owner, yet still too young for motherhood. There is no evidence whatsoever that the Tayloes practiced slave breeding in the sense that they mated Negroes forcibly, frequently, or promiscuously in order to sell the surplus progeny. But plainly the Tayloes did prefer male to female workers, and they maintained an artificially unbalanced sex ratio in their Mount Airy slave gang.

[18] Likewise at Mesopotamia the female slaves in scattered lists from 1786 to 1814 were priced at an average of £71.17.9 apiece as against £84.0.3 for the males.

The conditions described thus far did nothing to bolster family life among the slaves. The character of household and family structure at Mesopotamia and Mount Airy is difficult to discover, since the white men who compiled the slave inventories took small interest in such matters and seldom even identified husbands or wives. But it is certain that many slaves on both estates maintained conjugal family units. For family structure at Mesopotamia the best evidence comes in 1814, when the fifty-six newly purchased slaves from the Cairncurran estate are listed in family groups rather than by the usual division into males and females.[19] The first sixteen entries from this list are reproduced below to show the character of record keeping at Mesopotamia:

Name	Age	Occupation	Condition	Value ($£$)
Smart	37	Head Driver	Prime	200
Lettice	35	Field	Prime	145
Peggie	12	Field	Healthy	100
Job	5	Small Gang	Healthy	50
Camilla	33	Field	Able	160
Bob	3		Yaws	30
Leicester	5		Yaws	40
John Savey	9		Healthy	60
Exeter	55	Head Mason	Aged	140
Sally	37	House Cook	Prime	160
Bessie	13	House Wench	Healthy	130
Richard	11	Small Gang	Healthy	85
Joe	7	Small Gang	Healthy	70
Mary	5		Healthy	55
Jean	3		Healthy	40
Ann	1½		Healthy	30

These sixteen persons evidently belonged to three families: Smart and Lettice with two children; Camilla with three children and no mate; Exeter and Sally with six children. To be sure, Smart and Exeter are not specifically identified as husbands or fathers, but unless we are to suppose that the record keeper put down names at random—which is highly implausible—the list indicates that these men headed their respective families. A conspicuous feature of the list is that very young children worked in the field in the Small Gang, also known as the hogmeat or grass gang.

Camilla, without a mate on arrival at Mesopotamia, gave birth to her

[19] The list of Cairncurran slaves, dated Jan. 29, 1814, is in the Barham Papers, Box b. 34.

next child fourteen months later. Her small boys, Bob and Leicester, suffered from a common West Indian infectious disease, the yaws, characterized by skin eruptions and bone lesions. John Savey may have been a mulatto, named after his white father, which would explain why he was unemployed although a healthy nine year old. However, he was priced low for a mulatto, was never recorded as mulatto in the Mesopotamia lists, and soon went into the field gang in which mulattoes almost never worked. Exeter appears rather old for his wife and brood of young children, but he was evidently a robust person, still alive at age seventy-three when the last Mesopotamia list was made in 1832. Sally, a prolific breeder by Jamaican standards, had two more children after arrival at Mesopotamia. Viewed collectively, forty-five of the fifty-six Cairncurran slaves arrived in family groups.

How many of these Cairncurran families lived in nucleated households at Mesopotamia is unknown. Evidence from other contemporaneous Jamaican estates argues that rather few did so. Mating was often casual, parents frequently lived in separate establishments, and households containing children were more often headed by women than by men. In the Jamaican slave kinship network, the maternal bond was the key element, for a grown son tended to live with his mother until her death or stayed as close as possible in the house next door.[20] Demographic conditions also powerfully affected family life. In the case of the Cairncurran slaves, by 1832 when the last Mesopotamia inventory was taken, eighteen years after their arrival, twenty-two people from this group of fifty-six had died, and nineteen of the survivors were weak, diseased, or invalided. Of the twelve family groups in 1814, eight had lost one or both parents by 1832, and four had lost one or several children. The one stalwart exception was Exeter's and Sally's family of eight, all still alive, the father nearly blind and the mother caring for him, while their six grown children labored in the cane fields.

The other great impediment to family life among the Mesopotamia slaves was the white overseers' and bookkeepers' sexual exploitation of the black women. Fourteen of the 124 babies born at Mesopotamia between 1799 and 1818 were mulattoes or quadroons—11 percent of the total births. This ratio may not seem high, but it must be remembered that only about six white men lived on the estate at any one time as against some ninety black men between the ages of seventeen and fifty. A white man living at Mesopotamia was twice as likely as a black man to sire a slave baby, a

[20] See B. W. Higman, "Household Structure and Fertility on Jamaican Slave Plantations: A Nineteenth-century Example," *Population Studies*, XXVII (1973), 527-550. Compare Charles B. Dew's analysis of slave family life at a Virginia ironworks, 1811-1813, in "David Ross and the Oxford Iron Works: A Study of Industrial Slavery in the Early Nineteenth-Century South," *WMQ*, 3d Ser., XXXI (1974), 189-224.

finding which provides some idea of the frequency of interracial sexual intercourse. The whites preferred their slave mistresses to be young: of the nine women who bore mulatto or quadroon infants during this twenty-year span, one was only fifteen years old and four others were under twenty. The whites also preferred light-complexioned women, such as Mulatto Ann, who worked in the overseer's house from age ten on, and bore two quadroon children when she was sixteen and eighteen. Neither Ann nor any of the other women used by the whites at Mesopotamia was manumitted. A twenty-three-year-old field slave named Judy, the mother of two Negro children, bore a mulatto boy named Archibald; she remained in the field gang and bore six more Negro children. Her son Archibald, being a mulatto, was placed in the overseer's house at age six and trained as a carpenter at age sixteen, but he must have been an unhappy person for he became a chronic runaway and died of the yaws when he was twenty-seven. Another sad story is the case of Batty, a field slave who caught the eye of the overseer, Patrick Knight, when she was a young mother in her twenties. Batty had two daughters by Knight, and in 1803, when she was twenty-nine, he manu-mitted both girls, took Batty out of the field gang, and installed her in his house. For the next thirteen years Batty lived with Knight and bore him two more children. Her sixth baby was a Negro child, and at about the age of forty she contracted the Coco Bays, a disease akin to leprosy. So Batty was sent back to the Mesopotamia work force, though she was sick, to toil her declining years as a washerwoman and grass cutter.

In Virginia mulattoes and quadroons were not identified as such in the records; thus there is no direct evidence of miscegenation at Mount Airy. But the evidence of disrupted family life is abundant. In 1816, when the Tayloes sold Hopyard Kesiah and Hopyard Patty with eight of their children, two of Patty's teenage children stayed at Hopyard and no male mates went with Kesiah and Patty. Similarly, in 1820, when Bob and his wife Betty were sent from Oakenbrow quarter to Windsor farm with their three youngest children, their older three teenage children stayed at Oakenbrow. A fuller sense of the disjointed nature of family life at Mount Airy comes from inspection of the inventory for 1835, a few years beyond our period. This is an exceptionally interesting list because it identifies both parents of all the small children on the estate and thereby records many of the slave marriages.[21] The following extract shows the character of this 1835 list:

[21] The inventory for 1835 is in the first inventory book kept by William Henry Tayloe, John III's third son, who inherited Mount Airy and four adjoining farms in 1828 (Tayloe Papers, MSS 1 T2118d13410, 43-46). William Henry Tayloe's invento-ries for 1844 and 1845 are likewise useful, since they identify the parents of almost all the adult slaves living at Mount Airy in those years. *Ibid.*, MSS 1 T2118a13.

Car[penter]. Bill and his wife Esthers .... wife Winney Jr.

Children		Urias	7
Winney	8	Paul	5
Anne	7	China	3
Juliet	5	Prince	Inf[ant]
James	3		
Charlotte	Inf[ant]	Marilla's—Husband Decd.	
		Rose	8
Tom and his wife Winneys		Jacob and his wife Mary	
William .... out in field		Kate	10 in Ala[bama]
Grace	7		
Chapman	4		

Altogether, thirty-five Mount Airy slave families can be reconstructed by combining this inventory of 1835 with the earlier lists.

The five Mount Airy families shown in the illustration above are not listed completely. Esther had a ten-year-old daughter working at the Tayloe house in Washington; Mary had a fourteen-year-old son working in a field gang; and Marilla had five grown children, three of whom lived on the same quarter with her in 1835. Except for Winney's twelve-year-old son William, this list excludes working children, but when Mount Airy boys and girls did enter the work force they sometimes were sent far away—like ten-year-old Kate in the example above, who went to Alabama in 1836. When this list was drawn up, the Tayloes were in the process of moving Negroes from several of their Virginia estates to Alabama in order to open new cotton plantations there. By 1836 William Henry Tayloe had transferred forty-seven of his Mount Airy slaves—mainly young unmarried men and women—to Alabama, and by 1855 he had more slaves there than in Virginia.

The Mount Airy kinship network was pervasive in 1835; almost every slave had several blood relatives living on the estate. Yet of the thirty-five identifiable slave families, fifteen were lacking one or both parents, and in most families the children were widely dispersed. Furthermore, in the twenty families where husband and wife were both still living, only five couples regularly lived together. The others worked at separate quarters, often many miles apart, which doubtless helped to depress the Mount Airy fertility rate. Carpenter Bill in the illustration above was a polygamist who lived at Mount Airy while his two wives, Esther and Winney, lived at Landsdown with parallel sets of young children. Another polygamist in 1835 was a man named Oliver who was owned by a neighboring planter. Oliver had two wives and eight children at Doctors Hall quarter. Three other outside males were married to Mount Airy women; one of them was a free black named David, by whom Forkland Criss bore a family of ten slave children. As at Mesopotamia, most young Mount Airy children seem to have lived with their mothers but not with their fathers. And since the Tayloes kept more male than female slaves, a great many Mount Airy men had no marriage partners unless they mated with women from neighboring estates. According to the 1835 list, almost all the eligible Mount Airy women had husbands, while only a third of the men in their twenties and thirties had local wives—a fact that must have contributed powerfully to masculine feelings of inadequacy and frustration.[22]

We turn now to the employment pattern on the two estates. Table III compares the distribution of jobs at Mount Airy and Mesopotamia in 1809. According to these figures, Barham employed his slave force much more fully than did Tayloe. At Mesopotamia four-fifths of the Negroes were allotted tasks, and many more women and children worked than at Mount Airy.

Tayloe designated as working hands only those slaves mature and strong enough to do a full "share" or a half "share" of labor apiece—in practice, all able-bodied Negroes over the age of ten[23]—but the younger children also must have had light tasks to keep them occupied, if not productive. At Mesopotamia boys and girls were put to work at age six, generally in the hogmeat or grass gang, to gather grass and straw from the fields to feed the livestock. At age ten they usually graduated to harder assignments, such as hoeing the young cane and carrying dung in the third field gang. At fifteen or sixteen they might move up to the second field gang and spend the next few years weeding the cane and cleaning the pastures. At about twenty they would be ready for the Great Gang and its backbreaking toil of digging the cane holes and cutting the ripe cane. Slaves who started out as field laborers were rarely switched to craft or domestic jobs. Only workers in their prime did the heavy field labor. At Mesopotamia men who were past forty and sickly became jobbers or watchmen; old or ailing women became field cooks, nurses, or washerwomen. Very likely some of the older Mount Airy slaves listed as nonworkers performed similar marginal tasks.

On both plantations a majority of the laborers in 1809 were field hands, but there were a good many skilled and favored job holders. At Mesopotamia a small managerial elite—the drivers of the field gangs, the chief craftsmen, and Quasheba the African female doctor—received special rations of rum each week. The Mesopotamia craft workers were all male; almost all of them

[22] For a considerably more positive picture of the slave family in 18th-century Maryland see Allan Kulikoff, "The Beginnings of the Afro-American Family in Maryland," in Aubrey C. Land et al., eds., Law, Society, and Politics in Early Maryland: Essays in Honor of Morris Leon Radoff (Baltimore, 1976).
[23] The overseer on each Rappahannock farm got one or more "shares" of the crop, encouraging him to extract maximum output from the workers, who in 1809 produced an average about 50 bu. of wheat and 100 bu. of corn apiece.

TABLE III
LABOR PATTERNS AT MOUNT AIRY AND MESOPOTAMIA IN 1809

| | Mount Airy | | | Mesopotamia | | |
	Males	Females	%	Males	Females	%
A. *Workers*						
Drivers	0	0	0.00	4	1	1.55
Craftworkers	33	14	12.24	25	0	7.76
Domestics	18	17	9.11	8	15	7.14
Field Cooks	0	0	0.00	0	6	1.86
Fieldworkers	86	58	37.50	45	92	42.55
Jobbers	7	0	1.82	7	0	2.17
Transport	5	0	1.30	6	0	1.86
Stockkeepers	0	0	0.00	14	2	4.97
Watchmen	0	0	0.00	19	0	5.90
Nurses	0	0	0.00	0	11	3.42
Total	149	89	61.98	128	127	79.19
B. *Nonworkers*						
Too young	61	63	32.29	20	16	11.18
Too old	2	5	1.82	4	6	3.11
Too sick	7	8	3.91	11	10	6.52
Total	70	76	38.02	35	32	20.81
C. Totals	219	165	100.00	163	159	100.00

had learned their jobs as boy apprentices and pursued the same routine for years. The fact that nearly half of them were over the age of forty in 1809 indicates—as one might guess—that craft workers survived longer than field laborers. No fewer than ten houseboys, maid servants, and cooks waited on the overseer and the bookkeepers, and four slaves assisted the Moravian missionaries at their chapel. At Mount Airy the proportion of skilled and semi-skilled workers was considerably higher—34 percent of those employed, as compared with 21 percent at Mesopotamia.[24] Because the Tayloes lived at Mount Airy, they had twenty-six domestics, and the overseers at the outlying farms had one or two house servants each. As at Mesopotamia, the Mount Airy artisans and domestics entered their jobs as children and, once established, were far less likely to be transferred or sold than were the field laborers.

[24] This figure at Mount Airy is unusually high. Fogel and Engerman, in their analysis of southern U.S. slave occupations around 1850, claim that 26.3% were in skilled or semi-skilled jobs (*Time on the Cross*, I, 38-40), but Gutman argues that the true figure was 15% or lower ("The World Two Cliometricians Made," *Jour. of Negro Hist.*, LX [1975], 111-128).

The labor pattern at Mount Airy was designed to achieve almost total self-sufficiency. The field workers raised corn and pork—the staple slave foods in Virginia—and tended their vegetable gardens in off hours. Using cotton grown and ginned on the estate, and wool sheared from local sheep, the seventeen spinners and weavers made coarse cloth for slave apparel and fine cloth for household linen. The four shoemakers tanned and dressed leather from Mount Airy cattle to make coarse shoes for the slaves and custom shoes for the Tayloes, as well as harness for the horses, mules, and oxen.[25] The nine smiths and joiners built and repaired wagons, ploughs, and hoes, and shod horses, while the twenty-two carpenters, masons, and jobbers moved about the estate erecting and repairing buildings. Tayloe's wagoner carted goods from one unit to another, and his schooner, *The Federalist*, manned by four slave sailors, carried his cash crop of Rappahannock wheat, flour, corn, and oats to Baltimore or Alexandria.

By contrast, the Mesopotamia labor pattern was by no means designed for self-sufficiency. In order to keep his slaves alive and working, Barham shipped food, tools, and clothing from Britain. On the mountain land bordering the estate the slaves cultivated crops of cocco roots and plantains—an equivalent to Mount Airy's cornmeal—but quite often these provision crops were ruined by tropical storms or drought. In 1815 and again in 1816 the Mesopotamia overseer bought a ton of cocco roots as emergency rations to prevent starvation. For protein the slaves depended largely on meager allotments of salt herring shipped from England—150 barrels in 1817, or half a barrel per slave per year.[26] Livestock were plentiful on this estate—448 cattle in 1809, for example—but they were used to produce manure for fertilizer or as draft animals, and only three steers were slaughtered annually for the slaves as a special Christmas treat. No cloth was made at Mesopotamia; instead, Barham bought about two thousand yards of coarse oznaburgh linen annually, or seven yards per slave, together with thread, scissors, and needles, so that his Negroes could make their own clothes. There were no shoemakers—unneeded since slaves wore no shoes—and no local ironworks to supply ironmongery and nails. The three Mesopotamia blacksmiths did not manufacture farm implements as at Mount Airy, so that every tool and piece of machinery had to be imported. Not even the labor force was self-sufficient. Whenever major repairs were needed at the sugar factory, managers hired white masons and coppersmiths rather than trust the work to their slave craftsmen. And during the two years 1816-1817 they paid £930—the cost of a dozen new slaves—in order to hire extra Negro laborers to hole

---

[25] The Mount Airy artisans also did custom work for the Tayloes' white neighbors. See Tayloe Account Book, 1789-1828, Tayloe Papers, MSS 1 T2118d357.

[26] The Mesopotamia expense accounts for 1816-1817 are in the Barham Papers, Box b. 33.

the cane fields, clean the pastures, and plant provisions, since the regular work gangs could not handle all the necessary field tasks.

Another big difference between the employment patterns of the two estates is that the female slaves did much more of the basic labor at Mesopotamia. Table III shows that two-thirds of the agricultural laborers on that estate were women and girls. Even on the Mesopotamia Great Gang, where the hardest work was done, there were thirty-one women and twenty-two men in 1809. Females did much of the heavy labor at Mount Airy also, but more of them worked in craft or domestic jobs, and nearly half were excused from employment. Motherhood was no excuse, however. Thirty-eight Mount Airy women had one or more living children under the age of six in 1809, and all but two of them had full-time jobs. Sally, a twenty-nine-year-old field hand at Doctors Hall, had five young children in 1809 and gave birth to eight more by 1826, while continuing to do her "share" of farm labor. Motherhood was more honored at Mesopotamia, because the birth rate was so alarmingly low. Here the overseer made a practice of moving pregnant members of the Great Gang to the second field gang, where the work was lighter. Matura, the mother of five children, was taken off the Great Gang permanently in 1809 so that she could look after her youngsters. At Mesopotamia all mothers of newborn infants were paid a bonus of £1 in cash "for raising their children," and nursing mothers received a quart of oatmeal and a pint of sugar each week.[27]

Not surprisingly, the Mesopotamia management favored those mulatto and quadroon slaves who had been sired by the white staff. Of the seventeen mulattoes and one quadroon living on the estate in 1809, six were house servants, two were carpenters, one attended the Moravian missionaries, and the rest were too young for employment. Mulattoes at Mesopotamia generally began work when they were nine years old, three years later than the Negroes, and they never labored in the fields. At the opposite end of the spectrum, the management discriminated particularly against native Africans. Of the sixty-two persons at Mesopotamia in 1809 who had come via the slave trade, only Quasheba the doctor was recognized as an important figure. Over 80 percent were relegated to gang labor in the fields.[28]

But how meaningful were these occupational titles? Did the field hands really spend all their time in the fields or the blacksmiths at the forge? Fortunately, the Tayloe plantation records include three work logs dated just before and after 1809, showing the actual tasks performed each day of the

[27] Mesopotamia food allotments, June 1802, *ibid.*, Box b. 36; expense accounts, 1816-1817, *ibid.*, Box b. 33.

[28] Of these Africans, 43% were field workers in 1809, and another 39% were jobbers, watchmen, nurses, or invalids who had formerly worked in the field gangs. Craton and Walvin find much the same pattern for mulattoes and Africans at Worthy Park (*A Jamaican Plantation*, 138-140).

year by the Mount Airy craft workers, and each week of the year by the
Rappahannock farm gangs.[29] From these logs it is evident that the Tayloe
slaves did indeed have distinct occupations. The 144 field workers labored
almost exclusively on agricultural tasks, spending more time on the corn crop
than on any other job—some twenty weeks during the course of the year.
They spent ten weeks on the wheat crop and three weeks on the oats crop.
The artisans joined in the grain harvest for two weeks in June and July but
otherwise worked exclusively at their crafts. Work assignments were variegated, with new tasks assigned every two or three days. Throughout the year
the slaves were kept busy six days a week. Apart from Sundays, they had nine
days of vacation: Easter Monday, Whit Monday, two free Saturdays in May
and July, and a five-day Christmas break from December 25 to 29.

Though the Mount Airy artisans and field hands had separate and
specialized functions, their work rhythms were closely synchronized. During
the coldest six weeks from mid-December to the end of January, when the
previous season's crops had all been harvested and the winter wheat was in
the ground, the field workers and jobbers shucked and beat corn, cut and
hauled timber to the saw mill for fence rails and posts, and cut ice from the
Rappahannock creek. The carpenters meanwhile operated the saw mill,
while the smiths and joiners repaired ploughs, wagons, and harnesses for
spring ploughing. In February the field hands worked with the carpenters
and joiners in putting up fencing, with the jobbers in clearing and manuring
the fields for ploughing, and with the sailors in loading the previous year's
corn on *The Federalist* for shipment to Alexandria. In March the field gangs
planted oats, in April corn, and in May cotton and peas, while the smiths and
joiners repaired their tools. In mid-April, just before the Tayloe family
arrived for the summer from Washington, eighty-five laborers from five of
the Rappahannock farms came to Mount Airy to dress up the mansion lawn.
In late May the field workers began to weed the corn, while the smiths,
joiners, and carpenters were making and mending rakes, cradles, and scythes
for the coming harvest. In mid-June the wagoner went to Kinsale, a nearby
town, to fetch five barrels of whiskey for the harvest. The wheat crop at Old
House, Doctors Hall, and Forkland was harvested in one frenzied week
during mid- or late June; forty-five extra hands were pressed into service—
the smiths, masons, joiners, carpenters, and jobbers cut and cradled the grain,
while the spinners, shoemakers, and weavers raked and bound it into sheaves.
John Tayloe III personally supervised operations; in June 18, 1801, he com-

<hr>

[29] John Tayloe III's Minute Book for Jan. 1-Dec. 7, 1805, Tayloe Papers, MSS 1
T2118a8, records craft work daily and field work weekly. His Minute Book for 1811-
1812 does the same for Jan. 9-Sept. 4, 1811, and Feb. 10-Dec. 31, 1812, *ibid.*, MSS 1
T2118a10. His Spinning Minute Book itemizes the amount of cotton and wool spun
at Mount Airy every week for Jan. 1806-Dec. 1807, *ibid.*, MSS 1 T2118a9.

plained to a correspondent of being "just from my harvest field and fatigued to death."[30]

In July the seasonal pressure continued, as all hands joined for a week to cut and rake the oats crop at Old House. During the next weeks the field gangs worked mainly in the corn fields, hilling and hoeing the plants. In August they cut the hay and threshed the wheat. The jobbers helped with the hay, the carpenters made grain barrels, and the smiths and joiners worked as usual on ploughs and wagons. In September the wagoner and sailors helped the field hands to load Tayloe's schooner with wheat for the Baltimore market. Now it was time to gather the corn leaves as fodder, and to start the long process of seeding the winter wheat. With the fall racing season approaching, the smiths set to work to shoe Tayloe's racehorses. Shortly after the races, the Tayloes departed for Washington, and the craft workers could now make necessary repairs on the mansion house—as in 1805, when the carpenters, joiners, masons, and jobbers worked for a month reshingling the mansion roof under the supervision of a hired white builder. In October the spinners joined the field hands at picking cotton, and from mid-November to mid-December, with the wheat fields finally seeded, the field hands harvested the corn and hauled the stalks to the saw mill. Just before and after Christmas, the slackest work period of the year, Tayloe's masons, carpenters, and jobbers were sent to repair the Richmond County courthouse.

For the Mesopotamia labor force no equivalent work logs have survived. But a field labor book, dated 1796-1797, for Newton plantation in Barbados—a sugar estate of about the same strength as Mesopotamia—records the daily tasks of field and craft workers throughout the year.[31] The work pattern recorded at Newton did not necessarily hold true for Mesopotamia, since Barbadian and Jamaican planting practices differed significantly. Nonetheless, these Barbados work logs are certainly of some help. For one thing, they suggest that craft workers on a Caribbean sugar estate were less clearly differentiated from field workers than they were on a big Virginian estate like Mount Airy. The coopers and masons at Newton estate spent a full two months each year working with the field hands on the sugar harvest, and once the cane was processed, the specialists in the sugar factory labored in the fields for the next six months. Field laborers were ranked by ability in both systems, categorized in Virginia as full "shares" or half "shares," and were sorted in the Caribbean into three gangs, with the first gang (Great Gang) always assigned the hardest jobs. As at Mount Airy, work assignments were

[30] John Tayloe III to John Rose, John Tayloe Letter Book, 1801, *ibid.*, MSS 1 T2118d170.

[31] Newton Plantation Field Labor Book, May 5, 1796-Apr. 26, 1797, Newton Papers, MS 523/110, University of London Library. A second field labor book for the adjoining Barbados plantation of Seawalls, running from Jan. 1 to Sept. 4, 1798, is *ibid.*, MS 523/122.

changed every few days, and it would be a mistake to suppose that slaves on a sugar estate spent all their time planting and cutting cane. The Newton logs show that the first and second gangs spent the equivalent of six months per year in sugar production, three months raising guinea corn for cattle and slave food, two months repairing the cattle pens, and another month at such miscellaneous tasks as cultivating yams, potatoes, and peas.[32] On one day each year all plantation work was stopped, and every man, woman, and capable child was given cloth, a needle, and thread, and set to work stitching together his or her set of clothes for the following year.

At Mount Airy the Tayloes stretched seasonal employment into year-round employment by letting their slaves work at a leisurely pace. Three masons took fifteen working days to build a cottage chimney; thirty working hands at Old House took eight weeks to sow 258 bushels of wheat. Only at harvest time did people work under extreme pressure for several weeks. But in the Caribbean the sugar harvest lasted for four months or more, from January or February to May or June. And while at Mount Airy the heaviest labor was done by horses, mules, and oxen, at Newton—or Mesopotamia— the slaves did the work of draft animals. The Newton first-gang slaves spent nearly one week in every month at the brutal task of cane holing by hand. Crop time was the period of prime pressure, since the various stages in the sugar-making process were so closely synchronized. At Newton the fifty strong-est members of the first gang cut the cane and ten members of the second gang loaded it into carts and took it to the mill where another ten workers from the first and second gangs ground it, while fourteen workers processed the cane juice at the boiling house, and three still-house workers converted molasses from the boiling house into rum. This was not a continuous four-month process; every few days the cutting gang was shifted to lighter tasks in order to recruit strength. But the work clearly took its toll. At Newton, in relatively slack periods, only 3 or 4 percent of the field workers reported sick, but after a week of holing or cutting cane the number rose to 9 or 10 percent. Even the holidays were fewer at Newton than at Mount Airy—only four days off per year: Good Friday, a free day in mid-October, and two days at Christmas.

We are now in a better position to examine the demographic contrast between Mesopotamia and Mount Airy, which is the most mysterious and also the most crucial aspect of our inquiry. Why did the Mesopotamia slave population suffer such pronounced natural decrease while the Mount Airy slave population enjoyed pronounced natural increase? Why in particular did the Mesopotamia women produce so few children, only half as many as the

---

[32] There were 155 workers on average in the three Newton plantation field gangs in 1796-1797, compared with Mesopotamia's 137 field workers in 1809.

TABLE IV
MOTHERHOOD AT MOUNT AIRY AND MESOPOTAMIA

	Mount Airy, 1809-1828		Mesopotamia, 1799-1818	
	Number	%	Number	%
A. Childless Women	50	32.67	100	50.00
Mothers	103	67.32	100	50.00
	153		200	
B. Size of Completed Families:				
1 child		4.55		36.84
2-3 children		9.09		26.32
4-6 children		40.91		26.32
7-9 children		36.36		8.77
10-13 children		9.09		1.75
		100.00		100.00
Average no. live births per mother	6.36		3.07	
Average age of mother at first live birth	19.32		20.47	
C. Infant and Childhood Mortality:				
Percent died during first year		6.94		10.09
Percent died aged 1-10		15.28		16.06
Percent surviving past 10th birthday		77.78		73.85

Mount Airy women? Table IV compares the females aged seventeen and over who lived on these two estates during our twenty-year span. There are 200 potential mothers at Mesopotamia and 153 at Mount Airy. The smaller number at Mount Airy reflects the fact that many females on that estate were sold or transferred before they reached child-bearing age. Of the 200 Mesopotamia women, exactly half appear to have borne no live children. The other 100 are identified in the estate records as mothers—including seventeen women who bore some or all of their children on other Jamaican plantations before coming to Mesopotamia. At Mount Airy two-thirds of the women can be identified as mothers. This percentage is undoubtedly too low, for the Mount Airy records fail to pick up either the mothers of children who were grown by 1809 or the young future mothers who had children after they were transferred off the estate in their late 'teens or twenties. Of the 153 Mount Airy women in Table IV, only seven can definitely be categorized as sterile. In my opinion, close to 90 percent of the Mount Airy women bore children, compared with about 55 percent at Mesopotamia.

The other striking difference is that the Mesopotamia women who did bear children had much smaller families. As Table IV shows, only 37 percent of the Mesopotamia mothers had four or more children, whereas 86 percent of the Mount Airy mothers had families this large. The average Mesopotamia mother had less than half as many children as her Virginia counterpart. She entered into her first successful pregnancy a year later. If she bore more than one child, the births were spaced five months farther apart than at Mount Airy, and she had her last baby three years earlier. These averages conceal much significant variation. If we focus for a moment on those women who lived through the entire thirty-year period of possible reproduction (ages fifteen to forty-four), we find enormous range in age at first birth, child spacing, and age at last birth. The youngest mothers on both estates were only fourteen years old, while two Mesopotamia women had their first babies at age thirty-two. About 20 percent of the Mount Airy mothers gave birth before they were seventeen, twice the percentage at Mesopotamia, which suggests a possible difference in the age of menarche. At the other end of the cycle, nearly half of the Mount Airy mothers bore children into their forties—again twice the percentage at Mesopotamia. The presence of the white managerial staff was clearly a factor in the Mesopotamia fertility schedule, since more than half of the babies produced by mothers under the age of seventeen on this estate were mulattoes. Minny, a seamstress at the overseer's house, was the most prolific Mesopotamia mother; she bore eight sons and two daughters in twenty-five years, and three of these children were mulatto. Minny was forty-five when her last boy (a Negro) was born in December 1815, and to honor the occasion the baby was named Joseph Foster Barham. But Minny was a rarity in a community of small families.

According to Table IV, relatively few infants died on either estate, reflecting the incompleteness of infant birth and death records, especially at Mount Airy. The figures for children over age one are more reliable, especially for Mesopotamia with its immobile population. Unless the Mesopotamia infant records are completely misleading, newborn babies and young children died at about the same rate on the two estates, thus ruling out infant mortality as a factor in explaining the demographic difference between the two plantations. The key issue is clearly fertility—the low fertility of the Mesopotamia slave women.

There is no simple explanation for the low fertility at Mesopotamia. At least half a dozen separate factors contributed to the problem. In the first place, women lived less long than at Mount Airy, and experienced fewer years at risk of pregnancy. Half of the childless Mesopotamia women and a third of the mothers died in their twenties or thirties, during the prime child-bearing years. At Mount Airy only about a tenth of the women died at this age. Yet longevity is certainly not the only factor in our equation, nor probably the most important one, for the chief point to be made here is that the Mount Airy slaves had quite long life expectancy, and even the Mesopotamia slaves had longer life expectancy than many populations with stronger birth rates. At age seventeen a Mount Airy female could expect to live thirty-nine more years, a Mesopotamia female thirty-one years. Over 80 percent of the Mount Airy women lived long enough to reach menopause. Even at Mesopotamia the childless women averaged twenty-one years at risk of pregnancy without producing a live birth, and 40 percent of them lived on the estate throughout the years of possible reproduction. Likewise, most Mesopotamia mothers of one or two children lived on for many years after their babies were born. Nearly 60 percent reached the age of menopause, and the average mother bore her children within a space of seven years while experiencing twenty-three years at risk of pregnancy. While the longevity of the Mount Airy women thus helps to explain their large families, life expectancy at Mesopotamia was not sufficiently restricted to account by itself for the low birth rate in this community.

A second factor is the sex and age ratio, which in Caribbean slave populations is frequently seen as the chief reason for low fertility. As Table II has shown, however, neither the sex nor the age structure at Mesopotamia was unfavorable. The sexes were always much better balanced on this estate than at Mount Airy, where the young men consistently outnumbered the young women by nearly two to one. There was always a larger number of women of child-bearing age at Mesopotamia than at Mount Airy. Indeed, the age structure of the Mesopotamia population was seemingly very favorable to high fertility. Between 1799 and 1818 the proportion of females aged fifteen to forty-four averaged 24.5 percent of the total Barham slave force. At Mount Airy, because so many girls were sold or transferred, the proportion of potentially fertile females was significantly smaller: between 1809 and 1828 it averaged 19.4 percent. Thus if imbalance between the sexes and a low proportion of young women depress the birth rate, one should look for problems at the Tayloe estate rather than at Mesopotamia.

A third factor is the presence at Mesopotamia of African-born women with African child-rearing habits. It has been argued that Caribbean slave populations had low birth rates because so many of the women were Africans. Fertility rates in West Africa are thought to have been generally low; and when African women were shipped to America they reproduced less actively than creole slave women, being habituated to a long nursing period with a resultant wide spacing between births.[33] At Mesopotamia, however,

[33] This line of argument is advanced by Michael Craton, "Jamaican Slave Mortality: Fresh Light from Worthy Park, Longville and the Tharp Estates," Journal of Caribbean History, III (1971), 1-27, and by Russell R. Menard, "The Maryland Slave Population, 1658-1730: A Demographic Profile of Blacks in Four Counties," WMQ, 3d Ser., XXXII (1975), 29-54.

the differences between African-born and creole women were not pronounced. Of forty-two African women during the 1799-1818 span, twenty-three (55 percent) were childless, and the nineteen African mothers averaged 2.42 children each. They bore their children at no wider intervals than the creole women, so the probability is that all the mothers followed the same nursing practices. The Mesopotamia women collectively did space their children more widely than at Mount Airy, with an average interval between live births of three years and three months, compared with two years and ten months at Mount Airy.[34] But there is little evidence that this was because they nursed their infants longer. If we compare the most fecund mothers on both estates—those who bore seven or more children—we find no difference whatsoever in child spacing. The Mesopotamia and Mount Airy mothers in this category both averaged two years and six months between births. In fact, these women generally gave birth every two years, with an occasional shorter gap when the nursing period was broken off by the death of the last-born infant, and an occasional longer gap perhaps caused by a miscarriage or stillbirth. Mothers of small families, especially at Mesopotamia, had extremely irregular birth intervals, ranging up to ten years, and such eccentric spacing is better explained by sexual abstinence, intermittent fecundity, miscarriages, and abortions than by nursing habits.

A fourth factor is the debilitating work regimen imposed upon the Caribbean slaves, which presumably robbed them of vitality and dulled their sexual instincts. As we have seen, the labor pattern was more punishing at Mesopotamia, and women of child-bearing years performed much more heavy work than at Mount Airy. Unfortunately, there is no way of demonstrating a correlation between this debilitating labor and slave infertility. Analysis of job distribution at Mesopotamia during the 1799-1818 span shows that mothers and childless women held the same range of jobs in almost exactly the same proportions. The heaviest labor was done by the Great Gang, and on an average 34 percent of the Mesopotamia women over seventeen were assigned to this gang. Of the childless women in Table IV, 36 percent worked in the Great Gang; of the mothers with one to three children, 32 percent worked in the Great Gang; of the mothers with four or more children, 35 percent worked in the Great Gang. Similarly, at the other end of the spectrum, the lightest work was done by the domestic servants who attended the white staff; 6 percent of the Mesopotamia women were assigned to these jobs—5 percent of the childless women, 7 percent of the mothers with one to three children, and 6 percent of the mothers with four or more

[34] Herbert S. Klein and Stanley L. Engerman, who stress the difference between U.S. and British West Indian nursing practices in an unpublished paper, "The Demographic Study of the American Slave Population," find a U.S. child-spacing interval of only 2.5 years and a British West Indian rate of 3.5-4.0 years.

children. These figures seem to show that work assignments had no effect whatsoever on the birth rate. Yet it remains difficult to believe that years of rugged labor in the cane fields did not reduce slave procreation, increase the chance of miscarriage, and lower slave fertility.[35]

A fifth factor, possibly the most important one, is inadequate nutrition, which can depress fertility by impairing female reproductive development. Biologists have established that the timing of the adolescent growth spurt and menarche, the maintenance of regular menstrual function, the recovery of reproductive ability after childbirth, and the timing of menopause are all directly affected by the female's state of nourishment. A severely under-nourished woman, with inadequate fat storage in her body, will achieve menarche belatedly, will experience irregular menstrual cycles or none at all, and will enter menopause early. If she manages to conceive and bear a child, pregnancy and lactation will draw thousands of calories from her meager energy stores, so that she will be slow to recover reproductive ability for another pregnancy.[36] Certainly the Mesopotamia women betray symptoms of impaired reproductive development: delayed first births, long and irregular birth intervals, and early final births.

The estate death records contain some evidence of dietary deficiency, as well as bad sanitation, which further undermined the health of the Barham slaves. By the manager's own reckoning, 11 percent of the slaves died "bloated" or from "dropsy." These vague terms covered a wide range of bodily swellings, undoubtedly caused in many cases by protein and vitamin deficiencies. Another 9 percent died of "flux" or various forms of dysentery, promoted by unsanitary living conditions. This was a larger number than the 8 percent who died from malaria and other tropical fevers. Another 11 percent of the deaths were attributed to such African diseases as hookworm, guinea worm, yaws, leprosy, and elephantiasis, which were much more common in Jamaica than in Virginia. Among the remaining chief causes of death were—in rank order—tuberculosis, pleurisy, smallpox, epilepsy, and venereal disease. Nearly 3 percent of the slaves were said to have died in plantation accidents, but only two men in eighty years committed suicide, and

[35] It is perhaps significant that 40% of the Mesopotamian live births were concentrated in the four months October-January and only 25% in the four months April-July. A number of the pregnancies that should have come to term in April-July may have resulted in fetal deaths because of the mothers' field labor during the sugar harvest season.

[36] Rose E. Frisch, "Demographic Implications of the Biological Determinants of Female Fecundity," *Social Biology*, XXII (1975), 17-22.

[37] A comparable set of death records for Worthy Park estate in Jamaica has been analyzed by Michael Craton, with findings very similar to mine. I am indebted to Mr. Craton for the use of his unpublished essay, "Death, Disease and Medicine on Jamaican Slave Plantations: The Example of Worthy Park, 1792-1838."

only five women died during childbirth. Obviously, these mortality statistics cannot be taken too seriously, especially since 17 percent died of "old age" and another 9 percent died as "invalids." In any case, the correlation between ill health and infertility is inexact. A woman named Esther suffered continuously from "weakness" and yaws during her life at Mesopotamia, but she bore six children. Luna was incapable of employment because of her bad sores, but she gave birth to seven children. Ophelia contracted venereal disease when she was thirty and was retired from the field gang, but she had two more children and lived another twenty years. And Sabina began to experience epileptic seizures at twenty-eight but bore three more children and died at sixty-three.

Still another factor that could have contributed to low fertility at Mesopotamia is the aggressive role of the white overseers and bookkeepers, who requisitioned the sexual services of a good many young slaves. These women, if they wished to prolong their status as concubines, may have aborted their mulatto offspring in order to keep physically attractive. The large number of mulatto births at Mesopotamia, however, makes this proposition unlikely. Other Mesopotamia women may have practiced sexual abstinence or committed abortion because they could not stand the prospect of bringing babies into a world of enslavement. Several of the Mesopotamia children who died during infancy were "overlaid" by their mothers. Were such events accidental or intentional?

Finally, we should not forget the Mesopotamia men. It is surely a mistake to focus exclusively on the female slaves, for the males must have had much to do with the low birth rate. If longevity was a factor, the men had shorter life expectancy than the women, and many Mesopotamia females must have stopped bearing children when their mates died. If the work regimen was a factor, it was the men who were forced into the most exhausting jobs. If nutrition was a factor, the men suffered more than the women from chronic debility. Frequently weak or sick, flogged and maimed far more often than the females when they resisted or malingered or ran away, humiliated by an arrogant cadre of white masters who took their women, the Mesopotamia men had lost all powers of leadership and independence—and this loss in psychic power may well have drained their sexual potency.

Thus, despite the wealth of statistical information about slave life at Mesopotamia and Mount Airy, many questions cannot be answered and many issues cannot be settled. Ultimately the observer who wonders why Jamaican slaves behaved differently from Virginian slaves is reduced to armchair psychology. But at least we can document telling differences—some of them rather surprising—between the two communities. At Mesopotamia the slave population was cooped up; at Mount Airy it was in constant movement. Mesopotamia families were more inbred than Mount Airy families, and less disrupted by sales and transfers. Mesopotamia women were tougher than their men and dominated the work force, whereas Mount Airy women were reckoned to be more marginal than their men and were frequently sold. Vocational opportunities were narrower at Mesopotamia than at Mount Airy, the work load was harder, the food and clothing were less adequate, the disease environment was more threatening. In consequence, Mesopotamia slaves died earlier than at Mount Airy and produced fewer children.

The owner of Mesopotamia, Joseph Foster Barham, was a conscientious master by the Jamaican standards of the day. Few other sugar magnates paid missionaries £70 per year to instruct their slaves in the Christian religion, or published arguments for the abolition of West Indian slavery,[38] or required their agents to keep meticulous track of the blacks who inhabited their estates. During the eighty years of record keeping the Mesopotamia slaves never rebelled; very few of them ran away permanently; and during a smallpox epidemic the white managers showed their humanity by inoculating even the aged invalids in order to keep them alive. Nonetheless, the Mesopotamia records give us a deeply depressing picture of slave life on this estate, a picture reaffirming the universal opinion of modern scholars that Caribbean slavery was one of the most brutally dehumanizing systems ever devised.

John Tayloe III likewise emerges from his letter books and account books as a thoroughly benevolent and well-intentioned master. Working and living conditions on his Rappahannock estate must have been exceptionally relaxed, for Tayloe was no profit-maximizing entrepreneur. His well-worn fields produced modest yields, his work force was far larger than necessary, and the rhythm of the place evoked leisured gentility rather than business efficiency. And yet this paternalistic planter manipulated and exploited his slaves to a high degree. Thus my portrait of slave life at Mount Airy is ambiguous, and just how it fits into the general debate about the character of slavery in the United States is rather hard to say. As Stanley Elkins has recently pointed out, a long scholarly tradition that stressed white brutality and white damage has been superseded by a new emphasis on black achieve-

---

[38] While Barham was Wilberforce's ally in the British abolition movement, his tract, *Considerations on the Abolition of Negro Slavery*, was studded with pejorative remarks about the Negro as a person and a worker. In 1806 he offered Wilberforce a solution to the West Indian labor problem: substitute Chinese coolies for Negro slaves. Robert Isaac Wilberforce, *The Life of William Wilberforce*, III (London, 1839), 272.

ment and black resistance.[39] The Mount Airy evidence can be used to buttress either side of this debate, but on the whole I believe that it better supports the older tradition. While Tayloe was not a brutal master, his slave regimen was, it seems to me, designed to thwart black achievement and to defuse black resistance. His system offered extremely little scope for the dynamic economic, cultural, and social slave achievements currently celebrated by Robert Fogel, Stanley Engerman, Eugene Genovese, and Herbert Gutman.[40] But however noxious Tayloe's system, if one had to be a slave, Mount Airy was a better place to live than Mesopotamia.

[39] Stanley M. Elkins, "The Slavery Debate," Commentary, LX (Dec. 1975), 40-54.

[40] I am thinking here of Fogel and Engerman's Time on the Cross, Eugene D. Genovese's Roll, Jordan, Roll: The World the Slaves Made (New York, 1974), and Herbert G. Gutman's The Black Family in Slavery and Freedom; 1750-1925 (New York, 1976).

"Not Only Extreme Poverty, but the Worst Kind of Orphanage": Lemuel Haynes and the Boundaries of Racial Tolerance on the Yankee Frontier, 1770–1820

RICHARD D. BROWN

I

Day after day in December 1819 Stephen Boorn lay huddled, chained to the floor of an unlighted, solitary cell in the jail at Manchester, Vermont, awaiting his execution. According to the confession he had voluntarily written and signed, Boorn had, without intending to, killed his deranged brother-in-law, Russel Colvin, by striking him on the back of the head with a two-foot beechwood limb. The fatal blow, Boorn swore, had resulted from a quarrel with the good-for-nothing "little tory" Colvin in the presence of Stephen's brother Jesse Boorn and the deceased's ten-year-old son, Lewis, on a day seven years and seven months past, when the four had been working as day laborers clearing stones from a farmer's field. Now, barely a month before the fatal sentence would be visited on him, Stephen Boorn cried out against the injustice he was suffering. "I am innocent as Jesus Christ!" he exclaimed to the one man who was his frequent visitor. When this visitor "reproved" the "extravagant expression," Boorn retreated, but only slightly: "I don't mean that I am guiltless as he was, I know I am a great sinner; but I am as innocent of killing Colvin as he was." Although Boorn had previously sworn to a confession of guilt, he now asserted his innocence. The man who prayed

*The author wishes to thank Professor Donald Spivey of the University of Connecticut Department of History for his constructive advice.

502

with him for divine deliverance and salvation was the town's only clergyman and pastor at the meeting-house where hundreds had flocked to watch as Boorn was tried and condemned. He was the Reverend Lemuel Haynes, a black man.[1]

By the time of Stephen Boorn's imprisonment, the sixty-six-year-old Haynes was in his fourth pastorate, respected as an experienced, widely-published, evangelical Calvinist preacher. It was in this most traditional of clerical roles—that of pleading for the conversion of the condemned—that Haynes regularly visited with the aggrieved Boorn. For decades Haynes had been preaching the way of Christ, quoting sacred texts, and reminding his listeners that they were all sinners in need of Christ's saving grace. Consequently, it was natural for Haynes to stand in prayer beside the condemned murderer. Guilty or not, every soul was worth saving.

On Wednesday, 22 December, however, Haynes was not prepared for a miracle, though that is precisely what his jail-cell prayers seemed to have yielded, for on that day the live, flesh-and-blood Russel Colvin strolled into town, crazier than ever but unmistakably alive. He recognized and greeted everyone he had known, except his wife Sally Boorn, who had become pregnant to another man during his absence, and bragged of being a prosperous landowner in New Jersey. In truth, Colvin was a farmhand and had been brought back to Manchester by decent men bent on saving the innocent Boorn from the gallows. That autumn the trial of Stephen and his brother Jesse Boorn, who was also convicted and sentenced to life imprisonment, had become a major national news story, and a native of Manchester who was keeping a

---

[1] The story is related by Lemuel Haynes, in *Mystery developed; or Russel Colvin (supposed to be murdered), in full life: and Stephen and Jesse Boorn, (his convicted murderers,) rescued from ignominious death by wonderful discoveries.* (Hartford, 1820), p. 8. See also Sherman Roberts Moulton, *The Boorn Mystery: An Episode from the Judicial Annals of Vermont* (Montpelier: Vermont Historical Society, 1937). Jesse Boorn, also convicted, was sentenced to life imprisonment because he was an accomplice, rather than the supposed murderer, and for other mitigating factors.

store in New York City read about the case and remembered that he had recently seen Colvin among the living.

Stephen Boorn's and Lemuel Haynes's prayers were thus answered: Boorn was freed and converted to Christ. The townspeople of Manchester rejoiced, as boys ran from farm to farm to spread the good news, and the reports of muskets echoed off the nearby mountains. That evening the revelers crowded Captain Black's inn to celebrate the miraculous circumstances that had "restored" both Boorn and Colvin to life.

Two weeks later the Reverend Haynes commemorated the event with a sermon called "The Prisoner Released," which centered "on the remarkable interposition of divine providence." He presented a text from Isaiah, "That thou mayest say to the prisoners, go forth; to them that are in darkness, shew yourselves," through which he contrasted the liberation provided by salvation with the bondage inherent in sin.[2] Whatever else this remarkable episode in the annals of Vermont criminal justice might be, it was an occasion for preaching God's Word.

For an orthodox Congregational church in rural New England in 1820, this performance was impressive but not remarkable for either style or substance. What was surprising and, moreover, unique was that an all-white congregation in a white town of 1,500 people, in a county and state that were more than 99.5 percent white should be led by a black clergyman.[3] Exploring who this man was and why he was in Manchester, Vermont, in 1820 brings us into contact with a remarkable person and also helps us understand the complexity of whites' attitudes towards blacks in the New England of the early republic.

Lemuel Haynes's temperament, character, and sheer ability had early enabled him to distinguish himself. Con-

[2]Lemuel Haynes, *The Prisoner Released. A Sermon, delivered at Manchester, Vermont, Lords Day, Jan. 9th, 1820. On the remarkable interposition of divine providence, in the deliverance of Stephen and Jesse Boorn, who had been under sentence of death, for the supposed murder of Russel Colvin* (Hartford, [1820]).

[3]Data from 1810, 1820, and 1830 U.S. censuses.

Here Haynes's fortunes turned. Rose, a separatist, was "a man of singular piety," and though he and his wife had several children, Haynes recalled that Mrs. Rose "had peculiar attachment to me: she treated me as though I was her own child, I remember it was a saying among the neighbors that she loved Lemuel more than her own children." In this environment, notwithstanding his origins and indentured status, Haynes became one of the Rose family. Deacon Rose was carving a farm out of the wilderness and it was a hard life; but Lemuel was subject to the same discipline, the same meager schooling, the same labors as others in a home where family prayer and weekly discussion of Sunday sermons were routine. Significantly, it was in this context that Haynes first distinguished himself by his prodigious memory, for "at night, whenever requested by Deacon Rose, he gave him from memory a copious analysis of the sermons and other religious services."[6] With the Rose family Haynes safely excelled at piety, outdistancing his white peers with full encouragement from his master and mistress.

In a Christian community no one could be faulted for devoting himself to learning Holy Scripture; and because Haynes thoroughly exemplified the ideal of humility, his religious acquirements appeared seemly, and his ambitions quietly grew. His rule, he said, was "to know something more every night than I knew in the morning," so when a "professional gentleman" moved to Granville around 1770 and offered the indentured servant "the privilege of using his books," Haynes seized it. He had already learned not to thrust himself forward but to allow others the gratification of discovering his merits. A boy of "extreme poverty" and "the worst sort of orphanage" raised in a Yankee household, he had learned not only patience and humility, but to employ indirection. Deacon Rose gave the boy's wits the highest compliment a farmer could give by making it his own rule that "if a horse was to be purchased, Lemuel was the purchaser."[7]

[6]Cooley, *Lemuel Haynes*, pp. 30, 39–40.
[7]Cooley, *Lemuel Haynes*, p. 31.

The manner in which Lemuel's career was chosen was consistent with his coupling of humility, ambition, and indirection. After attaining his majority in 1774, and with it his freedom, Haynes remained with the Rose family, departing only twice—once with the Granville men who joined General Washington's army during the siege of Boston in 1775, and again in the fall of 1776 when he served in the garrison at Fort Ticonderoga. Haynes's experiences as a Revolutionary soldier evidently touched him deeply and awakened him politically. Upon his return from Boston in April 1775, he composed a patriotic ballad, "The Battle of Lexington," which, in a style reminiscent of the Isaac Watts hymns he had memorized, proclaimed the Whig views that were sweeping New England. That Haynes was already hoping to see his work published is suggested by the title page he created for his manuscript, whereon he identified the author in bold letters as "Lemuel a young Mollato."[8] In the following year or so, perhaps after he returned from Fort Ticonderoga, Haynes went on to compose a bold essay attacking slavery called "Liberty Further Extended." This substantial tract, which survives only in an incomplete forty-six-page second draft, argued that *The practice of Slave-Keeping, which so much abounds in this Land, is illicit.* Drawing not on abstract theory but on his own personal knowledge, Haynes pronounced that "Liberty is Equally as pre[c]ious to a *Black man*, as it is to a *white one*."[9] His forcefully stated arguments, which drew upon antislavery pamphlets by Anthony Benezet and by Samuel Hopkins, called on slaveholders to liberate their bondsmen and to free themselves from the inherent corruption and sin of slavery.[10] For Lemuel

[8] "The Battle of Lexington': A Patriotic Ballad by Lemuel Haynes," ed. Ruth Bogin, *William and Mary Quarterly*, 3d ser. 42 (October 1985): 499–506.

[9] "Liberty Further Extended': A 1776 Antislavery Manuscript by Lemuel Haynes," ed. Ruth Bogin, *William and Mary Quarterly*, 3d ser. 40 (January 1983): 95.

[10] "Liberty Further Extended," pp. 90, 93, 94, 95. Although Haynes is not known to have made any further sustained, public attacks on slavery, he continued to be critical of it and to express sympathy with the plight of Afro-Americans. See his *The Nature and Importance of True Republicanism with a few suggestions, favorable to independence. A discourse delivered at Rutland, the Fourth of July, 1801* ([Rutland,

Haynes, joining in the struggle for American liberty was an inspiring, psychologically enfranchising experience.

Back in Granville, however, not much had changed. Self-employed, Haynes supported himself in the Rose household by his farm labor, and he continued to share in the pious customs of the family as well. So it was that one evening preceding the sabbath, a time given to prayers or to Haynes reading aloud a sermon from the works of Isaac Watts, George Whitefield, Philip Doddridge, or Samuel Davies, he was asked to read as usual. This time, however, an eyewitness recalled:

he slipped into the book his own sermon which he had written, and read it to the family. The deacon was greatly delighted and edified by the sermon. . . . His eyes were dim, and he had no suspicion that anything out of the ordinary course had happened; and at the close of the reading, he inquired very earnestly, "Lemuel, whose work is that which you have been reading? Is it Davies's sermon, or Watts's, or Whitefield's?" It was the deacon's impression that the sermon was Whitefield's. Haynes blushed and hesitated, but at last was obliged to confess the truth—"It's Lemuel's sermon."[11]

As word of this incident spread in Granville, neighbors remembered that even as a youth Haynes had displayed exceptional "amiableness and ingenuity," "retiring humility," and "unspotted purity of character." Because the local pulpit was currently vacant, they called on the young Haynes to read sermons and to lead the parish in weekly worship. As he became more self-assured in the pulpit, the conviction grew that the illegitimate mulatto was one whom God had "raised up . . . for more than common usefulness"; some even pro-

---

1801]), and his *Dissimulation Illustrated: A Sermon Delivered at Brandon, Vermont, February 22, 1813; Before the Washington Benevolent Society* (Rutland, 1814). Haynes's continuing racial consciousness is further revealed by his ownership of a copy of Samuel Stanhope Smith's *An Essay on the Causes of the Variety of Complexion and Figure in the Human Species*, 2d ed., enlarged and improved (New Brunswick, 1810). His copy is inscribed with his name and the date 1823 (from a list of books owned by Haynes, Rutland Historical Society).

[11]Cooley, *Lemuel Haynes*, p. 48.

posed to raise money for a scholarship so that Haynes could train for the ministry at Dartmouth College.[12]

Although Haynes declined this offer of a college education, he did move toward a ministerial career in 1779 by going to live with the Reverend Daniel Farrand in Canaan, about twenty-five miles west of Granville in the northwest corner of Connecticut. Farrand, a 1750 graduate of Princeton who had known Jonathan Edwards and was friendly to the new Divinity, taught Haynes Latin, theology, and homiletics in exchange for the young man's help on his farm.[13] Farrand was an otherwordly mentor, whose own humility, tact, and gentle, indirect humor reinforced the same qualities in his student. In the following year Haynes moved to nearby Wintonbury, where the Reverend William Bradford instructed him in Greek and found him a job teaching in a district school. Near year's end, on 29 November 1780, Farrand and two other clergymen examined the fledgling clergyman and certified him as a minister of the gospel, so that he could take up a position as a temporary pastor of a new parish that had been created in his hometown of Granville.

Haynes's return to Granville after a two-year absence was something of a triumph. As a boy, Timothy Mather Cooley witnessed the event. Cooley, who was later to be directly influenced by Haynes and who served for fifty-nine years in a Granville pulpit, remembered Haynes's appointment as "one of the wonders of the age" because "he had been known from infancy only as a servant-boy" and was now a "spiritual teacher in a respectable and enlightened congregation." In a village community so keenly attuned to distinctions of rank, Cooley noted, "that reverence which it was the custom of the age to accord to ministers of the gospel, was cheerfully rendered to Mr. Haynes. All classes and ages were carried away with the sweet, animated eloquence of the preacher. . . . You might see children by the wayside, or near the vil-

[12]Cooley, *Lemuel Haynes*, pp. 59–60.
[13]James McLachlan, *Princetonians, 1748-1768: A Biographical Dictionary* (Princeton: Princeton University Press, 1976), pp. 29–30.

lage school-house arranging themselves in due order to welcome him as he passed, and vying with each other in tokens of reverence."[14]

If perhaps not quite one of the wonders of the age, it was nonetheless a remarkable, indeed a unique, American scene—a community of whites selecting a young black man as their spiritual leader. Should we infer that New England Yankees did not share the well-known Anglo-American prejudices toward blacks or that somehow the people of Granville, having known Haynes, were free of such bigotry?[15] The evidence will not sustain such conclusions. Yankees did share the common prejudices, and they were manifested wherever Haynes went. How they were expressed and how white people and Haynes himself—who did not become an outspoken antislavery advocate—dealt with them is instructive.

Long after Haynes had passed from the scene, one man remembered that during Haynes's ministry in West Rutland, Vermont, boys from the neighboring parish had taunted their playmates because they had a "nigger preacher." Rejecting this taunt, the boys had defended Haynes as a better preacher, whose soul was "all white! Snow white!"[16] The children's exchanges expose the tension that fueled Haynes's career, the community's conflict between common ethnocentric bigotry and the aspiration for a meritocratic Christian republic.

The test Haynes repeatedly faced was to vindicate Christian meritocracy by proving his legitimacy in the clerical office. Rather than confronting racism explicitly, he had to demonstrate that he was an exemplary Christian—generous, sober, loving, cheerful, and humble—as well as an effective pulpit performer. In Torrington, Connecticut, where he was

[14]Cooley, Lemuel Haynes, p. 66.

[15]Winthrop D. Jordan, White Over Black: American Attitudes Toward the Negro, 1550-1812 (Chapel Hill: University of North Carolina Press, 1968), esp. pts. 3, 4, 5.

[16]Paul Douglass, Black Apostle to Yankeeland: Egalitarian Catchcolt who overlived his Caste (Brandon, Vt.: The Sullivans, 1972), p. 28; Cooley, Lemuel Haynes, p. 81.

ordained in 1785, a step up from Granville, some parishioners refused to attend church because they opposed a Negro appointment. One such individual who, like many others, eventually returned out of curiosity, sat down in the crowded meeting-house determined to express publicly his disrespect by keeping his hat on. Haynes deliberately ignored this affront and spoke with his characteristic "impassioned earnestness." The black minister had mastered a technique that disarmed bigotry: "The preacher had not proceeded far in his sermon . . . before I thought him the *whitest* man I ever saw. My hat was instantly taken off and thrown under the seat, and I found myself listening with the most profound attention."[17] Here, as elsewhere, common prejudice against blacks enlarged Haynes's audience. A black preacher was exotic, a novelty, like women preachers who drew crowds that came to wonder and to scoff as much as to listen. But because what the crowds heard was a convincing evangelical Calvinism, Haynes touched responsive chords in rural New England and so permitted a partial victory over prejudice that was based solely on color. For Haynes, after all, was culturally and ethnically at one with his audience; though literally black, he could be viewed as "the *whitest* man" and a Yankee of exceptional piety and presence. Because he was raised in isolation from other blacks, he became an instrument to liberate whites from their customary prejudices.

Haynes's role in this conflict between prejudice and Christianity is illustrated by his experience at ministerial association meetings. These gatherings of up to a dozen clergymen were held in clergymen's homes. The wife of one commented that whenever "it was necessary to put two in one bed, one and another would say, '*I will sleep with Mr. Haynes!*'"[18] The alacrity with which Haynes's colleagues volunteered to share his bed, while intended to give Haynes a feeling of inclusion, was also, of course, an indication of their racial self-consciousness. By expressing their readiness to extend followship beyond professional association and mealtime

[17]Rev. Milton Huxley, in Cooley, *Lemuel Haynes*, p. 73.
[18]Reported by F. Skinner in Cooley, *Lemuel Haynes*, p. 214.

collegiality, by actually sharing the same bed with the black minister, these white clergymen could feel a surge of moral elevation from the triumph of Christian love over their residual bigotry. That Haynes understood the full ramifications of such situations can scarcely be doubted. The deft manner in which he handled the subject of his own matrimony reveals his appreciation of the delicacy of his relationship with whites.

Lemuel Haynes met and married Elizabeth Babbit, a white native of Dighton, in southeastern Massachusetts, while he was preaching in Granville. Babbit, who was ten years younger than Haynes, had come to teach at the village school. She regularly listened to Haynes preach and in time experienced conversion. Afterwards, "looking to Heaven for guidance, she was led . . . to make him the overture of her heart and hand as his companion for life." Although it was most irregular for a woman to propose to a man, it would have been totally improper for Haynes to seek marriage with a white. Although Haynes was "highly honoured" by Babbit's proposal, he hesitated. Only after consulting "a number of ministers" and only after "he received their unanimous advice and sanction" did he accept Babbit's invitation. When the marriage was performed in 1783 by the Reverend Samuel Woodbridge at Hartland, Connecticut, just south of Granville, the ceremony was not just the joining of two individuals but also a victory of tolerance over prejudice, of enlightened virtue over customary vice.[19] Now it seemed foreordained that Haynes's role included preparing Yankees to become better Christians by helping them to overcome their racial bigotry. First in the Rose family, then in Granville, and now with Elizabeth Babbit and the wedding assembly, Haynes had become an exemplar of what a black person born to "the worst kind of orphanage" could achieve.

III

It was during his third pastorate, at West Rutland, Vermont, where he was made the settled minister in 1788, that

[19]Cooley, *Lemuel Haynes*, pp. 69, 70.

Haynes first began to enjoy genuine eminence among evangelical Calvinists. By all accounts he was a compelling pulpit performer whose exotic race only increased popular interest. The West Rutland pastor was in considerable demand throughout Vermont and in the neighboring New York towns. He exchanged pulpits, preached ordination, funeral, and Independence Day sermons, several of which were published nearby, and became the instructor of a number of poor white divinity students who sought apprenticeship training.

Haynes's most significant honors, however, did not arrive until early in the new century, when he was already in his fifties. In 1804, the newly founded evangelical college at Middlebury, Vermont, presented him with an honorary master's degree.[20] During the following year his most widely read sermon, *Universal Salvation*, an extemporaneous attack on Hosea Ballou's doctrine of universal salvation, was published. This orthodox Calvinist sermon, which satirically refuted the Universalist doctrine that was gaining adherents in frontier New England—namely, that there was no eternal damnation and that in time all souls would go to heaven— was a spectacular success. It was reprinted all over New England and New York state and as far south as Philadelphia and west as Cleveland and Marietta, Ohio, and it went through some seventy editions from its first publication at Rutland in 1805 to its final appearance at Fairhaven, Vermont, in 1860.[21]

Largely because he was known as the author of this attack on Universalism, in 1814 Haynes was invited to preach at one of the prestigious churches on the green in New Haven

[20]Hileman, "'*Poor, Hell-Deserving Sinner,*'" pp. 4–11.

[21]*An Entertaining Controversy between Lemuel Haynes and Hosea Ballou . . . Universal Salvation, a very ancient doctrine . . . *, 2d ed. (Rutland 1805). The sermon was most commonly published with the title *Universal Salvation*. For a full bibliography of Haynes's publications, see Newman, *Lemuel Haynes*, p. 3 and pt. 3. Helen M. McLam, "Black Puritan on the Northern Frontier: The Vermont Ministry of Lemuel Haynes," in *Black Apostles at Home and Abroad: Afro-Americans and the Christian Mission from the Revolution to Reconstruction*, ed. David W. Wills and Richard Newman (Boston: G. K. Hall, 1982), pp. 11–12, reports that the sermon was extemporaneous.

where he reportedly brought tears to the eyes of President Timothy Dwight of Yale, one of orthodoxy's greatest champions. On this same journey, at Fairfield, where Haynes was the Vermont delegate to a meeting of the General Association of Congregational Clergy, he was asked to address the nearly one hundred clergymen in attendance. Haynes appeared "simple and child-like in his manners—sociable and shrewd in his observations upon men and things, but rather inclined to keep himself in the back-ground, notwithstanding the marked attention he received"; thus he somewhat astonished his colleagues when, speaking without notes, he delivered a sermon "rich in Scriptural thought" and so filled with "striking illustrations" that it "produced a powerful effect upon the great congregation." By the time Haynes had finished, "hundreds were melted into tears."[22] In this setting, for a person of Haynes's talent and experience, the question of his race and origins, while significant, was not paramount.

Yet in spite of Haynes's talents and his strategy for conquering racial prejudice through exemplary Christianity, the dissonance between his color and his stature as a clergyman remained. Just a few years after Haynes's great triumphs at New Haven and Fairfield, in 1818, he was dismissed from his parish after three decades of service. Race, it would appear, was among the factors contributing to the growing alienation between the pastor and his flock.

The foremost reason for the dismissal was apparently the widely held view that the sixty-five-year-old Haynes no longer inspired the religious sensibilities of the new generation. He had led his last great revival in 1808, when 109 parishioners had owned the covenant; but in succeeding years there was a falling away and a dullness toward piety, a growing "stupidity," as Haynes put it. The generation that had first welcomed Haynes to West Rutland had, with few exceptions, either died or departed. Because Haynes was a

---

[22]Rev. Heman Humphrey to T. M. Cooley, 5 April 1836, in Cooley, *Lemuel Haynes*, pp. 167–68.

decided and caustic old-school Federalist who denounced office-seekers as traitors comparable to Benedict Arnold, he did not endear himself to the rising generation of local politicians.[23] Such conflicts between aging clergymen and their parishes were common enough in the early republic and might have led to Haynes's ouster even if he had been white.[24] The fact that he was black also apparently played a part in his opponents' agenda, for years later Haynes was reported to have said that "he had lived with the people in Rutland thirty years, and they were so sagacious that at the end of the time they found out he was *a nigger*, and so turned him away.[25] In a frontier town where salvation mattered more than social stature, a black evangelist could be welcome; less so in a prosperous parish striving for genteel respectability. Even for one so accomplished as Haynes, race mattered.[26]

Haynes's departure (by "mutual consent" after a church council) was peaceful but embittered. In a farewell sermon he challenged the piety of the parish and noted that, after all, he had "many calls to labour elsewhere" and no desire to preside over a divided church.[27] Among the churches calling

[23]McLam, "Black Puritan on the Northern Frontier," pp. 12, 15, 16; Newman, *Lemuel Haynes*, p. 7; Cooley, *Lemuel Haynes*, p. 170; Henry G. Fairbanks, "Slavery and the Vermont Clergy," *Vermont History* 27 (October 1959): 309. Haynes's acerbic wit is evident in the anecdote told by Asa Fitch, who remembered Haynes from the 1820s. Fitch reports that Haynes was asked to offer a toast in celebration of Andrew Jackson's election to the presidency. Haynes lifted a glass and said "Andrew Jackson, Psalm 109, verse 8." After Haynes had departed the celebrants learned the meaning of the citation: "Let his days be few, and let another take his office" (Newman, *Lemuel Haynes*, p. 14).

[24]Donald M. Scott, *From Office to Profession: The New England Ministry, 1750–1850* (Philadelphia: University of Pennsylvania Press, 1978), pp. 119–22.

[25]Asa Fitch, quoted by Newman, in *Lemuel Haynes*, p. 16.

[26]Zadock Thompson, *History of Vermont* (Burlington: Chauncey Goodrich, 1842), pt. 3, pp. 153–54. It is noteworthy that two Universalist rejoinders to Haynes's criticism of Ballou explicitly called on their readers' racism. David Pickering, *A Calm Address to the Believers and Advocates of Endless Misery, Designed for the Benefit of Youth* (Hudson, N.Y., 1821), compared Haynes's "shade" of mind to his skin color. Joseph H. Ellis, *A Reply to Haynes' Sermon* (n.p., 1821), referred to the devil as "this black gentleman" and made other adverse references to Haynes's "dark" complexion. (See Newman, *Lemuel Haynes*, p. 14.)

[27]Haynes to Deacon Atkins, Rutland, 20 May 1818, in Cooley, *Lemuel Haynes*, pp. 172–73.

Haynes was one in Manchester, about twenty-five miles south of Rutland, where after a number of visiting appearances Haynes, in spite of his advanced years, was asked to reside for the indefinite future. Thus, Haynes arrived in Manchester, long after the fracas between Stephen Boorn and Russel Colvin, and about a year before the famous murder trial. That it was Haynes who prayed with Stephen Boorn as he awaited execution was fortuitous since, had Haynes remained in Rutland, there is no reason to suppose he would ever have been mixed up in this strange and sorry affair.

Yet as one reviews Haynes's career—from his boyhood in the humble and pious Rose family, through his triumphs in New Haven and Fairfield, to his decision to leave his parish of thirty years peacefully, it is in no way surprising that he would reach out to the condemned man. Praying with him for salvation, instructing him, following Christ's path in seeking out the scorned, the shunned, and the sinners, Haynes had come to terms with his own depravity long ago through Christ; and his own humility, even more than his remarkable memory and speaking gifts, had been the key to his success. As a poor, illegitimate black servant boy in a world of New England Yankees, he had learned from the beginning that he could have no pretensions that the world would treat as legitimate. Conscious that he had begun as the lowest of the low, he saw Boorn as his brother whether the man had killed Colvin or not. Consequently if Haynes's presence in Manchester was fortuitous, his attentions to the convicted murderer were by no means coincidental.

For his gravestone at Granville, New York (which ironically bears the name of the hometown of his youth in Massachusetts), just over the Vermont border, where Haynes had died on 28 September 1833, he had long before composed an epitaph revealing his sentiments. It explains why he prayed with Boorn and supplies clues about why this black man was able to succeed in a bigoted society. "Here," Haynes wrote,

lies the dust of a poor Hell-deserving sinner, who ventured into eternity trusting wholly on the merits of Christ for salvation. In the full belief of the great doctrines He preached while on earth, he invites his children, and all who read this, to trust their eternal interest on the same foundation.[28]

This exquisitely straightforward, humble statement of the universal Christian message made it impossible for anyone who professed belief in that message to reject Haynes. Perhaps it was for this reason that this man, Lemuel Haynes, choosing this particular career path, could become, as a black newspaper reported in 1837, "the only man of *known* African descent who has ever succeeded in overpowering the system of American *caste*."[29]

[28]Cooley, *Lemuel Haynes*, p. 312.

[29]*Colored American*, 11 March 1837, quoted in Fairbanks, "Slavery and the Vermont Clergy," p. 309, and in Newman, *Lemuel Haynes*, p. 3. It is ironic that in the first U.S. Census (1790), the Haynes household was listed as white (see Newman, *Lemuel Haynes*, p. 111).

Richard D. Brown, *Professor of History at the University of Connecticut, is a longtime student of New England history and is the author of the forthcoming* "KNOWLEDGE IS POWER": THE DIFFUSION OF INFORMATION IN EARLY AMERICA, 1700–1865.

"We Dwell in Safety and Pursue Our Honest Callings": Free Blacks in New York City, 1783–1810

Shane White

In August 1814, as the British naval blockade of New York tightened, the "free people of color" called a public meeting and resolved to offer their services to the city's Committee of Defense. To that end, they inserted a notice in the *New York Evening Post*, instructing the blacks to assemble in the park at five o'clock on Monday morning and to proceed from there to Brooklyn Heights where they would assist in erecting fortifications. The subsequent labors of the group were of little practical value as the expected attack did not materialize; later that week the British forces sailed up the Potomac and burned the Capitol and White House. But the symbolic importance of the involvement of New York's free blacks in the defense of their city was considerable. The vast majority of those who crossed the East River to help fortify Brooklyn Heights were either ex-slaves or the sons of slaves. The looming crisis threatened to bring down a regime that recently had enslaved them and that still held many of their compatriots in bondage. But instead of showing hostility or indifference, New York's free blacks had publicly seized the opportunity to demonstrate their allegiance to the city.

A letter by a "Citizen of Color" printed in the *Evening Post* under the caption "A Test of Patriotism" made that very point. It was, he declared, the "duty of every colored man resident in this city to volunteer." Under New York's liberal laws, the writer continued, "we dwell in safety and pursue our honest callings, none daring to molest us, whatever his complexion or circumstances." Such statements were probably dictated as much by pragmatism as by patriotism, by blacks' desire to convince white New Yorkers of their civic worth and thus to win better treatment. Hindsight has shown that such hopes would eventually prove naive. Leon F. Litwack and others have demonstrated that free blacks were not in the end able to live as independent and equal citizens in a society paying no heed to "complexion or circum-

Shane White is a tutor in the department of history at the University of Sydney, Australia.
    I would like to thank Ira Berlin, Richard Bosworth, Thomas J. Davis, Paul Gilje, Graham Hodges, Charles Joyner, Michael Kammen, Ian Mylchreest, Daniel Walkowitz, and especially Stanley Engerman, Philip Morgan, and Gary Nash for their helpful comments on various versions of this article. My largest debts, however, are due to Graham White (no relation) and Richard Waterhouse (my patient thesis supervisor).

stances."[1] But that was by no means clear in 1814. The later emphasis of historians on white discrimination has imbued the story with an air of inevitability and diverted attention from the achievements and experiences of the first generation of free blacks in New York. Optimistic though they may appear from our perspective, the claims of the "Citizen of Color" provide a starting point for reassessing the formation of the free black community in New York City during the three decades following the Revolution.

Shifting the focus from the whites to the blacks reveals, as it has elsewhere, that blacks were not passive ciphers, helplessly swept along by currents of repression and discrimination and controlled solely by whites. The recently freed slaves, in particular, were exceptional men and women. The story of their emancipation illustrates their ingenuity and strength. In marked contrast to southern slavery, slavery in New York City and the surrounding countryside ended gradually, over several decades, and the slaves themselves played a large role in determining just when they would become free. New York's Gradual Manumission Act of 1799 compelled slave owners to free any children born to slaves after July 4, 1799; New Jersey passed similar legislation in 1804. Slaves born in New York before 1799 were eventually set free on July 4, 1827, under the provisions of an act passed in 1817, while in New Jersey there was still a handful of slaves at the time of the Civil War. But this is not the whole story. Although some slave owners—particularly those of Dutch extraction on Long Island, on the west bank of the Hudson River, and in New Jersey—held on to their slaves as long as they possibly could, many others, though not legally obliged to do so, freed their slaves. Once it was certain that slavery would eventually end, slave owners became more susceptible to pressure from their slaves and often agreed to arrangements whereby slaves were freed in consideration of a number of years' trouble-free service or cash or both. To a large extent the details of the end of slavery in New York and New Jersey were worked out on an individual basis, by bargaining between slave and owner, rather than by legislative fiat. Success in such negotiations, and an early release from slavery, were partly the result of luck, but the process also favored the most industrious, tenacious, and skilled of the slaves.[2] Having gained for the first time, and largely through their own efforts, substantial control over their lives, many New York and New Jersey blacks exercised their newfound power by leaving the places where they had been slaves and starting new lives in New York City. The years of slavery's slow demise fell well short of being a "golden age" for those blacks, but that brief period in the city's history was characterized, not so

[1] *New York Evening Post*, Aug. 20, 1814; Leon F. Litwack, *North of Slavery: The Negro in the Free States, 1790–1860* (Chicago, 1961); George M. Fredrickson, *The Black Image in the White Mind: The Debate on Afro-American Character and Destiny, 1817–1914* (New York, 1972), 1–42, 97–129; Leonard P. Curry, *The Free Black in Urban America, 1800–1850: The Shadow of the Dream* (Chicago, 1981).
[2] The best account of the legislative end of slavery in New York and New Jersey is Arthur Zilversmit, *The First Emancipation: The Abolition of Slavery in the North* (Chicago, 1967), esp. 175–200; for an analysis of the negotiations between slaves and owners, see Shane White, "Somewhat More Independent: The End of Slavery in New York City, 1770–1810" (Ph. D. diss., University of Sydney, 1988), 126–34, 168–76.

much by discrimination and repression (although they were present), as by the sense of optimism and hope captured in the words of the "Citizen of Color."[3]

The main aim of this essay is to shed light on a little-known part of the black experience—the lives of the first generation of free blacks in New York City (and Armstead Robinson's recent assertion that "emancipation studies" are at the cutting edge of scholarly inquiry into black history and will maintain their preeminence at least until the end of this decade makes such an endeavor particularly apposite). My inquiry may suggest issues of method and substance to those interested in urban studies as well.[4] The "peculiar institution" is most commonly associated with the South, but thousands of blacks lived in bondage in key urban centers such as New York, as well as elsewhere in the North. Among eighteenth-century American cities, New York City generally ranked second only to Charleston, South Carolina, in the number of slaves owned by its inhabitants. In the first half of the nineteenth century, the city was either the largest or second largest center of free blacks in the United States. Restoring New York's free blacks to their rightful position as a significant element in the life of the city not only involves an attempt to write blacks back into the mainstream of American history but also adds an important dimension to our understanding of urbanization. In the decades after the Revolution, New York was rapidly emerging as the most important and vital city in the new nation. The lives and activities of its inhabitants have been a focus of interest for historians, particularly in the last five years. Sean Wilentz has written about class formation, Christine Stansell about gender relations, and Paul A. Gilje about popular disorder and violence. The following account of the first generation of free blacks is a contribution to the historiography of black Americans; it should also reveal something new about New York City itself.[5]

[3] The principal sources employed in this study—the early United States censuses, city directories, newspapers, and court records—contain a surprising amount of detail about the ordinary inhabitants of New York City. Similar sources were, of course, exploited by Theodore Hershberg and his associates in their pioneering study of Philadelphia in a later period of the nineteenth century. But the daunting scale and expense of the Philadelphia Social History Project—with at least nine grants from federal agencies, the employment of over five hundred undergraduates, and the work of numerous graduate students and other academics—may have discouraged historians from working with such material. This study demonstrates that, by combining and matching sources, admittedly a tedious process, an individual historian can add to our knowledge of such important topics as the occupational structure, position of women, demography, and residential patterns in late eighteenth- and early nineteenth-century cities. See Theodore Hershberg, "Prologue," in *Philadelphia: Work, Space, Family, and Group Experience in the Nineteenth Century: Essays toward an Interdisciplinary History of the City*, ed. Theodore Hershberg (New York, 1981), xiii–xiv.

[4] Armstead L. Robinson, "The Difference Freedom Made: The Emancipation of Afro-Americans," in *The State of Afro-American History: Past, Present, and Future*, ed. Darlene Clark Hine (Baton Rouge, 1986), 51–74. The transition from slavery to freedom, the topic of excellent studies focused on the South, has been relatively ignored by historians looking at New York. The end of slavery is dealt with only cursorily in Edgar J. McManus, *A History of Negro Slavery in New York* (Syracuse, 1966); and Edgar J. McManus, *Black Bondage in the North* (Syracuse, 1973). Leonard P. Curry's study includes New York, but it focuses mostly on the latter part of its period, as it extensively analyzes the 1850 census. See Curry, *Free Black in Urban America*. The only extensive examination of the issues raised in this article is Gary B. Nash, "Forging Freedom: The Emancipation Experience in the Northern Seaport Cities, 1775–1820," in *Slavery and Freedom in the Age of Revolution*, ed. Ira Berlin and Ronald Hoffman (Charlottesville, 1983), 3–48. Nash's article is much stronger on Boston and Philadelphia than on New York.

[5] The quantity and high quality of recent work on New York City is remarkable. See Hendrik Hartog, *Public Property and Private Power: The Corporation of the City of New York in American Law, 1730–1870* (Chapel Hill,

Table 1
New York City Population, 1790–1810

Year	Free Blacks	Slaves	Total Black Population	Enslaved Percentage of Black Population	Total Population	Black Percentage of Total Population
1790	1,036	2,056	3,092	66.5	31,225	9.9
1800	3,332	2,533	5,865	43.2	57,661	10.2
1810	7,470	1,446	8,918	16.2	91,659	9.7

SOURCE: See Appendix.

Although there were some free blacks in New York City in the seventeenth and eighteenth centuries, they were of little significance. Even the census takers failed to differentiate them from slaves, using the category "Negro" for both. Probably there were never more than one hundred free blacks in the city during the colonial period. After the Revolution, the free black population expanded rapidly, and by 1810 there were 7,470 blacks in that category, who made up 8.1 percent of New York's population. (See table 1.)[6] The 1790s and early 1800s saw the genesis, therefore, of the most important urban black center in nineteenth- and twentieth-century America.

From where had the free blacks come? The sources of the sharp rise in population were diverse. Although the enslaved percentage of the black population dropped from 66.5 percent in 1790 to 43.2 percent in 1800, the increase in the number of free blacks cannot be attributed simply to the activities of New York City slaveholders who, swayed by the egalitarian rhetoric of the Revolution and influenced by the New York Manumission Society, dutifully freed their slaves. The decline in the enslaved percentage of the black population was caused, not by a drop in the number of slaves, but by a sharp increase in the number of free blacks. Slavery did not simply fade away in those years. On the contrary, there was a 23 percent increase in the number of slaves in the 1790s and a massive 33 percent increase in the number of slaveholders—probably one of the largest decadal increases in the history of the city. Individual manumissions did occur, but they had little impact on the total slave population until the nineteenth century.[7]

The reasons for the growth of the free black population can be understood only by examining the larger context. In the years after the Revolution, New York, over-

1983); Amy Bridges, *A City in the Republic: Antebellum New York and the Origins of Machine Politics* (New York, 1984); Sean Wilentz, *Chants Democratic: New York City & the Rise of the American Working Class, 1788–1850* (New York, 1984); Peter George Buckley, "To the Opera House: Culture and Society in New York City, 1820–1860" (Ph.D. diss., State University of New York, Stony Brook, 1984); Graham Russell Hodges, *New York City Cartmen, 1667–1850* (New York, 1986); Christine Stansell, *City of Women: Sex and Class in New York, 1789–1860* (New York, 1986); Thomas Bender, *New York Intellect: A History of Intellectual Life in New York City, from 1750 to the Beginnings of Our Own Time* (New York, 1987); and Paul A. Gilje, *The Road to Mobocracy: Popular Disorder in New York City, 1763–1834* (Chapel Hill, 1987).

⁶ The sources for the figures in the tables and text of this article are explained in the Appendix.
⁷ On slavery in New York City during this period, see White, "Somewhat More Independent," 10–66.

Table 2

Population in Richmond County and the Rural Part of Kings County, 1790–1810

Year	Slaves	Free Blacks in White Households	Blacks in White Households	Free Blacks in Black Households	Total Black Population	Total White Population
1790	1,782	138	1,920	21 (6)	1,941	4,782
1800	1,736	208	1,944	11 (3)	1,955	5,998
1810	1,167	681	1,848	48 (8)	1,896	7,352

SOURCE: See Appendix. Brooklyn has been excluded from the Kings County figures. The figures in parentheses give the number of black households.

taking both Boston and Philadelphia, emerged as the biggest and most important city in the United States. Its population nearly doubled between 1790 and 1800. Even more remarkable was the increase in the black population, both slave and free. Not only did that population keep up with the city's very high rate of demographic growth, but blacks marginally increased their share of the population, from 9.9 percent to 10.2 percent. The main factors in the growth of the black population turn out to be similar to those influencing white population—migration from the surrounding countryside and from overseas.[8]

In 1803 an irate "Citizen" wrote to the *New York Gazette and General Advertiser* objecting to the "whole host of Africans that now deluge our city." Census records are not nearly detailed enough to allow us to analyze this influx of blacks with any precision, but the gross figures give some idea of what happened. Throughout the colonial and early national periods the hinterland of New York City had the heaviest concentration of slaveholding north of the Mason-Dixon Line. For example, in 1790 more than one in every two households on Staten Island (Richmond County) and in the rural parts of Kings County on the western end of Long Island contained slaves.[9] Slavery died hard in the area, but by 1810 the Gradual Manumission Act was beginning to have an effect and the number of blacks living in white households was diminishing. (See table 2.) Newly freed blacks did not, however, settle in the area: in 1810 there were only eight free black households, an increase of two from 1790. In fact, far from expanding with natural growth, the total black population there was shrinking. In a pattern repeated all across New York State and New Jersey, those blacks who were able left the areas where they had been held as slaves. They probably did so for many related reasons—the unavailability and high cost of land in slaveholding areas, the hostility of former owners, and the blacks' own desire to escape from a constrictive rural society in which they would always be stamped as

[8] The black population growth was so dramatic that it does not seem due to natural growth. See *ibid.*, 180.
[9] *New York Gazette and General Advertiser*, Jan. 3, 1803. In order to focus on the rural hinterland of New York City I have excluded Brooklyn from the Kings County figures. In 1790, 456 out of the 888 white households in Richmond County and the rural part of Kings County owned slaves.

slaves. The city of New York was a magnet to many such blacks, offering them not only work but also anonymity.[10]

The other major source of black migration to New York was Saint Domingue. Although historians have recognized the importance of black immigration in the 1790s from Saint Domingue to the American South, particularly to Charleston and New Orleans, the impact on New York of refugees from there has gone relatively unnoticed. By 1793 about ten thousand people had fled the great slave rebellion in the French West Indian colony and had settled in the United States. Although the majority of them migrated to the South, a substantial minority, particularly the French Royalists, went to New York after 1793, and among them were many blacks—either free mulattoes or slaves who came with their masters. It is not possible to estimate the actual number of blacks who came from Saint Domingue.[11] But there can be little doubt about their presence, indeed their prominence, in New York: they appear to have been involved in most of the black unrest in the city in the following decade. For instance, French-speaking blacks made up a surprisingly high proportion of the runaway slaves advertised in New York newspapers in the 1790s. In 1792 Zamor, a native of Guinea just arrived from Port au Prince, ran away from his master and was "supposed to be lurking about this city among the French negroes." In 1796 a wave of arson was widely attributed to the French blacks.[12] Even more disturbing to the white population, French blacks instigated a major riot in 1801. About 20 "French negroes" gathered outside the house of Madam Jeanne Mathusine Droibillan Volunbrun in Eagle Street to prevent the removal of 20 slaves to the South. That evening the crowd, swelled now to 250, threatened to "burn the said Volunbrun's house, murder all the white people in it and take away a number of Black Slaves." The mob was dispersed only by the forcible action of fifty members of the watch. In 1801 Thomas Eddy pointed out, in his account of the state prison, that one-third of the black prisoners were immigrants from "European colonies, in the West Indies and Africa." There can be little doubt that most of those blacks came from Saint Domingue.[13]

---

[10] Not all the free blacks went to the city. For an account, relying on historical archaeology, of a rural black community that formed in New Jersey in the aftermath of the Gradual Manumission Act in 1804, see Joan H. Geismar, *The Archaeology of Social Disintegration in Skunk Hollow: A Nineteenth-Century Rural Black Community* (New York, 1982).

[11] Ira Berlin, "The Structure of the Free Negro Caste in the Antebellum United States," *Journal of Social History*, 9 (Spring 1976), 297–318; John Baur, "International Repercussions of the Haitian Revolution," *Americas*, 26 (April 1970), 394–418; for an estimate that four thousand refugees may have come to New York, see Ira P. Rosenwaike, *Population History of New York City* (Syracuse, 1972), 22. Quantifying the number of free blacks with French names in the census would be of little value—the census takers and/or the blacks anglicized the surnames very quickly. This process can be observed when the directories listed French names. The surnames Arnauld and Pierre, for example, became Arnold and Peer.

[12] For example, in the six-month period from July 1, 1794, to Dec. 31, 1794, the *New York Daily Advertiser* contained advertisements describing thirty-nine runaways, of whom at least eleven were French-speaking. *New York Daily Advertiser*, July 3, 1792. On the 1796 fires, see Shane White, "Impious Prayers: Elite and Popular Attitudes toward Blacks and Slavery in the Middle-Atlantic States, 1783–1810," *New York History*, 67 (July 1986), 261–83, esp. 271–72.

[13] Statement of J. M. Gervais, *People v. Marcelle, Sam, Benjamin Bandey and 20 Others*, filed Oct. 9, 1801, box 9, District Attorney's Indictment Papers (Municipal Archives, New York, N.Y.); [Thomas Eddy], *An Account*

Table 3
Free Black Population in New York City, 1790–1810

Year	Free Blacks in White Households	Free Black Households	Blacks in Free Black Households	Free Black Population	Percentage of Free Blacks in White Households
1790	349	157	678	1,036	33.7
1800	1,152	676	2,115	3,332	34.6
1810	2,495	1,228	4,815	7,470	33.4

SOURCE: See Appendix. Columns 1 and 3 in this table do not add up to column 4 because of the free blacks in institutions such as the prison, almshouse, hospital, and debtor's prison. That category included 9 in 1790, 65 in 1800, and 160 in 1810.

In the first decade of the nineteenth century, the total population of New York City continued to increase rapidly, and by 1810 there were over ninety thousand people living there. The black population also grew quickly, though at a lower rate than the total population. In 1810 the percentage of blacks in the population had fallen to 9.7. The sources of the free black population increase gradually changed in the first decade of the nineteenth century. Migration from the surrounding countryside continued to play an important role, but as the situation in Saint Domingue stabilized, immigration from the Caribbean dwindled.[14] By 1810, however, the Gradual Manumission Act was beginning to have an effect, and for the first time freed city slaves had an appreciable impact on the size of the free black population. The number of slaves declined both absolutely and relatively until by 1810 only 16.2 percent of New York's black population were still slaves.

What did free blacks in New York do? About one in three lived in white households. (See table 3.) Some, who were genuinely free, did so by choice or because of the nature of their work, usually domestic service. But many, although classified as free by the census taker, were actually restricted by some form of indenture. In 1788, for example, the New York Daily Advertiser reported that Mr. John Henry, "a worthy theatric character," had manumitted his three slaves. A few days later the

---

of the State Prison or Penitentiary House in the City of New York (New York, 1801), 84–87. Some of the West Indian arrivals who caused trouble appear to have been deported. One newspaper report, for example, related that the captain of an American schooner had been taken before a magistrate in Kingston, Jamaica, for bringing in a "foreign negro of a description dangerous to the welfare of the community." The black had been sent "on board at New York by the Police of that city." The captain had apparently been instructed to take the black to St. Thomas, but the authorities there refused to allow him ashore. See New York Daily Advertiser, April 26, 1803.

14 There was another alarm about French blacks in 1802. See New York Evening Post, Sept. 10, 1802, and Sept. 13, 1802. The rumors were reprinted all over the state. A Catskill newspaper, for example, included a report of French blacks swimming ashore from the French frigates moored near Staten Island. The numerous blacks were illuminated by flashes of lightning and looked like "flocks of ducks making for the land." See Western Constellation, Sept. 13, 1802.

Table 4
Occupations of the Heads of White Households Containing
Free Blacks in New York City, 1800

Occupation	Number of Heads of Households	Percentage of All Slaveholding Households	Number of Free Blacks in White Households	Percentage of Free Blacks in White Households
Merchant	256	40.0	398	41.6
Professional	56	8.7	82	8.5
Retail	53	8.3	63	6.6
Official	21	3.3	39	4.1
Service	42	6.5	62	6.5
Maritime	18	2.8	19	2.0
Artisan	93	14.5	132	13.8
No occupation/widow	83	13.3	140	14.6
Miscellaneous	17	2.6	22	2.3
	639	100.0%	957	100.0%

SOURCE: See Appendix. The 1800 census listed 778 white households containing 1,152 free blacks; 139 (17.9 percent) of the households, containing 195 (16.9 percent) of the free blacks, were not found in the directories.

newspaper published a letter pointing out that Mr. Henry had taken out a fourteen-year indenture on each of the slaves "whereby he has restrained them actually more firmly in his power than before they were bound."[15] Such arrangements, whereby the master freed the slaves but retained control of their labor, were institutionalized in the Gradual Manumission Act of 1799. Under the terms of the act, the children born of slaves after July 4, 1799, were free. But such children had to serve the owners of their mothers until they were twenty-five (females) or twenty-eight (males).

The occupations of the heads of white households containing free blacks strongly suggests that most free blacks were employed as domestic servants. (See table 4.) Sixty percent of the households in which free blacks lived were headed by merchants, retailers, officials, and professionals (mostly lawyers and doctors). Free blacks in those residences typically lived in the attic rooms and cellars and performed duties similar to those of slaves. In both 1790 and 1800 one in three of the white households containing free blacks also owned slaves, and it is difficult to believe that the treatment of the two groups varied significantly.

Little is known of the occupational structure of the blacks living in free black households in the late eighteenth and early nineteenth centuries. Historians have generally relied on a few sporadic comments from travelers' accounts to cover the period before the 1850 federal census, in which, for the first time, occupations were

[15] *New York Daily Advertiser*, Aug. 5, 1788, Aug. 16, 1788, Sept. 1, 1788.

Table 5

Occupations of Male Free Black Heads of Household in New York City

	1800			1810	
Occupation	Number	Percentage	Mulattoes	Number	Percentage
Laborer (for example, mariner, laborer)	43	38.8	8	114	43.5
Service	6	5.4	2	20	7.6
Food (for example, oysterman, fruiter)	14	12.6	3	22	8.4
Artisan	42	37.8	15	75	28.6
Retail	2	1.8	1	18	6.9
Professional	0	—	—	5	1.9
Miscellaneous	4	3.6	2	8	3.1
	111	100.0%	31	262	100.0%

SOURCE: See Appendix.

included. However, by linking the early federal censuses with the city directories, it is possible to extract a surprising amount of information about the heads of free black households.[16] In table 5 the occupations of 111, or about one in five, of the black males heading households in the 1800 census, and 262, or about one in four, of the black males heading households in the 1810 census are tabulated. Obviously there are problems in using statistics that represent only a minority of the total black male work force: free black heads of household were more likely to be skilled than dependent members of households, and the bias of the directories toward the skilled further skews the figures. On the other hand, they are probably the best figures we are ever going to have. Though they must be interpreted with caution, the statistics in table 5, used in conjunction with other material, allow access to an important part of the black past that has previously remained obscure.

What, then, do these statistics show? First, that about four of every ten male blacks who appeared in both a census and a directory were either laborers or mariners. Those figures undoubtedly underestimate the number of blacks involved in such work. Mariners and laborers are notoriously underrepresented in sources like the directories; in fact, it is surprising that so many were included. In the quarter century after the Revolution over a third of the trade of the United States went through New York, providing work for many blacks in the merchants' warehouses, on the docks loading cargoes, and on the ships themselves. Also, William Strickland, one of the more observant travelers who visited New York in that period, noted that most of the "inferior" labor about town was done by blacks. Ira Dye's analysis

16 See Litwack, *North of Slavery*, 153–86; and Curry, *Free Black in Urban America*, 15–36. For a more detailed account of the methodology, see the Appendix.

of the protection certificate applications suggests that about one-fifth of Philadelphia's maritime work force in this period was made up of blacks, and although a similar study cannot be attempted for New York, there seems little reason to assume any substantial difference between the two cities.[17]

Many newly freed blacks pieced together an existence from day-laboring jobs. Since they were often accused of petty crimes, court records occasionally allow us a glimpse of their lives. John, a free black man accused of theft in September 1801, "kept house" up at the collect (the freshwater pond on map 2). He was married but his wife had been forced to leave New York to find work. For the previous three months she had been employed by a Mrs. Lawrence in Newark. A little over a year before John had gone as a sailor on a voyage to Cadiz, Spain. More recently he had been hired by Icard and Stafford's, where he had "wrought" as a laborer. He quit Icard and Stafford's, probably after being accused of theft, worked for half a day for a Mrs. Hio, then traveled to Newark to visit his wife for a week or so. On his return he was arrested on the charge of grand larceny but was later acquitted. The combination of laboring and working as a sailor seems to have been quite common. But such an existence was always marginal, and those blacks were extremely vulnerable each winter and whenever there was a downturn in the economy. The coroner's report on John Richards, a black man found dead in New York in January 1804, succinctly noted that he had languished and died "from the Want of Bedding, Cloathing, and the Common Necessaries of Life and the too frequent use of Spirituous Liquors."[18]

Probably the most surprising result to emerge from table 5, however, is the number of free black males who did other work. In 1800 more than one in three were classified as artisans, and by 1810, after the hard years of the embargo, nearly three in ten blacks were still in that category. Even allowing for the caveats about the bias of such statistics toward skilled blacks, the figures are high. It is clear from the directories that blacks possessed a wide variety of skills. They worked, for example, as carpenters, coopers, cabinetmakers, upholsterers, sailmakers, butchers, and bakers. Many skilled blacks probably worked for whites, but at least a few set up their own businesses. Timothy Weeks, who lived at 4 Reed Street, "followed shoemaking" in some sort of partnership with William Johnson, another black, who lived on Prince Street in the Fifth Ward.[19] Black artisans often appeared in white

---

[17] On New York's economic growth and its impact, see Hartog, *Public Property and Private Power*, 82–100; Thomas C. Cochran, "The Business Revolution," *American Historical Review*, 79 (Dec. 1974), 1449–66; Thomas C. Cochran, *Frontiers of Change: Early Industrialism in America* (New York, 1981); Michael Kammen, "'The Promised Sunshine of the Future': Reflections on Economic Growth and Social Change in Post-Revolutionary New York," in *New Opportunities in a New Nation: The Development of New York after the Revolution*, ed. Manfred Jonas and Robert V. Wells (Schenectady, 1982), 109–43; William Strickland, *Journal of a Tour in the United States of America, 1794–1795*, ed. J. E. Strickland (New York, 1971), 63–64; Ira Dye, "Early American Merchant Seafarers," *Proceedings of the American Philosophical Society*, 120 (1976), 331–60; see also Nash, "Forging Freedom," 8–10.

[18] Statements of Gabriel Theriot and John, *People v. John (a Black)*, filed Oct. 8, 1801, box 9, District Attorney's Indictment Papers; Coroner's Report for John Richards, a Black Man, Jan. 20, 1804 (Historical Documents Collection, Queens College, City University of New York, New York, N.Y.).

[19] I have based my definition of *artisan* on Howard B. Rock, *Artisans of the New Republic: The Tradesmen of New York City in the Age of Jefferson* (New York, 1979), 9–14. I agree with Sean Wilentz's criticisms of Rock,

business records. Alexander Anderson, white engraver, noted a number of times in his diary that he had cut tobacco stamps for many of the black tobacconists in the city. Some black artisans became quite well known. Years later John Francis, a New York antiquarian, remembered that Peter Williams, sexton at the John Street Methodist Episcopal Church, was "striving to sustain a rival opposition in the tobacco line, with the famous house of the Lorillards." Peter Williams, a free black, was listed as a tobacconist in both 1800 and 1810.[20]

The figures in table 5 provide an instructive contrast with the only comparable material from any city in this period. Gary B. Nash has analyzed the special listings of free blacks in the Philadelphia directories of 1795 and 1816. Nash's material suffers from the same shortcomings and distortions as do the figures in table 5. His definition of "artisan" is narrower than mine, excluding, for example, sawyers, whom I have included. But even if the narrower definition is used, New York blacks were more than twice as likely to possess a skill than Philadelphia blacks.[21] A number of factors explain the large discrepancy. Unlike their Philadelphian counterparts, who had used mainly white indentured servants, New York artisans had relied heavily on slave labor throughout the eighteenth century. As late as 1790, artisans were actually the largest slaveholding group in New York, outnumbering both the merchants and retailers. Undoubtedly, therefore, blacks in New York were more likely to be trained in artisan skills under slavery than blacks in Philadelphia. It should also be remembered that slavery still existed in New York: free blacks were not necessarily representative of the whole black population. Blacks who managed to buy their freedom or were manumitted for other reasons or who came from Saint Domingue were probably exceptional individuals possessing unusually high levels of skill.

Support for the contention that the black artisans were an exceptional group can be found in the high number of skilled blacks who were mulattoes. For some unknown reason, the census taker for New York City in 1800 added, in brackets after the name of the black head of the household, the term "mulatto" or the term "black." As far as I know, this is the earliest extensive listing of the racial origins of blacks in America, and it is interesting to note that this unusual concern with color occurred in the midst of the substantial migration from Saint Domingue,

---

but there were no blacks in the occupations in dispute. See Wilentz, *Chants Democratic*, 27; Statement of Timothy Weeks, *People v. Sally Gale*, filed June 7, 1798, box 3, District Attorney's Indictment Papers. Free blacks even appeared in the debtors' prison; according to the 1810 census there were fourteen black inmates. For an account of a black barber in the debtors' prison who carried on his trade, see Statement of John Albert, *People v. John Albert*, filed Feb. 9, 1804, box 16, District Attorney's Indictment Papers.

[20] See Diary of Alexander Anderson, 1793–1799, June 25, 1793, April 22, 1794, July 3, 1795, Aug. 15, 1795 (New York Historical Society, New York, N.Y.); John W. Francis, *Old New York: or, Reminiscences of the Past Sixty Years* (New York, 1858), 150.

[21] Nash, "Forging Freedom," 15–19. Nash is not explicit about his definition of artisan, but as far as I can tell, the sawyers are the only group in dispute. In New York there were eleven free black sawyers in the 1800 figures and thirteen in 1810. If these are taken out of the New York figures the artisan percentage drops from 37.8 to 27.9 in 1800, and from 28.6 to 23.7 in 1810. The new percentages are still substantially larger than Nash's figures for Philadelphia—12.0 percent in 1795 and 12.6 percent in 1816.

where racial distinctions were always much finer than in the United States. Nearly half the mulattoes identified in the directories had a trade. (See table 5.) More than one in three of the artisans were mulattoes, and if the less skilled sawyers, all of whom were "black," are taken out, this figure rises to nearly one in two.[22]

Free blacks and slaves were heavily involved in selling goods in the streets and markets, many coming from Long Island and New Jersey to sell their produce. Free blacks living in New York were also prominent in the market, although the directories again underestimate their importance. The blacks' presence was most noticeable in the oyster trade, which they dominated. The 1810 directory listed twenty-seven oystermen, of whom at least sixteen, or 60 percent, were free blacks. Most of those black oystermen probably hawked their wares in the streets, but two of the blacks in the 1810 directory had both home and work addresses, which among whites was a sign of relative well-being. The figures in table 5 do not allow an extensive analysis of the differences between 1800 and 1810. Nevertheless, the material does support the tentative conclusion that between 1800 and 1810 blacks began to become small proprietors and to move into some of the lesser professions. The black shift into the oyster houses was the logical extension of their dominance of the trade. The 1810 directory included only two oyster houses, one of them owned by a black. In the 1811 directory another black-owned oyster house appeared. The oyster house was to become a fashionable haunt of nineteenth-century New Yorkers, and those blacks were the forerunners of Thomas Downing, who ran a famous and luxurious establishment in the 1830s. Free blacks also ran small establishments such as taverns, which provided food and drink. By 1810 there were also two black teachers and, for the first time, a black clerk.[23]

Although analysis of directory and census material yields much new and valuable information on the occupational structure of the free blacks, it provides only snapshots of that structure at ten-year intervals. What is missing is any element of dynamism or mobility. Yet it is impossible to work for any length of time with the material without being impressed by the shifting nature of the population. Free blacks appear in the directory one year but are omitted in the next. Only a handful of blacks listed in the census of 1800 can be identified with any degree of certainty in that of 1810.[24]

---

[22] The census taker probably categorized the blacks by shades of color, but in this case, as only one census taker was involved, the problems of inconsistent application are minimized. For an account of such problems, see Theodore Hershberg and Henry Williams, "Mulattoes and Blacks: Intragroup Color Differences and Social Stratification in Nineteenth-Century Philadelphia," in *Philadelphia*, ed. Hershberg, 392–94. Unfortunately it is impossible to test the reliability of this data, as there is no other list separating blacks and mulattoes. On mulattoes, see Joel Williamson, *New People: Miscegenation and Mulattoes in the United States* (New York, 1980).

[23] The Jersey blacks, for example, frequented the "Buttermilk" market on the Hudson. See Thomas F. De Voe, *The Market Book: A History of the Public Markets of the City of New York* (New York, 1970), 322; John M. Kochiss, *Oystering from New York to Boston* (Middletown, 1974), 24–40. One of the first and best-known of the black tavern owners was Samuel Fraunces, about whose color there is controversy. See Kym S. Rice, *Early American Taverns: For the Entertainment of Friends and Strangers* (Chicago, 1983), 125–33. Rice concludes, not very convincingly, that Fraunces was not black.

[24] A very few blacks can be matched with the directories in both years and traced from census to census — William Hamilton was a carpenter in both 1800 and 1810, as was Edward West; Francis Paulin was a "segar" maker

Occasionally information that allows a more detailed reconstruction of black lives has survived. For example, Alexander Whistelo, a free black, was involved in a notorious trial in 1807 after the commissioner of the alms house sued him for support of his alleged bastard child. The published account of the case not only provides fascinating insights into the racial ideas of prominent New York doctors, who tried to establish whether the father of the child was black or white, it also reveals interesting details of Whistelo's employment patterns. At the time he was supposed to have fathered the child Whistelo was a mariner. From the testimony of Lucy Williams, the mother, it appears that between August 1805 and January 1807 Whistelo made four voyages, the longest lasting three months, from May 1, to August 4, 1806, and the shortest lasting eight days in January 1807 at about the time the child was born. His employment as a sailor was sporadic. Presumably in the slack time he either lived off his earnings or followed the pattern discussed earlier and found work laboring. When brought to trial in mid-1807, he was working as a coachman for Dr. David Hosack. Whistelo won his case and faded back into obscurity, but he turns up in the 1810 census and is listed in the directory as the owner of a small grocery shop. Many free blacks probably experienced similar occupational mobility, although the generally upward nature of Whistelo's movement was perhaps unusual.[25]

Though little is known about black female occupations, many of the black women living in male-headed households were doubtless also active in the work force, supplementing the household income. Most such women did domestic work, usually as servants. In addition, a large number of women were themselves heads of households. Women headed somewhere between one in five and one in six of the black households in the three censuses. (See table 6.) That figure may exaggerate the number of female-headed households, since at any time some husbands were away at sea. For example, in 1803 Diana Lawrence, who lived on Fayette Street and worked as a servant for a Mrs. Hazelton, was married but her husband, Samuel Lawrence, was listed in the court records as "at Sea now." However, many of those women did act for long periods of time as the virtual heads of their households. Some coped with this status rather too well. William Thomas arrived back from a voyage to the East Indies to discover that his wife Mary "had not been as true to his bed as she ought to have." He accused her of committing adultery, "which She admitted to be true and in some Measure boasted in what She had been guilty." Among the migrants from the surrounding countryside, there were single women

in 1800 and a tobacconist in 1810; and John Boyd was a hairdresser in both years. However, because the majority of heads of household cannot be matched with the directories and because of the very common surnames of many blacks (in the 1810 census almost 11 percent of the free black heads of household in New York City were called Williams, Smith, or Johnson), it was impossible to trace blacks through with any degree of certainty. Of the blacks heading households and listed with a surname in the 1800 and 1810 censuses, an absolute maximum of 147 were present in both lists. This is 23.1 percent of the blacks listed with a surname in the 1800 census and 13.1 percent of those in the 1810 census. The actual figures were probably much smaller.

[25] *The Commissioners of the Alms-house, vs. Alexander Whistelo, a Black Man; Being a Remarkable Case of Bastardy, Tried and Adjudged by the Mayor, Recorder and Several Aldermen of the City of New York Under the Act Passed 6th. March 1801, For the Relief of Cities and Towns from the Maintenance of Bastard Children* (New York, 1808), 4, 9–13.

Table 6
Female-Headed Black Households in New York City, 1790–1810

Year	Female-Headed Black Households	Black Households	Female-Headed Households as Percentage of Black Households	Free Blacks in Female-Headed Households	Free Blacks in Black Households	Free Blacks in Female-Headed Households as Percentage of Free Blacks in Black Households
1790	27	157	17.2	84	678	12.4
1800	127	676	18.8	325	2,115	15.4
1810	214	1,228	17.4	711	4,815	14.8

SOURCE: See Appendix.

attracted by the prospect of work and life in the city. Sally Gale, born and brought up in Huntington on Long Island, moved to New York in 1797. A week after she arrived she obtained a job at the New York Hospital, where she worked as a nurse for about seven months. The city was one of the few environments where such unattached women could earn a living.[26]

Unfortunately the directories are of little use in determining the occupations of free black women. In 1800 twelve, or nearly one in ten, of the females heading black households were listed in the directories. In 1810 the figure rose marginally to twenty-six, or about one in eight. The occupations of those women were all domestic. Some were seamstresses, one was a "pye-baker," and others were mantua-makers. By far the most important occupation, however, was "washer," with seven of the twenty-six women identified in 1810 in that category. The figures vastly underestimate the number of working women in the free black population. Only one was identified as a market woman, yet black women were very prominent as sellers of produce in New York markets and streets.[27]

Information on black women and their occupations is scarce. Thomas F. De Voe, a New York antiquarian, recorded an account of a remarkable woman, supposedly a slave freed by George Washington, who near the turn of the century lived on the corner of John and Cliff streets. She opened a store in the basement of the house and sold milk, butter, eggs, and "cookies, pies and sweetmeats of her own manufacture; and she also took in washing for several bachelor gentlemen in the neighborhood." On Washington's Birthday she baked her "Washington cake" and fed "some of the first men, old and young." During the yellow fever epidemics, the butchers

[26] Statement of Diana Lawrence, People v. Diana Lawrence, filed Dec. 7, 1803, box 14, District Attorney's Indictment Papers; Statement of William Thomas, People v. William Thomas, filed Feb. 4, 1802, box 11, ibid.; Statement of Sally Gale, People v. Sally Gale, filed June 7, 1798, box 3, ibid. On the black family in New York, see Vivienne L. Kruger, "Born to Run: The Slave Family in Early New York, 1626 to 1827" (Ph.D. diss., Columbia University, 1985).
[27] For an account of black women and their cries as they sold hot corn and baked pears, see Charles H. Haswell, Reminiscences of an Octogenarian of the City of New York (1816–1860) (New York, 1897), 35.

gave her sacks of sheep heads, enabling her to feed the scores of abandoned cats with the brains.[28]

Many free black women lived a precarious existence, and inevitably some turned to petty crime. Nancy, formerly the slave of Francis Van Dyck, a chocolate maker, stole a striped cotton apron from a line and "Carried it off to a Cook Shop in East George and there pledged it for something to eat as she was hungry." The slightest misfortune could invite disaster. The child of Betsey Miller, who lived near the New Furnace on Greenwich Street, caught measles. Having "no money to help herself with and not being able to go out to work on account of her sick child," Miller stole from an unattended money drawer and was quickly apprehended.[29]

Out of necessity or from choice, others turned to an occupation that did not appear in the directories—prostitution. Médéric Moreau de Saint-Méry, who paid more attention to such matters than most travelers, noted that "women of every color can be found in the streets, particularly after 10 o'clock at night, soliciting men and proudly flaunting their licentiousness in the most shameless manner." Alexander Anderson, the engraver, encountered an example of such "shameless" behavior when, on his way home one night, he stopped to relieve himself. "As I was busy against the wall, a mulatto wench came up to me in a very familiar manner, but finding I was not too disposed to make free with her begg'd my pardon, pretending she mistook me for some other person." There were many brothels in New York, and black women ran quite a few of them. Neighbors protested about the presence of such establishments, as court records show, but the unchecked flow of complaints strongly suggests that brothels were an accepted part of the city. Asked in court where he resided, the free black Anthony Delacroix bluntly replied: "in a whore house near the New Market." In 1802 Amos Curtis, a city marshal, finally decided to do something about the brothel in the cellar kitchen in his own residence at 83 Chambers Street. On entering the premises he had "found in one part of the said Nancy Cobus' House a White Man in the very fact of Committing adultery with a Black Woman and in another Room in the said Nancy's House he found one White Man undressed and in bed with two Black Women."[30]

Women were much more restricted in their choice of occupations than men. Skilled jobs, which a proportion of free black men could obtain, paid more and were less tedious than the domestic tasks to which women were largely consigned. Nevertheless, the availability of work, whether it was washing or prostitution, made the city a viable, if precarious, place in which women who headed households could live.

The material from the city directories suggests that the free black occupational

[28] De Voe, *Market Book*, 219–20.

[29] Statement of Nancy, *People v. Nancy (a Black)*, filed June 5, 1804, box 17, District Attorney's Indictment Papers; Statement of Betsey Miller, *People v. Betsey Miller*, filed April 5, 1802, box 11, *ibid*.

[30] Kenneth Roberts and Anna M. Roberts, trans. and eds., *Moreau de St. Méry's American Journal, 1793–1798* (Garden City, 1947), 156; Diary of Alexander Anderson, Oct. 21, 1793; Statement of Anthony Delacroix, *People v. Anthony Delacroix*, filed Dec. 1803, box 14, District Attorney's Indictment Papers; Statement of Amos Curtis, *People v. Nancy Cobus*, filed Aug. 6, 1802, box 13, *ibid*.

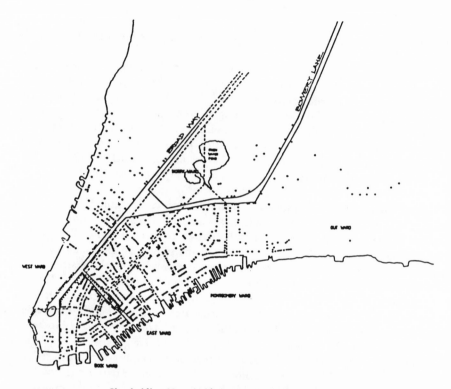

Slaveholding Households in New York City, 1790.

structure, particularly for males, was more open than historians have assumed. Not surprisingly, a large proportion of the newly freed blacks performed laboring jobs about New York. At the bottom of the social structure in the port city was a constantly changing and shifting pool of blacks who, often by combining short-term laboring jobs with work as sailors, eked out an existence. But by comparison with contemporary Philadelphia or, more poignantly, with New York later in the century, New York in the immediate postslavery period afforded a black male a much greater chance to work at a skilled trade. Of course, such mobility was limited—there were no black merchants or lawyers. However around the turn of the century New York offered recently freed blacks considerably more opportunities than other American cities to make a reasonable living and even, in a few instances, to establish their own businesses. Analysis of the directories suggests that the industrialization that impacted so strongly on New York City in the first half of the nineteenth century actually diminished the occupational opportunities available to free blacks.

Little is known about free black residential patterns in New York City in the late eighteenth and early nineteenth centuries. Historians, relying mainly on the occa-

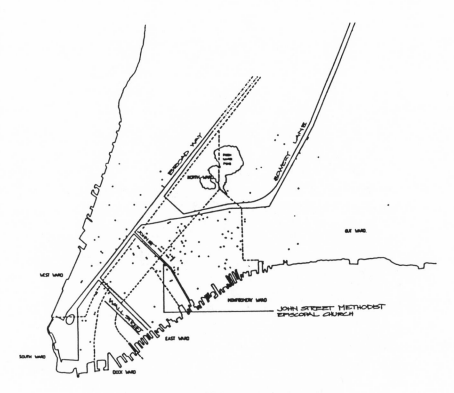

Free Black Households in New York City, 1790.

sional comments of travelers, have glossed over the subject, attempting no more than a few generalizations about the concentration of black housing in what are seen as embryonic ghettos.[31] A much more detailed picture comes into focus, however, if one analyzes the data contained in the city censuses of 1790, 1800, and 1810.

The most striking point, particularly for readers familiar with the ghettos of twentieth-century America, is that black households were well distributed throughout the city. Figures from the index of dissimilarity, which measures the amount of segregation in the city, are very low by later nineteenth- and twentieth-century standards.[32] The colonial city was a "walking city" of mixed neighborhoods and rela-

---

[31] Litwack, *North of Slavery*, 168–70. One historian has stated that Bancker Street "lay at the heart of a large black ghetto spreading between City Hall and the East River," but a glance at map 3 suggests that this is incorrect. See Raymond A. Mohl, *Poverty in New York, 1783–1825* (New York, 1971), 21. The most detailed discussion of black residential patterns in northern cities is in Curry, *Free Black in Urban America*, 49–95. But his analysis centers on the 1850 census and the directories from that period.

[32] The index of dissimilarity measures the number of black households (as a percentage of all black households), that would have to move into another ward in order that black households constitute the same percentage of the total number of households in each ward. See Ira Berlin, *Slaves without Masters: The Free Negro in the Antebellum South* (New York, 1974), 254–55; Curry, *Free Black in Urban America*, 54–55. The figures were 22.17 in 1790, 11.26 in 1800, and 22.29 in 1810.

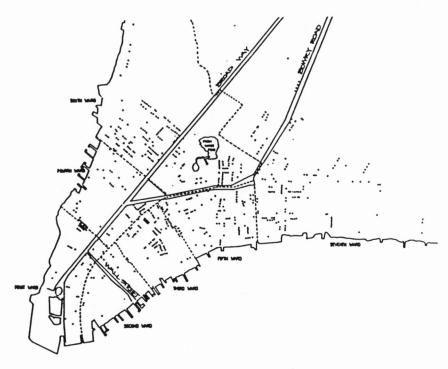

Free Black Households in New York City, 1800.

tively little spatial segregation of classes, and the distribution of free black households reflected those characteristics. As one goes through the census it becomes clear that black households were usually clustered in groups of between two and five, but the clusters were often very close to the houses of prominent members of the New York elite. In the years after the Revolution, however, and just as free blacks emerged as an important and statistically significant element in the population, the spatial organization of the city began to change. That change was related to economic developments. As the production of goods and services in that rapidly expanding urban center was divorced from the household and wage labor was introduced, the laboring classes were forced into rented accommodation. It became less common for employees to live and work under their masters' roofs. The old mixed neighborhoods began to give way to the more rigid class segregation of the "industrial city."[33]

[33] The clustering is similar to the pattern found in Cincinnati. See Henry Taylor, "The Use of Maps in the Study of the Black Ghetto-Formation Process: Cincinnati, 1802–1910," *Historical Methods*, 17 (Spring 1984), 44–58; Henry L. Taylor, "On Slavery's Fringe: City-Building and Black Community Development in Cincinnati, 1800–1850," *Ohio History*, 95 (Winter-Spring 1986), 5–33; and Henry L. Taylor, "Spatial Organization and the Residential Experience: Black Cincinnati in 1850," *Social Science History*, 10 (Spring 1986), 45–69. On the mixed neighborhoods of the colonial city, see Carl Abbott, "The Neighborhoods of New York City, 1760–1775," *New York*

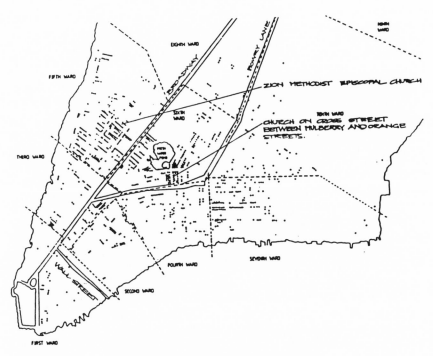

EIGHTH WARD

FIFTH WARD

SIXTH WARD

THIRD WARD

FIRST WARD

SECOND WARD

FOURTH WARD

SEVENTH WARD

NINTH WARD

ZION METHODIST EPISCOPAL CHURCH

CHURCH ON CROSS STREET BETWEEN MULBERRY AND ORANGE STREETS.

TENTH WARD

WALL STREET

BOWERY LANE

Free Black Households in New York City, 1810.

The industrial city did not emerge fully for some time, but its antecedents can be discerned early in the nineteenth century in New York's black residential patterns.

Like freed rural slaves, free urban blacks apparently chose not to live in areas where slavery was still entrenched. In 1790 there were only four black households in the Dock and East wards. Those were by far the heaviest slaveholding wards in the city; in 1790, 41 percent of the white households in the East Ward and 37 percent in the Dock Ward contained slaves. Farther north in John Street, on the other hand, a significant group of black households clustered around the John Street Methodist Episcopal Church. The link between that important institution in black community life and the black households was clear to at least one slaveholder who advertised that his runaway was probably being sheltered "in some negro house near the Methodist meeting house in John Street."[34]

History, 55 (Jan. 1974), 35–53. On the spatial transformation of the city, see Betsy Blackmar, "Re-Walking the 'Walking City': Housing and Property Relations in New York City, 1780–1840," Radical History Review, 21 (Fall 1979), 131–48; Elizabeth Strother Blackmar, "Housing and Property Relations in New York City, 1780–1850" (Ph. D. diss., Harvard University, 1980); and Allan R. Pred, The Spatial Dynamics of U.S. Urban-Industrial Growth, 1800–1914: Interpretive and Theoretical Essays (Cambridge, Mass., 1966). For a brilliant and provocative account of the larger process of which this was a part, see Wilentz, Chants Democratic.

34 New York Daily Advertiser, May 11, 1798.

The majority of free blacks who, over the next two decades, attempted to find housing in the city appear to have moved into the area north of John Street. By 1810 most free blacks were settled in a broad band from the Hudson River in the Fifth Ward, through the collect (or freshwater pond) in the Sixth Ward, and down to the East River. Increasingly, free blacks were concentrating in the emerging working-class wards. Much of the land in the working-class area was at best marginal. It was marshy, ill drained and, particularly in the Fourth and Sixth wards, was used for such semi-industrial activities as tanning, a trade notorious for its bad odors. Black settlement in the area was centered around that pillar of black community life—the church. In 1796 black members of the Methodist church in New York had obtained permission from the Reverend Francis Asbury, bishop of the American Methodist Episcopal church, to set up a separate church in a house on Cross Street, between Mulberry and Orange streets (just southeast of the freshwater pond on the maps). Subsequently the area attracted many black households; later, in the 1830s, it attained worldwide notoriety as the Five Points slum. In 1800 members of the new congregation built the Zion Methodist Episcopal Church on the corner of Leonard and Church streets in the Fifth Ward. That area had been owned by the Anglican church and had opened up for settlement relatively late; but by 1810 many blacks had established residences there near their place of worship. The census data suggests that the pattern was common; churches were built, and the establishment of black households followed. In this particular area black institutions, notably the church, appear to have fostered the development of a strong sense of community among blacks who, consequently, were probably better off in some ways than their white neighbors.[35]

When free blacks first entered the housing market the city was expanding rapidly in population and physical size. Slaves had nearly always lived in their masters' houses, usually in the attics or cellars, but newly freed and immigrant blacks had to find their own accommodation and to do so at a time when housing was in short supply. Blacks fresh from the countryside often stayed with friends or relatives. Robert Havens came to the city from Cow Harbor on Long Island and spent a short time "with his Aunt Peggy Banks in a Cellar three Doors from Frankfort Street in William Street." Others lived in households as lodgers. Silvia, a slave from Brunswick, New Jersey, who came to New York for a few days, boarded with Jane White on Rector Street. In 1801 Jacob Spellman, a sailor who had arrived from Newbern,

[35] See Jonathan Greenleaf, A History of the Churches of All Denominations, in the City of New York, from the First Settlement to the Year 1846 (New York, 1846), 321–22; New York American Citizen, March 21, 1800, July 29, 1800. On the importance of the black church in the northern cities, see Nash, "Forging Freedom," 43–48; Gary B. Nash, "'To Arise Out of the Dust': Absalom Jones and the African Church of Philadelphia, 1785–1795," in Race, Class, and Politics: Essays on American Colonial and Revolutionary Society, ed. Gary B. Nash (Urbana, 1986), 323–55; Doris Elisabett Andrews, "Popular Religion and the Revolution in the Middle Atlantic Ports: The Rise of the Methodists, 1770–1800" (Ph.D. diss., University of Pennsylvania, 1986), 218–68; Carol V. R. George, Segregated Sabbaths: Richard Allen and the Emergence of Independent Black Churches, 1760–1840 (New York, 1973). On community, see, for example, the case of an eighty-year-old black woman who had been burnt out in a fire. On being asked if she was all right, she replied, "O a sister in the church has promised to take me in." Ezra Stiles Ely, Visits of Mercy: Being the Journal of the Stated Preacher to the Hospital and Alms House in the City of New York for the Year of Our Lord, 1811 (New York, 1812), 101–2.

North Carolina, the previous winter, lodged in a house on Orange Street. Many of the single transient blacks at the bottom of the social hierarchy lived in places that were little more than flophouses. Details brought out in a court case in 1799 suggest the nature of their life-styles. At least five black males lived in one room in a house on Mulberry Street. Figaro, a French black, was probably a longtime resident. Peter Mathew had been in the room two days, John Jersey and Jacob Claire for about three weeks, and John Caesar for two months. Similar establishments appear to have existed for women. Nancy Cooke testified at the trial of Alexander Whistelo that Lucy Williams, mother of Whistelo's alleged child, had lived with her for six weeks in a room that contained little apart from two beds. Evidently the two women had little to do with one another. Nancy Cooke did not feel qualified to comment on Lucy Williams's character, although she was able to remember that a very "light" man had stayed one night.[36]

Even as early as the 1790s a few blacks owned the houses in which they lived. In 1796 William Platt, a black sawyer, willed his house at 49 Cedar Street to his wife. But, like an increasing number of white New Yorkers, the vast majority of free blacks lived in rented accommodation. Information contained in the directories and censuses shows that black households typically occupied only a portion of a house. Some blacks lived in the outbuildings at the rear (Ruth Dusenbury, a free black woman, lived in a "backhouse" on Cliff Street near John Street), others rented apartments, but the part of the house most closely associated with free blacks was the cellar. The prevailing architectural style in New York featured high-ceilinged cellars under the raised front stoop. The cellars, which were half underground, were easily separated from the rest of the house to allow multiple occupancy.[37]

Occasionally the testimony given in court cases furnishes particulars of the lives of black cellar occupants. When Thomas Cooney was charged with grand larceny in 1804, he and his wife Margaret were operating a grocery store at 22 Harman Street in the Seventh Ward. The cellar kitchen in this house was rented to Ruth Smith, a "yellow woman," for five shillings a week. She in turn had taken on a boarder, John Young, a black man. In his testimony John Young mentioned an equally complicated arrangement that had occurred just down the street. Young had bought a pair of pantaloons for two dollars from James Anderson, a black. Anderson had gone to sea about three weeks previously, but during his stay in New York he had lived "at Clarry Brown's who lives under a grocery store in Harman Street beyond George Street."[38]

---

[36] Statement of Robert Havens, *People v. Robert Havens*, filed June 4, 1800, box 4, District Attorney's Indictment Papers; Statement of Silvey, *People v. Silvia (a Slave)*, filed Aug. 11, 1800, box 5, *ibid.*; Statement of Jacob Spellman, *People v. Jacob Spellman*, filed Nov. 12, 1801, box 10, *ibid.*; Statements of Mathew, Caesar, Jersey, and Clair, *People v. Newall*, filed Dec. 1799, box 4, *ibid.*; *Commissioners of the Alms-house, vs. Alexander Whistelo, a Black Man*, 15.

[37] *Abstracts of Wills on File in the Surrogate's Office, New York City, 1665–1800* (17 vols., New York, 1892–1909), 330; Statement of Ruth Dusenbury, *Coroner's Report on Aury Slater*, Feb. 17, 1802, box 11, District Attorney's Indictment Papers; Blackmar, "Housing and Property Relations in New York City, 1780–1850," 148–52.

[38] Statements of Ruth Smith and John Young, *People v. Thomas Cooney and Others*, filed April 7, 1804, box 16, District Attorney's Indictment Papers.

Such details deepen our understanding of the black residential pattern shown on the maps. Although the concentration of black households became more marked over the twenty-year period, the blacks did live among white households. In 1800 the largest consecutive listing of black households, that on Ann Street, contained only eight. By 1810 there were three streets in the Fifth Ward with nine or ten black households in a row, but only two areas of any size were almost exclusively black. By the early years of the nineteenth century, Theatre Alley (near Broadway at the top of the Third Ward) was recognized as a black neighborhood. In 1802 the manager of the theater complained bitterly about the "noisy mob of Negroes and vulgar boys" hanging around the door begging for checks from patrons, which they then "promptly sell again at half price, or for what they can get."[39] The 1810 census listed, as far as I can make out, nineteen black and two white households in the alley. The other substantially black neighborhood was in the area later called the Five Points. In 1810 there were twenty-four black and two white households (totaling eighty-nine blacks and seven whites) near the corner of Little Water and Cross streets, eleven black households in a row further down Cross Street near Orange Street, and ten black households in a row on the adjoining Mulberry Street.

Generally, however, free blacks were not segregated in black enclaves. The type of segregation that did occur was of a curious vertical kind, foreshadowing the existence of Ralph Ellison's Invisible Man, whose basement residence was not in Harlem but in a border area. A medical report about the area near Bancker Street in the Fourth Ward graphically illustrates one consequence of such segregation.

> Out of the 48 blacks, living in ten cellars, 33 were sick, of whom 14 died; while, out of 120 whites, living *immediately over their heads* in the *apartments of the same houses, not one* even had the fever.

Conditions in the cellars were often appalling. Medical reports on the numerous epidemics that ravaged New York in the early nineteenth century speak of the cellars accumulating water and every type of refuse in rainy weather, and of the threat they posed to health. One of the first victims in the 1805 yellow fever epidemic was a black woman who lived in a "very filthy cellar" on Greenwich Street.[40]

But there is a more obvious point: black and white, far from being separated, lived in one another's pockets. That pattern is further established by numerous complaints in the court records. In 1800 for example Susan Brasher, a free black woman who lived at the corner of Ferry and Cliff streets, complained about John Stoddart. Stoddart, a white laborer who lived in the upper part of the same house, was perpetually drunk and cruelly beat and abused his pregnant wife. In 1804 several whites protested about the behavior of York, a resident of Gold Street. York apparently spent most of his time drunk and was given to cursing, swearing, and quarreling,

[39] New York Evening Post, March 13, 1802.
[40] Ralph Ellison, Invisible Man (Harmondsworth, 1986), esp. 9; James Ford, Slums and Housing with Special Reference to New York City (Cambridge, Mass., 1936), 86. For another example of vertical segregation, see Peter A. Coclanis, "The Sociology of Architecture in Colonial Charleston: Pattern and Process in an Eighteenth-Century Southern City," Journal of Social History, 18 (Summer 1985), 607–23, esp. 610; New York Evening Post, Aug. 23, 1805. Extracts from many of the medical reports are reprinted in Ford, Slums and Housing, 60–71.

so that "the whole neighborhood is continually disturbed by the disorderly behaviour of the said York."[41]

Blacks may have lived in cellars, but as Ellison's invisible protagonist reminds us, there are "warm holes" as well as "cold holes." In spite of the squalor in which they often had to live, New York's blacks were able to create a vibrant underground culture. Cellars and cellar kitchens allowed easy, and for the slaves unsupervised, access to the streets and fostered the development of complex networks of relationships.[42] Occasionally we get a glimpse of that urban black culture, which flourished in the area around Bancker Street. In 1799 an advertisement for Peter, a mulatto runaway slave, described him as a "great dancer and a very quarrelsome fellow, and is noted as such in the negro dancing cellars in the city." Peter was evidently captured and sold, but within a few months he absconded again. A second advertisement informed readers that Peter was well known in the vicinity of Lumber Street and "in the negro dancing cellars on Bancker Street by the appellation of Hazard's Peet." In 1802 Henry Thompson, a black, was convicted of keeping a disorderly house on Oliver Street near the intersection with Bancker Street. Day or night, the complainant alleged, up to twelve or fourteen men could be found playing dice, cards, and "Divers other games" in Thompson's establishment. Women, too, were drawn to the area. One night in 1805, Caty Thomas, Phoebe Brown, and Grace Kelley went uptown to a tavern and dance house on East George Street, run by Gilbert Williams, a black. Here they encountered Harry and Benjamin Dunbar and danced until about half past ten. Moving on to another tavern on Cheapside Street, also run by a black, they continued dancing until two o'clock in the morning.[43] Those blacks, some slave, some free, came to the Bancker Street area from all over town. Here they could gamble, drink, listen to music, meet members of the opposite sex, and most importantly, for it appears to have been an especially valued medium of self-expression, dance.

We are now in a better position to understand that there were grounds for the "Citizen of Color" to claim, in 1814, that free blacks were advancing under the protection of New York's liberal laws. Not only was slavery gradually ending but free blacks

[41] The numerous complaints surviving in the District Attorney's Indictment Papers testify to a strong faith in the efficacy of the legal system on the part of both black and white members of the lower classes in New York City. On that phenomenon in nineteenth-century Philadelphia, see Allen Steinberg, "'The Spirit of Litigation': Private Prosecution and Criminal Justice in Nineteenth Century Philadelphia," *Journal of Social History*, 20 (Winter 1986), 231–49. Statement of Susan Brasher, *People v. John Stoddart*, filed Feb. 8, 1800, box 4, District Attorney's Indictment Papers; Statements of George Duryee and John White, *People v. York Loyal*, filed Oct. 8, 1804, box 19, *ibid.*

[42] See, for example, a case where Jake sought out Ben, the slave of Van Zandt, by going to the cellar kitchen, knocking on the window, and getting a black woman to pass on a message. Statement of Jake, *People v. Jake, a Slave of Cornelius Brinkerhoff*, filed Dec. 4, 1804, box 19, District Attorney's Indictment Papers.

[43] *New York Daily Advertiser*, Feb. 15, 1799, May 7, 1799; Statement of Daniel Course, *People v. Henry Thompson*, filed April 9, 1802, box 11, District Attorney's Indictment Papers; Statement of Caty Thomas, *People v. Harry (a black)*, filed April 4, 1805, box 22, *ibid.* On the development of black culture in the North, see Ira Berlin, "Time, Space, and the Evolution of Afro-American Society in British Mainland North America," *American Historical Review*, 85 (Feb. 1980), 44–78. For a more specific analysis of New York City, focusing on black language, naming patterns, clothing, and bodily movements, see White, "Somewhat More Independent," 204–32.

were moreover flourishing in the urban environment. Blacks attended the African School and the African Church, and as recently as 1813 a city election, it was said, had been decided by black votes.[44] Blacks were also being given a chance to pursue their "honest callings," and to an extent not seen in any other northern urban center, they were finding their way into the ranks of the artisans and petty proprietors. The satisfaction that came from knowing that they were playing an important role in the life of the city, the air of celebration that marked the black response to the Committee of Defense's call for help, seemed justified despite the clear danger presented by the English.

Yet with the benefit of hindsight it is clear that the position of the free black was precarious. Several small, but nevertheless disturbing, incidents boded ill for the future. One evening in September 1801, Louis Cooney, a black man who ran a small shop adjoining the Museum on Greenwich Street, was accosted by three men of the watch. Roughly, they ordered him home. Cooney retorted that he *was* home and showed them his door. The watch began shoving him against the window of the house. Determined to stand up for his rights, Cooney insisted that it was not ten o'clock; he was a free man and would go inside when he pleased. Eventually William Waldron, the keeper of the Museum, came to Cooney's rescue, but by that time he had been badly bashed, particularly about the kidneys. That night he lost much blood through his penis. A similar incident occurred in June 1803. Louis Hart, a black hairdresser who lived on Water Street, was standing outside his house when Lewis Humphrey, a mariner, began beating the black woman who lived in Hart's cellar. The woman pushed the sailor away and ran into the cellar. When Humphrey then attempted to open the door with a knife, Hart protested. Humphrey then asked Hart "if the House was his to which he replied that it was whereupon he immediately struck the deponent who not being willing to fight with him went into the House." Humphrey left but returned half an hour later with six shipmates. They broke into the cellar and assaulted the black woman. They then moved upstairs into Hart's house, beat him with sticks, smashed up some of his property, and stole a quantity of silver teaspoons. The reactions of the black men involved in these assaults may have been different, but the significance of the violence was the same: poor whites from the neighborhood had attacked those free blacks who, as evidenced by their ownership of property, were managing to get ahead.[45]

The critical days of August 1814 were one of the last occasions when the optimism of the "Citizen of Color" was plausible. New York blacks had become free just as

[44] See the comments of Erastus Root cited in Dixon R. Fox, "The Negro Vote in Old New York," *Political Science Quarterly*, 32 (June 1917), 252–75, esp. 257.

[45] Statement of William Waldron, *People v. Henry Stanton*, filed Nov. 14, 1801, box 10, District Attorney's Indictment Papers; Statement of Lewis Hart, *People v. Lewis Humphrey*, filed June 9, 1803, box 14, *ibid*. The members of the watch in Cooney's case were listed in the indictment papers as laborers. On the background of the watch in this period, see James F. Richardson, *The New York Police: Colonial Times to 1901* (New York, 1970), 19–21. On similar behavior by poor whites in Philadelphia in the 1830s, see Emma Jones Lapsansky, "'Since They Got Those Separate Churches': Afro-Americans and Racism in Jacksonian Philadelphia," *American Quarterly*, 32 (Spring 1980), 54–78.

the social organization of the city was undergoing a fundamental transformation. The movements of blacks from their masters' houses to the cellars and from slave to wage labor are telling examples of the dislocations accompanying the transformation. Initially some blacks prospered in the uncertain transition between the gradual ending of slavery and the onset of what Sean Wilentz has labeled "metropolitan industrialization." But over the ensuing decades the opportunities available to the first generation of free blacks, opportunities they had eagerly exploited, would disappear under a relentless barrage of discrimination and prejudice, a dismal story that has been treated comprehensively elsewhere. Increasingly blacks became part of the emerging working class, and the heightened competition for jobs between blacks and whites had its inevitable result. The violence directed at Hart and Cooney was unusual at the turn of the century. By the 1820s and 1830s it had become common.[46]

APPENDIX
The statistics in this article are taken from the 1790, 1800, and 1810 federal censuses. My figures differ from the totals used by other historians for a number of reasons. Anyone who has worked with the early censuses soon discovers that they are riddled with errors. I have assumed that the individual entries are correct and the errors lie in the additions. (It is sometimes possible to see where the census taker has made mistakes, such as, for example, omitting the totals from one page in his computations.) I have reworked the statistics for New York State in the three censuses on that basis. I have then adjusted the figures for the total population by incorporating the corrected figures for the black population, both slave and free. Undoubtedly errors exist in the figures for the white population, but those, I am afraid, are someone else's problem. The errors in the figures for New York City are generally small; those for the rest of the state are sometimes more serious.[1]

Another source of discrepancy between these and other statistics is that I have eliminated from the city census returns data relating to the part of Manhattan Island north of the city. That area contained mostly small farms and the country estates of the rich, which are not relevant to a study

[46] See, for example, Litwack, *North of Slavery*; Curry, *Free Black in Urban America*. This suggested connection between "industrialization" and a savage attack on the status and persons of the blacks has strong resonances with later developments in the South and in South Africa. See John W. Cell, *The Highest Stage of White Supremacy: The Origins of Segregation in South Africa and the American South* (Cambridge, Eng., 1982), esp. 131–35; Robert J. Norell, "Caste in Steel: Jim Crow Careers in Birmingham, Alabama," *Journal of American History*, 73 (Dec. 1986), 669–94, esp. 694; Robinson, "The Difference Freedom Made," 52. On racial violence, see Leonard L. Richards, *Gentlemen of Property and Standing: Anti-Abolition Mobs in Jacksonian America* (New York, 1971); Paul O. Weinbaum, *Mobs and Demagogues: The New York Response to Collective Violence in the Early Nineteenth Century* (Ann Arbor, 1979); the best and most detailed account is Gilje, *Road to Mobocracy*, 145–70.

[1] Bureau of the Census, *Heads of Families at the First Census of the United States Taken in the Year 1790: New York* (Washington, 1909); Bureau of the Census, Second Census of the United States, 1800, M32, RG 29 (National Archives); Bureau of the Census, Third Census of the United States, 1810, M252, *ibid*. For example, in 1800 the census taker for Kings County calculated that the total population was 5,740 and that there were 1,479 slaves. However, if one adds up the slaves recorded in the manuscript census against individual heads of households in Kings County the total is 1,506. According to my reckoning, the census taker made the following errors—in Flatbush he counted 10 too many slaves, in Flatlands, 1 too many; but in Bushwick, he omitted 8 slaves, and in New Utrecht 30 slaves. Consequently I have entered Kings County in my calculations as having 1,506 slaves and a total population of 5,767.

of patterns in the city. As part of a related study on New York City slaveholders, I have "matched" the 1789 tax list and the 1790 census. That procedure has enabled me to work out which households, listed in the Out Ward of the 1790 census, lived "north of the line."[2] For 1800 I used the city directories to work out approximately where in the Seventh Ward the limits of the city were. For 1810 I excluded the Ninth Ward completely. There is one other major source of discrepancy. Free blacks were listed in a column in the census entitled "all other free persons." Generally that description signified free blacks, and many census takers actually used it rather than the official title. However, sometimes the census takers included nonblacks in that total. For example, in 1810 in the Sixth Ward, the census taker included 204 inmates of the prison. Some of them were undoubtedly black: the majority were not. I have excluded all such entries from the total, a procedure that does the least injury to the accuracy of the total.

Each census entry began with the name of the head of the household and then, in columns across the page, gave the numbers of members of the household in different age and sex categories. Free blacks and slaves were listed in the last two columns, undifferentiated until 1820 by either age or sex. Thus the censuses make it possible to identify the black heads of households in New York City. The city directories contained in alphabetical order the names, addresses, and occupations of a large proportion of working adults.[3] The New York directories made no mention of race. Many historians have used these directories, and for a variety of purposes, but no one seems to have noticed that many free blacks were listed, although names like Pompey Valentine and Congo Clark are rather conspicuous. By linking the names of the heads of black households in the census with the names in the directories it is possible to find out the occupations and addresses of many free blacks. Most of the heads of free black households in the 1790 census were identified only by their given or first names, so only a couple can be matched with the directories. But by 1800 most were listed with a surname. Table 5 was constructed by matching the 1800 census with the 1799, 1800, and 1801 directories and the 1810 census with the 1810 and 1811 directories. Table 4, listing the occupations of the white heads of households containing free blacks, was constructed by matching the 1800 census with the 1799, 1800, and 1801 directories.

The census and directory material was also the basis for maps 1, 2, and 3. The comparison between the census and the directories provided the addresses of a small proportion of the free black heads of household. These black households can be plotted on a map. If the census were no more than a random list of household heads in a particular ward, that would be all one could do with the material. The census, however, is not random. There is a system behind the 1790, 1800, and 1810 New York City censuses. The census taker made his entries while walking up and down the streets, and it is possible to use the city directories to follow his path. By checking the addresses of thousands of other households, particularly those around black households, I have been able to locate the street in which every black household included in the three censuses lived. Further, by using the cross streets (the census takers tended to walk up one side of a street, and then turn at the first cross street, often working their way around the block) I have been able to estimate the positions of the black households on those streets. Though I cannot claim 100 percent precision, I think that the maps provide a reasonably accurate picture of the residential pattern of *all* free black households listed in the 1790, 1800, and 1810 New York City censuses.

---

[2] See White, "Somewhat More Independent," 10–33.

[3] *The New York Directory, and Register, for the Year 1789* (New York, 1789); *The New York Directory, & Register, for the Year 1790* (New York, 1790); *The New York Directory, & Register, for the Year 1791* (New York, 1791); *Longworth's American Almanack, New-York Register, and City Directory, for the Twenty-Fourth Year of American Independence* (New York, 1799); *Longworth's American Almanack, New-York Register, and City Directory, for the Twenty-Fifth Year of American Independence* (New York, 1800); *Longworth's American Almanack, New-York Register, and City Directory, for the Twenty-Sixth Year of American Independence* (New York, 1801); *Longworth's American Alamanack, New-York Register, and City Directory; For the Thirty-Fifth Year of American Independence* (New York, 1810); *Elliot & Crissy's New-York Directory, For the Year 1811, & 36th of the Independence of the United States of America* (New York, 1811).

American Indians on the Cotton Frontier: Changing Economic Relations with Citizens and Slaves in the Mississippi Territory

Daniel H. Usner, Jr.

The popular view of how the Cotton South began tells us that Eli Whitney's cotton gin overcame the only real barrier to the expansion of commercial agriculture and slavery into "unsettled" parts of the Deep South. With industrialized textile factories demanding larger quantities of cotton, manufacturers and merchants indeed began during the 1790s to encourage cotton agriculture in North America as well as in Asia, West Africa, Brazil, and the Caribbean. Their demand for more cotton supplies coincided with a sharp drop in the prices of tobacco, rice, and indigo due to glutted markets and the removal of bounties by European importers. To avert financial losses from declining prices of those staples, more and more cultivators attempted to grow cotton in upland areas of the South. Influenced by the promotional campaign of English industrialists, governments in the British Caribbean, the American state of Georgia, and the Spanish colony of Louisiana rewarded experimentation on gins that could accelerate the separation of seeds from the tightly clinging fiber of green-seed, short-staple cotton—the variety that grew best in the southern interior.[1]

Little is known, however, about the less benign economic changes wrought within regions undergoing that agricultural expansion, especially those experienced by American Indians. The takeoff of cotton production in the Mississippi Territory coincided with a decline in the deerskin trade still important to most Indian communities during the early nineteenth century. The United States government, with cooperation from merchants familiar with Indian commerce, accelerated both processes by manipulating trade debts of Choctaw, Chickasaw, and Creek leaders into cessions of land from the tribes. Indian peoples coped with their diminishing land base through different

Daniel H. Usner, Jr., is assistant professor of history at Cornell University.

[1] Michael M. Edwards, *The Growth of the British Cotton Trade, 1780–1815* (Manchester, 1967), 75–106; Paul W. Gates, *The Farmer's Age: Agriculture, 1815–1860* (New York, 1960), 1–21. On the shift to cotton cultivation in the Natchez area, see Jack D. L. Holmes, *Gayoso: The Life of a Spanish Governor in the Mississippi Valley, 1789–1799* (Baton Rouge, 1965), 96–101; and D. Clayton James, *Antebellum Natchez* (Baton Rouge, 1968), 48–53.

economic strategies. Some groups migrated out of the territory, but most remained and tried to diversify trade with the United States, became itinerant laborers and vendors, or intensified their own horticultural production. Concentration on the territorial period of Mississippi history allows us to examine initiatives taken by Indians in face of rapid change and, furthermore, at a time preceding the influence of Protestant missionaries.

Changing economic relations with American settlers and Afro-American slaves also shaped Indian life on the cotton frontier. With noteworthy irony many of these newcomers, who are usually cast by historians in a one-dimensional shove against Indians, relied on economic exchange with Indians or on other economic activities resembling Indian livelihood. Nevertheless, a widening separation between racial groups occurred during the territorial years as laws and patrols tried to restrict economic relations and activities among Indians and blacks. The transformation of the region into the cotton states of Mississippi in 1817 and Alabama in 1819 also involved the use of military force to quell slave rebellion and Indian resistance. Examination of Indians' economic relations with both citizens and slaves in the Mississippi Territory, therefore, reveals significant dimensions of the incipient cotton economy in the early nineteenth-century South.

By 1793, when use of Whitney's patented gin began to spread across the southern hinterland, the region between the Chattahoochee and the Mississippi rivers was still very much Indian country. The Indian population in that area numbered at least 30,000 individuals, most of whom lived in the more than one hundred villages that constituted the Creek, Choctaw, and Chickasaw nations. Within the same territory were only about 2,500 whites and 2,000 blacks, mostly concentrated in settlements along the lower Tombigbee River and around the Natchez banks of the Mississippi.[2] In order to counteract the United States' claims to territory and its demands for navigating the Mississippi River, Spanish officials made serious efforts during the 1790s to attract American settlers to Louisiana. A generous land policy offered immigrants sizable grants of free land in proportion to the size of their families and the number of their laborers. Larger diplomatic considerations, however, compelled Spain in the Treaty of San Lorenzo, 1795, to cede to the United States all lands east of the Mississippi River and above the thirty-first parallel. In 1798 the United States Congress organized that cession into the Mississippi Territory, which was by the turn of the century occupied by nearly 5,000 whites, 3,500 black slaves, and 200 free blacks, in addition still to more than 30,000 Indians.[3]

---

[2] My estimate of an Indian population of at least 30,000 includes 15,160 Creeks, 11,447 Choctaws, and 2,400 Chickasaws. These tribal counts do not include separate Indian communities such as the Chickamauga Cherokees in the Tennessee Valley. Lawrence Kinnaird, trans. and ed., *Spain in the Mississippi Valley, 1765-1794* (3 vols., Washington, 1946-1949), III, 229-33; Jack D. L. Holmes, "The Choctaws in 1795," *Alabama Historical Quarterly*, 30 (Spring 1968), 33-49; U.S. Congress, *American State Papers: Indian Affairs* (2 vols., Washington, 1832-1848), I, 39; Census of the District of Mobile, Jan. 1, 1787, Works Progress Administration transcript, vol. 3, doc. 226, Favrot Papers (Louisiana Historical Center, New Orleans); Holmes, *Gayoso*, 115.

[3] Holmes, *Gayoso*, 23-24; James, *Antebellum Natchez*, 41-42; "Schedule of the whole Number of Persons in the Mississippi Territory, 1801," manuscript, Mississippi Territorial Census

Indian nations not only comprised the majority of the new territory's population in 1798 but held title, guaranteed by treaties with both Spain and the United States, to most of its land. Indian policy, therefore, was an integral priority in the United States government's territorial organization of Mississippi. The United States entered the nineteenth century with four major goals in Indian affairs. The first goal of establishing and maintaining alliances with tribes required, in compliance with Indian customs, a well-regulated, steady trade relationship. In the Mississippi Territory the task was especially difficult because Spain, which had developed strong political and commercial ties with the tribes of the area, possessed adjacent territories—Louisiana until 1803 and Florida until 1819. To enforce a second policy goal, the maintenance of peace and order among Indian peoples and between them and American citizens, United States agents in the Mississippi Territory entered a highly volatile world shaped by two decades of Anglo-American encroachment into Indian country and of intertribal struggle over diminishing resources. As reported by Gov. Winthrop Sargent in 1799, the Choctaws already felt "that their Country once affording abundance had become desolate by the hands of a People who knew them not but to increas their Wretchedness." Partially to diffuse resentment among Indians over such conditions and to make them more tractable, the government also pursued a third goal of reforming Indian societies by teaching "the Arts of husbandry, and domestic manufactures" and encouraging, as Secretary of War Henry Dearborn further suggested to Choctaw agent Silas Dinsmoor, "the growth of Cotton as well as Grain." Finally and most importantly, the goal of acquiring land cessions from Indian nations shaped policy in the Mississippi Territory. "[T]he time will come when a cession of land may be necessary to us and not injurious to them," Secretary of State Timothy Pickering informed Sargent. Suggesting how bribery might work as a means toward effecting that end, he mentioned that when the time came "the grant of an annuity should be the consideration."[4]

An important instument for implementing all of those goals was the establishment of government trading posts among the many tribes of the eastern

Returns, Territorial Governor RG 2 (Mississippi Department of Archives and History, Jackson); C. Richard Arena, "Land Settlement Policies and Practices in Spanish Louisiana," in *The Spanish in the Mississippi Valley, 1762-1804,* ed. John Francis McDermott (Urbana, 1974), 51-60. On political relations among the United States, Spain, and the Indian nations, see Arthur Preston Whitaker, *The Mississippi Question, 1795-1803: A Study in Trade, Politics, and Diplomacy* (New York, 1934), esp. 51-97; and Thomas P. Abernethy, *The South in the New Nation, 1789-1819* (Baton Rouge, 1961), 43-101, 169-216.

[4] W[illiam] C[harles] C[ole] Claiborne to Silas Dinsmoor, Jan. 28, 1803, Indian Department Journal, 1803-1808, Territorial Governor RG 2 (Mississippi Department of Archives and History); Dunbar Rowland, ed., *The Mississippi Territorial Archives, 1798-1803: Executive Journals of Governor Winthrop Sargent and Governor William Charles Cole Claiborne* (Nashville, 1905), 148-49; Clarence Edwin Carter, ed., *The Territorial Papers of the United States,* vol. V: *The Territory of Mississippi, 1798-1817* (Washington, 1937), 58, 146. For a general discussion of United States Indian policy during the Mississippi territorial period, see Francis Paul Prucha, *American Indian Policy in the Formative Years: The Indian Trade and Intercourse Acts, 1790-1834* (Cambridge, Mass., 1962); Martin Abbott, "Indian Policy and Management in the Mississippi Territory, 1798-1817," *Journal of Mississippi History,* 14 (July 1952), 153-69; and Joseph T. Hatfield, *William Claiborne: Jeffersonian Centurian in the American Southwest* (Lafayette, La., 1976), 41-66.

woodlands and midwestern prairies. The first two having been legislated into existence by Congress in 1795, those stores or trade factories provided Indians with fixed exchange rates and ample supplies of merchandise and thereby facilitated regulation of Indian trade. A factory among the Creeks began at Colerain on the St. Mary's River in 1795 and moved in succeeding years to more western locations. In 1802 a Chickasaw store was constructed at Chickasaw Bluffs near present-day Memphis, and a Choctaw post opened at Fort St. Stephens on the Tombigbee River. Daily records for those trade houses reveal that on a local level Indian commerce and trading practices were important facets of frontier life in early nineteenth-century Mississippi. Indians daily exchanged deerskins, beeswax, and small animal skins for cloth, blankets, ammunition, and steel implements. During the first decade of the century, when the United States factories purchased deerskins at twenty cents per pound, the Choctaw post alone exported over twenty thousand dollars' worth of peltry each year.[5]

Although on a day-to-day basis the trade houses allowed traditional economic activities to continue, their function of extending credit to individual chiefs and traders actually facilitated the displacement in the South of an Indian trade economy by a cotton export economy. Most transactions were carried out by barter, but certain persons were allowed goods in advance of payment. Chiefs, captains, interpreters, and traders—many of mixed ancestry—fell into increasing debt to the factories. In the Choctaw nation, for example, of the $3,875 due to the United States trade house at the end of 1809, Mushulatubbee, son of the recently deceased Mingo Homastubbee, owed $1,059; Capt. Tisho Hollatlak owed $616; Mingo Pushmataha, $499; mixed-blood traders John Forbes and William Jones, $290 and $229 respectively; and interpreter John Pitchlynn, $180. Between 1802 and 1815, deerskins passed through Fort St. Stephens in abundance, but by the end of that period the Choctaws still owed $7,500 to the United States. The drop in the price paid for deerskins in 1812 from twenty to seventeen cents per pound made it even more difficult to meet their obligations: The Choctaws produced 2,317 more pounds in 1812 than in 1811, but they earned $158 less. While the literature on United States trade houses has tended to emphasize losses incurred by the government, the impact of a deteriorating trade position upon Indian livelihood evidenced at the factories has remained poorly understood.[6]

At a time when prices for deerskins were dropping in Europe and when supplies of game were diminishing in the southeastern woodlands, the economic position of Indians was further exacerbated by the fiscal tightening exerted by their private and public trading partners. Through most of the eighteenth cen-

[5] Ora Brooks Peake, *A History of the United States Indian Factory System, 1795-1822* (Denver, 1954), 11-15; Aloysius Plaisance, "The Choctaw Trading House—1803-1822," *Alabama Historical Quarterly*, 16 (Fall-Winter 1954), 393-423; Nella J. Chambers, "The Creek Indian Factory at Fort Mitchell," *Alabama Historical Quarterly*, 21 (1959), 15-53; Choctaw Factory Daybooks, 1808-19, Records of the Office of Indian Trade, RG 75 (National Archives).

[6] Choctaw Factory Daybooks, 1808-19, Records of the Office of Indian Trade; Peake, *History of the United States Indian Factory System*, 204-56; Herman J. Viola, *Thomas L. McKenney: Architect of America's Early Indian Policy; 1816-1830* (Chicago, 1974), 47-70.

tury, colonial officials and merchants had followed Indian trade protocol, which included the practices of offering presents, smoking the calumet, and sharing food. By the end of the century, however, the United States began to discourage outright gift giving and, through its trade houses, to replace what had been political obligations with accountable debts. Influential leaders and intermediary traders still received extra merchandise for their peltry, but each advance was now carefully recorded in the debt column of the tribe's account book. In the Mississippi Territory the results of that practice materialized first among the Creeks in the Treaty of Fort Wilkinson, 1802. Of the $25,000 received by the tribe for a cession of land between the Oconee and the Ocmulgee rivers, $10,000 went "to satisfy certain debts due from Indians and white persons of the Creek country to the factory of the United States."[7]

After sending the Creek treaty to Congress, President Thomas Jefferson turned his attention to that portion of Chickasaw territory "of first importance to us" and evaluated several means through which the United States "may advance towards our object." One means was to encourage plow agriculture, which would reduce the acreage of farmland needed by Indians; another was to nourish their allegiance "by every act of justice & of favor which we can possibly render them." But a third approach involved selectively extending credit to draw the Chickasaws into debt. Jefferson realized it would be beneficial "to establish among them a factory or factories for furnishing them with all the necessaries and comforts they may wish (spirituous liquors excepted), encouraging these and especially their leading men, to run in debt for these beyond their individual means of paying; and whenever in that situation, they will always cede lands to rid themselves of debt." Within a few months Gov. William C. C. Claiborne of Mississippi instructed agent Samuel Mitchell to sound "some of the chiefs" of the Chickasaws on whether "the nation is willing to assume and pay the debts of individuals . . . by a sale of some of their lands to the United States." In July 1805 the Chickasaw tribe signed a treaty ceding all claim to lands north of the Tennessee River in exchange for $20,000 "for the use of the nation at large, and for the payment of the debts due to their merchants and traders." Of that sum, $12,000 went to merchant Forbes, who had participated directly in the treaty negotiations.[8]

The firm Panton, Leslie and Company in Spanish West Florida, renamed John Forbes and Company in 1804, had been trading for deerskins with Indian villagers across the Deep South since 1783. After the Treaty of San Lorenzo was made in 1795, the company initiated appeals to the United States for assistance in collecting approximately $170,000 claimed from the Creeks, Chickasaws, Choctaws, and Cherokees. As its commerce shifted to buying

---

[7] Congress, *American State Papers: Indian Affairs*, I, 669; Dorothy V. Jones, *License for Empire: Colonialism by Treaty in Early America* (Chicago, 1982), esp. 157–86.

[8] Thomas Jefferson, "Hints on the Subject of Indian Boundaries, suggested for Consideration. December 29th, 1802," in *The Writings of Thomas Jefferson*, ed. Andrew A. Lipscomb and Albert Ellery Bergh (20 vols., Washington, 1902–1904), XVII, 373–74; Claiborne to Samuel Mitchell, March 23, 1803, Indian Department Journal, 1803–1808; Congress, *American State Papers: Indian Affairs*, I, 697; "John Forbes & Co., Successors to Panton, Leslie & Co., vs the Chickasaw Nation: A Journal of an Indian Talk, July, 1805," *Florida Historical Quarterly*, 8 (Jan. 1930), 131–42.

and exporting cotton through Mobile and Pensacola, the firm became less dependent on Indian trade and more determined to force payment of outstanding Indian debts. In 1797 partner Forbes visited Gov. William Blount of Tennessee, "in order to arrange the affairs of the Panton firm and to prevent the ruin of its trade." John McKee, a confidant of Blount later to be appointed United States agent to the Choctaws, was welcomed at the company's houses in Mobile and Pensacola shortly after Forbes returned to the coast. In a letter to Benjamin Hawkins, United States agent to the Creeks, William Panton tossed out the idea of extinguishing the debts of Indians "by a sale of some part of their lands." Recognizing the federal government's prohibition against any land cession without its sanction, Panton appealed for such support. If a cession to the company proved "inadmissible," he requested that "some other means will be pointed out equally commensurate with the object."[9]

Like the Chickasaw treaty of 1805, the Treaty of Mount Dexter made with the Choctaws that same year illustrates pointedly how, to their mutual benefit, the company and the United States worked out "some other means." With the cotton boom underway at the opening of the nineteenth century, officials of the Jefferson administration sought from the Choctaw nation some of the fertile land that stretched between the Alabama and the Mississippi rivers and discerned a convenient means of acquiring such a cession in the nearly fifty thousand dollars owed by the Choctaws to the Forbes company. In 1803 Dearborn signaled to Gen. James Wilkinson in the Mississippi Territory that "if no other consideration will induce the Chocktaws to part with any of their lands but that of paying off the debt they owe Panton & Co.," agent Dinsmoor should inquire into the willingness of tribal divisions to pay their respective shares out of lands sold west of the Yazoo River and east of the lower Tombigbee. Ephraim Kirby, first sent to the territory as land commissioner and then appointed judge, observed that lands on the east bank of the Tombigbee are fertile and not subject to inundation, "in all respects suitable for the most extensive operations of husbandry." Noting "poverty and distress" among the Choctaws due to scarce game and debauching contacts with settlers, the Connecticut Republican suggested that "through the agency of the white traders settled among them, they may be pursuaded to exchange their country for a portion of the wilderness of Louisiana."[10]

By the time the United States began to pursue aggressively a Choctaw cession, the Forbes company was already employing its influence "in procuring the assent of the Indians." As recalled by partner William Simpson, "we exerted ourselves with the Chiefs of the Nation & spent much time, labor & Money" in encouraging a sale of land to the United States. We still need to un-

[9] Robert S. Cotterill, "A Chapter of Panton, Leslie and Company," *Journal of Southern History*, 10 (Aug. 1944), 275–92; Manuel Gayoso de Lemos to Conde de Santa Clara, Sept. 24, 1797, Papeles Procedentes de Cuba transcripts (North Carolina State Archives, Raleigh); William Panton to Benjamin Hawkins, June 11, 1799, Papers of Panton, Leslie and Company (University of West Florida Library, Pensacola). See also William S. Coker, *Historical Sketches of Panton, Leslie and Company* (Pensacola, 1976).

[10] Carter, ed., *Territorial Papers of the United States*, V, 189; Ephraim Kirby to Thomas Jefferson, April 20, 1804, Ephraim Kirby Papers (Manuscript Department, Perkins Library, Duke University, Durham, N.C.); Kirby to Secretary of the Treasury Albert Galatin, July 1, 1804, *ibid*.

cover more details about the company's intrigue with the federal government and its brokers in the Choctaw nation and about the dissent and discord that it incited among the Choctaw people. But we already know that during 1804 Forbes corresponded with and even visited the secretary of war, having already convinced Choctaw leaders one year earlier to request the United States to purchase land for the purpose of paying their debts to the firm. The Jefferson administration had declined that offer because portions of territory designated by the tribe were not those specifically desired. But with pressure from its creditors persisting, the Choctaw nation sent a petition to President Jefferson in August 1804 proposing a cession acceptable to the government.[11]

Arrangements for a treaty council with the Choctaws proceeded quickly and suspiciously. According to the instructions written by the secretary of war to the treaty commissioners, the cession designated in the Choctaw petition covered the highly fertile land between the Big Black and the Mississippi rivers. In an earlier letter to Dinsmoor, however, Dearborn had advised him "to prepare the minds of the Chiefs" for extending their cession over that very same area, indicating that the petition, at the very least, did not represent any consensus among Choctaw leaders. When the Choctaw chiefs met the United States commissioners at Fort St. Stephens in June 1805, they refused to cede any land near the Mississippi, prompting months of deadlock. That stand finally drove the commissioners, following a round of heated negotiations in November, to accept an offer of different lands—a huge tract comprising the southern border of Choctaw country and extending eastward from the Homochitto River to the watershed between the Tombigbee and the Alabama rivers.[12]

Of the $50,500 offered the Choctaws for those four million acres of land, $48,000 were reserved for discharging their debt to the Forbes company. The United States also promised the tribe an annuity of $3,000 in merchandise. Each of the three "great medal mingoes"—Puckshenubbee, Homastubbee, and Pushmataha—was granted $500 "in consideration of past services in their nation" and was offered an annuity of $150 "during their continuance in office." Villagers who used the ceded area directed most of their opposition to the treaty against those leaders, but to little avail. Because the Treaty of Mount Dexter produced lands in the less fertile pine barrens and swamps of southern Mississippi rather than in the rich Yazoo River delta targeted in the commissioners' instructions, Jefferson did not submit it to the Senate for ratification until 1808, when foreign affairs made "a strong settlement of militia along our southern frontier" and the "consolidation of the Mississippi territory" important considerations. By April 1809, the Forbes company

---

[11] Congress, *American State Papers: Indian Affairs*, I, 748, 750; Clarence Edwin Carter, ed., *Territorial Papers of the United States*, vol. VI: *The Territory of Mississippi, 1798-1817, continued* (Washington, 1938), 123; "Memorial of John Forbes & Co. to the President of the United States," [1807], Papers of Panton, Leslie and Company; David H. White, "The John Forbes Company: Heir to the Florida Indian Trade, 1801-1819" (Ph.D. diss., University of Alabama, 1973), 64-77.

[12] Carter, ed., *Territorial Papers of the United States*, V, 343; Congress, *American State Papers: Indian Affairs*, I, 748-50.

received most of what it claimed against the Choctaws' account, minus $4,304.25 disputed by agent Dinsmoor.[13]

The Treaty of Mount Dexter and other Choctaw, Creek, and Chickasaw treaties made during the first decade of the Mississippi Territory's existence reflected the entanglement of Indian villagers in the region within a chronic cycle of trade indebtedness and land cessions, a cycle that would steadily weaken their power and eventually culminate in removal. By 1822 the Choctaw nation, for example, ceded nearly thirteen million acres of land but still owed approximately thirteen thousand dollars to the United States trade house. The transfer of Indian land to the United States was, as the Choctaw and Chickasaw treaties of 1805 explicitly illustrate, further accelerated by cooperation between the federal government and merchant companies—a lesson that would not be lost on future administrators of Indian affairs.[14]

Indian inhabitants of the Mississippi Territory responded to their deteriorating economic position in a variety of ways, evincing a resourceful adaptability among native Americans too often neglected by historians. Beginning in the late eighteenth century, numerous Choctaw families and even some Creek villagers migrated across the Mississippi River and settled in the still-plentiful hunting grounds of the Ouachita, Red, and Atchafalaya river basins. As government trade-house records reveal, those who remained in their homelands continued to produce, although at a diminishing rate, deerskins and other furs. Still hoping to perpetuate their traditional exchange economy through adaptation, Indian men and women provided an array of other goods and services to the trade stores. During the five years from 1809 through 1813, the Choctaw factory received $22,877 worth of raw deerskins (44,232 skins), $4,109 worth of dressed deerskins, raccoon, lynx, and other miscellaneous pelts, $1,749 worth of beeswax (7,958 pounds), $145 worth of tallow (1,161 pounds), $249 worth of corn (443 barrels), and $24 worth of snakeroot (96 pounds). Indians occasionally sold their labor to the trade house in exchange for merchandise, working as boat hands, messengers, and boatbuilders. In January 1809, for

[13] Congress, American State Papers: Indian Affairs, I, 748–49, 751–52; Carter, ed., Territorial Papers of the United States, V, 434, VI, 123; Arthur H. DeRosier, Jr., The Removal of the Choctaw Indians (Knoxville, 1970), 29, 32; Cotterill, "Chapter of Panton, Leslie and Company," 289–91.

[14] U.S. Congress, American State Papers: Public Lands (3 vols., Washington, 1860–1861), III, 461–62; "A List of Individual debts Due to the Chaktaw Trading House, March 31st 1822," Choctaw Factory Miscellaneous Accounts, 1803–25, Records of the Office of Indian Trade. For summaries of Creek, Choctaw, and Chickasaw treaties with the United States during the Mississippi territorial period, see Michael D. Green, The Politics of Indian Removal: Creek Government and Society in Crisis (Lincoln, 1982), 36–73; DeRosier, Removal of the Choctaw Indians, 27–52; and Arrell M. Gibson, The Chickasaws (Norman, 1971), 80–105. For the role that government-business cooperation played in accelerating Indian land loss during the nineteenth century, see Paul W. Gates, "Indian Allotments Preceding the Dawes Act," in The Frontier Challenge: Responses to the Trans-Mississippi West, ed. John G. Clark (Lawrence, 1971), 141–70; James L. Clayton, "The Impact of Traders' Claims on the American Fur Trade," in The Frontier in American Devlopment: Essays in Honor of Paul Wallace Gates, ed. David M. Ellis et al. (Ithaca, 1969), 299–322; and Robert A. Trennert, Jr., Indian Traders on the Middle Border: The House of Ewing, 1827–54 (Lincoln, 1981), esp. 55–57, 77–84, 96–115.

example, the Choctaw factor "Bartered with an Indian" two yards of strouds valued at \$3.50 for a "Canoe" (pirogue) that he gave to the trade house.[15]

Many Indians became seasonal laborers or itinerant peddlers around the towns and plantations of the Mississippi Territory. As early as 1808 Choctaw women picked cotton during the harvest season for cloth, blankets, utensils, and even cash wages. John A. Watkins first became acquainted with the Choctaws in 1813–1814, "as they came into Jefferson Co. in the fall and winter in large numbers, the women to pick cotton, the men to hunt in the Louisiana swamps." From bark-covered huts that were always left open on the south side, hunters pursued deer and bear across the Mississippi while women worked in cotton fields east of the river. Those seasonally mobile camps of Choctaw families—the cotton economy's first migrant labor force—also sold dressed deerskins, bear oil, and venison at landings along the Mississippi or took those and other products to Natchez, where according to Watkins "they were usually exchanged for blankets, stroud & calico supplemented by a jug of whiskey."[16]

To maintain an economic base within their diminishing tribal domains, the Indian peoples also changed their farming and settlement patterns. Many Creeks, Choctaws, and Chickasaws had been raising livestock for some time, but at the opening of the nineteenth century that activity became a more important means of livelihood. As more grazing land was needed and as immigrants and travelers created a demand for foodstuffs, Indian villages began to spread outward from their previously more compact centers. The process was most visible among the Upper Creeks, many of whom settled on the outskirts of their towns as they became more attentive to cattle, hogs, and horses. The inhabitants of Hoithlewalli, for example, formed new settlements with fenced-in fields along the small tributaries of the Oakfuskee Creek, once reserved by the town for bear hunting and now providing "delightful range for stock." Choctaw and Chickasaw farmers also homesteaded outward from their villages during the early territorial period. Traveling from Natchez to the Chickasaw nation in the summer of 1805, Dr. Rush Nutt observed some Choctaws "building log houses & cultivating the earth in corn, cotton, & other garden vegetables." Farther along the Natchez Trace—at Chukasalaya, Estockshish, and Bear Creek—he found Chickasaws establishing supply stations for travelers, raising "plenty of hogs & cattle," and farming grain crops.

[15] John Sibley, *A Report from Natchitoches in 1807*, ed. Annie Heloise Abel (New York, 1922); Richard White, *The Roots of Dependency: Subsistence, Environment and Social Change among the Choctaws, Pawnees, and Navajos* (Lincoln, 1983), 97–146; Choctaw Factory Daybooks, 1808–19, Records of the Office of Indian Trade; Choctaw Factory Miscellaneous Accounts, 1803–25, *ibid.*

[16] John A. Watkins, "Choctaw Indians," John A. Watkins Manuscripts (Howard-Tilton Memorial Library, Tulane University, New Orleans); Reuben Gold Thwaites, ed., *Early Western Travels, 1748–1846*, vol. IV: *Cuming's Tour to the Western Country (1807–1809)* (Cleveland, 1904), 351–52; John McKee to Andrew Jackson, Nov. 19, 1814, microfilm reel 14, Andrew Jackson Papers (Library of Congress).

Chickasaw families were also settling westward in the Yazoo delta in order to use better range for their horses, cattle, and hogs.[17]

The Indian trade economy that had grown around the exchange of deerskins for European manufactures was not impervious to accommodating the cotton economy, although the latter did threaten to displace the former entirely. During the eighteenth century Indians in the Lower Mississippi Valley had adopted European and African food crops, developed their own herds of livestock, and traded those and other items to colonists. In keeping with that pattern of adaptation, Indian villagers in the Mississippi Territory began to grow their own cotton for the export market. Traders Abram Mordecai and John and William Price established cotton gins at "Weathersford's racetrack" and "the Boat Yard," both along the Alabama River, where they purchased cotton produced by Creek farmers. Chickasaw chiefs inquired as early as 1803 whether the United States factor at Chickasaw Bluffs would accept their cotton for cash.[18]

But even though the cotton economy began to replace the deerskin trade economy, Indian communities in the Mississippi Territory continued to create economic niches for some settlers and slaves. Before the region became a United States territory, many French and English traders had established their deerskin commerce in particular villages by marrying Indian women. Into the nineteenth century many of their offspring continued to play prominent roles in the regional economy and were joined by American newcomers licensed by the territorial government. As transportation on roads through Indian country increased, some of those traders even opened facilities that provided food and lodging to travelers. In addition to the actual traders who dealt directly with Indian villagers, Indian commerce employed black as well as white laborers at several different tasks: transporting products by packhorses or by boats, helping to preserve and to pack the deerskins, and doing construction work on the facilities. At both private trade firms and government factories, settlers worked for wages, and slaves were hired out by their owners. The experience among Indians gained by some black slaves, particularly those owned by whites and Indians engaged in trade, was evident to early territorial witnesses by the presence of blacks in settlements and villages who could interpret between the various Indian languages and English.[19]

[17] *Mississippi Herald and Natchez City Gazette*, June 15, 1804; Dinsmoor to Cato West, June 10, June 15, 1804, Indian Department Journal, 1803–1808; Benjamin Hawkins, "A Sketch of the Creek Country, in the Years 1798 and 1799," *Collections of the Georgia Historical Society*, vol. III, pt. 1 (Savannah, 1848), 26–66, esp. 32–33; Jesse D. Jennings, ed., "Nutt's Trip to the Chickasaw Country," *Journal of Mississippi History*, 9 (Jan. 1947), 40–45, 60–61.

[18] Claiborne to Mitchell, April 29, 1803, Indian Department Journal, 1803–1808; Albert James Pickett, *History of Alabama, and Incidentally of Georgia and Mississippi, from the Earliest Period* (2 vols., Charleston, 1851), II, 189–90.

[19] Pickett, *History of Alabama*, II, 123–35; Hawkins, "Sketch of the Creek Country," 26–48; Jennings, ed., "Nutt's Trip to the Chickasaw Country," 41–44; Bonds of Tax Collectors, Sheriffs and Indian Traders, 1802–1817, Territorial Governor RG 2 (Mississippi Department of Archives and History); Dawson A. Phelps, "Stands and Travel Accommodations on the Natchez Trace," *Journal of Mississippi History*, 11 (Jan. 1949), 1–54; Dawson A. Phelps, ed., "Excerpts from the Journal of the Reverend Joseph Bullen, 1799 and 1800," *ibid.*, 17 (Oct. 1955), 262–63, 273;

Obstacles to landownership and uncertainties of cotton production during the territorial years challenged settlers in Mississippi to find means of livelihood that resembled the Indian mixture of hunting, farming, and herding. That adaptation by whites to the cotton frontier, more than the production of cotton itself, brought them face to face with local Indians. Before the United States even began to survey land in the Mississippi Territory, an estimated two thousand settlers had already squatted on unused lands. Governor Claiborne expressed hope in late 1802 "that these Citizens may be secured in their improvements, and that the Government will sell out the Vacant land in this district upon moderate terms and in small tracts to actual settlers." United States land policy, however, was committed to selling large rectangular tracts of land for revenues drastically needed by the treasury. Thus in March 1803 Congress extended to the Mississippi Territory the prescription that a minimum of 320 acres had to be purchased at two dollars per acre with one-fourth of the cost paid in cash at the sale or the registration. For people actually migrating into the territory, that system caused much anxiety because it encouraged speculation by land companies and required a minimum purchase unaffordable to many settlers.[20]

Many of them drawn to the region by the prospects of growing cotton, several hundred Mississippi petitioners in 1803 asked Congress to encourage small holdings instead of large holdings, to prohibit land speculation, to reduce the national army, and to inhibit the spread of slavery. Congress responded to appeals by discontented territorial settlers both north and south of the Ohio River with new legislation in 1804 instituting the public sale of smaller tracts, 160 acres in quarter-sections, and reducing the minimum auction price to $1.25 per acre. Conditions in the Mississippi Territory, however, militated against a speedy and democratic distribution of land. Surveyal of lands languished for a long time, and public auctions of available tracts did not begin until August 1809. As reported by William Lattimore in 1806, the expectation by families moving into the region "of being able to purchase lands of the Government . . . has not been realized." Not enough cleared land existed for them to rent from those who already owned landed property, and the cost of purchasing land from private sellers "was beyond their resources." The only other alternatives available to settlers were to return to their home states, to acquire land "upon the easiest terms" in the Spanish colony of Florida, and to squat on vacant lands of the United States in hope of securing preemption rights to their improvements; most migrants to the Mississippi Territory chose the last, although an unknown number did resort to the other alternatives. But just when claimants were allowed to begin purchasing their

receipts, July 15, Oct. 6, 1803, March 9, 1807, Choctaw Factory Miscellaneous Accounts, 1803-25, Records of the Office of Indian Trade; Rowland, ed., *Mississippi Territorial Archives*, 164-65, 233-34; Jack D. L. Holmes, "The Role of Blacks in Spanish Alabama: The Mobile District, 1780-1813," *Alabama Historical Quarterly*, 37 (Spring 1975), 5-18.

[20] Dunbar Rowland, ed., *Official Letter Books of W. C. C. Claiborne, 1801-1816* (6 vols., Jackson, 1917), I, 219; Carter, ed., *Territorial Papers of the United States*, V, 192-205, esp. 203; Malcolm J. Rohrbough, *The Land Office Business: The Settlement and Administration of American Public Lands, 1789-1837* (New York, 1968), esp. 26-70.

preempted lands in 1809, the price of cotton began to drop sharply mainly because of the embargo imposed by the federal government in 1808. Although cotton in New Orleans had been dropping slightly from a high of 25 cents per pound in September 1805, after the embargo the price plummeted to 12 cents by September 1809.[21]

Having counted on a promising income from cotton produced for the English market to pay off the installments due on their lands, farmers now faced the bleak prospect of forfeiting their newly acquired property. As the territory entered the second decade of the nineteenth century, mounting hostility from the Creek Indians and impending war against Great Britain deepened uncertainty and instability, pushed down the value of cotton even more, and slowed the sale of public lands. In one petition sent to Congress by inhabitants of the Mississippi Territory, the trap that cotton already set for the South—an economy highly sensitive to the price of a single commodity—was clearly defined: "Confiding as we have done on the measures of Government which were intended to restore foreign intercourse, and which held out the probability of success, we have continued to cultivate the article of cotton, to the growth of which our soil is so propitious, and omited all or most other pursuits calculated to command money."[22]

Under those circumstances, squatting on the periphery of private landholdings and Indian villages or on federal lands and then raising livestock to sell to planters, townspeople, and newcomers became a pervasive means to economic security. Already familiar with open grazing in the backwoods of Georgia and the Carolinas, many settlers in Mississippi's promising pine forests acquired cattle, horses, and hogs from Indians. Some bought the animals; others sequestered strays. In time, a family of squatters might earn enough from its own herding to purchase title to the land, or, if not, the mobility of livestock eased their relocation to another tract when threatened with eviction. Meanwhile, competition over grazing lands and ambiguity between trading and rustling heightened antagonism in their relations with Indians. Symbiotically, the success of some farmers in producing cotton and buying slaves—by creating a growing market for food—allowed those who were unable or unwilling to grow the staple a distinct avenue to economic security and social autonomy. From that process, among others, emerged the yeoman farmers of the nineteenth-century South, whose intermittent participation in the cotton economy through livestock trade buffered them from

[21] Carter, ed., *Territorial Papers of the United States*, V, 279-87, 455; Benjamin Horace Hibbard, *A History of the Public Land Policies* (New York, 1924), 75; Rohrbough, *Land Office Business*, 35-59; Frederick Kimball to Nephew and Niece, May 23, 1808, Frederick Kimball Letters (Department of Archives and History, Louisiana State University, Baton Rouge); Flower & Faulkner to John Pintard, May 20, 1809, John M. Pintard Papers, *ibid.*; *Louisiana Gazette*, Aug. 30, 1805, Aug. 26, 1806, June 30, 1807; *Louisiana Gazette and New Orleans Daily Advertiser*, June 21, 1808, Sept. 1, 1809. Uncertainty over land titles and animosity toward land speculators were greatly exacerbated in the Mississippi Territory by claims to the Yazoo River valley sold by the Georgia state legislature. See Abernethy, *South in the New Nation*, 136-68; and C. Peter Magrath, *Yazoo: Law and Politics in the New Republic: The Case of* Fletcher v. Peck (Providence, 1966).

[22] Carter, ed., *Territorial Papers of the United States*, VI, 226.

the risks of cotton agriculture and yet perpetuated their hopes of becoming slave-owning cotton farmers themselves.[23]

By the second decade of the nineteenth century, the Mississippi Territory was fast becoming a cotton export region. Within a decade the non-Indian population had surpassed the number of Indians, increasing nearly fivefold to more than 23,000 settlers and 17,000 slaves. Although most white settlers still contended with obstacles to land acquisition and relied on multiple means of subsistence, planters who already possessed land or who could afford to purchase some in the private market committed more slaves to the production of more cotton. As one such individual described the process, "here you will ask, what do they want with so many negroes, the answer is, to make more Money—again, you will ask what do they want with so much Money, the answer is to buy more Negroes.... A Mans merit in this country, is estimated, according to the number of Negroes he works in the field."[24]

The influx of Afro-American slaves into the territory affected the economic life of Indians as deeply and equivocally as did white migration. More vulnerable to territorial laws than were Indians, Afro-Americans also struggled to preserve some economic autonomy and resilience within the narrowing interstices of a slave-labor, cotton economy. By trading among themselves and with Indians and whites—in foodstuffs, home manufactures, and even forbidden horses—slaves tried to secure for themselves what has been lately called an "internal economy," distinct from but tied to the larger regional system of staple agriculture.[25] But legislation and slave patrols discouraged forms of economic exchange and social interaction that had previously brought blacks

[23] Frank Lawrence Owsley, "The Pattern of Migration and Settlement on the Southern Frontier," *Journal of Southern History*, 11 (May 1945), 147–76; Frank Lawrence Owsley, *Plain Folk in the Old South* (Baton Rouge, 1949), esp. 1–90; Forrest McDonald and Grady McWhiney, "The Antebellum Southern Herdsman: A Reinterpretation," *Journal of Southern History*, 41 (May 1975), 147–66; Forrest McDonald and Grady McWhiney, "The South from Self-Sufficiency to Peonage: An Interpretation," *American Historical Review*, 85 (Dec. 1980), 1104–111; John D. W. Guice, "Cattle Raisers of the Old Southwest: A Reinterpretation," *Western Historical Quarterly*, 8 (April 1977), 167–87; Terry G. Jordan, *Trails to Texas: Southern Roots of Western Cattle Ranching* (Lincoln, 1981), 25–82; John Solomon Otto, "Southern 'Plain Folk' Agriculture: A Reconsideration," *Plantation Society in the Americas*, 2 (April 1983), 29–36; Gavin Wright, *The Political Economy of the Cotton South: Households, Markets, and Wealth in the Nineteenth Century* (New York, 1978), 69–74; Steven Hahn, *The Roots of Southern Populism: Yeoman Farmers and the Transformation of the Georgia Upcountry, 1850–1890* (New York, 1983), esp. 50–85, 239–89.

[24] John Mills to cousin Gilbert, May 19, 1807, John Mills Letters (Department of Archives and History, Louisiana State University); U.S. Census Bureau, *Aggregate Amount of Each Description of Persons within the United States of America and the Territories thereof, agreeable to actual enumeration made according to law, in the year 1810* (Washington, 1811), 83. On changing life on the cotton frontier, see Ulrich Bonnell Phillips, *Life and Labor in the Old South* (Boston, 1929), esp. 95–111, 274–304; Malcolm J. Rohrbough, *The Trans-Appalachian Frontier: People, Societies, and Institutions, 1775–1850* (New York, 1978), 93–114, 192–217; William B. Hamilton, Jr., "American Beginnings in the Old Southwest: The Mississippi Phase" (Ph.D. diss., Duke University, 1938); and W. B. Hamilton, "Mississippi 1817: A Sociological and Economic Analysis," *Journal of Mississippi History*, 29 (Nov. 1967), 270–92.

[25] Philip D. Morgan, "The Ownership of Property by Slaves in the Mid-Nineteenth-Century Low Country," *Journal of Southern History*, 49 (Aug. 1983), 399–420, esp. 414–17. See also Peter H. Wood, *Black Majority: Negroes in Colonial South Carolina from 1670 through the Stono Rebellion* (New York, 1974), 103–30, 195–217; and Eugene D. Genovese, *Roll, Jordan, Roll: The World the Slaves Made* (New York, 1974), 535–40.

and Indians together—for example, in weekend marketing on the streets of Natchez. Meanwhile, some individuals within the Indian nations—principally members of mixed-blood, trade families—were themselves becoming owners of black slaves and planters of cotton. Although those developments eventually generated greater racial separation and stratification between southern Indians and blacks, they were too nascent before 1820 to close all channels of interethnic communication.[26]

Throughout the colonial period slaves had perceived Indian country as potential refuge from bondage, and the increasing presence there of blacks owned by tribal members during territorial years may have even encouraged some runaways to take advantage of the confusion accompanying the movement of slaves to and from Indian jurisdictions. Cases of slaves being arrested by United States Indian agents for "want of a passport" and disputes over ownership of slaves who "ran away or were stolen" suggest that the blacks involved were playing an active role in creating their uncertain status within Indian country. Whether as slaves or as runaways, blacks who interacted closely with Indians during the early nineteenth century contributed to the formation of multiracial families and even of scattered communities across the South. One such community, whose members became known as "Cajuns of Alabama," grew rapidly during the territorial period along the west bank of the Mobile River; another group known as "Freejacks" took shape on the Tchefuncte River in Louisiana, along the Natchez-to-New Orleans road.[27]

Given the potential for increasing ties with blacks, Indians found their own activities and mobility being curtailed by the Mississippi territorial government's efforts to reinforce the institution of slavery. In addition to federal laws requiring licenses and prohibiting alcohol in Indian trade, which were enforced by all territorial governors, Governor Sargent issued an ordinance in May 1800 to strengthen control jointly over commerce with Indians and slaves in Mississippi. The mere sight of an Indian or slave carrying into a house or store

[26] On slavery in the Indian nations of the Mississippi Territory, see Wyatt F. Jeltz, "The Relations of Negroes and Choctaw and Chickasaw Indians," Journal of Negro History, 33 (Jan. 1948), 24–37; Arthur H. DeRosier, Jr., "Pioneers with Conflicting Ideals: Christianity and Slavery in the Choctaw Nation," Journal of Mississippi History, 21 (July 1959), 174–89; Michael F. Doran, "Negro Slaves of the Five Civilized Tribes," Annals of the Association of American Geographers, 68 (Sept. 1978), 335–50; and Daniel F. Littlefield, Jr., Africans and Creeks: From the Colonial Period to the Civil War (Westport, 1979), 26–109. For a provocative explanation of the biological and cultural significance of Indian-black interaction, see J. Leitch Wright, Jr., The Only Land They Knew: The Tragic Story of the American Indians in the Old South (New York, 1981), 248–78.

[27] Archives of the Spanish Government of West Florida, 1782–1810, Works Progress Administration typescript translations (18 vols.), Louisiana Historical Center, New Orleans), vol. 4, 165, vol. 7, 345–80; Gilbert Russell to Governor Holmes, April 30, 1811, Correspondence and Papers of Governor David Holmes, Territorial Governor RG 2 (Mississippi Department of Archives and History); Dinsmoor to Holmes, May 4, 1811, ibid.; John Pitchlynn to Dinsmoor, May 30, 1811, ibid.; Dinsmoor to Secretary of War William Eustis, Sept. 27, 1812, microfilm reel 5, Andrew Jackson Papers; Horace Mann Bond, "Two Racial Islands in Alabama," American Journal of Sociology, 36 (Jan. 1931), 552–67; J. Anthony Paredes, "Back from Disappearance: The Alabama Creek Indian Community," in Southeastern Indians since the Removal Era, ed. Walter L. Williams (Athens, Ga., 1979), 123–41; Darrell A. Posey, "Origin, Development and Maintenance of a Louisiana Mixed-Blood Community: The Ethnohistory of the Freejacks of the First Ward Settlement," Ethnohistory, 26 (Spring 1979), 177–92.

"any article which may be supposed for sale, or any bottle, jug or other thing in which liquor may be conveyed" was sufficient evidence for convicting the storekeeper cr housekeeper. An initial law requiring slaves who participated in the Natchez marketplace to carry permits issued by their owners was extended over the entire territory in 1805 to declare that "no person whatsoever shall buy, sell, or receive of, to or from a slave, any commodity whatsoever without the leave or consent of the master, owner or overseer of such slave, expressive of the article so permitted to be bought, sold or bartered." Guilty persons would pay to slave owners four times the value of the item exchanged, the slave would receive ten lashes, and owners who allowed a slave "to go at large and trade as a freeman" had to pay a fine of fifty dollars. A statute enacted in 1810 further increased the risk of independent marketing to slaves by making it lawful for any citizen to apprehend a slave suspected of carrying goods without written consent.[28]

The exchange of two items in particular—cotton and horses—threatened the property of planters and received special attention from lawmakers. In the spring of 1800, slaves were prohibited from the "raising and Vending of Cotton" and from "holding property in horses." Although some owners apparently permitted those activities, both the need to prevent theft of those valuable products and the desire to limit avenues of financial independence activated a comprehensive prohibition against possession of cotton and horses by slaves. To reduce the chances of petty rustling by black and Indian herdsmen, an act of March 4, 1803, prescribed that "no person whosoever shall send or permit any slave or Indian to go into any of the woods or ranges in the territory, to brand or mark any horse, mare, colt, mule, ass, cattle, hog, sheep, under any pretence whatsoever; unless the slave be in company, and under the direction of some reputable white person."[29]

In southern folklore and history, Natchez and the road linking it with Nashville became legendary for crime and violence during the early nineteenth century. As the oldest and largest town in the territory (until Mobile was annexed in 1813), Natchez resembled urban places in other frontier or colonial regions in its very real function as a nexus of underground exchange activity and of volatile ethnic contact. "Ebriety of Indians and Negroes on Sundays," complained Sargent on arriving in Natchez, made it "a most Abominable place"—a message that signaled his and subsequent governors' commitment to reversing customary trends. The seasonal encampment of one hundred or so Choctaw families around Natchez, where they bartered for ammunition and other supplies for hunting trips, had become a familiar part of the cultural landscape before the end of the eighteenth century. Under United States territorial control, however, officials and propertied residents loathed what they

[28] William D. McCain, ed., *Laws of the Mississippi Territory, May 27, 1800* (Beauvoir Community, Miss., 1948), 237–40; *Statutes of the Mississippi Territory* (Natchez, 1816), 384, 388–89. For examples of licenses issued and of violations penalized, see Bonds of Tax Collectors, Sheriffs and Indian Traders, 1802–1817; and West to John Kincaid, Feb. 15, 1805, Indian Department Journal, 1803–1808.

[29] McCain, ed., *Laws of the Mississippi Territory*, 237–40; *Statutes of the Mississippi Territory*, 385–86, 393.

saw as pilfering, loitering, and carousing; thus they discouraged Indians from visiting the area. In 1807 Gov. Robert Williams even tried, with little effect, to require that Indians leaving their tribal lands carry passports to be issued at the discretion of government agents.[30]

Incidents of drunken affrays and robberies among Choctaws, blacks, and whites, of violent and often fatal assaults committed against Indians, and of Indian thefts of livestock and crops were too numerous and various to describe here, but they all involved a confrontation between two different systems of justice. Much of the aggravation and theft perpetrated by Indians represented a form of banditry committed to protest against and compensate for the abandonment of protocol and respect by the growing American population. Because Choctaws traveling to hunt or to trade, for example, encountered more and more settlers unwilling or unable to share some corn or meat with them, as had traditionally been the case, they would simply take what was available from a field or pasture. Whenever an Indian was killed by a white or black assailant, an acute clash between tribal and territorial laws ensued. Although officials often expressed concern over the Indians' "Spirit of Retaliation," territorial courts rarely convicted and punished white men who murdered Indians on the pretense that guilt was difficult to prove in such crimes.[31] Meanwhile, Indians followed their own rules of retributive justice, which required the kin of a victim to avenge his death by killing either the guilty person or some surrogate. As those of other United States territories, the early government of Mississippi tried, with great difficulty, to replace tribal systems of law and order with its own codes of trial and punishment. But in some cases of homicide against Indians, officials compromised by paying merchandise to relatives in compensation for their loss. In January 1809, for example, the Choctaw agent gave two hundred dollars' worth of strouds, blankets, and ammunition to the uncle and brother of an Indian killed the previous summer by William Bates. Bates reimbursed the agency in August. A revealing case of territorial conflict with Indian jurisdiction occurred in 1810, when two young Choctaws who executed another Choctaw under blood law outside the tribal boundary were arrested and imprisoned at Fort Stoddert. Fearful of "unpleasant consequences," Gov. David Holmes pardoned them but urged Judge Harry Toulmin "that they should be made sensible that they have been guilty of an infraction of our laws and that in future such conduct will not be tolerated."[32]

[30] Rowland, ed., *Official Letter Books of W. C. C. Claiborne*, I, 13–14, 67–70; Abbott, "Indian Policy and Management in the Mississippi Territory," 159–60; Rowland, ed., *Mississippi Territorial Archives*, 82.

[31] Mills to cousin Gilbert, May 19, 1807, Mills Letters; White, *Roots of Dependency*, 97–112; Rowland, ed., *Mississippi Territorial Archives*, 123–24; entry for April 15, 1803, Indian Department Journal, 1803–1808; Claiborne to Mitchell, April 29, 1803, *ibid.*; Claiborne to Ochchummey, May 17, 1803, *ibid.*; Holmes to Mr. Newman, coroner, Dec. 15, 1812, Correspondence and Papers of Governor David Holmes.

[32] Rowland, ed., *Official Letter Books of W. C. C. Claiborne*, I, 13–14; receipt, Jan. 9, 1809, Choctaw Factory Miscellaneous Accounts, 1803–25, Records of the Office of Indian Trade; entry for Aug. 18, 1809, Choctaw Factory Daybooks, 1808–19, *ibid.*; Claiborne to Dearborn, June 28, 1803, Indian Department Journal, 1803–1808; West to Dearborn, June 2, 1804, *ibid.*; J. R. Wilson,

Behind all of the legislative and police action directed against slaves and Indians reigned a deep anxiety over black insurrection, Indian warfare, and even combined rebellion by the two groups. News of the Gabriel Prosser revolt that was barely averted in Virginia drove Sargent to address a circular letter of November 16, 1800, to slave owners in the Mississippi Territory, exhorting "the utmost Vigilance" toward all slaves. Recent assaults on two overseers were evidence enough that greater attention to the slave laws had to be given by "all good Citizens." Fear that the increasing in-migration of slaves would introduce experienced insurgents from other slave regions nearly produced in the territorial legislation a law that would have prohibited the importation of "Male Slaves, above the age of Sixteen."[33]

The self-conscious endeavor by white Mississippians to establish slavery safely in the midst of a large Indian population elicited from their officials an obsessive concern with well-organized and trained militias, adequate weaponry, and a responsive federal army—all overtly effective means of controlling subjugated ethnic groups. Although military officials repeatedly assured the government that the army and the militia were prepared to quell any outbreak of Indian or black hostility, the very prospect of having to mobilize against rebellion in one part of the territory heightened the fear of exposing another part to concurrent attack. In January 1811 hundreds of slaves in the adjacent territory of Louisiana turned their hoes and axes against planters outside New Orleans. Their march toward the city was quickly and violently stopped by troops of the United States Army's Southern Division, led by the cotton planter Gen. Wade Hampton. That revolt, which resulted in the brutal and speedy killing of nearly one hundred blacks in Louisiana, intensified apprehension in the Mississippi Territory over thinly stretched defenses against both external and internal enemies. The declaration of war against Great Britain in 1812 then brought the fear of racial war on different fronts to a climax. In a letter to General Wilkinson concerning possible withdrawal of troops from the territory for action elsewhere, Governor Holmes recited his faith in the friendship of the Choctaws but warned that "knowledge of our defenceless state . . . may tempt them to commit aggressions." Regarding blacks, Holmes continued, "Of the slaves, who compose so large a portion of our population I entertain much stronger apprehensions. Scarcely a day passes

---

"A Statement of violence done to my person and property by the Choctaw Indians, Jan. 21, 1811," Correspondence and Papers of Governor David Holmes; Harry Toulmin to Holmes, May 27, July 7, 1810, ibid.; Carter, ed., Territorial Papers of the United States, VI, 69-70.

[33] Rowland, ed., Mississippi Territorial Archives, 311-12; Rowland, ed., Official Letter Books of W. C. C. Claiborne, I, 39. It is important to note that the expansion of cotton agriculture in the lower Mississippi Valley coincided with a tightening of slave codes and a heightening of racial barriers across the South that reflected in large part a reaction to the contagion of rebellion among blacks in the Americas sparked by the slave revolution in St. Domingo. Many historians, however, continue to neglect or downplay the authenticity of this spreading rebelliousness and thereby miss its influence on the renewed codification of race relations that occurred during the early nineteenth century. See Winthrop D. Jordan, White over Black: American Attitudes toward the Negro, 1550-1812 (Chapel Hill, 1968), 375-426; and Vincent Harding, There Is a River: The Black Struggle for Freedom in America (New York, 1981), 46-74.

without my receiving some information relative to the designs of those people to insurrect."[34]

The Creek War of 1813-1814, waged in the eastern valleys of the Mississippi Territory, has recently received skillful attention in regard to both its wide context of international affairs and its internal dimension of tribal politics. But the function of the military conflict in expanding the cotton economy and in enforcing concommitant racial control is not yet fully appreciated. As already indicated, the territorialization of Mississippi imposed multiple pressures upon Indian societies. In the Creek nation, those pressures provoked increasing rebelliousness from a large segment of its population. Persistent demands by the Forbes company and the United States government that trade debts be paid through cessions of land severely tested the patience of Creek villagers. Indian leaders contested debts that were accounted to the nation but that actually had been incurred by individuals whose tribal status they did not recognize. When the company tried to add interest to their account, the Creeks grew angrier, insisting that "there was no word for it in their language" and accusing their old trade partner of wanting "to tear the very flesh off their backs."[35]

Further aggravating those issues, settlers were sprawling from the Tennessee and Tombigbee-Alabama valleys, and territorial militiamen were making frequent border patrols into Creek country. The government's program of reforming, or "civilizing," Indian societies, which was aggressively implemented among the Lower Creeks by agent Hawkins, undermined the ability of the Creek nation to respond effectively to such pressures by expediting the emergence of a new class of assimilated Creek citizens who were themselves becoming cotton planters and slave owners. The tour of the rising Shawnee leader, Tecumseh, among the southern tribes during the summer and fall of 1811 injected into the already factionalized Creek nation a surge of religious nativism and political militance, which took hold most strongly among the angry young men of the Upper Creek towns. In the summer of 1812, the tribal council ordered the execution of a group of Red Sticks, as the rebels were called, who were accused of killing settlers in Tennessee on their return from the town in Indiana where Tecumseh and his brother, the "Shawnee Prophet," resided. And in November it agreed to pay some $22,000 of debts owed the Forbes company by turning over to the firm each year the tribe's

[34] John Hope Franklin, *The Militant South, 1800-1861* (Cambridge, Mass., 1956), 25-32; Tommy R. Young II, "The United States Army and the Institution of Slavery in Louisiana, 1803-1815," *Louisiana Studies,* 13 (Fall 1974), 201-22; Rowland, ed., *Official Letter Books of W. C. C. Claiborne,* I, 42-43; Carter, ed., *Territorial Papers of the United States,* V, 217, VI, 298-99, 301, 328-29; James H. Dormon, "The Persistent Specter: Slave Rebellion in Territorial Louisiana," *Louisiana History,* 18 (Fall 1977), 389-404.

[35] Frank Lawrence Owsley, Jr., *Struggle for the Gulf Borderlands: The Creek War and the Battle of New Orleans, 1812-1815* (Gainesville, 1981), 6-94; Green, *Politics of Indian Removal,* esp. 35-43; Michael Paul Rogin, *Fathers and Children: Andrew Jackson and the Subjugation of the American Indian* (New York, 1975), esp. 165-205; "John Forbes' record of his talks with chiefs of Creek, Cherokee, Choctaw, and Chickasaw tribes, held at Hickory Ground, 27 May-3 June 1803, concerning Indian debts," manuscript (Howard-Tilton Memorial Library); "Account of trip made into the Indian Country by John Innerarity, Oct. 14-Nov. 1, 1812," Papers of Panton, Leslie and Company.

annuities from the United States. Those two explosive developments helped bring civil war to the Creek people by 1813.[36]

United States intervention against the rebellious Creeks came swiftly and forcefully, making the Mississippi Territory the theater of one of the nation's bloodiest and most costly Indian wars. In July 1813 a party of Red Sticks, carrying ammunition and other supplies from Pensacola, was attacked by a joint force of territorial militiamen and Lower Creek adversaries. In retaliation Creek rebels attacked Fort Mims at the confluence of the Alabama and the Tombigbee rivers. On August 30, 1813, approximately 250 of the men, women, and children who had sought refuge inside the fort were killed during a siege that lasted five hours. News of the "massacre," which included reports that black slaves had joined the Red Sticks, threw the Mississippi Territory and adjacent states into an alarm that speedily mobilized soldiers and citizens into action.[37]

The invasion of Upper Creek country by four separate armies of militiamen and federal troops proved to be a painful experience for Indians and non-Indians. Red Stick fighters and their families managed to evade United States soldiers and their Indian allies, who in turn resorted to burning abandoned villages to the ground. After suffering ten months of sickness, hunger, desertion, and severe discipline, the invasionary armies backed the Creek rebels into a bend of the Tallapoosa River. On March 27, 1814, approximately 1,000 Red Sticks stood up against a combined force of 1,400 whites, 500 Cherokees, and 100 Lower Creeks in the Battle of Horseshoe Bend, losing by the end of the day approximately 800 tribesmen killed. Having led personally the western Tennessee volunteers and provided much of the strategy in the Creek War, Andrew Jackson—a merchant, planter, and land speculator long interested in the Mississippi Territory—received command of the United States Army's Seventh Military District and proceeded to impose a peace treaty on the Creek nation. The beleagured Creek leaders who signed the Treaty of Fort Jackson on August 9, 1814, agreed to cede fourteen million acres of land—more than one-half of present-day Alabama—even though most of them were Lower Creeks who had not rebelled against the United States.[38]

The military subjugation of the Creek Indians greatly accelerated the transformation of ethnic relations already underway in the Mississippi Territory. Indian trade in deerskins and other frontier commodities would never recover in the Deep South, forcing most Indian villagers to become marginal participants in the emerging cotton economy while allowing some to accumulate their own property in cotton lands and Negro slaves. Although banditry and violence would continue to serve many Indians in Mississippi and

[36] Theron A. Nunez, Jr., "Creek Nativism and the Creek War of 1813-1814, Part 2 (Stiggin's Narrative, continued)," *Ethnohistory*, 5 (Spring 1958), 145; Green, *Politics of Indian Removal*, 39-42.

[37] H. S. Halbert and T. H. Ball, *The Creek War of 1813 and 1814* (Chicago, 1895), 125-76; Rogin, *Fathers and Children*, 148; Owsley, *Struggle for the Gulf Borderlands*, 30-41.

[38] Halbert and Ball, *Creek War of 1813 and 1814*, 177-286; Rogin, *Fathers and Children*, 149-64; Owsley, *Struggle for the Gulf Borderlands*, 42-94.

Alabama as means of resistance, the Creek War demonstrated the futility and danger of military confrontation and drove surviving militants out of the territory and into Florida. The Creek land cession that resulted from their defeat drastically contracted the area of Indian country and intensified the physical isolation of Indian villages from other inhabitants. Furthermore, the sudden availability of so much land to settlers, coinciding with the post-Napoleonic expansion of the demand for cotton in Europe, set in motion the great wave of public land sales and immigration that guaranteed the dominance of cotton agriculture over the territory's political offspring—the states of Mississippi and Alabama.

The "Alabama Fever," as the postwar boom in land sales and cotton production was called, revived the conflict between immigrant settlers and land speculators. As the average price of public land in the Creek cession rose above five dollars per acre by 1818, crowds of angry squatters assembled at land auctions to push for registration of their claims at the minimum price. Hostility toward large purchasers was tempered, however, by the heady climb of cotton prices above thirty cents per pound. Eager to produce for such an export market, small farmers and wealthy planters alike borrowed more and more money in order to purchase both land and labor. In 1817, the year in which Alabama became a separate territory and Mississippi acquired statehood, cotton annually exported from the region exceeded seventeen million pounds. The fragile financial basis of the expansion, though, soon reached its breaking point. Just as Alabama was becoming a state, cotton prices plummeted in the panic of 1819 well below twenty cents per pound and stranded Alabamians with a land debt of eleven million dollars .But the cotton-export economy had already taken hold of land and labor across the South. Following a short period of contraction and adjustment, white Mississippians and Alabamians proceeded to import more slaves from eastern states and to expand cotton production across more land, of course borrowing more money to finance both.[39]

Development of a cotton economy drastically altered the economic relations of Indian peoples with citizens and slaves in the Mississippi Territory. The United States government, through its own trade houses and with cooperation from private companies, pressured Indian tribes into making repeated cessions of land. In the concomitant transfer of public land into the private market, the federal government allowed speculation by land companies and made ownership difficult for early nineteenth-century migrants. Settlers coped with that obstacle and with the uncertainty of cotton production through means of livelihood similar to those of neighboring Indians. Territorial laws meanwhile restricted the economic activities of slaves and limited their interaction with free individuals, confining them more to the production of cotton for their

[39] Thomas Perkins Abernethy, *The Formative Period in Alabama, 1815-1828* (University, Ala., 1965), 34-71; Charles S. Davis, *The Cotton Kingdom in Alabama* (Montgomery, 1939), 25-32; Rohrbough, *Land Office Business*, 97-126; J. Mills Thornton III, *Politics and Power in a Slave Society: Alabama, 1800-1860* (Baton Rouge, 1978), 6-20; Lewis E. Atherton, *The Southern Country Store, 1800-1860* (Baton Rouge, 1949), 18-37, 113-44; Harold D. Woodman, *King Cotton and His Retainers: Financing and Marketing the Cotton Crop of the South, 1800-1925* (Lexington, Ky., 1968), 129-95.

owners. The Creek War, more than any other action, accelerated the physical confinement of Indians into ethnic enclaves. By 1820 an American Indian population of more than 30,000 persons was surrounded by 42,000 whites and 33,000 blacks in the state of Mississippi and by another 85,000 whites and 42,000 blacks in Alabama.[40]

While a new socioeconomic order originated from those processes, the strategies used to mitigate or to avert them created undercurrents of resistance that have been only slowly and inadequately uncovered by historians. The different economic adaptations selected variantly by Indian inhabitants of the Mississippi Territory greatly influenced impending struggles over removal, with some committed to commercial agriculture becoming the most staunch defenders of tribal homelands.[41] Slaves in Mississippi and Alabama, meanwhile, continued to take economic initiatives in defiance of their owners' economic interests, maintaining a market in self-produced and pilfered goods reminiscent of earlier exchange with Indians and settlers. Although they had greater freedom of choice, nonslaveholding whites also struggled to secure a safe, albeit uneasy, relationship with the cotton export market. Becoming endemic to life in the nineteenth-century South, those widespread attempts to minimize dependence on the expanding cotton economy made the conquest of peoples and places by King Cotton more tenuous and complex than perhaps the participants themselves believed it to be. Old Carothers McCaslin bought the land, as portended by William Faulkner, "with white man's money from the wild men whose grandfathers without guns hunted it, and tamed and ordered or believed he had tamed and ordered it for the reason that the human beings he held in bondage and in the power of life and death had removed the forest from it and in their sweat scratched the surface of it to a depth of perhaps fourteen inches in order to grow something out of it which had not been there before and which could be translated back into the money he who believed he had bought it had had to pay to get it and hold it."[42]

[40] U.S. Department of Commerce, *Historical Statistics of the United States: Colonial Times to 1970* (2 vols., Washington, 1975), I, 24, 30; John R. Swanton, *Early History of the Creek Indians and Their Neighbors* (Washington, 1922), 443–52.

[41] This suggestion defies a general impression, produced by removal historiography, that proponents of change within Indian societies tended to accept removal. Alignments in favor of removal treaties, however, did not automatically form around people of mixed ancestry who practiced commercial agriculture. See Mary Elizabeth Young, *Redskins, Ruffleshirts, and Rednecks: Indian Allotments in Alabama and Mississippi, 1830–1860* (Norman, 1961), 3–46; and White, *Roots of Dependency*, 110–46.

[42] William Faulkner, *Go Down, Moses and Other Stories* (New York, 1942), 254.